THE SKEPTICAL TRADITION

MAJOR THINKERS SERIES

General Editor

Amélie Oksenberg Rorty

1. John M. Rist (editor), *The Stoics*
2. Amélie Oksenberg Rorty (editor), *Essays on Aristotle's Ethics*
3. Myles Burnyeat (editor), *The Skeptical Tradition*

eds ord 2·27·85

THE SKEPTICAL TRADITION

Edited by Myles Burnyeat

UNIVERSITY OF CALIFORNIA PRESS

Berkeley   Los Angeles   London

University of California Press
Berkeley and Los Angeles, California

University of California Press, Ltd.
London, England

Library of Congress Cataloging in Publication Data
Main entry under title:

The Skeptical tradition.

    1. Skepticism—Addresses, essays, lectures.
I. Burnyeat, Myles.
B837.S56   1983   149'.73   78-62833
ISBN 0-520-03747-2

Printed in the United States of America

1 2 3 4 5 6 7 8 9

quae sine eruditione Graeca intellegi non possunt

CICERO

Contents

1

Introduction

M. F. Burnyeat

Skepticism is one of the few subjects which every philosopher thinks he knows a good deal about. The skeptical arguments in the classic texts of Descartes and Hume are so familiar a part of a philosophical education that every philosopher has given some consideration to the radical challenge to our knowledge of the world which these arguments present.

Equally familiar is the way in which the modern philosopher feels free to construct skeptical arguments of his own and to describe them as "what the skeptic says," without worrying whether any historical skeptic did make himself vulnerable to the crushing refutation which then follows. For it is not as widely known as it should be that once upon a time there were real live skeptics, quite a number of them, and that it is the tradition they founded of which Descartes and Hume are the foremost modern representatives.

By a "tradition" I mean a succession of thinkers whose thought is conditioned in one way or another by a knowledge of their predecessors in the line, and I would include in this description not only those who develop and modify previous ideas, but also those who attempt to overthrow a particular tradition and make a revolutionary break with the past. Hume comes into the skeptical tradition under the first heading, Descartes under the second: Hume was making creative use of, Descartes attempting to eradicate, a skeptical tradition that reaches back to Pyrrho of Elis in the fourth century B.C. (Descartes's handling of ancient skepticism is discussed by Bernard Williams in chapter 13, Hume's by Robert Fogelin in chapter 16.)

It is thanks to the researches of Richard Popkin that we know so much about the formative role in the birth of modern philosophy played by Pyrrhonian skepticism, following the rediscovery and publication of the works of Sextus Empiricus in the sixteenth century.[1] In the sixteenth and seventeenth centuries Sextus was an immediate presence, read and studied and argued with in intense seriousness. To mention just two of the high points in the fascinating story that Popkin tells, he was the inspiration of Montaigne and the Fideist defense of Catholic tradition against Calvinist individualism, for his skeptical arguments showed the vanity of merely human attempts to understand the mysteries of religion and man's relation to God (Fideism from Montaigne to Wittgenstein is discussed by Terence Penelhum in chapter 11); and he was a potent influence on Gassendi's attempt to build one of the first modern empiricist theories of knowledge (discussed by Ralph Walker in chapter 12). But Sextus's *Outlines of Pyrrhonism* and *Adversus mathematicos* are themselves a compendious summing up of some five hundred years of skeptical argumentation, as well as a rich source of information on the positive philosophies that ancient skeptics took as their target. It is this whole tradition of philosophical debate which Sextus transmitted to the sixteenth century, achieving an impact far greater than he ever had in antiquity.

As Sextus represented Pyrrhonian skepticism to the modern world, so the other mainstream of ancient skepticism, Academic skepticism, was represented by Cicero. Interest in Cicero's *Academica* was beginning to grow some while before the first modern publication of Sextus. Thanks to Charles Schmitt, we know a good deal about where and how this interest manifested itself,[2] while in Lisa Jardine's essay on Lorenzo Valla in chapter 10 we now have an extended study of the influence of Ciceronian skepticism on Renaissance Humanism and the introduction of new approaches to the teaching and use of logic.

Thus Sextus and Cicero are the two great sources by which Greek skepticism helped in a fundamental way to shape the course of modern philosophy. One of the aims of this volume is to take *philosophical* stock of the historical findings set before us by Popkin and Schmitt. (An up-to-date account of the present state of historical research is given by Schmitt in chapter 9.) I believe that it ought to make a philosophical difference to our reading of Descartes and Hume and other modern philosophers to realize how much history lies behind their references to skeptics and skepticism: a history, moreover, which was a living force in the culture of their times in a way it can no longer be for us.

Consider, for example, the following characterization by Descartes of the purpose of the First *Meditation*:

Nothing conduces more to the obtaining of a secure knowledge of reality than a previous accustoming of ourselves to entertain doubts especially about corporeal things; and although I had long ago seen several books written by the Academics and Sceptics about this subject and felt some disgust in warming over again that old cabbage, I could not for the above reasons refuse to allot to this subject one whole meditation.[3]

What Descartes is telling us is that the First *Meditation* is a rehash of ancient skepticism, deriving (directly or indirectly) from Cicero and Sextus. Descartes's aim, of course, as the passage explains, is to ground positive knowledge on his examination of skepticism. But it is the skeptical materials transmitted from antiquity which are to be thus transformed into positive certainty: "Although the Pyrrhonians reached no certain conclusion from their doubts, it does not follow that no one can."[4] In virtue of this novel strategy Descartes claimed to be the first philosopher in history to refute "the Skeptics."[5] What he in fact achieved was to bring about a permanent enlargement of our conception of the power and scope of skeptical doubt, with the result that Hume, for example, lists "Cartesian doubt" as a species of skepticism alongside, and more fundamental than, Pyrrhonism and "the Academical philosophy."[6] This was indeed a transformation of the ancient materials, but in a sense quite opposite to that which Descartes intended.

Montaigne and Gassendi, Descartes and Hume make explicit references to ancient skepticism. With Locke and Berkeley, discovering the importance that Pyrrhonism had for them is more a question of reconstructing the background to their thinking; this task is undertaken for Locke by Martha Bolton in chapter 14 and for Berkeley by Richard Popkin in chapter 15. There remains Kant, who set out to show the inadequacy of all previous attempts to grapple with the challenge of skepticism. Barry Stroud argues in chapter 17 that Kant's introduction of the distinction between "the transcendental" and "the empirical" was a decisive turning point for the meaning of skepticism in philosophy. One small but telling measure of the change Kant wrought is that, while many of Kant's own references to skepticism show a knowledge of its ancient history, in philosophical writing after Kant "skepticism" and "the skeptic" increasingly become schematic, ahistorical notions. If I may venture an editorial opinion, it is that Stroud's essay explains why Kant brought the skeptical tradition to an end. Not that there is nothing left for contemporary philosophers to say about various kinds of skepticism. But the skepticisms they are talking about are a free creation of the modern philosophical imagination. They no longer descend from the ancient lineage of Pyrrho and the Academy.

CHRONOLOGICAL TABLE

Academy	Pyrrhonists	Stoics	Others
347: Plato dies	c. 365: Pyrrho born		
	c. 344-324: Pyrrho in East with Alexander	344: Zeno of Citium born	341: Epicurus born
	c. 325: Timon born		c. 322: Aristotle dies
		312: Zeno arrives in Athens	312: Diodorus Cronus teaching in Athens until 290s
			307: Epicurus founds Garden in Athens
c. 295: Arcesilaus arrives in Athens			
c. 273: Arcesilaus becomes head of the Academy and institutes skepticism	c. 270: Pyrrho dies	Ariston of Chios, fl. c. 270-250	271: Epicurus dies
		262: Zeno dies, succeeded by Cleanthes	
242: Arcesilaus dies, succeeded by Lacydes	c. 235: Timon dies	c. 232: Cleanthes dies, succeeded by Chrysippus	
c. 219: Carneades born		c. 206: Chrysippus dies, succeeded by Zeno of Tarsus	
(?): Carneades becomes head of Academy		(?): Zeno dies, succeeded by Diogenes of Babylon	
155: Carneades on embassy to Rome with Peripatetic Critolaus and Stoic Diogenes		c. 152: Diogenes dies, succeeded by Antipater	

CHRONOLOGICAL TABLE (*Continued*)

Academy	Pyrrhonists	Stoics	Others
129: Carneades dies		c. 129: Antipater dies, succeeded by Panaetius	
c. 128: Clitomachus becomes head of Academy			
c. 110: Clitomachus dies, succeeded by Philo of Larissa		109: Panaetius dies	
c. 87: Antiochus breaks away to found old Academy	c. 90-80 (probably): Aenesidemus breaks away from Academy and revives "Pyrrhonism"		
c. 79: Philo dies		Posidonius, 135-151	
c. 67: Antiochus dies			
45-44: most of Cicero's philosophical works written			
	Agrippa (1st cent. A.D. ?)		A.D. 129-c. 199: Galen
	Sextus Empiricus, fl. c. A.D. 200		
			A.D. 354-430: Augustine

But this very freedom which philosophy now enjoys to dispose of the concept of skepticism as it will is at the same time an opportunity to dip into the distant past to gain a richer understanding of what skepticism has been, and hence of what it can be. I hope that philosophical readers will find food for thought in the first half of this volume, devoted to the ancient skeptical tradition from around 300 B.C. to A.D. 400. The vitality and philosophical interest of the centuries-long controversy between skeptics and their opponents in antiquity has not been as well understood or appreciated as it deserves. So the second aim of this volume is to summon the resources of modern, philosophically trained scholarship to further the understanding of these debates, from both the skeptic and the antiskeptic points of view. It may help readers unfamiliar with the period if, without anticipating David Sedley's discussion of the motivation and development of ancient skepticism in chapter 2, I introduce the leading names and tabulate their chronological relations.

In the beginning was Pyrrho; just what kind of a beginning he marks is one of the topics of Sedley's chapter. Pyrrho himself, who was some twenty years younger than Aristotle, wrote nothing, but an account of his teaching was circulated by his pupil Timon. There is not at this period (third century B.C.) anything that could be called a Pyrrhonist school. But already within Timon's lifetime Plato's Academy has turned skeptical under the leadership of Arcesilaus and is engaged in dispute with Zeno, the founder of Stoicism. The controversy between Academic skepticism and the Stoa continues unabated for two centuries, with notable contributions by Chrysippus on the Stoic side and then, in the second century B.C., by Carneades for the Academy. But early in the first century B.C. the old patterns of thought start to give way. Both skepticism and Stoicism go soft; a *rapprochement* between the two schools becomes inevitable. (The reasons why Academic skepticism could so easily turn toward Stoicism are explained by Pierre Couissin in chapter 3; the reasons why Stoicism was always close to skepticism are explained by Michael Frede in chapter 4.) It is about this time that the Pyrrhonist movement properly so called is founded by Aenesidemus, a renegade Academic determined to resist the new developments.

Aenesidemus is thus an important character in our story. As the man who put Pyrrhonism on the map and equipped it with systematic methods of argument, he is a major unsung figure in the history of philosophy. (His Ten Tropes for inducing suspension of judgment are discussed by Gisela Striker in chapter 5, and he features also in chapters 6 and 7.) The movement he began lasted for over two hundred years and had important connections with antidogmatic tendencies in medicine. Then, soon after the time of Sextus Empiricus (around 200 A.D.), the traces begin to fade out. Aenesidemus could still be read in Byzantium in the ninth century, and manuscripts of Sextus survived there to be brought to Italy in the early fifteenth century. But so far as antiquity is concerned, Sextus's writings are virtually the end, as they are the climax and culmination, of the Pyrrhonist tradition. For us now, these writings serve a double role. They are our chief text for the character and aims of ancient Pyrrhonism (discussed by the editor in chapter 6). And they are also a record of the numerous deeply interesting, as yet largely unstudied philosophical debates in which skeptics were involved, such as the debate about causation which Jonathan Barnes investigates in chapter 7.

It remains to say a word about Cicero. Although the Pyrrhonist tradition faded out in later antiquity, Cicero continued to be an important author. This was for literary and cultural reasons that were unconnected with the *Academica*, but the effect was that Academic skepticism could retain a "presence" long after it had ceased to have living adherents. When Augustine in the fourth century A.D. struggles with the temptations of skepticism and overcomes them with a striking anticipation of Descartes's *Cogito* (discussed by Christopher Kirwan in chapter 8), the skepticism he is contending with is Academic skepticism as presented by Cicero.

Now Cicero attended the Academy in the first century B.C., the period of a general softening in philosophy; he knew Philo and Antiochus, two chief agents of this process (for their roles, see Sedley, chapter 2, and Couissin, chapter 3). There are, in consequence, two layers to his account of Academic skepticism, one deriving from the original dialectical strategies of Arcesilaus and Carneades, the other representing the more positive directions which these strategies received from Philo. But it is only recently that these two layers have been clearly distinguished. For a long time the idea prevailed that Academic skepticism was a "mitigated skepticism," to use Hume's phrase,[7] and that Carneades taught a probabilistic theory of knowledge. (Lisa Jardine in chapter 10 displays a wide range of Ciceronian texts on which Lorenzo Valla, for example, could mount an interpretation of this kind.) The first serious breach in the traditional reading of Academic skepticism was made by Pierre Couissin in a pioneering paper of 1929. I have included an English translation of that paper in this volume (chapter 3) because for years it lay unread and ignored by the scholarly community and it is still not as widely known as it should be. Only quite recently has it been acknowledged as the foundation of modern research on Academic skepticism, which is now seen, thanks to Couissin, as primarily a dialectical critique of other philosophies, operating in Socratic style with premises taken from the opponent of the day.[8] Not until Philo do the positions worked out in dialectical debate come to be recommended by the Academy as its own teaching, and even then they do not, in my own view, constitute anything that could be called a probabilistic theory of knowledge.

So much by way of an introductory glance at the history of ancient skepticism. It is a history well worth getting into, both for its own intrinsic interest and for the light it can cast on later developments. Skepticism, as this volume shows, has not been a single nor a stationary phenomenon. But there have been recurring themes and questions, recurring patterns of argument and counterargument. Descartes's antiskeptical appeal to clear and distinct ideas can profitably be compared to its counterpart in ancient Stoicism (Williams, chapter 13, and Frede, chapter 4). The question whether it is possible to live in a state of skeptical doubt is important both for Hume, who says "No," and for Sextus, who says "Yes" (Fogelin, chapter 16; the editor, chapter 6), and it is a central topic in Penelhum's discussion of Fideism (chapter 11). The familiar fact that things appear differently to different observers, depending on their circumstances, is a perennial starting point for skeptical arguments: it forms the basis for the Ten Tropes of Aenesidemus (Striker, chapter 5), but it recurs again in chapter 12 on Gassendi (Walker), chapter 14 on Locke (Bolton), and chapter 15 on Berkeley (Popkin), for each of these philosophers offers his own evaluation of skeptical arguments from conflicting appearances.

These are just a few of the issues on which comparative illumination can be hoped for when ancient and modern treatments of skepticism are set side by side. The reader who considers this volume as a whole will find many more. He will find, I hope, that a historical perspective which sees the skeptical tradition as a continuous development from ancient into modern times leads to a better understanding of skepticism. If it does, this collection of essays will have achieved its aim. And it is perhaps permissible to hope that a richer historical understanding will bring renewed philosophical interest and significance to discussions of skepticism in the contemporary world.

NOTES

1. See Richard H. Popkin, *The History of Scepticism from Erasmus to Spinoza* (Berkeley, Los Angeles, London, 1979 [1st ed. 1964]), and the essays collected in his *The High Road to Pyrrhonism*, ed. Richard A. Watson and James E. Force (San Diego, 1980).

2. See Charles B. Schmitt, *Cicero Scepticus: A Study of the Influence of the "Academica" in the Renaissance* (The Hague, 1972).

3. II *Replies*, in *The Philosophical Works of Descartes*, ed. E. S. Haldane and G. R. T. Ross (corr. ed., Cambridge, 1934), II, 31; translation amended to restore the echo of Juvenal, *Satires* VII 154. By "Sceptics" the reader should understand "Pyrrhonists," for it was Pyrrhonists rather than Academics who claimed the title of "skeptic."

4. Letter to Reneri for Pollot, April 1638, in *Descartes: Philosophical Letters*, trans. and ed. Anthony Kenny (Oxford, 1970), p. 53.

5. VII *Replies*, Haldane and Ross, II, 336.

6. David Hume, *Enquiry Concerning Human Understanding*, sec. XII, §116.

7. Ibid., §129.

8. See in this volume Sedley (chap. 2) and Frede (chap. 4). Also Gisela Striker, "Sceptical Strategies," in *Doubt and Dogmatism: Studies in Hellenistic Epistemology*, ed. Malcolm Schofield, Myles Burnyeat, and Jonathan Barnes (Oxford, 1980), and my own "Carneades Was No Probabilist," in *Riverside Studies in Ancient Skepticism*, ed. David K. Glidden (forthcoming).

2

The Motivation of Greek Skepticism

David Sedley

By Greek skepticism I shall mean, for the purposes of this article,[1] not the widespread expressions of doubt or ignorance found among Greek philosophers in general, but the philosophical movement which spans the half millennium or so from Pyrrho and Arcesilaus at the opening of the Hellenistic age down to Sextus Empiricus, conventionally dated to the late second century A.D. During those five centuries skepticism weathered numerous upheavals, heresies, and schisms, and emerged at the end of it all looking recognizably like the original product. It is certainly not my intention to present Greek skepticism as a static system. The differences between its various exponents are both many and important. But recognition of these differences should not blind us to one highly individual characteristic that unites the leading Hellenistic skeptics and distinguishes them sharply both from the predecessors from whom they drew so much inspiration and from the later skeptics whom they in turn inspired. It is, moreover, a characteristic that should bring into sharper focus Pyrrho's enigmatic role in the history of Greek skepticism.

Of the earlier philosophers to whose authority the Hellenistic skeptics often appealed, some deserved the honor less for any lack of dogmatism than because they had provided arguments useful to the skeptic. Heraclitus, the Eleatics, Anaxagoras, and Protagoras are prominent examples. Others, such as Xenophanes, Empedocles, Democritus, and Socrates, earned it by their admission, at any rate in their gloomier moments, that knowledge is unattainable, or as yet unattained, by man. In some cases controlled doubt may, rather as it later did for Descartes, have served a methodological function: the recognition that you do not know what you thought you knew can be considered a necessary precondition of a proper search for the truth, and some such propaedeutic purpose underlies Socrates' aporetic method as portrayed in, for example, Plato's *Meno*.[2] Usually, however, the assertion of doubt is nothing more than a disarmingly frank acknowledgment by a committed system-builder that his conclusions are necessarily hazardous and unproven, a self-imposed counterweight to excessive didacticism and dogmatism, a modest sacrifice at the altar of intellectual honesty. There is no suggestion that any of these pre-Hellenistic philosophers derived much comfort from his admission of ignorance or thought of it as anything more than a regrettable expedient. Indeed, it is hard to see what comfort it could afford anybody who was not prepared to renounce a rather fundamental human trait, the desire for knowledge.

What above all characterizes Hellenistic skepticism is, I would claim, its abandonment of that desire—its radical conviction that to suspend assent and to resign oneself to ignorance is not a bleak expedient but, on the contrary, a highly desirable intellectual achievement. I do not mean to discount a second distinguishing feature, the systematic collection of arguments against the possibility of knowledge. But the former characteristic is the more fundamental of the two, in that without a prior faith in the intrinsic value of suspension of assent there would have been little motivation to seek arguments that might lead to it.

Two questions immediately suggest themselves. What positive value was suspension of assent thought to have? And how could a skeptic assign such value to it without thereby compromising his skepticism? My thesis, to be illustrated first in the New Academy and then in the later Pyrrhonist tradition, will be that the founder of a skeptical sect must inevitably steer a dangerous course on these questions, whereas his later followers can afford a rather more relaxed approach.

We can start by considering Arcesilaus, the founder of Academic skepticism and probably the first champion of *epochē*, suspension of assent,[3] who became head of the Academy around 273 b.c. Arcesilaus saw himself as a true Platonist, and his method of including "*epochē* about all things" was in essence borrowed from Plato's early Socratic dialogues. A pupil would be asked to argue some positive current thesis, usually one emanating from the Stoa, and Arcesilaus would produce counterarguments, while allowing the pupil to maintain a defense.[4] The intended result was a stalemate, and the withholding of assent both from the thesis itself and from its denial.

It was not in his methodology that Arcesilaus's originality lay. Quite apart from the acknowledged Platonic precedent, a rhetorical exercise of balancing argument with counterargument was already established in the Peripatos, and similar procedures had been the stock-in-trade of Protagoras and some of his contemporaries in the late fifth century. But Plato had harnessed his method to the search for knowledge, the Peripatetics had valued theirs as a rhetorical training device, and Protagoras had probably put his to work in support of his relativistic theory of truth. No one before Arcesilaus had thought of using equipollence of arguments as an antidote to belief. And by common consent it was the calculated quest for *epochē*, coupled with the denial that certainty can be achieved, that gave Arcesilaus's school its distinctive philosophical coloring.[5]

I have assumed the equation of suspension of assent with avoidance of belief, and a brief terminological excursus is necessary to show why Arcesilaus would have shared that assumption. His ideal of *epochē* is, by origin, the "withholding" or "suspension" of *synkatathesis*. It is well recognized that the terminology of skepticism arose directly out of Stoicism, and "*synkatathesis*," "assent," was established by Zeno, the founder of Stoicism, as the term for accepting as true any impression, *phantasia*, about the world. Merely to have a *phantasia* is not yet to believe anything, but to entertain an idea which you are still at liberty to believe or disbelieve. Belief is located in the three varieties of assent, the three ways in which you can accept an impression as true: (1) "opinion" (*doxa*), weak or fallible belief; (2) "cognition" (*katalēpsis*), infallible belief; and (3) "understanding" (*epistēmē*), the wise man's brand of cognition, irreversible even by reason. Our word "assent" is often taken to imply voluntary commitment, a deliberate decision that such-and-such is the case, and among the Stoics Zeno, at least, regarded it in the same light. This might appear to leave the proponent of *epochē* with all sorts of involuntary beliefs (assuming, being under the impression that, and so on) without the need for assent. It is important therefore to appreciate that the Stoics, Zeno included, in fact recognized no kinds of belief beyond the three varieties of assent listed above, and in consequence that when Arcesilaus advocated suspension of assent about everything, he meant suspension of all belief—refusal to regard any impression whatever, or its contradictory, as true.

How then could Arcesilaus justify his championship of *epochē* without *eo ipso* contravening it? He had certainly given some thought to the charge that skepticism refutes itself, already leveled by his older contemporary Epicurus;[6] for he expressly opted out of the Socratic solution of making the assertion "I know nothing" uniquely exempt from its own scope,[7] and must therefore have offered some alternative reply to the charge—no doubt that it is precisely because we do not actually know that we know nothing that we need to conduct the dialectical investigation which, in the event, leads to *epochē*. So we ought not to imagine him as insensitive to the parallel danger that "We should suspend assent" similarly applies to itself and therefore should not be asserted at all. He could reply that a skeptic might indeed, in convincing himself of its truth, have simultaneously to withdraw his assent from it for the sake of consistency, but that by then he would no longer be required to believe it, since he would already be successfully purged of all assent—just as (to borrow a simile from the later Pyrrhonist skeptics)[8] a medical purge eliminates first the bodily matter against which it is aimed, and then itself. It is conceivable that Arcesilaus was thinking along these lines. But such a move, handy though it is for defusing the self-refutation argument against skepticism,[9] is of little tactical use to someone who, if only for didactic reasons, still has to argue positively for *epochē*. For taken on its own it would render the *epochē* theory self-consistent only by robbing it of all normative force. (Why should I pursue an end that I will not value once I have achieved it? Has skepticism no more positive attraction than suicide?) It is not surprising that it does not feature among Arcesilaus's recorded arguments.

The question therefore remains, what positive case could Arcesilaus make out for *epochē*? How, in addition to conducting individual debates that resulted in *epochē*, could he put across the idea that the result was not a defeat but an intrinsically worthwhile one? It seems natural to start from his own recorded arguments in its support. The trouble here, however, is that these are now recognized as *ad hominem* dialectical gambits that work from Stoic premises, not premises of Arcesilaus's own. The Stoics upheld as the ultimate guarantee, or "criterion," of truth an allegedly infallible species of impression which they called "cognitive" (*phantasia katalēptikē*). Arcesilaus constructed an elaborate set of arguments to show that there could be no such impression. This conclusion he then coupled with the Stoic tenet that the wise man never holds a mere "opinion" (technically defined as "assent to a noncognitive impression"), with the consequent inference that "in the Stoics' view too"[10] the wise man suspends assent. This argument, together with others that appear to offer surrogate principles of action,[11] can be fitted coherently into a strategy by which Arcesilaus defended the skeptical position against Stoic objections.[12] But it is hard to see how it could have lent any credence to Arcesilaus's own espousal of *epochē*—unless, that is, he himself subscribed to the tenet that the wise man does not hold "opinions."

Cicero, indeed, does attribute such a positive starting point to him: "No earlier thinker [earlier, that is, than the Stoic Zeno] had worked out or even stated the view that it is possible for a man to hold no opinions, and not just possible but actually essential for the wise man. To Arcesilaus the view seemed true, as well as honorable and worthy of the wise man."[13] It is tempting to agree. That the wise man holds no opinions—no beliefs that fall short of certainty—was, as Cicero says, a radical new doctrine (albeit with antecedents in Plato, *Republic* V-VII), and was currently being marketed by Arcesilaus's older contemporary Zeno. Might we not envisage the young Arcesilaus being seduced by this ideal but, as time went on, disillusioned by his own failure to attain certainty about anything? If this could be established, Stoic theory might even turn out to have supplied some genuine motivation for Arcesilaus's philosophy, and not just the jargon in which it was set out.[14]

The suggestion might seem to find some support in Arcesilaus's failure fully to disguise his objective moral commitment to *epochē*. Sextus, in what is by far his fairest set of comments on the skeptical Academy,[15] grants an almost complete philosophical concord between Arcesilaus and his own Pyrrhonist school; but he adds the qualification that, when Arcesilaus says that individual acts of *epochē* are goods and individual acts of assent are evils, he might be accused of treating this as an objective truth, whereas when the Pyrrhonist says more or less the same thing[16] he is merely describing the way things appear to him. One is attempted to dismiss this as idle nitpicking. But Sextus is not here in a nitpicking mood, and I am inclined to believe that the criticism has some basis in fact. Arcesilaus is too regularly represented in our sources as positively recommending *epochē*, even apparently naming it as the ethical goal (*telos*).[17] Of course, such remarks are likely to derive, once again, from dialectical contexts in which Arcesilaus made skeptical positions seem to follow from Stoic premises. That *epochē* is the goal, for example, could have been argued from the Stoics' definition of the goal as "to live in accordance with nature" coupled with a refutation of their view that the nature of things is discoverable. But even that exercise would have had little point unless he had taken the conclusion to represent the actual position of his New Academy.

Nor, in the historical context, would the indiscretion be surprising. To lead the Academy off into the uncharted wilderness of *epochē*, to deprive it of all its authority on doctrinal questions, required powerful advocacy, and Arcesilaus's reportedly eloquent championship of *epochē* fills the bill admirably. If a century later Carneades could (as we shall see) afford to play his cards close to his chest on this issue, it was thanks to the hard work Arcesilaus had already done in establishing the philosophical credentials of *epochē* in the Academy. Perhaps, then, the fairest gloss on Arcesilaus's strategy is this: he always retained the escape route of being able, if challenged, to disown whatever premises he happened to be arguing from; but he must have hoped that his regular conclusion, the need for *epochē*, would take on an autonomous authority which the status of his premises did not strictly warrant.

Are these considerations sufficient to corroborate the Ciceronian story of Arcesilaus taking a single Stoic ideal, the need for infallibility, and deriving from it a recommendation abhorrent to any Stoic, that of total *epochē*? No, there is still something unsatisfying or incomplete about Cicero's picture of Arcesilaus's motivation. The most that it would lead us to expect, psychologically speaking, is saddened resignation to a life without beliefs, hardly Arcesilaus's enthusiastic elevation of *epochē* to the status of an end desirable for its own sake. And Cicero is oversimplifying when he speaks of the possibility and desirability of a life without opinions as a radical new idea which Arcesilaus learned from Zeno. Zeno only considered such a life possible and desirable insofar as "opinion" could be supplanted by a more satisfactory kind of belief, namely, infallible cognition. What can have put into Arcesilaus's head the preposterous idea that a life devoid of *any* kind of belief was desirable, or even possible?

At this point Pyrrho of Elis can no longer be kept out of the picture. Pyrrho (c. 365–c. 270), an older contemporary of Arcesilaus, is often spoken of as the founder of Greek skepticism. As far as the theoretical side of skepticism is concerned, I believe this to be an exaggeration. Pyrrho belonged, if loosely, to a long line of Democritean philosophers who denied the possibility of knowledge. But there was already within that tradition a version of skepticism methodologically closer to Hellenistic skepticism, encapsulated in the pronouncement with which Democritus's pupil Metrodorus of Chios had opened his cosmological work *On Nature*:

"None of us knows anything, not even whether we know anything or not."[18] Metrodorus's avoidance of a dogmatic assertion that nothing is known presumably licensed the series of investigations to which he proceeded; and in this strategy, if in nothing else, he was anticipating the leading Hellenistic skeptics.[19] Pyrrho took the quite different course of asserting a single dogmatic truth about the world, that it is in its own nature "undifferentiated, unmeasurable, and unjudgeable."[20] It followed that further inquiry about the world need not even commence, and Pyrrho was praised in the verses of his leading pupil and propagandist Timon for accepting this consequence: "Aged Pyrrho, how and whence did you find escape from slavery to the opinions and empty thought of the sophists, and break the bonds of all deceit and persuasion? You were not concerned to inquire what winds blow over Greece, and the origin and destination of each thing."[21]

So far we are a long way from the dialectical skepticism of the Hellenistic age, whose lifeblood was the investigation of truth claims about the world. But Pyrrho also preached, and practiced, a way of life consistent with his theory—a life with no positive beliefs or assertions, but only dispassionate acquiescence in appearances and social conventions. Through his total lack of commitment Pyrrho was said to have achieved an enviable state of equanimity, described by the negative term *"ataraxia,"* "imperturbability" or "freedom from disquiet." The practical model which this unopinionated life-style offered was, I believe, Pyrrho's unique contribution to Hellenistic skepticism. Its revolutionary impact may be explicable partly in terms of its exotic origin, for Pyrrho was said to have come under the influence of the Indian "naked philosophers" during his travels with Alexander the Great. It is hard to piece together any sort of description of it, but his mental disposition was characterized as *apragmosynē*, "detachment from worldly matters," and its many emulators and admirers included even the dogmatist Epicurus, who adopted Pyrrho's *ataraxia* as one of his own ethical ideals.[22] The comparison with Socrates is inescapable. For Pyrrho, like Socrates, wrote nothing, but by his personal example inspired those who knew him or read about him to set the values which he embodied on a firm theoretical foundation.

This brief sketch inevitably does less than justice to so enigmatic a figure as Pyrrho. But it should be sufficient to underline my present point, that nothing less than Pyrrho's practical model of a life without beliefs could have suggested to Arcesilaus the positive value which he found in *epochē*. Indeed, it seemed obvious to at least two of Arcesilaus's contemporaries that Pyrrho was the chief inspiration of his skepticism. Pyrrho's pupil Timon satirized him as a hanger-on of Pyrrho and Diodorus Cronus (the dialectician who had helped shape Arcesilaus's argumentative technique).[23] And the Stoic Ariston of Chios brilliantly summed him up in a mock-Homeric line as a philosophical chimaera: "Plato in front, Pyrrho behind, Diodorus in the middle."[24] That is, behind his formal pose as Plato's heir in the Academy lay Pyrrho's philosophy, while Diodorus's dialectical technique held the two heterogeneous creatures together.

There is a difficulty about this view. If Arcesilaus was inspired by Pyrrho's embodiment of the skeptical ideal, why did he not proclaim the debt? After all, to draw attention to Pyrrho's example would have been an excellent approach to the problem already discussed, how to recommend *epochē* without thereby dogmatizing. Moreover, Arcesilaus is said to have had no qualms about invoking philosophical precedent. As Plutarch puts it,

Arcesilaus was so far from cherishing any reputation for originality or plagiarizing anything from the ancients that he was charged by contemporary sophists with foisting on Socrates, Plato, Parmenides, and Heraclitus the doctrines about *epochē* and the impossibility of cognition. They did not need him to do this, but he was, as it were, confirming his doctrines by appeal to men of repute.[25]

It may then be suspected that Arcesilaus's apparent silence about Pyrrho is only explicable if he was either ignorant or misinformed about him.

But I am not so sure. There is nothing haphazard about Arcesilaus's list of illustrious forerunners—Socrates, Plato, Parmenides, and Heraclitus. Plato was the founder of the Academy, and the other three were plausibly represented as Plato's own leading philosophical forebears.[26] No appeals to philosophical precedent outside these four are recorded elsewhere,[27] not even to Democritus, whom others ranked foremost among the precursors of skepticism. So Arcesilaus's invocation of his skeptical forerunners was not the modest (if historically misguided) acknowledgment of a debt nor a self-effacing appeal to higher authority. It looks more like a political gesture designed to furnish skepticism with an Academic pedigree and thus reinforce Arcesilaus's well-attested claim that he was restoring the true philosophy of Plato.[28] Squabbling about philosophical pedigrees was unfortunately a common failing of the Hellenistic Academy.

Arcesilaus, then, had a political motive for keeping skepticism within the Academic family, and his silence about Pyrrho's contribution may now appear in a less innocent light.[29] It was in all probability Pyrrho's example that set him on his skeptical path, but political considerations deterred him from exploiting its considerable propaganda value. Pyrrho may, on an extreme view, have been no more a skeptic (in the Hellenistic sense) than Socrates was a Platonist. Yet it was he alone who gave Hellenistic skepticism what I have described as its most distinctive feature, its positive commitment to the eradication of belief. No doubt Arcesilaus's own valuation of *epochē* put more stress than Pyrrho's on intellectual integrity. Where Pyrrho had been praised by Timon above all for his tranquillity, a *summum bonum* already possessing strong antecedents within the Democritean tradition, and for his lack of vanity, Arcesilaus emphasized freedom from the unbecoming rashness of ill-founded belief. And here at least Socrates' model of "wisdom," consisting in the recognition of his own ignorance, can be acknowledged to have had a genuine influence. But the core commitment common to both thinkers, the elimination of all belief, was a revolutionary innovation which, barring an astonishing coincidence, Arcesilaus must have picked up from Pyrrho. His dialectical defense of *epochē* against the Stoics, and his appeals to precedent, represent not so much the origin of that commitment as an attempt to put it on the philosophical map, to develop its implications, and to liberate it from dependence on Pyrrho.

The next major figure in Hellenistic skepticism is Carneades, head of the Academy in the mid second century B.C. Methodologically he was very close to Arcesilaus, devoting his main energy to combating the current tenets of Stoic philosophy, particularly its defense of an infallible criterion of truth. On some central issues his critique claimed to cover all actual and all possible philosophical positions. He was also quite prepared, if the occasion demanded, to argue both sides of a case, as we know he did during his celebrated ambassadorial visit to Rome in 155 B.C. Having delivered one speech in favor of justice, he shocked his Roman audience the next day by delivering a second speech, against justice.[30] All this supports the assumption that Carneades was continuing Arcesilaus's quest for *epochē*. But even his own disciples were divided on that very point. His dialectical techniques, and in particular perhaps his practice of sometimes arguing both sides of a case, could give the misleading impression that he himself favored a thesis which he happened to be defending.[31] It seems best to accept the judgment of his trusted amanuensis Clitomachus, himself a later head of the school, who said that he had never been able to find out what Carneades himself believed,[32] and revered him as a champion of *epochē*.[33] But Carneades was not one for putting his cards on the table. *Epochē* barely features in his recorded arguments, and the most he seems to have offered in explanation of his strategy was the occasional riddling simile. He likened *epochē* to a boxer's guard, or to a charioteer reining back his horses;[34] and dialectic to an octopus which first grows its tentacles, then (allegedly) consumes them, just as dialecticians eventually overturn their own arguments.[35] Even at Rome he did not stoop to explaining *why* he had argued both sides of the case. One can perhaps detect here a reluctance to preach *epochē* overtly, for fear of appearing to take a dogmatic stance. But, as I suggested earlier, this reticence was a luxury which Carneades could afford only because Arcesilaus had already done the hard work and established *epochē* as an Academic ideal. And just because Carneades was able to concentrate his inventive brilliance on the nuts and bolts of skeptic dialectic, it should not be supposed that the normative aspect of *epochē* was now dormant. Rather it was taken for granted. Clitomachus could still praise Carneades for "performing a Herculean labor when he rid our minds of assent, that is, opinion and rashness, like some wild and frightful monster."[36]

Whether the full-strength Pyrrhonian ideal of a life without beliefs still exercised any pull might be doubted by some on the score of Carneades' own proclamation of a criterion, the "convincing impression"[37] (*pithanē phantasia*, or, for short, the *pithanon*), which he argued to be, while fallible, adequate for the conduct of life, especially when certain confirmatory checks were carried out on it. In one version this theory did not involve an abandonment of *epochē*, because it was argued that one could follow a convincing impression without assenting to it—without, that is, accepting it as true.[38] But it is clear, as Sextus saw,[39] that once an Academic admitted that he found some claims about the world more convincing than others, he would rapidly distance himself from the Pyrrhonian spirit of Arcesilaus's skepticism, the quest for disinterested neutrality on all issues.

Fortunately there is now a growing consensus, with which I am in agreement, that Carneades did not put forward the *pithanon* theory as one to which he himself was comitted,[40] but as a dialectical gambit. One may feel with Couissin, dal Pra, and Burnyeat[41] that it was intended as a deflationary parody of Stoic theory, a demonstration to the Stoics that on their own premises nothing better than a highly fallible "criterion" is available;[42] or with Striker that it represents Carneades' *ad hominem* defense against the Stoic charge that skepticism makes life unlivable.[43] The suspicion to which I myself incline is that here, as on his visit to Rome, Carneades was arguing both sides of the case; for we know from Sextus that he first argued against the existence of any criterion whatsoever, then went on to argue that there is a criterion—namely, the "convincing impression."[44] His defense of this latter criterion is essentially an appeal to experience, an analysis of the way in which we arrive at judgments in everyday life. Such a pairing of the arguments against and for— the one a dialectical refutation, the other an appeal to experience—would bear a close resemblance to Sextus's regular method of creating *isostheneia*, equipollence of opposed arguments, in the cause of *epochē*. If Carneades was as secretive about his purpose on this occasion as he had been when first praising and then attacking justice at Rome, it would hardly be surprising if some took him to be expressing his own doctrine.[45]

On any of these views we are at liberty to accept at face value Clitomachus's judgment that Carneades never put forward his own beliefs and was a true champion of *epochē*.[46] The subsequent history of the New Academy, from Carneades' retirement in 137 down to the headship of Philo of Larissa (died c. 79 B.C.), is a depressing one of rapid drift into dogmatism. It was difficult to live in Carneades' shadow. Academic philosophy became largely a matter of interpreting Carneades,[47] and Clitomachus's view of him as a hard-nosed skeptic was rivaled by the meatier dogmatizing interpretation marketed by his fellow disciple Metrodorus of Stratonicea, whose chief tactic was to claim that he had gained a more intimate acquaintance with Carneades' thoughts than anyone else.[48] Clitomachus's successor Philo, who had himself never known Carneades, was strongly influenced by Metrodorus, and developed a dogmatist philosophy whose only vestige of skepticism was its denial of infallible cognition. The *pithanon* was incorporated as an official Academic doctrine. It was even claimed that truths not infallibly known might be "self-evident,"[49] and that the wise man could assent to them—that is, hold opinions—so long as he realized that he might be mistaken.[50] Indeed, Philo held it to be the job of philosophy to substitute correct for incorrect opinions.[51]

It is clear that despite Clitomachus's stand the post-Carneadean Academy was rapidly shedding its positive commitment to *epochē*,[52] and it may seem that my characterization of Hellenistic skepticism must here grind to a halt. But there ensued an event which on the contrary illustrates and confirms that characterization. Aenesidemus, a disaffected member of Philo's Academy, broke away to form his own hard-line skeptical movement. Although he undoubtedly derived much of his methodology from Arcesilaus and Carneades, he bitterly attacked the dogmatic tendencies of the contemporary Academy; and, significantly, it was Pyrrho whom he chose as his sect's figurehead. This "Pyrrhonist" movement was the most prominent flagbearer of skepticism from the early or mid-first-century B.C. down to Sextus Empiricus around 200 A.D.

Why Pyrrhonism? The claim (deriving from Aenesidemus himself?) that the school could be traced back through an unbroken sequence of teachers and pupils to Pyrrho himself,[53] finds too little independent support, and looks like a political gesture to establish the historical priority of Aenesidemus's school over Arcesilaus's New Academy. The more serious purpose behind his choice is undoubtedly Pyrrho's propaganda value as a practical embodiment of the *epochē* ideal. Thus Aenesidemus took it on himself to set the historical record straight about Pyrrho's lifestyle. He dismissed the popular picture of him as a reckless eccentric constantly being snatched by his friends from precipices and the paths of vehicles: Pyrrho's innocence of all belief had been no bar to his living, as he did, in noncommittal conformity with appearances.[54] Aenesidemus spoke openly of "philosophizing in Pyrrho's way" as a means to happiness;[55] and by this he must above all have meant *epochē*, for he even followed Timon in naming it as, in some sense, the skeptic's goal (*telos*),[56] and his major contribution to the skeptical tradition was his ten "Methods of *epochē*," a systematic catalogue of the arguments that lead to suspension of assent.

A terminological note is needed here. It is clear from Sextus Empiricus's usage that *epochē* for the Pyrrhonist is no longer suspension of assent, since despite his "*epochē* about all things" he does assent to appearances, over which he has no control. That is, while he reserves judgment on whether things actually are the way they appear, he cannot doubt that they do appear that way. Assent regarding the former kind of question is called "*doxa*," "belief," and it is *doxa* that the Pyrrhonist explicitly claims to have eliminated from his life.[57] So it seems safer to call the Pyrrhonist's *epochē* "suspension of belief," while bearing in mind that it is essentially equivalent to Academic "suspension of assent," since what is suspended in both cases is the acceptance of some impression, or appearance, as true.

Just as Arcesilaus, in establishing *epochē* as a desirable condition of the intellect, had had to add an evangelical note to his otherwise disinterested dialectic, so too Aenesidemus now tackled the task of reestablishing *epochē* at a time when its positive value had been forgotten. His inestimable advantage over Arcesilaus was his willingness to draw attention to the example set by Pyrrho, and thus to publicize his ideal without thereby compromising it.

This Pyrrhonism is, by and large, the philosophy which Sextus Empiricus was teaching two and a half centuries later. But I think a change of emphasis is detectable. It will be recalled that Carneades, while staying loyal to Arcesilaus's philosophy, had taken the end for granted and concentrated almost exclusively on the means. My claim is that a parallel development is detectable in the Pyrrhonist school. Superficially the change is evidenced by the introduction of a new name for the movement; and this innovation, I shall argue, reflects a guarded reassessment of the skeptic's attitude to his own ultimate goal.

Many readers of Sextus must have noticed how disappointingly little we learn about Pyrrho from his works. Sextus is still a "Pyrrhonist," and for the right reason ("because it seems to us that Pyrrho applied himself to skepticism in a more bodily and manifest way than his predecessors"),[58] yet in practice he pays no more than lip service to his movement's patron saint.[59] The title that Sextus uses far more often than "Pyrrhonist" is "*Skeptikos*," literally "Inquirer." This usage certainly does not antedate Aenesidemus,[60] and there is good reason not to attribute it to Aenesidemus himself either.[61] It is, I believe, in the mid second century A.D. that "Skeptic" emerges as an equivalent for "Pyrrhonist."[62] One step in the process by which the new term partially eclipsed the old can be seen around this date when Theodosius, a member of the movement who wrote a work called *Skeptical Chapters*, maintained in a rare attack of historical scruples that Skepticism should not be called Pyrrhonism,[63] (a) because if one person's thoughts are inaccessible to another[64] we will never know Pyrrho's disposition, and (b) because Pyrrho was not the first discoverer of Skepticism, and indeed had no doctrines at all.[65] However, he added, someone whose external behavior resembles that of Pyrrho might reasonably be called "Pyrrhonian."

One can detect here that once Pyrrho's personal example had served its purpose in launching a new phase of skepticism, it itself fell victim to skeptical doubts. A skeptic could draw attention to it in a noncommittal fashion, but if a particular account of it was challenged, there was no way of defending that account without seeming to dogmatize. Anyhow, Skepticism was by now a living philosophy no longer reliant on a distant historical precedent. The Skeptics, not Pyrrho, are Sextus's real heroes.

More important, however, is the methodological emphasis brought out by the new name "Skeptics." Why "Inquirers"? An inquirer, normally understood, is someone who sees at least an outside chance of finding the truth. Yet a Skeptic, although he might start out with this expectation, could hardly be recognized as a Skeptic until he either abandoned it or at the very least had some hopes of doing so.[66] The solution, I think, is to see the notion of open-mindedness as dominant in the word "inquirer." For in this way "Skeptic" would naturally suggest itself for the role it in fact often plays, the direct antithesis of "dogmatist." A dogmatist is someone who holds *dogmata*—not merely beliefs but theoretical doctrines, tenets, or principles.[67] The least misleading translation of *"dogmatikos"* might be "doctrinaire thinker," and the Skeptic would then be a mere inquirer in the sense that he is as yet unshackled by theoretical commitment.

Such a story, which Sextus does indeed sometimes seem to have in mind,[68] presents the Skeptic with a problem. If he is really an open-minded inquirer, it may be that he has always up to now found every dogmatist argument to be equally balanced by a counterargument,[69] but why should he suppose that the same will hold of theses he has yet to investigate? Some Skeptics responded to this problem by suggesting that in the Skeptic formula "To every argument an equal argument is opposed" the noncommittal infinitive form of the verb used in the Greek should be thought of as expressing an injunction—to every argument *let us* oppose an equal argument—in order to avoid being misled into dogmatism at some future time.[70] The move is ingenious, for an injunction is not an assertion at all, let alone a doctrinaire one. But it reveals the hand which the Skeptic most wants to conceal: he is committed in advance to the goal of suspension of belief.

Aenesidemus, indeed, had made no bones about this commitment. Seeing *epochē* as the hallmark of Pyrrho's life-style and the source of his *ataraxia*, he had named it as the Pyrrhonist's goal (*telos*). Sextus, on the other hand, makes *ataraxia* the goal and *epochē* the means to it. A small difference, but a crucial one. A man's *telos* is the ultimate focus of all his desires and intentions, and there is a world of difference between aiming from the outset for *epochē*, which only a skeptic would contemplate doing, and aiming for so nonsectarian a goal as freedom from disquiet.

The former option might be *stated* undogmatically as a description of the way things appear ("Up to now *epochē* has appeared to us the ultimate end to aim for"),[71] but it is hard to see how it could be *defended* undogmatically—without, that is, appealing to some further doctrine or doctrines about what sort of thing should be aimed for. The latter option scarcely needs defense, since the Skeptic supposes freedom from disquiet to be already a common, nonpartisan philosophical goal. As Sextus puts it, if clever men in the past have sought knowledge, it has been in the hope of freedom from the disquiet which they have felt at the contradictory nature of the world.[72] The Skeptic has up to now been motivated by just the same goal of *ataraxia*, but has got there by a different route. He too starts out by searching for the truth, but once he has discovered that there are equally strong arguments on either side of any dispute, he gives up and suspends belief; whereupon it dawns on him that, as luck would have it, he now *is* free from disquiet.[73] This story has considerable evangelical force, yet it can be stated as a mere description of appearances without any doctrinaire claim that things will necessarily continue to appear so or that the state achieved is objectively good.

It may seem that while on the explanation of "Inquirer" discussed earlier the Skeptic is a lifelong inquirer, since he always remains openminded,[74] on the story just told his inquiry is a pre-Skeptic phase, succeeded by the *epochē* which alone distinguishes him from the dogmatists.[75] However, the two explanations coalesce satisfactorily if we take it that what eventually leads the Skeptic to *epochē* is precisely the fact that he alone has conducted his inquiry in an open-minded way, without putting it at the service of this or that doctrine. Nor is it really likely that the onset of *epochē* signals the cessation of inquiry: resistance to the snares of doctrine must involve lifelong open-minded investigation and reinvestigation of doctrinaire arguments.

"Inquirers," then, emerges as a title chosen by the successors of Aenesidemus in the second century A.D. in order to shift the emphasis from the "Pyrrhonian" goal of suspension of belief to the "Skeptical" method which serves that goal. Aenesidemus's Pyrrhonism, his unequivocal recommendation of the *epochē* ideal that Pyrrho had embodied, had been a practical expedient in the formative years of a skeptical school. The parallel with Arcesilaus is unmistakable. Later Skeptics will have felt uncomfortable about it because of their growing independence of Pyrrho's example coupled with their sensitivity to the charge that they themselves were governed by an ethical doctrine. Nor is the latter consideration a merely diplomatic one, for in advance commitment to a partisan ideal they would see a genuine threat to their own skeptical equanimity. Doctrinaire ethics, according to Sextus, creates disquiet because by setting up objective goods it foments in us an intense feeling of deprivation when we do not have them and a terror of losing them when we do.[76] If the Skeptic is to escape the penalties of this dogmatist failing, then he had better simply get on with the job by pursuing the method of noncommittal inquiry, "Skepticism" in its true sense, instead of striving from the start to emulate Pyrrho. Withholding belief, like learning to walk a tightrope, is easier when you do not try too hard.

NOTES

1. Although this article represents by and large my own views, I have learned a lot about Greek skepticism from the conversation and writings (both published and unpublished) of Myles Burnyeat and Tony Long. I am also grateful to both, and to David Glidden and Malcolm Schofield, for their criticisms of an earlier draft.

2. Plato, *Meno* 84a-c, echoing 79e-80a.

3. See Couissin, "L'origine et l'évolution de l'*epochē*," *Revue des études grecques* 42 (1929), 373-397, for a plausible, though not watertight, defense of Arcesilaus's precedence over Pyrrho and Timon in the use of "*epochē*."

4. Cic. *Acad.* I 45; *De or.* III 80; *Fin.* II 2, V 10.

5. For assertions of Arcesilaus's positive commitment to *epochē* see note 17 below.

6. Cf. Lucretius IV 472; and M. F. Burnyeat, "The Upside-Down Back-to-Front Sceptic of Lucretius IV 472," *Philologus* 122 (1978), 197-206, for its significance and Epicurean origin.

7. Cic. *Acad.* I 45.

8. DL IX 76.

9. See M. F. Burnyeat, "Protagoras and Self-refutation in Later Greek Philosophy," *Philosophical Review* 85 (1976), 44-69.

10. SE *M* VII 155.

11. These are the "reasonable" (*eulogon*), SE *M* VII 158; and the possibility of bypassing assent, Plutarch, *Col.* 1122b-d.

12. As admirably demonstrated by Gisela Striker, "Sceptical Strategies," in *Doubt and Dogmatism*, ed. M. Schofield, M. Burnyeat, and J. Barnes (Oxford, 1980), pp. 54-83.

13. Cic. *Acad.* II 77. Cf. ibid. I 44-45 (a passage which reads rather like a précis of II 72-77), where Arcesilaus is said to defend his skepticism by appeal to the rashness and shamefulness of fallible belief. Also SE *M* VII 157; Augustine, *C. Acad.* II 5.11.

14. Cf. Couissin, "L'origine et l'évolution de l'*epochē*."

15. SE *PH* I 232-233.

16. Strictly speaking, Sextus makes the ethical goal *ataraxia*, and *epochē* purely instrumental (see below), but for present purposes he is prepared to overlook the difference, since, as he says at *PH* I 23, the former follows the latter "like a shadow."

17. Cic. *Acad.* I 45; II 59, 77-78; Numenius ap. Euseb. *Praep. ev.* XIV 4.15, 7.14; SE *PH* I 232; Augustine, *C. Acad.* II 5.11.

18. 70 B 1 Diels-Kranz = Euseb. *Praep. ev.* XIV 19.9; SE *M* VII 88; Cic. *Acad.* II 73.

19. Cf. Cic. *Acad.* I 45 for Arcesilaus; ibid. II 28 for Carneades.

20. Aristocles ap. Euseb. *Praep. ev.* XIV 18.3. The world possesses these characteristics "in its own nature" because Timon reports them as Pyrrho's answer to the question "What are things like by nature?"

21. Timon, *Silloi*, fr. 48 Diels, *Poetae Philosophi Graeci* (Berlin, 1901) = DL IX 64.

22. DL IX 64; cf. D. N. Sedley, "Epicurus and His Professional Rivals," in *Etudes sur l'Epicurisme antique*, ed. J. Bollack and A. Laks, *Cahiers de philologie* 1 (1976), 136-137. For Indian influences on Pyrrho, see now Everard Flintoff, "Pyrrho and India," *Phronesis* 25 (1980), 88-108.

23. D. N. Sedley, "Diodorus Cronus and Hellenistic Philosophy," *Proceedings of the Cambridge Philological Society* 203 (1977), 74-120. For Timon's lines see frr. 31-32 Diels = DL IV 33, and A. A. Long, "Timon of Phlius: Pyrrhonist and Satirist," *Proceedings of the Cambridge Philological Society* 204 (1978), 68-91.

24. SE *PH* I 234; Numenius ap. Euseb. *Praep. ev.* XIV 5.13.

25. Plutarch, *Col.* 1121f-1122a.

26. In Diogenes Laertius's life of Plato his first three teachers are Socrates, the Heraclitean Cratylus, and the Parmenidean Hermogenes (DL III 6). The first is certainly correct, and the second probably has some truth in it (cf. Aristotle, *Met.* A, 987a32-b1). The third is unlikely, but no reader of Plato's later dialogues can doubt Parmenides' influence. A full list should have mentioned the Pythagoreans, but there was no way that they could be represented as skeptics. (For a similar interpretation of the Plutarch evidence, see now J. Glucker, "Antiochus and the Late Academy," *Hypomnemata* 56 [1978], 36.)

27. I owe to A. A. Long the interesting suggestion that Colotes, in the work attacked by Plutarch in *Adversus Colotem*, derived his entire list of skeptically inclined philosophers from Arcesilaus. As Long points out, there is a remarkably close correspondence between Colotes' list and those given on behalf of the New Academy by Cicero (*Acad.* I 44-46; II 14, 72-76). I agree that a common source looks likely, but my reasons for hesitating to identify it as Arcesilaus is that Colotes seems to have followed Epicurus in accusing Arcesilaus of feigning originality for his doctrines (Plutarch, *Col.* 1121f-1122a)—a transparently dishonest charge if Colotes was in that very same work drawing on Arcesilaus's appeals to philosophical precedent.

28. Cf. Cic. *Acad.* II 15; *De or.* III 67.

29. Arcesilaus's cold-shouldering of Pyrrho clearly became an Academic orthodoxy. Cicero's *Academica,* whose main Academic sources are Clitomachus and Philo, maintains a studied silence about him, omitting him altogether from its lists of skeptically inclined philosophers (I 44-46; II 14, 72-76), and mentioning him only in a list of outmoded ethical dogmatists (II 129). The irony is that Pyrrho was by this date the figurehead of a breakaway movement of hardline skeptics which rapidly eclipsed the New Academy (see below).

30. Cic. *Rep.* III 8; Lactantius, *Inst. div.* V 14.3-5; *Epitome* 50 [55] 5-8.

31. Cic. *Acad.* II 78, 139; *Fin.* V 20.

32. Cic. *Acad.* II 139. Carneades himself considered Clitomachus to be true to his own teachings: Cic. *Or.* 51.

33. Cic. *Acad.* II 108.

34. Cic. *Ad Att.* XIII 21.

35. Stob. *Ecl.* II 2.20.

36. Cic. *Acad.* II 108.

37. Against the conventional translation "probable" see M. F. Burnyeat, "Carneades Was No Probabilist," in *Riverside Studies in Ancient Skepticism*, ed. D. K. Glidden (forthcoming).

38. Cic. *Acad.* II 104. Sextus Empiricus's version does involve assent (*M* VII 188), no doubt because its immediate source is Antiochus (see, e.g., Burnyeat, "Carneades Was No Probabilist"), who had studied in the Academy at a time when *epochē* had been superseded by a doctrine of provisional assent (see below, esp. note 52).

39. SE *PH* I 226-232.

40. Cicero in the *Academica* does treat the *pithanon* as the Academics' own criterion of conduct (see especially II 32, referring to the Academic positions set out in the lost Book I of the *Academica priora*), as indeed it was under Philo of Larissa, his teacher. But it is instructive to see what a mess he gets into in II 98-105 when he tries to establish Carneadean authority for this position. Admitting at the outset that his claim will be disputed, he cites two texts of Clitomachus in its support. The first (99) summarizes Carneades' analysis of the *pithanē phantasia*; but the crucial comments about its value as a bona fide criterion in the conduct of life (from "etenim contra naturam . . .") are not part of the quotation. The second (103-104) may possibly be speaking of the *pithanon* as a criterion actually accepted by the Academy (for well-founded doubts about this, see Burnyeat, "Carneades Was No Probabilist"), but even if that is so, there is this time no attribution to Carneades himself, only to the "Academics."

41. P. Couissin, "Le stoïcisme de la Nouvelle Académie," *Revue d'hist. de la philos.* 3 (1929), 241-276, an English translation of which appears as chap. 2 of this anthology; M. dal Pra, *Lo scetticismo greco*, 2d ed. (Rome, 1975), pp. 270-281; M. F. Burnyeat, "Carneades Was No Probabilist."

42. I cannot here do justice to Burnyeat's illuminating and penetrating investigation. My doubts about his thesis rest mainly on my feeling that the *pithanon* doctrine is too good an epistemological theory in its own right to have been devised as a mere leg-pull.

43. G. Striker, "Sceptical Strategies."

44. SE *M* VII 159-189.

45. Sextus's source, apparently Antiochus (see note 38 above), naturally puts his own gloss on Carneades' motivation: after first denying the existence of any absolute criterion, Carneades was "virtually compelled" by practical needs to offer some sort of criterion on his own account for the conduct of life (*M* VII 166; cf. Cic. *Acad.* II 34, also from Antiochus, "convicio veritatis coacti"). But the rest of *M* VII 159-189 can stand as a reasonably accurate report of Carneades' argu-

ments (with the probable exception of 179, which both the elaborate medical example and the reference to "the Academic," whom Carneades would not have brought into the argument in this way, suggest to be Sextus's own padding).

46. Gisela Striker's comment ("Sceptical Strategies," p. 69) that in respect of *epochē* Arcesilaus is "unanimously" described as having been more strict than Carneades seems to me an overstatement. Cicero (*Acad.* II 59) says that this would be so according to the claim of "some" that Carneades allowed provisional assent. These "some" are Metrodorus and Philo (whose interpretation plainly lies behind Euseb. *Praep. ev.* XIV 7.14 as well; cf. Cic. *Acad.* II 32, from a passage attacking Philo's Academy [note 49 below]), and their mistake was readily pointed out by Clitomachus (*Acad.* II 78, cf. 67). I see no sign that Clitomachus ever questioned Carneades' complete commitment to *epochē*.

47. Cf. Cic. *Fin.* V 6, where even as late as 79 B.C. to attend New Academy lectures is to "hear about Carneades."

48. Cic. *Acad.* II 16, 78; *De or.* 45; Augustine, *C. Acad.* III 41; *Index Acad. Herc.* col. 26 (Mekler).

49. *"Enargēs"* (= Latin *perspicuum*), "obvious" or "self-evident," was for the Stoics, followed by Carneades and Clitomachus (Cic. *Acad.* II 99), an epithet restricted to the cognitive impression. But the Academics attacked by Antiochus (as represented by Lucullus at *Acad.* II 34) divorce the "self-evident" from the "cognitive"—presumably by overinterpretation of purely dialectical moves like those attributed to Carneades at SE *M* VII 160-164, 402-403. The innovation must be Philo's, since Antiochus is attacking the version of skepticism that he himself had espoused while Philo's pupil (cf. his inclusion of Philo at II 17 as an orthodox New Academic; the exclusion of Philo from his main attack, announced at II 12 fin., refers only to the heretical doctrine of 87 B.C., cf. II 18).

50. Cic. *Acad.* II 59, 78, 148: a clumsy extraction of a positive doctrine from one of Carneades' anti-Stoic gambits, see ibid. 67.

51. Stobaeus, *Ecl.* II 6.2.40.

52. Despite numerous mentions of *epochē* in Cicero's *Academica*, it was not, I think, an ideal of Philo's Academy. It occurs mainly in connection with Arcesilaus, Carneades, and Clitomachus (I 45; II 59, 67, 78, 98, 104, 108). In the lost *Acad. pr.* I Catulus, almost certainly representing the orthodox Philonian Academy (see Glucker, "Antiochus and the Late Academy," pp. 417-418), defended qualified assent as the proper Carneadean doctrine (*Acad.* II 59, 148, cf. 78). Lucullus, reporting Antiochus's attack on the Philonian Academy (see note 49 above), focuses almost entirely on the question of certainty; he allots only one short section to assent (II 37-39), and even there he avoids any outright assertion that his current opponents advocate its suspension. Cicero in his reply does advocate *epochē*, but only in the parts where his source seems to be Clitomachus (II 64-68, 72-109), and not in the two unmistakably Philonian sections (II 69-71, 109-146; for these attributions, see my "The End of the Academy," *Phronesis* 26 [1981], 67-75, n. 1). And he says explicitly at II 78 that the Academy of his own day maintains the impossibility of cognition but not, any longer, *epochē*.

53. DL IX 115-116.

54. DL IX 62, 106.

55. Photius, *Bibl.* 212, 169b26-27.

56. DL IX 107; cf. SE *PH* I 30. In his *Pyrrhonian Arguments*, Book VIII, he argued that there is no *telos* (Photius, *Bibl.* 212. 170b30-35); but no doubt his assignment of that status to *epochē* would be a description of the way things appear to the skeptics, not a truth claim (cf. SE *PH* I 232-233).

57. Cf. SE *PH* I 25, *M* XI 118 (comparing *PH* I 13, 19) for the scope of *doxa*, and *PH* I 23 for the life without *doxa*. Michael Frede's "Des Skeptikers Meinungen," *Neue Heft für Philosophie* 15/16 (1979), 102-129, now offers a powerful challenge to a central assumption of my paper, that the Skeptical life is one without beliefs. In defense of that orthodoxy I can hardly do better than refer to Burnyeat's paper, "Can the Skeptic Live His Skepticism?" (chapter 6 of this anthology). For my own part I shall merely explain how I understand the text that Frede himself considers crucial to any interpretation, SE *PH* I 13. This is Sextus's definitive statement, not on the question whether the Skeptic holds beliefs, but on the question whether he holds *dogmata*, which as a term in Hellenistic philosophy always means theoretical tenets, doctrines, or principles (see note 67 below; the question is a serious one for a skeptic, because Philo's Academy had considered skepticism itself a *dogma*, Cic. *Acad.* II 29, 109). Before answering "No," Sextus notes a broader, nontechnical sense of *"dogma"* (literally "seeming," from *"dokein," "to seem"*), which some define as "acceptance (*eudokein*) of something"; and he allows that in that sense the Skeptic does have some *dogmata*, to the extent that when he gets hot he does not deny that he seems (*dokein*) to be getting hot. That remark is a brief aside, and one not very carefully thought out in that it leaves it unclear whether we are to connect *"dogma"* etymologically with the word for "acceptance" (picked up by "does not deny") or with that for "seems." The point is only fully explained—and in explicit resumption of the earlier remark—in its proper context at *PH* I 19-20, to which we should therefore turn for enlightenment. Here it emerges that when the Skeptic assents to an "appearance" (*phainomenon*) he is conceding only the fact of the appearance itself ("that it appears, we grant") and explicitly excluding the statement (*ho legetai, legomenon, logos*) which interprets the appearance—e.g., the statement that the honey which appears sweet *is* sweet.

58. SE *PH* I 7.

59. The only traces of interest in Pyrrho as an individual are *PH* I 7; *M* I 272, 281-282 (where he is no more exemplary than Epicurus!), XI 1 and 141 (not named, but the verses quoted from Timon are about him). Even if Sextus may have spoken more about Pyrrho in a lost work (cf. *M* I 282), the silence about him in *PH* I, the skeptic manifesto, cannot be other than surprising.

60. Philodemus (*Rhet.* I 191.4 Sudhaus) says that everybody conceives of philosophers as being "the most unerring and inquiring (*skeptikōtatous*)" of men—comically inappropriate if the adjective had by then (c. 80 B.C.) gained any inkling of its modern sense. Timon fr. 55 Diels, sometimes cited, is not direct quotation, and I doubt whether Timon would have welcomed the label (cf. frr. 48, 59).

61. Later references to Aenesidemus as a "Skeptic" (e.g., SE *PH* I 36), and indirect quotations (e.g., DL IX 107; SE *PH* I 210), carry little weight, since the

word became a standard doublet for "Pyrrhonist." Photius's extended summary of Aenesidemus's *Pyrrhonian Arguments* (*Bibl.* 212) uses "Pyrrhonist" throughout, and Philo of Alexandria (c. 35 B.C. to A.D. 40), who was certainly familiar with Aenesidemus's ten Tropes, uses "*skeptikoi*" of philosophers in general (interchangeably with "*dogmatikoi*"!): see K. Janáček, "Das Wort *Skeptikos* in Philons Schriften," *Listy Filologicke* 101 (1979), 65-68; G. Striker, "Sceptical Strategies," p. 54, n. 1. However, its application to the Pyrrhonists was perhaps just beginning to surface in Philo's day: it is probably included in a group of relatively unfamiliar-looking titles for the school at Philo, *Quaestiones et solutiones in Genesin* III 33, extant only in Armenian (see R. Marcus, Loeb ed. supp. 1, *ad loc.*).

62. Theodosius ap. DL IX 70; Lucian, *Vit. auct.* 27; Gellius, *NA* XI 5. Gellius's source here, almost certainly Favorinus (c. A.D. 80-160), apparently used "Skeptics" as a title for the Pyrrhonist school (*appellantur*, XI 5.1), but was prepared to describe even the Academics as "Skeptics" (*dicuntur*, XI 5.6). *Scepticus* does not occur in Latin, despite Lewis and Short, who falsely cite it from Quintilian X 1.124.

63. DL IX 70.

64. I translate "the movement of the mind, so far as concerns another person, is inaccessible" in preference to Hicks's "the movement of the mind in either direction...." I am not sure whether to take "*to*" with "*kinēma*" (so, presumably, A. Russo, *Scettici antichi* [Turin, 1978], p. 69, "il movimento del pensiero concepito da un altro"), or just with "*kath' heteron*" as a unitary phrase meaning "so far as concerns another person" on the lines of the familiar "*to kat' eme*" (cf. Plato, *Phlb.* 17c1; Kühner-Gerth I, 479).

65. Strictly speaking, of course, having no doctrine (*dogma*, see note 67 below) is a prerequisite of, not a bar to, being a skeptic; but "*dogma*" here is being used of philosophical teaching in a sense broad enough to embrace skepticism itself (cf. DL IX 69; Cic. *Acad.* II 29, 109; Plutarch, *Col.* 1122a). Pyrrho did not have a philosophy at all, Theodosius means.

66. The only Hellenistic precedents for arguing both sides of the case in order to find out which is true, or "truer," seem to belong to the semidogmatist post-Carneadean Academy, being, for example, the basis of Cicero's methodology (e.g., *ND* I 11, III 95; cf. Galen, *De opt. doctr.* c. 1, p. 41 K.). The "truth" which Arcesilaus sought, according to Cicero (*Acad.* II 76), turns out to be merely that of the *epochē* theory. Cicero (*ND* I 4) may appear to attribute a desire to find the truth to Carneades, but the subordinate clause ("ut excitaret," etc.) is probably consecutive, not final.

67. I must here dissent from Myles Burnyeat's view (expressed in n. 50 of "Can the Skeptic Live His Skepticism?") that *dogma* (Latin *decretum*) is merely "belief" in the broadest sense. It seems to have that meaning in Plato and early Aristotle, but thereafter its philosophical usage is confined exclusively to principles, theories, or doctrines (e.g., Aristotle, *Phys.* 209b15 on Plato's "unwritten *dogmata*," and innumerable Hellenistic instances), and it is defined accordingly (Seneca, *Ep. mor.* 94.31; SE *PH* I 13, 17, 147).

68. E.g., *PH* I 2-3.

69. Cf. ibid. 200.
70. Ibid. 204-205.
71. Cf. note 56 above.
72. SE *PH* I 12. Cf. ibid. 210-211: a Skeptic is not dogmatizing when he employs as a premise a concept common to all other philosophers and to mankind in general.
73. Ibid. 25-30.
74. Cf. DL IX 70: they are named "Skeptics" because they are always searching and never finding.
75. Cf. SE *PH* I 7: *epochē* comes after the inquiry.
76. Ibid. 27-28; *M* XI 141-167.

3

The Stoicism of the New Academy*

Pierre Couissin

The recent translation of Mr. Edwyn Bevan's work, *Stoics and Sceptics*,[1] has once again attracted public attention in France to the conflict between the Stoa and the Academy. At the same time, a monograph by Herr Helfried Hartmann[2] has appeared in Germany, dealing with this same struggle and underlining the extent to which the two schools influenced each other. I have already discussed these works;[3] their publication is an indication of the growing importance, in studies of the New Academy, of the connection between its teachings and the teachings of the Stoa. Since antiquity, people have been struck by the manner in which the Academics singled out the Stoics for attack. On the whole, this has been seen as a kind of unspoken homage to Stoicism, taken to be the most perfect dogmatism and so representing, in the eyes of the skeptics, dogmatism *par excellence*. Where the New Academy is concerned, however, we must examine the problem more closely, in the hope of shedding fresh light on certain of the theses maintained by Arcesilaus and Carneades. The New Academics are not only opponents of the Stoics, but, if we can believe Aenesidemus,[4] they themselves seem just like Stoics; this description applies above all to Aenesidemus's contemporaries (*malista tēs nun*), but also to the whole Academy after Arcesilaus. Determined to be a pure skeptic and to claim this purity for Pyrrhonism alone, Aenesidemus lan-

*"Le Stoïcisme de la Nouvelle Académie," *Revue d'histoire de la philosophie* 3 (1929), 241-276. Translated by Jennifer Barnes and M. F. Burnyeat.

guidly dismisses the discussions between Stoics which, according to him, is all the Academics' teaching amounts to. Of course, we shouldn't take too literally this remark from a turncoat attempting to decry those rivals whom, for all that, the Pyrrhonians did not scruple to ransack. It may be, however, that insufficient attention has been paid until now to the relative character of the doctrines maintained by the Academics. Too often, people have attributed to them, as doctrines they actually held, remarks or arguments that were really no more than polemic. For in the war they waged against the Stoa, not content to attack the conclusions of their adversary, they opposed him with other conclusions that were themselves derived from Stoic principles:"They sometimes concur with Stoic opinions," says Aenesidemus (*ibid.*). In this sense, they might well seem to be Stoics: they are posing as Stoics in order to confound Stoicism. It is not that they invented or taught on their own account a theory of knowledge or of action; rather, they borrowed from their opponents the material for their counterattacks. This is the interpretation I propose of what might be called the skeptic Stoicism of the New Academy. I shall not be concerned to criticize alternative explanations, differing from my own, which have been advanced by historians of ancient skepticism, nor to repeat what is generally known of the Academic theses; that would exceed the limits of an article. I simply want to stress the Stoic elements in these theses and to try to grasp their meaning, staying as close as possible to the texts that have come down to us.

I. ARCESILAUS

1. Akatalēpsia. It is indisputable, and often attested, that Arcesilaus's critique was directed, historically speaking, against Zeno's teaching, and that it consisted of a refutation of the Stoic theory of knowledge.[5] Its sole purpose was to demonstrate that knowledge, as the Stoics conceived it, apprehension (*katalēpsis*), which is their criterion of truth, does not exist. The criticism is derived from definitions and principles laid down by the Stoics, and works only for them, as if it were aimed at them alone. Sextus (*M* VII 153-155) has preserved for us a summary comprising three arguments. The first argument is founded on the relations Zeno established between opinion, knowledge, and apprehension.[6] Arcesilaus labors to prove that between knowledge, limited to the Sage, and opinion, limited to the fool, there is no room for any intermediate reality, and that apprehension as an intermediate between the two is only a word. The other two arguments draw the same conclusion from the Stoic definition of apprehension: assent to an apprehensive presentation. (1) Assent is not given to a presentation but to a proposition (second argument); (2) there is no such thing as an apprehensive presentation (third argument). The third argument presupposes much discussion: it asserts that an apprehensive presentation that fits Zeno's definition is not to be found (*heurisketai*). Arcesilaus's method is purely dialectical: granted that an apprehensive presentation is such that it could not be false, he defies the Stoics to produce one single incontestable example. In the second argument, he seems to be appealing to a theory of his own—namely, that assent is only given to a proposition. We are ill informed about Zeno's conception of assent, but Chrysippus's is more familiar to us; it might have been identical to Zeno's or implicit in it. Now, for him, a proposition is what is true or false;[7] consequently, accurately speaking, it isn't the presentation that is true, but the proposition, and we only give our assent to the proposition.[8] Arcesilaus could therefore have deduced this last formula from a Stoic dogma put out in his time; or it might even have been expressly maintained by Zeno or Cleanthes. At any rate, it is not unique to him, since we find it reported by Stobaeus:[9] we assent, he writes, to a proposition, and our impulse relates to the predicate contained in the proposition to which we assent.

2. *Epochē*. But the real problem is the supposed "positive" or "constructive" part of Arcesilaus's philosophy. If one goes by what Sextus says (*PH* I 232), his acknowledged end was *epochē*, the suspension of judgment; he even (ibid. 233) held individual acts of suspending judgment to be good and individual acts of assent to be bad. On this point, Sextus contrasts him with the Pyrrhonists, for whom *epochē* is only a means, the end being *ataraxia*.[10] It would perhaps be more skeptical not to propose any end;[11] still, once accept the need for an end and one can conceive tranquillity playing the role, whereas it is very odd that *epochē* should be thought desirable in itself, independently of the tranquillity that accompanies it as its shadow. Is it likely that a man with the critical acuity of Arcesilaus should have perpetrated such a crass error[12] and that his contemporary opponents failed to jump on it? Sextus, it is true, is precise, and his evidence seems to be confirmed by that of Cicero (*Fin.* III 31), and Clement of Alexandria (*Strom.* II 21, p. 129, 8 Stählin). But Cicero and Clement must have drawn on the same source;[13] Clement speaks of "safe suspension of belief in the face of presentations" (*tēn asphalē pros tas phantasias epochēn*), where Cicero writes *obsistere visis assensusque suos firme sustinere*. Both of them use a guarded manner of expression (*quidam Academici... dicuntur*, "certain Academics are said..."; *axiousi tines*, "some people hold"), and neither names Arcesilaus. Now if we examine closely the argument on which Arcesilaus founds *epochē*, as it is reported by Cicero and Sextus, we will see that it is

only valid against the Stoics.[14] It is a demonstration of how incapable
Stoicism is of grounding assent: if we work from Stoic principles, we end
up with universal suspension of belief. In Cicero's version,[15] the argument is Stoic in form: if ever the Sage assents to something, he will also at
some time have an opinion: now, he will never have an opinion, therefore he will not assent to anything. This Stoic form, clearly indicated by
the conditional that forms its major premise, is apparent also from Chrysippus's having assigned this type of argument to the second class of
indemonstrables.[16] On the other hand, Sextus's report (*M* VII 155-157)
carries on almost every line an explicit indication that this critique is
leveled solely against Stoicism: "Everything being inapprehensible *in
consequence of the nonexistence of the Stoic criterion (dia tēn anuparxian
tou Stoikou kritēriou)*, if the Sage assents, the Sage will have an opinion." When Arcesilaus says "the Sage," he is therefore not referring to a
Sage of the Academy, to whom he might attribute suspension of belief as
his end; for what difference would the nonexistence of the Stoic criterion
make to *him*? Arcesilaus claims to prove that the *Stoic* Sage, demigod of
the founders of the Stoa, is driven either to error or to suspension; which
is to say, to suspension, since the Sage is by definition infallible. And
Arcesilaus proves the major premise of his argument by working from
Stoic definitions: "Since nothing," he says, "is in fact apprehensible, if
the Sage assents to anything, he will assent to something inapprehensible; but to assent to what is inapprehensible is to have an opinion."
This definition of opinion is Stoic.[17] The minor premise is also established by this method: the Sage has no opinion, for that, according to
them (*kat' autous*), would be a cause of unreason and error. The testimony of the Stoics is adduced as the only argument, and the result is that
the Sage has to withhold his assent (*asunkatathetein*) on everything—in
other words, suspend belief (*epechein*). And the author concludes in the
future tense: "So the Sage will suspend judgment on everything." It is
plain from the above that this cannot mean, as Sextus claims in the *Outlines* (where he tries to contrast Arcesilaus with the Pyrrhonists, perhaps
influenced by Aenesidemus),[18] that Arcesilaus thinks *epochē* is an end
and teaches it as such to his disciples, but that the *Stoic* Sage, faithful to
Stoic principles, will end up in *epochē*. It is a *reductio ad absurdum* of the
Stoic theory of knowledge. Besides, before setting out this argument (*M*
VII 155), Arcesilaus states it thus: "Everything being inapprehensible, the
result will be that, *even according to the Stoics*, the Sage suspends judgment." We cannot therefore properly conclude from this passage that
Arcesilaus has, *in propria persona*, upheld and professed *epochē*; he has
shown that it is the end result of Stoic doctrine. What Sextus says (*PH* I
233-234) is mere chicanery: it is not *pros tēn phusin* ("by reference to

nature") that Arcesilaus has dubbed *epochē* a good and assent an evil, it is *pros tēn Stoan* ("by reference to the Stoa"). But at all costs he had to be dissociated from the Pyrrhonists, although Sextus himself (ibid. 232) recognizes that he appears to profess exactly the same theses.

Did Arcesilaus invent *epochē*? Diogenes Laertius (IV 28) says so, but perhaps this should be taken to mean that he was the first *in the Academy* to suspend judgment. Besides, Diogenes elsewhere echoes another tradition, which credits Pyrrho with the introduction of *epochē*.[19] In any case, Arcesilaus's *epochē* fits in well with Stoic philosophy and presupposes a voluntarist theory of assent. Suspension means to suspend assent. For the Stoics, some presentations are true and others are false, but among the true ones, some bear the incontrovertible mark of their truthfulness; these are the apprehensive presentations. If the Sage will give his assent to these and these alone, he will never be mistaken; but when confronted with an inapprehensive presentation, he withholds his assent.[20] If no presentation were apprehensive, he would obviously have to withhold assent from everything; it is to this *epochē peri pantōn* that Arcesilaus is guiding them. Now *epochē* would be unacceptable to people who thought that presentations are imposed on the mind with no possibility of resistance. It would scarcely be admissible in the *Canonic* of Epicurus, who accepts that all presentations are true and that only an opinion added to them (*prosdoxazomenōi*) can be false.[21] The radical remedy against error is then to cling fast to the phenomena without appending any opinion: such is the Pyrrhonian solution;[22] it is only by an abuse of language that it is called *epochē*. Or if you like, it isn't the same *epochē*; the Pyrronian *epochē* is the mental attitude that neither assents nor denies:[23] it is doubt. The Academic *epochē* is the withholding of assent, not only according to Arcesilaus, who identifies *epochē* with nonassent,[24] but also according to Carneades, whose disciple Clitomachus wrote a work on *epochē* in four books, which Cicero (*Acad.* II 98) quotes under the title *De sustinendis adsensionibus*. When an Academic says "the Sage suspends" (*epechei ho sophos*), we must understand "assent" (*tēn sunkatathesin*). *Epochē* is only meaningful in a theory of knowledge where knowledge includes not only presentation, a passive state, but the free and voluntary act of assent. The Sage can only withhold his assent if it depends on him to give it or not; and this is exactly the Stoics' idea. They were the first to maintain this, and it is one of the points on which, according to Antiochus of Ascalon,[25] Zeno diverged from earlier philosophers, notably the Old Academy: "To presentations he adds assent of the mind, which he affirms to be voluntary and dependent on us."

3. *The eulogon.* But perhaps you will say that the "constructive part" of Arcesilaus's philosophy is not *epochē* but the *eulogon*. Very well; but

it should be pointed out that if we allow that for him the end is *epochē*, *epochē* belongs to this "constructive part." Besides, the important thing here is that the *eulogon* is a consequence of *epochē* and cannot exist without it. "After this (*sc.* after having shown that the Sage suspends belief on everything) it was also necessary," reports Sextus (*M* VII 158), "to investigate (*zētein*) the conduct of life." So for Arcesilaus it was a question of investigation, and not of teaching a doctrine already discovered. When Sextus adds that the conduct of life is not the sort of thing that you can give an account of without a criterion, on which depends the belief which happiness—that is, the end of life—requires,[26] he is plainly reproducing ideas not of Arcesilaus but of a Stoic opponent, which Arcesilaus may perhaps have adopted dialectically for the sake of argument. We have already seen that elsewhere (*PH* I 232) Sextus claims that for Arcesilaus the end was not happiness but *epochē*; and we also know that he spurned all belief (ibid.) or persuasion (Numen. *ap.* Euseb. *Praep. ev.* XIV 6.5). Sextus's text itself shows that this is so since, having delivered himself of this sentence, he adds: "Arcesilaus says that . . . ." So it is only under pressure from his opponents that Arcesilaus states his doctrine of the *eulogon*, because he cannot wriggle out of explaining just how the Sage can be happy; this presupposes that happiness requires belief and is in no way consistent with universal suspension of judgment. Stoic principles led him to *epochē* and will lead him also to the *eulogon*. It is again from Stoicism that he borrowed his "practical criterion:" for the Stoics, that proposition is *eulogon* which one has more reason to think true than false.[27] For example, "I shall be alive tomorrow": I have no reason to think that I shan't be alive tomorrow, but the supposition is not absurd. We may presume that I shall be alive tomorrow, it is plausible, indeed probable; the reasons I have for considering this proposition true are stronger than those which would make me think it false; but it is in no way evident. For the needs of his dialectic Arcesilaus allows, with Zeno, that the Sage must, above all, avoid error (Cic. *Acad.* II 66): but the only way for this sage to achieve that is by withholding his assent on every matter. Forced by the nonexistence of the Stoic criterion to abandon certainty, he is reduced to regulating his conduct by mere presumptions. Reading between the lines of his argument, we sense a biting irony that will reduce the Sage to a mere mortal, a man like everyone else, lacking a talisman by which to know what others don't know, and so like them forced to weigh the pros and cons and to choose—though without assent —the most likely possibility and its attendant risks.

This method of Arcesilaus's is even more apparent in his idea of the *katorthōma*. He introduces it by the following sorites: "Happiness is achieved by prudence: prudence is found in right actions (*katorthōmata*):

a right action is one that, once performed, has a probable justification"
(Sextus, *M* VII 158). It is impossible that a skeptic as radical as Arcesilaus, whom Sextus considers to be at bottom a straight Pyrrhonist,
should have upheld on his own account these three dogmatic assertions.
In reality his reasoning is an argument *ad hominem*, formed from Stoic
propositions. The first proposition might seem Epicurean, if several texts
in Plutarch (*SVF* I 200-201) did not suggest a Stoic interpretation. Zeno,
says Plutarch, distinguishes several virtues as Plato does; but when it
comes to defining them, he inserts the word "prudence" into the definition of each one; the result is that in the end there is only one virtue (*hōs
mian ousan aretēn*), prudence. Certainly Zeno never said that every virtue comes down to prudence in the end. On the contrary, he asserts that
the virtues are many, and on this point he is supported by Chrysippus.
But his definitions of virtues imply the contrary doctrine, and so he
appears (*eoike*) to be agreeing with his disciple Ariston of Chios, who
claimed that virtue, in its essence, is one. Plainly, Zeno has tripped up
here, much to Arcesilaus's advantage. Certain later apologists attempted
to explain that when Zeno says "prudence" in his definitions, he really
meant "knowledge," thus equating his definitions with those formulated
by Chrysippus. But Ariston, Arcesilaus's contemporary and great opponent, blithely reduced all virtues to just one, which he called health,
while his disciple Apollophanes (Athenaeus VII 281d), who lived probably at the time of Lacydes, considered prudence the only virtue (DL VII
92). Arcesilaus allowed himself a deduction that the Stoics did not forbid; and if Zeno implicitly equates "virtue" and "prudence," his theory
"that virtue is sufficient for happiness" (*SVF* I 186-189) might just as well
be put: "prudence is sufficient for happiness"; whence the corollary,
almost identical: "Happiness is achieved by prudence."[28] It is true that
happiness is not an end, but an additional benefit. Nonetheless, we must
not forget that we now possess no more than Sextus's skeletal account of
this discussion on the *eulogon.* This three-sentence argument implies
fuller treatments, of which there may well be a distant echo in Plutarch.
Arcesilaus wanted to humble the Stoic sage, to show that in the end he
was not superior to the ordinary man or the Epicurean, who strives in all
modesty to find a happy life through prudence. For the Stoics are perfectly willing to discuss this additional benefit; they impart the news that
"the much-vaunted prudence of which they dream" is identical with a
happiness which is as great in the Sage as in the gods.[29] What's new in all
this? What need is there for wisdom based on understanding if prudence
is enough and if it is attainable by those who practice universal suspension of judgment?

An act accomplished by virtue is a right action, a *katorthōma.*[30] If we admit that prudence is the only virtue, a *katorthōma* is an act accomplished by prudence. Prudence is not distinct from the law that instructs us to act with rectitude: *recte facere* = *katorthoun* (Cic. *Leg.* I 18: cf. Chrysippus, *De lege*: SVF III 314). Prudence is sometimes defined as knowing what we must do and also what we must not. The things that we must do are *katorthōmata* (*SVF* II 1005): so Arcesilaus expresses Stoic thought very well when he says that prudence lies[31] in *katorthōmata*. But, and this is even more characteristic, he defined the *katorthōma* exactly as Zeno defined the *kathēkon*.[32] Let us recall briefly the difference between the *katorthōma* and the *kathēkon*. A *katorthōma*, or right action, is a perfect or complete act of duty, and is the monopoly of the Sage. A *kathēkon*, or *officium*, is not reserved for the Sage alone, nor even for humans and the moral life (*en biōi*); it extends to irrational animals as well and even to plants; it is that which conforms to nature in organic life (*en zōēi*). So one and the same act can be both a *katorthōma* as done by the Sage and a *kathēkon* as done by the fool; what characterizes the *katorthōma* is that it is accomplished by virtue. Thus, to repay a debt of money is a *kathēkon*; but to repay a debt out of justice is a *katorthōma*, for only the Sage is just. The outward action is therefore identical in the Sage and the fool, and the difference rests in the right intention, found only in the Sage. Arcesilaus could not fail to underline the contradiction between seeing everyone but the Sage as a fool, and yet simultaneously allowing that between good and evil there are things more or less estimable (*aestimabiles*, Cic. *Fin.* IV 56; *axian echonta* DL VII 105), and similarly that between right and wrong actions there are *media officia*. That was how Zeno, the crafty Phoenician (*ille Poenulus . . . homo igitur acutus*, Cic. loc. cit.), hit on the means of judging Plato superior to the tyrant Dionysius, even though they were both fools. Now we see why Arcesilaus preserved the *katorthōma* while attributing to it the definition of the *kathēkon*. He set out from Stoic principles and wants to show that the Sage, as portrayed by the Stoics, is in no way distinct from or superior to the fool; he is simply a prudent man who is guided by probability and doesn't step outside the territory of *media officia*. And so the *katorthōma* is no great mystery; it is simply the *kathēkon*, and the Stoic Sage who claims to be quite different from the man in the street is just the same as he is and indeed acts the same: this right action of his, supposedly almost divine, is exactly like the biological functions of plants and animals. In this way, Arcesilaus wrenches Stoicism away from its rigor and opens the way to the Stoics who succeeded Chrysippus. He did not teach the doctrine of the *eulogon*; that was a thesis he derived from Stoicism in order to attack and wound it in its weakest part. He behaved as a nihilist, a fifth columnist inside the Stoa.

It remains to be seen why Arcesilaus, as head of the Academy, adopted this skeptical anti-Stoic attitude and why, having adopted it, he maintained the *eulogon* thesis instead of remaining faithful to *epochē*. The ancients themselves asked the first question, and gave a variety of answers; it would require a lengthy study to review them. Let us just say that Platonic dogma should be distinguished from the spirit of investigation implicit in the Dialogues. The Early Academics favored the dogma, while Arcesilaus wanted to revive the *viva voce* method of investigation practiced by Socrates and Plato.[33] Hence his skeptic interpretation of Platonism, an interpretation which confirms that he refrained from dogmatizing, whether it be that he had no opinions or beliefs, or that he considered beliefs or opinions were not the sort of thing one can undertake to teach. He wanted, like Socrates, to rouse men's souls and, like him, to ridicule pretension and complacency. Zeno's self-assurance, overturning the principle that we should only pass judgment after having heard both sides of a question (Plut. *Stoic. rep.* 1034e), marked the split with Socratic midwifery. If the Stoics were in truth diametrically opposed to the Sophists so decried by Socrates and Plato, there was nonetheless something reminiscent of the Sophists in the Stoics' arrogance and in the sensationalist basis of their theory of knowledge. Arcesilaus's polemical fury was fueled by a vital urgency. "The Academy, as a result of the great success of the Lyceum and the new schools, notably the Stoa, saw itself completely relegated to the background" (Arnim, in Pauly-Wissowa, II, 1165, lines 25-29). It could only make a comeback by staging a fierce counterattack against these victorious innovators. Besides, contrary to what is often said, the first blows had been struck by Zeno, who had written against Plato's *Republic* (Plut. *Stoic. rep.* 1034f) and had revived the old polemic against the Theory of Ideas (Stob. *Ecl.* I, p. 136, 21W); his disciple Perseus of Citium, a contemporary of Arcesilaus, also wrote a work in seven volumes against Plato's *Laws* (DL VII 36).

Now it is true that in his critique of the Stoics Arcesilaus could have kept to *epochē* without going on to the *eulogon*. Surely he would have been in a much stronger position if he had asserted that no practical action can be based on Stoic principles? A close examination of the texts that introduce and explain the *eulogon* thesis will lead us to see that in his many and various debates with the Stoics, Arcesilaus was sometimes drawn to keep to *epochē* (and this is why Sextus reports that he accepts it as an end), and was sometimes tempted to go further and deduce a practical criterion from it. Perhaps he did prefer the first solution, but there were serious reasons why he could not always be content with it. First, the real existence of the Stoic Sage was a massive objection of fact to any nihilist interpretation of Stoicism. The new school plainly gave birth, precisely through its intractable rigor, to a splendid flowering of virtues. Zeno enjoyed universal esteem, his endurance and temperance were proverbial. Cleanthes was well known for his diligence, for his imperviousness to insult, and for the dignity of his life. Impossible to appear to deny these men's morality: so Arcesilaus preferred to divest it of its divinity, to reduce it to the level of ordinary decency. He labored to prove that, contrary to Stoic doctrine, assent was not necessary for action[34] and that in consequence, the Stoic theory of knowledge was not only inconsistent but useless. Himself a critic of the ideas of other men, he was unwilling to lay himself open to criticism, and so he kept his thoughts to himself. Accordingly, he would not agree to profess a practical criterion. But if under the pressure of objections he had said that he had nothing to propose for action, he would have been playing into his enemies' hands. Accordingly, by borrowing their own ideas, he was killing two birds with one stone; for on the one hand he was attacking the essential doctrines of the Stoa without incurring the reproach of doing away entirely with morality. (The Stoics could not deny all worth to a doctrine that was after all their own, and to intermediate duties which they credited with a certain value.) On the other hand, this was an opportunity for a renewed attack on Zeno, the false innovator, who, like a true Phoenician, had made off with other people's ideas (cf. DL VII 25).

Besides, if Arcesilaus was seeking to restore the Academy to its erstwhile standing, he had to try to provoke defections among the disciples of Stoic teachers. He stood a good chance of succeeding since he was working from their own principles, but would risk failure if he appeared to concede to them that no doctrine of action could be reconciled with *epochē*. Maybe he himself would not have dared admit, successor and professed imitator of Socrates as he was, that he was abandoning all concern with ethics. In fact, Aenesidemus was perhaps the only skeptic to have dispensed with an end altogether, and that was more than two centuries later, at a time when the great moral doctrines had become outmoded and when Stoicism in particular had abandoned the ideas that constituted its originality. So it is not impossible that Arcesilaus did, consciously or unconsciously, accept an end, and that, assailed by doubts, he nonetheless kept faith with certain convictions shared by all his philosophical contemporaries (for example, that happiness is a good or desirable thing). This is why Cleanthes, charging him with inconsistency, accused him of maintaining the *kathēkon* in his actions while condemning it in his words (DL VII 171). But whatever he really thought, he was diplomatic enough not to reject openly all practical notions and so risk losing new recruits. The theory of the *eulogon*, borrowed from the Stoics, bridged the gap between the Stoa and the Academy.

And it remained a Stoic theory: Arcesilaus does not prove, he argues. He is a dialectician. He does not oppose his own principles to others' contrary principles, he works from his adversary's principles themselves. We are only familiar with the *eulogon* thesis from a single text of Sextus, in the treatise *Against the Logicians* (M VII 158). There is no mention of it in the book *Against the Moralists* (M XI), nor in the first book of the *Outlines of Pyrrhonism*, where it would have been natural to speak of it, in a chapter where Sextus cites the *pithanon* of Carneades in an attempt to prove the originality of Pyrrhonism in relation to the Academy. He struggles, albeit sometimes without much conviction, to find differences between Arcesilaus and the Pyrrhonists, and this would have been an appropriate place to draw our attention to the doctrine of the *eulogon*. If Sextus (or his source) failed to do so, it was because he knew that Arcesilaus did not subscribe to this thesis on his own account; and he actually says this quite explicitly, in an oddly neglected sentence at the beginning of the passage where he explains the thesis of the *eulogon*: "Arcesilaus did not, in principle, establish any criterion; but those who think he did establish one ascribed it to an attack (or a counterattack, *antiparexagōgēn*) against the Stoics" (M VII 150).[35]

There are thus two traditions about Arcesilaus: according to one, he laid down no criterion; according to the other, he did it to counterattack against the Stoics. These two traditions are by no means incompatible; Arcesilaus accepted no criterion, but in discussion he was induced to answer objections by drawing on his opponents' own principles for a practical criterion—a very modest one—which they could not take exception to. Besides, if he had allowed a criterion and described an ideal Sage who performed right actions, he would have been accused of dogmatizing himself. Now, he was indeed accused both of being a secret dogmatist and of being a complete skeptic, but never of having publicly professed dogmas—as, for example, Carneades was alleged to have done. His teaching method was to ask his audience to set out their view, which he then systematically disproved (Cic. *Fin.* II 2). Both the pros and cons had thus been put forward and the equal force of the opposing arguments had been established, without any judgment being made one way or the other (DL IV 28; Cic. *Acad.* I 45).

THE ROLE OF ARCESILAUS

To sum up, Arcesilaus's main achievement was to apply Socratic irony to Stoicism in order to force it into a confession of universal ignorance. Deduced from the definitions of the Sage and of apprehension, *epochē* and the *eulogon* are only valid for those who accept these definitions.

This applies in particular to the *eulogon,* since, because Arcesilaus criticized and refuted everything without drawing a conclusion, the true consequence, perhaps even the aim, of these discussions was *epochē.*[36] It is in this sense alone that we must understand Sextus's claim that the end for Arcesilaus was *epochē*; and if he is credited with the assertion, as a kind of dogma, that every *epochē* is a good and every assent an evil, it is in fact because in his teaching his dialectic tracked down assent in each particular case and ended up every time with nothing but *epochē.* If the Stoics then condemned him for refuting everything without drawing any conclusions and challenged him to reveal his practical criterion, Arcesilaus evaded the trap they had laid for him. He refrained from suggesting any moral principle for his own part but took the offensive himself by maintaining that assent was by no means essential for action, and that the Stoic Sage himself could spurn the fine words of his own school and attain decency and happiness in the accomplishment of ordinary duties and in conducting himself by the probable. Arcesilaus thought he was following in the steps of Socrates by making men confess their ignorance. In the heat of the debate, he may appear to have put a very high value on *epochē,* but he never made it an end. For picking up Socrates' words: "I only know one thing, which is that I know nothing," he used to add: "And I don't even know that" (Cic. *Acad.* I 45). So he did not give his assent to the suspension of assent any more than to anything else. He was wise enough to doubt his own doubt. Perhaps, in so acting, his aim was to maintain the rights of the critical spirit at a time when the pressure of practical problems threatened to undermine theoretical philosophy.

II. CARNEADES

1. Antilogy. Carneades is above all the successor to Arcesilaus: *in eadem ratione permansit* ("he kept to the same standpoint," Cic. *Acad.* I 45). Like Socrates and Arcesilaus, his aim was to awaken men's intelligence; like them, he wrote nothing. But he spoke much, and perhaps his dazzling eloquence would have been exercised on subjects quite different from those which in fact brought him fame if he had not been preceded by Chrysippus, the second founder of the Stoa so rudely shaken by Arcesilaus. Chrysippus responded to Arcesilaus, expounding and refining Stoic doctrine to such an extent that it could be said that "if there had been no Chrysippus, there would have been no Stoa" (DL VII 183). Carneades, however, who had read attentively the works of the Stoics and especially of Chrysippus, was happy to parody this remark: "If there had been no Chrysippus, there would have been no Carneades" (DL IV 62).

The Stoics rejoiced as though at a stroke of great good fortune that the gods had seen fit to place Chrysippus between Arcesilaus and Carneades; for by refuting the former, he had silenced the garrulous quibbles of the latter (Plut. *Comm. not.* 1050b; *SVF* II 33). It is true that they also grumbled that Carneades drew his arguments from the works of Chrysippus. Chrysippus had produced six books *Against Common Experience* in which he set out the pros and cons of the reliability of the senses, and, eager as he was to be impartial in expounding the case against the senses and to outdo even Arcesilaus, he succeeded beyond his wildest dreams, since his refutation of the case against seemed woefully inadequate. Thus Carneades was saying nothing that was personal to himself. Rather, attacking Chrysippus with his own weapons, he could say to him as Andromache did to Hector: "Unhappy one, your courage will be your undoing!" (Plut. *Stoic. rep.* 1036b-1037a; Cic. *Acad.* II 75 and 87; *SVF* II 32 and 109). These testimonies (which obviously we must not take literally) show that Carneades' method was the same as Arcesilaus's: the application of antilogy to Stoicism. This is not to say that Carneades did not occasionally take issue with other philosophies, but his work did mainly and essentially consist in a highly unsympathetic critical study of Stoicism according to Chrysippus. Sextus (*M* IX 1) rebukes Clitomachus and the Academics in general for lingering over particular questions of detail. They plunge, he says, into other people's material; and basing their arguments on points conceded by various dogmatists,[37] they prolong the refutation interminably. Certainly this is the way Carneades works, but the alien material into which our evidence shows him plunging is invariably Stoicism. His method is clearly revealed in the debate about the *Summum Bonum*, where, if we are to believe Diogenes Laertius (IV 62), he must have shone with especial brilliance: "He was stronger in ethics." Here he classifies the conceptions of the Good, opposes them to each other, criticizes them, upholding now some, now others, but always attacking the Stoic conception. Let Antipater, pressed by a renewal of the arguments of Arcesilaus, take refuge in the *eulogistos eklogē* ("the most reasonable choice"): Carneades will track him to his lair, refuting this theory and pleading the cause of the *prōta kata phusin* ("the primary things in accordance with nature"), not because he supports it, but in order to contradict the Stoics (Cic. *Acad.* II 13; *Fin.* V 20; Plut. *Comm. not.* XXVII). In physics, he speaks out against God and against the gods, against providence, against divination, and against fate, providing on various points factual support for the Epicureans, whose refutation would nevertheless have given him the opportunity of easy success. In the part of the *Academica* (II 118-128) concerning physics, Cicero gives us a bird's-eye view of the philosophers' theories about the sun, moon, and earth, about the body and the soul, about fate and divination: Carneades accepts none of these theories; he opposes some to others to make them destroy each other, but he keeps returning to Stoicism, to attack it in particular, arriving finally at universal *akatalēpsia*. This *akatalēpsia* is at the root of his detailed criticisms; when he broaches so many questions of ethics and physics, his intention is principally to force the Stoics to admit the emptiness of their criterion. Sextus (*M* VII 159; cf. 166) does in fact say that on the subject of the criterion Carneades opposed not only the Stoics, but all his predecessors. However, we cannot leap to the conclusion that he refuted in detail the criteria of all schools, because his argument as it is reported to us is in fact directed against the criterion of the Stoa. It is true that he extended the discussion, that in refuting the Stoic criterion he showed that no other criterion seemed preferable to him and that he tried to stop up his enemies' bolt-holes by proving not only, as Arcesilaus had done, the unreality of the Stoic criterion but the impossibility of any criterion at all. He approached the criterion as he did the *Summum Bonum*: this method was dictated to him by the development of Stoic thought, which tried to escape Arcesilaus's critique by indulging in innovations. Carneades took his example from Chrysippus himself, who did not absolutely forbid himself the practice of arguing the opposite sides of a question (Plut. *Stoic. rep.* 1035f), and who larded his works with testimonies and even quotations from nonphilosophical authors (DL VII 180; Galen, *De Hipp. et Plat.* II 2). However, the focal point of Carneades' discussion remained Stoicism, and if he criticizes other philosophers, it is always in connection with Stoic doctrines, just as it is in relation to the *katalēpsis* ("apprehension") of the Stoa that he expresses his *akatalēpsia*.

2. *The Pithanon.* But with Carneades as with Arcesilaus it is in what is taken to be the positive part of their philosophy that the influence of the Stoa is especially characteristic. It is unfortunate that a thorny problem arises here, caused by disagreement among the ancients themselves over the meaning and significance of the theses expounded by Carneades. His teaching, entirely oral as it was, was transcribed by an excellent interpreter, his faithful companion and a man, moreover, whose outstanding wisdom was matched only by his diligence—namely, the subtle Semite Clitomachus (Cic. *Acad.* II 98). However, we do not possess any of his numerous works, and so Carneades' thought on the point at issue is scarcely known to us except from Cicero and Sextus Empiricus. Now, Cicero associated chiefly with Antiochus,[38] the disciple and adversary of Philo; from him he heard the echo of the most recent discussions between the Academy and the partisans of the Stoa; his account does not refer to Carneades, nor, save at certain places, to Clitomachus, but to Metro-

dorus and to Philo, pupils of Carneades who differed on certain points
with Clitomachus, since even Antiochus was shocked by Philo's innovations. Carneades could maintain theses by way of controverting the
Stoics in which certain of his disciples spotted, as they thought, convictions of his own and which certain modern writers have attributed to him
as such. As for Sextus, perhaps he is more trustworthy, at least in the
work *Against the Dogmatists* (M VII-XI); but in his *Outlines of Pyrrhonism*, he is following an author who is hostile to the Academics and concerned principally to distinguish them from the Pyrrhonists.

Arcesilaus used to end up at *epochē* and from there at the *eulogon*.
Carneades, however, ends up at *doxa* ("opinion") and from there at the
pithanon. At this point we are faced with the question Hirzel posed, a
question whose implications have perhaps been somewhat exaggerated
by him and Brochard,[39] the question of a difference of opinion between
Clitomachus on the one hand and Philo and Metrodorus on the other on
the subject of *epochē*. There is no shadow of doubt that Philo and
Metrodorus softened Carneades' skepticism, but it is because Hirzel had
faith in Sextus's testimony about *epochē* being the end for Arcesilaus that
he gave it such importance. *Epochē*, as we have seen, was for Arcesilaus
a consequence of the nonexistence of the Stoic criterion; it was the attitude forced upon that infallible Sage, who in fact avoids error on condition that he pronounces upon nothing. Where the criterion is concerned,
Carneades backs up Arcesilaus's position again; accordingly, he must
have made *epochē* the conclusion of a large number of arguments against
the Stoics, and this is the origin of Clitomachus's work on suspension of
judgment. But in the reasoning on which *epochē* is founded, Arcesilaus
had posed a choice, from which he took up only one of the options. He
used to say: "Since everything is inapprehensible, the Sage can only give
assent to the inapprehensible, so he will withhold assent." However,
there was another hypothesis—namely, that the Sage should assent to
the inapprehensible (Cic. *Acad.* II 78). This hypothesis, which would
deprive the Sage of his wisdom, was accordingly much less worthy of
him than the conclusion "Therefore, the Sage will suspend judgment
about everything." So Carneades adopted it, without, however, accepting it as his view; or rather, he kept Arcesilaus's argument while adding
one of his own, so as to catch the Stoics on the horns of a dilemma.
Everything is inapprehensible, so the Sage will either withhold his assent
(that is *epochē*) or will assent to what is inapprehensible and so perhaps
false (that is *doxa*, "opinion"). But in fact, since the Stoic Sage is a man,
since he lives and claims to act, he has opinions. With or without assent,
but in any case without apprehension, he behaves according to his conviction in conformity with the simple appearance of truth, since he is

denied certain knowledge of what is true: "Even the man whom you present as the Sage follows many things that are convincing but not apprehended or perceived or assented to—things with verisimilitude: and if he were not to approve them, all life would be done away with" (Clitomachus, *De sustin. adsension.* I ap. Cic. *Acad.* II 99). The thesis "that the Sage will have opinions" is thus derived from Stoic definitions, and the Stoics are cornered in this conclusion, which is in fact contrary to the doctrine they constantly reiterated.[40] According to the needs of his discussion, Carneades resorted sometimes to *epochē*, sometimes to *doxa*, leaving his opponents no means of escape from the dilemma. For it is patently absurd that the Sage should have opinions. Opinion is defined by the Stoics in two ways: as assent to what is inapprehensible, and as weak and false assent; both are equally foreign to the Sage.[41] For if the Sage holds opinions, he is mistaken, indeed he sins.[42] So he follows the *pithanon* or the persuasive. Carneades borrows the persuasive presentation from Chrysippus in order to refute the Stoic dogma of the infallibility of the Sage. He distinguishes presentations: on the one hand apprehensive from nonapprehensive, on the other persuasive from nonpersuasive; his critique is only aimed at apprehension and leaves persuasion intact (Clitomachus, *De sust. adsens.* I, *loc. cit.*). This classification is Stoic; it is almost identical with the following more complete classification which Sextus (*M* VII 241-248) explicitly attributes to the Stoa: 1) classification of presentations in general with regard to persuasion (subjective point of view); 2) classification of persuasive presentations with regard to truth (objective point of view); 3) classification of true presentations with regard to apprehension (their objective validity is guaranteed for the subject or it is not). Carneades leaves aside the presentation which is true and not apprehensive because, since its truth remains unknown to the subject, it is devoid of interest in a discussion on the criterion. Carneades describes as persuasive the presentation which appears true, and this does not mean that which resembles the true (a meaningless phrase) but that which in a natural way persuades us (*peithein hēmas pephuken*, SE M VII 169) and which draws us to assent (ibid. 172). The Stoics also fix the label "persuasive" to a proposition that leads us to assent (Diocl. Magn. *ap.* DL VII 75); it is true that Carneades speaks of presentations and not of propositions, but we must recognize that the Stoics sometimes use these two words interchangeably; besides, not all presentations are sensible (DL VII 51), and assent is given to a proposition, not to a presentation, so that a persuasive presentation is one that induces us to assent to the proposition involved in it. In the Stoic classification of presentations, persuasive ones are defined as "those which produce a gentle, even (literally: smooth, *leion*) movement in the soul," as opposed to the powerful imprint marked by the apprehensive presentation. Their definition of nonpersuasive (or dissuasive) presentation is clearer: "One that deflects us from assent." So Carneades understands the *pithanon* as the Stoics did, and the *pithanon* implies assent; which tallies with Sextus's claim (*PH* I 230) that the *pithanon* does not comprise solely a pupil's practical compliance with his schoolmaster, but a strong assent; and we should note that Sextus here links the names of Clitomachus and Carneades. I should also remark in passing that the Stoics present as neither persuasive nor dissuasive a presentation such as "The stars are even (or uneven) in number" (SE *M* VII 243). This same presentation is cited by Sextus (*M* VIII 147) as an example of *kathapax adēlon*, that is, something that is absolutely concealed from our perception. Now in the *Academica* (II 32) Lucullus leaves out of the discussion, *quasi desperatos aliquos* ("like some desperate characters"), those for whom universal inapprehensibility (*panta estin akatalēpta*) means that everything is as uncertain as the number of stars (that is, *panta estin kathapax adēla*). Lucullus is here gunning for those, Pyrrhonists or dissident Academics, who assert that everything is "neither persuasive nor dissuasive"; those, then, who do not call on the notion of the *pithanon*. These divergences are also expressed in Stoic terms.

In their classification, the Stoics distinguish true presentations from apprehensive presentations. The first derive from and conform to the real; the second in addition have a character that they would not have had if they derived from the unreal. Carneades accepts the existence of the true but denies the existence of the apprehensive.[43] But the Stoics considered true, nonapprehensive presentations as pathological; they are only to be found in melancholics or frenetics, whose presentations are true only by chance; often, however, they mistrust them and so do not assent to them (SE *M* VII 247-248). Carneades, who stresses so heavily the illusions of dreams and of madness in the course of abolishing the apprehensive and keeping the true, reduces all men to the level of frenetics and melancholics. Sometimes presentations derive from the real and conform to their object, sometimes they do not; and we never know whether they are true or false. There is no concession to dogmatism here, rather the reverse. This theory even goes so far as to abolish the Sage's superiority. For the Stoics, the true is distinct from truth. The true has only an incorporeal existence and is found even in the fool; truth, or sense of the true, possesses a corporeal existence and is the prerogative of the Sage (SE *PH* II 80-84; *M* VII 38-42). To admit the true, without apprehension—the condition of knowledge—without the criterion of truth is to render knowledge impossible and to confound the Sage with the fool.

The persuasive presentation hardly gives guarantees of truth; but people attribute to Carneades a theory of degrees of probability, which could be more precisely described as a scale of criteria: (1) persuasive presentation; (2) persuasive presentation which is not drawn in a contrary direction (*aperispastos*); (3) persuasive presentation which is not drawn in a contrary direction and which has been subjected to detailed scrutiny (SE *M* VII 176-189).[44] We do not know whether Carneades borrowed this scale from the Stoics or whether it is his own invention. But the verb *"perispō,"* to which *"aperispastos"* corresponds, was used in the same sense by Chrysippus (*Peri logou chrēseōs*, fr. 2: *SVF* III, p. 201, 14), and precisely in connection with the *pithanon* and the practice of arguing the opposite sides of a question. He advises his disciples against producing arguments for opposite sides. For, he says, they might draw in a contrary direction, deflect or divert their apprehension: *perispōntas tēn katalēpsin*. The hearers, diverted (*perispasthentes*) by the arguments, abandon their comprehension: that is the result of expounding contrary persuasive views (*Peri biōn* IV fr. 10: *SVF* III, p. 194, 34). Thus Chrysippus says that by a persuasive expounding of contrary theses, the hearers are diverted from a thesis. Carneades suggests as a second criterion the presentation which is persuasive and not diverted, that is, one that is not opposed by a contrary persuasion. The third criterion is the presentation which has been subjected to a detailed scrutiny, known as *periōdeumenē* or *diexōdeumenē*. The Stoics were not unaware of the term *"diexodos"*; indeed, they used it to distinguish rhetoric from dialectic: dialectic is conducted by dialogue, rhetoric by consecutive speeches that are delivered *en mēkei kai diexodōi*, that is to say, in a detailed exposition (SE *M* II 6-7). This would encourage us to think there is some relation between the *diexōdeumenon* and the *eulogon* (rhetoric is the science *tou eu legein*): the *diexōdeumenon* would be that for which one could give a justification by a detailed exposition; and in fact the epithet *eulogos* had been applied to the *diexodos* by Chrysippus (*Peri psuchēs*: *SVF* II, p. 250, 27-28). The orator's *diexodos* is perfectly well placed in the service of the *pithanon*; and Carneades was able to find the elements of his scale of the persuasive in Stoicism itself. Nonetheless, these elements had little importance in the Stoa, where they were usually devoid of any characteristic significance: so it is impossible to assert that Carneades borrowed them from there.

Be that as it may, the scale of criteria is a development of the notion of the persuasive, which Carneades, as we have seen, understood in the Stoic sense. Now the Stoics often referred to the persuasive as a source of error. In his attempt to show that presentation does not *ipso facto* (*autotelōs*) lead to assent, Chrysippus remarks that Sages often resort to lies (*pseudei chrōntai*) in dealing with fools and offer them a persuasive presentation. The latter is not, however, a cause of assent, since it will be the cause of a false supposition or of a mistake.[45] Elsewhere (*Peri biōn* IV: fr. 10: *loc. cit.*), Chrysippus voices the fear that a persuasive exposition to support a thesis under attack may distract our minds from apprehension. Finally, Diocles of Magnesia (DL VII 75) gives as an example of a persuasive proposition "If someone has given birth to something, she is its mother," and he adds: "Now this is false, for the bird is not the mother of an egg." This source of error is Carneades' criterion, and an odd one it is too: how is he going to explain and defend it? He cites examples, but a noteworthy point here, too often overlooked, is that these examples reveal less the probability of the persuasive presentation than its chances of being false. Carneades cites four examples: first, a presentation which is merely persuasive; then two examples of a persuasive presentation which is not drawn in a contrary direction; third, a persuasive presentation which is not drawn in a contrary direction and which is scrutinized in detail. (1) A man pursued by enemies takes refuge in a cave; he experiences the persuasive presentation that he has enemies in the cave and so takes to his heels. The likelihood of error is about as great as that of truth. (2) Hercules leads Alcestis, returned to life, back to Admetus; Admetus experiences the persuasive presentation that it really is Alcestis (and indeed it is); but the notion that she is dead diverts him from this presentation. So the presentation is not *aperispastos*, although it is true. (3) Menelaus has been sailing with the (false) image of Helen. Reaching the island of Pharos, he sees the real Helen, but cannot credit this presentation, because it is inconsistent with the other one, following which he believes he left Helen in the ship. (In these two examples, the second criterion, supposedly more credible than the other, is the more surely misleading.) (4) A man in a dark house finds a coiled rope and supposes it to be a snake. If he hasn't had time to make sure, he will hold on to this false persuasive presentation of a snake; but the stillness of the rope diverts him from this persuasion. However, this second criterion is inadequate, for it would tempt him to a fatal mistake if the rope were in fact a snake hibernating during cold weather. It is only after a close and detailed scrutiny that the truth appears from every side;[46] in other words, the presentation seems true from whatever side one takes it.

These examples throw an interesting light on the meaning of the *pithanon*: two out of four are misleading. Carneades admits that there are true presentations and that certain presentations impel us to assent. But we can be impelled to assent by a false presentation, because subjectively a false presentation is in no way distinguishable from a true one. For the same reason, a presentation may be true and yet divert us from assent. Consequently, what the Stoics call *apprehension* is really only persuasion. We may consider in the presentation either the subjective or the objective aspect, but there is no bridge between the two. We can, if we wish, compare presentations among themselves, and use them to confirm each other; we can advance to ever more detailed examinations and arrive at beliefs that are ever more firm; still our presentation, however true it may appear to us, will be in no way distinguishable from what it would be were it false. So the theory of the *pithanon* is an exegesis of the facts that destroy Stoic dogmatism much more than it is the founding of a mitigated dogmatism.

Indeed, even more than Arcesilaus's *eulogon*, the *pithanon* makes apprehension useless for action, and action is the goal of philosophy; the Stoic theory of knowledge is therefore pointless. The theory of the *pithanon* also shows that the Stoic pretension to establishing a science of the true and the false, starting out from sense data, is vain. Their dialectic leads to the persuasive, neither more nor less than Aristotle's does; basically, indeed, it is nothing more than rhetoric, whose object is the *pithanon* (SE M II 61-63). Since the *pithanon* often leads to error, Carneades made play with it. If Arcesilaus is a dialectician, he is a rhetorician; not only does he debate, he discourses. The *pithanon* is his end in the sense that he is setting out to convince his audience now of this thesis, now of the contrary thesis—not to prove one or the other of these theses but to win approval for it. Carneades is an advocate, supporting now the pros, now the cons, by a method of antilogy that results in evenly balanced arguments; this balance or equipollence is the equal persuasive force of arguments. Everything is inapprehensible, but everything is, in a sense, persuasive. That is why Numenius[47] portrays Carneades as a clever conjuror, whose sleight-of-hand juggles truth away, making us take the false for the true and the true for the false.

Was Carneades the dupe of his own theory? Having elaborated it to undermine Stoic logic, did he end up by believing it himself and applying it in action? These questions go beyond the scope of the present article; so I shall confine myself to a few remarks. Not only do we not know a single thesis, no matter what the subject, of which it can be said that Carneades professed it as his sincere belief; but where the central problem of philosophy is concerned, that of the *Summum Bonum*, his friend and disciple Clitomachus could never tell what he really thought. On the other hand, we have abundant evidence that Carneades often supported some doctrine or other for mere polemic. The opponents of the Academy rebuked them for concealing their doctrines, not for favoring one particular doctrine. Further, a large number of the texts that provide us with what knowledge we have of Carneades emanate either from Philo of Larissa, an innovator already tending toward dogmatism, or from Pyrrhonist opponents bent on arrogating to themselves the title of skeptic.

Numenius (loc. cit.) asserts in so many words that Carneades was elusive, that he never committed himself and doubted his own arguments. Finally, it seems that it was with some reluctance that Carneades decided to work out this theory of the *pithanon* and its degrees, and above all to apply it to moral action with a view to happiness. He did not do it of his own accord; rather, because he was questioned (*apaitoumenos*) about the criterion he would adopt for practical life, he too was obliged, indeed virtually forced (*dunamei epanagkazetai*), to speak out on the criterion (SE M VII 166). It is true that Sextus's report (ibid. 182-189) is set in an affirmative style, but it is in the indicative, not in the imperative. It is a chapter on the psychology of belief, inserted, moreover, like Arcesilaus's theory of the *eulogon*, in the work *Against the Logicians*, not that *Against the Ethicists*. We must assume that Carneades, whether because he really didn't believe in anything, or because as a skilled and cunning orator he didn't want to expose himself to criticism, refused to commit himself to any positive doctrine.

III. ECLECTICISM

1. *The Middle Stoa.* The critical analysis of Stoicism seems to have failed in its bid to weaken the Stoa, if we measure it by the development of the Academy. Thirty years after the death of Carneades, Philo is already yielding; then Antiochus capitulates and joins the enemy. The least we can say is that the Stoics gained a Pyrrhic victory. It is an eclectic doctrine, stripped of its characteristic content, that takes possession of the Academy; it is in Stoicism revised and corrected by Carneades that Antiochus thought to find again, beneath novel terminology, the dogmas that had been shared in common by the Lyceum and the Old Academy. The Stoics rallied to some extent to the *eulogon* and the *pithanon*, abandoning their original attitude to the end and the criterion.[48]

Diogenes of Babylon, Carneades' colleague on the embassy to Rome, says that the end consists in "calculating well in the choice of that which is in accordance with nature" (DL VII 88). "Calculating well" is to *eulogistein* (from *eu* and *logizomai*); *eulogistia* is the science which establishes the balance sheet (*antanairetikē*) of facts and actions; it figures in the same class as prudence, to which it is subordinate (Stobaeus, *Ecl.* II 60, 9 W: *SVF* III, p. 64, 21 and 26). It is similar to Epicurus's prudence; he uses the word in his letter to Menoeceus (DL X 135), when he states that it is better to be subject to misfortune *eulogistōs* ("after calculating well") than to good fortune *alogistōs* ("without calculating"). This "calculating well" and "balance sheet" cannot fail to evoke Bentham's felicific calculus. Antipater combines the idea of choice and the *eulogiston*: the end is "the well-calculated choice of natural things."[49] It is true that Antipater added that this choice had to be continual and unbreached, which preserves the Stoic idea of the impeccable Sage, but which nonetheless reduces his wisdom to calculation (though this word does not imply the negation of disinterestedness), where you weigh up the pros and the cons and choose the one that carries most weight. So Diogenes' and Antipater's *eulogiston* is close to Arcesilaus's *eulogon*. We know that Antipater, under pressure from Carneades' argument, had implicitly abandoned the doctrine that virtue is the sole good (Cic. *Fin.* III 57). Archedemus goes further: he adopts the thesis put forward by Arcesilaus. The latter assigned to the *katorthōma* the Stoic definition of the *kathēkon*; Archedemus made the *kathēkon* the ethical end. For him, the end consists in accomplishing all the *kathekōnta* (DL VII 88; Stobaeus *Ecl.* II 75, 11 W: *SVF* III, p. 264, 16-21): there is no longer any difference between the Sages depicted by Arcesilaus and by Archedemus, since the *kathēkon* is that for which a probable justification can be given. It is true that, like Antipater, Archedemus insists on the choice of the greatest and highest natural goods and on not breaching the choice (Clem. *Strom.* II 21; *SVF* III, p. 264, 22-24). It is still true, however, that Stoicism is here coming down from the elevated sphere of perfect acts to search for ordinary duties, for what is fitting, thereby yielding to Arcesilaus's critique, which Carneades had reinforced.

The Stoics even went so far as to adopt Carneades' criterion; they merely dress it in their own style and translate it into their own language. For these "younger Stoics," says Sextus,[50] contrasting them with the old Stoics, the criterion is not apprehensive presentation pure and simple, but apprehensive presentation that has no obstacle (*mēden echousan enstēma*). Sextus sets out their doctrine for us, working on Carneades' examples, which they had doubtless annexed as well. It may happen, they say, that a presentation, although apprehensive, may be incredible (*apistos*), because of concomitant external circumstances. So Admetus, faced with Alcestis brought back from Hades by Hercules, has an apprehensive presentation of her; he ought to believe in this presentation, but doesn't because of the obstacles set in his path by the following thoughts: Alcestis is dead; the dead do not return; ghosts sometimes appear to our minds. Similarly, Menelaus will not accept the apprehensive presentation that he has of Helen on Pharos: (a) because he thinks that Helen is on the ship; (b) because the idea that the Pharos Helen is not the real Helen is not dissuasive (*apithanon*), that is, of a kind to discourage persuasion. Thus, an apprehensive presentation may be believed false; the apprehensive presentation does not drag us by the hair to give assent. In the examples cited, a true presentation is *katalēptikē* ("apprehensive") but not *mēden echousa enstēma* ("having no obstacle"); in Carneades' scheme the same thing was *pithanē* but not *aperispastos.* There is therefore an identity between the impression which is apprehensive and without obstacle and the impression which is persuasive and not diverted. According to this new criterion, the Sage may take what is true for false (Admetus, Menelaus); but he must avoid at all costs taking what is false for true. For this, when he experiences an obscure (*amudran*) presentation of a visible object, he intensifies his gaze, goes nearer to it, rubs his eyes, until he has achieved a perceptive and striking (*tranēn kai plēktikēn*) presentation of the object in question. He makes a detailed examination that leads him to establish in the presentation the credibility of the apprehension (*tēn tēs katalēpseōs pistin*): in sum, it is Carneades' *phantasia periōdeumenē* ("thoroughly scrutinized presentation") with the belief or credibility that results from it. This doctrine of the *enstēma* ("obstacle") aims to refute the *pithanon* thesis insofar as it is destructive and to preserve it insofar as something positive can be got from it. The Younger Stoics' reply to Carneades, or rather, perhaps, to Philo, was that Carneades' second criterion (*to aperispaston*) assumes that we attribute some validity to the presentation. They condemn the absurd notion of admitting things that we only know by presentations and simultaneously rejecting presentations. They themselves, however, leave the door open to Academic doubt, the moment they no longer accept apprehensive presentation as a sufficient criterion but demand instead a stringent critique that is liable to dissolve apprehension.

2. *Philo and Antiochus.* Were these concessions enough for the Academics? One might well think so, to see Clitomachus's successors, instead of profiting from their advantages, sketching in their turn a tentative withdrawal, a withdrawal that is already detectable in Philo and is confirmed in Antiochus. It is, besides, Antiochus whom we may see as the more faithful of the two to the Academic tradition. There has been much discussion about the innovations for which he rebukes Philo; we do not know exactly what they are, but are nonetheless fortunate to possess a few precise texts. We have two pieces of clear information: (1) Philo is less skeptical than Arcesilaus and Carneades (*est adversarius lenior, minus acer est adversarius* ["he is a milder adversary"]: *Acad.* II 12); (2) he claims that his mitigated skepticism is indeed that of Carneades (*ista quae sunt heri defensa, negat Academicos omnino dicere* ["the things defended yesterday are not what the Academics say at all"][51]). It is this last claim that makes Antiochus see red; infuriated, he loses all his usual sweetness. This is very understandable: Antiochus was attacking Carneades' philosophy, from which Philo had originally not deviated; his system of argument was elaborated to counter a radical skepticism. It was only natural that he should have felt disappointed when he saw that he

had to start all over again. If Philo attenuated or limited *akatalēpsia,* it
was after all his right, and Antiochus ought not to have resented it; but
that he should dare lay this attenuation or limitation at Carneades' door
was really intolerable; it was a downright lying interpretation (*mentitur*).
This information only makes sense if Philo kept to Carneades' teaching
but endowed it with a new meaning. Now this meaning is not unknown
to us: Philo taught, says Sextus (*PH* I 235), that things, although knowable in themselves, are not knowable so far as concerns the Stoic criterion. In this way he reduces Carneades' critique to a refutation of this
criterion, and when he says that things are *akatalēpta* ("inapprehensible"), he means that the Stoics' "apprehensive presentation" does not
lead to apprehension. Philo was right to see in Carneades' philosophy a
critical approach to Stoicism: Sextus (*PH* I 226) reproduced a mistake,
possibly deliberate, by his source when he claimed that the New Academics "affirmed" (*diabebaiountai*) the inapprehensibility of things. Carneades refuted the Stoic theory of knowledge, but was content with that,
putting forward no theory of his own. Thus Antiochus could denounce
him as a nihilist. But Philo, faithful to Carneades on the critical and anti-
Stoic side, diverges from him in teaching that a doctrine of knowledge remains possible outside Stoicism. Antiochus replies that if things are inapprehensible for the *phantasia katalēptikē,* then they are absolutely inapprehensible, whereas Philo wants to preserve the apprehensibility of
things without the *phantasia katalēptikē* (SE *PH* I 235; Cic. *Acad.* II 18).
For Philo, as for Carneades, there is no presentation derived from a real
object which is such that it could not have derived from an unreal object.
Carneades also allowed that presentations could be true and that things
could be perceived; but he did not consider them *katalēpta* ("apprehensible"), since we never know whether or not our presentation comes from
a real object. Philo yields more ground, admitting that things are *katalēpta;* he attempts to keep knowledge while abandoning certainty. But
what is uncertain knowledge if not probable knowledge? Philo will be a
probabilist, and therein lies his innovation. Carneades' only thought was
to persuade, without concerning himself with truth; he was an orator as
well as a philosopher. Philo also cultivated rhetoric, which he taught con-
currently with philosophy (Cic. *Tusc.* II 9). He abided by the letter of
Carneades' teaching, but, thoughtful and circumspect rather than original in spirit, he could not revel in Carneades' sleight-of-hand. Unlike his
brilliant predecessor, he could not move at ease among contradictions.
He therefore abandoned Carneades' purely combative point of view; and
since Carneades had expressed this point of view in Stoicism, Philo bids
farewell to Stoicism, condemning it to oblivion, to construct outside it a
new doctrine of knowledge. When he attributed a philosophical value to
the *pithanon,* until then a mere subject of rhetoric, Philo became the true

founder of the "probabilism of the New Academy," the probabilism that Antiochus refuted, not without some success.[52] Philo produced the scholastic version of Carneades' philosophy. In some respects, he was poles apart from Carneades, because he was gulled by his argumentation and took for serious the theses he maintained—because he dissociated himself from Stoicism and discoursed in absolute terms, whereas Carneades was talking for his opponents and arguing in relation to their assertions.

Antiochus, on the other hand, Stoic though he be, remains by contrast the continuator of the Academy. The Academy is a place of perpetual motion. Between Socrates, Plato, Arcesilaus, Carneades, and Antiochus there are points in common, thinking in common. As Socrates awoke men's souls, Arcesilaus and Carneades labored to shape their spirits. Plato was faithful to his master's living dialectic, but he "never ceased to look for the higher vantage-point, from which he could overcome apparent contradictions and reduce them to harmony."[53] According to Albert Rivaud, "Plato set out to draw up the balance sheet of his time, sifting through everything he found by way of ideas and sentiments."[54] Antiochus, keeping everything in perspective, tried to reach the same goal. He does not appear to accept the theory of Ideas; but what seems to him essential for Plato is his commitment to establish certain knowledge as distinct from mere opinion. The Stoics achieved this, so the Stoa was a continuation of the Old Academy. Antiochus took arms against the New Academy and its *akatalēpsia*, which was further removed than Stoic dogmatism from Plato's main preoccupation. But just like Arcesilaus and Carneades, he argues in a Stoic framework; no longer, it is true, as an opponent but as an ally, for the Stoicism before him is by no means the same as the Stoicism that was harassed by Arcesilaus and Carneades. All that the Stoa could offer in the way of strength or originality became diluted or vanished altogether. Stripped of its excesses, Stoicism is no longer itself but becomes acceptable; in the end, its doctrine is no different from the teaching of the first Academics, and of the Peripatetics. Why, then, persist in the attack? Besides, the Stoics had ceased hostilities against Plato and Aristotle, finding that they occasionally had something to contribute. Why should the Academy not imitate them? By borrowing what he saw as the best in their theories and formulae, Antiochus, like Plato, imagined he was achieving a higher synthesis.

SUMMARY AND CONCLUSION

Plato's immediate successors were not, properly speaking, dogmatists. The Pyrrhonists distinguished them from other philosophers: in his general classification of the schools, Sextus (*PH* I 3) only cites as *idiōs kalou-*

menoi dogmatikoi ("dogmatists specially so called") the Aristotelians, Epicureans, and Stoics; that is to say, those who were rivals of the Platonists around 300 B.C. Aenesidemus and Menodotus strove to prove that Plato wasn't *always* a skeptic; even if he only dogmatized once, or preferred one presentation to another in terms of credibility, he should be considered a dogmatist (SE *PH* I 222-223). This really doesn't mean much. Plato's works are full of life and variety; it would be pointless to try to impose a system on his continually moving thought. This is why his followers interpreted him each in his own way and why a fixed orthodox doctrine was never established at the Old Academy as it was at the Lyceum, the Garden, and the Stoa. This aspect of Platonism explains the skepticism of the New Academy, but it should not blind us to the fact that the New Academy was really new, and recognized as such by its contemporaries. The divergences and oppositions which one can establish in the teachings of the first Platonists do not prevent there being a certain doctrinal unity; until Arcesilaus a Platonic tradition free from any skepticism remained in force at the Academy. How are we to account for the great change that Arcesilaus wrought? What new fact produced this transformation? It was the founding of the Stoa. From Arcesilaus to Antiochus, the Academy was pervaded by an interior dialectic that developed along these lines: granted that Stoicism is there, what are we to make of it? Nothing was more distasteful to the freedom of discussion that was favored at the Academy, or to its preference for moderate sentiments, than the spiritual rigor of the first Stoics. Arcesilaus and Carneades were implacable toward the Stoa; Philo denied that they were able to lead us to *katalēpsis*. Stoicism bent under these attacks; it adapted itself to the criticisms, and changed, becoming in its turn ponderous and "academic"; its masters went so far as to put into practice the works of the Platonists. Then Antiochus welcomed this humanized Stoicism, for it was no longer an insolent cynic but a lost child returning to its father's house in a spirit of humility and repentance. Antiochus recalled that Plato's followers had devoted themselves to morals and that Xenocrates had had a powerful influence on the philosophers at the Stoa; as a result he saw more similarities between the Stoics and the Old Academics than between the latter and their successors. Besides, in his time, the old enemies had mended some of their quarrels. If Antiochus taught the Stoic theory of the *enstēma* ("obstacle"), the different between him and Philo was almost entirely verbal, and the conflict between the two, while it was indeed a conflict between two Academics, was equally a conflict between two Stoics of different persuasions, since the *pithanon* used by Philo was a Stoic idea.

That is what Aenesidemus meant. Doubtless Arcesilaus and Carneades, implacably opposed to the Stoa as they were, hardly deserve the description of Stoics as much as the Academics at the beginning of the first century. But they too discussed the *phantasia kataleptike* and assent, the *katorthoma*, the *eulogon* and the *pithanon*. It may be that they were aiming to destroy Stoicism, but on their own admission they only existed by and because of it. Their first teacher, Socrates, claimed that he had invented nothing new but was merely using questions to help his interlocutors regain the truth. Arcesilaus and Carneades had the Stoics as their interlocutors and were in their debt, presenting themselves as heterodox Stoics rather than independent philosophers. They failed to destroy Stoicism, but they did make it evolve, to the point where, under Antiochus, it could be admitted into the Academy. The stature it thus achieved by becoming the constant subject of their discussions shows that, consciously or not, they were submitting to its ascendancy. Accordingly, Aenesidemus thought, the Academic philosophy has less scope than Pyrrhonism, since it is a stance taken toward Stoicism, while Pyrrhonism is a universal attitude. That is why the Academic philosophy leads nowhere: to suspend assent, to persuade us of this or of that—these, for the Academic, are just exercises in dialectic. The Pyrrhonist does not envisage a goal; but suspension of belief ensures that he is blessed with unruffled indifference and unshakable calm. Aenesidemus applied himself, therefore, to giving his arguments and his Modes of doubt (*tropoi tes epoches*) a general scope. He was not satisfied with antilogy and equipollence, nor did he limit his critique of sense perception to any particular past philosophy. He is not acataleptic but aporetic. It is not the criterion he disapproves of, nor certainty, but the knowledge of everything that goes beyond momentary appearance. However, when the New Academy was no longer active, the awareness of such distinctions became dulled. The skeptics were delighted to find in the Academic writings a whole battery of arguments against dogmatism. These arguments piled up in their archives, and sometimes no one could remember where they came from. This accounts for the anti-Stoic tone in the work of Sextus. The *Outlines of Pyrrhonism* shows immense concern for Pyrrhonian orthodoxy, particularly in the first book, but when Sextus embarks on refutation, it is nearly always Stoic logic that he takes as his target; in his works, dogmatism usually means Stoicism. This substitution of the Academic method of antilogy for the truly skeptic method of the Modes is a kind of adulteration of the original Pyrrhonism, against which Sextus tried to react, although he gave in to it himself.

NOTES

1. Edwyn Bevan, *Stoics and Sceptics* (Oxford, 1913); French translation by Laure Baudelot (Paris, 1927).

2. Helfried Hartmann, *Gewissheit und Wahrheit: Der Streit zwischen Stoa und akademischer Skepsis* (Halle-a-S., 1927).

3. *Revue d'histoire de la philosophie* 2 (1928), 186 ff. and 418 ff.

4. Πυρρωνίων Λόγοι, Book I (Photius, *Bibl.* 212, 170a).

5. See, among others, Cic. *Acad.* II 16: *Arcesilas Zenoni, ut putatur, obtrectans;* SE M VII 153: ταῦτα δὴ λεγόντων τῶν ἀπὸ τῆς Στοᾶς ὁ Ἀρκεσίλαος ἀντικαθίστατο.

6. See, in Arnim, *Stoicorum Veterum Fragmenta*, I, 67-69, the testimonies of Cicero, Sextus, Diogenes Laertius, and Stobaeus.

7. This definition must predate Chrysippus, because, having reported it, Diocles of Magnesia (DL VII 65: *SVF* II 193) adds: "*or*, as Chrysippus says (*Def. dial.*)," and quotes another more precise definition.

8. A presentation is true if a true assertion (κατηγορία) may be drawn from it; for example, the presentation that it is day is true at the moment when it is day, because then we may draw the assertion, conforming to reality, that it is day (SE M VII 244). The truth of the presentation derives from that of the proposition; to affirm that a presentation is true is to give our assent to the proposition involved in it.

9. *Ecl.* II 88, 1W (*SVF* III 171). A. Levi, "La teoria stoica della verità e dell' errore," *Rev. d'hist. de la Philos.* 2 (1928), 116, considers as Stoic the doctrine that assent relates, properly speaking, not to the presentation, but to the proposition.

10. The distinction Sextus draws here is not very solid: he accepts (*PH* I 30) that some famous skeptics also allowed as an end the suspension of judgment in inquiries. Diogenes Laertius (IX 107) states roundly: "The skeptics say that the end is *epochē*." It is not true, as Fabricius was the first to believe, that Diogenes attributes this thesis to Timon and Aenesidemus; he only says: "The skeptics accept *epochē* as end, which *ataraxia* follows like a shadow, as Timon and Aenesidemus declare." It is not impossible that this tradition, which has filtered into the skeptic school itself, derives from authors who made no distinction between Pyrrhonism and the Academy, and that by these "famous skeptics" one should understand simply Arcesilaus.

11. This seems to be what Aenesidemus did (*Pyrrh.* VIII, according to Photius, *Bibl.* 212, 170b).

12. I agree entirely with the remarks of Goedeckemeyer, *Die Geschichte des griechischen Skeptizismus* (Leipzig, 1905), p. 41 and n. 4. In his view, if Arcesilaus claimed that every *epochē* was a good and every assent an evil, it could only be in a spirit of mockery.

13. According to Usener, *Epicurea*, p. 399, this source would be Antiochus. Döring, "Doxographisches zur Lehre vom Τέλος ," *Zeitschrift für Philosophie und philosophische Kritik*, 1893, pp. 180-195, thinks the question is not so simple.

14. My interpretation of *epochē* and of the *eulogon* is close to H. von Arnim's (Pauly-Wissowa, *Realenzyklopädie*, II, 1166-68). However, I cannot quite share his view that Arcesilaus "subscribed in his heart to Platonic idealism" but "thought it inopportune to give doctrinal expression to his adherence."

15. *Acad.* II 67. A related version in Sextus *M* VII 157.

16. Diocles of Magnesia ap. DL VII 80.

17. Plutarch, *Stoic. repugn.* 1056e; Stobaeus, *Ecl.* II 111, 18W (SVF II, p. 291, 12 and III, p. 147, 4). These texts concern Stoics in general, but Stobaeus links the definition of opinion to the doctrine that the Sage has no opinion—a doctrine we know, from various reports (SVF 53-54 and 59), to have been taught by Zeno.

18. Aenesidemus does not accept any end; he groups the Academics among the dogmatists and so is keen to attribute an end to them. However, Cicero's report (*Fin.* III 31) shows that this interpretation of Arcesilaus did in fact exist in the Academy without being generally accepted there (*quidam*), at the time of Philo and Antiochus.

19. DL IX 61 tells us that Ascanius of Abdera, a character who seems otherwise completely unknown, credited Pyrrho with the introduction of *akatalēpsia* and of *epochē*. Now the term *akatalēpsia* is particularly appropriate for the Academics, adversaries of the *phantasia kataleptikē*; which is why Goedeckemeyer, *Geschichte d. Skept.*, p. 12, n. 3, who accepts the testimony of Ascanius, is induced to reject that of Aenesidemus (Photius, *Bibl.* 212, 169b). In any case, we are constantly told that Arcesilaus spoke of *epochē*; Pyrrho seems to have attached importance above all to indifference and to *ataraxia*, and his attitude is governed by reference to things rather than thoughts.

20. Clem. *Strom.* VIII 5 (*SVF* II, p. 37, 12-14). This text is certainly referring to a Stoic later than Arcesilaus, but it shows that the Stoa considered *epochē* compatible, in certain cases (ἔν τισι), with their doctrine.

21. Epicurus, *Letter to Herodotus* (DL X 50-51); Lucr. IV 463: *opinatus animi, quos addimus ipsi*. Cf. Cic. *Acad.* II 83.

22. Sextus, *PH* I 19. It is not always possible to make out, in Sextus's work, what belongs to original Pyrrhonism and what the Pyrrhonists borrowed later from the Academy. However, Sextus's phrase ἀβουλήτως ἡμᾶς ἄγοντα εἰς συγκατάθεσιν ("leading us involuntarily to assent"), although it seems to have been more or less borrowed from the Stoics or the Academics, is in fact contrary to Stoicism, which makes assent dependent on our will.

23. Sextus, *PH* I 10. Pyrrhonian *epochē*, closely linked to the formula οὐ μᾶλλον ("no more"), leaves no room for the *eulogon*.

24. Sextus, *M* VII 155-157: τὸ δὲ ἀσυγκαταθετεῖν οὐδέν ἕτερόν ἐστιν ἢ τὸ ἐπέχειν. Cf. Cic. *Acad.* II 67-68 and 78.

25. Cic. *Acad.* I 40. Clement, *Strom.* II (*SVF* II 992) says, on the contrary: "Not only the *Platonists* but also the Stoics say that assents depend on us." But this report, which cites no proper name, is vague indeed. Carneades, speaking in Stoic fashion, says that a presentation is apprehensive insofar as it leads to assent (Sextus, *M* VII 405). But that does not mean that it produces it automatically; Chrysippus is up in arms at the idea that a presentation could be the sufficient cause of assent (Plut. *Stoic. rep.* 1055f; *SVF* II 994; cf. Cic. *Acad.* II 37 *in fine*). See Levi, "La Teoria stoica della verità e dell' errore," pp. 124-125.

26. "on which . . . requires" reproduces Couissin's rendering of a difficult passage in Sextus's Greek which might alternatively mean: "on which happiness, that is, the end of life, depends for its assurance."—Ed.

27. Diocles of Magnesia (DL VII 75). Strictly speaking, the *eulogon*, like the *pithanon* and the true, is an attribute of a *proposition*; but in the broader sense, the Stoics spoke of presentations as *pithanai*, true, *eulogoi*, which is to say, as involving propositions of the same quality. The term *eulogos phantasia* is found in the end of an anecdote about Sphaerus (Athenaeus VIII 354c: DL VII 177). This anecdote also shows how a disciple of Zeno and Cleanthes understood the term *eulogon*. King Ptolemy Philopator had served to him some wax pomegranates; deceived by their appearance, he replied, without embarrassment, that he had assented not to their being pomegranates but to its being *eulogon* that they were pomegranates. I think, therefore, contrary to the interpretation of Goedeckemeyer, *Geschichte d. Skept.*, p. 43, that already Cleanthes and Arcesilaus understood the term *"eulogon"* in accordance with the definition of Diocles of Magnesia.

28. Arnim, *SVF* III 284 reproduces Arcesilaus's argument and writes, "Arcesilaus e Stoicorum placitis profectus contra Stoicos disputat." As for the proposition "prudence is sufficient for happiness," it is genuinely Stoic, since Seneca (*Ep.* 85.2), having deduced happiness from prudence by a sorites, formulates this conclusion: *Prudentia ad beatam vitam satis est.*

29. It is Chrysippus, according to Plutarch (*Stoic. rep.* 1046d), who identifies happiness and prudence. And this, the author adds, leads him to contradictions that would never arise if he thought, like Epicurus, that prudence is a good that creates happiness. We can sense the Academic's effort to reduce the Stoic doctrine to the Epicurean doctrine. There is no lack of texts where the Stoics describe prudence as an "end" (Plut. *Comm. not.* 1065d), as an "art of life," as the "knowledge of things good and evil and indifferent" (SE *M* XI 170 *passim*). Carneades uses this last definition in his refutation of Stoic theology (SE *M* X 163). It is plain that prudence played an important part in the philosophy of the Stoa and in the Academic critique.

30. Chrysippus, *De lust. demonstr.* fr. 2 (*SVF* III 297). Zeno knows the *katorthōma* (Cic. *Acad.* I 37); nothing allows us to suppose that he saw it any differently from Chrysippus, even if he did not at once find such an exact definition.

31. Instead of "lies"(κεῖσθαι) certain manuscripts have "moves" (κινεῖσθαι). Stobaeus (*SVF* III, p. 64, 16) relates prudence to *kathēkonta*, not to *katorthōmata*; but this passage must refer to Stoics after Chrysippus—for example, Archedemus (*SVF* III 19-20) or Antipater.

32. DL VII 107-108; Stob. *Ecl.* II 7-8; Cic. *Fin.* III 58 (*SVF* I 230). Zeno, the author of a book *About the kathēkon*, was said to have been the first to have used this word in this sense (DL VII 4, 25, 108).

33. See Arnim, in Pauly-Wiss., II, 1165, lines 8-61; Albert Thibaudet, *Le Bergsonisme*, 7th ed. (Paris, 1923) II, 250-251; Rivaud, "Platon auteur dramatique," *Rev. d'hist. de la Philos.* 1 (1927), esp. pp. 150-151. A recent interpreter of Antiochus denies that Plato was a dogmatist: "Plato himself did not want to be dogmatic; every ten years he searched for a new formula, and many of his dialogues,

for example the *Theaetetus* and the *Phaedrus*, are explicitly antidogmatic" (Hans Strache, *Der Eklektizismus des Antiochus von Askalon* [Berlin, 1921], p. 2, n. 1). See below, Summary and Conclusion.

34. According to the Stoics, an action presupposes impulse (*hormē*), without which nothing can be accomplished (Sen. *Ep.* 113, 1; *SVF* III 307); now impulse is an assent, practical assent (Stob. *Ecl.* II 88, 1W; *SVF* III 171). These texts are attributed to the Stoics in general, but Zeno and Cleanthes had already written *About Impulse* (*SVF* I 41, and p. 107, 4).

35. "but those . . . attack" reproduces Couissin's rendering of a difficult passage in Sextus's Greek which might alternatively mean: "but those [associates of Arcesilaus] who are thought to have established one produced it as an attack."—Ed.

36. Plutarch's *Against Colotes* contains a defense of Arcesilaus and of *epochē* (chaps. 26-27, 1121e-1123a). This does not prove that the theses put forward there are those of Arcesilaus; if Plutarch names only him, it is because he is replying to one of his contemporaries, but he may be influenced by later Academic teaching. This does not in any way detract from the interest of the work, because: 1) The principal objection of the Epicurean Colotes is borrowed from the Stoa, which is proof of the fiery quarrel between Arcesilaus and the Stoics. 2) This objection is that inaction follows upon *epochē*. Now or never is the moment to counter with the theory of the *eulogon*, but a Stoic reply is inappropriate for an Epicurean; and since no probabilism exists in Epicurus, the Academic professes none when he replies. Epicurus teaches that the objects of presentation are real; Arcesilaus's defender concludes from this that impulse follows presentation, with no need of assent; it is an apology for *epochē* in Epicurean style. 3) The Epicureans are rebuked for invoking common opinion, while going against it when they reject providence and the art of divination. The insult would be odd for an Academic, were it not polemical. 4) Epicurus accused Arcesilaus (before he was scholarch) of saying nothing of his own, and indeed his method demanded this. But let us add that, far from attempting to pass for an innovator, Arcesilaus attributed his theses on *epochē* and *akatalēpsia* to famous ancients: the "sophists" of his time (τοὺς τότε σοφιστάς) reproached him for it. It is strange and significant that Arcesilaus's adversaries (doubtless Stoics) should be called Sophists.

37. "Basing . . . dogmatists" reproduces Couissin's rendering of a difficult passage in Sextus's Greek which might alternatively mean: "basing their arguments on a concession [by themselves, for a dialectical end] of various dogmatic views."—Ed.

38. *Acad.* II 11-12: *Dedi Antiocho operam diligentius, ut causam ex eo totam cognoscerem* ("I gave my attention more closely to Antiochus, in order to learn from him his whole case"). Cf. *Ad fam.* IX 8.1.

39. Hirzel, *Untersuchungen zu Cicero's philosophischen Schriften* (Leipzig, 1883), III, 162-180; Brochard, *Les Sceptiques grecs* (Paris, 1887), pp. 132-135.

40. *SVF* I 53-54 (Zeno); 625 (Sphaerus); II 110; *passim* (Chrysippus). Chrysippus had devoted an entire work to this question (*SVF* II, p. 9, 27).

41. SE M VII 151: Cic. *Tusc.* IV 15; Stob. *Ecl.* II 111, 18W. Ganter (*Philologus*, 1894, pp. 498-500) remarks that opinion thus has two causes: one subjective, the

weakness of assent, the other objective, its falsity. I think that just one of these causes is enough for assent to be an opinion: assent to a presentation that is true but not apprehensive (SE *M* VII 247) is an opinion.

42. Cic. *Acad.* II 59: *opinatorum, id est peccatorum* |= ἁμαρτήσειν|, *esse sapientem*.

43. Cic. *Acad.* II 73, 111, 119. Carneades is not named in any of these texts, but he is at the head of the passage from Sextus (*M* VII 169) which implies the admission of truth. The third text of the *Academica* (II 119) seems also to be in a part borrowed from Clitomachus. See Lorcher, *Das fremde und das eigene in Ciceros Büchern de finibus bonorum et malorum und den Academica* (Halle-a.-S., 1911), pp. 276-281, and "Bericht über die Literatur zu Ciceros philosophischen Schriften aus den Jahren 1902-1922," in *Jahresbericht über die Fortschritte der klassischen Altertumswissenschaft* 162 (1913), 84-85.

44. Sextus's texts contain some obscurities: in *PH* I 227-229, he inverts the order of the second and third criteria. Reasons for preferring this latter order are to be found in Mutschmann, "Die Stufen der Wahrscheinlichkeit des Karneades," *Rhein. Mus.*, 1911, pp. 190-198; reasons against in Arnim, in Pauly-Wiss., s.v. Karneades, I, B.

45. Plut. *Stoic. rep.* 1055f (*SVF* II 994). This passage is explained by the fact that assent is up to us. If persuasive presentation leads to assent, it does not mean that we cannot withhold assent: thus the *pithanon* is not irreconcilable with *epochē*. Perhaps the word ἄγον (DL VII 75) forces the meaning of *pithanon*. Ἐπισπᾶσθαι (SE *M* VII 172) εἰς συγκατάθεσιν seems to be more suitable for the *pithanon*: persuasive presentation draws us toward assent, but apprehensive presentation leads us to it (ἐπάγονται, SE *M* VII 405).

46. περιφανῶς. The term "περιφάνεια" is also applied by the Stoics to persuasive presentations (Sextus *M* VII 242).

47. *De Acad. cum Plat. dissens.*, ap. Euseb. *Praep. ev.* XIV 8.

48. They also abandoned it on other questions. See Schmekel, *Die Philosophie der mittleren Stoa* (Berlin, 1892), pp. 304-384, and Bréhier, *Chrysippe* (Paris, 1910), pp. 280 (cf. p. 91, n. 2 and p. 100, n. 2).

49. Stob. *Ecl.* II 75, 11W; Clem. *Strom.* II 21; Plut. *Comm. not.* XXVII (*SVF* III, p. 252, 35-253, 23).

50. *M* VII 253-260. Hirzel (*Untersuch.*, III, Exc. 1, pp. 514-517) has spotted characteristics of Antiochus in this text. The ἐνστημα reappears in *quae obstant et impediunt* (Cic. *Acad.* II 19); other striking similarities are to be found in *Acad.* II 38 and 46. But did Antiochus invent his arguments and theories? If he borrowed them from the Stoics, as Schmekel thinks (*Die Philos. d. mittleren Stoa*, pp. 392-399), even this link in no way proves that Sextus's source is here Antiochus. It would be most unusual to describe a scholarch of the Academy, even *germanissimus Stoicus*, by the appellation "the younger Stoics." Schmekel (pp. 353-356) sees the author of the passage as a contemporary of Clitomachus, none other, according to him, than Panaetius.

51. The reference is to the lost Book I of the first edition of Cicero's *Academica*, in which Catulus expounded the skepticism of Carneades. The *Academica* as we have it now consists of (part of) Book I from the second edition and Book II from the first.—Ed.

52. Cic. *Acad.* II 111. Among presentations, says Carneades, some are true, others false; but true presentations and false ones are indistinguishable. But how, if the presentations are indistinguishable, can we say that the first are true and the others false? This objection is awkward for Philo, who asserts the existence of such presentations, but Carneades asserts nothing. He starts from Stoicism, conceding to it for the sake of argument that there are true and false presentations; but then he shows that they are indistinguishable. Antiochus's argument works against Philo, not against Carneades.

53. Léon Robin, *La pensée grècque* (Paris, 1923), p. 283.

54. "Platon auteur dramatique," *Rev. d'hist. de la Philos.* 1 (1927), 146.

4

Stoics and Skeptics on Clear and Distinct Impressions

Michael Frede

The history of Hellenistic philosophy is dominated by the rivalry between Stoics and skeptics, first Academic skeptics and later Pyrrhonian skeptics who tried to revive a more radical form of skepticism when in the second and first centuries B.C. Academic skeptics seemed to have softened their stand to a degree that made it difficult to distinguish them from their Stoic rivals. The debate between Stoics and skeptics primarily concerned the nature and possibility of knowledge. If the skeptics also tried to attack the Stoic position on all other questions, the point of this, at least originally, was in good part to show that the Stoics themselves had failed to attain the knowledge they claimed to be attainable.

Both Stoics and skeptics saw themselves as followers of Socrates, but they took a different view as to the moral to be drawn from Socrates' experience. Socrates by his dialectical practice had shown that, in spite of claims to the contrary, nobody actually possesses the kind of knowledge which would guarantee a rational and happy life, and that, if he himself had any claim to wisdom, it only rested on his ready recognition that he was no less ignorant than anybody else. But Socrates had not resigned himself to his ignorance. And the Stoics seem to have assumed that the reason for this was that Socrates thought that the special kind of knowledge which he had shown people to lack is in fact attainable. They assumed that nature must have constructed human beings in such a way as to make it possible for them to lead a rational and good life. And if this, as Socrates was thought to have shown, is a matter of being wise, nature must also have provided us with the means to gain the kind of knowledge which constitutes wisdom. The skeptics, on the other hand, thought that it remained an open question whether such knowledge could be attained and that hence all one could do meanwhile was go on looking for the truth and subject all claims to the kind of dialectical scrutiny Socrates had subjected them to. Since the Stoa was rapidly developing into the most influential school, it was only natural that the skeptics would turn their dialectical skill in particular against the Stoics who claimed to be on the way to the kind of knowledge Socrates had searched for in vain.

Now when the Stoics claimed that such knowledge is attainable, they also thought that they had to construct an epistemology in terms of which they could show that and how such knowledge is to be gained. On this account nature has provided us with a firm basis for knowledge by providing us with clear and distinct impressions, the so-called kataleptic or cognitive impressions, which by their very nature cannot be false and hence constitute an unfailing guide to the truths one has to know in order to have the wisdom that guarantees the good life. Thus the Stoic theory of knowledge is based on a doctrine of clear and distinct impressions. Given that the skeptics not only were not persuaded that such knowledge had been attained, but even questioned whether such knowledge was attainable, they naturally focused their attack on the Stoic theory of knowledge and in particular on the Stoic doctrine of clear and distinct impressions by means of which we are supposed to be able to acquire the knowledge in question. As a result a lively debate ensued which lasted for more than two centuries and which attracted the best philosophers of the time.

Tradition, though, has developed a view of the Stoic position which makes it so vulnerable to skeptical attacks that it becomes very difficult to understand how the Stoics, through centuries, were able to sustain the criticism without having to concede defeat. If the Stoics had defended the position that tends to be ascribed to them, their school should have been deserted in no time. That instead it was defended by men of the ingenuity of a Chrysippus should encourage us to take a fresh look at the Stoic position to see whether it might not be more attractive or at least easier to defend than tradition would make us believe.

THE STOIC POSITION

IMPRESSIONS

Animals and human beings are constructed in such a way that their survival and well-being depends essentially on the adequacy of their cognitions. They have to be able to recognize and to shun what is bad for them, and they have to be in a position to realize and seek out what is conducive to their preservation and well-being. For this purpose they are equipped with a sensory apparatus and a soul which, via the senses, receives impressions of the outside world, and thus provides them with some kind of awareness of the world around them. There is a crucial difference, though, between the impressions of rational beings and the impressions of animals. The impressions of rational beings are called "rational impressions" (DL VII 51). Rational impressions have a propositional content, they are impressions to the effect that something is the case very much in the sense in which we might say ordinarily, "the impression which one gets, if one looks at the evidence, is that. . . ." Thus rational impressions are thoughts (DL VII 51; Ps.-Gal. *Def. med.* XIX 381 K.) which present themselves to the mind and which the mind either accepts or refuses to accept. To accept or give assent to a thought or impression is to have the belief that the proposition which forms the content of the impression is true, to refuse to accept a thought is to suspend judgment. Thoughts may present themselves to the mind in all sorts of ways. They may come to mind when one considers the evidence concerning a question in doubt. But many of them are brought about by the causal agency of an external object which, through the sense organs, gives rise to an impression in us. Thus to see something, on this view, is to have a certain kind of thought generated in a certain way. But thoughts may also be generated in all sorts of other ways.

Now the Stoics follow Socrates, Plato, and Aristotle in the view that it is a mark of moral knowledge that one never has a mistaken view in moral matters. The Stoics even take the stronger view that the wise man will never have any false beliefs at all (Stob. *Ecl.* II 111, 18 W.), because, for reasons we will see later, any false belief might stand in the way of one's acquiring the kind of knowledge we are after. One way in which nature could construct a mind which has the ability to avoid any false beliefs whatsoever would be to endow the mind with the ability unfailingly to sort the true impressions from the false ones. But such a mind would be superhuman; nothing like the human physiology would be able to support such a powerful mind. Instead nature provided human beings with the ability unfailingly to distinguish true impressions of a certain kind—namely, clear and distinct impressions—from all other impressions whether they are true or not. In this way human beings are not in a position to know all truths but only those whose truth is guaranteed by clear and distinct impressions. But then we do not need to know all truths to lead a good life, and the clear and distinct impressions we receive in the ordinary course of events provide an ample basis for what we need to know. If our ability to know is restricted this way, our ability to avoid false belief is unlimited: all we need to do is not to accept as true any impression that is not guaranteed to be true by clear and distinct impressions. Thus there will be many true impressions which we nevertheless will not give assent to, but there will be no false impressions which we accept as true.

All this presupposes that there is a class of impressions which by their very nature cannot be false and that the mind can discriminate between these and other impressions. Our main task in the following will be to explain how the Stoics could make these assumptions. In order to understand this, we first have to have a closer look at the Stoic doctrine of rational impressions quite generally.

On the one hand rational impressions are not mere sensory affections. This distinguishes them from the impressions of irrational animals. There are several passages according to which the Stoics distinguish rational impressions from mere sense-impressions (cf. Cic. *Acad.* II 21; SE *M* VII 345). Even the most primitive rational impression, like the impression that this is white, already involves the representation of the object by means of a concept, in this case the concept "white." It is in this way that they require a rational mind and manage to be thoughts and to have a definite propositional content. Sometimes commentators talk as if we applied concepts to objects on the basis of impressions which in themselves are preconceptual. But this cannot be the way the Stoics think of rational impressions. For given an impression which does not yet involve the conceptualization of the object, we could have any number of beliefs about the object on the basis of such an impression. Hence there would not be any one definite proposition that forms the content of the impression, and assent to the impression would not constitute a definite belief. It may be objected that impressions are supposed to be passive affections of the mind, whereas the mind's conceptualization of an object would be an active contribution of the mind to the impression. But it has to be kept in mind that the Stoics characterize an impression as a passive affection of the mind to contrast it with the act of assent and not to deny that the mind has any part in the formation of a thought. As we will see, the Stoics think that the kind of impression which we have very much depends on whether our mind is in normal working order; and part of what an object does, when it gives rise to an impression in a rational mind that is in working order, is that it makes the mind conceptualize the object in a certain way. In this sense the rational impression is a passive affection of the mind, though it does involve the operation of the mind. It will also be objected that impressions only give rise to concepts and hence cannot themselves already presuppose concepts. This objection overlooks the developmental character of the Stoic account. Human beings, according to the Stoics, start out as irrational animals. As such they have the kind of sense-impressions which animals have. But in the case of human beings these impressions give rise to concepts of very simple perceptual features like colors, shapes, tastes, and the like, and thus reason slowly starts to grow. Once we have these simple concepts, we can have corresponding rational impressions and, what is more important, corresponding cognitive impressions. These will naturally give rise to more complex concepts, like that of a man or a tree, which in turn will enable us to have more complex rational and in particular cognitive impressions (cf. Cic. *Acad.* II 21). Thus these common notions that arise in us naturally on the basis of more primitive impressions turn out to be truly anticipations (Cic. *nd* I 44; *prolēpseis*); for they are needed to form the impressions that afford us a grasp on things (*katalēpsis*); it is in terms of them that the mind has a grasp on things. Thus rational impressions and in particular cognitive impressions do presuppose concepts, but these arise from more primitive impressions that do not presuppose these concepts, and ultimately from sense-impressions that do not presuppose any concepts whatsoever but that are not rational either. Given this developmental account, it is easy to see how the Stoics can claim that concepts only arise from the appropriate impressions and nevertheless maintain that a rational impression involves the conceptualization of the object.

On the other hand, there is more to a rational impression than just the propositional content. We cannot identify an impression by just specifying the proposition it is a thought of. To have a rational impression is to think a certain proposition in a certain way. The kind of impression we have depends not only on the propositional content, but also on the way in which this content is thought. For the same proposition may be thought in any number of ways, and depending on the way it is thought we get different kinds of impressions. One way they differ is the way in which the subject of the proposition—that is, the object of the thought—is represented in the impression. The thought that this (a book in front of me) is green which I have when I look at the book differs considerably from the thought that this (the very same book) is green which I have when I close my eyes and touch the book, though the propositional content, at least in Stoic logic, is exactly the same. The thought that John's cat is gray is quite different depending on whether I see the cat or whether I am just told that John bought a gray cat, though, again, the propositional content may be exactly the same. But thoughts may also differ in the way in which the feature that is attributed to the object is represented. I may be in the habit of thinking of death as something bad and dreadful, in which case it would be a pain for me to accept the thought that I am dying. If, on the other hand, death is a matter of indifference to me, the thought that I am dying would be a rather different kind of thought, whose acceptance would not be a pain. In fact, the Stoics seem to think that all emotions and passions are a matter of accepting thoughts thought in a certain way, and that the way these thoughts are thought is entirely a matter of certain further beliefs we have—in particular, beliefs about what is good and what is bad—which we draw on to represent the object of the impression and the feature attributed to it in the thought. Thus all contents of the mind turn out to be thoughts. And it becomes even more apparent why the Stoics should be so concerned with our ability to distinguish between true and false impressions; for on this view even our feelings and desires turn out to be nothing but a matter of accepting true or false thoughts of a certain kind.

For our purposes one difference in the way objects may be represented in our thoughts deserves special emphasis. If one perceives an object, it tends, at least under normal conditions, to be represented in one's thought in such a way that just on the basis of this very representation one could go on to say lots of things about the object in addition to what one thinks about it, and these things that one could say about it may or may not be things one antecedently believed to be true of the object. In cases in which one neither is perceiving the object nor even has perceived it, the object will be represented in one's thought entirely in terms of what one antecedently believed to be true of it. And thus it will be represented in terms of general concepts each of which might equally apply to other objects. But if I see the object and think that it is green, the object may not be represented by general concepts at all, except for the concept "green," though it will be represented in such a way that, just on the basis of the impression, we could go on to represent it in terms of a host of concepts.

From what has been said it should be clear that there is some sense in which impressions have parts corresponding to the various features that are represented in the impression—more particularly, a part or parts corresponding to the features in terms of which the object of the thought or the subject of the proposition is represented, and a part or parts corresponding to the feature or features the object is represented as having—that is, a part or parts that correspond to the predicate of the proposition the impression is a thought of. The Stoics seem to be willing to call such parts of impressions "impressions," too. For they call general notions "impressions" (SE *M* VII 246; Plut. *Comm. not.* 1084F; cf. Cic. *Acad.* II 21). But this seems to be misleading, since parts of impressions are not true or false in the way impressions properly speaking are. Hence it might be better to call such parts of impressions "ideas" and to distinguish the way ideas have a propositional content and are true or false from the way impressions properly speaking are propositional and true or false. The Stoics also seem to distinguish between generic, or abstract, and specific, or concrete, ideas (cf. SE *M* VII 246). The idea of man in general, for example, is abstract, whereas the idea of Socrates and the idea of his complexion may be specific, or concrete. The fact that we represent an object in an impression by means of a general concept is reflected by the fact that the corresponding part of the impression is an abstract idea. Moreover, we have to assume that the parts of rational impressions are ordered so that their combination in the appropriate order amounts to the thought of a proposition, whereas their combination in a different order might amount to the thought of a different proposition or to no thought at all.

To sum up: impressions are impressions of an object; in the case of rational impressions this impression consists in a thought concerning the object; such a thought involves the conceptualization of the object, but it need not be, and in the case of perception is not, entirely conceptual; nevertheless, the thought is the thought of a proposition; but it is characterized not only by the proposition it is a thought of, but also by the way this proposition is thought; the way a proposition is thought depends on the way the constituents of the proposition are represented in the thought; this representation does not have to be entirely conceptual— that is, it does not have to consist entirely of abstract ideas—in order to represent a constituent of a proposition and in order to be constitutive of a thought; in the case of perception the thought is partly nonconceptual; it nevertheless is a thought, because it does involve the conceptualization of the object, and in particular because it minimally involves the kind of conceptualization of its object which gives it a propositional content that is true or false, as a result of which the thought itself can be said to be true or false.

COGNITIVE IMPRESSIONS

How could there be impressions that cannot fail to be true, not for the trivial reason that they are true or correspond to the facts, but because of some other feature that is logically independent of their truth? It seems that there could be such a feature, namely the property of having a certain kind of causal history, and that the Stoics are relying on this feature.

Impressions have a certain causal history. In the course of this history all sorts of things can go wrong. The mind, for example, may be defective and hence produce the wrong impression. In the case of vision the light may be wrong, the distance too big or too small, the sensory apparatus malfunctioning, and as a result we may get a false impression. On the other hand, it stands to reason that nature has constructed things in such a way that under normal conditions the impression we receive is true. If under normal conditions something appears to be red or appears to be a human being, then it is red or is a human being. Thus impressions with the right kind of history cannot fail to be true, though the fact that they have this kind of history is logically independent of their truth. Let us call such impressions "normal."

There are different kinds of normal impressions. In particular it seems useful to distinguish two kinds. If, for example, I have the impression that $2 + 2 = 4$ because I have a proof for the proposition that $2 + 2 = 4$, my impression will have the right kind of causal history that will guarantee its truth. But it is not a causal history that links the object of the impression, say the number 4, with my impression; the impression, though produced in an appropriate, normal way, is not produced or caused by the object of the impression itself. It is, at least according to the Stoics, only in cases of perception that the normal impression is caused by the object itself. Hence it will be useful to treat normal impressions of this particular kind as a separate class and to call them "perceptual impressions."

That the Stoics think of cognitive impressions as normal is suggested by the following. Sextus Empiricus (*M* VII 247) characterized noncognitive impressions quite generally as those one comes to have because of some abnormal condition (*pathos*). "Abnormal condition" here can hardly refer just to abnormal states of mind; for even in a normal state of mind one will have noncognitive impressions—for example, if one is seeing something from too far away. Hence "abnormal conditions" here has to be understood as referring to a whole set of normal conditions. And in SE *M* VII 424 we are in fact given such a set of conditions for the case of vision. Five conditions have to be met for a visual impression to be cognitive: conditions on the sense organ, on the object of vision, on how the object is placed, on how the impression comes about, and on the state of mind. And though this is not said explicitly, it is strongly suggested that if these conditions are met, the impression will be cognitive. Similarly Cicero (*Acad.* II 19) refers to such a set of sufficient and necessary conditions for cognitive impressions.

Moreover, though this is a matter of considerable controversy, it also seems that the Stoics think of cognitive impressions as perceptual. Aetius (*Plac.* IV 8.1) explicitly says that cognitive impressions come about through a sense organ. Cicero talks of cognitive impressions as if they originated in the senses (*Acad.* II 83). And the way the Stoics define cognitive impressions (they are supposed to arise from an object) and what they have to say about the clearness and distinctness of impressions make straightforward sense only for perceptual impressions.

What seems to stand in the way of this assumption is the following. The Stoics clearly assume that there are nonperceptual cognitions, namely, in those cases where we have a proof of a theorem (DL VII 52). But it also is the case that even nonperceptual cognitions according to the Stoics involve impressions (SE *M* VII 370). Hence, it seems natural to assume that the impressions involved in cognitions, whether they are perceptual or not, are cognitive. Moreover, there are texts which claim that a cognition consists in the assent to a cognitive impression (SE *M* VII 151; VIII 397). Hence, if there are nonperceptual cognitions, there should be nonperceptual cognitive impressions. Finally, cognitive impressions are supposed to be the criterion of truth. Whatever else this may mean, it must mean that the truth of cognitive impressions is the guarantee of the truth of whatever impressions the wise man accepts as true. But if we restrict cognitive impressions to perceptual impressions, it is difficult to see how their truth would suffice as a basis to guarantee the truth of all other impressions the wise man will accept as true.

To deal with the last point first, we have to take into account that the Stoics seem to think that all features of objects—that is, of sensible bodies—are perceptible. Thus they think that we can even learn to see that something or somebody is beautiful, good, or virtuous (Plut. *Comm. not.* 1062C; *Stoic. rep.* 1042E-F; Cic. *ND* II 145), just as we have to learn to see that something is a man or a horse (Cic. *Acad.* II 21). If this at first sight seems strange, we have to remember that according to the Stoics, qualities of bodily objects like virtue are bodies themselves that form a mixture with the bodies they are the qualities of and hence cannot fail to affect our perception of the objects, given that our perception, at least if trained, is extremely discriminatory; a virtuous body must look quite different from a vicious body to a trained eye. Thus perception, as the Stoics understand it, provides a much broader basis than we would assume. And it will also turn out, when we consider the doctrine of the criterion, that the Stoics do in fact think that all other impressions can be accepted as true to the extent that their truth is guaranteed by the truth of perceptual impressions. Thus Cicero (*Acad.* II 21-22) points out that at some time in our development we come to have the (nonperceptual) cognition that if something is a man, it is a mortal rational animal. But when he explains why this cannot but be true, he does not say that the corresponding impression is cognitive; instead he says that it cannot be false because it is due to impressions that cannot be false, namely, cognitive impressions that are perceptual.

Once we realize that all truths available to us are supposed to be certified by the truth of perceptual impressions, it seems fairly clear that our problem about the scope of cognitive impressions is not so much a problem concerning Stoic doctrine but rather a problem concerning terminology. In fact, it is rather similar, and materially related, to the problem which we have about the scope of "clear" or "evident" and which it seems best to solve by distinguishing between self-evident impressions and impressions whose evidence depends on the evidence of other impressions. Similarly it seems that the Stoics take the view that only perceptual impressions are cognitive in their own right. Thus other impressions can only be called cognitive to the extent that they have a cognitive content which depends on the cognitive content of impressions which are cognitive in their own right. Thus we may distinguish between self-evident impressions which are cognitive in a narrow sense, and evident impressions which are cognitive in a wider sense. And if we do so, we can say with Sextus Empiricus that a cognition consists in the assent to a cognitive impression, and we can also say that any cognition, whether perceptual or not, involves a cognitive impression, and nevertheless assume that cognitive impressions, strictly speaking, are perceptual.

Perceptual impressions, in addition to being normal and hence true, have certain other features that are of interest for our purposes. In the case of perceptual impressions the impression represents the object the way it does because the object is this way—that is, all representational features of the impression are due to the object and not to some abnormal condition that would cause the mind to produce an impression different from the one it would produce normally. Thus a perceptual impression in no way misrepresents its object. But considering the purpose for which we have been endowed with cognition, it also stands to reason that nature has constructed things in such a way that under normal conditions we not only have an impression which does not misrepresent things but have one which represents them clearly, that is, affords us a clear answer as to what kinds of objects we are facing. And under normal conditions we do in fact have a clear view of an object we are confronted with, and we can tell without difficulty what its visual features are. Let us call such an impression "clear" or "evident."

The term "evident" has been used, misused, and misunderstood in many ways. To guard against such misunderstanding of the Stoic position some remarks may be in order. The adjective "evident" (*enargēs*) can be used in ordinary Greek to qualify a term "A" to refer to something as being obviously as A; thus an evident robber is somebody who quite obviously is a robber (Soph. *O.T.* 535). But even in ordinary Greek the term can be used in cases in which appearances are deceptive; the evident ox may not be an ox at all, but Zeus in disguise (cf. Soph. *Tr.* 11). Things also can be said to evidently appear to be a certain way. And hence it is easy for philosophers to move on to talk of evident appearances or evident impressions, though by this they obviously do not mean to suggest that some of our impressions are such that it is evident that they are impressions. This move must have been facilitated by the fact that even in ordinary Greek, dream images can be said to be evident (Aesch. *Pers.* 179). Given the ordinary use of the term, evidence suggests but does not guarantee truth. Thus Platonists (cf. SE *M* VII 143) and, of course, Academics (cf. Cic. *Acad.* II 34) do not take evidence to be a criterion of truth. Theophrastus, on the other hand, seems to have been the first philosopher to assume that it does guarantee truth (cf. SE *M* VII 218), and in this he was followed by the Epicureans and the Stoics. Since they cannot rely on ordinary usage for this assumption, we have to look for some argument that would justify this restricted use of the term "evident" or the assumption that even given the ordinary use it turns out that only true impressions are evident. The Stoics may have argued along the following lines: we can learn to see whether something is an ox or a robber; and under normal conditions, if nothing impedes our seeing things clearly, we do see whether something is an ox or only an ox in disguise; for the only things that can really look and move like oxen are oxen; thus something cannot be an evident ox without being a real ox. For it could appear to be an ox without being one only if we had not yet learned to see oxen properly or if our view was somehow impeded because one of the normal conditions was not met; but in this case the ox would not be evident. Evidence is an objective feature of impressions which is not to be confused with a subjective feeling of conviction or certainty, however strong that feeling may be, just as having a clear view of something is a matter of objective fact and not of subjective feeling. How we know that an impression is evident is a different matter, to which we will turn later; for this, our "feeling" may very well be relevant, but it seems, even in optimal circumstances, to be no more than a symptom of the evidence of an impression.

To get clearer about the notion of evidence which is in question here, it may be useful to consider the connection between truth and evidence. Impressions are true, because their propositional content is true, and not because of the way this propositional content is thought, that is, represented in the impression. The same propositional content, as we have seen, can be thought in all sorts of different ways, and correspondingly we get different kinds of impressions; but this difference between the impressions is of no relevance for their truth, which entirely depends on the truth of the proposition. Evidence, on the other hand, is primarily a feature of impressions which does depend on the way a proposition is represented in thought. Thus the same proposition that this is octagonal can be thought by an evident thought when I see an octagonal tower under normal conditions, and by a nonevident thought, if I just know from a book that the tower is octagonal. Propositions only secondarily may be called evident, if there should be any propositions that cannot be thought at all except by evident thoughts. What makes a thought or an impression evident is that it is already part of the representation of the subject of the proposition that the predicate should be true of it and that the representation of the subject is entirely due to the subject itself. Thus evidence is not what makes an impression or a proposition true, but an evident impression cannot but have a true proposition for its content and hence be true itself.

So far it would seem that for the impression that S is P to be evident, the representation of S already has to represent S as being P. But it seems that under normal conditions, when we have a clear view of an object, more than one of its features is clearly represented. And, in fact, Sextus (*M* VII 248, 250, 251) talks as if a cognitive impression captured all the characteristics of the object in precise manner. Cicero on the other hand explains that a cognitive impression does not pick up all the features of an object, but only all those features which are appropriate for its kind, visual features in the case of vision, auditory features in the case of hearing, etc. (*Acad.* I 42). Since even the weaker claim is extraordinarily strong, it will be safer to follow Cicero. In this case a cognitive impression will be evident in that it involves a representation of the object which clearly represents all the features of the object that are appropriate for the kind of impression it is; and since it represents all the features of the object in question, it will also represent the particular feature which it represents it as having, that is, the feature attributed to it in the proposition.

Cognitive impressions are not only clear, as opposed to obscure (*amudros*; cf. Alex. Aphrod. *De an.* 71.5 f.), they also are distinct (*ektupos*; cf. DL VII 46), as opposed to confused (*sugkechumenos*; cf. SE *M* VII 171). To see what their distinctness is supposed to consist in, it will be useful to refer to a doctrine which is never explicitly attributed to the Stoics but which we do find in Hellenistic dogmatic medicine and of which we have some reason to believe that it is in part of Stoic origin. According to this doctrine, the discriminatory power of the senses far outruns the ability of the mind to conceptualize the object. Thus, if under normal conditions we see an object clearly, its features are represented in the impression in such detail that our concepts do not capture them in all their detail. Hence, though a normal impression, as a rational impression, has a propositional content, the way it represents the subject of the proposition cannot be exhausted by any number of propositions (cf. Gal. *De loc. aff.* VIII 86.12 ff., 87.4, 117.6, 339.13, 355; *De praesag. ex puls.* IX 366.10K; *De sanit. tuenda, CMG* V 4.1, p. 185, 16). Now the Stoics assume that the properties of bodies themselves are particular (Cic. *Acad.* II 56). Hence they are called "*idiōmata,*" that is, properties (SE *M* VII 248). And they seem to be particular not in the sense that Socrates' wisdom is Socrates' wisdom rather than Plato's wisdom, but in the sense that they are qualitatively different individuals. After all, on the Stoic theory, Plato's wisdom and Socrates' wisdom quite literally are two particular bodies which, by the law of the identity of indistinguishables which the Stoics adhere to, should be internally distinct and not just differ in their relational properties. A property, given its intimate connection and interdependence with the whole body it is the property of, cannot but take a certain form reflecting the idiosyncrasy of the object and hence be peculiar to it. Moreover, both Sextus and Cicero emphasize the artistic precision with which the features of the object are represented in a cognitive impression down to their last detail (SE *M* VII 248, 250-251; cf. "*subtiliter impressa*" in Cic. *Acad.* II 34). Hence a cognitive impression of an object will involve a representation of this object which is so articulate that the only object which will fit this representation is the very object the impression has its origin in (cf. SE *M* VII 252). This feature of cognitive impressions, that they represent their objects in such detail as to fit only them, is their distinctness. Since the Stoics assume that clear impressions represent all the relevant features of an object, cognitive impressions will be highly distinct.

Now normal impressions in general and perceptual impressions in particular have been characterized in such a way that their normality or perceptuality is a relational feature of these impressions, a feature which these impressions do not have by themselves, but only in virtue of the fact that they stand in a certain relation to the world. Hence it would seem that to determine whether an impression is cognitive or perceptual it will not suffice just to consider the impression by itself, that we also have to consider its relation to the world.

But the Stoics also seem to assume that cognitive impressions by themselves differ from all other impressions, that there is some internal characteristic that serves to mark them off from other kinds of impressions and allows the mind to discriminate between cognitive and noncognitive impressions without having to consider their relation to the world (Cic. *Acad.* I 41). Cognitive impressions are supposed to differ from noncognitive impressions in the way in which horned serpents differ from all other kinds of snakes, that is, by some internal differentiating mark (SE *M* VII 252). The reason why the Stoics postulate such a mark is easy to see. All the mind has to go by is its thoughts or impressions. If there is not a privileged set of impressions which we can rely on to be true, we will be reduced to considerations of plausibility and coherence, to inferences to the best available explanation for our impressions, to decide which of them to accept as true and which to reject as false or to suspend judgment on. But even in the best of all circumstances such considerations could not fail to occasionally produce wrong conclusions, and there is nothing to guard us against the possibility that they generate conclusions which are so much off the mark that they would disrupt our life radically. But the Stoics want to argue that we are entirely responsible for our life and that for that reason nature has put us into the position to avoid any false beliefs at all. And the only way to do this, it seems, is to provide us with impressions which cannot but be true and which we can discriminate.

Most of us will be thoroughly disinclined to believe that there is such a qualitative difference between our impressions. But one has to keep in mind that its postulation fits in with Stoic physics without any difficulty. Given that according to Stoic physics all states of the world and all parts of a state of the world are closely interdependent, any variation of the conditions under which an impression arises should affect the impression itself. Thus the assumption that normal impressions have a distinctive character seems not to be ad hoc but to be required by Stoic physics anyway. Even if this were not so, it would not be much of a problem for an omniscient nature to ensure that only impressions which have a normal history have a certain distinctive character which is the effect of the kind of history they have. Moreover, we have to take into account that it is part of the Stoic position that we are so corrupted that we tend to give assent to and to act on cognitive and noncognitive impressions rather indiscriminately. Hence our awareness of their difference is not just seriously retarded but also very distorted. And in any case it does not follow from the fact that we have such difficulties in telling whether an impression is cognitive or not, that there is no clear difference between them. Finally it has to be kept in mind that already Plato and Aristotle had made very strong claims as to the power of the knowledge they attributed to the wise man; the man of practical wisdom always is right in practical matters. The Stoics explicitly refer to this Aristotelian doctrine (Pap. Herc. 1020, col. 1 n., *SVF* II, p. 41, 25), and they just seem to try to provide a theory that would explain how the wise man might manage to invariably get things right. If one gives up this conception of the wise man, one will, of course, not have the motivation the Stoics had to resort to such a strong assumption. But this conception of wisdom was too firmly embedded to be given up lightly in the face of epistemological difficulties.

STOIC DEFINITIONS OF COGNITIVE IMPRESSIONS

On the basis of what has been said, it should be relatively easy to understand the force of the Stoic definitions of cognitive impressions. These come in basically two versions. In a shorter version, which we find in DL VII 46 and SE *M* XI 183, cognitive impressions are defined by two clauses, whereas on the other, more common, version a further clause is added to the two clauses of the shorter version. There may be some truth in Cicero's claim (*Acad.* II 77) that the shorter definition is the one Zeno originally gave, before he went on to add a third clause to avoid an Academic objection, especially since this notice gets some support from Sextus's remark (*M* VII 252) that the Stoics only added the third clause to block an Academic objection based on an assumption which the Stoics did not share.

Let us, then, first consider the definition in its shorter version. To follow the formulation in DL VII 46, an impression is cognitive exactly if (i) it comes about from what is (*apo huparchontos*) and (ii) it is imprinted and impressed in exact accordance with what is. Though this is by no means obvious from the formulation of the second clause by itself, Sextus's comments on this clause in *M* VII 250-251 show that it is supposed to amount to the requirement that the impression be clear and distinct. And this interpretation is borne out by the characterization of noncognitive impressions which in DL follows immediately on the definition of cognitive impressions. According to this definition an impression is noncognitive if "it either is not from what is or, though it is from what is, is not in exact accordance with what is; one which is not clear nor distinct." Here the phrase "one which is not clear nor distinct" looks like a gloss on "is not in exact accordance with what is," that is, the negative counterpart to the second clause in the definition of cognitive impressions. And if this is correct, the second clause of the definition of a cognitive impression should amount to the requirement that cognitive impressions be clear and distinct.

It is tempting to think that the first clause amounts to the requirement that a cognitive impression have its origin in a real object rather than some disturbance or affection of the mind, that the object the impression presents itself as an impression of be a real object rather than a mere figment of the mind. And this seems to be the way Sextus interprets the clause, as one can see from his comments on the first part of the second clause in *M* VII 249. Nevertheless the interpretation of the first clause has been the subject of considerable controversy, which mainly turns around the force of the term "what is" (*huparchon*). It has been pointed out that Cicero in this context again and again renders "*huparchon*" by "what is true," that is, understands "what is" in the sense of "what is the case" (cf. *Acad.* II 42, 112), and that the Stoics do use *"to huparchon"* for a true proposition. Against this it has to be remembered that there is a great number of examples in which Sextus talks of impressions that have their origin in something or other, and that in his examples the something or other in question never is a proposition but always a real or a fictional object.

Nevertheless, there is some reason to think that Cicero's rendering is not a mere mistranslation or due to misinterpretation, but rests on the correct assumption that the first clause was not meant to amount to the requirement that the impression should have its origin in a real object, but to the stronger requirement that it be altogether true. That this assumption may be correct is suggested by M VII 402 ff. There Sextus, following Carneades, argues that there are impressions which have their origin in what is not, but which present themselves as impressions which have their origin in what is just as much as purportedly cognitive impressions do. And as an example of such an impression Sextus adduces the case of Heracles who in his madness took his own children to be those of Eurystheus. Heracles here is explicitly said to have an impression that has its origin in his own children who are standing in front of him, that is, in a real external object. And nevertheless this impression, too, is supposed to be an example of an impression that has its origin in what is not. The reason for this must be that the impression is false in that it represents Heracles' children as being Eurystheus's children. In what sense could such an impression be said to have its origin in what is not? The answer seems to be that the impression does not as a whole have its origin in what is; part of it—namely, the part that represents Heracles' children as being Eurystheus's children—is made up by the mind and is not due to the object. We saw earlier that it is characteristic of perceptual impressions that all their representational features are due to the object. In this sense, only true impressions, and more particularly impressions that are true not by accident, have their origin in what is. If we interpret the first clause in this way, not only do we not have to assume that Cicero has misunderstood the Stoic definition, it also will be easy to explain why the third clause of the longer version of the definition—which runs, "it is such that it could not come about from what is not"—is standardly interpreted as meaning that a cognitive impression has to be such that it could not be false (cf. SE *M* VII 152, 252; Cic. *Acad.* II 42, 112). But even a confused and obscure impression may be entirely true, and true not by accident but because all of its representational features are due to the object that has given rise to it. Hence, to single out cognitive impressions, the second clause is added. So much about the shorter version of the Stoic definition of cognitive impressions.

Standardly, though, the Stoics define cognitive impressions by adding a third clause. A cognitive impression is supposed to satisfy the further requirement that it be "such that an impression of this character could not come about from what is not" (SE *M* VII 248, 252; DL VII 50). This, as we noted above, is taken to imply that an impression of this character could not be false (cf. SE *M* VII 152, 252). Given the strong reading of "has its origin in what is," it is easy to see how the clause would have this implication. The main question concerning the third clause is the identity of the character referred to. Is this a further characteristic of cognitive impressions which is postulated, but not specified by the definition, or is it the property of satisfying the first two conditions, or is it perhaps just the property of being clear and distinct? The phrase "of this character" (*hoia*) is ambiguous in this respect.

Given what we said earlier about cognitive impressions, it seems most plausible to take this to refer to the distinctive inherent feature that cognitive impressions are supposed to have. And this seems to be confirmed by remarks in Sextus (*M* VII 252) and in Cicero (*Acad.* II 77) which suggest that the Stoics think that any impression which satisfies the first two conditions will in fact also satisfy the third condition, but that they add the third clause because this implication is denied by the Academics, though both agree that cognitive impressions, in order to play the role assigned to them by the Stoics, would have to satisfy the third condition, too. And this dispute about the third clause turns out to be a dispute as to whether cognitive impressions have an internal differentiating feature (cf. SE *M* VII 252). Hence it would seem that the third clause refers to this distinctive feature of cognitive impressions, which is postulated, but not specified.

THE CRITERION

To get a clearer notion of this feature and of the role it is supposed to play in cognition, it will be useful to briefly consider in which way cognitive impressions are supposed to constitute the criterion or canon of truth. We already have seen that they are not a criterion of truth in the sense that they put us in a position to determine the truth of any proposition whatsoever. There are lots of propositions that cannot be certified by them. Nor are they the criterion of truth in the sense that whenever the truth of a proposition is in question, we at least consider the corresponding impression and try to determine by introspection whether it has the distinctive mark of a cognitive impression. There are several reasons why this can hardly be the Stoic view of the matter.

First of all, cognitive impressions will directly guarantee only the truth of their own propositional content. And if it is true that cognitive impressions are perceptual, the only propositions whose truth they can guarantee directly are propositions that attribute a perceptual feature to a particular object. If they nevertheless are called *the* criterion of truth, it is because in an indirect way they also guarantee the truth of all other propositions that are known to be true by human beings. And they do this in the following way. They give rise to general ideas, the so-called common notions which the mind forms naturally on the basis of cognitive impressions and which in turn allow us to have further cognitive impressions. And since cognitive impressions do represent things as they are, the common notions based on them will represent things as they are. Thus if the common notion of a man represents a man as a biped rational animal, the proposition that man is a biped rational animal will be certified not by an impression that man is a biped rational animal, which is cognitive in its own right, but by the common notion, and this in turn will be certified by the cognitive impressions which give rise to it and which it gives rise to, and these will be cognitive in their own right (cf. Cic. *Acad.* II 22). And the truth of propositions certified by cognitive impressions and of propositions certified by common notions in turn will guarantee the truth of further propositions derived by deductive inference from the former propositions. It is for this reason that Chrysippus sometimes can say that perceptions and common notions constitute the criterion (DL VII 54). Cognitive impressions, then, are the criterion of truth in the sense that their truth guarantees the truth of whatever can be known by human beings. It is only through them that we have any knowledge as to what is true and what is not true.

Second, we have to remember that there is no such thing as the impression that corresponds to a given proposition, and therefore, when the truth of a proposition is in question, we may have to go through a number of impressions all of which have the proposition in question as their propositional content till we hit upon a cognitive impression. Thus we may not be certain of the color of an object we see in the distance. As we move nearer we have a series of different impressions which all may be impressions that the object is blue. Similarly in the case of a theoretical problem our impression of the proposition in question will change as we consider the matter. The impression we have when we have a proof for a proposition is quite different from the impression that we had to start with. Thus cognitive impressions cannot be the criterion in the sense that we just have to look at our impressions to determine whether a proposition is true. It is rather by considering the proposition that we may get a clearer and clearer impression.

Most importantly, though, we have to avoid thinking of Stoic impressions as pictures or images of the world which can be looked at introspectively, with the mind's eye, as it were, to see whether they have this feature that guarantees their truth. What we see and grasp, according to the Stoics, are objects in the world, and not pictures or images of them, though grasping objects does involve the awareness of their representations in the mind, just as it involves an awareness of the mind itself. For we have to take into account that impressions for the Stoics are mental states that are identified as highly complex physical states, as we can see from the fact that originally they were conceived of quite literally as imprints. When Chrysippus objected to this, it was because he thought that they were much more complex than the term "imprint" suggested; in calling them "alterations" or "modifications" (cf. SE *M* VII 229-230; VIII 400; *PH* II 70; DL VII 50) of the mind instead, he deliberately, it seems, left it open what their precise nature consists in. There is no suggestion that we could observe them to find out what exactly they are like. It is, of course, true that the Stoics think that impressions reveal themselves along with the object they are impressions of (Aetius, *Plac.* IV 12.2). But all that this means is that we can tell what our impressions are; after all, they are our thoughts. But we do not know our thoughts by introspection, nor is there any reason to believe that the Stoics think so. Moreover, if the Stoics thought that we could see by introspection whether an impression has the distinctive feature of a cognitive impression, we would expect them to say, at least on occasion, that the criterion of truth is this feature. But they never say anything of this sort. Also, if they had taken this view, they would have opened themselves to the charge of an infinite regress. For we would have to ask what is supposed to guarantee the truth of the impression that a given impression has this distinctive feature. Quite generally, the criterion will only fulfill its role if it does not require the judgment that an impression is of a certain kind. For this will always raise the question how this judgment is to be certified.

The Stoic theory, I want to suggest, escapes this difficulty because it assumes that the distinctive feature of cognitive impressions is a causal feature of impressions such that cognitive impressions play their criterial role not through our awareness of their distinctive feature, but through the causal effects they have on our minds in virtue of this feature. The word "to discriminate" is ambiguous. It is used in cases in which one recognizes things to be of different kinds and, in virtue of this awareness of the difference, treats them differently. But there also are cases in which somebody reacts differently to things of a different kind not in virtue of an awareness of their difference and perhaps even without knowing that there is such a kind of thing which he systematically reacts to in a distinctive manner; there is a causal link between a feature of the object and the behavior of the person, but the awareness of the feature on the part of the person is not an essential part of the causal chain; and nevertheless such a person can be said to discriminate or to discern the feature. Many forms of discrimination in the pejorative sense are of this kind. The suggestion then is that the distinctive mark of cognitive impressions is a causal feature in that it makes the mind react in a distinctive way and that it is in this sense that the mind can discriminate cognitive and noncognitive impressions. It also can learn to tell whether an impression is cognitive or not, but that is a different ability not at issue at this point of our argument.

What reason do we have to think that this is the Stoic position? The Stoics assume that cognitive impressions give rise to common notions. Common notions have their privileged status exactly because the mind forms them naturally on the basis of cognitive impressions. Nobody, so at least the Stoics think, can help but end up with the notion of a tree and the notion of a human being and the notion of the color green if he grows up normally in a normal environment. This formation of common notions is not something we engage in deliberately according to certain rules and precepts; if we did, we could make mistakes and end up with the wrong notions. The Stoics clearly assume that the mind sorts out cognitive impressions to form concepts on the basis of them without our being aware of this at all; we just find ourselves having certain concepts that we did not have to start with. Thus the Stoics also must assume that the mind can discriminate cognitive impressions without our being aware of it.

We also have to find some explanation of the fact that the mind gives assent to some impressions but not to others. As soon as the mind has acquired all sorts of beliefs, it is easy to see how it would accept or reject impressions against the background of the beliefs it already has. But in the beginning, it would seem, the mind has no more reason to accept than not to accept any given impression. This problem would be solved if we assume that cognitive impressions cause the mind to accept them. And there is some evidence, though by no means decisive, that this is in fact the Stoic position (cf. SE *M* VII 405, 407; Cic. *Acad.* II 38; Plut. *Adv. Colot.* 1121E, 1122C). This is perfectly compatible with the further Stoic claim that we are responsible for our acts of assent, for it is explicitly not part of the Stoic doctrine of responsibility that we are only responsible for those things which we could have done otherwise. But it clearly cannot be the Stoic view that we acquire our first beliefs by scanning our impressions and by being caused to assent to those which we detect to have the distinctive mark of cognitive impressions. It rather must be the case that the Stoics assume that the mind does this without our being aware of it.

Moreover, the Stoics point out (SE *M* VII 258; Cic. *Acad.* II 19) that if we do not have a clear impression we take the appropriate steps to receive an evident impression, in case the subject is of any importance to us; that is, not having a clear impression naturally makes us consider the matter further till we have a clear impression. The suggestion does not seem to be that we recognize that our impression is confused and obscure and hence decide to get a clearer one, but rather that there is a causal mechanism that sets us going and would naturally make us stop once we had a clear impression. For these reasons, then, it seems that the differentiating mark of cognitive impressions is a causal feature rather than a phenomenological character to be detected by introspection.

But this is not to say that we cannot be aware of the fact that an impression is cognitive or noncognitive, that we cannot learn to tell whether an impression is clear and distinct or obscure and confused. In fact the Stoic view seems to be that this is a matter of practice and that in principle one can get so good at it that one will never take a noncognitive impression to be cognitive. But to learn this is not to acquire a mysterious sixth sense which, unlike the other senses, is not subject to the possibility of abnormal conditions and hence unfailingly gives us notice of an equally mysterious feature of cognitive impressions. Judgments as to the evidence of an impression notoriously are as fallible as any other judgments, and there is no reason to saddle the Stoics with the assumption that this is not so. But we can get better and better at seeing how variations in the conditions under which our impressions arise, especially variations in our mental state and the beliefs we have, do affect our impression.

COGNITION, KNOWLEGE, AND THE WISE MAN

Whereas their predecessors had only distinguished between knowledge and mere opinion, the Stoics distinguish between knowledge, cognition, and mere belief (SE *M* VII 151 ff.). Cognition consists in the assent to, or acceptance of, the appropriate kind of impression, that is, an impression that is at least cognitive in the wider sense. A mere opinion, on the other hand, even if it is true, may or may not involve the appropriate kind of impression; if it does, it also is a cognition; but whether it does or not is not what one focuses on when one calls it an opinion. Knowledge differs from cognition in that it involves not only the appropriate kind of impression but also the appropriate kind of assent—namely, the kind of firm assent that one cannot be persuaded to withdraw by any argument to the contrary. This presumably is one reason why we have to try to avoid having any false beliefs whatsoever. For if we do accept a false premise we might be led by a chain of reasoning to accept the contradictory of what we already had believed to be true, even if we had accepted it on the basis of a cognitive impression. And as long as one is susceptible to this, one's assent will not be firm. On the other hand, once one has learned to accept true impressions only, no amount of dialectical skill will suffice to make one withdraw one's assent from impressions that are cognitive in the wider sense; and then one's assent will be stable and firm or certain; in this sense of "certain" one will have certain knowledge.

All cases of cognition are cases either of knowledge or of opinion. For though they all involve the appropriate kind of impression, they will be a matter either of opinion or of knowledge depending on whether or not they also involve the appropriate kind of assent. Nevertheless, there is a point to the distinction. It emphasizes the fact that the conditions on knowledge are so strong that only the wise man will have knowledge (SE M VII 152, 432). In fact, his wisdom will consist in this kind of knowledge. The ordinary person will have nothing but mere beliefs, for he is not yet able to avoid any false belief and hence his assent is not yet firm. But it is important that many of his beliefs are at least cognitive. For they will afford him a basis to acquire the knowledge that constitutes wisdom.

This view has one consequence that hardly seems to have been noticed, but which is highly relevant to our topic. For the Stoics also assume that there are no wise men or at least that not even the members of their own school have attained the blissful state of wisdom (SE M VII 432-433). It immediately follows that there is no knowledge or at least that the Stoics do not have any knowledge. And once we realize this, all sorts of Stoic texts with a strong skeptical flavor come to mind. Thus Seneca (*De ben.* IV 33.2) says: "We never expect completely certain cognition of things, since the exploration of truth is extremely difficult; we follow where likelihood guides us." The Stoic claim is not that they have attained the knowledge Socrates tried to find, but rather that the knowledge Socrates was after is attainable by human beings.

THE SKEPTICAL ATTACK

It should be clear then that skepticism did not arise as a reaction to overly confident claims to knowledge on the part of the Stoics. The Stoics were in no mood to make such claims. But the Stoics did claim some expertise, and on the authority of this expertise tried to put forth views as to the nature and the material content of the knowledge Socrates had been looking for in vain. Hence the central role of the notion of a dogma and the charges of dogmatism in skeptical attacks on Stoicism. Moreover, the view the Stoics did adopt turned out to be extremely revisionist and literally paradoxical. Thus it would easily occur to one to subject the Stoic claims to exactly the kind of dialectic that Socrates had used to test and expose unfounded claims to expertise. And this is precisely what the skeptics did.

Now there are some crucial features of Socratic dialectic which it is worthwhile to recall if we want to understand the skeptical position. The Socratic method allows one to test expertise in a subject without being oneself an expert in this subject—in fact, without committing oneself to or even having any views on the subject. All one has to do is to show that the person who claims expertise or makes statements with the air of authority involves himself in contradictions concerning the very subject he claims to be an expert in or that he is unable to discard a thesis which is the contradictory of a thesis he has put forth with the air of expertise. For if he were an expert, he should be able to defend his position against theses to the contrary, and he certainly should not involve himself in contradictions. Hence such dialectical arguments are not meant to establish the truth or falsehood of some thesis. All they are meant to show is that the opponent is no authority on the matters in question.

It is important to keep this in mind, because otherwise one might be misled into thinking that the skeptics themselves accept either the premises or the conclusions of their arguments. Thus one might think that the ancient Academic skeptic fits the prevailing modern notion of what a skeptic is, in that he believes that all that is given to us are our impressions and that he tries to convince us that since this is so, there is no way in which we ever can have certain knowledge of what the world that gives rise to these impressions really is like. The skeptic may argue this way, but if he does so, it is just another *ad hominem* argument against those who believe that all that is given to us immediately are our impressions. There is no reason why the skeptic himself should feel committed to this very dogmatic, speculative, unskeptical assumption and the dualism between the mental and the physical, the subject and the object which tends to go with it. Thus it is not surprising that in other contexts the skeptic is quite willing to challenge the dogma of the impression as a given (Gal. *De diff. puls.* VIII 710, 18 ff. K.; *De praenot.* XIV 628, 14 ff.). He is quite willing to say that some things evidently appear to be the case, as we ordinarily do, but he does not think that this commits him to the view that there are such entities as impressions, assents, and evidence. Nor are the skeptics committed to the conclusions of their arguments— for example, the conclusion that there is no knowledge or the conclusion that nothing can be known, or the conclusion that the wise man will suspend judgment on all questions. He is not even committed to the view that the conclusions of his arguments follow from their premises. For, as he will emphasize, he does not subscribe to the canons of logic worked out by his opponents, either (cf. Cic. *Acad.* II 91 ff.). He just is prepared, for the sake of argument, to meet whatever standards of logic are met or required by his opponents. For otherwise his arguments will not have the desired effect on them.

What is the envisaged effect of such arguments? Reporting his experience the skeptic might say that they tend to leave one with the impression that the Stoics have not successfully argued their case concerning the nature and the attainability of knowledge. They may also tend to leave one with the impression that it is doubtful whether such a case can be made at all. More generally, it will appear doubtful whether the case for any revisionist conception of knowledge can be made; we might just have to accept the fact that all that is available to us is the kind of everyday knowledge the vulgar have. Even more generally, it may appear doubtful whether the case for any position can be made. On the other hand, it would not be desirable, from the skeptic's point of view, if one was left with the impression that the positions attacked by him are false, or that, even if they are true, there is no way to definitively establish them as true. This would lead to a dogmatic pseudoskepticism quite alien to true Academic or Pyrrhonean skepticism (cf. SE *PH* I 200, 226, 236; Gal. *De subf. emp.* 84, 22 D.).

Given the central position of the doctrine of cognitive impressions in Stoic epistemology, it is not surprising that the skeptics focused their attack on this doctrine. And here the main point at issue was whether cognitive impressions differ qualitatively from all other impressions. This, as we saw, is an assumption so central to the Stoic position that already Zeno added it to his definition of cognitive impressions. The skeptics were quite willing, at least for the sake of argument, to accept the first part of the definition and to grant that there may be impressions that have their origin in what is and that represent their object faithfully and clearly (SE *M* VII 402). But they took issue with the added assumption that such an impression, just given internal characteristics, could have no other origin than the object it faithfully represented, that there could not be an impression exactly like it which was nevertheless false. Already Arcesilaus attacked the further assumption (Cic. *Acad.* II 77; SE *M* VII 154), Carneades pursued the same line of attack (SE *M* VII 164, 402 ff.), and it was to remain the main point of contention throughout the debate (Cic. *Acad.* II 33, 78; SE *M* VII 252).

We only have a rather general idea of the form this debate took, since its details have not been studied with the care they deserve. Apparently the skeptics adopted the strategy of arguing for the more general thesis that for any true impression there could be another impression exactly like it which is false (Cic. *Acad.* II 40, 41, 42; 44, 84, 90; SE *M* VII 154, 164, 252, 402, 415, 438), or at least one which differs so minimally from the true one that we cannot distinguish between it and the true one and which, nevertheless, is false (Cic. *Acad.* II 40, 85). More particularly they seem to have argued the matter for the various kinds of true impressions, kind by kind (Cic. *Acad.* II 42). In the case of cognitive impressions they did so in at least two ways. To start with, they tried to show that there are impressions which, as far as their representational features are concerned, differ in no way, or at least in no discriminable way, from cognitive impressions, though they themselves are not true. But then they also tried to show that there are impressions which have all the supposed characteristics of cognitive impressions—which, for example, are vivid or striking, or which at least could not be distinguished from a cognitive impression by the person who has the impression at the time he has them, and which nevertheless are false (SE *M* VII 408).

Let us first turn to the impressions that are supposed to be exactly like, or at least indistinguishable from, cognitive impressions in the way in which they represent their object (cf. Cic. *Acad.* II 84 ff.; SE *M* VII 408 ff.). Suppose that Socrates is standing in full view in front of one; in this case one may have the cognitive impression that this is pale or that this is a man or even that this is Socrates, if one has learned to grasp his Socraticity and has a corresponding idea of Socrates. Now also suppose that Socrates has a twin brother, whom we do not know anything about, but who is exactly like Socrates, or who at least looks exactly like Socrates. In this case, the skeptic rightly claims, the impression one would have of Socrates' twin brother under identical normal conditions would be exactly like the cognitive impression one has of Socrates. Hence, he goes on to argue, it is not the case, as the Stoics claim, that an impression which has all the characteristics of a cognitive impression can only have its origin in the object which gives rise to it and that there could not be another impression exactly like it which does not have its origin in this object. Moreover, suppose (i) that we first see Socrates and have the cognitive impression that this is Socrates and (ii) that then Socrates disappears and his twin brother takes his place. We would have an impression exactly like our first impression and on the basis of it judge again that this is Socrates. But this impression and the corresponding judgment would be false.

The Stoic answer to this relies on the assumption that no two objects are exactly alike (cf. Cic. *Acad.* II 85). Thus Socrates and his twin brother will differ from each other at least minimally. Hence a cognitive impression of Socrates, being by definition distinct, could not be exactly like an impression that had its origin in his twin brother. If the impression one received of Socrates were exactly like the one which one received of his twin brother, both impressions would be confused and hence not cognitive. But the impressions we receive of Socrates and his twin brother do not need to be indistinguishable and hence confused. For, the Stoics assume, the two brothers do differ from each other at least minimally, and by sufficient training we can learn to distinguish perceptually any two perceptible objects (cf. Cic. *Acad.* II 20; 56; 57; 86). Thus we can learn to distinguish Socrates and his twin brother however much they may look alike, and only if we have learned this can we have the cognitive impression that this is Socrates. Hence it cannot happen that we first have a cognitive impression of Socrates and then a false impression exactly like it that this (Socrates' twin brother) is Socrates.

The crucial issue here is the metaphysical principle of the internal distinctness of different objects or the identity of indistinguishables. Since this principle is firmly embedded in Stoic metaphysics, their reliance on it here cannot be discounted as an *ad hoc* move. And once this principle is granted, the claim that for any object there could be another object so much like it that we could not possibly discriminate the two is considerably weakened. For though the skeptics can point to lots of cases in which we would find it exceedingly difficult, if not impossible, to distinguish different objects from each other because of their similarity, the Stoics point out, not without plausibility, that if we just put our mind to it we would also learn to tell these objects apart (Cic. *Acad.* II 56, 57). It also may be mentioned that according to Stoic logic the two impressions one receives when one sees Socrates and his twin brother would differ in one crucial respect even if the two brothers were exactly alike: if they are impressions that this is Socrates, they would differ in propositional content since the demonstrative has a different reference.

Now one may think that the skeptic's case gets a good deal of its force from the fact that it seems to show that even under normal conditions we do not know whether our impression is cognitive, since we do not know whether it is an impression of the object it presents itself as an impression of, or whether it is in fact an impression of an object very much like it which we have not yet learned to distinguish from it. But we have to keep in mind that the Stoics do not deny that we can make the mistake of thinking that an impression is cognitive when it is not. They are committed only to the view that under normal conditions we will have a cognitive impression of the object in view, that the mind can discriminate the impression as cognitive, and that we could not have the cognitive impression that this is Socrates without being able to distinguish Socrates from all other objects. But this does not mean that we cannot have all sorts of other cognitive impressions of Socrates without being able to distinguish him from all other objects. Similarly we will have a cognitive impression of Socrates' twin brother if we see him under normal conditions, even if we do not know him at all, let alone are able to distinguish him from all other objects. But this impression, whichever it is, will be quite different from the cognitive impression that this is Socrates. There is also nothing to prevent us from having the impression, concerning Socrates' twin brother, with him in full view, that this is Socrates. But this impression will not be any of the *cognitive* impressions we have when we have the brother in full view, though we may make the mistake of thinking that it is.

The other line of attack the skeptics choose seems more promising. They point out that even the patently false impressions of dreamers, madmen, and drunkards seem to have all the features supposed to be characteristic of cognitive impressions, or that they at least seem to be indistinguishable from them for the person who has them.

The first thing to notice is that these impressions are due to nonnormal or abnormal states of mind; and it does seem far from obvious that such states of mind do not have an effect on the internal character of the impressions they produce; in fact, often it seems obvious enough that an abnormal state of mind systematically changes the character of our impressions. And, for reasons indicated above, Stoic physics would seem to require that the internal character of impressions implies a certain state of mind. Second, it needs to be noticed that even if it were the case that in certain abnormal states a person is not in a position to tell whether his impressions are cognitive or not, because the noncognitive ones seem to him to have all the features of cognitive ones, this would not show that he does not have cognitive and noncognitive impressions which differ from each other qualitatively and which his mind discriminates accordingly. And correspondingly we do not find the Stoics arguing that even dreamers and madmen can tell that their dreams and hallucinations are noncognitive, but that even dreamers and madmen react differently to cognitive and noncognitive impressions (cf. SE *M* VII 247). And this seems true enough, if we consider the matter in general. The Stoics are, of course, committed to the view that the mind in each case manages to discriminate between cognitive and noncognitive impressions, but their theory also seems to allow them to explain apparent counterexamples. It is exactly a sign of a severely abnormal state of mind, if the mind treats cognitive and noncognitive impressions almost indiscriminately so that in particular cases there may seem to be no difference in observable behavior.

Thus, it seems that the skeptics fail to show that cognitive and noncognitive impressions do not differ from each other qualitatively and that hence the mind cannot discriminate between them on the basis of their inherent difference. They even fail to show that it is impossible to tell absolutely reliably whether one's impression is cognitive or not. What they perhaps do show is that we, in our present state, cannot invariably tell whether an impression is cognitive or not. But then the Stoics would be the last to deny that.

CONCLUSION

Academic skepticism is not characterized by a certain philosophical posi-tion, by a set of philosophical views Academics are expected to subscribe to, but by a certain dialectical practice and the impression the pursuit of this dialectical practice left on them. Now it seems that earlier Academic skeptics like Arcesilaus and Carneades were left with the impression that they had no reason to accept philosophical beliefs. Whatever reasons they may have had when they had started out had been neutralized by arguments to the contrary. Later Academic skeptics, though, starting with Metrodorus and Philo, seem to have had the impression that how-ever much one argued on both sides of any philosophical or theoretical question, one still may find in the end that, as a matter of fact, one is still inclined toward one side of the matter, that there is no reason to think that this is just due to the fact that one is lacking in dialectical skill or has not considered the matter carefully enough, and that there is no reason not to report which view one feels inclined to, at least as long as one is among one's peers and there is no danger that one's report is mistaken for an authoritative statement, as it might be, for example, by young stu-dents. As a result many Academic skeptics came to articulate quite elabo-rate philosophical beliefs. And given the dominance of Stoicism and the syncretism of the time, these often hardly differed from the views of their Stoic rivals. And since the Stoics did not claim knowledge for their either, the two positions became more and more difficult to distinguish, as soon as one left the field of epistemology. But given that both sides now tended to have more or less the same beliefs on the basis of the same considerations anyway, the epistemological debate must have started to look somewhat academic and futile, especially since it seemed to have ended in a deadlock. Galen (*De dogm. Plat: et Hipp.* 796, 8 ff. M) could even claim the following: the younger Academics say that everything should be judged by means of plausible, tested, incontrovertible impres-sions (the Carneadean "criterion"), Chrysippus maintains that matters should be judged by cognitive impressions, and common sense tells us that it is all a matter of perception and evident thought; but their disagreement is only verbal: if one considers the matter more closely, Galen says, one will see that they all advocate the same epistemic practice.

Thus it is not surprising that some skeptics thought that the Academy had become unfaithful to its skeptical tradition and that they tried to revive the radical skepticism of the early Academics, but now under the name of "Pyrrhonism" to distinguish themselves from their Academic contemporaries. But by this time, it seems, the Stoics were no longer inclined to engage in a real debate on the matter and to refine their position accordingly. And thus orthodox Stoicism itself was soon a matter of the past, whose views only lived on in the more or less distorted form in which they were assimilated into other systems. And in this distorted form the Stoics' views on cognitive impressions and their clarity and distinctness, in fact the whole Stoic epistemology, have exercised through surviving Greek and Latin authors like Cicero and Sextus Empiricus an enormous influence well into modern times.

5

The Ten Tropes of Aenesidemus

Gisela Striker

The Ten Tropes of Skepticism are, as histories of philosophy tell us, a systematic collection of all or the most important arguments against the possibility of knowledge used by the ancient Pyrrhonists. The list of eight, nine, or ten "tropes," or modes of argument, presumably goes back to Aenesidemus, the reviver of the Pyrrhonist school in the first century B.C. Very little is known about Aenesidemus as a person.[1] He seems to have lived in Alexandria (Aristocles ap. Eusebius, *Praep. ev.* XIV 18. 22). Photius tells us (*Bibl.* Cod. 212) that he dedicated a book to a "fellow Academic," the Roman L. Tubero, and this may indicate that he started off as a student of the skeptical Academy, but later decided to argue for a different form of skepticism associated with the name of Pyrrho. From Photius's account it appears that he may have been dissatisfied with the dogmatic turn the Academy seemed to take during his lifetime, and hence decided to appeal to the more or less mythical founder of the skeptic movement. We do not know how he became acquainted with the Pyrrhonist tradition, nor whether his collection of arguments had any predecessor; but since later authors tend to associate the list of Tropes with his name, it seems likely that he was the first who tried to present a systematic repertoire of Pyrrhonist arguments. The purpose of the systematization would have been to provide the skeptic with an arsenal of weapons against all temptations of dogmatism.

In view of the central importance thus ascribed to these arguments, it is surprising to see that they are rather perfunctorily treated by most commentators. While there are a number of useful and learned investigations of their historical origin, order, and number,[2] the arguments themselves are mostly just summarized. It is then said that they all follow the same strategy, leading to the conclusion that nothing can be found out about the real nature of things because of what is alternatively and indiscriminately called the undecidable conflict between mutually inconsistent views or the relativity of all impressions.

Now it seems to me that undecidability and relativity can hardly come to the same, since the first leaves open the possibility that one of the conflicting views may be right, while the other seems to imply either that nothing is absolutely or unrestrictedly true or at least that none of the "relative" impressions can be. So either there must be more than one strategy, or the common strategy is not as easily detectable as commentators seem to think.

It may be that the apparent neglect of the Tropes by recent scholars is due, as one colleague has suggested to me, to the fact that they are quite bad arguments. I suppose they are, in the sense that they are not likely to convince a modern reader of the correctness of their conclusions; but then this could equally well be said of the arguments of Parmenides or St. Anselm, to cite only two prominent examples. It is perhaps easy to see that something must be wrong with these arguments, but I submit that it is not so easy to say just what is wrong with them, or how they arrive at their patently unpalatable conclusions. Some of them, at least, have proved intriguing enough to occupy philosophers well beyond antiquity, and even modern commentators do not agree in their diagnosis, if they attempt one at all. Hence a closer study of their strategy may not seem superfluous even to a modern philosopher who is not tempted to become a convert to Pyrrhonism.

I

Since my primary concern in this paper is with the structure of the Tropes as they are presented in our sources, I may perhaps be forgiven for dealing very briefly with the traditional questions of their origin, order, and number. We have three fairly full accounts of the Tropes from Philo Alexandrinus (*De ebr.* 169-202), Sextus Empiricus (*PH* I 36-163), and Diogenes Laertius (IX 79-88), plus a very short résumé by Aristocles (ap. Euseb. *Praep. ev.* XIV 18. 9-10). Philo, who does not number them, seems to have eight arguments, Sextus Empiricus and Diogenes Laertius each have ten, and both state that Aenesidemus had ten; Aristocles says Aenesidemus had nine, but his summary does not show clearly which of the customary ten would not have been included. There have been some speculations about the development of the list; for example, Philo, who was probably a contemporary of Aenesidemus and also lived, like Aenesidemus, in Alexandria, might have used an early book by Aenesidemus himself which did not yet have all the Tropes. But then Philo was using these arguments for his own purposes and might easily have omitted things that did not seem important or useful to him. Diogenes (IX 87) says that there were several lists differing in order though apparently not in number. Since he ascribes to Sextus an order that is not in fact to be found in *PH* I, the likeliest conclusion seems to be that there were many lists around, mostly containing ten arguments, but that their order and sometimes also the number of Tropes was considered to be more or less irrelevant—as indeed it is, as far as the argumentative purpose is concerned. With regard to the origin of the Tropes, von Fritz has shown on the basis of examples recurring in all three versions that some of the materials used go back beyond Pyrrho to Democritus and Protagoras, but that later skeptics like Sextus felt free to add new examples, and of course also to present their arguments in a form that need not have been that of their predecessors. Philo, who was of course not a skeptic, uses these arguments to remind his readers of the unreliability of wordly wisdom (as against revelation). Hence he leaves out the skeptical framework, and some of his formulations are probably influenced by his change of purpose. We do not know what source Diogenes was using, but since he states (IX 87) that the order he gives differs from those of Sextus, Aenesidemus, and Favorinus, none of these authors is likely to have been his model. Diogenes' version is by far the shortest. Since he does not seem to depend on Sextus, a comparison between the two may perhaps sometimes show where Sextus elaborated on the traditional arguments for himself. Sextus's account is naturally the fullest, and, as coming from a prominent representative of the school, also the most authoritative. However, he lived presumably about two hundred years later than Aenesidemus, and so it is likely that the form in which he presents the Tropes is not exactly the one given them by Aenesidemus. For example, Sextus invokes the so-called Five Tropes of Agrippa,[3] which are certainly later than Aenesidemus, to support the argument of the older Tropes. Since neither Philo nor Diogenes brings them up in this connection, this addition may well have been Sextus's own idea.

In speaking about *the* Tropes of the Pyrrhonists, then, we are simplifying and generalizing about a tradition that need not have been altogether uniform. However, since the common factors of our main sources are far more striking than their divergences, it should not do too much harm to treat them collectively.

As far as I can see, the only attempts to analyze the Tropes in detail are by R. Richter (1902) and Ch. Stough (1969),[4] who unfortunately ignores

Richter. Both commentators assert that the Tropes all follow one and the same strategy, but while Richter seems to subsume them all under relativity, Stough goes on to describe two different types of argument. Richter, who sets out to discover the tacit presuppositions underlying the skeptics' arguments, claims that the Pyrrhonists drew out the consequences of what he calls naïve realism—that is, the view that holds that if we are to find out the truth about the nature of things, appearances or impressions must be exact images of what they represent. The skeptics, according to Richter, pointed out that the obvious conflict between different appearances of the same objects or types of objects rules out the possibility of their correctness in the naïve sense, and hence concluded that things in themselves were unknowable. Stough suggests that the Tropes start from a theory of perception which is aimed at discovering reality behind or through appearances (sense-impressions), but which defines perception in such a way as to make the attainment of this aim impossible. Thus the skeptical arguments turn out to be a priori refutations of something very much like the Stoic theory of perception, rather than the kind of inductive argument based on observation which the large number of examples might lead one to expect, and which the skeptics themselves thought they were offering.

Now while it is plausible to suppose that unacceptable conclusions in what appears to be a formally correct argument must be due to some tacit presuppositions, I suspect that these are not as unified as Richter's naïve realism or Stough's representative theory of perception. The skeptics, for one thing, did not consider themselves to be arguing from or against a specific philosophical position; that type of argument belonged, according to Sextus Empiricus (*PH* I 5-6), to the special (*eidikos*) part of the Pyrrhonist exposition, in which they argued against "each part of so-called philosophy," as against the general account, in which they set out the characteristics of skepticism itself.

In what follows I shall try to show that there are indeed two forms of argument used in the Tropes, neither of which coincides with the classical argument of modern skepticism based upon the representative theory of perception. Both types can, I think, be found explicitly formulated in our sources. In the end I will venture a suggestion as to how they came to be used together.

II

Both Diogenes Laertius and Sextus Empiricus present the Tropes as ways of inducing suspension of judgment. If we look at the particular arguments to see how this is supposed to be achieved, we note that the argument is nowhere fully set out. Most of the Tropes, in fact, seem to consist of a collection of examples chosen to illustrate the existence of conflicting perceptual impressions or beliefs concerning various types of features. The last Trope (in Sextus's order) is concerned with value judgments rather than with perceptual impressions. This does not show, as some have been inclined to think, that the skeptics illegitimately treated "good" and "bad," "just" and "unjust" as perceptual predicates, or treated value judgments as some kind of perception statements. Rather, it shows that perceiving is treated as one, perhaps the most important, case of having things appear to one. In both the perceptual and the evaluative cases the alleged conflict is said to arise from the fact that the same things appear different to different observers or kinds of observers, and for this it makes no difference whether the appearance is due to perception or some other kind of awareness. Actually this comes out already in the earlier Tropes: not only are "pleasant"/"unpleasant" often treated as prime examples—they might still be thought to come under perception in some broad sense—but we also get predicates like "healthy" and "harmful," "desirable" and "to be avoided," which can hardly be said to introduce perceptual qualities. And Sextus is clearly aware of this: at *PH* I 100 he says, "In order to arrive at suspension of judgment . . . *even leaving aside the senses . . .*" What the examples show, then, is that the same objects appear different to different observers, which is a part, but clearly not the whole, of the skeptics' argument.

In Diogenes' account the conclusion is often left out entirely (82; 86; 87), sometimes stated as *"ephekteon"* ("we must suspend judgment") or similar formulae (81; 84) which do not give the reason for suspension supposedly provided by the argument. In three cases the conclusion given suggests that the argument is built upon the contrast relative-absolute (85 *kat' idian;* 86 *phusis;* 88 *pros ti* vs. *kath' heauta;* cf. Philo 187, 192). In one place (81) Diogenes states the conclusion as "it follows then that the thing appearing is no more such than otherwise," which is ambiguous between (1) "the thing is neither such nor otherwise" and (b) "the thing might just as well be such as otherwise"—an interpretation missing from Diogenes' list of senses of *"ou mallon"* (no more this than that) at IX 75, but emphasized by Sextus (*PH* I 213, cf. 189), who declares it to be the only correct Pyrrhonist interpretation, while Diogenes as categorically asserts that the skeptics used *"ou mallon"* in the sense of "neither-nor." Sextus always states the conclusion (with slight variations corresponding to the examples) as, "We can say how things appear (to different observers, in relation to certain conditions, and so on), not how they are by nature or in themselves." This formula is ambiguous in the same way as *"ou mallon"*: it may be taken to mean either that we cannot decide whether things really are as they appear, or that we can only grasp the apparent, not the real, properties of things. The ambiguity is no accident: we can find arguments for both interpretations of the conclusion in the Tropes. To fill the gap between first premise and conclusion, I will rely mainly upon Sextus, since Diogenes' versions are usually all too elliptic.

The first type of argument is most fully, though not consecutively, given by Sextus in the course of his exposition of the first Trope. Taking together §§ 59 and 61, we get the following argument:

1) The same things produce different impressions in different kinds of animals;

2) it is impossible to decide which (impressions) are correct (both in 61);

   hence

3) we can say how the underlying thing appears to us, but we will suspend judgment as to how it is with regard to nature. (59; cf. DL IX 79)

By far the greatest part of Sextus's exposition is as usual devoted to establishing, by means of numerous examples, the first premise. Sextus claims —rightly, I think—that 1) is not a dogma of skepticism but a fact that presents itself to other philosophers as well and indeed to all human beings (*PH* I 210-211), a "common notion" that does not involve any special theory. It is to be taken simply as a generalization of such observations as that the same wind appears hot to the one, cold to the other, and so on. It must be the second premise, then, which sets us on the road to skepticism. This premise tacitly rules out the possibility that all of the conflicting impressions might be true together. This is ruled out, as appears from *PH* I 88 (cf. DL IX 78; 101), on the ground that we would have to accept contradictory propositions as true together. As no contradiction would be forthcoming if the differences in impressions were due to changes in the underlying objects, another tacit assumption here seems to be that what holds of a thing "by nature" holds of it permanently— and that is indeed a standard implication of expressions like *"phusei"* ("by nature"). It is then argued at length that it is impossible to adjudicate the claims of the disputants. Sextus has three main arguments for this: first, the equal-authority argument, to the effect that each party to the dispute has as good a claim to be correct as any other; second, the argument that reason cannot be invoked to decide where the senses cannot (*PH* I 99; 128); and third, the argument that no proof can be produced on behalf of any view since it would lead either to an infinite regress or to a vicious circle (60-61; 114-117; 121-123). The last of these is an application of the Tropes of Agrippa and hence can hardly have belonged to the oldest versions of the Tropes (it does not occur in Diogenes Laertius or Philo). The second is barely mentioned and hardly adequate as it stands, since no suggestion as to how reason might proceed to settle the dispute is discussed. Besides, it seems to assume—wrongly, as we saw earlier—that the conflict is only between perceptual impressions, and the idea that reason is dependent upon the senses sounds suspiciously like Stoic or Epicurean doctrine. In short, I think that it has been imported—possibly by Sextus himself—from Carneades' argument against the Stoic theory of knowledge (cf. SE M VII 165). Much better arguments against the use of reason were produced by Aenesidemus in his Eight Tropes against causal explanations, which were, I suspect, drawn up to show that attempts by the dogmatists to resolve the puzzles set out in the old Tropes would not work.[5] I assume, therefore, that the first argument—equal authority—is the one originally associated with the examples in the Tropes. It proceeds on the assumption that the question which of the conflicting impressions may be correct must be decided on the basis of the authority of the observer. It shows that no party to the dispute can claim greater authority than any other: majority won't do, since it is impossible even to establish what is in fact the majority view (we would have to ask every single observer: 189). Nor is it possible to appeal to the "normal" or "healthy" observer, since impressions come as naturally to the madman as to the sane person, and may in fact be as "normal" for his state as the healthy person's impressions are for his (102-103). Nor will it do to invoke the superior wisdom of some, philosophers for example, since philosophers notoriously disagree among themselves (88; 98); and besides, who is to decide whether the allegedly wise man really is wise (*PH* II 39-41)? Finally, every point of view may be a source of distortions, and it is not possible to judge without belonging to a certain group, being in a particular state of mind or body, so no one can be presumed to be an impartial judge (*PH* I 112f.; 121). Hence we are led to the conclusion that we can only say how things appear to the various observers, not how they are in themselves.

This argument is often labeled as *isosthenēs* or *anepikritos diaphōnia* (undecidable conflict between—equally strong—conflicting views), and I shall for brevity's sake refer to it as the undecidability argument.

The situation envisaged by the skeptic has a close parallel in the modern discussion about objectivity in history. Having noticed that each historian judges from his own particular viewpoint, historical situation, educational background, and so on, which influence him and possibly involve a bias, some theoreticians have argued that there can be no such thing as objective truth in history. Now with regard to objectivity it has been argued, against this, that if objectivity is demonstrably unattainable, then the contrast between objectivity and, say, subjectivity becomes vacuous. In order to find out what the original point of the contrast might have been, we should turn to paradigmatic cases of both subjectivity and objectivity and try to see what distinguishes them. Similarly one could object to the skeptics' argument that if, on their showing, it is impossible to establish correctness, we should try to see how disagreements between different observers are in fact typically resolved. And then we should find, I suppose, that it is not, or not always, a question of authority, or who is or is not biased, but—depending on the type of case —a question of which methods were used (measuring for quantities, for example), or what standard is implicit in our concepts (so, for example, "red" might be defined as "what appears in a certain way to a normal observer under standard conditions"). This would serve to bring out the important point that conflicts between different impressions cannot always be settled in the same way. In some cases, there may indeed be no method available—for example, in the skeptics' favorite cases of likes and dislikes. But then we could still avoid the undecidability argument by saying—as indeed the dogmatic opponents of skepticism were quick to point out—that the predicates involved are relational, so that no decision is called for because no contradiction arises.

The thought-provoking character of these puzzles has been rightly emphasized by Richter.[6] However, since the Pyrrhonists seem to blandly ignore some of the more obvious solutions (for measuring cf. Plato, *Prot.* 356c-e), he concludes that they are tied to a naïve world view—more naïve, indeed, than anyone could have expected after the fourth century B.C. But since they do, for example, raise the question why we should take the healthy person's impressions to come closer to the truth than the sick one's, thus picking up one of the accepted standards to which Aristotle (*Met.* Γ 5. 1010b1-10; 6. 1011a3-13) and Theophrastus (*De sens.* 70 p. 519 Diels) so confidently appeal, why shouldn't we expect them to raise the same question about our accepted ways of measuring quantities? In a way, a little reflection will do to resolve most of the apparent conflicts; in another way, perhaps they cannot be resolved: not if we accept the stringent conditions of objectivity apparently presupposed by the Pyrrhonists' argument.

The force of the undecidability argument, then, lies in the assumptions a) that different impressions contradict one another, and b) that the question which view is correct is a question of establishing authority. It does not, as far as I can see, rely upon any specific theory about perception to the effect that the only adequate way of establishing the truth would be to compare impressions with objects, as Stough supposes. As indeed befits the skeptics, no theory of perception seems to be involved at all; there is not the slightest suggestion as to how the "underlying object" produces an impression in the observer, or whether that impression should be taken to be an image of the object.[7] Given that the examples do not discriminate between particular objects (the wind) and types of objects or stuffs designated by mass terms (honey, water, oil, and so on), it is not even very plausible to suggest an image theory. There is then also no good reason to conclude that the "underlying objects," the nature of which is said to remain obscure, cannot be the commonplace things like ships, towers, honey, and so on constantly cited as examples, on the grounds that these are identified by means of impressions, and the "real object" cannot be identical with any phenomenal object.

Stough's argument seems to be that if the skeptics don't know which features go with what, they are not entitled to their assumption that it is the same thing—namely, honey, or the wind—which produces different impressions in different observers.

I think there are two remarks to be made with regard to this suggestion. The first is an observation: as a matter of fact, the examples of conflicting appearances given in the Tropes do not involve disagreement about sortal predicates like "man," "house," "tree" or about mass terms like "water" or "honey." This is probably to be explained by the simple fact that these do not lend themselves easily to the type of observation adduced: it is not generally the case that what appears as an apple to me appears as a cherry to you, or that what I take to be a house on one occasion I take to be a mountain on another. Of course such things do happen occasionally, but it would be difficult to associate such differences in appearance with certain types of observers or perceptual circumstances. Now we might remind ourselves that the Pyrrhonists restricted their skepticism explicitly to "the obscure things investigated in the sciences" (*PH* I 13, cf. 19 f.; DL IX 103-104). "Whether this is a man or a statue" is not a scientific question; and the famous argument from doubt, which shows that we can never be certain of facts of this kind, seems to belong to the Academic rather than the Pyrrhonist tradition. The Pyrrhonists seem much more concerned with rejecting attempts to answer questions of the type "whether honey is really sweet or not" (*PH* I 19) or "whether fire burns *by nature*" (DL IX 104). They do not intend to deny *that* we see; they suspend judgment, however, as to *how* it is that we see (DL ibid.). In one significant passage (*PH* I 20), Sextus says that "when we present arguments against the *phainomena* (appearances), we do not set these out in order to overthrow the *phainomena*, but only by way of exhibiting the rashness of the dogmatists." So one might be tempted to say that they accepted it as a fact that there are people, trees, and houses around them; they only insist that we cannot establish the "real nature" of these things.

On the other hand, it seems unlikely that they should have limited their skepticism in this way. Disagreements immediately arise once we start asking, not indeed "Is this a man or a statue?" but "What is a man?"; and Sextus has no trouble at all (for whatever his arguments are worth) in showing that man is unknowable, given the widely differing views of philosophers about his nature (*PH* II 22-33). If the requirement for identifying objects or kinds of objects is to be that one must know the kind of thing the object is, then the skeptics would presumably have to admit that they did not fulfill the requirement.

But is this really required? Identifying an object, or even a kind of thing, does not seem to be a matter of determining its "real nature." In the case of the historians mentioned above, it seems not at all absurd to suggest that they might all agree about the identity of their object—a historical event, say, or a personage, or, for that matter, wars in general— and yet be unable to reach an agreement about its "real" (objective) nature. Similarly, Locke thought that we could identify and recognize pieces of gold on the basis of their "secondary qualities," sometimes even using widely different clues, and yet be totally ignorant of the "real essence" of gold. All that seems to be needed here is a modest degree of similarity in appearances—and the skeptics do not mean to deny *that*.

I suspect it is only when we begin to think of appearances as entities intervening between the observer and the object of his observation that we are tempted to ask how we can say that there is one object, or any object at all. But while the skeptics obviously distinguished between the way a thing appears and the way it really is, I see no reason to attribute to them the view that this distinction must be made in terms of special entities—images or otherwise—mediating between observers and observed objects. Hence I also see no reason to take their arguments as a *reductio ad absurdum* of a certain theory about perception.

If the Tropes, then, are not a *reductio ad absurdum* of a specific theory, we should perhaps try to take them at their face value, that is, as arguments directed against the thesis denied by their conclusion, namely, the thesis that we can indeed say how things really are, not only how they appear to different observers—or, to use Diogenes' version of the conclusion, that things are one way rather than another. This thesis, which may be considered to be the essence of dogmatism as the skeptic sees it (*PH* I 13 f.), does not appeal to any theory of perception, since what things appear to be like cannot be identified with sense data or sense impressions, as we saw. The motivation for the dogmatist attitude is well brought out by the skeptics when they rule out the possibility that things might really be as they appear in each case, on the ground that this would lead us to accept contradictions as true. But if reality cannot be as it appears to be, then, as the skeptics point out, there seems to be no way left to find out what it really is like. In other words, the Tropes are denying the possibility of establishing a consistent account of the world "as it really is by nature," where "by nature" would seem to imply at least that a thing's nature must be permanent enough to be observed by different observers or at different times. Some further restrictions on what one could ascribe to a thing by nature will come out below when we consider the second strategy of argument.

Now if we disregard for a moment the superficial character of some of the skeptics' examples (such as pleasantness and unpleasantness, features which nobody would presumably wish to ascribe to things as belonging to their nature), it seems that the issue raised by the Tropes—whether we can say how things really are—is still an important one, not lightly to be dismissed as based on a mistaken conception of perception or naïve assumptions about how features are ascribed to things. While there may be accepted methods of settling some of the disputes to which the skeptics appeal, and even, perhaps, justifications for these methods, one might point to the field of value judgments as an example of a case where no method has been found as yet. And to deny that justice or goodness are features generally attributable to action types, as one might be inclined to do (cf. Epicurus at DL X 151-152) to avoid the charge of contradiction, will only transfer the disagreement to a different level, where the skeptic, of course, is already waiting for the dogmatist with his method of showing how the opposite of every philosophical thesis can be argued for on equally good grounds. We have little reason, then, to think with Richter that the puzzles will disappear together with the sometimes naïve assumptions underlying the examples.

But let us return to the strategies of the Tropes. The conclusion of the undecidability argument leaves open, as I noted before, the possibility that one or another of the conflicting views might be true. All it tries to establish is that we have no way of finding out which one is true, and that is of course sufficient to bring about suspension of judgment with regard to the nature of the object. This argument, then, is in accordance with Sextus's favored interpretation of the skeptic formula *"ou mallon."* The second type of argument, as we will see, is not.

III

The second type of argument is strangely introduced by Sextus as no. 8 of the Tropes (*PH* I 135). He describes the Trope *apo tou pros ti* (from relation) as follows: "According to this [Trope] we conclude that since everything is relative, we will suspend judgment as to what things are absolutely, and with regard to nature." The argument he has in mind seems to be:

1) all things are relative (that is, all things are whatever they are in relation to some other things);
2) what a thing is relatively (in relation to some other thing) it is not absolutely or by nature (not stated).

From these two premises it seems to follow that nothing is anything absolutely—that is, there is no nature of things in the sense of a way in which they are in themselves. However, Sextus reminds us immediately that the "are" in the first premise should be read as "appear," following the skeptics' policy of avoiding assertions about how things really are. This has the effect of limiting the scope of the first premise to cases encountered by the skeptic so far. If we keep the second premise as it stands, since it seems to be needed to make the transition from "relative" to "not by nature," we get the conclusion that nothing appears to be anything absolutely, which can be taken to mean that, as far as the skeptics can see, no feature seems to belong to anything by nature; so while there might indeed be a nature of things, we cannot find out what it is and hence must suspend judgment about it.

This is still not very illuminating, since we have not been told how it is that "all things are (appear to be) relative" or why their being relative precludes our finding out about their nature. Sextus goes on to tell us that "relative" is said in two ways, namely, either in relation to the subject judging (*pros to krinon*) or in relation to things considered together with the first thing (*pros ta suntheōroumena*), and that the first premise is established through the other Tropes, which show that everything is relative in one or the other of these two senses. (I disregard the argument in 137-140, which is patently eristical, and shows, if anything, only that all things fall under some relational predicate.) This seems to indicate that relativity is not on the same level as the other Tropes: it is, rather, another way of using the materials collected there to establish, this time, a totally negative conclusion regarding things "as they are by nature."

Given that some version of this Trope seems to have been on the list from the start, as is shown by its presence in Philo, Diogenes, and the list of Aristocles, and that Sextus claims in his introduction to the Tropes that this one is "the most general" (*genikōtatos, PH* I 39), one is led to suspect that there might have been an older version, based on a restricted class of examples like the other Tropes, which is supplanted here by a version showing how it can be made to comprehend all the others.

Such a version seems indeed to be preserved in Philo and Diogenes, and it may serve to show us how we get from "relative" to "not by nature." Diogenes calls this Trope "by the comparison with other things" (*kata tēn pros alla sumblēsin*, IX 87). Both Philo and Diogenes begin by introducing a list of pairs of terms most of which are not explicitly relative but could easily be argued to be so: big and small, dry and wet, hot and cold, heavy and light, strong and weak, and so on. This suggests that the Trope originally dealt only with the class of relations identified by Sextus as "to things considered together with the first thing." It is not quite clear, however, how the argument about these is to be construed. In Philo's version the point seems to be that relatives cannot provide knowledge of a thing in itself since things can be recognized as having relational features only with regard to some other things. This would seem to rule out relational features as sources of knowledge about things simply because they are relational, and hence do not belong to the thing by itself. Diogenes seems to introduce a different point. He outlines an argument as follows: "What is to the right is not by nature to the right, but is thought (to be so) in virtue of its disposition in relation to the other. Now if the other thing is displaced, it will no longer be to the right. Similarly father and brother are relative, and day relative to the sun, and everything relative to the mind. Now relatives (*ta pros ti*) are unknowable in themselves."

On the lines of Philo's argument, one might take the conclusion to mean that relatives can only be recognized as such in relation to other things, not in themselves. But then this does not seem to make any use of the example, which seemed to point out that a relational predicate may cease to be true of a thing merely because some other thing changes. What one expects after this would be an argument to the effect that relational features cannot belong to the nature of a thing because it may lose them without undergoing a change. And such an argument is indeed provided by Sextus in *M* VIII 455-457, where he argues that "the relative does not really exist" (*ouch huparchei*).[8]

So the Trope about the comparison with other things might be either an argument to the effect that relational features do not tell us anything about things in themselves just because things have them only in relation to other things, or that relations do not reveal the nature of a thing because they may cease to hold without a change in the thing. In either case the result seems to be different from that of the undecidability argument: it is not that we cannot decide which relational feature belongs to the thing by nature, but that since no relation belongs to a thing by nature, and all observed features seem to be relative, we cannot say anything about the nature of things.

Now it is easy to see how the pattern of this argument can be taken to cover the examples from all the other Tropes, and Sextus shows us how this is done: alongside the class of things "considered together," which seems to cover the examples cited by Diogenes, we introduce the class of relatives *pros to krinon* (to the subject judging). Then we point out that the predicates introduced in the other Tropes can all be brought under one of these headings, thus showing that all predicates thus far considered are relational, and use the rest of the relativity schema to conclude that no predicate holds of a thing in itself. This generalization may be indicated by Diogenes' phrase "and everything relative to the mind" (cf. Philo 187).

This may be the pattern intended by Sextus. However, before we go on to consider the argument itself, we should note that there might be a different form of the relativity argument, more closely related to the examples of alleged contradictions collected in the other Tropes. Such a connection is indicated, for example, in *PH* I 177: "Intelligibles are relative; for they are said to be intelligible in relation to the intellect, and if they were by nature such as they are said to be, they would not be controversial" (*ouk an diephōnētē*). Setting aside the specific case for which the argument is used here, we seem to get the general premise: If anything is by nature F, then there will be no controversy about its being F. This premise recurs in what appears to be a standard skeptical argument about good and bad. Both Sextus and Diogenes present the following argument: "If there is anything which is by nature good and bad, this must be good or bad for all, as snow is cold for all;[9] but nothing is good or bad for all in common; therefore, there is no good or bad by nature" (DL IX 101; cf. SE *PH* III 179 ff.; *M* XI 69). The term "relative" does not occur here, but a connection can easily be made if we suppose that we can go from "nothing is F for all" to "things are F only for some, not for others," and hence to "things are F only in relation to certain persons." This argument differs from the one presented above in that it does not seem to use the premise that relational predicates may cease to hold without a change in the relata, or that they don't hold of the thing in itself. Instead, it asserts, rather dogmatically, that things are F by nature only if they are (or, as Sextus puts it in *PH* III, appear) F for all observers. One might suspect, however, that some assumption about change is at work here too. The idea that a feature belongs to a thing by nature only if the thing appears to have it for all observers might be based on some argument to the effect that what a thing is by nature, it must be at all times, so how can the fact that it is judged by a different observer affect it? Hence the fact that it is judged differently by different observers must be due, not to the nature of the thing, but to the observers—the thing has the feature only in relation to certain people or, as it is often put, only by convention or by habit (*nomōi, ethei*: cf. DL IX 61).[10] So if there is disagreement among different observers about certain features of a thing, this may be taken to show that the relevant features do not belong to the thing by nature, but only relatively.[11] Hence this argument provides a way of getting from disagreement among subjects to relativity and thence to the impossibility of finding out about the nature of things.

Clearly the relativity argument is not another candidate for a specific Trope, but rather a scheme for using the examples of conflicting appearances to show that nothing can be known about the nature of things. Since Sextus does not tell us how he gets from "relative" to "not by nature," it is not clear which strategy he means to introduce as the most general of the Tropes.

But I think he probably does not have to choose, because in fact these two arguments are two sides of the same coin, and the classification of relations into those that are to a subject and those that are to a thing considered with the other may have served to bring them together. They start from different sets of examples—comparisons between things on the one hand, conflicting appearances on the other—to arrive at the same conclusion, namely, that certain features do not belong to things by nature. In both cases the crucial assumption seems to be that what holds "by nature" or "absolutely" must hold of a thing in itself irrespective of any other things to which it might be related either by comparison or by being observed.

The first of them, in Diogenes' version, arrives at its conclusion by generalizing from cases like right and left, inferring that all relations can cease to hold without a change in the relata, and hence that relations cannot be among the features a thing has "in itself." Now the generalization is certainly mistaken—not all relations are like right and left, above and below, and some are such that they will not cease to hold unless one of the relata undergoes an internal change. For example, if I am susceptible to polio, that relation between me and the polio will hold until I am vaccinated. Some relations seem indeed to be based on the nature of the things involved: thus water will presumably remain translucent so long as it and light remain unchanged, and aspirin will be good for headaches until one or the other changes its nature. However, Philo's version seems to suggest that the skeptics want to exclude relatives not only because relations between the same relata may change without a change in the relata, but also because things do not bear the same relations to all other things (cf. the example of equal and unequal in SE *M* VIII 456). That is, they might wish to say that what holds true of a thing in itself ought to be true of it regardless of everything else. If the conditions of a feature belonging to something by nature were only that it should hold always with regard to the same relatum, then some relations might arguably be by nature. If the condition is that it belong to the thing regardless of all other things, then one would have to argue, against the generalized version of the relativity argument, that not "everything" is relative. And this is, of course, what the dogmatists of all times have tried to do.

The second argument, which maintains that only those features belong to things by nature which appear the same to all observers, looks at first sight even less convincing than the first. Why should one not simply say that if there is a disagreement about whether a thing is really F, this may be due to a mistake on the part of one of the subjects? Sextus and Diogenes seem to anticipate such an objection and hence bring in the undecidability argument at this point (DL IX 101; *PH* III 182; *M* XI 72-78).

The source of the argument, however, and of its suggestion that what is or appears the same to all is really so, may not have been a discussion of perceptible qualities, in which it might not look very plausible, but a contrast between mass terms on the one hand, value terms on the other. Such a contrast appears in an argument which the Epicurean Polystratus denounces in his treatise *De contemptu inani* (col. XIIb, p. 20f Wilke). Commentators tend to say, on the strength of such parallels as DL IX 61 (about Pyrrho) that the argument must come from Pyrrho or one of his immediate disciples. According to Polystratus, the argument is as follows: "They say that neither beautiful nor ugly nor anything else of the kind is, since it is not the case that, like stone and gold and the things similar to these, which we say exist (*huparchei*) by nature, not by convention, so these too are the same for all, but rather others for others. For none of these (they say) is truly. . . . "

Polystratus's reply to this argument is remarkable—both for its incisiveness and as an illustration of the state of the question in the second half of the third century B.C. First he points out that what is supposed to show that beautiful and ugly and the like are not (real) also holds for greater and smaller, heavier and lighter, healthy and its opposite, thus bringing in the well-known examples of relatives (col. XV a, b). The upshot is that "relative predicates are not in the same field as things said according to proper nature and not relatively, but it is not the case that the ones truly exist, the others not" (col. XVI b 1-8). In fact, as he goes on to argue, one might as well say that stone and gold do not really exist because they are not different to different people as that relatives are not real because they are. That is, there are categorical facts and there are relational facts, and it is no use denying the reality of the latter on the ground that they are not the former.

This argument effectively refutes the suggestion that relational predicates cannot really belong to a thing just because it has them only in relation to other things. It does not purport to show that such features can also be "by nature"; but at the end of his list of relatives Polystratus mentions "capacities in general" (col. XVI b 6: *kai epi tōn loipōn d'haplōs dunameōn*), apparently as instances of relational features that are undoubtedly real, and one might suspect that these could also be argued to be natural. Some evidence for arguments of this kind can be found in Sextus, *M* VIII 194 ff. (on the *dunameis* of fire) and *M* IX 237-243 (on the relativity of *dunameis*).

With these distinctions once established, the relativity argument would seem to have lost much of its force. If the Pyrrhonists still went on using it, they were indeed using premises that should have been obsolete by the time of Aenesidemus.

IV

Thus far I have tried to extract, from the accounts of Sextus and Diogenes and some parallels, what might have been the strategy or strategies of argument employed in the Tropes. I have also mentioned that Sextus is right about the most general form: we could subsume all examples under the relativity type but not under undecidability, because once we realize that many of the examples involve relational predicates, we see that no contradictions arise, so that there would be no basis for the undecidability argument. This being so, should we perhaps conclude that relativity is the original strategy? Or rather that it was introduced later than undecidability to answer the objections about relational predicates? Neither of these is very likely; in fact, there seems to be evidence to show that both types of argument are considerably older than Pyrrho, and that both were used in the Tropes from the beginning.

Undecidability occurs, without a label but with the most common examples supporting it, in *Met.* Γ 5, 1009b2-11, and Aristotle adds that Democritus was so impressed by it that he concluded that either nothing is true or at least the truth is hidden from us. Plato introduces a version of it, though not as fully spelled out, in *Tht.* 158b-e, as an argument for relativism. So the argument must be as old as Democritus and probably Protagoras.

Relativity—again without the terminology, of course, but notably with both types of examples—also occurs in the *Theaetetus* (154b ff.), as an argument in support of Protagoras. And if Theophrastus's report is correct, Democritus argued that the sensible qualities are not by nature because "the same does not appear to all" (*ou pasi tauta phainesthai, De sens.* 70 p. 519 Diels; cf. 63, p. 517 and 69, p. 519).

That both types of argument were used in the Tropes seems to be confirmed by the fact that Agrippa uses the labels *"diaphōnia"* (disagreement) and *"pros ti"* (relation) in what appears to be an attempt to integrate the material from the old Tropes in his new list of five.

And so long as we consider the Tropes only as ways of inducing suspension of judgment, there seems to be nothing wrong with employing both types of argument together. In fact, we have already seen how undecidability could be brought in to help with the suggestion that some disagreements among observers could be resolved on the assumption that one of them might be wrong. On the other hand, relativity could have been used to help with the objection that some of the contradictions adduced in the Tropes are only apparent because the terms involved are relatives—though I cannot cite a case in which this actually happened.[12] What is surprising about Sextus's claim that relativity is the general strategy of the Tropes is, however, the fact that it does not seem to sit at all well in the general framework of Pyrrhonism as outlined by Sextus himself. Sextus declares in *PH* I (8; 26; and many other places) that Pyrrhonism is based on *isostheneia*, the equal force of conflicting propositions, which leads the skeptic first to *epochē*, then to peace of mind. He finds that what distinguishes the Pyrrhonists from the Academics is that while the Academics dogmatically assert that truth cannot be found, the Pyrrhonists are still searching (*PH* 13, cf. 226). In accordance with this, Diogenes also explains how Aenesidemus wanted to show that the opposite of what tends to convince us can be argued for just as convincingly (IX 78). Also, Aenesidemus apparently ascribed this reason for *epochē* to Pyrrho, saying that he asserted nothing dogmatically *dia tēn antilogian* (because of the controversy; DL IX 106). But while the undecidability argument clearly tries to establish *isostheneia*, the relativity argument does not; it shows that we are never right about the nature of things because all we have come to find out is relative and hence does not belong to the nature of the thing. In short, it conforms to the negative interpretation of *"ou mallon"*—neither the one nor the other—ascribed to the skeptics by Diogenes (IX 75).

I do not know how to resolve this apparent inconsistency in Sextus's account of the matter. With regard to the skeptic slogan *"ou mallon"* he insists, against Democritus, on the interpretation "we don't know whether both or neither of the appearances are the case" (*PH* I 213). On the other hand, Diogenes clearly says the skeptics used *"ou mallon"* in the negative sense.

The truth might be that the skeptics used both—the one going with undecidability, the other with relativity—but Sextus and Aenesidemus preferred to stress undecidability. Nor is it very hard to see why they should have preferred this.

First of all, the relativity argument seems to belong to a tradition of negative dogmatism, if not of a universal kind, at least with regard to certain features of things—as is in fact shown even by the two occurrences of the argument about good and bad which Sextus explicitly introduces as belonging to the skeptics. Now a negative dogmatist, as Aenesidemus certainly knew from Academic debates, will soon be faced with the question how he knows that the nature of things cannot be known. Surely he must know at least the premises of the argument he uses to demonstrate his thesis, and of course the thesis itself? So even apart from the fact that the relativity argument might seem to involve some rather dubious premises, a negative dogmatist could be argued into either admitting that he knows these things, thereby apparently contradicting himself, or into retracting his argument. However, relativity can be adapted as a strategy, as Sextus also shows, if the premise "everything is relative"—or, in a particular case, "things are F only relatively"—is changed to read "everything appears to be relative," thus stating only how the world has presented itself to the skeptic so far. The conclusion then becomes, as we noted, "nothing appears to be anything absolutely or by nature," which leaves the possibility that things do have a nature, saying only that the features things appear to have do not seem to belong to it.

But the undecidability argument might look more promising: it does not involve an assumption like "only that is by nature which is the same for all," or "relational predicates cannot hold of a thing by nature"— premises which, judging from the evidence of passages like the one quoted above from Polystratus, may not have appeared as innocent by the time of Aenesidemus as the simple observation that the same things appear different to different people. Besides, the undecidability argument also covers the case of conflicting theoretical views which is not very prominent in the Tropes, but was obviously the most important antidogmatic weapon of the later skeptics (and of course of the skeptical Academy). There seem then to be good reasons for the Pyrrhonist to base his case on undecidability.

But this may not have been so clear to Pyrrho himself or his early followers who used the arguments put together in the Tropes. So the old relativity argument, which was after all a part of the Democritean tradition and seems to offer quite a good case for *epochē*, was probably handed on with the others before Aenesidemus undertook to rebuild Pyrrhonism on the basis of *isostheneia*. It is possible that Aenesidemus was more cautious than Sextus in not giving relativity the prominence Sextus seems to ascribe to it by making it the most general of the Tropes. It might also be that the unknown author of the "Two Tropes" (*PH* I 178-179), which are in effect Agrippa's Tropes nos. 2, 4, and 5 (where undecidability is covered by the first of the two, but relativity is left out), saw that relativity did not fit in with *isostheneia* and proposed to drop it altogether.

But of course the old Tropes would have to be kept in order to establish the vital contrast between appearance and reality on which the skeptics continued to rely. Moreover, it might have been hard to keep up the general case for the conclusion "we can only say how things appear" if all the examples involving relational terms had been left out. So the skeptics presumably preferred to leave them there, thinking that not-so-good arguments may still do their job if people don't see what goes wrong (cf. *PH* III 280-281).

NOTES

Earlier versions of this paper were read at Pittsburgh, Princeton, Riverside, and Berkeley. I am grateful for the criticisms and clarifications arising out of the discussion at all these places, and in particular for Richmond Thomason's acute objections. Special thanks are due to Anthony A. Long and Myles Burnyeat for reading and commenting upon the first draft.

1. The best account of the chronology of Pyrrhonism, and of Aenesidemus's biography, is in V. Brochard, *Les sceptiques grecs*, 2d ed. (Paris, 1932; reprint ed., Paris, 1969), pp. 227 ff., 242 ff.

2. Cf. E. Pappenheim, "Die Tropen der griechischen Skeptiker," *Wissenschaftliche Beilage zum Programm des köllnischen Gymnasiums Berlin*, 1885, pp. 1-23; H. v. Arnim, "Quellenstudien zu Philo von Alexandria," *Philologische Untersuchungen* 11 (1888), 53-100; K. v. Fritz, "Pyrrhon," in Pauly-Wissowa, *Realencyclopädie der classischen Altertumswissenschaft*, 34 (1963), 89 ff.; U. Burkhard, *Die angebliche Heraklit-Nachfolge des Skeptikers Aenesidem* (Bonn, 1973), pp. 175-193. A. E. Chatzilysandros, *Geschichte der skeptischen Tropen* (Munich, 1970) is disappointing.

3. Sextus introduces these as belonging to "the younger skeptics" (*PH* I 164); Diogenes ascribes them to "Agrippa and his school" (IX 88).

4. R. Richter, "Die erkenntnistheoretischen Voraussetzungen des griechischen Skeptizismus," *Philosophische Studien* 20 (1902), 246-299. Cf. also his *Der Skeptizismus in der Philosophie*, vol. I (Leipzig, 1904); Ch. Stough, *Greek Skepticism* (Berkeley and Los Angeles, 1969), pp. 67-97.

5. For the Eight Tropes cf. SE *PH* I 180-186. One, perhaps the most promising way of dealing with conflicting perceptual appearances would seem to be explaining them as the results of a consistent set of causal factors. The best example for such an attempt in ancient times is probably Epicureanism. But as the Tropes against causal explanation show, such attempts had not been successful: they only served to reproduce the conflict on the theoretical level.

6. *Der Skeptizismus in d. Philos.*, I, 121 ff.

7. Such a theory of perception is indeed refuted at *PH* II 74-75 and *M* VII 357-358. In both places Sextus has *the dogmatist* suggest that "the affections of the senses" might be similar to the external objects.

8. The crucial lines are as follows: "So whatever really exists ($\dot{\upsilon}\pi\acute{\alpha}\rho\chi o\nu$) does not admit of a change into something else without an affection. But the relative changes apart from any affection and without any alteration occurring about it; for example, a piece of wood of a cubit's length, when another piece of a cubit's length is put next to it, is said to be equal to that, while if a piece of two cubits' length is put alongside, it is no longer said to be equal, but unequal, without any change or alteration having occurred about it. . . ."

9. Of course the assertion that snow is cold for all—and hence cold by nature—is incompatible with the skeptical attitude as officially set out by Sextus and Diogenes, but it seems to go with this argument, as is shown by the presence of this or similar examples in all our sources.

10. For the combination of *nomōi* and *pros ti* cf. SE *PH* III 232: οὐδὲ τῶν προειρημένων τι ἐστὶ φύσει τοῖον ἢ τοῖον, νομιστὰ δὲ πάντα καὶ πρός τι (nor is any one of the things mentioned before by nature such or such, but they are all [such] by convention and relatively).

11. Actually there are several versions of this argument, depending on whether the conclusion is read as a) nothing is F by nature (things are F only relatively), or b) there is no such thing as the F by nature (the F does not really exist). Both can be taken to be expressed by the formula "οὐκ ἔστι (τι) φύσει . . ."; and so the argument about good and bad is sometimes treated by Sextus as leading to a), sometimes as leading to b), as Richter pointed out ("Die erkenntnistheoretischen Voraussetzungen," pp. 278-284). A third version, in which the conclusion is c) there is no nature of F, discussed by Aristotle (*Met.* Γ 5, 1010b19-30) and Theophrastus (*De sens.* 70-71, pp. 519 f. Diels), does not seem to have been taken over by the Pyrrhonists. While Sextus seems to waver between a) and b), Theophrastus in his report on Democritus wavers between a) and c). Plato seems to combine b) and c) at *Tht.* 172b4: ὡς οὐκ ἔστι φύσει αὐτῶν οὐδὲν οὐσίαν ἑαυτοῦ ἔχον. Though it might be interesting to pursue the connections between these, I will not discuss versions b) and c) here, since only a) seems to be relevant in the context of the Tropes.

12. But cf. perhaps Plutarch, *Adv. Col.* 1110 D-E, against Epicurus.

6

Can the Skeptic Live His Skepticism?*

M. F. Burnyeat

HUME'S CHALLENGE

A Stoic or Epicurean displays principles, which may not only be durable, but which have an effect on conduct and behaviour. But a Pyrrhonian cannot expect, that his philosophy will have any constant influence on the mind: or if it had, that its influence would be beneficial to society. On the contrary, he must acknowledge, if he will acknowledge anything, that all human life must perish, were his principles universally and steadily to prevail. All discourse, all action would immediately cease; and men remain in a total lethargy, till the necessities of nature, unsatisfied, put an end to their miserable existence. It is true; so fatal an event is very little to be dreaded. Nature is always too strong for principle. And though a Pyrrhonian may throw himself or others into a momentary amazement and confusion by his profound reasonings; the first and most trivial event in life will put to flight all his doubts and scruples, and leave him the same, in every point of action and speculation, with the philosophers of every other sect, or with those who never concerned themselves in any philosophical researches. When he awakes from his dream, he will be the first to join in the laugh against himself, and to confess, that all his objections are mere amusement, and can have no other tendency than to show the whimsical condition of mankind, who must act and reason and believe; though they are not able, by their most diligent enquiry, to satisfy themselves concerning the foundation of these operations, or to remove the objections, which may be raised against them. [David Hume, *An Enquiry Concerning Human Understanding*, Sec. XII, 128].[1]

*Reprinted from *Doubt and Dogmatism: Studies in Hellenistic Epistemology*, ed. Malcolm Schofield, Myles Burnyeat, and Jonathan Barnes (Oxford, 1980), a collection of papers presented at a conference on Hellenistic philosophy held at Oriel College, Oxford, in March 1978.

I begin with Hume, both in deference to the vital influence of Pyrrhonian skepticism on modern thought, following the rediscovery and publication of the works of Sextus Empiricus in the sixteenth century,[2] and because Hume is so clear on the philosophical issues I wish to discuss in connection with Sextus Empiricus. Pyrrhonism is the only serious attempt in Western thought to carry skepticism to its furthest limits and to live by the result, and the question whether this is possible, or even notionally coherent, was keenly disputed in ancient times and had been a major focus of renewed debate for some two hundred years before Hume wrote. My purpose is to return to those old controversies from the perspective of a modern scholarly understanding of Sextus Empiricus.

The background to the passage I have quoted is Hume's well-known contention that our nature constrains us to make inferences and to hold beliefs which cannot be rationally defended against skeptical objections. He has particularly in mind the propensity for belief in external bodies and for causal inference, but not only these. And he has a particular purpose in showing them to be rationally indefensible. Since exposure to the skeptical objections does not stop us indulging in belief and inference, it does not appear that we make the inferences and hold the beliefs on the strength of the reasons whose inadequacy is shown up by the skeptical arguments; for when a belief or a practice is genuinely based on reasons, it is given up if those reasons are invalidated. Since we do not give up the inferences and the beliefs in the face of overwhelming skeptical objections, there must be other factors at work in our nature than reason—notably custom and imagination—and it is to these, rather than to man's much-vaunted rationality, that the beliefs and the inferences are due.[3] In the passage quoted, Hume's claim is a double one: first, that what the skeptic invalidates when his arguments are successful, and hence what he would take from us if such arguments could have a "constant influence on the mind," is nothing less than reason and belief; second, that what makes it impossible to sustain a radical skepticism in the ordinary business of life is that "mankind . . . must act and reason and believe." A brief comment on each of these claims in turn will give us a philosophical context in which to consider what Sextus Empiricus has to say in defense and advocacy of his Pyrrhonist ideal.

All too often in contemporary discussion the target of the skeptic is taken to be knowledge rather than belief. Skeptical arguments are used to raise questions about the adequacy of the grounds on which we ordinarily claim to know about the external world, about other minds, and so on, but in truth there are few interesting problems got at by this means which are not problems for reasonable belief as well as for knowledge. It is not much of an oversimplification to say that the more serious the inadequacy exposed in the grounds for a knowledge-claim, the less reasonable it becomes to base belief on such grounds. To take a well-worn, traditional example, if the evidence of our senses is really shown to be unreliable and the inferences we ordinarily base on this evidence are unwarranted, the correct moral to draw is not merely that we should not claim to know things on these grounds but that we should not believe them either. Further, in the normal case, that which we think we should not believe we do not believe: it takes rather special circumstances to make intelligible the idea that a man could maintain a belief in the face of a clear realization that it is unfounded. If skepticism is convincing, we ought to be convinced, and that ought to have a radical effect on the structure of our thought.

It is very clear that Hume appreciated this. He presses the Pyrrhonist not on the matter of knowledge-claims, which are easily given up, but on the question whether he can stop holding the beliefs which his arguments show to be unreasonable. Sextus appreciated the point also. The objection that a man cannot live without belief was familiar, indeed much older than the Pyrrhonist movement, since it goes right back to the time when Arcesilaus in the Academy first urged *epochē* about everything.[4] Accordingly, Sextus defends exactly the proposition Hume challenged the Pyrrhonist to defend, the proposition that he should, can, and does give up his beliefs in response to the skeptical arguments; and out of this continuing resignation of belief he proposes to make a way of life. Likewise with the Pyrrhonist's abandonment of reason: that too, according to Sextus, is not only desirable but practicable, subject to the complication that the abandonment of reason is itself the result of argument, i.e. of the exercise of reason. Consequently—and here I come to my second point of comment—Hume has no right to assume without argument that it is impossible to live without reason and belief. No doubt it seems an obvious impossibility, but Sextus claims otherwise, and he purports to describe a life which would substantiate his claim. That description ought to be examined in detail before we concede Hume's dogmatic claim that the Pyrrhonist cannot live his skepticism.[5] We ought to try to discover what the life without belief is really meant to be.

BELIEF, TRUTH, AND REAL EXISTENCE

We may begin, as the skeptic himself begins, with the arguments. *Skepsis* means inquiry, examination, and Pyrrhonian skepticism is in the first instance a highly developed practice of argumentative inquiry, formalized according to a number of modes or patterns of argument. The Ten

Modes of Aenesidemus (*PH* I 36 ff., DL IX 79 ff.) and the Five of Agrippa (*PH* I 164-177, DL IX 88-89) are the most conspicuous of the patterns, but there are others besides, all of which recur with quite remarkable regularity on page after page of the skeptic literature, and always with the same result: *epochē*, suspension of judgment and belief. These patterns of argument, with this outcome, constitute the essence of skepticism (*skepsis*, inquiry) as that is defined by Sextus Empiricus in the *Outlines of Pyrrhonism*; it is, he states, "a capacity for bringing into opposition, in any way whatever, things that appear and things that are thought, so that, owing to the equal strength of the opposed items and rival claims, we come first to suspend judgment and after that to *ataraxia* (tranquillity, freedom from disturbance)" (*PH* I 8; cf. 31-34). The definition delineates a journey which the skeptic makes over and over again from an opposition or conflict of opinions to *epochē* and *ataraxia*.

The journey begins when he is investigating some question or field of inquiry and finds that opinions conflict as to where the truth lies. The hope of the investigation, at least in the early stages of his quest for enlightenment, is that he will attain *ataraxia* if only he can discover the rights and wrongs of the matter and give his assent to the truth (*PH* I 12, 26-29, *M* I 6). His difficulty is that, as skeptics through the ages have always found, in any matter things appear differently to different people according to one or another of a variety of circumstances, all catalogued in great detail by the Ten Modes of Aenesidemus. We are to understand, and sometimes it is explicitly stated (e.g. *M* VII 392, VIII 18, IX 192, XI 74), that conflicting appearances cannot be equally true, equally real. Hence he needs a criterion of truth, to determine which he should accept. But the skeptic then argues, often at some length, that there is no intellectually satisfactory criterion we can trust and use; this is the real backbone of the discussion, corresponding to a modern skeptic's attempt to show we have no adequate way of telling when things really are as they appear to be, and hence no adequate insurance against mistaken judgments. Assuming the point proved, the skeptic is left with the conflicting appearances and the conflicting opinions based upon them, unable to find any reason for preferring one to another and therefore bound to treat all as of equal strength and equally worthy (or unworthy) of acceptance. But he cannot accept them all, because they conflict. Hence, if he can neither accept them all (because they conflict) nor make a choice between them (for lack of a criterion), he cannot accept any. That is the standard outcome of the skeptic discovery of the equal strength (*isostheneia*) of opposed assertions. So far as truth is concerned, we must suspend judgment. And when the skeptic does suspend judgment, *ataraxia* follows: the tranquillity he sought comes to him, as if by chance, once he stops actively trying to get it—just as the painter Apelles only achieved the effect of a horse's foam when he gave up and flung his sponge at the painting (*PH* I 26-29).

All this is compressed into Sextus's definition of skepticism. The sequence is: conflict—undecidability—equal strength—*epochē*—and finally *ataraxia*. The arguments bring about *epochē*, suspension of judgment and belief, and this, it seems, effects a fundamental change in the character of a man's thinking and thereby in his practical life. Henceforth he lives *adoxastōs*, without belief, enjoying, in consequence, that tranquillity of mind (*ataraxia*, freedom from disturbance) which is the skeptic spelling of happiness (*eudaimonia*).[6] But note: the conflict of opinions is inconsistency, the impossibility of being true together (cf. *M* VII 392); the undecidability of the conflict is the impossibility of deciding which opinion is true; the equal strength of conflicting opinions means they are all equally worthy (or unworthy) of acceptance as true; *epochē* is a state in which one refrains from affirming or denying that any one of them is true; even *ataraxia* is among other things a matter of not worrying about truth and falsity any more. All these notions depend on the concept of truth; no stage of the sequence would make sense without it. And it is a fact of central importance that truth, in the skeptic's vocabulary, is closely tied to real existence as contrasted with appearance.[7]

When the skeptic doubts that anything is true (*PH* II 88 ff., *M* VIII 17 ff.), he has exclusively in view claims as to real existence. Statements which merely record how things appear are not in question—they are not called true or false—only statements which say that things are thus and so in reality. In the controversy between the skeptic and the dogmatists over whether any truth exists at all, the issue is whether any proposition or class of propositions can be accepted as true of a real objective world as distinct from mere appearance. For "true" in these discussions means "true of a real objective world"; the true, if there is such a thing, is what conforms with the real, an association traditional to the word *alēthēs* since the earliest period of Greek philosophy (cf. *M* XI 221).[8]

Now clearly, if truth is restricted to matters pertaining to real existence, as contrasted with appearance, the same will apply right back along the sequence we traced out a moment ago. The notions involved, consistency and conflict, undecidability, *isostheneia*, *epochē*, *ataraxia*, since they are defined in terms of truth, will all relate, via truth, to real existence rather than appearance. In particular, if *epochē* is suspending belief about real existence as contrasted with appearance, that will amount to suspending all belief, since belief is the accepting of something as true. There can be no question of belief about appearance, as opposed to real existence, if statements recording how things appear cannot be described as true or false, only statements making claims as to how they really are.

This result is obviously of the first importance for understanding the skeptic's enterprise and his ideal of a life without belief. Sextus defines "dogma"—and, of course, the Greek word *dogma* originally means simply "belief" (cf. Plato *Rep.* 538c, *Theaet.* 158d)—as assent to something nonevident, that is, to something not given in appearance (*PH* I 16).[9] Similarly, to dogmatize, as Sextus explains the term, is what someone does who posits the real existence of something (*hōs huparchon tithetai, PH* I 14, 15, from a context where it has been acknowledged that not everyone would use the word in this restricted sense).[10] Assent is the genus, opinion or belief that species of it which concerns matters of real existence as contrasted with appearance. The dogmatists, the endless variety of whose opinions concerning real existence provides the skeptic with both his weapons and his targets, are simply the believers; to the extent that it is justified to read in the modern connotation of "dogmatist," viz., person with an obstinate and unreasonable attachment to his opinions, this belongs not to the core meaning of the Greek term but to the skeptic's argued claim, to which we shall come, that *all* belief is unreasonable. All belief is unreasonable precisely because, as we are now seeing, all belief concerns real existence as opposed to appearance.

HISTORICAL INTERLUDE

We can trace this polemic against belief at least as far back as Aenesidemus, the man who was chiefly responsible for founding, or at any rate reviving, Pyrrhonism in the first century B.C.—some two hundred years or more before Sextus compiled his *Outlines of Pyrrhonism*. Aenesidemus's own *Outline Introduction to Pyrrhonism* was presumably the first work to bear such a title, and we know something of it from a report in Diogenes Laertius (IX 78 ff.; cf. also Aristocles ap. Euseb. *Praep. evang.* XIV 18.11). Aenesidemus set out to classify the various modes or ways in which things give rise to belief or persuasion[11] and then tried to destroy, systematically, the beliefs so acquired by showing that each of these modes produces conflicting beliefs of equal persuasiveness and is therefore not to be relied upon to put us in touch with the truth.[12] Most obviously, where our senses deliver consistent reports we tend to be persuaded that things really are as they appear to be,[13] but if we take full account of the different impressions which objects produce on different animals and different people and people in different conditions or circumstances, and all the other considerations adduced under the Ten

Modes, we will see that in any such case as much evidence of the same kind, or as good, can be adduced for a contrary opinion; each type of evidence can be matched by evidence of the same sort but going the other way, each source of belief is a source of conflicting beliefs.[14] The moral, naturally, is *epochē* about what is true (DL IX 84); but this is also expressed by saying we must accept our ignorance concerning the real nature of things (DL IX 85, 86), which confirms once again the intimate connection of truth and reality. Then there is the additional consideration that some of the modes in which beliefs are acquired have little or no bearing on truth and falsity, as when we believe something because it is familiar to us or because we have been persuaded of it by an artful speaker. In sum,

We must not assume that what persuades us (*to peithon*) is actually true. For the same thing does not persuade every one, nor even the same people always. Persuasiveness (*pithanotēs*) sometimes depends on external circumstances, on the reputation of the speaker, on his ability as a thinker or his artfulness, on the familiarity or the pleasantness of the topic. [DL IX 94, tr. Hicks][15]

Now this talk of persuasion and persuasiveness has an identifiable historical resonance. In a context (*M* VIII 51) closely parallel to the passage just quoted, and not long after a mention of Aenesidemus (*M* VIII 40), Sextus equates what persuades us (*to peithon hēmas*) with the Academic notion of *to pithanon*. "*Pithanon*" is often mistranslated "probable," but what the word normally means in Greek is "persuasive" or "convincing," and Carneades defined a *pithanē* impression as one which appears true (*M* VII 169, 174).[16] The important point for our purposes is that in the skeptic historiography, as in most history books since, Carneades was supposed to have made *to pithanon* the Academic criterion for the conduct of life (*M* VII 166 ff.): a fallible criterion, since he allowed that in some instances we would be persuaded of something which was actually false (*M* VII 175). He also said that our belief is greater—and the Pyrrhonists read him as meaning that it should be greater—when our senses deliver consistent reports (*M* VII 177); this idea, which we saw to be one of Aenesidemus's targets, is the basis for the second and stricter criterion in Carneades' three-level criterial scheme, the impression which is not only *pithanē* but also not "reversed" by any of the associated impressions. If, then, *to peithon* is the Academic *pithanon*, and if I am right to detect Aenesidemus behind the passages in Diogenes and Sextus where *to peithon* is under fire, then his campaign against persuasion and belief was at the same time a polemic against the Academy from which he had defected.[17] The general purpose of the Ten Modes is to unpersuade us of anything which persuades us that it represents truth and reality. Aenesi-demus's more particular target is the idea, which he attributes to the Academy (whether rightly or polemically),[18] that one has a satisfactory enough criterion of action in taking to be true that which is persuasive in the sense that it appears true. In Aenesidemus's view, one should not take anything to be true, and he had arguments to show that, in fact, nothing is true (M VIII 40 ff.).

I conclude, then, not only that the life without belief was a funda-mental feature of Pyrrhonism from Aenesidemus onwards, but that it was put forward by Aenesidemus in conscious opposition to (what he represented as) the teaching of the New Academy. If the Ten Modes have their intended effect, we will be weaned from the Academic criterion for the conduct of life to Aenesidemus's new Pyrrhonist ideal of a life with-out belief. It is quite possible, however, that this was not so much a new proposal as the revival of one much older.

The idea that one should live without belief (the word used is adoxas-tous, as in Sextus) is prominent in the most extended doxographical account we possess of the philosophy of Pyrrho himself: the quotation in Eusebius (Praep. evang. XIX 18.2-4) from Aristocles, a Peripatetic writer of the second century A.D., which gives what purports to be a summary of the views attributed to Pyrrho by his follower Timon.[19] We should not put any trust in our perceptions or beliefs, says the summary, since they are neither true nor false, and when we are thus neutrally disposed, with-out belief, tranquillity results. It is possible that Aristocles received this report through Aenesidemus himself,[20] but that need not mean it gives a distorted interpretation of Timon's account of Pyrrho. Quite a few of the fragments of Timon which have come down to us are at least suggestive of later Pyrrhonism.[21] Moreover, various stories relating how Pyrrho's friends had to follow him about to keep him from being run over by carts or walking over precipices (DL IX 62: the precipice fantasy may derive from Aristotle, Met. 1008b15-16) are exactly of the type one would expect to grow up around a man known for teaching a life without belief. And these stories are old. They are cited from the biography of Pyrrho written by Antigonus of Carystus in the late third century B.C., well before Aenesidemus; in fact Aenesidemus felt it necessary to combat the idea that a philosophy based on suspending belief would make Pyrrho behave without foresight (DL ibid.). This seems rather clear evidence that for Aenesidemus himself the life without belief was the revival of a much older ideal.

It is not difficult, moreover, to guess something of the philosophical reasons why Aenesidemus should have resorted to Pyrrho for his model. On the one hand, the Academy at the time of Philo of Larissa appeared less sharply skeptical than it had been; in particular, on Philo's controversial interpretation of Carneades (cf. Cic. *Acad.* II 78, *Index Acad. Herc.* XXVI, 4), *to pithanon* could be and was offered as a positive criterion for life.[22] On the other hand, the great difficulty for Academic skepticism had always been the objection—Hume's objection—that total *epochē* makes it impossible to live.[23] The tradition concerning Pyrrho offered a solution to both problems at once. The way to live without belief, without softening the skeptical *epochē*, is by keeping to appearances. This was the plan or criterion for living that Aenesidemus adopted (DL IX 106), again not without some support in the fragments of Timon,[24] and we shall find it elaborated in Sextus Empiricus. It is a pleasing thought that not only does Sextus anticipate Hume's objection, but also, if I am right about the philosophical context which prompted Aenesidemus to his revival of Pyrrhonism, it was in part precisely to meet that objection more effectively than had been done hitherto that Aenesidemus left the Academy and aligned himself to Pyrrho.

LIVING BY APPEARANCES

A skeptical restructuring of thought, a life without belief, tranquillity— these are not ideas that we would nowadays associate with philosophical skepticism, which has become a largely dialectical exercise in problem-setting, focused, as I noted earlier, on knowledge rather than belief. Even Peter Unger, who has recently propounded a program for a skeptical restructuring of thought,[25] does not really try to dislodge belief. Having assiduously rediscovered that skepticism involves a denial of reason, and the connection between skepticism and the emotions, as well as much else that was familiar to Sextus Empiricus, he agrees that all belief is unreasonable, and he even has an argument that in fact no one does believe anything—belief itself is impossible. But he does not really believe this last refinement, since his program envisages that concepts like *knowledge* and *reason* be replaced by less demanding assessments of our cognitive relation to reality, rather in the spirit of Academic fallibilism; thus it seems clear that, while a great number of our present beliefs would go (for a start, all those beliefs having to do with what is known and what is reasonable), believing as such would remain firmly entrenched at the center of our mental life. The ancient Greek Pyrrhonist would not let it rest there. He is skeptical about knowledge, to be sure: that is the burden of all the arguments against the Stoics' cataleptic impression—the impression which, being clear and distinct (DL VII 46), affords a grasp of its object and serves as a foundation for secure knowledge. But his chief enemy, as we have seen, is belief. So the question arises, What then remains for a man who is converted by the skeptic arguments to a life without belief, where this means, as always, without belief as to real existence? This is the question we have to ask if we want to probe the secret of skeptic tranquillity.

The skeptic's answer, in brief, is that he follows appearances (*PH* I 21). The criterion by which he lives his life is appearance. In more detail, he has a fourfold scheme of life (*PH* I 23-24), allowing him to be active under four main heads, as follows. First, there is the guidance of nature: the skeptic is guided by the natural human capacity for percipience and thought, he uses his senses and exercises his mental faculties—to what result we shall see in due course. Second comes the constraint of bodily drives (*pathōn anagkē*): hunger leads him to food, thirst to drink, and Sextus agrees with Hume that you cannot dispel by argument attitudes the causal origin of which has nothing to do with reason and belief (*M* XI 148). In this respect, indeed, perfect *ataraxia* is unattainable for a human being, physical creature that he is, and the skeptic settles for *metrio-patheia* (*PH* I 30, III 235-236): the disturbance will be greatly moderated if he is free of the additional element of belief (*to prosdoxazein*) that it *matters* whether he secures food and drink. Third, there is the tradition of laws and customs: the skeptic keeps the rules and observes in the conduct of life the pieties of his society.[26] Finally, the fourth element is instruction in the arts: he practices an art or profession, in Sextus's own case medicine, so that he has something to do. All of this falls under the criterion of appearance, but Sextus does not really aim to develop the scheme in practical detail. Once he has pointed us in these four directions, his main concern, and therefore ours here, is with the general criterion of appearance.

In the section of the *Outlines of Pyrrhonism* where it is formally stated that the criterion by which the skeptic lives his life is appearance (*PH* I 21-24), not only does appearance contrast with reality, but living by appearance contrasts with the life of belief. Evidently, the mental resources left to the skeptic when he eschews belief will be commensurate with whatever falls on the side of appearance when the line is drawn between appearance and real existence. So it becomes important to ask, as I have not so far asked, just what the skeptic is contrasting when he sets appearance against real existence. By the same token, if appearance is identified with some one type of appearance—and the most likely candidate for this is sense-appearance—that will have restrictive implications for the mental content of the life without belief.

Let us go back briefly to the passage where Sextus gave his definition of skepticism as a capacity for bringing into opposition things that appear and things that are thought, etc. When Sextus comes to elucidate the terms of his definition, he says that by "things that appear" (*phaino-mena*) we *now* mean sensibles (*aisthēta*) in contrast with things thought (*nooumena* or *noēta*) (*PH* I 8-9). This surely implies that he does not always or even usually mean sensibles alone when he speaks of what appears (cf. *M* VIII 216). Some scholars, most recently Charlotte Stough, have taken the skeptic criterion to be sense-appearance, in the narrow meaning, because when Sextus says the criterion is what appears (*to phainomenon*), he adds that the skeptics mean by this the impression (*phantasia*) of the thing that appears (*PH* I 22).[27] But the point here is simply to explain that what the skeptic goes by in his daily life is not, strictly, the thing itself that appears, but the impression it makes on him, and in Sextus's vocabulary (as in Stoic usage: cf. DL VII 51) there are impressions (*phantasiai*) which are not and could not possibly be thought to be sense-impressions. I need only cite the impression, shared by all opponents of Protagoras, that not every impression is true (*M* VII 390). As for *to phainomenon*, what appears may, so far as I can see, be any-thing whatever. Sextus is prepared to include under things appearing both objects of sense and objects of thought (*M* VIII 362), and sometimes he goes so far as to speak of things appearing to reason (*logos*) or thought (*dianoia*) (ambiguously so *PH* II 10, *M* VIII 70, unambiguously *M* VII 25, VIII 141). Finally, there is a most important set of appearances annexed to the skeptic's own philosophical utterances; as Michael Frede has emphasized,[28] these are hardly to be classed as appearances of sense.

Time and again Sextus warns that skeptic formulae such as "I deter-mine nothing" and "No more this than that" (*PH* I 15), or the conclusions of skeptic arguments like "Everything is relative" (*PH* I 135), or indeed the entire contents of his treatise (*PH* I 4), are to be taken as mere records of appearance. Like a chronicle (*PH* I 4), they record how each thing appears to the skeptic, announcing or narrating how it affects him (his *pathos*) without committing him to the belief or assertion that anything really and truly is as it appears to him to be (cf. also *PH* I 197). Clearly it would be impossible to regard all these appearances as impressions of sense.[29] But the practice of argumentative inquiry is so considerable a portion of the skeptic's way of life that they must certainly be included under the skeptic criterion. They are one outcome, surely, and a most important outcome, of his natural capacity for percipience *and thought*. Sense-appearance cannot be all that is involved when the skeptic says he follows appearances.

It may be granted that the conclusion of a skeptic argument is typically that the real nature of something cannot be determined and that we must content ourselves with saying how it appears, where this frequently does mean: how it appears to the senses. But essentially the same formulae are used when the subject of inquiry is, say, the existence of species and genera (PH I 138-140), the rightness or wrongness of certain customs and practices (PH I 148 ff.), or, quite generally, objects of thought (noēta) as contrasted with sensible things (PH I 177). Further, the conclusion of a skeptic argument may be also that a certain concept cannot be formed: for example, the concept of man (PH II 27). In this connection Sextus contrasts asserting dogmatically that man really is, e.g., a featherless two-footed animal with broad nails and a capacity for political science and putting forward this same definition as something merely persuasive (pithanon); the former is the illegitimate thing which is the target of his argument, the latter what he thinks Plato would do (PH II 28). I think it would be wholly in keeping with the spirit, if not the letter, of this text to add the properly Pyrrhonist alternative of saying what man appears to one to be. For Sextus insists[30] that the skeptic is not prohibited from noē-sis, the forming of conceptions. He can form his own conceptions just so long as the basis for this is that things he experiences appear clearly to reason itself and he is not led into any commitment to the reality of the things conceived (PH II 10).

I suggest, therefore, that the skeptic contrast between appearance and real existence is a purely formal one, entirely independent of subject matter. The skeptic does not divide the world into appearances and realities so that one could ask of this or that whether it belongs to the category of appearance or to the category of reality. He divides questions into questions about how something appears and questions about how it really and truly is, and both types of question may be asked about anything whatever.

In his chapter on the skeptic criterion Sextus says: "No one, I suppose, disputes about the underlying subject's appearing thus or thus; what he inquires about is whether it is such as it appears" (PH I 22). The point is one familiar in modern philosophy, that how a thing appears or seems is authoritatively answered by each individual. When Sextus says that a man's impression is azētētos, not subject to inquiry (PH I 22), the claim is that his report that this is how it appears to him cannot be challenged and he cannot properly be required to give reasons, evidence, or proof for it. It is only when he ventures a claim about how something really is that he can be asked for the appropriate justification. It follows that the skeptic who adheres strictly to appearance is withdrawing to the safety of a position not open to challenge or inquiry. He may talk about anything under the sun—but only to note how it appears to him, not to say how it really is. He withdraws to this detached stance as the result of repeatedly satisfying himself that inquiry as to the real nature of a thing leads to unresolvable disagreement. We can understand, now, why the only use the skeptic has for reason is polemical. Quite simply, nothing he wants to say in his own person is such as to require a reasoned justification.[31] Reason is one more important notion which is tied to truth and real existence.

It turns out, then, that the life without belief is not the mental blank one might at first imagine it to be. It is not even limited as to the subject matter over which the skeptic's thoughts may range. Its secret is rather an attitude of mind manifest in his thoughts. He notes the impressions things make on him and the contrary impressions they make on other people, and his own impressions seem to him no stronger, no more plausible, than anyone else's.[32] To the extent that he has achieved *ataraxia*, he is no longer concerned to inquire which is right. When a thing appears in a certain light to him, that no more inclines him to believe it is as it appears than would the fact of its so appearing to someone else. It is merely one more impression or appearance to be noted. Thus the withdrawal from truth and real existence becomes, in a certain sense, a detachment from oneself.

ASSENT AND CONSTRAINT

With this conclusion we reach, I think, the real point of skepticism as a philosophy of life. So thoroughgoing a detachment from oneself is not easy to understand—indeed, it is here that I would locate the ultimate incoherence of the skeptic philosophy—but the attempt must be made if we are to appreciate the kind of restructuring which the skeptic arguments aim to produce in a man's thought, and thereby in his practical life. To this end I must now broach the difficult topic of assent and the will.

I have already explained that assent is a wider notion than belief. The skeptic's nonbelief, his *epochē*, is his withholding assent to anything not given in appearance (*PH* I 13). But there are things he assents to: *ta phainomena*, anything that appears. This doctrine is stated in full generality at *PH* I 19-20, with no restriction to any specific class of appearances; although the example to hand is a sensible appearance, the taste of honey, I hold, as before, that Sextus means any kind of appearance and hence that the important further characterization he gives in this connection is to be applied to all appearances without exception.

The further characterization is as follows: things that appear lead us to assent (sc. to them) *aboulētōs*, without our willing it, in accordance with the impression they affect us with (*kata phantasian pathētikēn*). Much the same is said on numerous occasions elsewhere. When the skeptic assents, it is because he experiences two kinds of constraint. First, what he assents to are *kata phantasian katēnagkasmena pathē*, states with which we are forcibly affected in accordance with an impression (*PH* I 13). He can assent to an impression, or, as Sextus also puts it (*PH* II 10), he can assent to what is presented in accordance with an impression he is affected with insofar as it appears, because the impression itself, the way the thing appears, is a passive affection not willed by the person who experiences it and as such is not open to inquiry or dispute (*en peisei kai aboulētōi pathei keimenē azētētos estin*) (*PH* I 22); in other words, it is merely what is happening to him now. But second, besides having the impression forced upon us, we are also constrained in these cases to assent. The skeptic yields to things which move us affectively (*tois kinousin hēmas pathētikōs*) and lead us by compulsion to assent (*kai anagkastikōs agousin eis sunkatathesin*) (*PH* I 193).

What then, is the content of the skeptic's assent? Assent is described as assent to something insofar as it appears, or to the state/impression which is its appearing to us, but the expression of this assent is propositional: e.g. "Honey appears sweet" (*PH* I 20). In another place (*PH* I 13) Sextus puts the point in a negative way: when the skeptic is warmed or chilled, he would not say "I think I am not warmed/chilled."[33] Arne Naess takes the negative formulation to be an attempt to articulate the idea that the skeptic does not accept or reject "It now seems cold to me" as a proposition.[34] I do not find in Sextus any evidence of a contrast between assenting to a state or to the impression of a thing and assenting to a proposition about how something appears to one. We concede, says Sextus (*PH* I 20), that honey appears sweet because we are sweetened perceptually (*glukazometha aisthētikōs*), which I take to mean: we have a perceptual experience featuring the character of sweetness. The skeptic's assent is simply the acknowledging of what is happening to him, and the compulsion to assent, to acknowledge what is happening to him, is equally simple. It is not that there is resistance to overcome, but that there can be no dispute about what the impression is; it is *azētētos*, not open to inquiry. The impression is just the way something appears to one, and assent to it is just acknowledging that this is indeed how the thing appears to one at the moment.

So far, I have illustrated these points, as Sextus does, by reference to impressions of sense. As it happens, however, at least one of the statements cited occurs in a context describing the attitude of mind which the skeptic brings to the practice of argumentative inquiry. This is the statement (*PH* II 10) that the skeptic assents to things presented to him in accordance with an impression which they affect him with (*kata phantasian pathētikēn*), insofar as they appear to him. Given the context, it is natural to refer the remark to the appearances annexed to the skeptic's various philosophical pronouncements. That the *phantasia*, the impression, is characterized as *pathētikē*, something one is affected with, is no hindrance to this; we have already seen that an impression need not be an impression of sense, and to call it *pathētikē* simply means it is a passivity (*peisis*) or *pathos*, as at *PH* I 22. Sextus is perfectly prepared to speak of a *pathos*, affection, annexed to the skeptic formula "I determine nothing" (*PH* I 197; cf. I 203). As he explains, when the skeptic says "I determine nothing," what he is saying is, "I am now affected (*ego houtō pepontha nun*) in such a way as not to affirm or deny dogmatically any of the matters under inquiry." At *PH* I 193 this is generalized to all expressions of skeptical nonassertion (*aphasia*) and linked with the topic of compulsory assent to states of appearance. Clearly, "I determine nothing," as an expression of the skeptic's nonassertion, does not indicate a sense-impression. But it does indicate a *pathos*, a passive affection. It would seem, therefore, that this *pathos*, and assent to it, is forced upon the skeptic as the outcome of his arguments just as much as a sense-impression is forced upon him by an encounter with some sensible object and then forcibly engages his assent.

I think this is right. Look through a sample of skeptic arguments and you will find that a great number of them end by saying that one is forced to suspend judgment, the word most commonly used being "*anagkazō*," the same word as describes our passive relationship to an impression of sense and the assent it engages. The skeptic assents only when his assent is constrained; and equally, when he withholds assent, suspends judgment, this is because he finds himself constrained to do so. A marked passivity in the face of both his sensations and his own thought processes is an important aspect of the skeptic's detachment from himself. But, once again, there is neither mystery nor effort involved in the constraint.

We are all familiar with the way in which an argument or overwhelming evidence may compel assent. In just this way, the skeptic's arguments are designed to check assent ("*epechein*" has a transitive use, "to check," as well as the standard intransitive meaning, "to suspend judgment"). Imagine a man so placed that he really can see no reason at all to believe *p* rather than not-*p*; the considerations for and against each of them seem absolutely equal no matter how hard he tries to resolve the question. Then, as Sextus puts it, he will be checked (*epischethēsetai*: *PH* I 186; cf. I 180, *M* VII 337). If it was a matter of acting where he could see no reason to choose this rather than that, he could toss a coin or simply do whatever one has been brought up to do in the circumstances. In effect, that is what the skeptic does do when he adheres to the conventions of whatever society he lives in without himself believing in them or having any personal attachment to their values. But believing is not like that. Of course, it is a good philosophical question whether it is not possible in some circumstances to decide or will to believe something, but these will have to be circumstances more auspicious than those I have described, where one can literally see nothing to choose between p and not-p. To quote Epictetus (*Diss.* I 28. 3), just try to believe, or positively disbelieve, that the number of the stars is even.[35]

I repeat: try it. Make yourself vividly aware of your helpless inability to mind either way. *That* is how the skeptic wants you to feel about everything, including whether what I am saying is true or false (you are not to be convinced by the reputation or the artfulness of the speaker). That is *ataraxia*. If a tyrant sends a message that you and your family are to perish at dawn unless you commit some unspeakable deed, the true skeptic will be undisturbed both about whether the message is true or false and about whether it would be a good thing or a bad thing to comply with the command. You will be undisturbed not because your will has subjugated the tendency to believe and to be emotionally disturbed, but because you have been rendered unable to find any reason to think anything is true rather than false or good rather than bad. This is not to say that you will do nothing—Hume's charge of total lethargy. Sextus meets this old complaint, first by acknowledging the role of bodily drives like hunger and thirst and by the rest of the fourfold scheme of activity, and in the case of the tyrant (*M* XI 162-166) by saying that of course the skeptic will have his preconceptions, the result of being brought up in certain forms of life (cf. *PH* II 246), and these will prompt him to act one way or the other. But the point is that he does not identify with the values involved. He notes that they have left him with inclinations to pursue some things and avoid others, but he does not believe there is any reason to prefer the things he pursues over those that he avoids.[36]

The assumptions at work here are reminiscent of Socrates, as is much else in Hellenistic moral psychology. The emotions depend on belief, especially beliefs about what is good and bad. Remove belief and the emotions will disappear; as fear, for example, fades when one is dissuaded of one's belief that the thing one was afraid of is dangerous. At least, to the extent that emotions derive from reason and thought, they must disappear when judgment is suspended on every question of fact and value. This will not eliminate bodily disturbances such as hunger and thirst, nor the tendencies to action which result from the endowments of nature and from an upbringing in human society (cf. *PH* I 230-231). For they do not depend on reason and thought. But they will be less disturbing without the added element of belief about good and bad, truth and falsity (above, p. 126). One may feel that this added element of belief is the very thing that gives meaning and sense to a life, even if it is also the source of trouble and disturbance. Without it, the skeptic's life will be a hollow shell of the existence he enjoyed, and was troubled by, prior to his skeptical enlightenment. Such is the price of peace and tranquillity, however, and the skeptic is willing to pay it to the full. Or rather, he is constrained by argument to suspend judgment and belief, and then finds that this just happens to bring tranquillity (*PH* I 28-30; above, p. 120-121). He exercises no deliberate choice in the matter, any more than when hunger leads him to get food.[37] So far from relying on the will to control assent, the skeptic panacea, beginning with the Ten Modes of Aenesidemus, is to use reason to check all the sources of belief and destroy all trust in reason itself, thereby eliminating the very inclination to believe. The life without belief is not an achievement of the will but a paralysis of reason by itself.[38]

CONTROVERSIAL INTERLUDE

It is time to take stock. A life has been described, and we want to know whether it is a possible life for man. But there is a prior question of some moment to face first: Is the life described a life without belief, as Sextus so often claims (*adoxastōs bioumen*, etc., *PH* I 23; 226; 231; II 246; 254; 258; III 235)?[39] The skeptic is supposed to content himself with appearances in lieu of beliefs, but it may be objected that, whatever Sextus may say, at least some of these appearances are beliefs in disguise. "Honey tastes sweet" may pass muster as the record of a perceptual or bodily experience, but when it comes to "All things appear relative" (*PH* I 135) or "Let it be granted that the premises of the proof appear" (*M* VIII 368) or "Some things appear good, others evil" (*M* XI 19), we can hardly take "appear" (*phainesthai*) otherwise than in its epistemic sense. That is, when the skeptic offers a report of the form "It appears to me now that *p*," at least sometimes he is chronicling the fact that he believes or finds himself inclined to believe that something is the case.

This epistemic reading of the skeptic's talk of appearances may be presented in either of two forms: as an objection to Sextus or as an objection to my interpretation of Sextus. In the second version, which I take up first, the claim will be that the skeptic's assent to appearance, as Sextus describes it, is not the assertion of the existence of a certain impression or experience but the expression of a nondogmatic belief about what is the case in the world. It will then follow that what the skeptic eschews, when he suspends judgment about everything, is not any and every kind of belief about things, but belief of a more ambitious type, which we may call (pending further elucidation) dogmatic belief.[40]

I do not doubt that a good number of the appearance-statements in Sextus Empiricus *can* be read epistemically. But if this fact is to yield an objection not to Sextus but to my interpretation of him, it needs to be shown that the epistemic reading has the approval of Sextus himself. The passage which comes closest to showing it is *PH* I 13. There Sextus says that some people define a broad sense of "*dogma*" meaning to accept something or not contradict it,[41] and with this he contrasts a narrower sense explained by some (? the same) people as assent to one of the non-evident things investigated by the sciences. The point of this distinction is to clarify the sense in which the skeptic does not dogmatize: he will have nothing to do with *dogma* in the second and narrower sense, "for the Pyrrhonist does not assent to anything that is nonevident." But he does assent to states with which he is forcibly affected in accordance with an impression, and such assent (we are given to understand) is or involves *dogma* in the broader sense to which the Pyrrhonist has no objection. For example (an example we have met before), "He would not say, when he is warmed or chilled, 'I think I am not warmed or chilled.'" Two questions now arise. First, does Sextus's tolerance of the broad sense signify approval of an epistemic reading for appearance-statements generally? Second, does his account of the narrower sense restrict his disapproval to what we have provisionally called dogmatic belief?

(1) What the skeptic accepts or does not contradict is "I am warmed/chilled." This is a *dogma* (in the broad sense) inasmuch as the skeptic thinks, or it seems to him, that he is warmed/chilled.[42] But it does not follow that it is an epistemic seeming, in the sense relevant to our discussion, unless its content "I am warmed/chilled" is a proposition about what is the case in the world rather than a proposition about the skeptic's experience.

We must be careful here. The Greek verbs *thermainesthai* and *psuchesthai* do not normally *mean* "I feel hot/cold," although translators (Bury, Hossenfelder) have a tendency to render them in such terms here, just because Sextus is illustrating an affection (*pathos*). They normally mean "be warmed/chilled."[43] On the other hand, neither does "I am warmed/chilled" necessarily refer to an objective process of acquiring or losing heat. And my own view is that to insist that Sextus's illustrative *pathos* must be either a subjective feeling or an objective happening is to impose a Cartesian choice which is foreign to his way of thinking.

Sextus's terminology here is probably Cyrenaic. *Thermainesthai* and *psuchesthai* appear (by a well-motivated editorial insertion) on a list of Cyrenaic terms for *pathē* of perception in Plutarch, *Col.* 1120e, along with *glukainesthai*, "to be sweetened," which Sextus uses at *M* VIII 211 (cf. *glukazesthai*, *PH* I 20, 211; II 51, 72; *M* VIII 54; IX 139); *leukainesthai*, "to be whitened," and the like, applied by Sextus to the activity of the senses, look to be of similar provenance (*M* VII 293 with 190-198). As Plutarch describes the Cyrenaic doctrine which was the original home of this peculiar terminology,[44] it is that I can say *thermainomai*, "I am warmed," but not *thermos ho akratos*, where this does not mean "Neat wine is warm" but "Neat wine is warming" (*thermos* = *thermantikos*, *Col.* 1109f). The case is exactly comparable to one we find in Aristocles (ap. Euseb. *Praep. ev.* XIV 19.2-3): according to the Cyrenaics, when I am being cut or burned I know I am undergoing something (*paschein ti*), but whether it is fire that is burning or iron that is cutting me, I cannot say. Do they mean, when they talk of undergoing something, the physical event or the way it feels? To that question *there is no clear answer*, and the terminology makes it impossible to decide. It is the same with Sextus. The reference of these funny verbs is plainly to a perceptual process rather than to the transmission of heat (cf. the case of the neat wine: conversely, the warming of a man so chilled that he could not feel a thing when you rubbed his hands would not illustrate Sextus's point at all), but we should keep the translation "be warmed/chilled." The man is being affected perceptually (cf. "we are sweetened perceptually," *glukazometha aisthētikōs*, at *PH* I 20 and the uses of *thermainein* at *PH* I 110; II 56; *M* I 147; VII 368; IX 69), but we cannot "split" the affection (*pathos*) into separate mental (subjective) and physical (objective) components. The moral to draw is not that the Pyrrhonist allows himself some beliefs about what is the case, but that skepticism is not yet associated with a Cartesian conception of the self.[45]

If this is correct, *PH* I 13 offers no justification for an epistemic reading of the skeptic's appearance-statements. The broader sense of *dogma* is simply the accepting of a perceptual experience as the experience it is, in the manner we have found amply attested already (above, p. 130-131).[46] Sextus is not going out of his way to leave room for a nondogmatic type of belief about matters of real existence. On the contrary, he says that when as a skeptic he makes statements with the verb "to be," he is to be understood as meaning "to appear" (*PH* I 135, 198, 200), and he glosses this use of "to be" at *M* XI 18 in terms which are unmistakably nonepistemic:

The word "is" has two meanings: (a) "is actually (*huparchei*)," as we say at the present moment "It is day" in place of "It is actually day," (b) "appears," as some of the mathematicians are accustomed to say often that the distance between two stars "is" a cubit's length, meaning this as equivalent to "It appears so and doubtless is not actually so"; for perhaps it is actually one hundred stades, but appears a cubit because of the height and distance from the eye.

He then applies this elucidation to one of the statements that troubled us earlier, "Some things appear good, others evil" (M XI 19).

(2) Moving on to the narrower sense of *"dogma,"* the point to observe is that *anything* which is nonevident is something for the sciences to investigate, the nonevident being by definition that which can only be known by the mediation of inference.[47] The scope for investigation or inquiry will be determined by the extent of things nonevident, "for," as Sextus says, "the Pyrrhonist does not assent to anything that is nonevident." But the Pyrrhonist attack on the criterion of truth abolishes the evidence of everything that the dogmatists consider evident (PH II 95, M VIII 141-142). Take one of the dogmatists' favorite examples of things too patently obvious to be doubted, "It is day," which turns up both in connection with the criterion (M VIII 144) and in the passage just quoted: the skeptic denies it is evident and, as we have seen, he accepts it only as a nonepistemic statement of appearance, "It appears to be day (sc. but may not actually be so)." *Anything* which goes beyond (nonepistemic) appearances is subject to inquiry (PH I 19; above, p. 128; cf. M VIII 344-345).

In sum, I do not think that one solitary reference to the sciences (for it is not repeated elsewhere in Sextus) in a definition borrowed from someone else[48] is sufficient basis to credit Sextus with a distinction between dogmatic and nondogmatic belief. It is not sufficient even when we add to the scales that Sextus frequently restricts what he suspends judgment about to the question how things are "in nature" (*pros tēn phusin,* etc., PH I 59, 78, 87, et al.) or how things are "so far as concerns what the dogmatists say about them" (PH II 26, 104; III 13, 29, 135; M VIII 3) or, ambiguously, how things are "so far as this is a matter for *logos* (statement, definition, reason)" (PH I 20, 215).[49] Just how restrictive these qualifications are depends on what they are contrasted with, and in every case the contrast is with how things appear, where this, as we have seen, is to be taken nonepistemically. All we are left with, then, is a passive impression (*phantasia*) or experience (*pathos*), expressed in a statement which makes no truth-claim about what is the case. As Sextus sums up the skeptic's avoidance of dogmatism, at the end of the passage which has detained us so long, it is simply this: "He states what appears to himself and announces his own experience without belief, making no assertion about external things" (PH I 15).

To which we may add that if the skeptic did allow himself some belief, opponents of Pyrrhonism would be guilty of serious *ignoratio elenchi* when they bring up the simple instinctive beliefs which, they claim, are inseparable from the use of the senses and from everyday actions (see the arguments from Aristocles and Galen cited in n. 4). Aristocles repeatedly takes his target to be a philosophy which pretends to eschew all judgment and belief whatever, so that he can say that it is inconsistent for the Pyrrhonist to advance any assertion or argument (ap. Euseb. *Praep. ev.* XIV 18.8-9; 15; 16-17; 24). Sextus, as we have seen, connects dogmatism with claims that something is (simply) true, and he needs to do so if he is to undercut the ordinary man's hopes and fears. For clearly, hope and fear can come from any type of belief about what is or will be the case; it need not be dogmatic belief in some more stringent sense. What is at issue here is the ordinary man's ordinary belief that it is good and desirable to have money, say, or fame or pleasure, and bad to be without them (*M* XI 120-124, 144-146; cf. *PH* I 27-28). Belief, in the sense Sextus is attacking, is responsible for *all* the things men pursue and avoid by their own judgment (*M* XI 142, using *doxa*). The internal logic of Pyrrhonism requires that *dogma* and *doxa*—Sextus does not differentiate between these two terms—really do mean: belief.[50]

Behind this issue of interpretation lies a philosophical question of considerable interest, the question whether and in what terms a distinction between nondogmatic and dogmatic belief can be made out. One promising line to start might be to distinguish a belief that honey is sweet and a belief that honey is *really* sweet in the sense that sweetness exists in the honey, as part of its objective nature. Such talk has a familiar philosophical ring where the sensible qualities are concerned, but it would need to be explained what it amounted to when applied to such examples as "It is day," "I am conversing" (*M* VIII 144), or "This is a man" (*M* VIII 316). Again, one may suggest that nondogmatic belief is belief not grounded in or responsive to reasons and reasoning—but that will bring with it a breaking of the connection between belief and truth. What Sextus objects to is the accepting of anything as true. Any such acceptance he will count as dogmatizing (*PH* I 14-15; above, p. 121). I do not myself think there is a notion of belief which lacks this connection with truth and, in a more complicated way, with reason.[51] Nor, at bottom, did Hume: else he would not have found it paradoxical that the skeptical arguments fail to dislodge belief. But all I have contended here is that Sextus has no other notion of belief than the accepting of something as true.

DETACHMENT AND PHILOSOPHICAL BELIEF

It remains to consider whether it is an objection to Sextus that many of his appearance-statements seem to demand the epistemic reading which he refuses. One instance out of many would be the following: "To every dogmatic claim I have examined there appears to me to be opposed a rival dogmatic claim which is equally worthy and equally unworthy of belief" (freely rendered from *PH* I 203). Sextus insists that this utterance is not dogmatic, i.e., not expressive of belief. It is an announcement of a human state or affection (*anthrōpeiou pathous apaggelia*), which is something that appears or is apparent to the person who undergoes it (*ho esti phainomenon tōi paschonti*). And this would be all right if "It appears to me to be so" meant here "I have some inclination to believe it is so." Perhaps there could be an experience it was appropriate to record in those terms. But an inclination to believe is the last thing the skeptic wants to enter in his chronicle. The verb "appears" in the above statement, and dozens like it, is to be taken nonepistemically, as we have seen. At times, no doubt, the nonepistemic reading is sheer bluff on Sextus's part, but the objector's opposition will itself be no better than bare counterassertion unless he can muster more to say. I think there is more to say about the appearances annexed to the skeptic's philosophical pronouncements. They form a class of appearances which lie at the center of the skeptic's conception of himself and his life.

Remember that we know perfectly well *why* it appears to the skeptic that any dogmatic claim has a contrary equally worthy or unworthy of acceptance. It is the result of a set of arguments designed to show, compellingly, that this is in fact the case. Such arguments can compel him to suspend judgment because they compel him to accept their conclusion—to accept, that is, that in each and every case dogmatic claims are indeed equally balanced and hence that one ought to suspend judgment. (Which is often enough, of course, the way Sextus does conclude his arguments.) But accepting the conclusion that *p* is true on the basis of a certain argument is hardly to be distinguished from coming to *believe* that *p* is *true* with that argument as one's *reason*. In being shown that there is as much, or as little, reason to believe the first-level proposition that honey is bitter as that it is sweet, the skeptic has been given reason to believe the second-level proposition that the reasons for and against are equally balanced. In being shown, both on general grounds and by the accumulation of instances, that no claim about real existence is to be preferred to its denial, he has, again, been given reason to believe that generalization true. Certainly it appears to him that dogmatic claims are equally balanced, but this appearance, so called, being the effect of argument, is only to be made sense of in terms of reason, belief and truth—the very notions the skeptic is most anxious to avoid.[52] He wants to say something of the form "It appears to me that *p* but I do not believe that *p*," with a nonepistemic use of "appears," but it looks to be intelligible only if "appears" is in fact epistemic, yielding a contradiction: "I (am inclined to) believe that *p* but I do not believe that *p*." How is this result to be avoided?

The difficulty is not to be overcome by suggesting that the skeptic emerges from his arguments in a state of bafflement rather than belief. Bafflement could be the effect of arguments for and against; you are pulled now this way, now that, until you just do not know what to say (cf. *M* VII 243). The problem is to see why this should produce tranquillity rather than acute anxiety.[53]

Nor should we allow Sextus to deny that the skeptic's philosophical appearances are the effect of argument. He does on occasion claim that the skeptical arguments do not give demonstrative disproof of the dogmatists' views but mere reminders or suggestions of what can be said against them, and through this of the apparently equal strength of opposed positions (*PH* II 103, 130, 177; *M* VIII 289). In the technical terms of the period the arguments are not indicative but commemorative signs. I need not enlarge on the technicalities because (to be blunt) Sextus offers no elucidation whatever of the crucial notion of something's being said *against* a doctrine or belief but not by way of reasons or evidence against it. If the skeptic works through reasoned arguments to the point where the reasons on either side balance and reason stultifies itself, if his arguments are (in the now famous phrase) a ladder to be thrown over when you have climbed up (*M* VIII 481), then we must insist that they make their impact through the normal operations of our reason. *Epochē* is not a blind, mechanical effect but, supposedly, the natural and intelligible outcome of following with our human capacity for thought along the paths marked out by the skeptical arguments.

Another suggestion might be that what the skeptic records as the outcome of his arguments is an interrogative rather than an assertive frame of mind: "Is it the case, then, that contrary claims are equally balanced?" This would fit the skeptic's characterization of himself as *zētētikos*, one who goes on seeking (*PH* I 2-3; 7; II 11), and Sextus does at one point say that some skeptics prefer to take the formula "No more this than that" as a question, "Why this rather than that?" (*PH* I 189; cf. *M* I 315). But again we must be careful about *ataraxia*. The skeptic goes on seeking not in the sense that he has an active program of research but in the sense that he continues to regard it as an open question whether *p* or not-*p* is the case, at least for any first-level proposition concerning real existence. But this should not mean he is left in a state of actually *wondering* whether *p* or not-*p* is the case, for that might induce anxiety. Still less should he be wondering whether, in general, contrary claims are equally balanced. For if it is a real possibility for him that they are not, that means it is a real possibility that there are answers to be found; and it will be an immense worry to him, as it was at the very beginning of his skeptical education, that he does not know what these answers are.

In other words, if tranquillity is to be achieved, at some stage the skeptic's questing thoughts must come to a state of rest or equilibrium.[54]

There need be no finality to this achievement; the skeptic may hold himself ready to be persuaded that there are after all answers to be had. He is not a negative dogmatist furnished with a priori objections that rule out the possibility of answers as a matter of general principle once and for all (cf. *PH* I 1-3). But *ataraxia* is hardly to be attained if he is not in some sense satisfied—so far—that no answers are forthcoming, that contrary claims are indeed equal. And my question is: How can Sextus then deny that this is something he believes?

I do not think he can. Both the causes (reasoned arguments) of the state which Sextus calls appearance and its effects (tranquillity and the cessation of emotional disturbance) are such as to justify us in calling it a state of belief. And this objection to Sextus's claim to have described a life without belief leads on to an answer to our original question about the possibility, in human terms, of the life Sextus describes.

The source of the objection I have been urging is that the skeptic wants to treat "It appears to me that *p* but I do not believe that *p*," where *p* is some philosophical proposition such as "Contrary claims have equal strength," on a par with perceptual instances of that form such as "It appears (looks) to me that the stick in the water is bent but I do not believe it is." The latter is acceptable because its first conjunct describes a genuine experience—in Greek terms, a *pathos*, a *phantasia*, which awaits my assent. And it is important here that assent and impression are logically independent. For they are not independent in the philosophical case. In the philosophical case, the impression, when all is said and done, simply *is* my assent to the conclusion of an argument, assent to it as true. That is the danger of allowing talk about appearances or impressions of thought: it comes to seem legitimate to treat states which are in fact states of belief, presupposing assent, as if they were independent of assent in the way that sense-impressions can be. For if, beneath its disguise as a mere passive affection, the philosophical impression includes assent, it ought to make no sense for the skeptic to insist that he does not assent to it as true. That would be to contemplate a further act of assent to the assent already given. If the skeptic does insist, if he refuses to identify with his assent, he is as it were detaching himself from the person (namely, himself) who was convinced by the argument, and he is treating his own thought as if it were the thought of someone else, someone thinking thoughts within him. He is saying, in effect, "It is thought within me that *p*, but *I* do not believe it." In the right circumstances, that could be said. But not all the time, for every appearance/thought one has.[55] Yet that is what it will come to if absolutely every appearance, higher-level as well as lower-level, is construed nonepistemically.

One of the more memorable sayings attributed to Pyrrho is a remark regretting that it is difficult to divest oneself entirely of one's humanity.[56]

(As the story goes, this was his reply to a charge of failing to practice what he preached when once he was frightened of a dog.) Sextus makes out that the skeptic ideal preserves all that is worth preserving in human nature. But it seems to me that Hume and the ancient critics were right. When one has seen how radically the skeptic must detach himself from himself, one will agree that the supposed life without belief is not, after all, a possible life for man.[57]

NOTES

In these notes the following works are referred to by number:
[1]   V. Brochard, *Les sceptiques grecs*, 2d ed. (Paris, 1923, reprint ed., 1969)
[2]   U. Burkhard, *Die angebliche Heraklit-Nachfolge des Skeptikers Aenesidem* (Bonn, 1973)
[3]   M. F. Burnyeat, "Protagoras and Self-refutation in Later Greek Philosophy," *Philosophical Review* 85 (1976), 44-69
[4]   Idem, "Tranquillity without a Stop: Timon Frag. 68," *Classical Quarterly* 72 (n.s. 30) (1980), 86-93
[5]   Idem, "Carneades Was No Probabilist," in *Riverside Studies in Ancient Skepticism*, ed. D. Glidden (forthcoming)
[6]   Idem, "Idealism and Greek Philosophy: What Descartes Saw and Berkeley Missed," in *Idealism Past and Present*, ed. G. Vesey, Royal Institute of Philosophy Lectures, vol. 13 (1982)
[7]   K. Deichgräber, *Die griechische Empirikerschule* (Berlin, 1930)
[8]   H. Diels, *Poetarum Philosophorum Fragmenta* (Berlin, 1901)
[9]   J.-P. Dumont, *Le scepticisme et le phénomène* (Paris, 1972)
[10] M. Frede, review of Stough (no. [19] below), *Journal of Philosophy* 70 (1973), 805-810
[11] Idem, "Des Skeptikers Meinungen," *Neue Hefte für Philosophie* 15/16 (1979), 102-129
[12] M. Hossenfelder, *Sextus Empiricus: Grundriss der pyrrhonischen Skepsis* (Frankfurt a.M., 1968)
[13] K. Janáček, *Sextus Empiricus' Sceptical Methods* (Prague, 1972)
[14] Idem, "Zur Interpretation des Photios-Abschnittes über Aenesidemos," *Eirene* 14 (1976), 93-100
[15] A. A. Long, "Freedom and Determinism in the Stoic Theory of Human Action," in *Problems in Stoicism*, ed. A. A. Long (London, 1971), pp. 173-199
[16] Idem, "Timon of Phlius: Pyrrhonist and Satirist," *Proceedings of the Cambridge Philological Society* 204 (n.s. 24) (1978), 68-91
[17] A. Naess, *Scepticism* (London, 1968)
[18] C. L. Stough, *Greek Skepticism* (Berkeley and Los Angeles, 1969)
[19] G. Striker, "Sceptical Strategies," in *Doubt and Dogmatism: Studies in Hellenistic Epistemology*, ed. Malcolm Schofield, Myles Burnyeat, and Jonathan Barnes (Oxford, 1980), pp. 54-83

[20] C. C. W. Taylor, "'All Perceptions Are True,'" in *Doubt and Dogmatism* (see [19] above), pp. 105-124

[21] A.-J. Voelké, *L'idée de volonté dans le stoïcisme* (Paris, 1973)

[22] E. Zeller, *Die Philosophie der Griechen in ihrer geschichtlichen Entwicklung*, III, Abt. 1 and 2, *Die nacharistotelische Philosophie*, 4th ed. (Leipzig, 1903-1909)

1. Cited from the third edition of Selby-Bigge's edition, with text revised by P. H. Nidditch (Oxford, 1975). One of Nidditch's revisions is restoring the word "only" to the first sentence of the quoted passage.

2. The exciting story of this influence has been pursued through the ins and outs of religious and philosophical controversy in a series of studies by Richard H. Popkin. See, in particular, *The History of Scepticism, from Erasmus to Descartes*, rev. ed. (New York, Evanston, and London, 1968); "David Hume: His Pyrrhonism and His Critique of Pyrrhonism," *Philosophical Quarterly* 1 (1951), 385-407; "David Hume and the Pyrrhonian Controversy," *Review of Metaphysics* 6 (1952-53), 65-81.

3. On the role and importance of this argument within Hume's general program for a naturalistic science of man, see Barry Stroud, *Hume* (London, Henley, and Boston, 1977), esp. chap. 1.

4. Witness the title of the polemical tract by Arcesilaus's contemporary, the Epicurean Colotes, "On the fact that the doctrines of the other philosophers make it impossible to live" (Plut. *Col.* 1107d, 1108d). The section dealing with Arcesilaus borrowed the Stoic argument that total *epochē* must result in total inaction (*ib.* 1122ab)—essentially, Hume's charge of total lethargy. For the controversy around this issue in the period of Academic skepticism, see the references and discussion in Striker [19]. Subsequently, the Pyrrhonist *epochē* encountered similar criticism: (1) Aristocles ap. Euseb. *Praep. evang.* XIV 18.23-24 argues that judgment, hence belief, is inseparably bound up with the use of the senses and other mental faculties; (2) Galen *De dignosc. puls.* VIII 781, 16-783, 5, K = Deichgräber [7] frag. 74, p. 133, 19-p. 134, 6, asks scoffingly whether the Pyrrhonist expects us to stay in bed when the sun is up for lack of certainty about whether it is day or night, or to sit on board our ship when everyone else is disembarking, wondering whether what appears to be land really is land; (3) Sextus has the lethargy criticism in view at *M* XI 162-163.

5. I call it dogmatic because Hume offers no argument to support his claim against the alternative, Pyrrhonist account of life and action, available in Sextus or in modern writers like Montaigne.

6. The claim that skeptic *ataraxia* alone is *eudaimonia* is argued at length in *M* XI 110-167.

7. Cf. Stough [18], pp. 142 ff.

8. If the modern reader finds this an arbitrary terminological narrowing, on the grounds that if I say how things appear to me my statement ought to count as true if, and only if, things really do appear as I say they do (cf. Stough [18], pp. 142 ff.), the answer is that his objection, though natural, is anachronistic. The idea that truth can be attained without going outside subjective experience was

not always the philosophical commonplace it has come to be. It was Descartes who made it so, who (in the second *Meditation*) laid the basis for our broader use of the predicates "true" and "false" whereby they can apply to statements of appearance without reference to real existence. See Burnyeat [6].

9. The notion of that which is evident (δῆλον, πρόδηλον, ἐναργές) is a dogmatist's notion in the first instance. Things evident are things which come to our knowledge of themselves (*PH* II 97; *M* VIII 144), which are grasped from themselves (*PH* II 99), which immediately present themselves to sense and intellect (*M* VIII 141), which require no other thing to announce them (*M* VIII 149), i.e., which are such that we have immediate noninferential knowledge of them, directly from the impression (*M* VIII 316). Examples: it is day, I am conversing (*M* VIII 144), this is a man (*M* VIII 316). Sextus declares that this whole class of things is put in doubt by the skeptic critique of the criterion of truth (*PH* II 95; *M* VIII 141-142). Consequently, any statement about such things will be dogma in the sense the skeptic eschews.

10. The reader should be warned that some interpretations take *PH* I 13-15 as evidence that "dogma" and "dogmatize" are still more restricted than I allow, with the consequence that the skeptic does not eschew all belief. It will be best to postpone controversy until the rest of my interpretation has been set out, but meanwhile the examples in the previous note will serve as well as any to illustrate the sorts of things about which, in my view, the skeptic suspends judgment.

11. DL IX 78: καθ᾽ οὓς τρόπους πείθει τὰ πράγματα.

12. DL IX 79: ἐδείκνυσαν οὖν ἀπὸ τῶν ἐναντίων τοῖς πείθουσιν ἴσας τὰς πιθανότητας.

13. DL IX 78: πείθειν γὰρ τά τε κατ᾽ αἴσθησιν συμφώνως ἔχοντα.

14. Note the partial overlapping between the τρόπους in DL IX 78 and the δέκα τρόπους, καθ᾽ οὓς τὰ ὑποκείμενα παραλλάττοντα ἐφαίνετο in 79 ff.: cf. τά τε κατ᾽ αἴσθησιν συμφώνως ἔχοντα with Modes I-IV, VII, τὰ νόμοις διεσταλμένα with Mode V, τὰ μηδέποτε ἢ σπανίως γοῦν μεταπίπτοντα and τὰ θαυμαζόμενα with Mode IX.

15. I should explain why, without explicit textual warrant, I attribute the content of this last paragraph also to Aenesidemus. The paragraph is one of two (IX 91-94) which intrude into a sequence of arguments announced earlier at IX 90. Not only is it likely, therefore, to derive from a different source, but the sequence of arguments follows immediately on the account of the Five Modes of Agrippa (IX 88-89), and its argumentation is largely Agrippean in construction, while the intruding paragraphs have a certain affinity of content and expression with the section 78-79, which is definitely associated with the name of Aenesidemus. For example, both passages are dismissive of belief due to something being familiar (σύνηθες) or pleasing (79: τέρποντα, 94: κεχαρισμένον). Perhaps the most telling affinity is in the use of the verb πείθειν to denote the dogmatic belief which the author opposes: the verb does not occur in (what I suppose to be) the Agrippean sequence IX 88-91, 94-101, nor is it usual for Sextus to employ it as part of his own technical vocabulary for the key concept of dogmatic belief. Where he does use it is in discussing Academic fallibilism, as we are about to see. Cf. also *PH* I 226, 229-230.

16. For the correct translation of πιθανός, see Couissin, chap. 3 above, p. 46, Striker [19], section III. Getting the translation right is a first step towards undoing the myth of Carneades as a proponent of "probabilism": see Burnyeat [5].

17. The evidence for Aenesidemus's having begun his philosophical career in the Academy is that he dedicated his *Pyrrhonian Discourses* to L. Tubero, described as a fellow associate of the Academy (Photius, *Bibl.* 169b33). Zeller [22] Abt. 2, p. 23, n. 2, is perhaps right in suggesting that because Photius's report of this work (which is mentioned also at DL IX 106 and 116) says nothing of the Ten Modes, it is to be distinguished from the *Outline Introduction to Pyrrhonism* which Aristocles and Diogenes indicate as the place where the Modes were developed.

18. Both rightly and polemically if his target is Philo of Larissa: see below.

19. Timon frag. 2 in Diels [8]; translation and discussion in Stough [18], chap. 2.

20. The ground for this suspicion is a somewhat odd, textually disputed reference to Aenesidemus tacked on at the end of the summary. See Dumont [9], pp. 140-147.

21. For discussion, see Burnyeat [4]. The question of the historical accuracy of Timon's account of Pyrrho is a further matter which need not concern us here.

22. For the controversy about Carneades, see Striker [19]. That Aenesidemus's target was the Academy of Philo is indicated above all by Photius's report (*Bibl.* 170a21-22) that he characterized his Academic opponents as determining many things with assurance and claiming to contest only the cataleptic impression. This corresponds not to Carneades' skeptical outlook but to the distinctive innovation of Philo, according to whom it is not that in their own nature things cannot be grasped but that they cannot be grasped by the Stoics' cataleptic impression (*PH* I 235). The alternative target would be Antiochus, but he does not fit Aenesidemus's scornful description of contemporary Academics as Stoics *fighting* Stoics (Photius, *Bibl.* 170a14-17). It would appear that Aenesidemus was also provoked by Philo's claim (Cic. *Acad.* I 13) that there were not two Academies, but a single unified tradition reaching right back to Plato. This amounted to the assertion that Plato stood for skepticism as Philo understood it, and Aenesidemus was at pains to deny that Plato could rightly be regarded as a skeptic (*PH* 1 222), reading κατὰ τούς with Natorp and noting the disjunctive form of the argument: Plato is not skeptical if either he assents to certain things as true *or* he accepts them as merely persuasive. For a decisive defense of Natorp's reading against the alternative κατὰ τῶν, which would mean that Aenesidemus thought Plato was skeptical, see Burkhard [2], pp. 21-27.

23. Above, n. 4.

24. Esp. frags. 69: "But the phenomenon prevails on every side, wherever it may go"; and 74: "I do not assert that honey (really) is sweet, but that it appears (sweet) I grant" (tr. Stough).

25. Peter Unger, *Ignorance: A Case for Scepticism* (Oxford, 1975).

26. I have done a little interpretation here, taking τὸ μὲν εὐσεβεῖν παραλαμβάνομεν βιωτικῶς ὡς ἀγαθὸν τὸ δὲ ἀσεβεῖν ὡς φαῦλον in the light of such passages as *PH* I 226, II 246, III 12, *M* IX 49. Note the verb forms τὸ εὐσεβεῖν,

ἀσεβεῖν: not attitudes but practices (which were in any case the main content of Greek piety and impiety) are what the skeptic accepts. To say that it is βιωτικῶς, not as a matter of belief, that he accepts the one as good and the other as bad comes to little more than that he pursues the one and avoids the other; in short, he tries to observe the pieties of his society. If custom demands it, he will even declare that gods exist, but he will not believe it (*PH* III 2) or mean it *in propria persona* as do both the dogmatists and the ordinary man (*M* IX 49-50): on the existence of the gods, as on any question of real existence, the skeptic suspends judgment (*PH* III 6, 9, 11; *M* IX 59, 191).

27. Stough [18], pp. 119 ff. Stough's initial mistake (as I think it) is to treat the statement as a contribution to a theory of experience. She then elicits the consequence that one perceives only one's own impressions, not the external object, since that which appears *is* (according to Stough's reading of the present passage) our impression. This goes flatly against the innumerable passages where that which appears is the very thing whose real properties cannot be determined, e.g., the honey at *PH* I 20. A further undesirable and unwarranted feature of Stough's interpretation is the divergence it leads her to postulate between Aenesidemus and Sextus (pp. 124-125).

28. Frede [10].

29. *Contra* Stough [18], p. 146 n. 83.

30. *Contra* Naess [17], p. 51.

31. In keeping with this, Sextus does not claim knowledge or (*pace* Hossenfelder [12], pp. 60-61) certainty about how things appear to him. If pressed, the radical Pyrrhonist will actually deny that he knows such things (Galen, *De diff. puls.* VIII 711, 1-3 K = Deichgräber [7], frag. 75, p. 135, 28-30. See further Burnyeat [6].

32. It is of the essence of skepticism, as defined *PH* I 8 and as practiced throughout the skeptic literature, to set one person's impressions against those of another. Questions could be raised about the skeptic's entitlement to talk of other people's impressions, and suitable answers could be devised. But on the whole such questions are not raised, any more than the skeptic inquires into the basis for his extensive historical surveys of the views of other philosophers. The radically first-person stance of the skepticisms we are familiar with is a distinctively modern development (cf. n. 8 above).

33. On the translation of θερμαίνεσθαι and ψύχεσθαι, see below.

34. Naess [17], p. 8. Naess, however, has a rather special theory about what it is to accept or reject something as a proposition, a theory which is claimed to rescue Pyrrhonism from Hume's critique: see Alistair Hannay, "Giving the Sceptic a Good Name," *Inquiry* 18 (1975), 409-436.

35. The example is traditional, i.e., much older than Epictetus. It is a standard Stoic example of something altogether nonevident, which can be discerned neither from itself nor through a sign (*PH* II 97; *M* VII 393; VIII 147, 317; cf. VII 243; XI 59). It occurs also in Cicero's reference (*Acad.* II 32) to certain *quasi desperatos* who say that everything is as uncertain as whether the number of the stars is odd or even, a reference which is sometimes taken to point to Aenesidemus: so Brochard [1], p. 245, Striker [19], p. 64.

36. Compare, perhaps, Feyerabend's reply to the question why his "epistemological anarchist" does not jump out of the window: Paul Feyerabend, *Against Method* (London, 1975), 221-222. He notes his fear, and its effect on his behavior, but he does not endorse any reasons for the fear. See further n. 37 below.

37. According to Timon frag. 72, quoted *M* XI 164, the follower of Pyrrho is ἀφυγὴς καὶ ἀναίρετος. According to Sextus (*PH* I 28) he does not pursue or avoid anything eagerly (συντόνως), i.e., he does not mind how it turns out. This detachment in action is interestingly discussed by Hossenfelder [12], esp. pp. 66-74. On Socratic assumptions, it is the logical outcome of the skeptical conclusion that nothing is by nature good or bad, i.e., nothing is really *worth* pursuit or avoidance (Timon frag. 70 = *M* XI 140, discussed in Burnyeat [4]; *PH* I 27; III 235-238; *M* XI 69 ff).

38. The passivity of the skeptic's *epochē* has not, I think, been appreciated in the modern scholarly literature, Hossenfelder [12] excepted. One reason for this is the tendency to read appearance as sense-appearance wherever possible, with the consequence that Sextus's remarks about compulsion are taken to extend no further than bodily and perceptual sensation. That I have already taken issue with. The other reason is that it has been widely held to be common ground to philosophers of different persuasions in the period we are concerned with that "assent is free" (so, e.g., Brochard [1], pp. 138, 391). If that is so, it is easy to assume that, except when the skeptic is compelled to assent, he is free to give his assent or withhold it, and always chooses—chooses of his own volition—to withhold it.

The idea that assent is free is Stoic doctrine in the first place, and there are indeed plenty of Stoic texts which say that assent is voluntary or in our power. But there are also texts which say that at least some impressions compel assent. The cataleptic impression lays hold of us almost by the hairs, they say, and drags us to assent (*M* VII 257; cf. 405); in another image, the mind yields to what is clear as a scale yields to the weights (*Acad.* II 38; cf. Epict. *Diss.* II 26.7). Assent in such cases is still voluntary because, it would seem, all that is meant by saying it is voluntary is that it depends on my judgment, hence on me, whether I assent or not. At any rate, that is all there is to Sextus's account of the Stoic view in a passage (*M* VIII 397) which explicitly contrasts voluntary assent with involuntary impression. The impression is involuntary (ἀκούσιος), not willed (ἀβούλητος), because whether or not I am affected by an impression does not depend on me but on something else, namely, the thing which appears to me; the impression once received, however, it does depend on me whether I assent to it, for it depends on my judgment. This leaves it quite open what factors influence my judgment, and how, and therefore leaves it open whether the influence could be regarded as in any sense a type of compulsion. In fact, recent studies on the Stoic side have pursued with illuminating results a line of interpretation according to which assent is determined internally, by a man's character and the education of his mind, and is voluntary just because and in the sense that it is internally determined in this way: see Long [15], Voelké [21], and cf. Epict. *Diss.* I 28.1-5. If that is the content of the doctrine that assent is free, it fits perfectly well with the emphasis I have placed on the passivity of the skeptic's *epochē*. He does not and could not choose *epochē* for the sake of *ataraxia*.

39. Cf. the talk of stating or assenting to something ἀδοξάστως at *PH* I 24, 240; II 13, 102; III 2, 151.

40. For the challenge to try to meet this objection I am indebted to the conference and to discussions with Michael Frede. In the space available I cannot hope to do justice to the subtlety with which Frede [11] expounds a very different interpretation of Sextus from that advocated here.

41. εὐδοκεῖν, on which see Frede [11].

42. Sextus evidently intends to bring out the semantic connection between δόγμα and δοκεῖν.

43. See Frede [11].

44. Plutarch's report shows that the Cyrenaic terminology was caricatured as peculiar.

45. This is a topic that has come up before: see n. 8 above and Burnyeat [6].

46. δοκῶ θερμαίνεσθαι is thus parallel to φαίνεται ἡμῖν γλυκάζειν τὸ μέλι at *PH* I 20.

47. See n. 9 above.

48. That the two definitions of *"dogma"* are borrowed from some previous skeptic writer is evidenced not only by Sextus's saying so, but by the structurally parallel *PH* I 16-17. Here too we have a contrasting pair of "someone's" definitions, this time of the term αἵρεσις ("philosophical system"), to one of which the skeptic objects and one he does not, and the first definition, couched (it would appear) in terms of the narrower sense of dogma, can be found almost verbatim in an unfortunately truncated passage of Clement (*SVF* II, p. 37, 8-10), where it is again attributed to "some people."

49. ὅσον ἐπὶ τῷ λόγῳ: it is a nice question for interpretation how to take λόγος here. Bury translates "in its essence" at *PH* I 20, while *PH* III 65, *M* X 49, XI 165 ὅσον ἐπὶ τῷ φιλοσόφῳ λόγῳ may seem to favor "reason," but Sextus's own elucidation at *PH* I 20 (what honey is ὅσον ἐπὶ τῷ λόγῳ is what is said about the thing that appears) has decided several scholars for "statement": Janáček [13], chap. 2; Hossenfelder [12], p. 64 n. 124. Perhaps "theory" would do justice to the resonances of ambiguity (cf. e.g., *PH* III 167; *M* VII 283; VIII 3), provided we remember that what counts as theory and what as evidence is itself part of the dispute between Sextus and his opponents.

50. The same is implied by the original sense of several key words in the skeptical vocabulary. Προσδοξάζειν is the Epicurean term for the judgment or belief which is added to perception, where perception is ἄλογος, involving no judgmental element at all (see Taylor [20]). Ἀδόξαστος credits the Stoic sage with the capacity to avoid *all* belief falling short of certainty (DL VII 162). Δογματίζειν may again be Epicurean, as at DL X 120 (the earliest occurrence I can find), where it appears to mean nothing more stringent than not being in a state of puzzlement (ἀπορεῖν). The first instance I can find of δογματικός is attributed to Aenesidemus, who calls the *Academics* δογματικοί because they affirm some things without hesitation and deny others unambiguously, whereas the Pyrrhonists are aporetic (N.B.) and free of all belief (παντὸς ἀπολελυμένοι δόγματος) and do not say that things are such rather than such (Phot. *Bibl.* 169b36-170a2; on the general accuracy of the relevant sections of Photius's report, see Janáček [14]). Equally, it is Aenesidemus's contention, as it is Sextus's, that one dogmatizes if

one gives credence to what is *pithanon* (ibid. 170a18-20; *PH* I 222, 230).

Δόγμα itself may look harder since, although it originally means just "belief" (above, p. 122), some contrast with δόξα is indicated by Cicero's translating the terms *decretum* and *opinio* respectively. But the reason for this contrast would seem to be that the Stoics contrast δόξα(mere opinion, defined as assent to something uncertain or to something false: *Acad.* II 59, 68, 77; *M* VII 151) with κατάληψις and ἐπιστήμη. They therefore need another word than δόξα for the wise man's belief. The wise man avoids δόξα (opinion as opposed to knowledge), but he has δόγματα, every one of them unwavering and true (*Acad.* II 27, 29; cf. *SVF* II, p. 37, 10-11). Notice that in Cicero's account it is not part of the meaning of δόγμα that it should be firmly held, but rather the consequence of its being the wise man who holds it: for the Academics say that all their *decreta* are *probabilia non percepta* (*Acad.* II 109-110). Readers of Plato are often perplexed by the way δόξα sometimes means "opinion" in contrast to knowledge and sometimes "belief" or "judgment" in the broad sense in which it is a component of knowledge: my suggestion is that δόγμα in Hellenistic usage conveniently takes over the latter role. It is a broader and more nearly neutral term than δόξα, not a term for a more stringently defined type of belief.

51. For a contrary view, see Striker [19], pp. 80-81.

52. Notice that it is for these higher-level generalizations that Sextus invokes the defense of cheerful self-refutation (*PH* I 14-15 and other passages discussed in Burnyeat [3]). Self-refutation presupposes that the propositions do make a truth-claim. Sextus would not need (and could not use) the defense if the generalizations were really the expressions of appearance which he simultaneously claims them to be.

53. Cf. Hume's marvelous description of the despair of skeptical doubt, *A Treatise of Human Nature*, Bk. I, pt. IV, sec. VII, pp. 268-269 in Selby-Bigge's edition (Oxford, 1888).

54. Στάσις διανοίας, *PH* I 10; ἀρρεψία, *PH* I 190; *M* VII 159, 332a; *DL* IX 74. Hossenfelder [12], pp. 54 ff., is excellent on this, but I do not think we need go along with him in detecting an ambiguity in the term "*epochē*."

55. It is instructive in this connection to read through section II x of Wittgenstein's *Philosophical Investigations*, which discusses among other things Moore's paradox "*p* but I do not believe that *p*."

56. *DL* IX 66; Aristocles ap. Euseb. *Praep. ev.* XIV 18.26: ὡς χαλεπὸν εἴη ὁλοσχερῶς ἐκδῦναι τὸν ἄνθρωπον. The source is Antigonus of Carystus, which means, as Long [16] has shown, that the remark probably derives from something in Timon.

57. This paper has benefited greatly, especially in its last two sections, from helpful criticism at the Conference and at various universities where earlier drafts were read (Amsterdam, Berkeley, Essex, Oxford, Pittsburgh, Rutgers, SMU Dallas, and UBC Vancouver). Among the many individuals to whom thanks are due I should like to mention Jonathan Barnes, David Sedley, Gisela Striker, and, above all, Michael Frede.   ·

7

Ancient Skepticism and Causation

Jonathan Barnes

INTRODUCTION

THE IMPORTANCE OF CAUSES

Modern philosophers of a skeptical bent have puzzled over the possibility of causal explanation, and they have nicely examined the notion of causality itself. The motives behind their scrutiny are not hard to divine; and it is no matter for surprise that the ancient Greek Skeptics evinced an equally profound interest in what Hume called the cement of the universe; for the Believers,[1] as the Skeptics liked to call their adversaries, troweled busily in that ubiquitous mortar.

Sextus Empiricus asserts, with pardonable exaggeration, that all the Believers "say that nothing occurs causelessly (*anaitiōs*)"[2] (*PH* III 67). Some of them plausibly supposed that the notion of causality enters essentially into our concept of a material substance; for "body is that which can act and be acted upon" (*PH* III 38; cf. *M* IX 366), that which can cause and be affected. Believers of all Schools investigated the nature of the causal relation; the Stoics developed a particularly thorough and subtle analysis of the varieties of causes and of their mutual interrelations.

Such metaphysical and conceptual speculations were invigorated by the demands of moral philosophy and given substance by a certain vision of the task of natural science. In moral philosophy, the Epicureans, the

149

Stoics, and the Skeptical Academy hotly debated the issues of determinism and freedom, of fate, divination, and human responsibility. In such debates, the concept of causation is of central importance; and as the intellectual warfare escalated, generals on both sides were supplied with ever more powerful armaments by the students of causality.

As for the scientists, "there is occasions and causes why and wherefore in all things": for the Stoics, *aitiologia* or the provision of causal explanations was one of the three divisions of natural science (DL VII 132); for the Peripatetics, *epistēmē* or scientific knowledge was by definition knowledge of causes. The surviving fragments of Posidonius, a Stoic who "Aristotelized," amply illustrate[3] Strabo's general judgment that "there is a great quantity of *aitiologiai*" in his works (II 3.8 = T 85 EK).[4] On this point at least, Stoics and Aristotelians might have agreed with their Epicurean rivals; for according to Epicurus himself the aim of natural science, *phusiologia*, is "to give a precise account of the causes of the most important things" (*Ad Hdt.* 78); and "we must give causal explanations (*aitiologēteon*) of what happens in the sky (*ta meteōra*) and of everything nonevident (*adēlon*)" (ibid. 80).[5] Without a doubt, the Believers, as Sextus puts it, "take an especial pride in their *aitiologiai*" (*PH* I 180).

Causation mattered to the Believers: even the Cyrenaics, who barely count as Believers and who rejected *phusiologia* as a futile exercise, were obliged to include a treatment of causes in their moral theorizing (*M* VII 11). Indeed, for many Believers, aetiology had a moral purpose: "Philosophical instruction removes the amazement and astonishment born of puzzlement and ignorance, by knowledge of and inquiry into the cause of each thing" (Plutarch, *Rat. aud.* 44BC); *felix qui potuit rerum cognoscere causas.* The Greek Skeptics had a vocation to cure mankind of rash Belief (*PH* III 280): they had every reason to compound therapeutic drugs against the chronic malaise of aetiologizing.

THE SOURCES OF SKEPTICISM

In his *Outlines of Pyrrhonism* Sextus twice tangles with causes: at *PH* I 180-186, he rehearses the Eight Modes of Aenesidemus "by which we raise puzzles about particular *aitiologiai*"; at *PH* III 13-29, he tries to induce suspension of belief on the general question of "whether anything is cause of anything." The second passage, but not the first, has a parallel in Sextus's more extended treatise: *M* IX 195-358 produces a string of arguments critical of agency and patiency, of cause and effect.

One of Sextus's prime sources was the fifth Book of Aenesidemus's *Pyrrhonian Discourses*; that work is lost, but the Byzantine patriarch

Photius has left us a summary of it, in which he records that "the fifth book sets out the skeptical attacks on causes, refusing to grant that anything is cause of anything, and asserting that those who aetiologize are deceived—enumerating modes in accordance with which he thinks that, having been led on to aetiologize, they have become entangled in such errors" (*Bibl.* cod. 212, 170b17-22).[6] What Aenesidemus "refused to grant" is what Sextus disputes in *PH* III and *M* IX; and what Aenesidemus "asserted" is what Sextus epitomizes in *PH* I.[7]

Sextus indicates that Aenesidemus was not his only source (see *M* IX 281);[8] but he does not name anyone else. Aenesidemus was not the first of the Skeptical tribe; and we might expect that he drew on the work of his philosophical predecessors: surely the Skeptical Academy, in its battles with the Stoa, must have raised doubts about causal explanation; surely the early Pyrrhonians, enemies of all Believers, must have attacked the Believers' notion of causation.[9] It is hard to imagine that philosophical skeptics did not begin to assault aetiologizing until the middle of the first century B.C. Yet if we abjure a priori speculation, a surprising fact emerges: skepticism about causation is not explicitly ascribed to any of Aenesidemus's philosophical precursors. That fact may of course point to nothing more than the paucity of our evidence for the early history of philosophical skepticism; but I am inclined to take seriously the possibility that the first philosophical opponents of Belief did not train their weapons upon causation.

However that may be, causation was under fire long before Aenesidemus wrote his *Pyrrhonian Discourses:* the attack was launched not from the murky groves of the philosophers but from the salubrious uplands of medical science. Greek medicine was always in close touch with philosophy; and from the earliest beginnings of their science in the fifth century B.C., doctors had been tempted to adopt a skeptical attitude to the pretentions of *phusiologia*. The long and often acrimonious debates among the medical theorists of the Hellenistic and Imperial ages occasioned arguments of great depth and ingenuity both for and against skeptical positions;[10] and in those debates causation and *aitiologia* were frequently at the forefront of the discussion.

Ancient historians of medicine conveniently divided their heroes into three main schools of thought: the Logical doctors, also known as the *dogmatikoi*; the Empirics; and the Methodics. The three schools differed fundamentally in their views on the place of causes in medical science. Logical doctors, who held that reason (*logos*) must infer from the evident symptoms of a disease to its underlying causes, naturally stood on the side of *phusiologia*; they held that practical medicine required "knowledge first of the hidden and containing causes of diseases; then of the evident causes; after that, of natural actions; and finally of internal parts" (Celsus, *Prooem.* 13). The Empirics relied solely on "experience"; they studied symptoms observed by themselves or recorded by others,[11] and grouped them into "syndromes"; they sternly rejected any inquiry into "the nonevident," *ta adēla.* They thus "embraced evident causes as being necessary, but contended that inquiry into hidden causes and natural actions was superfluous, since nature is not apprehensible" (ibid. 27 = F 14 D).[12] The Methodics, who held that diseases themselves, in virtue of the "common conditions," indicated their own treatment, and who claimed that a six-month course was sufficient to train a doctor, were happy to believe in causation but contended that "no knowledge of causes has any bearing on medical treatment" (ibid. 54[13]).

A patient comes to the surgery suffering from rabies: what causes his wretched condition? The Logical doctors will advert to the man's internal state—to the balance of his humors, the clearness of his pores, the disposition of his *pneuma,* or whatever; they will either dismiss or give little importance to the bite of the mad dog. The Empirical doctors will cite the dog's action as the cause, and show no interest in the patient's undiscoverable inner states. The Methodics will allow that both the bite and the inner state are causally relevant; but they will hold that such matters are therapeutically irrelevant, and therefore of no concern to the doctor.

The Empirical school was closely associated with skepticism: "Some say that the Skeptical philosophy is the same as medical Empiricism" (*PH* I 236); for "as the Skeptic is with regard to the whole of life, so the Empiric is with regard to medicine" (Galen, *Subf. emp.* 62. 25 = F 10b D, p. 82, 29).[14] That Sextus, surnamed "the Empiric," took some of his anticausal weapons from the well-stocked arsenal of his Empirical colleagues is scarcely to be doubted; but the threefold division of medical opinion, and the philosophy that goes with it, represent a relatively late schematization.

Long before the establishment of the three canonical schools of thought, doctors had argued about causation. Some of the positions they took up are described by Galen, in a passage from his treatise *On Antecedent Causes*: "Some [doctors] said that nothing is cause of anything, some—e.g., the Empirics—doubted whether there were causes or not, some—like Herophilus[15]—accepted causes hypothetically, others—of whom he [sc. Erasistratus[16]] was the chief—did away with antecedent causes as being wrongly believed in"[17] (*Caus. procat.* XIII 162 = *CMG* supp. II, pp. 41-42). Herophilus and Erasistratus take us back to the third century B.C., two hundred years before Aenesidemus; and there is abundant evidence to show that each of those eminent men engaged in lively and philosophical altercations on the subject of causation and causal explanation.[18]

It was the doctors, not the philosophers, who began the debate about causation and who first turned the weapons of skepticism against *aitiologia*. Some of the arguments which Sextus directs against causation can still be traced back to Herophilus and to Erasistratus,[19] and it is scarcely to be doubted that many more of the arguments in Sextus's text had a medical origin. It may be that Aenesidemus stood apart from that medical tradition, that his Pyrrhonian arguments were only later put between the same covers as those medical arguments with which they so happily combined; but it seems to me highly probable that Aenesidemus was aware of the medical tradition, and that his *Pyrrhonian Discourses* did not fear to borrow from it. However that may be, it is beyond dispute that the ancient physicians hold a prominent place in the history of skeptical argument against causation.

SEXTUS'S PROGRAM

In Aenesidemus's *Pyrrhonian Discourses* the Eight Modes against Aetiology and the general attack on causation were apparently two maneuvers in a unitary campaign; but what exactly is their interconnection? Every *aitiologia* cites an *aition* or cause, so that a completely general assault on causation will implicitly attack aetiologizing. But in fact, as we shall see, the skeptical attack on causes is presented as an attack on efficient causes —causes that produce or bring about effects; and it is not clear that every *aitiologia* must cite an efficient cause. Thus the Eight Modes are not superfluous, even if the attack on causes is successful. Again, it is not clear that every causal proposition will count as an aetiology: aetiologies are scientific explanations, and not every causal judgment offers a scientific explanation. Thus the attack on causation is not superfluous, even if the Eight Modes are successful.

However that may be, in Sextus's account the Modes appear as an appendix to his extended treatment of the Ten Modes of Suspension: they are not integrated into Sextus's overall strategy, and he shows relatively little interest in them.

The beginning of *PH* III is, by contrast, structurally solid: about to consider the scientific (*phusikon*) part of "so-called philosophy," and determined to deal only with "the more universal issues," Sextus will begin with "the account of first principles." Most philosophers distinguish between material and efficient principles;[20] and since the latter are held to be more important (cf. Seneca, *Ep.* LXV 23; Aëtius, I 11. 2), they are the better starting-point (III 1). God, in the opinion of many, is "a most efficient cause" (cf. [Galen], *Hist. phil.* XIX 240K = 16D), and III 2-12 therefore discuss the divine Effector. At III 13 the issue widens: "We shall puzzle more generally about active causes, having first tried to attend to the concept of cause." Thus III 13-29 contains Sextus's skeptical consideration of causation itself, 13-16 offering some preliminary remarks on the Believers' notion of *aition*,[21] 17-29 presenting the puzzle proper. That puzzle is an exercise of the skeptic's antithetical art (cf. *PH* I 8): first, in 17-19, come the positive considerations—three short arguments designed to show that "it is plausible that there are causes"; then 20-28 set down the negative considerations—three or four arguments, "few out of many,"[22] to indicate that "it is also plausible to say that nothing is a cause of anything." III 29 concludes that the arguments are all plausible, so that suspension of belief is the only admissible attitude to causation.

M IX also begins by distinguishing between efficient and material principles (4-11); and Sextus again elects to start with "the active principles, arguing first, in the fashion of the Believers as it were,[23] about god, and then more skeptically (*aporētikōteron*) about there being nothing which acts or is acted upon." IX 13-193 duly deals with god; and 194 oddly concludes that "suspension follows on what has been said in the fashion of the Believers about the efficient principles." Section 195 launches the main attack upon efficient causation: Sextus will not stop to discuss the concept of cause since "we have discussed it fairly precisely elsewhere" (the reference is presumably to *PH* III 17-19); nor does he spend much time on the arguments in favor of causes (196-206). The major part of his discussion (206-358) is occupied by a long series of anticausal arguments: 206-266 contain arguments that work against agent and patient alike, 267-357 contain arguments directed specifically against the patient; and so ends the treatment "concerning the efficient principles of the universe" (358).

SKEPTICISM AND COMMON SENSE

Sextus appeals to his attack on causation in later contexts. At *PH* III 38 and *M* IX 366 he raises doubts about the existence of body: according to some Believers, body is "that which can act and be acted upon"; but agency has been exploded along with causation. Elsewhere, doubts about causation are used to raise doubt in turn about change (*PH* III 113), about rest (ibid. 116), about place (*M* X 17), about generation and destruction (ibid. 322). The Skeptics doubt whether "anything is cause of anything"; and that doubt runs through the whole of their objection to "the scientific part" of philosophy.

For all that, Sextus's attitude to causal propositions is by no means uniformly hostile: in the course of his own skeptical arguments he frequently avails himself of premises from which his attack on causation must surely seem to debar him. Ordinary language—Greek no less than English—is shot through with causality: a multitude of common verbs advert to causal transactions, many common nouns and adjectives denote agency or patiency. Sextus makes no attempt to avoid that ordinary vocabulary, the causal import of which he must surely have recognized.[24] More specifically, Sextus from time to time permits himself an overtly causal sentence: a wound to the heart will cause death (*M* V 104); motion and rest must have causes (*M* X 16, 246); good things may be the cause of misery (*M* XI 120). Sextus was an Empirical doctor: he alludes approvingly to his own profession;[25] he adverts to "medical powers" (*PH* I 133; *M* XI 153; cf. I 255), prominent among which are the nutritive capacities of foodstuffs (*PH* I 53, 131) and the therapeutic capabilities of drugs (e.g., *PH* III 59).[26] More pertinent to his skepticism are the powers associated with the "humors" of the body; for it is irregularities and differences among our several humorous constitutions which cause irregularities and differences among our sensations—"we are affected in these ways because of the differing predominance of the so-called humors within us" (*PH* I 52; cf. 46, 51, 80, 102-103, 128)—and the Modes of Suspension depend largely on such sensational irregularities.

Medical *arcana* apart, Sextus unhesitatingly supposes that our perceptual affections are caused, and caused by external objects: those objects are said, generally, to "move (*kinein*)," to "act (*poiein*)," to be "causes (*aitia*)"; they are also said, specifically, to warm, to sweeten, to chill, to embitter. "No one would dare say that honey does not sweeten [i.e., affect sweetly] those in good health, or that it does not embitter [i.e., affect bitterly] those with jaundice" (*PH* I 211); and in general, "the presentation (*phantasia*) is an effect of the object presented (*to phantaston*), and the object presented is a cause of the presentation and is capable of impressing the faculty of perception" (*M* VII 383).[27]

It is tempting to discount all those causal pronouncements and to leave Sextus uniformly skeptical about causation. Some of the causal sentences he utters are no doubt mere carelessnesses. Others are not uttered *in propria persona* but borrowed from the Believers for the sake of polemical argument; thus, having illustrated at some length "the differences among men," Sextus once casually notes that "we shall content ourselves with stating a few of the many instances given by the Believers" (*PH* I 85).[28] Or again, perhaps the Skeptics will remind us that "here, as elsewhere, we use 'it is' instead of 'it seems'" (*PH* I 135), and that often, on hearing an apparently categorical statement, "we supply 'as it seems to me'" (*PH* I 202).[29] In Sextus's circle, as in the Army, things only seem to be things: Sextus's causes only seem to be causes, and the overt "it is" of his causal sentences must be construed as, or implicitly prefixed by, an innocuous "it seems." Whatever you do, don't call the bleeders *sheep*.

There is some force in each of those exculpatory points; but they fail to account for one crucial fact: Sextus's causal utterances are not embarrassing flaws on the smooth body of his philosophical system; on the contrary, they form part of the texture of that body itself. For Sextus presents himself as the champion of what he calls Life, *bios*. Life is contrasted with Philosophy and with Belief; it represents the wisdom of the plain man who is uncorrupted by esoteric and presumptuous speculation; Life, in short, is what later generations of philosophers came to call Common Sense.[30]

In a programmatic passage of central importance for the understanding of ancient Skepticism, Sextus announces that "we attend to phenomena and live unbelievingly (*adoxastōs*) in accordance with Life's observance (*kata tēn biōtikēn tērēsin*)" (*PH* I 23). According to Diogenes, the Skeptics "recognize that it is day and that we are alive and many other of the phenomena of Life (*ta en tōi biōi phainomena*)" (DL IX 103). Utterances of that kidney are neither rare nor casual.[31] Thus adherence to Life or Common Sense shapes the Skeptics' attack on the theory of "signs": Skeptics have no objection to "commemorative" signs, "for these are generally believed by everyone in Life (*pasi . . . tois ek tou biou*) to be useful" (*M* VIII 156), and "we do not fight with the common preconceptions of men, nor do we subvert Life" (ibid. 157; cf. *PH* II 102). By championing commemorative signs, the Skeptic is able to reject the Believer's charge that his stance on signs is self-defeating (*M* VIII 288-290).

"Life's observance" is fourfold (*PH* I 23); and its fourth part consists in "the teaching of the arts, in virtue of which we are not inactive in the arts we adopt" (ibid. 24). The arts a skeptic may adopt certainly include medicine (e.g., *PH* II 236 ff.), and such practical crafts as navigation and agriculture (*M* V 2; VIII 270); they also embrace the astronomy of "Eudoxus and Hipparchus and those like them" (*M* V 1). The most illuminating passage on the subject is *M* I 44-56, where Sextus discusses the art of "grammar": "grammar," he says, "is of two sorts—one promising to teach the elements and their combinations, and in general being an art of writing and reading; the other being in comparison a more profound power, lying not in mere knowledge of letters but in the investigation of their discovery and nature. . . ." (*M* I 49). The skeptics attack the latter art; they do not attack the former, "for it is agreed by everyone to be useful" (ibid.).[32] Utility is the key: the Skeptics will attack arts and sciences, but only those useless—and pretentious—skills on which the Believers plume themselves; the Arts of Life they defend.

Life and the arts love causation: Common Sense believes that the fire burns, and a Pyrrhonian must believe it too (DL IX 104)—if he really supports Common Sense; the doctors "have observed that the wounding of the heart is a cause of death" (*M* V 104),[33] and a Skeptic must believe so too—if he genuinely subscribes to the arts of Life. The fact that Sextus unhesitatingly commits himself to causal pronouncements is to be explained from within his philosophical system: Sextus sides with Life, and Life is committed to causation.

But if the Skeptics are friends of Common Sense, against what are their arrows directed? And how are we to understand their attack on causation and causal knowledge? The first question is readily answered: Skepticism is directed against Belief or *dogma*; and not every opinion or judgment—not every belief—qualifies as a *dogma*: *dogma* is defined as "assent to some item from among the nonevident (*adēla*) objects of inquiry in the sciences" (*PH* I 13). That is the official announcement of the Skeptic's target; and its message is echoed many times in the course of *PH*.[34] It emerges that the "nonevident objects" in question are things "which do not have a nature capable of falling under immediate observation (*enargeia*)[35]—e.g., the intelligible pores" (*PH* II 98).[36] The Skeptic, then, attacks unobservable entities and judgments ostensibly made about them; he fixes his sights on what by nature escapes our sight, and on the Believers' blind statements about such things: *ta adēla* are epistemologically indefensible, and the sciences that blather about them are profitless. *Dogma* must go; and with it the sport of *phusiologia*.[37] But Life remains; and none of our Common Sense beliefs is destroyed.

The attack on causation was a part of that general campaign against *dogma* and the unobservable. Sextus introduces the Eight Modes of Aenesidemus as those "in virtue of which we raise puzzles about particular *aitiologiai* and check the Believers—because they especially pride themselves on these" (*PH* I 180).[38] The First Mode remarks that "the whole business of *aitiologia* revolves around the nonapparent (*ta aphanē*)" (ibid. 181). The Modes are thus expressly aimed at the causal explanations of the Believers; and they assert that those explanations will always and fatally involve *ta aphanē* or *ta adēla*. There is no suggestion that causality as such is under fire.

Matters are less easy with *PH* III 13-29 and the corresponding sections in *M* IX; for there the aim seems uncompromisingly universal: the Skeptic will show that suspension should be our answer to the general question, Does anything cause anything? Yet here too a nearer inspection may discover hints of a less radical enterprise. First, we might ask ourselves why *PH* III and *M* IX discuss the gods: what place have they in a Skeptical treatment of causation? In particular, how can Sextus conclude that "suspension follows on what has been said dogmatically about the efficient principles" (*M* IX 194), when all that he has so far discussed is god? The answer is that god is a "most efficient cause" (*PH* III 2), that is to say, a putative cause of *everything*;[39] and, in *M* IX at least, Sextus is

quite explicit that the Skeptic's target is the Believer's claim to have laid
bare "the principles *of the universe*": the point is made both at the beginning and at the end of the attack (*M* IX 4, 358; cf. 331; X 310), and it is
echoed in Diogenes' account of Skepticism (DL IX 99).

Consider, secondly, Diogenes' report that "we perceive that fire burns,
but we suspend judgment over whether it possesses a nature (*phusis*)
capable of burning" (DL IX 104). Sextus makes the same point with the
same example: the Skeptics do not doubt that fire burns wood; they do
doubt the Believer's claim to have discovered the "nature" of fire, the
inner constitution in virtue of which it possesses that causal power (see *M*
VII 197-199). Speaking of drugs, Galen observes that "their power is a
sort of efficient cause. . . . That there are such powers . . . scarcely anyone
will dispute; but as to the substance (*ousia* = *phusis*) of that power, some
supposed it to be unknowable—namely, the skeptical philosophers and,
among the doctors, those called Empirics" (*Simp. med.* XI 380-381K).[40]
The Believers, in their tracts *Concerning Nature*, descanted upon the hidden "natures" or constitutions of things, in terms of which their superficial appearances and overt behaviors should be explained. That, after
all, is the very stuff of science. But it is stuff and nonsense in the Skeptic's
book: occult causes are inapprehensible, and the search for them is a
futile enterprise.

The thrust of the arguments in *PH* III and *M* IX is not against the everyday causes known to Common Sense: it is against the *recherché* causes
sought out by scientists or philosophers—grand and comprehensive
causes which, like god or the Vortex, pretend to explain everything; deep
and hidden causes which, like atoms or imperceptible pores, purport to
burrow beneath the surface of things, and to lay bare their inner and
explanatory natures.

There is a sober Skeptic struggling to emerge from Sextus's boozy
texts. He is eager to let the doctor hack away in his surgery and the gar-
dener cultivate his garden; he will not throw Everyman off the Clapham
omnibus. Rather, his general and philanthropical intention is to unseat
the Believer from his philosophical armchair, to curb the scientist's gran-
diose ambitions, to outlaw vain and pretentious claims to understand
"that which is by nature nonevident." In particular, the sober Skeptic lets
causation reign in the realm of Life: knives still cut flesh, fire still melts
wax; I can light my pipe with a match and warm my brandy with my
hands. Doubt is cast only on the causal claims of the Believers—claims to
teach the first principles of the universe and to have uncovered the hidden causes of natural phenomena. The sober Skeptic, like the Empirical
doctor, rejects occult causes, but embraces evident causes.[41]

THREE GRADES OF SKEPTICAL INVOLVEMENT

Sextus's skepticism is not always temperate; indeed, the arguments against causation in *PH* III and *M* IX do not apply only to the hidden causes of the Believers: if they work at all, they work against all causes. There is a mismatch between the extravagant proofs and the restrained *probandum*: the proofs prove nothing—or too much. Such a mismatch is, I think, a common feature of Skeptical argumentation. All Skeptics believe that some propositions are true; and their attack on "the true" (*PH* II 80-96; *M* VIII 2-140) is directed against the *dogmata* of the Believers. But their arguments against Believers' truth work, if they work at all, against all truths, whether of Believers or of Life. Or again, the assault on "signs" is explicitly restricted to the Believer's "indicative" signs (*PH* II 102; *M* VIII 157); yet the arguments deployed against indicative signs work, for the most part, with equal force against those "commemorative" signs which the Skeptic, loyal to Common Sense, promises to defend.

The fact is that there are several Skeptics beneath Sextus's skin.[42] They can best be distinguished with the aid of a fourfold division among types of propositions. (Sextus himself employs, sometimes confusingly, a twofold division between types of objects: the nonevident, *ta adēla*, and the evident, *ta enargē*.) A proposition is of *type (A)* if it contains a term purporting to refer to something "by nature nonevident"; for example:

(1) The tower is composed of atoms

—where atoms are those nonevident corpuscles hypothesized by some schools of Belief. Propositions of *type (B)* refer to evident objects and describe their evident characteristics; for example:

(2) The tower is square

Propositions of *type (C)* again refer to evident objects, but report on how they seem (how they look, feel, etc.); for example:

(3) The tower looks round

Finally, propositions of *type (D)* make no reference to any objects, but merely state how things seem to be; for example:

(4) It looks as though there's a round tower

Those distinctions might benefit from more detailed elaboration; but they will suffice, roughly drawn, for my present purpose.

Now Sober Skepticism in effect argues that suspension of belief is the proper attitude towards propositions of type (A): faced with an example of type (A), the appropriate response is a skeptical shrug. As for (B), (C), and (D), the Sober Skeptic will make room for them all; and in admitting (B) he is, in effect, doing his duty by Life—for (B) will include most of the propositions of Common Sense. Sextus does sometimes admit (B), (C), and (D), outlawing only (A); and then he is sober.[43] But sometimes he loses his sobriety. There are passages, indeed, where he appears quite blotto, admitting only (D) and rejecting (A)-(C); for he sometimes advocates suspension with regard to *ta phainomena*, and in propositions (2) and (3) the phrase "the tower" purports to refer to an evident object—to a *phantaston* or *phainomenon*.[44] More often Sextus is neither high nor dry, but betwixt and between: he will neither soberly accept (B), nor drunkenly reject (C); he draws the epistemological line between (B) and (C): (A) and (B) are alike rejected; (C) and (D) are alike permissible.[45]

The three grades of Skepticism form a hierarchy; and traces of each grade can be found in Sextus. Sextus was a systematizer rather than an original philosopher; and his thoughts are generally the thoughts of his authorities. It will already be clear that a main source of Sober Skepticism was the Empirical school of medical science. "The Empirics say that of things apprehended, some are apprehended by perception—for example, blushing—and others commemoratively, that is, those apprehended by way of certain signs; but nothing is apprehended indicatively" ([Galen], *Opt. sect.* I 149K = F 80D; cf. Galen, *Sect. introd.* I 77K = *Scr. min.* III 10 = F 24D). Like Sober Sextus, the Empirics reject indicative signs, and also "demonstration" or proof (see Galen, *Sect. introd.* I 77K); like Sober Sextus, they cling to *tērēsis* and the phenomena, and they rely on "commemorative" signs (see M VIII 204).[46] The Empirical doctor, in short, is the very model of a Sober Skeptic.[47] However that may be, it would be an error and an impoverishment to impose a single and uniform Skepticism on Sextus's writings: sobriety is philosophically challenging; but let me not deny the pleasures of the bottle.

AGAINST AETIOLOGY

THE EIGHT MODES

I turn now to the Eight Modes of Aenesidemus, and I rehearse them with the existence of Sober Skepticism in mind; for, as I have already observed, the First Mode states that "the whole business of *aitiologia* revolves around the nonapparent" (*PH* I 181). Before looking at the individual Modes, I shall pass a few general remarks on the set as a whole.

"Aenesidemus hands down eight modes by which he thinks that he can refute (*elenchōn*) and show to be unsound (*mochthēra*) every Believer's aetiology" (*PH* I 180). That might suggest that Aenesidemus wanted to *reject* every aetiology, that he judged all causal explanations to be *false*. But to make such a judgment is incompatible with the strict letter of Pyrrhonism, to which Aenesidemus himself subscribed;[48] and Sextus also offers a slightly different account of the purpose of the Modes: "Some propound modes in virtue of which we raise puzzles about particular causal explanations and check the Believers" (*PH* I 180). And at I 185-186 he argues that the Five Modes of Agrippa "themselves perhaps suffice against the *aitiologiai*," so that "through these too one can perhaps refute the rashness of the Believers in casual explanations." On that account, the Eight Modes, like the Ten Modes of Suspension, are designed to halt the rush to judgment: they do not disprove; they restrain—for they show *aitiologiai* to be "unsound" not in that they are false but in that they are unfounded. And that is surely what Aenesidemus meant to say.

The Modes are not eight arguments leading to the conclusion that every aetiology is unsound; rather, they are schemata, or argument-patterns, which can be applied to cast doubt on particular aetiologies. "Give me any aetiology," Aenesidemus claims, "and I have a Mode through which I can show it to be ill founded." When Sextus introduced the Ten Modes of Suspension, he did not vouch for their soundness or their completeness (see *PH* I 35); but he expresses no such reservations about the Eight Modes, and we are entitled to believe that Aenesidemus propounded precisely eight aetiological modes, and that he propounded them in the order in which Sextus reports them.[49] (But I can find no system behind Aenesidemus's ordering, and I shall not myself stick to it.) After the eighth mode Sextus adds: "He says that it is not impossible that some should fall down in their aetiologies because of certain mixed modes, dependent on those we have already described" (*PH* I 185). Presumably the "mixed" modes do not constitute additions to the Eight: to apply a "mixed mode" is to apply some conjunction or disjunction of the Eight.

There is one important vagueness in Sextus's account of the Modes: they can be used against "every Believer's aetiology"; but does "every aetiology" mean "every aetiology *so far proposed*" (cf. *PH* I 198, 200)? Or does it mean "every possible aetiology"? Did Aenesidemus claim, modestly, that he had the means to shed doubt on every scientific explanation which the Believers had so far suggested? Or did he claim, radically, that he could knock the props from under any aetiology which any Believer might conceivably come up with? That question can only be answered by looking at the Modes themselves.

SOME MODEST MODES

Some at least of Aenesidemus's Modes are mild in their power and moderate in their scope. Thus Mode Six remarks that "often they accept what is consonant[50] with their own hypotheses[51] but reject what tells against them and has equal plausibility" (*PH* I 183); and Mode Seven has it that "often they produce causes that conflict not only with the phenomena but also with their own hypotheses" (ibid. 184). No doubt scientists did and do ignore inconvenient facts, and overlook internal inconsistencies in their theorizing.[52] Aenesidemus rightly reminds us of the possibility of such unfortunate lapses; and the two Modes will enable him to unseat some careless Believers.

The same can be said of Mode Three: "They give causes which exhibit no order for things which happen in an orderly way (*tetagmenōs*)" (*PH* I 182). At *M* IX 111-113 Sextus reports an argument against Democritus's theory that "the universe is moved in accordance with necessity and by a vortex": a vortex is "unorderly (*ataktos*) and short-lasting"; but "if it is unorderly, it cannot move anything in an orderly way (*tetagmenōs*)"— and the universe is, of course, a model of orderly movement. Sextus ascribed the argument to "those from the Stoa and those who sympathize with them" (*M* IX 111); but it is a perfect application of Aenesidemus's third mode. For the primary point[53] of that mode is, I take it, simply this: many Believers do not explain the orderliness of events—their theories may perhaps show why *X* occurs, and why *Y* occurs, and why *Z* occurs; but they do not explain why *XYZ* occurs as a harmonious whole. There is surely something in that; and Mode Three, like Modes Six and Seven, offers a salutary warning to the scientist.

Next consider Mode Eight: "Often, when the things thought to be evident and the things being inquired into are equally puzzling (*aporos*), they produce teaching about what is equally puzzling on the basis of what is equally puzzling" (*PH* I 184). I find this Mode difficult to understand; and my interpretation is tentative. I think that "teaching" (*didaskalia*) is being used in its literal sense,[54] and that Aenesidemus is adverting to the commonplace that "teaching ought to proceed from what is agreed upon" (*PH* III 257; cf. *M* I 14; VII 426; XI 222). Moreover, I suppose that the teaching in question is "demonstrative" teaching or teaching by *apodeixis* (cf. *M* III 13; VII 396); for "it is absurd to demonstrate what is at issue on the basis of what is equally at issue" (*PH* II 122).

Thus some Believers, according to Aenesidemus, attempt to explain puzzling facts by deducing them from things that seem to be evident[55] but in reality are equally puzzling.[56] "Democritus, who teaches what is less puzzling by what is more puzzling, is not to be believed. For nature offers a great variety of indications as to how men acquired the concept of god; but the view that there are in the environment huge images having human shape (and in general such things as Democritus likes to invent for himself) is utterly unacceptable" (*M* IX 42). Democritus tried to explain how men gained the concept of god by positing gigantic anthropomorphic images; but the point he appeals to is actually more puzzling than the point he is trying to explain. And that is absurd.[57]

But what exactly is the absurdity here? It is natural to construe the word "puzzling" in a subjective sense: you cannot explain something to me by adverting to a point that I find equally puzzling; you cannot teach me anything if you take as your starting-point matters that perplex me. Now if we accept that account of the word "puzzling," then Mode Eight has force only against what I may call pedagogical aetiologizing—the attempt to explain something *to someone*. It has no bearing on *scientific* aetiologizing or on the aetiologies of the Believers. For, plainly, the fact that the General Theory of Relativity is as puzzling to me as the phenomena it is intended to illuminate does not tell at all against its adequacy as an explanatory hypothesis; and Democritus's gigantic images may be the correct explanation of our acquiring the concept of god, even if Democritus's enemies find them wholly unacceptable. Subjective puzzlement is neither here nor there.

Perhaps, however, the word "puzzling" has a different sense in Mode Eight; perhaps it does not advert to subjective bewilderment. Sometimes at least, Sextus appears to use *"aporos"* as a synonym for *"zētoumenos"*: things are *apora* if they are being puzzled over or investigated.[58] Suppose, then, that a scientist is investigating two problems; he wants to know why *p*, and he wants to know why *q*. He will not solve his first problem simply by suggesting that *p* because *q*. Thus we have an objective interpretation of Mode Eight.[59] Perhaps the objective interpretation is correct; but if it is, then Aenesidemus has simply made a mistake—for it may be true that *p* because *q*, even if we still want to ask why *q*.

"The fifth is that according to which pretty well all of them offer aetiologies on the basis of their own hypotheses about the elements,[60] and not on the basis of any common and agreed procedures (*ephodoi*)" (*PH* I 183). At first blush, Mode Five seems to suggest a large skeptical claim: does it not imply that there are *no* "agreed procedures" in science, so that the Believer can do no more than fix upon an arbitrary set of hypotheses and weave private aetiological fantasies? I do not think that that is the right reading of the Mode; for Aenesidemus says that "pretty well all" the aetiologists fall foul of it—and that implies that some of them do not. Hence we should adopt a more modest reading of the Mode: perhaps there are agreed scientific procedures; but scientists are prone to ignore them, and to jump precipitately to an explanation based upon their own principles. An Atomist for example, when faced by a problem in the theory of colors, may glibly trot out an Atomistic aetiology, bypassing proper scientific methodology.

The five Modes thus far considered are skeptical only in the most meager of senses: reflection upon them, and practice in their application, may lead us to be wary of precipitate assent to scientific theorizing; for even scientists may err. But the Modes are not likely to upset any honest Believer: a Believer may admit that he and his colleagues are fallible men, and that some proposed aetiologies do indeed succumb to the Modes; but he will still reasonably hope to produce explanations which avoid the errors Aenesidemus has so far described.

TWO RADICAL MODES

Mode Four is "that according to which they grasp how the phenomena come about and then think that they have comprehended how the *non*-phenomena come about—but what is nonapparent is perhaps accomplished similarly to the phenomena, and perhaps not similarly but in a way of its own" (*PH* I 182). The Mode refers to an assumption that *ta aphanē*—the putative causes—somehow *resemble* the phenomena they allegedly explain. Not all Believers held that the phenomena resembled their unseen causes in all respects: notoriously, the Atomists asserted that the microscopical world of corpuscles differed to a remarkable degree from the large world of everyday objects—atoms are not, for instance, colored or tasty. But Aenesidemus appears to have had a particular kind of resemblance in mind: it is a similarity in "how things come about" (*hōs ginetai*), in how they "are accomplished."

Dionysius of Cyrene argued for the Stoic view that the sun was very large on the basis of just such a resemblance: things in our experience reappear slowly from behind obstructions either because they move slowly or because they are large; the same, therefore, goes for the sun; but the sun is seen to move quickly, yet it reappears slowly from behind obstructions: *ergo*, it is large. Philodemus, an Epicurean, replied as follows: "Let it be granted that things in our experience make their reappearances slowly only if either they move slowly or they occupy large areas. But what necessity is there for *the sun*, when it reappears slowly, to do so from those causes? . . . Will not the sun be able to have that character not because of those causes but because of another cause, different from the things in our experience?" (*Sign.* X 1-XI 8). Dionysius assumes that terrestrial dynamics apply equally to celestial motion; Philodemus questions that assumption.

Aenesidemus agrees with Philodemus:[61] perhaps the dynamics of *ta aphanē* are "similar" to those of mundane objects; perhaps they are different, and *ta aphanē* move "in a way of their own." Now the word "perhaps (*tacha*)" is a technical term of Pyrrhonism (see *PH* I 194-195); and it suggests a strong reading of Mode Four: Aenesidemus is not merely advising the scientist to entertain the thought that nonevident objects move in accordance with the laws of a nonevident dynamics; he is suggesting that no scientist can ever know how *ta aphanē* "are accomplished"—our experience is limited to *ta phainomena*, and that experience can give no clue to the dynamics of a nonevident world.

The Believer cannot react to Mode Four as he can react to the five modest modes; he cannot accept Aenesidemus's strictures, but hope that he may yet find an aetiology which escapes them. Nevertheless, he should not be shaken by Mode Four: the mode denies that we can have knowledge of nonevident dynamics, but it gives no ground for that denial—and the Believer need not pay attention to an ungrounded skeptical denial. I shall return to that important point in a moment; meanwhile, let us advance to Mode One.

The first mode requires careful translation: "He says that the first is the mode according to which the whole business of aetiology, involving things nonapparent, *ouch homologoumenēn echei tēn ek tōn phainomenōn epimarturēsin*" (*PH* I 181). The clause I have left in Greek is translated in the Loeb as follows: ". . . is unconfirmed by any agreed evidence derived from appearances." That leaves Aenesidemus's point unclear: does he mean that no aetiology can be *confirmed*? that no aetiology can be confirmed by *agreed* evidence? that no aetiology can be confirmed *by the appearances*?

"*Epimarturēsis*" is a technical term in Epicureanism; Sextus elsewhere defines it as follows: "*Epimarturēsis* is apprehension by way of immediate observation (*enargeias*) that the thing judged is such as it was judged to be—for example, when Plato approaches, I conjecture, that is, judge, because of the distance, that it is Plato; and when he has drawn near, it is further confirmed, the distance being reduced, that it is Plato—that is, it is confirmed by immediate observation" (*M* VII 212). I judge that *p*; the situation improves, and further evidence confirms the judgment that *p*. "Confirmation" is thus the application of additional evidence, gleaned from immediate observation, to a judgment of whatever sort. An *epimarturēsis*, then, is by definition "derived from the phenomena (*ek tōn phainomenōn*)": Aenesidemus does not mean that an aetiology cannot be confirmed *by the phenomena* (but might perhaps be confirmed by something else); he means that no aetiology can be confirmed *at all*—for all confirmation is necessarily "by the phenomena."

But that is not quite right: Aenesidemus uses the definite article, *tēn . . . epimarturēsin*. He does not say that aetiologies receive *no epimarturēsis*; he says that they *do* receive *epimarturēsis*—but that such *epimarturēsis* is *ouch homologoumenēn*, "not agreed." Thus: "Since the whole business of aetiology involves things nonapparent, the confirmation from the phe-

nomena which any aetiology may receive will not be agreed upon."
Where and why does agreement fail?

In ordinary *epimarturēsis*, you judge that *p*, later observe that *q*, and
find that the observation that *q* confirms the judgment that *p*.[62] In aetiologies, the judgment that *p* will express the aetiology in question, and it
will be about things nonapparent; it will refer to atoms, or to imperceptible pores, or whatever. But the judgment that *q* will concern only phenomena.[63] Does Aenesidemus mean that people will not agree that *q*? Is
the confirmation "not agreed" in the sense that there will be disagreement
over the truth of the proposition advanced as confirmatory? I do not
think so. Galen says explicitly of the Empirics that "they say there is undecidable disagreement about what is nonevident, but not about the phenomena; for there each thing, having appeared as it is, bears witness to
those who speak truly and refutes those who speak falsely" (*Sect. intr.* I
78-79K = *Scr. min.* III 12 = F 24 D). Sextus has nothing as clear as that;
but it is plain enough from various passages that the Skeptics did not
hold that the phenomena are invariably subject to dispute.[64]

If the *epimarturēsis* is not agreed, that is not because the confirmatory
evidence is disputed: there need be no dispute about whether or not *q*.
The disagreement must therefore concern the relationship between *q* and
p; and the *epimarturēsis* will be "not agreed" in the sense that people will
not generally agree that the observation that *q* confirms or supports the
aetiological hypothesis that *p*. No doubt the sun reappears slowly; but
we need not agree that that confirms the hypothesis that the sun is large.

The Believer can no more accept the strictures of Mode One than he
could those of Mode Four; but why should he accept them? True, the
Skeptic frequently asserts, in many contexts, the existence of eternal dispute[65] and infers a skeptical conclusion. But even if the Believer allows
the assertion to be true (and there is no compelling reason for him to do
so), still he may question the inference. For, first, the existence of dispute
casts no doubt on the *truth* of an aetiology: the fact that people disagree
with a putative causal explanation is no evidence whatsoever that it is
unsound. Admittedly, if there is reasoned disagreement, then that may
cast doubt upon the explanation; but in that case it is not the disagreement itself, but rather the reasons for it, which cast the doubt. Secondly,
the existence of dispute does not show that the proponent of an aetiology
may not claim to *know* his thesis: the fact that you disagree with me does
not in itself give me a reason for doubt or uncertainty; your disbelief that
p is no reason for me to doubt that *p*. Again, if you have reasons for dis-
believing that *p*, then I may have reasons for doubt; but again, it is not
your disbelief, but the reasons for your disbelief, which may properly
lead me to doubt.

Modes One and Four have a different character from the five modes I have called modest: the Believing scientist may regard the modest modes as salutary warnings, and he may reasonably hope to produce aetiologies which avoid the dangers they signal. He cannot take the same benign view of Modes One and Four: in the case of those two modes he must challenge Aenesidemus to back up his claims that nonevident dynamics are unknowable and that disagreement is both ubiquitous and of such a sort as to prevent satisfactory *epimarturēsis*.[66] Has Aenesidemus any answer to that challenge?

THE UNDERDETERMINATION OF THEORY

"The second is that according to which often,[67] although there is an abundant opportunity to explain the matter at issue in many ways (*polutropōs*), some explain it in one way only" (*PH* I 181). The Mode can be illustrated from another passage in Sextus, which may well derive from Aenesidemus:[68] "In the case of those suffering from fever, flushing and the prominence of the vessels and the sweaty skin and the high temperature and the rapid pulse . . . do not seem the same to everyone: to Herophilus, e.g., they are signs of good [?] blood, to Erasistratus of transference of blood from veins to arteries, to Asclepiades of the blocking of imperceptible interstices by imperceptible particles" (*M* VIII 219-220; cf. 188). The symptoms of fever can be explained in many ways; yet the different doctors stick each to his own explanation. In general, there are many ways of explaining the fact that *q*; but most aetiologists cite just one of those ways.

Aenesidemus did not discover the phenomenon of multiple explanation; on the contrary, it was a commonplace of Epicurean thought. Thus Epicurus says of *ta meteōra* that "they have a multiple cause of their coming into being and a multiple cause of their existence that agrees with the perceptions" (*Ad Pyth.* 86); we may "discover several explanations of the turnings and settings and risings and eclipsings and things of that sort" (*Ad Hdt.* 79). In the case of celestial phenomena, multiple explanation (*aitia pleonachē*) is possible; you may cite several causes of the phenomena, each fully consistent with what is observed; and Epicurus regularly does so (e.g., *Ad Pyth.* 93, 95, 97, 98, 99, 100, 104).

It is not easy to determine the details of Epicurus's view; but two things can be asserted with some confidence. First, the scientist must report *all* the causes, not a selection of them: "When someone admits one account and rejects another, equally consistent with the phenomenon, it is clear that he has utterly abandoned natural science and has fallen into mythology" (*Ad Pyth.* 87).[69] Second, of the various causes recorded, only one is in fact explanatory: "There are a certain number of things for which it is not enough to cite a single cause, but several—of which, however, only one is actually the cause" (Lucretius, VI 703-704).[70] You must list a dozen causes, but your list is a catalogue of possibilities; only one of its items is explanatory in actuality.

Aenesidemus adapted the Epicurean story to his own ends. Epicurus's concern with multiple causation was primarily therapeutic: if you list all possible causes, you must have grasped the actual cause (even if you do not recognize it); and you will thus be freed from ignorance and superstitious fears. Aenesidemus was interested in attacking aetiologists, not in curing the superstitious. Again, Epicurus limited multiple causation to *ta meteōra*; for some things "have a unique (*monachōs*) agreement with the phenomena" (*Ad Pyth.* 86). Aenesidemus suggested that multiple causation was ubiquitous: whatever the *explanandum*, there are many ways to explain it.[71] In general, for any set of phenomena, Σ, there are always at least two *aitiologiai* or explanatory theories, T_1 and T_2, which can be adduced to account for Σ.

Now according to Mode Two, "often... some explain it in one way only": what is wrong with that? Sextus does not tell us; but it is easy to guess. Suppose an aetiologist adduces T_1 in explanation of Σ, when in fact T_2 is also available. Then Aenesidemus will point out that there is nothing to be said for T_1 which cannot equally be said for T_2, and vice versa; the selection of T_1 is arbitrary and unscientific, and the aetiologist cannot properly claim to have given "the explanation."

An Epicurean might agree up to that point; but Epicureans are Believers and claim to provide *aitiologiai*. Has Aenesidemus anything to say against them? Sextus's brief report of Mode Two gives him no answer to the Epicurean strategy; but an answer is provided in another Sextan passage: "The multiplicity (*to polutropon*) of their assertion certifies their ignorance of the truth; for there can be many ways of conceiving of god, and the true one among them is not apprehended" (*M* IX 29; cf. VIII 333a). It is no use citing both T_1 and T_2 in explanation of Σ, as the Epicureans would have us do; for at most one of the two theories is true, and we do not know which one.

I suggest that we fill out Mode Two with the aid of *M* IX 29, and produce a dilemma for the aetiologist. For any set of phenomena, Σ, there will be at least two explanatory theories, T_1 and T_2, at most one of which will be true.[72] If an aetiologist cites just one of those theories, he is making an arbitrary choice and cannot claim to have grasped the truth; if he cites both theories, he cannot claim to have put forward the explanation.

Mode Two can now be used to support Modes Four and One. Mode Four, indeed, turns out to be no more than a special case of Mode Two:

the aetiologist who assumes that ordinary dynamics belong in his nonevident aetiology is, in effect, arbitrarily picking upon T_1 and ignoring the equal claims of T_2. As for Mode One, Mode Two shows how there will always be a reasoned dispute of the sort which the first Mode postulates. For if I advance a theory, T_1, to explain Σ, and then adduce the observation that q as confirmation, you can always rationally deny that T_1 is thereby confirmed. For there is a rival theory, T_2, which copes equally well with the fact that q. Since the fact that q stands in the same relationship to T_2 as it does to T_1, it confirms neither theory or it confirms both; but, the two theories being incompatible, it cannot confirm both; hence it confirms neither.

That way of using Mode Two to support Mode One is admittedly not suggested by the text of Sextus; but it is not a modern construction. According to Galen, the Empirical doctors "say that inference begins from the phenomena and ends with what is forever nonevident, and it is for that reason multiform (*polueidēs*); for from the same phenomena one arrives at different *adēla*. And here they lay hold of the undecidable disagreement which they say is a sign of inapprehensibility" (*Sect. introd.* I 78 K = *Scr. min.* III 11 = F 24 D). The doctors are speaking in particular about inference to causes. They hold that such inference is always multiform, *polueidēs*; and that is what Aenesidemus's states in Mode Two. According to the doctors, multiformity is the ground for undecidable disagreement, the phenomenon to which Mode One appeals; and from that disagreement they infer the inapprehensibility of causes. Galen's doctors thus effectively support Mode One by Mode Two: the coincidence between their view and that of Aenesidemus is hardly accidental; I incline to believe that Aenesidemus borrowed from the Empirics, but the matter cannot be conclusively determined.

Aenesidemus's second Mode has a modern ring to it; for it calls to mind the familiar thesis of the underdetermination of theories by data: as Quine puts it, "Our own theories and beliefs in general are under-determined by the totality of possible sensory evidence time without end"; any set of data can be organized and explained by at least two (and in fact by infinitely many) different and incompatible theories. I suggest that Aenesidemus had a grasp of that thesis; and that he employed it to a skeptical end.

Several questions arise: did Aenesidemus argue for the thesis of underdetermination? If so, how? Did his thesis receive any criticisms (that, for example, T_1 might be preferred to T_2 not in virtue of any *epimarturēsis*, but on grounds of ontological economy, or of mathematical simplicity, or whatever)? It would be idle speculation to pursue such questions. Instead, I end by observing that Aenesidemus's Eight Modes do appear to offer a serious and general challenge to aetiologizing, and hence to the Believers' proud pursuit of *phusiologia*. The Modes are uneven in scope and power; but they are more than a collection of modest reminders of the fallibility of scientists: they contain intimations of a genuine Skepticism. But it must still be remembered that the skepticism they promote is Sober: they attack the temerity of the Believer and his pretensions to knowledge of *ta adēla*; they do not suggest a skeptical attitude to Life or Common Sense.

AGAINST CAUSATION

THE STRUCTURE OF CAUSES

Sextus begins his account of the concept (*epinoia*) of cause by observing, in standard Skeptical fashion, that there is disagreement on the subject among the Believers; but he thinks that he can offer a general definition of causation which will prove acceptable to everyone:[73] "It would seem that a cause, according to their common view, is that because of which, acting, the effect comes about (*di' ho energoun ginetai to apotelesma*)" (*PH* III 14; cf. 103).

A cause is that because of which, *di' ho*. It is sometimes said that Sextus is here adopting the standard Stoic view; for, according to Stobaeus, the Stoics defined cause as "that because of which": *aition einai di' ho*.[74] But of course there is nothing proprietorially Stoic about that: "*dia*" is the ordinary Greek preposition for expressing causality;[75] Aristotle talks regularly of an *aition* being *to dia ti*, "the because of what" (or, equivalently, *to dioti*); and the Stoics have simply sanctified a commonplace.

For all that, Sextus forgets the commonplace when it suits him. Two of the arguments in *M* IX explicitly rest upon a notion of causation from which the *di' ho* is missing: "A cause is that in the presence of which the effect comes about (*hou parontos ginetai to apotelesma*)" (*M* IX 228; 243).[76] But that definition fails to distinguish active causes from background conditions: the distinction was expressly made by the Believers;[77] and Sextus has no excuse for dropping the *di' ho* and ignoring the general definition of *PH* III 14.[78]

A cause is described as "acting," *energoun*. The participle can be taken in two ways: it may mean "being active" as opposed to "being passive" (Sextus is talking specifically of efficient causes); and it may mean "being actual" as opposed to "being potential."[79] A cause will surely be "actual": it will actualize or realize its potentialities in causing its effect: a cause is something possessed of what Sextus elsewhere calls an "active *power*," a *drastērios dunamis* (*M* IX 240, 256; cf. VIII 192-199, which refers forward to IX); and it operates *energoun*, by actualizing that capacity. Clement says that a cause must be "already actual" (*ēdē energoun*) as opposed to "possessing the power of being actual" (*dunamis . . . tou energēsai*) (*Strom.* VIII 25.5; cf. [Galen], *In Hipp. alim.* XV 302K). Again, efficient causes must certainly be active: it is a defining mark of the sort of cause Sextus is here discussing that it *does* things. Clement, in his notes on Hellenistic theories of causation, remarks that "a cause is thought of as consisting in being active and doing something (*to energein kai dran ti*)" (*Strom.* VIII 27.6); and numerous texts bear out the truth of what he says.[80]

Causes, as the Believers define them, are relational things, they fall into the category of *to pros ti*. The fact is evident, indeed trivial; but it assumes a crucial importance in the Skeptics' counterarguments.[81] "A cause is relative to something subsisting" (*PH* III 16);[82] "causes are among things relative to something" (*M* IX 207). As Clement puts it: "Causes are among things relative to something; for they are conceived of in respect of holding relatively to something else, so that we attend to two things in order to conceive of a cause as cause" (*Strom.* VIII 29.2).[83]

In *M* IX, the relational character of causes is explained as follows: "A cause is a cause of something and for something; for example, the scalpel is a cause of something, namely, the cutting, for something, namely, the flesh" (*M* IX 207; cf. 211; Clement, *Strom.* VIII 29.1).[84] Consider the paradigm causal sentences:

The scalpel cuts the flesh

The sun melts the wax

The cause (*aition*) or agent (*poioun*) is denoted by "the scalpel," or "the sun"; that *for* which it is a cause—the patient (*paschon*)—is denoted by "the flesh," or "the wax"; and that *of* which it is a cause—the effect (*apotelesma*)[85]—is introduced by the verb "cuts," or "melts."

PH reports a difference of opinion among the Believers over the nature of effects: "A cause . . . is that because of which, acting, the effect comes about, as, for example, the sun, or the heat of the sun, is cause of the wax being melted (*tou cheisthai ton kēron*) or of the melting of the wax (*tēs chuseōs tou kerou*). For here too they disagree, some saying that a cause is cause of *prosēgoriai* (e.g., of the melting), others that it is cause of *katēgorēmata* (e.g., of being melted)" (*PH* III 14). *Katēgorēmata* are predicates, not in the linguistic but the semantic sense: the predicate *being melted* is a potential component not of sentences but of propositions. *Prosēgoriai* are appellatives or common nouns: the appellative "melting" is a potential component not of propositions but of sentences. Both the predicate *being melted* and the appellative "melting" are distinct from the actual physical process of melting.

The Stoics, we are told, held that effects were *katēgorēmata*, or predicates;[86] and the view that effects are *prosēgoriai* or appellatives is ascribed to the Peripatetics (Clement, *Strom.* VIII 26.4). It is tempting to dismiss the dispute between those two views as compounded from a muddle and a triviality. The muddle consists in supposing that effects must be linguistic items, like *prosēgoriai*, or semantic entities, like *katēgorēmata*. Both suppositions are silly because, quite plainly, the fire is not the cause of the *noun* "melting"—it is a cause of melting; and the fire does not cause the *predicate, being melted*—it causes the wax to be melted. That silly muddle removed, the question in dispute can be posed in clear terms, as follows: in making causal judgments, should we properly express the effect by means of a noun (as in "The sun causes the melting [*chusis*] of the wax") or rather by means of a predicate (as in "The sun causes the wax to be melted [*cheisthai*]")? And *that* dispute is surely quite trivial: either mode of expression is perfectly admissible.

Having mentioned the dispute, Sextus himself ignores it: he generally prefers the language of *prosēgoriai*, but he is quite happy to employ *katēgorēmata*;[87] and he implicitly regards the difference between the disputants as immaterial to his Skeptical purposes. In doing so, he is largely correct; but it would, I think, be a mistake to dismiss the whole issue as a trivial muddle.

First, we must take at its face value the Stoic suggestion that effects are *predicates*; it is, after all, of a piece with their familiar contention that signs are propositions (*axiōmata*); and that contention, though peculiar, was not the result of a careless muddle but the conclusion of a self-conscious argument.[88] Second, and more importantly, even if it is cleansed of the "muddle," the dispute is by no means trivial: on the face of it, it raises difficult ontological issues to which modern philosophers have recently drawn fresh attention. For if we accept the "Aristotelian" view, we are apparently committed to an ontology of events (e.g., the melting of the wax); whereas if the Stoic view is right, causal judgments presuppose no more ontological furniture than substances (e.g., the wax) and their attributes (e.g., being melted).

For my part, I side with the Stoics and their latter-day followers; and henceforth I shall speak uniformly in the language of *katēgorēmata*. That will be of no great importance for my exposition of the Skeptical arguments against causation: Sextus correctly felt that the dispute over the nature of *apotelesmata* did not matter for his purposes. But in my final pages my preference for the language of *katēgorēmata* will assume some significance.

At *M* IX 195 a restriction is placed upon the class of effects: "The sophists who do away with change and locomotion[89] hold that there are no causes; for without the former, agents do not subsist." If there is no change, there are no agents and therefore no causes. Agency implies change in two ways: first, agents in acting are themselves in motion or process of change (see *PH* III 68); second, what an agent effects is, according to Sextus, a change or *kinēsis* of some sort: ". . . In that case, the cause will not possess that of which it is cause [i.e., it will have no effect], because neither generation nor destruction. . ."[90] nor *kinēsis* in general exists. . ." (*M* IX 209). If there is no *kinēsis*, there are no effects, and hence no causes.[91]

The restricting of effects to changes is unwarranted: keeping the wax liquid requires heat no less than melting it does; I exercise agency in holding the door open no less than in opening it; causes are required to conserve as well as to change. Sextus's text provides a few examples of such conservative causes: the soul is a cause of being alive (*M* IX 198);[92] the immobility of the base is (allegedly) a cause of the immobility of the column (IX 229). The definition of *PH* III 14 does not imply that effects must all be changes; and Sextus has no grounds, historical or philosophical, for the restriction he imposes in *M* IX 195.[93]

Thus far, we have reached the following position. Causal sentences express *relations*, and the relation in question is *triadic*; it binds together agent, patient, and effect. (The effect may be introduced by an appellative or a predicative expression; it may, but need not, be a change.) *PH* III introduces a variation on that analysis. There the terminology of agency and patiency is infrequent;[94] in place of the account in *M* IX of the relational character of *to aition*, *PH* makes the following observation: "A cause is relative to something subsistent, i.e., to its effect" (III 16); and effects are specified not by a simple noun or predicate ("melting" or "being melted"), but by complex phrases such as "the melting of the wax" or "the wax being melted."

A formal schema for the analysis of causation in *M* IX might be written as:

x causes ϕ-ing for y

An analogous schema for *PH* would be:

x causes y to ϕ

The difference between *M* and *PH* may seem slight: in both analyses, "x" picks out the agent and "y" the patient; and the effect is introduced by some form of the verb "ϕ." But whereas causation is a triadic relation in *M*, it is a dyadic relation in *PH* : two of the three *relata* of the *M* analysis are, as it were, amalgamated into a single complex *relatum* in the *PH* analysis "ϕ-ing" and "y," "being melted" and "the wax," are united into "y to ϕ," "the wax to be melted."

The complexity of the *apotelesma* in the *PH* analysis is a propositional complexity;[95] for "y to ϕ" is a syntactical transformation of the declarative sentence "ϕy." We can bring out the true character of this complexity by means of the schema:

x causes that ϕy

or more idiomatically:

x brings it about that ϕy

That schema shows at once the dyadic character of the causal relation[96] and the propositional complexity of its second argument.[97]

If effects are most fully expressed by complete sentences, perhaps the same is true also of causes? Perhaps instead of the simple term "x," we require, in a fully explicit statement of a singular causal judgment, a complex phrase, "x's ψ-ing," or " ψx"? Then we should have the formula:

that ψx brings it about that ϕy

Causation is still a dyadic relation; but now both its *relata* have the same propositional standing.[98]

Sextus nowhere expressly opts for, or even mentions, that schema; but it is implicit in a number of passages. First, there are one or two illustrative examples in *PH* and *M* where the cause seems to be specified not by a name[99] but rather by something with the complexity of a proposition. Thus the cause of the wax's melting is the sun or *the heat of the sun* (*PH* III 14); "*the fixing of the halter* is cause of the throttling" (ibid. 15); "*each of the oxen hauling the plough* is cause of the hauling of the plough" (ibid.); "*extended exposure to the sun*" causes fever (ibid. 16); "*the suitability of the logs*" is alleged—in a *reductio ad absurdum*—to be cause of their burning (*M* IX 243).

Again, according to Sextus causes must be themselves in motion, or changing (*PH* III 68; *M* X 76); indeed, they must come into contact with the patient on which they produce an effect (*M* IX 216, 253, 258; cf. 378). The change in the agent is symmetrical with the change effected in the patient; and it is by changing that the agent makes its mark: it is not the agent but the agent acting (as Aristotle might have put it) which is, properly speaking, the cause. And that same conclusion is suggested by the presence of the participle *energoun* in the general definition of cause: the plough is moved by the oxen—but by the oxen *acting*, i.e., by the hauling oxen.

Those passages are not prominent, and they are no more than straws in the wind; but they do suggest that a fully explicit causal sentence will have the form:

> that ψx brings it about that ϕy

Causes, like effects, are propositional in character: it takes a complete sentence to specify an effect, and a complete sentence to specify a cause.

A simple causal sentence like "The fire melts the wax" has the superficial form of a dyadic relation, xRy. A little reflection converts the simple sentence into the more explicit sentence, "The fire is cause of melting for the wax"; and that appears to be triadic in form, $C(x,y,\phi)$. Further reflection leads to the amalgamation of "the wax" and "melting," thus: "The fire brings it about that the wax melts." And the form of that may be given by: $xC: \phi y$. Finally, a fuller understanding of the causal relation produces something like this: "That the fire is hot brings it about that the wax melts." And the full or canonical formula for expressing causal judgments is thus: $C(\psi x, \phi y)$.

I have labored that point for two reasons. First, the matter is of some philosophical interest: in effect I have tried to father on the Believers—and on the Skeptics—the view that all causation is, at bottom, "event causation"; that "agent causation" is, so to speak, an elliptical version of event causation. For that view, as I understand it, is simply the thesis that "$xC: \phi y$" is always expandable into "$C(\psi x, \phi y)$." And the view seems to me to be both true and important. Second, the question of the appropriate form of causal sentences is crucial to an assessment of the most interesting of the Skeptical arguments against causation; and I shall eventually make use of the canonical formula which I have just extorted from the texts.[100]

ARE CAUSES CONCEIVABLE?

The arguments against causation in *PH* III occupy sections 20-28. First, in 20-22, comes an argument directed against the concept of causation and designed to show that we cannot even conceive of things as causes. Section 23 begins by remarking that "even if we grant that causes can be conceived of, they might be thought to be inapprehensible because of the dispute (*diaphōnia*)."[101] At this point there is a lacuna in the Greek manuscripts; and although the medieval Latin translation enables us to put something in the gap, the extent of the lacuna is uncertain:[102] it is possible that the end of 23, together with 24, represents part of a second argument, distinct from the argument based on *diaphōnia*. Sections 25-26a produce a further argument against causes. 26b-27 offers what I take to be a second version of the argument of 25-26a; 28, which is linked to 26b-27, urges that "in this way too the concept of cause is again overturned," and gives a brief résumé of the argument of 20-22.

I shall not discuss the whole of *PH* III 20-28; and I shall say nothing directly about any of the more numerous arguments in *M* IX. I find *PH* III more interesting than *M* IX, much of which is rude and mechanical; and I believe that I shall deal with most of the interesting parts of *PH* III. But I cannot pretend to have discussed more than a fragment of the skeptical case against causation.

PH III 20-22 is concerned with the legitimacy of the concept of causation. Modern readers, familiar with Hume's skeptical dissection of that notion, and recalling that the Believers' definition of cause implicitly introduced the notion of an active power, will perhaps expect to find in Sextus some anticipation of Hume's celebrated argument. After all, the basis of Hume's argument is his principle that all our ideas must be derived from impressions; and that principle is clearly and frequently expressed by Sextus, who asserts that all our concepts must come, directly or indirectly, from our perceptions.[103] Moreover, Sextus is capable of using the principle in a thoroughly Humean manner: thus at *M* III 37-59 he argues at length against the Believing geometers' notion of a line as "length without breadth," and the basis of his argument is the contention that such a notion cannot possibly be grounded in perceptual experience. "Then consider the notion of causation," we expect him to argue; "that contains implicitly the concept of an active power, a *drastikē dunamis*. But from what percept can such a concept have arisen? We do not directly observe active powers; nor yet can we derive a conception of them indirectly by any of the acceptable routes of 'transference'—similarity, composition, analogy. Hence active powers—and therefore causes—are inconceivable."

But that argument is not to be found in Sextus; nor do I know of any passage in his work which casts doubt on the concept of a power: "that there are powers . . . scarcely anyone will dispute" (Galen, *Simp. med.* XI 380K). Instead, Sextus fastens his claws on the relational character of causation. The nerve of the argument at *PH* III 20-22 is this:

It is impossible to conceive of (*ennoēsai*) the cause[104] before grasping (*katalabein*) its effect as its effect; for we only recognize that it is cause of the effect when we grasp the latter as an effect. But we cannot grasp the effect of the cause as its effect if we do not grasp the cause of the effect as its cause; for we think we know that it is its effect only when we grasp its cause as its cause. [*PH* III 20-21]

The verb *"katalambanein"* ("grasp") usually means "apprehend" or "know"; but the present argument employs it as a synonym for *"enno-ein,"* "conceive of" (cf. *PH* II 4). And Sextus's conclusion apparently rests upon two parallel propositions, namely: (a) you cannot conceive of *A* as cause of *B* before you conceive of *B* as effect of *A*; (b) you cannot conceive of *B* as effect of *A* before you conceive of *A* as cause of *B*. Sextus offers no argument for (a) or (b): perhaps he thought that the general definition of causation implied their truth; perhaps he found them self-evident. At all events, both (a) and (b) are very plausible: cause and effect are correlative notions, so that neither can be grasped without the other. Anyone who knows what it is for *A* to cause *B* knows equally what it is for *B* to be effected by *A*. For in a sense there is only one thing to know here, namely, what it is for a causal relation to hold between *A* and *B*. You could no doubt understand the *word* "cause" without understanding the word "effect"; but if you have the concept of *A*'s being cause of *B*, you thereby have the concept of *B*'s being effect of *A*. Thus Sextus's premises seem unexceptionable: how does he infer from them that causes are inconceivable?

Section 22 opens as follows: "If, therefore, in order to conceive of the cause it is necessary to recognize the effect beforehand (*proepignōnai*) and in order to recognize the effect, as I said, it is necessary to know the cause beforehand (*proepistasthai*), the circular mode of puzzlement shows that both are inconceivable...." In order to conceive of *A* as cause, you must *already* have conceived ob *B* as effect; in order to conceive of *B* as effect, you must *already* have conceived of *A* as cause: there is something here which might be described as a circle, and which, however described, does surely imply that cause and effect cannot be conceived, at least by temporally finite minds.[16]

But the argument in section 22 does not rely upon premises (a) and (b); rather, it rests on the following two propositions: (a') you cannot conceive of *A* as cause of *B* unless you have already conceived of *B* as effect of *A*; (b') you cannot conceive of *B* as effect of *A* unless you have already conceived of *A* as cause of *B*. (The adverb "already" corresponds to Sextu's prefix *"pro-."*) Sextus slips from (a) to (a'), from (b) to (b'); indeed, he implies that (a) is the samer as (a'), (b) the same as (b'). But (a) is distinct from (a'), and (b) from (b'); moreover, (a') does not follow from (a), and (b') does not follow from (b). Sextus's argument is based upon a confusion: (a) and (b) are true, but yield no skeptical conclusion; (a') and (b') yield a skeptical conclusion, but both are false. Sextus hopes to enjoy the truth of (a) and (b), together with the logical power of (a') and (b'): his hope is vain, and his argument against the concept of causation fails.

That may seem a little unsympathetic to Sextus: his argument is no doubt fallacious; but is there not a sound critical point hidden somewhere behind it? After all, the Believers' definition of "cause" includes the word "effect"; and there is surely something wrong about that, just as it would be wrong to define "parent" as "person who conspires to produce a child." Anyone who has the concept of *child* has the concept of *parent*; for those concepts are, as it were, two aspects of the single relational concept of generation. And anyone who has the concept of *cause* has the concept of *effect*; for those concepts are aspects of the single relational concept of causation. Thus to define "parent" in terms of "child," or "cause" in terms of "effect," amounts to defining a concept in terms of itself; and that is illegitimate.

Now whatever the validity of that argument, the Believer has an easy reply: he need only replace the word "effect" in his definition by the indefinite pronoun "something."[106] He should say: "A cause is that because of which, acting, something comes about"; in other words, *A* is a cause if something comes about because of *A*'s activity (and *A* is a cause of *B* if *B* comes about as a result of *A*'s activity). That definition is impervious to the argument of *PH* III 20-22.

I do not mean to suggest that the Believers' definition is beyond criticism: a Skeptic might well ponder the notion of an active power; and he might remark, with Hume, that "if a cause be defined, *that which produces any thing*; it is easy to observe, that *producing* is synonymous to *causing*. In like manner, if a cause be defined, *that by which any thing exists*; this is liable to the same objection. For what is meant by these words, *by which*?" (*Enquiry* VIII ii §74n).[107] But Sextus did not anticipate Hume; and his attempt to show the inconceivability of causes is a simple failure.

THE CAUSE OF CAUSES

The argument of sections 23-24 relies upon the Modes of Agrippa (see *PH* I 164-177). I shall concentrate upon one of its features. According to Sextus, "he who says that some things are causes of others either asserts that he says this baldly and without starting from any reasonable cause (*aitia eulogos*) or will say that he arrives at assent because of some cause." Given the first option, Agrippa's Hypothetical Mode applies: to the *mere* hypothesis that there are causes we may oppose the *mere* hypothesis that there are no causes—one bald statement is no better than its bald contradictory. Given the second option, both the Circular Mode and the Mode of Infinite Regress apply.[108]

Sextus's application of the Circular Mode[109] reads like this: "And if he actually states causes because of which he thinks that some things are causes of others, he will be trying to establish the matter at issue through the matter at issue; for we are inquiring whether anything is a cause of anything, and he, assuming that there are causes, says there is a cause of there being causes."[110] If you cite a cause for believing that there are causes, you are assuming the very thing you are trying to prove.[111]

The argument is an *ignoratio elenchi*. Sextus is discussing the existence of efficient causes. If the proponent of efficient causation is to ground his thesis, then he must indeed produce a "cause" or reason for believing that there are causes; but he is under no obligation to cite an *efficient* cause. The advocate of efficient causation must argue, in effect, that there are causes *because p*; but the "because" in his argument need not introduce an efficient cause. (His argument *might* refer to efficient causes of causation: he might allege that God created the universe with its tidy causal structure; but no plausible argument for the existence of efficient causes would in fact proceed in so crass a fashion.)

Oddly enough, Sextus's argument can evade the charge of *ignoratio elenchi* if it makes a bolder claim: let the Skeptic doubt not merely efficient causation, but causation *tout court*; let him raise general doubts applicable to *all* statements of the form "*q* because *p*." Now the proponent of causes is bound to "beg the question" if he attempts to ground his thesis; for his attempt must invoke, explicitly or implicitly, some proposition of the form "*q* because *p*"; and his task is precisely to show the legitimacy of that form.

The Believer might reply that the word "because" is ambiguous, that it adverts now to efficient causes, now to reasons, now to something else, and that those various referents cannot be subsumed under any generic notion of cause: there is no single concept under which all "because" relations fall. But even if that thesis is true, it will not cause the Skeptic much loss of sleep. For he will simply take all the multifarious referents of the equivocal term "because," whatever and however many they may be, and express his doubt conjunctively. Let those referents be denoted by the terms "cause$_1$," "cause$_2$," etc. Then the Skeptic doubts whether there are any causes$_1$, and whether there are any causes$_2$ and . . . and whether there are any causes$_n$. The Believer holds that there are causes$_i$, for at least some values of "*i*." If he is to ground his belief, he must in effect produce some sentence of the form "there are causes$_i$ because $_j p$." If $i = j$, then he assumes what he is trying to establish; if $i \neq j$, then he is vulnerable to a slightly more complex Skeptical objection.

Of course, that argument does not establish that there are no causes; but I think that it does establish something. If we are to justify a belief in causes, we cannot do so by any direct form of argumentation: either causes—or, if I may use the expression, "becauses"—are a fundamental

presupposition of thought;[112] or they are immediate *data* of experience—
things to be perceived, not to be argued for;[113] or their existence must be
shown by way of some "transcendental" argument.

CAUSES AND TIME

The argument of sections 25-26a is based upon the relation between
causes and time. Sections 26b-28 seem, as I have said, to contain a
slightly different version of the same argument; and a third version can
be found at *M* IX 232-236. Sextus no doubt transcribed the argument
from two or three different sources:[114] the differences are unimportant,
and I shall restrict myself to the version in *PH* III 25-26a.

The argument is presented as a dilemma:

> The cause produces the effect either [i] being and subsisting already (*ēdē*) as a
> cause or [ii] not being a cause. And [ii'] not being [sc. a cause], in no way [sc. will
> it produce the effect]. But [i'] if being [sc. a cause], then it must have subsisted
> earlier and have become beforehand (*progenesthai*) a cause, and then in this way
> have introduced the effect, which is said to be effected by it when it is already a
> cause. But since the cause is relative to something, that is, relative to the effect, it
> is clear that it cannot have subsisted before (*proüpostēnai*) it as a cause.
> [*PH* III 25]

Sextus's argument rests, I think, on two fundamental and indisputable
theses about efficient causes: first, efficient causes *produce* their effects;
second, efficient causes *are correlative with* their effects. Because causes
are productive, option [ii] is ruled out: *A* cannot produce *B* unless *A*
"already subsists as a cause." Because causes are correlative, option [i] is
ruled out: *A* cannot be correlative with *B* if *A* "subsists before it as a
cause." In effect, then, Sextus is inferring from the productive aspect of
causation that:

(1) Causes, as causes, precede their effects in time.

And he is inferring from the relative aspect of causation that:

(2) Causes, as causes, do not precede their effects in time.

From (1) and (2) it follows that there are no causes.

In *PH* III 16, Sextus observes that some Believers deny that there any
"antecedent (*prokatarktika*) causes," precisely on the grounds that "the
cause is relative to something actual, that is, to the effect, and so cannot
precede (*proēgeisthai*) it as cause."[115] Such Believers will deny the force
of Sextus's argument by rejecting proposition (1). Their position is hardly
satisfactory: unless they are prepared to do away with efficient causes
altogether, they must explain how causes can produce their effects without preceding them in time; and they are in any event committed to a

number of strange views: they must, for example, deny that dog bites cause rabies.

Other Believers will have sought to escape Sextus's argument by denying proposition (2): efficient causes, on their view, are always "antecedent" to their effects.[116] Such men must explain how antecedent causes can nonetheless be correlative with their effects. Since most modern readers will, I suspect, be initially inclined to reject (2), I shall begin by arguing that it is both true and a consequence of the correlative character of cause and effect.

Sextus's acceptance of proposition (2) is based upon a general thesis about the logical character of correlatives: "correlatives, as they [i.e., the Believers] say, insofar as they are correlatives, co-subsist (*sunuparchein*) and are co-conceived (*sunnoeisthai*) with one another" (*PH* III 27; cf. *M* IX 239; X 267). At first blush the notion that correlatives co-subsist seems outrageous: fathers and sons, husbands and wives, are correlative; but husbands rarely share a life span with their wives, and fathers cannot share a life span with their sons. But the thesis about correlatives is not insane. It states, not that correlatives co-subsist, but that correlatives co-subsist *as correlatives*; and it surely means that if x is relative to y at a time t, then y is relative to x at t. More precisely put, the thesis says that if x stands in a relation R to y at t, then y stands in the converse relation, $\check{R}$, to x at t.[117] Sophroniscus did not share a life span with his son; but Sophroniscus sired Socrates at t if and only if Socrates was sired by Sophroniscus at t. Socrates and Xanthippe were born and died at different times; but Socrates was husband of Xanthippe at t if and only if Xanthippe was wife of Socrates at t.

The general theorem is this: xRy at t if and only if $y\check{R}x$ at t. That theorem is true. Applied to the relation of causation, it yields the thesis that A causes B at t if and only if B is effected by A at t. That, I suggest, is the proper interpretation of Sextus's proposition (2); and it is both true and a direct consequence of the relational nature of causation.

If we accept proposition (2), then we must reject proposition (1)—unless we are to acquiesce in causal skepticism. The idea that causes must be temporally prior to their effects has often been regarded as incontestable: it is, after all, an essential part of Hume's celebrated analysis of causation. But in fact, many philosophers, both ancient and modern, have contested it: it is not unusual to assert that some causes are simultaneous with their effects, and the more audacious contend that a cause might, in principle, postdate its effect. Can we not save ourselves from causal skepticism by renouncing the Humean view, and with it proposition (1)?

That attempt to dispatch Sextus's argument is too hasty; for the argument does not invoke Hume's principle. Hume states, simply, that causes precede their effects; proposition (1) states that causes, *as causes*, precede their effects. The qualifying phrase "as causes" is no idle embellishment to the argument; and we shall not have done our duty by Sextus unless we take it seriously.

But what does the qualifying phrase mean? What is it for a cause to do something "as cause"? The obvious interpretation, suggested by Sextus's language, is this: *A* exists "as cause" of *B* just so long as *A* is actually causing *B*. The eagle caused Aeschylus's death by dropping a tortoise on his head. The eagle was cause of the poet's demise; and the eagle no doubt lived for many years; but it existed *as cause* just at the time when it was actually causing Aeschylus to die. If that is right, then to say that causes as causes precede their effects amounts to saying that causes cause their effects at some time prior to the existence or happening of those effects.

Proposition (1) can thus be rewritten as:

(1a)   If *B* is effected by *A* at *t*, then *A* causes *B* at
                  some time prior to *t*

Now (1a) certainly conflicts with proposition (2); but it is both ill grounded and false. It cannot be grounded on the productive aspect of efficient causes: if *A* is to produce *B*, then it is at any rate plausible to suppose that *A* must exist before *B* does: the father must be older than his son. But the productive relation does not require that producers should be producing before their products are being produced; and, of course, the truth of proposition (2) is enough to show the falsity of (1a): *A* cannot be causing *B* at any time when *B* is not being caused by *A*.

It is tempting to diagnose Sextus's error as follows. Sextus failed to see the significance of his own qualifying phrase, "as cause": omit the phrase from (1), and the resulting proposition is at any rate plausible; but it does not conflict with (2). Retain the phrase, and (1)—or (1a)—genuinely conflicts with (2); but it is evidently false. Sextus both wants and does not want the qualifying phrase; but he must make up his mind—and whichever way he makes it up, his argument fails.

It does not greatly matter if that diagnosis is right: Sextus's argument is certainly mistaken; and we can show it to be so without making the smallest concession to skepticism.

THE UNREALITY OF CAUSES

But it would be unadventurous to let matters rest there. Let me return, at last, to the canonical formula for expressing causal propositions, namely, that ψx brings it about that ϕy

Notice that every instance of the formula will contain three verbs: there will be the main verb, "brings it about," and there will be two subordinate verbs, one replacing "$\psi(\ )$" and expressing the agent's activity, the other replacing "$\phi(\ )$" and expressing the patient's new state. Thus there are, in principle, three points in any causal sentence at which temporal adverbs may be inserted; and since the argument we are considering turns on the relation between causation and time, it is worth rewriting the schematic formula with temporal adverbs attached to it, thus:

that ψx-at-t_1 brings it about at t_2 that ϕy-at-t_3

Now let us return to the qualifying phrase "as cause," and interpret it with the help of that formula. So far, we have supposed that the cause exists "as cause" just when it is actually causing; in other words, we have supposed that the cause exists as cause at t_2. But a different interpretation of the qualifying phrase may now come to mind: why not suppose that the cause exists as cause just when it is exercising its causal powers, when it is acting or *energoun*? The exercising of x's causal powers is represented by "ψx" in the canonical formula; so that, on this interpretation, the cause will exist as cause at t_1.

The difference is not trivial; for it breathes new life into Sextus's proposition (1). That proposition will now be construed as stating that causes exert their causal powers before their effects happen or exist; in other words, that t_1 is earlier than t_3. The fatal eagle exerted its causal powers when it dropped the tortoise; after that action, which took place at t_1, it did nothing that had any bearing upon Aeschylus' life span. But Aeschylus did not die at t_1: the tortoise had to fall a few hundred feet before it hit Aeschylus's head; and even then, I doubt whether death was instantaneous; indeed, Aeschylus may well have suffered for days at the hands of Hippocrates before finally legging it to the Elysian fields. In any event, t_3, the time of the effect, was surely appreciably later than t_1.

We can now produce a new, and rather more complex, version of proposition (1):

(1b)   If that ψx-at-t_1 brings it about at t_2 that ϕy-at-t_3,
         then t_1 is earlier than t_3

Unlike (1a), proposition (1b) is not evidently false; indeed, it has some of the plausibility of the simple Humean principle that causes precede their effects. Even if (1b) is in fact false (and I think that it *is* false), we can still salvage something that may encourage the Skeptic. For surely in *some* cases—for example, the case of Aeschylus's death—t_1 will indeed be prior to t_3. And we may then argue as follows: by a modified version of proposition (1), some causes as causes precede their effects; by proposition (2), all causes as causes are simultaneous with their effects; but that is impossible; therefore, there are no causes. That is not, of course, the argument which Sextus expounds; but it is an argument quite in the spirit of his skepticism.

But, alas, if we tinker with proposition (1), logic requires that we tinker likewise with (2); and if (1) is to be expressed by way of the canonical formula for causation, then the same must be done with (2). Now proposition (2) expresses a thesis about the time of causing, that is, about t_2; and it should therefore be rewritten as follows:

(2b)   That ψx-at-t_1 brings it about at t_2 that ϕy-at-t_3 if and only
             if that ϕy-at-t_3 is brought about at t_2 by the fact that
             ψx-at-t_1

That proposition, like (2), is surely true; and it follows from the general consideration about relational terms which I rehearsed earlier.[118]

The trouble is that (2b) and (1b) do not in any way conflict: the thesis about t_2 expressed in (2b) is compatible with *any* thesis about the relations between t_1 and t_3; and in particular, it is compatible with the thesis of (1b). The canonical formula has allowed us to connect time and causation at three points: it now emerges that proposition (2) talks about one of those points, while the modified version of proposition (1) talks about the other two; Sextus's two propositions lose their connection, and if Sextus is to make any skeptical headway he must contrive to join them together again; he must, in fact, somehow conflate the three temporal points which the formula distinguishes. How could he have done that? I sketch, on his behalf, a possible line of argument:

Consider, first, the relation between t_1 and t_2. The event that happens at t_2 is the causing of the effect; but what is that causing if not the exercise of the agent's causal powers? To exercise causal powers successfully[119] simply is to cause: *"energein"* and *"poiein"* denote one and the same event. (That is why the simpler formula *"xC: ϕy"* will often serve instead of *"C(ψx, ϕy)"*; for x's ψ-ing is already implicit in the *"xC:—"* of the simpler formula.) Since the time of the exercise is t_1 and the time of the causing is t_2, t_1 is the same as t_2.

Consider, second, the relation between t_2 and t_3. The event that happens at t_3 is the coming about of the effect; but what is that, if not its being brought about? If an event is brought about, then it comes about just when it is brought about—for its coming about and its being brought about are one and the same event. Now we know from proposition (2), or (2b), that the time at which the effect is brought about by the cause is the same as the time at which the cause brings about the effect. Since the time of the latter is t_2, the effect is brought about at t_2. Hence, by the previous argument, the effect comes about at t_2. But the effect comes about at t_3. Hence t_2 is the same time at t_3.

We have proved that $t_1 = t_2$, and that $t_2 = t_3$. It follows trivially that $t_1 = t_3$, that is, that causes exist as causes when and only when their effects exist as effects. But that contradicts the *datum* so laboriously recorded in proposition (1b). The argument against causation is complete.

I shall answer that argument indirectly, by asking how t_2 in fact relates to t_1 and t_3. Various views have been canvassed. Some urge that t_2 is to be identified with t_1, on the grounds that the event of bringing something about cannot be distinguished from the event of the successful exercising of the relevant causal powers. Others argue that t_2 is to be identified with t_3, on the grounds that the causing of an effect cannot be supposed to have occurred until the effect itself is actually present. A third party suggests that the causing may well be a long and complex process, made up of various events that link the exercise of the causal powers to its final achievement in the occurrence of the effect; and such thinkers propose that t_2 be identified with the *stretch* of time bounded by, and including, t_1 and t_3.[120]

All three of those proposals seem to me unsatisfactory; for each offers to answer a spurious question. The question is: When is t_2? or: When does the causing come about? And the question is spurious because it presupposes something false: it presupposes that causing is an event, and an event that is datable. But causing is not an event at all, and a fortiori not datable: there is no such time as t_2.

The statement that the eagle, by dropping the tortoise, brought about Aeschylus's death, adverts to precisely two events, namely, the dropping of the tortoise and the death of Aeschylus; there is no third event, the bringing about of the death. (Of course, there are indefinitely many events linking the drop to the death; but they are not referred to in the causal statement, even if a full causal explanation of Aeschylus's death would need to mention at least some of them.) The canonical formula for causal propositions is: $C(\psi x, \phi y)$. "$C(\dots, \underline{\quad})$" is read as an abbreviation for the verb "... causes—" or "... brings it about that—"; and the presence of a verb suggests the applicability of temporal adverbs, and hence the importation of a datable event. But not all verbs take temporal adverbs or import events. The verb "entail," for example, does not: there is no time at which one thing entails another. The same can be said of the verbs "prove" and "signify," which are intimately associated with causation in the philosophical systems of the Believers. I suggest that "cause" or " brings it about that" is similar, in this respect at least, to "entail," "prove," and "signify": "cause" does not take temporal adverbs; it does not introduce datable events.[121]

In the formula "$C(\psi x, \phi y)$," "$C(\dots, \underline{\quad})$" is, syntactically speaking, a sentential connective; for it has the syntactical function of taking two sentences and making a sentence. It leaps to the eye that the word "because" is a dyadic sentential connective, and that it is causal in nature: why not forget about the verb "cause," with its misleading suggestions of datable events, and read "$C(\psi x, \phi y)$" as: "ϕy because ψx"? (Remember that the general definition of *PH* III 14 explains "cause," *aition*, by way of the preposition "because of," *dia*: the present suggestion, that we replace the verb "cause" by the connective "because," has some affinity to that ancient move.) There is no temptation to attach temporal adverbs to the connective "because," or to think that the sentence "Aeschylus died because the eagle dropped a tortoise" adverts to three events.

In an outmoded jargon, causal relations are not real but rational. The fundamental error in Sextus's main argument against causation is that of treating causing as a datable event, an occurrence in the world. It is a piquant thought that we can refute a skeptical argument against causation by insisting that causation itself is unreal.[122]

BIBLIOGRAPHY

Surprisingly little work has been done on the Skeptics' attitude to causation. An introductory bibliography for ancient skepticism may be found in *Doubt and Dogmatism: Studies in Hellenistic Epistemology*, ed. M. Schofield, M. Burnyeat, and J. Barnes (Oxford, 1980).

Of the general handbooks on the Skeptics the best is still V. Brochard, *Les sceptiques grecs*, 2d ed. (Paris, 1923; reprint ed., 1969).

The texts bearing on medical Empiricism are collected and discussed in K. Deichgräber, *Die griechische Empirikerschule: Sammlung der Fragmente und Darstellung der Lehre*, 2d ed. (Berlin, 1930; reprint ed., 1965).

The corpus of Greek medical writings is of forbidding bulk, and students of ancient philosophy do not always pay it the attention it deserves. The essays collected in L. Edelstein, *Ancient Medicine* (Baltimore, 1967) provide an excellent introduction; of particular relevance to this paper are the pieces entitled "The Methodists" and "Empiricism and Scepticism in the Teaching of the Greek Empiricist School."

With my remarks on Skepticism and Common Sense, compare two contrasting papers: M. F. Burnyeat, "Can the Skeptic Live his Skepticism?" (chap. 6 above) and M. Frede, "Des Skeptikers Meinungen," *Neue Hefte für Philosophie*, 15/16 (1979), 102-209.

With my remarks on The Structure of Causes compare M. Frede, "The Original Notion of Cause," in *Doubt and Dogmatism*.

NOTES

Most references to ancient sources are made in a standard or self-explanatory form. In the case of the medical writers, I have appended, where applicable, a reference to Deichgräber's collection of Empirical texts; such references have the form "F x D." Citations of Galen's works begin with an abbreviated title, usually followed by volume and page number in Kühn's edition (*Galeni Opera*, 20 vols., Leipzig, 1821-1833). Where a work has been edited in the *Corpus Medicorum Graecorum* (*CMG*), I have added a reference to the appropriate volume, page, and line; similarly for the Teubner *Galeni Scripta Minora* (*Scr. min.*), 3 vols., ed. Marquardt, Mueller, and Helmreich (Leipzig, 1884-1893). *Med. Exp.* is cited from R. Walzer, *Galen on Medical Experience* (Oxford, 1944). Apart from a few pages, *Med. Exp.* survives only in Arabic translation; *Caus. procat.* and *Subf. emp.* are only known through a Latin translation; *Caus. cont.* and *Part. med.* are found in Arabic and Latin. None of those six treatises is found in Kühn.

1. "Οἱ δογματικοί" is normally Englished as "the Dogmatists." But although οἱ δογματικοί were deemed arrogant and inflexible by their opponents, they were decidedly not accused of preferring ex cathedra pronouncements to reasoned arguments, of setting authority above logic and evidence; for that reason, "the Dogmatists" is a mildly misleading nomenclature, and I prefer an unorthodox translation.

2. Cf. [Galen], *In Hipp. alim.* XV 303 K, quoted below, n. 18. I shall use "cause" to translate both "αἴτιον" and "αἰτία." According to Arius Didymus, fr. 18 = Stobaeus, *Ecl.* I 13. 1c, Chrysippus says that "an αἰτία is an account of an αἴτιον, or the account of the αἴτιον qua αἴτιον." Chrysippus's distinction is certainly not uniformly observed by Sextus, if he observed it at all; and Galen, *Syn. puls.* IX 458 K explicitly says that "αἴτιον" and "αἰτία" are synonyms. (The Loeb Sextus suggests that "αἴτιον" is normally used by Sextus of the general notion of cause, "αἰτία" of the particular instance; or that "αἴτιον" is used of the cause of existence, "αἰτία" of the cause of cognition: I find no evidence in the text for such general rules.) The modern orthodoxy has it that "cause" is a misleading translation of "αἴτιον": I dissent. There are, to be sure, subtle and important distinctions to be made in this area; but for the purposes of the present paper, a uniform use of "cause" will do no harm.

3. For the term "αἰτιολογία" in Posidonius see F 18.38 EK, F 176 EK, F 223 EK. The Index to EK, s.vv. αἰτία, αἴτιον, provides numerous references to Posidonian aetiologizing.

4. Strabo actually says: "There is a great quantity of aetiologizing and of Aristotelizing in him, to which our school (οἱ ἡμέτεροι) is averse because of the hiddenness of the causes"; the reference is specifically to the "more scientific (φυσικός) side of Posidonius's thought. By "οἱ ἡμέτεροι" Strabo means the Stoics (cf. I 2. 3, 34); and some infer from this passage that the old Stoa refrained from *aitiologiai*. We know, indeed, that Posidonius, in his treatise *On Passions*, fre-

quently upbraided Chrysippus for omitting to inquire into causes; and that Chrysippus explicitly allowed that some causes lie beyond human knowledge (Plutarch, *Stoic. repugn.* 1045C; cf., e.g., Cicero *Top.* XVII 63; *Div.* I 56. 127). But we should not make too much of all that. Chrysippus, who was speaking in connection with the theory of divination, did not imply that *all*, or even most, causes were hidden from us. (The Stoic view is clearly expressed by Artemidorus, the second-century-A.D. dream-interpreter, who was probably influenced by Skeptical as well as by Stoic thought: "Try to give a causal explanation (αἰτιολογεῖν) of everything, and to assign a reason and some persuasive proofs to each thing; for even if what you say is quite true, still, by stating the events (ἀποτελέσματα) in a bare and naked fashion you will seem less expert. But do not yourself be deceived into thinking that causal explanation is sovereign over the events. For many things happen continuously to certain things; and that they happen we know from the fact that they always happen similarly, but the causes because of which they happen in this way we cannot discover; hence we think that what happens has been discovered by experience, but that the causal explanations are found by us ourselves according to our individual capacities" (*Oneiroc.* IV 20). Cf. Cicero, *Div.* I 6. 12: "In these cases I think the events (*eventa*) should be sought for rather than their causes.") As for Posidonius, his treatise *On Passions* was a polemical work; and he charges Chrysippus, not with ignoring aetiology altogether, but with being an indolent aetiologist.

5. Cf. *Ad Hdt.* 82; *Ad Pyth.* 97; and, for the term "αἰτιολογία," [34, 28] 26, [34 30] 7, [34 33] 6 Arr. According to the Epicurean scholarch Polystratus, we should "study natural science (φυσιολογία) and consider the causes of all things and investigate them" (IVa-Va 5). And recall the celebrated aphorism of Democritus: "I would rather discover a single αἰτιολογία than become King of Persia" (68 B 118 DK = Eusebius, *PE* XIV 27. 4; cf. A 120 = Theophrastus, *Phys. op.* fr. 13 D).

6. Προβάλλεται αὐτῷ καὶ ὁ ε΄ λόγος τὰς κατὰ τῶν αἰτίων ἀπορητικὰς λαβάς, μηδὲν μὲν μηδενὸς αἴτιον ἐνδίδους εἶναι, ἠπατῆσθαι δὲ τοὺς αἰτιολογοῦντας φάσκων καὶ τρόπους ἀριθμῶν καθ᾽ οὓς οἴεται αὐτοὺς αἰτιολογεῖν ὑπαχθέντας εἰς τὴν τοιαύτην περιενεχθῆναι πλάνην.
In Book 2, "he discusses principles (ἀρχῶν Pappenheim: ἀληθῶν codd.) and causes and effects (παθῶν) and change, and generation and destruction and their opposites" (ibid. 170b4-7). Thus Aenesidemus dealt with αἴτια twice (note καὶ ὁ ε΄ λόγος). Sextus cites him explicitly at M IX 218: some scholars refer the passage to Aenesidemus's *second* Book; however that may be, the fifth Book surely contained Aenesidemus's major attack on causation, and was a prime source—direct or indirect—for Sextus's arguments.

7. Photius's text is not easy to understand: I think that "τρόπους ἀριθμῶν" must refer to the Eight Modes; but other scholars have other ideas.

8. M IX 218 contrasts τινές with Aenesidemus; and the arguments ascribed to τινές are largely identical with those reported at DL IX 97-99. Some infer that Agrippa lies behind Sextus's τινές; but it is by no means certain that οὗτοι of DL IX 90 (to whom the arguments of IX 97-99 are attributed) are to be identified with οἱ περὶ Ἀγρίππαν of DL IX 88. However that may be, I doubt whether Sextus's τινές represent a source *earlier* than Aenesidemus.

9. Such attacks might have been found, for example, in Carneades' objections to divination, in Timon's πρὸς φυσικούς (see M III 2), in Lacydes' περὶ φύσεως (see Suda, s.v. Λακύδης), in Aristippus's περὶ φυσιολόγων (see Numenius, fr. 26 = Eusebius, *PE* XIV 7. 14).

10. For accounts of those disputes, which are of great philosophical interest, see, e.g., Galen *Sect. introd., Subf. emp., Med. Exp.*; Celsus, *Prooem.* I should confess here that the various references made in the ensuing pages to the Greek medical *corpus* are not based on any systematic study: the doctors have much to offer the student of ancient philosophy; and more work on their texts could profitably be done.

11. The Empirics—or at any rate most of them (see Galen, *Part. med.* 2. 38-49 = *CMG Supp. or.* II p. 120 = F 39 D)—allowed that "experience" might be supplemented by analogical inference, ἡ τοῦ ὁμοίου μετάβασις: see, e.g., Galen *Sect. introd.* I 68 K = *Scr. min.* III 3-4 = F 15 D; [Galen], *Opt. sect.* I 152 K = F 63 D.

12. Compare the Empirics' objection to Asclepiades: "By reducing the whole of medicine to causes he made it a matter of guesswork" (Pliny, *NH* XXVI 7. 12-13). On evident and hidden causes see below, n. 41.

13. Cf. [Galen], *Opt. sect.* I 170 K: "The Methodics accept them as causes, since they are productive of the symptoms; but they say that they indicate not as causes but as common things(κοινότητες)"—i.e., they believe in hidden causes, but deny them any value in indicating the proper treatment of diseases (cf., e.g., Caelius Aurelianus *Morb. acut.* II 87, on pleurisy, or III 191, on cholera; *Morb. tard.* II 118, on hemorrhage, II 196, on phthisis). There is a long and instructive passage on the Methodics' attitude to causation in [Dioscorides], *Iob.* II, pp. 51-57 Spr.

14. Diogenes' list of Pyrrhonian philosophers (IX 115-116; cf. [Galen], *Intr.* XIV 683 K = F 6 D; Suda, s.v. Σέξτος), in many ways a puzzling document, describes three of his nineteen men as Empirics: (1) MENODOTUS, the most celebrated of the Empirical doctors (see F 291-295 D; note that Menodotus attacked "the dogmatists who preceded him, both doctors and philosophers," and that he praised Pyrrho [Galen, *Subf. emp.* 64.3, 13 = F 10b D, p. 84, 10, 31]; he also argued that Plato was really a skeptic [*PH* I 222, whereκατὰ τῶν περὶ Μηνόδοτου should be read]); (2) SEXTUS himself (see F 6-9 D); (3) the shadowy SATURNINUS, known only from Diogenes' list. Scholars have ascribed medical expertise to other Pyrrhonians in the list. (4) TIMON is said to have "taught medicine" to his son (DL IX 109); and the Empirics sometimes acknowledged him as one of the founders of their school (Galen, *Subf. emp.* 35. 12 = F 10b D, p. 43, 1). (5) PTOLEMY of Cyrene may be the doctor mentioned by Galen, *Comp. med.* XII 584 K = F 167 D, and Celsus, VI 7. 2b = F 166 D; although Ptolemy is included in Deichgräber's collection, the sources do not call him an Empiric. (6) HERACLIDES is often identified with the eminent Empiric, Heraclides of Tarentum (see F 168-248 D). (7) ZEUXIS ὁ Γωνιόπους is often identified with the Empiric Zeuxis (see, e.g., Galen, *In Hipp. prorrh.* XVI 636 K = *CMG* V 9.3, p. 73, II = F 332a D; *In Hipp. med. off.* XVIII B 631 K = F 319 D); but note that Galen's Zeuxis apparently lived before Heraclides of Tarentum (as a comparison of the two texts just cited reveals), whereas Diogenes' Heraclides lived before his

Zeuxis. (8) THEODAS of Laodicea is presumably the Empiric of that name (see, e.g., Galen, *Lib. prop.* XIX 38 K = *Scr. min.* II 115 = **F 1 D**; *Meth. med.* X 142 K = **F 32E D**). (9) HERODOTUS of Tarsus was perhaps the physician of that name and origin (see, e.g., Galen, *Simp. med.* XI 432 K); but the doctor was a Pneumatic, not an Empiric. Diogenes' list does not contain all known Pyrrhonians (the important figure of Agrippa is the most notable omission); and it does not purport to catalogue doctors with skeptical affiliations. Among the latter it is worth mentioning: (10) CASSIUS, "the most talented doctor of our age" (Celsus, *Prooem,* 69 = **F 30 D**), an Empiric described as a Pyrrhonian by Galen, *Subf. emp.* 40. 15 = **F 10b D**, p. 49, 31 (cf. "Cassius the Skeptic" at DL VII 32; see **F 285-90 D**). (11) THEODOSIUS, a Skeptic (DL IX 70; Suda, s.v. Θεοδόσιος) and Empiric (**F 7c D**). (12) DIONYSIUS of Aegae: his curious work, the **Dictyaca,** was a Skeptical Handbook to Medicine, its hundred chapters coming in antithetical pairs; the work is summarized by Photius (*Bibl.* cod. 185 ≏ cod. 211; text and annotations in Deichgräber, pp. 335-340; cf. Eustathius, *Ad Il.* 20. 2). (13) MNASEAS, a Skeptic (Numenius, fr. 25 des P = Eusebius, *PE* XIV 6. 5) and a Methodist (e.g., [Galen], *Intr.* XIV 684 K; Caelius Aurelianus, *Morb. tard.* II 97).

Note that the Academic Skeptic Philo of Larissa drew an elaborate analogy between the tasks of the (skeptical) philosopher and those of the doctor: Stobaeus, *Ecl.* II 6. 2. See further below, n. 47.

15. For Herophilus's position see Galen, *Caus. procat.* XVI 197-204 = *CMG Supp.* II, pp. 53, 16-55, 19. Galen accuses him of timidity: "Casting doubt on all causes by many powerful arguments, he is later to be found using causes himself, saying that many men believe in them" (ibid. 197 = 53, 20-24); Herophilus himself is quoted as remarking that "whether or not there are causes is by nature undiscoverable, but in opinion I think that I am made cold and hot, and am filled by food and drink" (ibid. 198 = 53, 27-31). See below, n. 19; but note that, according to Pliny, "earlier [sc. than Asclepiades] Herophilus had begun to inquire into the causes of diseases" (*NH* XXVI 8. 14).

16. For Erasistratus's rejection of antecedent causes see also Galen, *Caus. procat.* XII 161 = *CMG Supp.* II, p. 41, 20; XIII 171 = 44, 13; XIV 173 = 45, 9; and in general, VIII 96-XV 196 = 23, 19-53, 15 (see also below, n. 19). Note that Erasistratus wrote a work *Concerning Causes:* [Dioscorides], *Iob.* II, p. 49 Spr. = **F 25 D.**

17. Herodotus of Tarsus held a milder view: "Some people sometimes catch fever without any antecedent cause" ([Galen], *Phil. hist.* XIX 433 K = 131 D). I am not sure what to make of [Dioscorides], *Iob.* II, p. 47 Spr.: "the outcomes of venomous animals and fatal drugs are called inexplicable (ἀναιτιολόγητα)."

18. See also Diocles of Carystus, fr. 112 W = Galen, *Alim. fac.* VI 455-456 K [= *CMG* V 4. 2, pp. 202-203] = *In Hipp. alim.* XV 303 K (in the latter passage, [Galen] quotes Diocles in qualification of his own assertion that "one should certainly know causes, if nothing comes about causelessly—and that is commonly agreed by pretty well all the philosophers"). It is worth quoting Diocles at length: "Those who think that one should state a cause in each case . . . seem not to know, first, that such a thing is not often necessary from the point of view of utility, and second, that many of the things that exist are by their nature similar to principles

in a certain way, so that they do not admit an account of the cause; in addition, they sometimes go wrong when they assume what is unknown and not agreed upon and implausible and think that they have stated the cause satisfactorily. Now you should pay no attention to those who aetiologize in this way and who think one should state a cause for everything: you should rather put trust in the things that have been thought out over much time on the basis of experience (ἐμπειρία); and you should seek a cause for contingent things when that is likely to make what you say about them more familiar or more credible."

19. Herophilus is known to have employed the arguments found at M IX 210, 227-231, 232-236 (Galen, Caus. procat. XVI 199-200 = CMG Supp. II, pp. 53-54); Erasistratus championed the notorious argument of M IX 242-243 (see below, n. 76).

20. Sextus has the Stoics primarily in mind: "They hold that there are two principles of everything, the agent and the patient (τὸ ποιοῦν καὶ τὸ πάσχον)" (DL VII 134; cf., e.g., Seneca, Ep. 65. 2; Galen, Caus. cont. I 2 = CMG Supp. or. II, p. 133). The nomenclature for efficient causes and principles is rich: τὸ ποιοῦν αἴτιον (see Clement, Strom. VIII 28. 2; Posidonius, F 90 EK): M VII 383; IX 194, 216, 254, 267 (cf. II 54: "for the sake of clarity, we use 'agent [τὸ ποιοῦν]' in place of 'cause [αἴτιον]'"); ποιητικός (Clement, ibid. 25. 3, 27. 2, 33. 2): M IX 12; τὸ δρῶν αἴτιον (Clement, ibid. 27. 6, 28. 5): M VIII, 406; IX 330; X 277, 322; δραστικός (see Nemesius, SVF II 418; Galen, SVF II 405, 410): PH III 1, 2, 30, 55, 63; M V 5; δραστήριος (cf. Philo, SVF II 302): M VII 115; IX 4, 6, 194; ἐνεργητικός (Clement, ibid. 25. 5, 27. 6, 29. 3): PH III 13 (see below, n. 79). For αἰτίαι κινητικαί or κινοῦσαι (M IX 7, 115, 116; cf. 76) see below, n. 91.

21. For other examples of conceptual analysis preceding skeptical argumentation see, e.g., PH II 134-143; M I 57; II 1; VII 263; XI 21.

22. For this motif see, e.g., PH II 130; III 273. It might be thought that M IX offers the "many" from which PH III made its selection; but in fact only one of the arguments in PH III recurs in M IX—and that in a different form.

23. IX 12, οἷον δογματικῶς: that curious phrase presumably adverts to the fact that here the arguments on both sides of the question are borrowed from the Believers.

24. Some Empirics recognized it; see Galen, Caus. procat. VI 49-50 = CMG Supp. II, p. 13, 30-14, 1: certain "sophists" try to do away with causes while admitting that a diet or a drug may be harmful (βλαβερόν) or healthy (ὑγιεινόν); the Empiric observes that "harmful" is synonymous (ἰσοδυναμῶν) with "causing harm" (βλάβης αἴτιον), etc.

25. See PH I 133; II 238, 240 (perhaps taken from Theodas: Galen, Subf. emp. 66. 29 = F 10b D, p. 88, 13); III 280; M I 51, 72; II 13, 49; V 57; XI 136, 153 (see below, n. 47).

26. The Skeptical arguments themselves work like purgative drugs: PH I 206; II 188; M VIII 480; DL IX 76; Aristocles, ap. Eusebius, PE XIV 18. 21.

27. External objects κινεῖ: PH I 50, 51, 87, 106, 113, 130, 193; II 51; III 179 (cf. M I 147; XI 69); M VII 344; VIII 188, 240; ποιεῖ: PH I 93, 121; M VII 191, 365, 367, 386; are αἴτια: M VII 367, 387; "sweeten," etc.: PH I 20, 92; M I 147. See also, e.g., PH I 46, 59.

28. But Heintz plausibly excises the crucial phrase τῶν παρὰ τοῖς δογματικοῖς κειμένων. Cf. *PH* I 80: "The irregularity is brought about, *as they say* (καθάπερ φασίν). by the different predominance of the humors."

29. The Skeptics use "it is (ἐστι)" loosely or καταχρηστικῶς: "we do not fight over words" (*PH* I 195). Inexactitudes of this sort are tiresome: Sextus appears to allow them because he is averse to pedantry; Aenesidemus excused himself by appeal to *patrii sermonis egestas* (see Photius, *Bibl.* cod. 212, 170a13).—At *M* XI 18-19 Sextus attempts to justify the Skeptic's use of "ἐστι" for "φαίνεται": "'ἐστι' signifies two things—in one sense it means 'it is the case,' in the other 'it seems.'" But the usage he appeals to will not really support the *systematic* employment of "ἐστι" for "φαίνεται"; that remains catachrestical.

30. Stoics, Epicureans, and Peripatetics all claimed to base their philosophics on "common notions" or "preconceptions," and to that extent purported to side with Common Sense. (It is surprising how rarely philosophers will admit that they are, by profession, revolutionaries.) But the Skeptics make a stronger claim: the Believers may *start* from Common Sense; the Skeptics refuse to go *beyond* Common Sense.

31. See *PH* I 226, 231, 237; II 246, 254; III 2, 235; *M* XI 165 (but note the rejection of Life at *M* IX 50). Pyrrho collected and rejected the δόγματα of "the other sages" and subscribed to no δόγμα himself (Epiphanius, *Adv. haer.* III 18); but "he did not depart from common custom (μὴ ἐκβεβηκέναι τὴν συνηθείαν)" (Timon, fr. 81 D = DL IX 105). "Pyrrho the Skeptic..., seeking the truth and not finding it, suspended judgment about all things nonevident, following what is evident in day-to-day actions but suspending judgment about everything apart from that" (Galen, *Subf. emp.* 62. 20 = F 10b D, p. 82, 23). Note also Galen, *Diff. puls.* VIII 783 K = F 74 D: "I see you yourselves [i.e., the Empirics] making a great point of not overturning any of the things in Life on which all men agree" (cf. e.g., *Med. Exp.* XVIII 5).

32. The Skeptical rejection of γραμματική is closely linked to their defense of Common Usage (see *M* I 153, 176, 179, 189): the Greek defenders of Life, like the modern defenders of Common Sense, proclaimed a love of ordinary language.— *M* VIII 128-129 is amusing: the Stoics defend a point in their logic by appeal to "Life and Common Usage"; the Skeptics reply that Ordinary Language permits loose usage (κατάχρησις), but that "when we investigate the nature of things, then we must hold fast to precision (ἀκριβείαν)." "We do not fight over words" (above, n. 29): See also Galen, *Subf. emp.* 46. 25 = F 10b D, p. 59, 18: "But we ought to despise words, as Plato advised, but not neglect precision (*certitudinem* = ἀκριβείαν) of argument."

33. Cf. [Galen], *Opt. sect.* I 112-113 K; Galen, *Subf. emp.* 46. 8 = F 10b D, p. 58, 19—a passage with close affinities to *M* VIII 288.

34. See, e.g., *PH* I 16, 18, 193, 197, 198, 200, 202, 208, 210, 219, 223.

35. Ἐναργεία need not involve sense-perception: a thing is ἐναργές if it is known directly or immediately (i.e., not by inference), whether on the basis of perception or through some intellectual intuition. In an interesting passage, [Galen] reproves the Methodics for "not knowing how to use the Greek language": they use "φαινόμενον" in the sense of "apprehensible in itself" (ἐξ αὐτοῦ

καταληπτόν), and thus as a synonym for "ἐναργές" (*Opt. sect.* I 175-176 K; cf. *Meth. med.* X 35-9 K, see F 46 D). [Galen], following the Empirics, thinks that "φαινόμενον" should be reserved for what is directly apprehended *in perception*: Sextus's usage—and, I think, Greek philosophical usage in general—agrees with the Methodics (see *PH* I 19; at *PH* I 9 he uses the term in a narrower sense for the nonce (νῦν), and he thinks that that was Aenesidemus's normal use: *M* VIII 216). See further below, p. 159.

36. On τὰ ἄδηλα see esp. *PH* II 97-99; *M* VIII 141-151. The things ἄδηλα by nature are the things that we cannot perceive or intuit directly: the suggestion, at *M* VII 393 and VIII 267, that τὰ ἄδηλα are what we cannot *know* is only a carelessness; the suggestion, at *M* VII 366, that all external objects are ἄδηλα belongs to the Drunken side of Sextus's philosophizing.

37. For the Skeptic's attitude to φυσιολογία see, e.g., *PH* I 18; III 62, 63, 114. Note that the Empirics—and the Methodics—rejected φυσιολογία: [Galen], *Intr.* XIV 677 K = F 21 D.

38. The "because" clause, despite its position, should be attached not to ἐφιστῶμεν (with the Loeb) but to ἐκτίθενται.—For other areas of "special pride" see *PH* II 194; *M* VII 27.

39. According to the Stoics, God is the active principle of the universe, as matter is the passive principle (e.g., DL VII 134).—Note that Aenesidemus dealt with gods in the *fourth* Book of his *Pyrrhonian Discourses* (Photius, *Bibl.* cod. 212, 170b16): was it Sextus himself who subordinated the discussion of theology to the treatment of causes?

40. Cf. Galen, *Dig. puls.* VIII 781 K = F 74 D: "In all their arguments they [sc. the Empirics] lay down the phenomena and doubt with regard to the nature of the thing"; see also Galen, *Med. Exp.* IX 2, where the Empiric argues that ordinary men may know the "action and effect" of, e.g., foodstuffs without having to "inquire into their nature and substance"; Celsus, *Prooem.* 27 = F 14 D.

41. Ancient authors talk about the nonevidence of causes in three distinct ways: Suppose that *A* causes *B*, then (i) *A* may be ἄδηλον in the simple sense of not being known to us (in that sense, Chrysippus held that many causes are "nonevident": above, n. 4); (ii) *A* may be ἄδηλον in the sense that *A* can only be known indirectly or by inference (see above, n. 36); (iii) it may be ἄδηλον that *A* causes *B*, i.e., we may be able to know indirectly that *A* causes *B* (see below, n. 113). It is sense (ii) that is relevant here.

The distinction between evident and nonevident causes, in sense (ii), is a commonplace in the medical writers. [Galen] defines the notions thus: "Pre-evident (πρόδηλα) causes are those which are by themselves comprehended through perception as acting and being efficient (ἐνεργοῦντα). (Some say: pre-evident causes are those which both are evident (φαίνεται) themselves and make evident the effect that comes about consistently with them.) Not pre-evident are those which are comprehended not by themselves but through signs" (*Def. med.* XIX 344 K; cf. [Galen], *In Hipp. alim.* XV 303 K). For further references see, e.g.: Galen, *Sect. introd.* I 66 K; *Diff. feb.* VII 281 K = F 88 D, 302 K; *Simp. med.* XI 431 K; *Ther.* XIV 245 K; *In Hipp. nat. hom.* XV 162 K = CMG V 9. 1, p. 82; *In Hipp. epid.* XVII A 24 K = CMG V 10. 1, p. 17, 725 K; *Caus. cont.* 10. 4-6 = CMG

Supp. or. II, p. 141 = **F 78 D**; *Caus. procat.* XII 159 = *CMG Supp.* II, pp. 40, 30-41, 1; *Med. Exp.* XXV; *Subf. emp.* 49. 18 = **F 10b D**, p. 63, 29; [Galen], *Intr.* XIV 678 K; Caelius Aurelianus, *Morb. acut.* I 17, 170; [Soranus], *Quaest. med.* 50 = **F 12 D**; Philodemus, περὶ θεῶν III col. 10, 21 D; Clement, *Strom.* VIII 32. 4, 33. 5. Most of these texts bear witness to the fact that the Empirics rejected nonevident causes and accepted evident causes (above, p. 152).

The Empirics believed in antecedent causes (προκαταρκτικά); indeed, the antecedent cause of a disease would usually be an element in its "syndrome": see, e.g., Galen, *Sect. introd.* I 88 K = *Scr. min.* III 19 = **F 29 D**; *Meth. med.* X 244 K = **F 89 D**. And there is a tendency to identify antecedent causes with evident causes (e.g., Galen, *Comp. med.* XII 527 K = **F 90 D**; *In Hipp. epid.* XVII A 52 K = *CMG* V 10. 1, p. 30, 30; *Caus. procat.* I 6 = *CMG Supp.* II, p. 2, 20-21); but I have not come across an explicit identification—and it is surely not a logical truth that a cause is evident if and only if it is antecedent.

42. Galen explicitly distinguished different grades of Skeptics, the most extreme of whom he calls "rustic Pyrrhonians," ἀγροικοπυρρωνεῖοι: *Diff. puls.* VII 711 K = **F 75 D**; *Praenot.* XIV 628 K.

43. In addition to the evidence cited on pp. 156-157, see *M* II 65; III 9; VII 391; VIII 316 (all passages explicitly accepting propositions of type [B]).

44. See, e.g., *PH* II 72-73; *M* VII 354, 357-358, 365-366, 383: in all these passages Sextus *seems* to assert that the Skeptic will limit himself to propositions of type (D). But note *PH* I 20, which warns that when the Skeptic attacks "the phenomena," he does so for polemical purposes only; and observe that in some passages where Sextus says he is attacking "the phenomena," it is only propositions of type (B) that he is rejecting (e.g., *PH* II 95; *M* VII 25-26; VIII 142, 362).

45. E.g., *PH* I 20, 22, 32, 92; *M* VII 397; and the many passages in which φαντασίαι are said to come to different observers from *the same* source: *PH* I 40, 49, 58, 59, etc.; cf. Timon fr. 74D = DL IX 105: "That honey is sweet, I do not affirm; that it seems so, I agree."—In Sextus, "τὸ φαινόμενον" is generally synonymous with "τὸ φανταστόν ": τὰ φαινόμενα are (external) objects that cause our φαντασίαι or perceptual πάθη. Sextus's normal view is that we do have knowledge about τὰ φαινόμενα, i.e., about (external) objects, but that our knowledge is restricted to how they appear to us, i.e., to type (C) truths. Sometimes, however, "τὸ φαινόμενον" is synonymous with "φαντασία": φαινόμενα are the πάθη putatively caused by (external) objects (see esp. *M* VII 191-198 for a clear statement of these two interpretations of "τὸ φαινόμενον"—in connection with Cyrenaicism); in his drunken moods, Sextus restricts our knowledge to φαινόμενα in this latter sense, i.e., to type (D) truths.

46. The Empirics reject ἀναλογισμός, inference from the phenomena to what is nonevident (i.e., roughly, "indicative" signs); they accept ἐπιλογισμός, inference from phenomena to phenomena (i.e., roughly, "commemorative" signs): see, e.g., Galen, *Sect. introd.* I 78 K = *Scr. min.* III 11 = **F 24 D**; *Subf. emp.* 49. 1 = **F 10 b D**, p. 62, 27; *Med. Exp.* XXIII 3-XXVII; [Soranus], *Quaest. med.* 50 = **F 12 D**.

47. Sextus was himself an Empiric (above, n. 14); he sometimes appears to approve of the Empirics (e.g., *M* V 104; VIII 191; cf. *PH* II 245-246); and he certainly objects to Logical doctors (*M* VIII 156, 327). But at *PH* I 236-241 he

argues against the view that Pyrrhonism is the same thing as Empiricism—and he suggests instead that it is the Methodics who are true Skeptics (cf. *M* I 255). Sextus's argument is pedantic; and it does not show that there were not intimate connections between Empiricism and Pyrrhonism. (Of course, the Empirics were not the only doctors from whom the Skeptics learned: I have already mentioned their debt to Erasistratus and Herophilus (above, n. 19); and see, e.g., Galen, *Med. Exp.* VII 8-10 (cf. XVI-XVII), where a Logical doctor applies the sorites argument to show the absurdity of the Empirics' inductive epistemology.) It is a pity that Sextus's Ἰατρικὰ Ὑπομνήματα (*M* VII 202: identical with the Ἐμπειρικὰ Ὑπομνήματα of *M* I 61?) have not survived.

48. Photius, *Bibl.* cod. 212, 169b36-170a11; cf. *PH* I 193 ("We say that we do not accept or even reject (μηδὲν τιθέναι μηδὲ ἀναιρεῖν) any of the things the Believers say in respect of what is nonevident"). Galen accuses Menodotus of inconsistency on this point: in his Empirical writings, Menodotus claims to know nothing at all about the nonevident; in his violent attack on Asclepiades, he claims to know that all Asclepiades' remarks about the nonevident are false (*Subf. emp.* 64. 4-10 = F 10 b D, p. 84, 11-30).

49. Sextus speaks of "eight modes . . . of which [Aenesidemus] says that the first is . . .": "says (φησι)" does not introduce a quotation; but it implies a paraphrase—and must mean that the numbering of the Modes comes from Aenesidemus (cf. the participle "enumerating (ἀριθμῶν)" in Photius's report, above, n. 6).

50. σύμφωνα (Heintz, from the Latin translation: *convenientia*); the Greek MSS read φωρατά, which ought to mean "detectable by." The word is ἅπαξ λεγόμενον, and its sense is hardly appropriate in the context.

51. On the term "hypothesis" see esp. *M* III 1-17; at *PH* I 184 Sextus uses it in the sense of "principle of demonstration, being a postulation of something for the establishment of something" (*M* III 4)—a sense he illustrates by citing the three medical hypotheses of Asclepiades.

52. "Menodotus the Empiric gives an inescapable refutation of Asclepiades' views, pointing out their conflict both with the phenomena and with one another" (Galen, *Nat. fac.* II 52 K = *Scr. min.* III 139 = F 292 D); cf. Galen, *Med. Exp.* XII 8, XV 8.

53. There may be a secondary point, viz., that only what is orderly can be the cause of order in other things; for instances of the general principle of "causation by synonyms" (if *x* makes *y* to be *F*, then *x* is *F*) see, e.g., *M* III 76; IX 77.

54. For Skeptical adversions on teaching see *PH* III 252-269; *M* I 9-40; XI 216-256. Sextus reports on "the disagreement among the philosophers about learning, which is widespread and various" (*M* I 9).

55. The phrase τὰ φαίνεσθαι δοκοῦντα is odd; but it is paralleled at *PH* III 49 (where δοκεῖν should be retained, with Heintz); and cf. *PH* II 95: τὰ ἐναργῆ εἶναι δοκοῦντα. I take the phrase to mean: "the things that seem [to the aetiologist] to be perfectly plain"; not: ". . . that seem . . . to be objects of immediate observation."

56. Compare the third of Diocles' objections to those who try to explain everything: text quoted above, n. 18.

57. See, e.g., *PH* II 33; *M* VIII 66, 285 ("don't try to establish what is less at

issue by way of what is more at issue"); *M* VIII 86 ("don't teach what is unknown by way of what is unknown"); *M* X 180 ("don't try to grasp what is easily considered on the basis of what is hard to consider").

58. See, e.g., *PH* I 7, *M* VII 393, for the connection between ἀπορεῖν and ζητεῖν.

59. Some may hope to find an objective interpretation of Trope Eight which still gives the sense of "puzzling" to "ἄπορος": some facts are, objectively, more puzzling than others. (Perhaps we should take a leaf out of Aristotle's book and say that *x* is more puzzling than *y* if and only if *y* is "prior by nature" to *x*, elucidating natural priority in terms of greater generality.) But I can find no such suggestion in Sextus's writings, and I forbear from further speculation.

60. "Elements (στοιχεῖα)" usually has the restricted sense of "material principles" (e.g., *PH* III 33, 37, 63); but it can be used in a larger sense, equivalent to "ἀρχαί," "principles" (cf. *M* V 49), and it seems best to take it in that larger sense here.

61. I guess that Aenesidemus is consciously borrowing from the Epicureans (see further below, on Mode Two). The text of Philodemus is not certain; but it seems clear that he is arguing for a skeptical conclusion: he does not want to assert positively that the sun moves "in a way of its own." Some scholars have suggested that the Eight Modes were directed primarily against the Epicureans; I think, on the contrary, that Aenesidemus was drawing on Epicurean material to attack all Believers.

62. Some scholars suppose that ἐπιμαρτύρησις was applied by the Epicureans exclusively to the confirmation of τὰ ἐναργῆ, or even that the observation that *q* "confirms" nothing but the judgment that *q*. If that is so, then Aenesidemus is extending the use of the term "ἐπιμαρτύρησις"—in a thoroughly intelligible way.

63. I.e., "*p*" will belong to class (A) of the types of proposition distinguished on p. 159; "*q*" will belong to (C)—or perhaps (B) or (D).

64. See *PH* II 8; III 254, 266; *M* I 27, 36, 184; VIII 178, 215, 280, 322; XI 76, 240.

65. When Sextus talks of dispute (διαφωνία), he often seems to imply, and occasionally expressly states (see *PH* II 37; *M* I 170; VIII 177, 184, 186), that the διαφωνία will last forever. But he sometimes talks of a disagreement lasting "up to now" (see *M* VIII 257, 401, 427), thereby implying that disagreements may come to an end (or at any rate, cease to be undecidable). Under what conditions does διαφωνία exist? It is plausible to define διαφωνία thus:

> There is διαφωνία over the thought that *p* if and only if for
> some *x*, *y*, *t*, *t'*, *x* at *t* judges that *p* and *y* at *t'* judges that not-*p*

Given that definition, every διαφωνία is trivially eternal (or else timeless); the end of διαφωνία is a logical possibility only if the definition specifies that *t* = *t'*, and that *t* is also the time of the διαφωνία.

66. It has been suggested to me that a διαφωνία is precisely a *reasoned* dispute. If that is right, then the Believer must challenge Aenesidemus to show that reasoned dispute is always to be found. But I find the suggestion implausible; indeed, Agrippa's Hypothetical Mode is designed to cope with parties to a διαφωνία who provide *no* reason for their views.

67. I take "πολλάκις" with "αἰτιολογοῦσιν," not with "εὐεπιφορίας οὔσης" (compare the use of "πολλάκις" in Modes Six, Seven, and especially Eight). If "πολλάκις" modifies "οὔσης," then Aenesidemus's point is quite different from —and much weaker than—the one I ascribe to him in the text.

68. M VIII 215-243 discusses an argument expanded in the fourth Book of Aenesidemus's *Pyrrhonian Discourses* (the book against signs: Photius, *Bibl.* cod. 212, 170b12-14); but the material has been reworked, and it is not certain that the illustrative example of M VIII 220, which was a stock example in Empirical writings (e.g., Galen, *Med. Exp.* XXIV 6; Celsus, *Prooem.* 60-61), was used by Aenesidemus himself. Mode Two is often compared to the argument against indicative signs at M VIII 200 (cf. Galen, *Med. Exp.* XIII 1-3).

69. Cf. *Ad Pyth.* 113; Diogenes of Oenoanda, fr. 8 Ch; Lucretius, V 526-533, VI 703-711.

70.   sunt aliquot quoque res quarum unam dicere causam
           non satis est, verum pluris, unde una tamen sit.

71. Sextus does not explicitly say this in is statement of Mode Two (and if "πολλάκις" goes with "οὔσης"—above, n. 67—he implicitly denies it); but the parallel at M VIII 220, and also the passage from Galen cited on p. 169, makes it plausible to ascribe the generalization to Aenesidemus.

72. At M VIII 241, a passage deriving from Aenesidemus (above, n. 68), Sextus makes it explicit that T_1 and T_2 are incompatible: "They fall into variety (ποικιλία) and make statements which are πολυτρόποι and conflicting (μαχομέναι)."

73. That is the force of κοινότερον κατ᾽ αὐτούς: cf. *PH* II 118.

74. Arius Didymus, fr. 18 (= Stobaeus I 13. 1c) ascribes this definition to Zeno and to Chrysippus; of Posidonius he says: "A cause of something is that because of which it holds, or the primary agent, or the originator of agency" (= F 95 EK); Seneca, *Ep.* 65. 2: "There must be that from which (*unde*) something comes about, and that by which (*a quo*) it comes about: the latter is cause, the former matter"; [Galen], *Def. med.* XIX 392 K: "A cause is, as the philosophers say, that which is productive of something or that because of which something comes about."

75. See Apollonius Dyscolus, *Conj.* 242, 8-12; *Synt.* 459, 2-461, 12. And note his interesting remarks on causal connectives (αἰτιολογικοὶ συνδεσμοί): *Synt.* 234, 13-247, 21.

76. M IX 242-243 argues that if, e.g., fire is genuinely a cause of burning, then fire will *always* burn; but fire does not always burn; hence fire is not a cause. That argument is the first of the "sophisms" discussed by Galen in *Caus. procat.*, a treatise directed against doctors who are skeptical of antecedent causes (see, e.g., I 10, VI 46, XIII 165 = *CMG Supp.* II, pp. 3, 17-22; 13, 8-12; 42, 24-33). Celsus ascribes the argument to Erasistratus (*Prooem.* 54; cf. 58-61); Galen, while ascribing his second sophism to Erasistratus (VIII 104 = 25, 21-26, etc.), does not name the proponents of the first (but the obscure passage at XV 187-189 = 50, 17-51, 12 *may* associate the first sophism too with Erasistratus). The argument featured later in the disputes among the three medical schools (see Caelius Aurelianus, *Morb. acut.* I 22-30); and it was evidently borrowed by the philosophers

from the physicians (but its substance is to be found already at Theophrastus, *Caus. plant.* VI 2. 1).

77. "That without which a thing does not come about must be carefully distinguished from that by which it definitely comes about": Cicero, *Top.* XVI 61; cf. *De fato* 36; Seneca, *Ep.* 65. 11; Galen, *Caus. procat.* VII 84 = *CMG Supp.* II, p. 20, 28-33; Clement, *Strom.* VIII 25.1. (But perhaps Zeno did not make the distinction: see the run of the argument ascribed to him by Arius Didymus, fr. 18D, quoted below, n. 92.)

78. "Containing causes (αἴτια συνεκτικά)" are defined at *PH* III 15 as "those in the presence of which the effect is present (ὧν παρόντων πάρεστι τὸ ἀποτέλεσμα), and with the removal of which it is removed, and with the lessening of which it is lessened." But the antecedent of ὧν is αἴτια: the definition does not say that A is a containing cause of B if and only if B is present, etc., if A is present, etc.; it says that A is a containing cause of B if and only if (i) A is a cause of B and (ii) B is present, etc., if A is present, etc.

79. In Sextus, ἐνεργεῖν is normally contrasted with πάσχειν and synonymous with ποιεῖν or δρᾶν (e.g., *PH* III 5; *M* VII 293, IX 151); but for the contrast with δύνασθαι see, e.g., *M* VII 223, IX 248.

80. In addition to Arius Didymus and [Galen] (n. 74) see Athenaeus (below, n. 116); Cicero, *Top.* XIV 58 (equating *causa* with *res efficiens*); Seneca, *Ep.* 65. 4 ("the Stoics hold that there is only one cause, that which acts [*id quod facit*]"). At *Phil.* 26E Plato notes that "the nature of that which acts does not differ except in name from the cause; that which acts and the cause might properly be called one." There is some terminological confusion in ancient writers here: on the one hand, αἴτιον or *causa* might be used to denote *any* explanatory factor (that is Aristotle's normal usage); in that case it is properly connected with the δι' ὅ. On the other hand, αἴτιον or *causa* might be restricted to efficient causes (that was normal Stoic practice); and in that case αἴτιον is sometimes treated as only one species of δι' ὅ (cf. Clement, *Strom.* VIII 27. 2-3; Galen, *In Hipp. prorrh.* XVI 496 K = *CMG* V 9. 2, p. 6, 18-29). The two uses of αἴτιον can engender puzzlement: see, e.g., Damascius, *In Phil.* 114; Iamblichus, ap. Simplicius, *In Cat.* 327, 6-328, 25.

81. Similarly, the Skeptical attack on indicative signs fastens upon the relational character of the sign: see *PH* II 117-120, 125-126, 169, 179; *M* VIII 161-170 (cf. *DL* IX 97). Those arguments are worth comparing with the arguments in *PH* III 20-27. Note too that the Logical doctors based one of their criticisms of the Empiricists' attitude to causes upon the relative character of causation: [Galen], *Opt. sect.* I 121 K.

82. τὸ αἴτιον πρός τι ὑπάρχον: why does Sextus add "ὑπάρχον," "subsisting"? "Think of" (νοεῖν) is a relational verb, and Sextus would have recognized that "thoughts are relative to something" (cf., e.g., *PH* I 177); but we can think of things that do not exist (e.g., *PH* II 10; *M* VIII 381): thoughts, then are πρός τι but not πρός τι ὑπάρχον. Sextus writes ὑπάρχον at *PH* III 16 to show that (in the current argot) causation is not an intensional relation.

83. Cf. *DL* IX 98: "They [sc. the Skeptics] do away with causes in the following way: causes belong to the class of things relative to something; for they are rela-

tive to the thing caused." Retain the MSS reading πρὸς τῷ αἰτιάτῳ: the dative is perfectly normal here (e.g., *PH* II 119, 125), and Menagius's alteration to πρὸς τὸ αἰτιατόν is unnecessary.

84. αἴτιον τινὸς τινί is a perfectly normal Greek idiom (e.g., Lysias, XIII 57; Isocrates V 42, 117; Demosthenes, XV 18; XXIV 154).

85. The term "ἀποτέλεσμα," frequent in *PH* III, is not used at *M* IX 207; but see *M* IX 197, 201, 220, 228, 234, 235, 237-244, 249, 251.

86. See *M* IX 211; Arius Didymus, fr. 18 = Stobaeus, I 13. 1c (mentioning specifically Zeno and Posidonius); cf. Clement, *Strom.* VIII 26. 4, 30. 2. Soranus ascribes the Stoic view to Asclepiades, and he discussed in his lost *Aitiologoumena* the dispute to which Sextus refers (see Caelius Aurelianus, *Morb. acut.* I 10-11).

87. Effects are called "κατηγορήματα" at *M* IX 211, XI 32; Sextus uses κατηγορήματα in his examples at *M* IX 76, 198, 199, 201, 231, 244, 247. He uses προσηγορίαι in examples at, e.g., *PH* III 15, 17; *M* IX 22, 24, 72, 118, 160, 197. *M* IX 231 is instructive: "neither is what rests a cause of resting (μονή) for what rests, nor is what moves a cause of moving (κίνησις) for what moves, nor is what rests a cause of being in motion (τοῦ κινεῖσθαι) for what moves, nor is what moves a cause of being at rest (τοῦ μένειν) for what is at rest"—two προσηγορίαι, two κατηγορήματα, used indifferently.

88. See *M* VIII 254-256: signs must be ἀξιώματα because every sign has to be "a present sign of a present thing."

89. οἱ τὴν μεταβλητικὴν καὶ μεταβατικὴν κίνησιν ἀνελόντες σοφισταί: these are the two highest genera of κίνησις according to "the majority, among whom are included those about Aenesidemus" (*M* X 38).

90. The MSS here have μήτε πεῖσιν: that is unsatisfactory, and there is no convincing emendation. Perhaps the words should be excised.

91. Hence Sextus will sometimes refer to efficient causes as αἰτίαι κινητικαί / κινοῦσαι (see above, n. 20).

92. The example is Stoic; see Arius Didymus, fr. 18 D = Stobaeus, *Ecl.* I 13. 1c, referring to Zeno: "A cause is that because of which something comes about; e.g., because of wisdom being wise comes about, and because of soul being alive comes about, and because of moderation being moderate comes about; for it is impossible that a man should not be moderate when moderation is about him, or not alive when soul is, or not wise when wisdom is." Zeno, it is true, seems to have treated these examples as causes of *coming about*; but the Stoics' "containing causes" are all conservative. See, e.g., Galen, *Caus. cont.* I 3, IX 2-3 = *CMG Supp.* or II, p. 133, 15-19, p. 140, 6-17; *Syn. puls.* IX 458 K.

93. Galen sometimes distinguishes active (ποιητικά) from conservative (φυλακτικά) causes (e.g., *Ars med.* I 365-366 K); *he* may then say that all active causes are causes of change. But Galen's distinction is not found in Sextus; and if Sextus will not allow conservative causes to count as a sort of active cause, he has no room for them at all.

94. It is found only at III 38, 71, 103, 104, 106.

95. See Clement, *Strom.* VIII 26. 4: "On this view, causes are causes of κατηγορήματα or, as some say, of λεκτά (for Cleanthes and Archedemus call

κατηγορήματα λεκτά); or—what is actually better—some will be called causes of κατηγορήματα (e.g., of *cuts*, of which *being cut* is a case), and others of propositions (ἀξιώματα) —e.g. of *a ship comes about*, of which, again, *a ship's coming about* is a case." The report is not entirely clear (and Clement's text is uncertain in places); but the idea that effects may be propositional in nature is plain enough.

96. How is "*x* brings it about that *p*" to be parsed? (i) "brings it about" is a two-place predicate, having "*x*" and "that *p*" as its subject-terms; "that *p*" denotes (e.g.) the fact that *p*. (ii) "brings it about" is a two-place predicate, having "*x*" and "that" as arguments; "*p*" is a paratactic adjunct, supplying "that" with a denotation. (iii) "brings it about that" is a semi-verb, i.e., a part of speech which makes a sentence from a name and a sentence: "*x*" is the name, "*p*" the sentence. Purists will say that we can only talk of the causal *relation* given parsings (i) or (ii): if (iii) is right, causation is not, strictly speaking, a relation at all. But though I prefer (iii), I shall continue to talk—loosely—of causal relations.

97. The difference between *PH* and *M* precisely parallels the difference between Russell's two analyses of belief. On the one analysis, "*x* believes that *φy*" expresses a triadic relation among *x*, *y* and *φ*-ness; on the other, it expresses a dyadic relation between *x* and the proposition that *φy*.

98. How parse "that *q* brings it about that *p*"? (i) "that *p*" and "that *q*" as subject-terms for the two-place relation "brings it about"; (ii) "that" and "that" as subject-terms for the same relation, with "*p*," "*q*" in parataxis; (iii) "that . . . brings it about that—" as a dyadic sentential connective, i.e., a part of speech which makes a sentence from a pair of sentences. See below, p. 186.

99. In almost all of Sextus's examples, the cause is referred to by a simple noun or nominal phrase: "the gods," "the oxen," "the knife," "the son," and so on. But equally, in the vast majority of his examples the effect is referred to in the same way: in *M* IX 227, for example, he says that "if anything is cause of anything, either the motionless is cause of the motionless or the moving is cause of the moving or the moving is cause of the motionless or the motionless is cause of the moving." He immediately glosses the first of the four options by the sentence "the motionless is cause of motionlessness for the motionless": he certainly thought that "*x* is cause of *y*" was an elliptical or surface form of "*x* is cause of *φ*-ing for *y*," or "*x* brings it about that *φy*." I am now asking whether in "*x* causes *y*," "*x*" is no less elliptical than "*y*"; the form in which Sextus normally presents his examples does not provide any answer to that question.

100. It may be objected that the difference I find between *M* and *PH* (between "*x* causes being *φ* for *y*" and "*x* causes that *φy*") is illusory: Sextus's words may *suggest* such a difference, but Sextus did not *intend* to make any distinction. That may be so; and I cannot pretend that any ancient author explicitly discusses my canonical formula, "that *ψx* brings it about that *φy*," or recognizes it as canonical. But what matters for the rest of my argument is a recognition of the conceptual complexity of causal judgments, not a recognition of the canonical formula for expressing that complexity.

101. For this mode of procedure—arguing first against the conceivability of the subject, then against its apprehensibility—see, e.g., *PH* II 29, 71; III 63, 168; *M* IX 49, 366; X 50.

102. The Greek text reads: "... causes might be thought to be inapprehensible because of the dispute. For he who says that ..." After "dispute," the Latin translation proceeds: "For some say that one thing is cause of another, some deny it, and some suspend belief. For he who says that...." The connection is abrupt, even in the Latin version: perhaps several sentences have dropped out.

103. "In general, everything thought of is conceived in one of two primary modes—either in virtue of immediate impression (περίπτωσις ἐναργής), or in virtue of transference from what is immediate; and in the latter case, in one of three ways—either by similarity or by composition or by analogy" (*M* III 40); cf. *PH* I 99, 128; III 47, 48, 50; *M* I 25; III 25; VIII 56-60; 356; IX 393-396, 438; XI 250-252. (Strictly speaking, *M* III 40 need not refer to *perceptual* apprehension (see above, n. 35), but the other passages explicitly state that the ἐναργεία in question here is perceptual.)

104. Heintz proposes: τὸ αἴτιον < ὡς αἴτιον > ἐννοῆσαι ("to conceive of the cause as cause").

105. For similar applications of the Circular Mode to show inconceivability, see *M* III 97-99 (on "plane" and "straight line"); IX 47 (on "happy" and "god"); cf., e.g., Plutarch, *Comm. not.* 1072 B.

106. "A cause is that because of which the effect [comes about] or that because of which something results (συμβαίνει τι); for it suffices [to state the matter] descriptively (ὑπογραφικῶς)" (Aetius, I 11.1). Note that the word "ἀποτέλεσμα" does not occur in the Stoic definition (above, n. 74).

107. The Humean objection might be overcome if we could take seriously Aëtius's remark that "it suffices to state the matter descriptively" (above, n. 106). The Stoics distinguished between definitions proper (ὅροι) and "descriptions" (ὑπογραφαί): DL VII 60; cf. [Galen], *Def. med.* XIX 349-350 K. (The distinction was adopted by the Empirics: Galen, *Subf. emp.* 49. 5 = F 10 b D, p. 63, 3; *Diff. puls.* VIII 708 K, 720 K = F 75 D, F 172 D.) A ὑπογραφή is an elucidatory sketch rather than an analytical account of a notion; if what I have called the Stoic "definition" of αἴτιον was meant only as a ὑπογραφή, then Hume's footnote does not bear upon it.

108. Compare the περιτροπαί at *PH* III 19, *M* 204-206, designed to show that anyone who *denies* the existence of cause overthrows himself. This style of argument was probably first employed by the Believers to attack the Skeptics (cf. *M* VII 440; VIII 470): the Skeptics borrowed the weapon and used it in their counterattack.

109. In strict truth this is not the Circular Mode of *PH* I 169: the Circular Mode applies when a Believer argues for A_1 from A_2, for A_2 from A_3, ..., for A_n from A_1; the accusation made against the Believers at *PH* III 23 is simpler: they argue for *A* on the basis of *A* itself—but "it is absurd to try to establish what is at issue by way of what is at issue" (*PH* I 61: see above, n. 57). At *PH* II 36 Sextus distinguishes this Mode from the Circular Mode: we might regard the Mode as the limiting case of Circularity—if we do not, there will be a Mode that escapes the purportedly all-embracing grasp of Agrippa.

110. The Loeb translates: "He asserts that Cause exists since there exists a cause for the existence of Cause"; that is compatible with Sextus's Greek, but not with his argument.

111. "Isn't Sextus confusing reasons with causes here? Doesn't he confuse 'There are causes that explain why *x* believes that *p'* with '*x* has reasons for believing that *p'*?" Perhaps he does (certainly, *M* IX 204-206 seems confused: Sextus slides from talking of "a reasonable cause preexisting" to speaking of a man "*moved* by some cause"); but I think that the argument at *PH* III 23 can easily be cleared of that confusion.

112. Cf. Galen, *Caus. cont.* VI 2 = *CMG Supp. or.* II, p. 137, 6-8: "We hear many asserting that this is an indemonstrable and intrinsically credible proposition, viz., that no body in any state whatever can exist without a containing cause."

113. See, e.g., Posidonius, F 158 EK = Galen, *Plac. Hipp. Plat.* V 424 K = *CMG* V 4. 1. 2, p. 288: "the causes of the abatement of the passions are not beyond conjecture, as Chrysippus used to say; in fact, they are perfectly plain—to anyone whose aim is not to rival his predecessors. For nothing is so immediate (ἐναργές) as that there are certain powers (δυνάμεις) in our souls, striving one for pleasure and the other for power and predominance; Posidonius says that they can be seen immediately (ἐναργῶς ὁρᾶσθαι) in the other animals too." Note that, according to the Logical doctors, "causes are not apparent qua causes" ([Galen], *Opt. sect.* I 120 K): if *x* causes *y*, *x* may be evident; but that *x* causes *y* is never evident (see above, n. 41).

114. Sextus opens section 26b with the sentence: "Hence (ὅθεν) some (τινες) offer this argument too." The "τινες" indicates that he is using a different source in 26b from the source for 26-26a; the "ὅθεν" seems to imply that he takes the argument of 26b-27 to be virtually the same as that of 25-26a. Whether he used a third source for *M* IX 232-236 is unclear.

115. For doctors who rejected antecedent causes see Galen, *Caus. procat.* (above, n. 76); Galen's "sophisms" do not include the consideration cited at *PH* III 16.—I have written generally of "antecedent" causes: in fact, many (but not all) ancient sources distinguish αἴτια προκαταρκτικά from αἴτια προηγούμενα, and a doctor who rejects "procatarctic" causes need not be committed to rejecting *all* antecedent causes. The distinction is not easy to make out, however; and it has no direct bearing on the Skeptical positions which this essay considers.

116. "Athenaeus [the founder of the Pneumatic school] says this: a cause is what acts (τὸ ποιοῦν), and that is the antecedent (προκαταρκτικόν) cause": [Galen], *Def. med.* XIX 392 K (for a fuller account of Athenaeus's views on causation see Galen, *Caus. cont.* 2 = *CMG Supp. or.* II, p. 134, 3-36). The view that efficient causes are antecedent goes back at least to Plato, *Phil.* 26 E (cf. Damascius, *In Phil.* 115).

117. A dyadic relation, *S*, is the converse of *R*, if and only if, for any *x* and any *y*, *xRy* if and only if *ySx*. Thus ". . . is wife of—" expresses the relation converse to ". . . is husband of—"; ". . . is cause of—" expresses the relation converse to ". . . is effect of—."

118. If "brings it about that" is not a dyadic relation, properly speaking (see above, nn. 96, 98), then the earlier argument will need to be modified; but the truth of (2b) is not seriously in question.

119. "What if *x* unsuccessfully exercises its powers? Suppose the eagle misses,

what then?" In that case the causal proposition is false, and no question arises about the relation between t_1 and t_2.

120. If $t_1 = t_3$, then $t_2 = t_1 = t_3$; i.e., t_2 is an instant, not a stretch, of time in this limiting case.

121. "Then surely proposition (2b) turns out false; for it ascribes a date to the act of causing." No: (2b) remains true, but vacuously true.

122. An infant form of this paper was prepared for a Balliol Reading Party at the Chalet des Mélèzes; parts of the adolescent version were read to the B Club at Cambridge, and to a seminar at the University of Liverpool: on all three occasions I gained much from the critical comments of my audience. The argument of Part III owes a lot to the patient and subtle advice of Malcolm Schofield and Jim Hankinson—though neither, I fear, will be wholly satisfied with my final version. I am further indebted to Jim Hankinson for his kindness in checking a multitude of references for me. My greatest debt is to Myles Burnyeat: his detailed comments saved me from numerous errors; his editorial encouragement was a constant comfort; and it was his example—and his exhortations—which first led me to explore the lovely landscapes of later Greek philosoph: for all that, and more, my thanks.

8

Augustine against the Skeptics

Christopher Kirwan

THE DIALOGUE *CONTRA ACADEMICOS*

Augustine's attack on skepticism is largely confined to the *Contra Academicos*, his earliest surviving work, which he composed at the time of choosing between Christianity and pagan Neoplatonism. Fourteen years before, when he was an eighteen-year-old student at Carthage, Cicero's now lost protreptic *Hortensius* had attracted him to the pursuit of wisdom (*Conf.* III 4.7, *BV* I 4). He resolved, according to the account in the *Confessions*, "to bend my mind to the Holy Scriptures, to see what they were like. . . . But they seemed to me unworthy of comparison with the dignity of Tully" (*Conf.* III 5.9). There is little doubt that he was at that time already under the influence of Manichaeism, a religion which, while honoring Christ and St. Paul, derided the inconsistencies and crudities of the Bible, and especially the Old Testament. But the positive doctrines of Mani, which correspondingly claimed the authority of reason, gradually lost their hold on Augustine (*Conf.* V 6.10-7.13) until, some ten years later, "there began to arise in me the thought that those philosophers whom they call Academics were wiser than the rest, because they held that everything ought to be doubted, and they declared that no truth can be apprehended by man" (*Conf.* V 10.19, cf. *CA* III 20.43). That was in Rome in A.D. 383 or 384. There followed exposure to Neoplatonism (*CA* II 2.5, *Conf.* VII 13.26) and, connectedly (cf. *Ep.* VI 1), conversion to Christianity in 386 at Milan. Shortly afterward Augustine retired with some friends to a country villa at Cassiciacum, where the *Contra Academicos* was written. His conversion had had a strongly intellectual element. Confidence in reason reasserted itself together with a new conviction, perhaps due to Ambrose (*Conf.* VI 4.6), that the Bible could be defended (*Conf.* VII 21.27), a conviction that was to shape much of his subsequent literary output. At the end of his life he wrote of the *Contra Academicos*, "My purpose was to rid my mind, with the strongest reasoning I could, of the arguments (argumenta) of those who cause many to despair of finding truth. . . . For these arguments were also influencing me" (*R* I 1.1, cf. *Ep.* I 3, *Trin.* XV 12.21).

Augustine did not read Greek, or not until later in life (Bonner, Appendix A). His knowledge of the skeptical Academic philosophy was drawn mainly, perhaps only, from Cicero, and therefore mainly from Cicero's *Academica* (though evidently also the *Hortensius*, *CA* III 14.31). It is not possible to tell which of the two editions of that work was known to him, whether the first from which our Book II or "Lucullus" or *Prior Academics* survives, or the second incorporating our Book I or "Varro" or *Posterior Academics* (O'Meara, p. 156, n. 57). The plan of Augustine's response to Cicero in the *Contra Academicos* is loose. His Book I premises that the wise man alone is happy and asks whether wisdom consists in finding truth or in seeking it. Book II expounds the doctrine of the Academy that "philosophical" knowledge is impossible ("Nor is it possible for a man to achieve knowledge, at any rate of those things that pertain to philosophy," *CA* II 5.11) and that the wise man will assent to nothing (ibid.). Some objections are brought, but the main reply is reserved to a long discourse which Augustine puts into his own mouth and which occupies most of the final Book III (*CA* III 7.15-20.43).

Though ill read and sometimes artless as a philosopher, Augustine had an aptitude for philosophical controversy, which he conducted with commendable intellectual honesty. Several of his arguments in the *Contra Academicos* are well worth examining. I shall look at three of them. The third will lead eventually beyond that dialogue into regions where Augustine appears to be a remarkable pioneer.

THE ARGUMENT FROM BEATITUDE

In Book I of the *Contra Academicos* Licentius, who takes the skeptic's side, asserts that the search for truth, if conducted in the best possible way, will suffice to produce the only happiness that is proper to man: "The end of a man is to seek the truth perfectly" (*CA* I 3.9). "In that case," responds Trygetius, "a man cannot be happy. For how could he be, since he cannot attain (*assequi*) what he greatly desires? Yet a man can (*potest*) live happily. . . . Therefore he can find the truth (*verum*). Otherwise he must get a grip on himself and not desire the truth, to avoid the necessity of being miserable because he has not been able to attain it" (*CA* I 3.9). Both parties agree that this last alternative will not work: a man who abandons his desire for the truth will not be happy either. So it is a premise of the argument that

(1) Every happy man greatly desires the truth.

The other premises are

(2) Men can be happy;

(3) No man can be happy if there is something he greatly desires but cannot attain.

Let us take the conclusion as weakly as possible: "Some men can attain some truth." Is the argument a good one? A crude defense might go as follows. Suppose the conclusion's contradictory, that no man can attain any truth. Then by (3) all who greatly desire any truth will be unhappy. Hence by (1) all who are happy will be unhappy, that is, no one will be happy, contrary to (2). One objection to this defense is that its outcome is *not* contrary to (2), which only says that some men, perhaps all men, have a capacity for happiness. Even with the stronger of these two readings it seems that the argument will not go through. For if we construe (2) as "All men have a capacity for happiness" and (3) as

(3a) No man has a capacity for happiness if any of his strong desires are unfulfillable,

it will follow only that every *happy* man can attain some truth: the possibility will not be excluded that no men are happy. One way of meeting the objection is to read into (2) the stronger sense "Some men are happy," taking its "potest" for "some." Then the argument is valid. But is (3a) true? It is tempting to suppose that Augustine would have supported it with the thesis that

(T) No man is happy if any of his strong desires are unfulfilled.

But this support is illusory. For suppose none of us happy with any strong desires unfulfilled; we might still be capable of happiness though some of our strong desires are incapable of fulfillment, since we might still have the recourse of abandoning the unfulfillable desires. Just so it might be that in a perfect sports meeting everyone who jumps four feet jumps five feet, even though there is a sports meeting that could be perfect (by Billy Bunter's withdrawal from it) at which not everyone who does jump four feet can jump five feet—Bunter does and can't. So (T) does not entail (3a).

This prompts the suggestion that premise (3) of the argument should be understood differently, as

(3b) Happiness is incompatible with the presence of unfulfillable
desires.

(3b) does not entail (3a); the desires in (3a) would have to be, in addition,
ineliminable. But this does not matter, because (3b) itself validates the
argument, and could easily be the intended meaning of (3): we merely
have to take its "can" with wide scope, so that (3) proposes unhappiness
as a necessary consequence rather than necessary unhappiness as a consequence. Moreover, (2) can now be weakened to "Some men are capable
of happiness" without forfeiting validity, provided that (1) and (3b) are
taken as necessary truths, and "it can be" is cancelable from "it can be
that some men can attain some truth."

But is even (3b) really true? I suppose that Augustine, with his keen
sense of the affinity between love of truth and love of women, might well
have thought so (cf. *LA* II 13.35, and *Sol.* I 13.22, "[Wisdom] which . . .
you desire to see and hold as it were naked, without any veil intervening"): there is no joy in a hopeless passion. Unfortunately such a line of
thought is still not cogent, unless it presupposes (T). If we count it no bar
to happiness that an object of passion is unattained, there will still be no
bar, surely, if the object is unattainable, so long as the lover thinks otherwise. This last is not enough for (3b); or if we imagine that it is enough,
then the argument from it is no longer valid: we may only infer, unexcit-
ingly, that some men think they can attain some truth.

However, if (T) itself were asserted as a premise, the argument would
go through; and (T) is asserted in a version of the argument from *De
beata vita*, a dialogue whose setting and composition belong to the same
months as the *Contra Academicos*. There the Academics are offered a
choice of three consequences if they deny the attainability of truth. They
must either give up desire for the truth, or allow that a wise man need not
be happy, or treat as happy the man who lacks what he most ardently
wishes to have (*BV* II 15). The premises thus become:

Every happy man greatly desires the truth;

Some men can be wise, and all the wise are happy;

(T) All who are happy and greatly desire something have
attained it.

As before, it does follow that truth is attainable by some men, provided
that all these premises are taken as necessary.

An earlier section of *De beata vita* is plausibly read as asserting (T)
while denying its converse: "So is this agreed between us, I said, that no
one can be happy who does not have what he wants, though not everyone who has what he wants is happy? They granted it" (*BV* II 10). Denial
of the converse is later retracted, on the ground that what makes fulfilled
desire for something unsatisfactory is nothing but fear of its loss (*BV* II

11), and the fear is itself a kind of unfulfilled desire (*BV* IV 27). But (T) itself has meanwhile been questioned, with the suggestion that he who seeks the truth has God on his side, which is enough for happiness even without possession of the truth that is sought (*BV* III 20). Augustine's response is to reject the claim that all who have God on their side are happy (*BV* III 21).

Plainly, the little argument in *CA* I 3.9 needs some such assistance as is offered by the sister dialogue in defense of (T). And it is perhaps an innovation that Augustine sees the need of such assistance, since earlier thinkers, in the Aristotelian, Stoic, and skeptical traditions alike, had tended to assume that the only profitable response to the discovery of obstacles in the way of getting what one desires is to trim the desires. Nevertheless I find the assistance inadequate. We may admit that God's favor is not enough on its own: the important thing for happiness is to feel that you have that favor, or in some similar way to feel supported or self-confident, and hopeful. But it is wrong, as Tolstoy saw, to think that a happy man must have achieved his major goals.

Later in Book I we find the suggestion that wisdom is the knowledge of those human and divine things that pertain to a happy life (*CA* I 7.23). Perhaps this stems from the thought that you cannot be happy without the security of knowing that your projects really do conduce to happiness, a thought which makes the intellectual project of discovering wherein happiness consists special among a man's projects in needing to be accomplished before the man can be happy. I do not claim to have blocked that interesting route to the thesis that the attainment of some truth is necessary for happiness, but only the route from the premise that *desire* for some truth is necessary for it.

THE ARGUMENT FROM VERISIMILITUDE

Two arguments in the *Contra Academicos* concern credibility. In the second, Alypius puts forward the view that wise men have possession of things they have found approvable or credible ("Inventorum probabilium habitus," *CA* III 3.5), but do not know anything. Augustine gets him to retract this on the ground that wise men must know wisdom ("Si inveniri . . . sapiens . . . queat, poteat . . . scire sapientiam," *CA* III 4.9; cf. Cicero, *Acad.* II 24). The argument is confused and unconvincing, and its conclusion, that if there is no knowledge there is no wisdom, does no more than dent the bodywork of the Academic bulldozer.

The earlier of the two arguments is more interesting. Academics describe the credible as "like a truth" ("Probabile . . . scisne ab ipsis etiam verisimile nominari?" *CA* II 7.16; the Latin idiom "verisimile" is due to Cicero, *Acad.* II 32). If someone who had never seen your father asserted, on seeing your brother, that he was like your father, you would take him for a madman or a fool (*CA* II 7.16). In the same way the Academics make themselves ridiculous when they say that in life they follow the likeness of a truth ("Veri similitudinem sequi") although they do not know what the truth itself is ("Ipsum verum quid sit ignorent," *CA* II 7.19). To this the Academics are made to reply with an alternative, ostensive, definition of "credible": we expect a fine day after a bright night, and credible things are "like that" (*CA* II 11.26). But Licentius suggests that even the new definition can be applied only by comparison with instances of knowledge (*CA* II 12.27, cf. Cicero, *Acad.* II 32-34); and although the suggestion is received with scorn (CA II 12.28), Augustine continues to be attracted by the thesis it supports (*CA* III 18.40, and cf. *Sol.* I 2.7).

The thesis comes from Plato: "Whenever someone on seeing a thing thinks 'This that I now see wants to be like some other thing there is, but falls short of it and cannot be like it, but is inferior,' is it not necessary that he who thinks this should have known beforehand that thing which he says this one resembles but falls short of?" (*Phaedo* 74d9-e4). If the thought on seeing x "x falls short of y" requires previous knowledge of y, then so, clearly, does the implied thought "but x does (somewhat) resemble y." It is the latter requirement that Augustine takes over from Plato, and illustrates by the case of Licentius's father. I begin by examining the illustration.

"So that's Licentius's brother. How like Romanianus!" No one would seriously wish to say that a sane man making this remark must have *met* Romanianus. The thesis is that he must already know him, and in particular know how he looks. Moreover it is not asserted that the only way of getting to know that two people look alike is from knowledge of the looks of both. Augustine, like Plato, stresses that the route to knowledge of similarity requires knowledge of one of the similars *when* it is through knowledge of the other ("Fratrem tuum visum," *CA* II 7.16). Yet Licentius was right to deny (*CA* II 7.16) even this restricted claim, for there are cases of telling from how just one thing looks that it is part of a matching pair, or that something else, with whose looks one is not yet acquainted, matches it. For example, previous inspection of the outside of your garage block may allow me to infer, on entering your left garage, that your right garage is the same size and shape. The more natural expression of the knowledge so acquired would be "So your other garage must be just like this one"; but you would hardly mark me down as a madman if I chose instead to say "So this garage must be just like your other one."

In addition to this objection, there are problems about applying Plato's thesis to Augustine's purpose. Absurdity is supposed to arise from the Academic proposal to follow the verisimile while not knowing the verum ("Ipsum verum ignorare," *CA* II 6.15; "Verum . . . non novimus," II 9.20) or not knowing what the verum is ("Quid sit," *CA* II 7.19, 12.27). A complicated ambiguity lurks here, for we need to distinguish three possible conditions under which the Academic will assent to a proposition *P*: (a) he finds *P* like some truth or other, (b) he finds *P* like some particular truth, or (c) there exists some particular truth that he finds *P* like (cf. Grice, p. 145; Ackrill, pp. 194-195). (b) and (c) are genuinely analogous to the Romanianus illustration, where there is or is thought to be some particular person Romanianus to whom the young man present is found similar. But only (a) imputes a sensible procedure to the Academic. If we now consider the ignorance of verum which is supposed incompatible with that procedure, it follows that the ignorance cannot be of *that* true proposition whose likeness it is proposed to follow, since no such proposition is identifiable. Nor, in spite of the "quid sit," does it seem likely that Augustine means ignorance of what truth is. For one thing, that would be "ignorare veritatem," and Augustine is careful elsewhere to distinguish veritas from verum (*Sol.* I 15.27). For another, no defense is offered, or available, for the tacit inference that would then be required from "You know what truth is" to "You know some truths." Nothing remains then, against the Academic who opts for policy (a), but to construe his vaunted ignorance of verum, on Augustine's behalf, as ignorance of all true propositions: in fact, ignorance.

In view of this, a better analogy with the Academic claim would be, not regarding someone as like Romanianus while not knowing Romanianus, but regarding something as like, say, a bell while not knowing *any* bells. Why should that be thought impossible? We might try, forlornly, to help Augustine as follows. No one finds things alike without finding them alike in some, perhaps inarticulable, respect, such as shape or pitch, or more generally looks or sound. Suppose I am woken by what sounds to me like a bell. If that is to be a true description, I do not need, admittedly, to be acquainted with any bells, for no bells need exist or even be thought by me to exist. But I do need to know how a bell sounds, that is, how at least some bells would sound if there were any. If we now ask the Academic in what respect the propositions he assents to are required to be like a truth, he will answer merely that they must seem or appear true (cf. Cicero, *Acad.* II 33-34). Then what follows is that he needs to know how a truth would seem if there were any. But this, unfortunately for Augustine, he can do without having knowledge of truths, indeed without there being any truths for him to know.

WITHHOLDING ASSENT

We now come to Augustine's main attack on skepticism, in which he separates its two traditional elements of denying knowledge and prescribing what the Greeks called *epochē*, suspension of judgment. The long speech in Book III of the *Contra Academicos* attends to these elements successively, drawing sometimes on material from earlier chapters. Since my comments on the second element can be brief, I shall start with it.

The prescription of *epochē* is put forward as a consequence of the thesis about knowledge: "If [one] assented to uncertain things, one would necessarily be in error (erret necesse est), which is forbidden to the wise man" (*CA* II 5.11, cf. I 3.7). Since not all assent to the uncertain leads into error, this looks to be at best an argument against habitual assent (cf. Cicero, *Acad.* II 67). Probably Augustine, who was in some confusion about the nature of error (*CA* I 4.10-12), means "errare" here in the sense of "risk error" (cf. Cicero, *Acad.* II 66; Plutarch, *Adv. Col.* 1122b). If so, the argument for *epochē* he has in mind runs as follows:

It is unwise to risk error;
He who assents to what he does not know risks error;
No one knows anything;
So it is unwise for anyone to assent to anything.

The argument is valid. But Augustine rightly attacks its first premise, in a response that is none the less sound for being rhetorical and scornful. He points to Carneades' concession (Cicero, *Acad.* II 99, cf. ibid. II 104) that without some surrogate for assent—such as following the credible (*CA* III 15.34)—it is possible neither to act (e.g., to journey past a road junction, *CA* III 15.33-34) nor to settle disputes (e.g., in litigation, *CA* III 16. 35-36). Action risks error, and so does judgment by imputing it. But abstention from action is impossible, and from judgment absurd. So the risk of error is unavoidable, and cannot be forbidden to the wise man. In sum, withholding assent fails to secure the very advantage that the argument urged in its favor.

So understood, this is a thoroughly successful rejoinder, demolishing the supposedly Academic premise that it is unwise to risk error. But it has to be noticed that Augustine assumes, what Descartes may have wished away, that the seeker after truth lives in the real world where he must act and judge; so he is not a Pure Enquirer in the sense introduced by Bernard Williams (*Descartes*, pp. 46 ff.). It is also worth remark that there was another Academic argument for withholding assent apparently unknown to Augustine, namely, "from the conflict of arguments" (Diogenes Laertius IV 28).

KNOWLEDGE: THE AGREED CONDITIONS

In the remainder of this essay I shall examine Augustine's major argument against the Academic assertion that knowledge of interesting, "philosophical," matters is unattainable. The argument rests on what Augustine calls Zeno's definition, known in earlier antiquity as the Stoic criterion of truth, and goes as follows:

(4) Zeno's definition gives a sufficient condition of knowledge;
(5) Its definiens is satisfied by some things pertaining to philosophy;
   Therefore there is knowledge of some things pertaining to philosophy.

(4) is stated at *CA* III 9.21: "I for my part do not see how to refute [Zeno's definition], and I judge it to be entirely true." (5) is supported by various instances put forward by Augustine as satisfying the definiens, which are of two types: necessary truths—for example, "The world is either one or not one" (*CA* III 10.23)—and subjective truths—for example, "This smells delightful to me" (*CA* III 11.26).

He rightly sees his argument as having a dual role: it purports not only to prove that there is knowledge but also to show what is wrong with a famous Academic proof that there is not. That proof, set out in *CA* II 5.11, relied on the denial of (5) and took Zeno's definition as a necessary condition of knowledge. Thus Augustine's assertion of (5) both rebuts the Academic proof and has a place in his own counterproof.

In Augustine's treatment, as in that of his predecessors, the question answered by Zeno's definition contains some obscurities, and the answer is variously formulated. I begin with two remarks about the question. First, in the modern philosophical sense of "criterion" it asks for a criterion not of truth but of knowledge; for the definition offers not conditions, nor even recognizable conditions, for being true but rather conditions for recognizing or perceiving something to be true. "Perceive" covers more than sense-perception (cf. *Sol.* I 4.9, "Do you perceive these things by the senses or the intellect?"). Like Cicero before him, Augustine uses "perceptio" interchangeably with "comprehensio" (apprehension), which is Cicero's translation of the technical Stoic term "*katalēpsis*" (*Acad.* I 41, II 18; cf. John 1:5, "And the darkness comprehended it not," quoted by Augustine in a comparison with Neoplatonism at *Conf.* VII 9.13). He also assumes, unlike the Stoics (Cicero, *Acad.* I 42, and cf. *CA* I 7.19), that perception and apprehension are the same as knowledge (cf. Cicero, *Acad.* II 83, "There are four heads which purport to prove that nothing can be known, perceived or apprehended"). Second, the objects of perception are not described as propositions, in spite of the expectation aroused by Augustine's mode of exemplifying them (e.g., "This smells delightful to me," *CA* III 11.26). Usually he leaves their nature unspecified; but two versions of the definition give them as *visa*, appearances or presentations (*CA* III 9.18, 9.21), following Cicero's translation of another Stoic technical term, *"phantasia"* (*Acad.* I 40, II 18). In this, Augustine is once more following the main tradition: Cicero tells us that the Academics constructed, at no less length than the Stoics, an art of presentations ("Artem quandam de iis quae visa dicimus") in which their force and kinds were defined, and especially the nature of that which can be perceived and apprehended (*Acad.* II 40). The tradition had been interrupted by one Academic, Arcesilaus, who held that the criterion of truth was concerned with assent, which could be given only to propositions (*axiōmata*) and not *phantasiai* (Sextus, *M* VII 154); but we shall see that Augustine can evade this objection.

So the question is: Under what conditions will a presentation be perceived? Augustine in effect lays down two further conditions for perception—in addition to what is perceived being a presentation—the first of which is that the presentation be true. This is sufficiently obvious from his earliest formulation, where perception of a truth is defined as if no other kind of perception is thereby omitted (*CA* II 5.11). He also directly asserts that there cannot be knowledge of falsehoods: "Everyone is agreed that there cannot be knowledge of false things" (*CA* III 3.5, cf. 9.21). But what is truth in presentations? A presentation is something impressed on the mind by a feature in the world, which is its source ("Animo impressum ex eo unde esset," *CA* II 5.11). Between the impression and the feature there is a *relation* of truth when the impression presents the feature as it is; and an impression has the *property* of truth when it stands in that relation to its source (cf. Sextus, *M* VII 168). The relation was sometimes taken as symmetrical, so that Cicero can speak of a presentation "impressed from a true source" ("Impressum e vero," *Acad.* II 112). There is a tacit analogy here with such things as pictures, maps, and sentences. The representation on page 37 of my atlas might be true to Brazil, not at all true to Bulgaria; it will be true *simpliciter* if it is true to what it is a representation of. Of course the analogy is misleading in various ways. Information will flow from a map or a sentence, as from a witness, only if those sources are, so to speak, audible and intelligible as well as accurate. But a presentation is conceived as something that cannot fail to be "read" correctly: although even a true one can deceive a man, that must be because he distrusts its truth, not because he scans it incompetently or is ignorant of the mode (whether natural or conventional) in which it represents. In view of these peculiarities we may well wonder whether there are such things, as we may about sense-data. On the other hand it seems possible to interpret the project for an "art of presentations" innocuously. Understand "the presentation that *p* is true," sc. to its source, as meaning "it is presented that *p* because it is (from its being) true that *p*"; and understand "it is presented" to mean "it appears, or seems." Both these interpretations may well have been assumed by Augustine: for the past participle "visum" (unlike the Greek abstract noun *"phantasia"*) naturally refers to features or states of the world, not of the mind; and its derivation (like that of *"phantasia"*) from the common verb for "seem" gives little positive encouragement to the idea of a representative medium or mental correlate of external things.

If this is right, we can see the function of *visa* in Augustine's Zenonian definition as follows. If I perceive or know something, it must appear to me, and appear because it is true. So much, according to Cicero, had been admitted by those Peripatetics who said we can perceive what is impressed from a true source (*Acad.* II 112). The something will be a state of affairs, which might be identified with a proposition as Arcesilaus wanted. But already in Plato's *Theaetetus* we find roughly these two conditions rejected as insufficient; for, so far as seeming can be identified with being believed, and in spite of the causal connection they impute between seeming and being (which is absent from Plato), the two conditions fail to distinguish knowledge from certain kinds of lucky guess. We need, as Cicero says against his Peripatetics, some "magna accessio" (*Acad.* II 112), some important extra. It is the purpose of Zeno's definition to supply the extra.

KNOWLEDGE: ZENO'S CONDITION

Unfortunately the final, and controversial, condition of knowledge is expressed by Augustine in several different ways, all with precedents in the tradition. Initially he puts it like this: "[Zeno] says that that truth can be perceived, which is so impressed on the mind from the source it is from that it could not be from a source it is not from" ("Ait id verum percipi posse, quod ita esset animo impressum et eo unde esset, ut esse non posset ex eo unde non esset," *CA* II 5.11). Suppose it appears to Socrates that the leaves are quivering. Could the appearance have been caused by anything else? Since it is doubtful whether any particular event could have had a different cause, let us take the question to ask about the *actual* cause of *similar* events ("could not" in its generalizing sense): are suchlike appearances ever caused by states of affairs that are not suchlike? Well, evidently they are; and since Augustine agrees with the Academics in understanding Zeno's definition to constitute also a necessary condition of knowledge ("It is manifest that nothing else comes to be perceived," *CA* III 9.21), he would in this case have us deny to Socrates, I believe, the knowledge that the leaves are quivering. The reasoning that leads to such a denial seems to be as follows: F-type appearances come from sources that are not F-type if and only if those appearances are false (to their sources); and if an appearance, even a true one, belongs to a type with some false members, there's no knowing that it is not false itself. We find the reasoning in Cicero's comment on a formulation very close to this one of Augustine's: "We claim that that definition of Zeno's is quite correct, for who can apprehend anything so as to make you fully confident that it is perceived and known, if it is such as even a false one could be?" (". . . quod est tale quale vel falsum esse possit?" *Acad.* II 18; cf. "of the same kind," ibid. II 77; also ibid. II 40-41, 84, 112, Sextus, *M* VII 248, 252).

The Zenonian objection against a claim to knowledge can be met if the truth perceived is unlike every falsehood (cf. "Let Carneades show that *that* opinion [the number of worlds is finite or infinite] is like any false one!" *CA* III 10.23; ibid. III 12.27; Cicero, *Acad.* II 83, Sextus, *M* VII 164) and the unlikeness is detectable (cf. "It is so true that it can be distinguished from the false by unlike marks," *CA* II 6.14; also *CA* III 10.23, Cicero, *Acad.* II 90). In order to detect unlikeness we need a sign (signum, nota), and that is what Sextus has in mind when he reports the Stoics as asserting that "anyone who has an apprehensive presentation comes systematically in contact with the actual differences of things, since a presentation of that kind has some such peculiarity (*idiōma*) in comparison with others, like the horned snakes in comparison with other snakes" (*M* VII 252, cf. Cicero, *Acad.* II 84). Augustine concurs in the same requirement, continuing his first formulation of Zeno's definition, "Put more briefly and plainly, a truth can be apprehended by signs which cannot be possessed by anything false" ("His signis verum posse comprehendi, quae signa non potest habere quod falsum est," *CA* II 5.11). Since the efficacy of a sign depends on its being recognized as such, "cannot" here, as often in Cicero, needs to have an epistemic sense, "manifestly are not." I take Augustine to mean that the signs must be such that it is manifest that they belong to no falsehoods. This is the sense in which they must be distinguishing.

DOES ANYTHING PHILOSOPHICAL
SATISFY THE CONDITIONS?

A full examination of Augustine's epistemology would next inquire whether such distinguishing signs are, as he supposes, necessary for knowledge. Doubtless they are not. On the other hand their sufficiency, when they are conjoined with the uncontroversial conditions, is plain enough, and that is all that Augustine need assert, in premise (4), for his argument against the Academics. I pass therefore to premise (5).

Augustine sets himself to find not just instances of knowledge but instances that "pertain to philosophy" (*CA* II 5.11). Although his own discussion often ignores the restriction, he revives it in Book III, chapters 10-13, where Carneades is once more cited as concerning himself only with what philosophers inquire into ("Quae inter philosophos inquirun-tur," *CA* III 10.22). What is the force of this? In Carneades the restriction may have been dialectical, for the sake of argument. In Augustine's treat-ment it comes to little. He divides philosophy into physics, ethics, and dialectic, but allows subjective truths into the first two divisions and necessary truths into all three. Whether his instances would have passed muster with Carneades we cannot say, because the source of the ascrip-tion to Carneades is unknown. I shall give Augustine the benefit of this doubt, only remarking that subjective truths had not generally been cited on either side in earlier controversy about the existence of knowledge (Burnyeat, pp. 37 ff.).

On premise (5), and there alone, Augustine sees himself in contest with the Academics. He will win the contest if he finds a "philosophical" truth which, when—at least sometimes when—presented, is presented in con-junction with *some* sign manifestly *not* shared by any falsehood. He doesn't win, because he doesn't keep his eye on the ball. To begin with, *CA* III 9.18 misreports Zeno's definition as requiring only "is presented with *no* sign that *is* shared by any falsehood" ("Quale cum falso non haberet signa communia"): love-fifteen. Then in one of several limping discussions of self-refutation he claims that the definition will itself be an instance, satisfying its own condition for perceptibility, provided that it cannot be *shown* to be capable of falsity (". . . ostendas eam etiam falsam esse posse," *CA* III 9.21): love-thirty. He rallies at *CA* III 10.23, claiming to have found "disjunctions" that *have nothing* in common with a false-hood: fifteen-thirty. Better still, no one can *confuse* them with any like-ness to the false ("Nec similitudine aliqua falsi ea potest quisquam con-fundere," *CA* III 10.23): thirty all. Now it might seem that once we are given some truth that cannot be confused with—that is, mistaken for—a falsehood, we have a truth that can be distinguished as true, and Augus-tine is well on the way to victory. But "cannot be mistaken for a false-hood" is ambiguous as to the scope of both "cannot" and "mistaken" (cf. "The Argument from Verisimilitude," above). If Augustine means to say about each of his instances—for example, "the world is either one or not one"—that there is no falsehood it can be mistaken for, he may be right; perhaps the proposition is not misidentifiable. Yet its truth value might still be inscrutable. Augustine is not entitled to infer, as the trend of his argument requires, that such a proposition cannot be *mistaken for false*. Moreover, "cannot be mistaken for false" is still ambiguous, between "cannot be taken for false (which would be an error)" and "cannot be erroneously taken for false." That is, we have to ask whether Augustine means that his propositions cannot both *be* true and be taken for false, or both *are* true and cannot be taken for false. For necessary truths these conditions are equivalent, but for contingent truths like "This seems white to me" (*CA* III 11.26) the former may hold without the latter. We find the latter, stronger condition in yet another of his formulations of Zeno's definition: "That presentation can be apprehended which so appears that it cannot appear false" (*CA* III 9.21; here "cannot" means what it says).

Let us pause for review. Augustine has begun unpropitiously by looking for propositions having no sign in common with any falsehood, or even for propositions not provably capable of falsehood. I take him to be correcting these lapses when he substitutes the condition "unconfusable with any falsehood"; but the condition is still weaker than Zeno's. By a scope fallacy he then tacitly infers that what satisfies the condition will be incapable of being taken for false; with this fallacy the score moves to thirty-forty. Nevertheless we cannot be sure that the fallacy has led him yet into error. Since his specimen necessary truths are all simple (cf. Descartes, *Second Replies,* AT VII, p. 125) and his specimen contingent truths are subjective, it is a defensible view that none of them can be taken for false—that is, disbelieved—or even doubted: they compel assent. What he needs, then, is a reason for treating indubitability, or unrejectability, as a sign of truth. But unlike Descartes, Augustine offers us no such reason; so the game goes to the Academics.

DOES "SUM" SATISFY THE CONDITIONS?

In looking for propositions that compel assent and cannot be doubted, Augustine was following in the Stoic tradition (Sextus, *M* VII 257). His well-known adumbrations of Descartes's "cogito ergo sum" (see Gilson, pp. 191-201) seem to be original. Even if Descartes thought it impossible to doubt one's own existence, it was not that feature that he exploited in the *Second Meditation* but rather the fact that a man's doubt of, or other mental attitude toward, the proposition that he exists ensures that the proposition is true ("Quoties a me . . . mente concipitur necessario esse verum," "As often as it is mentally conceived by me it is necessarily true," AT VII 25). Likewise when Augustine offers "I am," "I am alive," and "I think" as instances of knowledge, he eschews mention of literal indubitability. These instances are absent from the *Contra Academicos* (perhaps as "not pertaining to philosophy"—Carneades is made to concede knowledge that he is a man and not an ant, *CA* III 10.22); but they occur, without argument, in works from the same period (*BV* II 7, *Sol.* II 1.1). An argument appears in the *De Trinitate*: "Even if someone doubts, he is alive... if he doubts, he thinks... therefore whoever doubts on another matter ought to doubt about none of these things; if they were not [true], he could not doubt about anything" (*Trin.* X 10.14). Such doubts ought to be dispelled, then, because it is a condition of their existence that they be unfounded. We must notice that this is presented as an argument against *epochē*, not as a proof of knowledge.

A passage in *De vera religione* has an even more limited purpose, aiming to establish not that there are some truths one ought not to doubt but that one ought not to doubt that there are some truths: "Everyone who observes (intelligit) himself doubting observes a truth (verum), and about that which he observes he is certain; therefore he is certain about a truth. Everyone therefore who doubts whether truth exists (utrum sit veritas) has in himself a truth on which not to doubt.... Hence one who can doubt at all ought not to doubt about [the existence of] truth" (*VR* XXXIX 73). Let us call the man who doubts about the existence of truth, that is, whether there are truths, an *ephektikos*. The argument appears to rest on the assumption that one who is certain of anything ought not to be *ephektikos*. But this is admissible only if the "ought" has wide scope, that is, as saying that it would be inconsistent, and so wrong, to be both certain of some truth and doubtful whether there are truths ("of some *truth*" is actually redundant). The assumption so understood, namely,

(6) One ought not to be both certain of some truth and *ephektikos*

will validate Augustine's argument if it is joined by two others:

(7) If someone is doubtful (about anything), it follows that he is certain he is doubtful,

and

(8) What follows from something that ought to be, ought itself to be.

Since if someone is doubtful it follows trivially that it is true that he is doubtful, we can infer from (7) that if someone is doubtful it follows that he is certain of some truth. From that we can infer, by simple modal logic, that if he is not both certain of some truth and *ephektikos*, it follows that he is not both doubtful and *ephektikos*; and hence (because he cannot be *ephektikos* without being doubtful about something) that he is not *ephektikos* at all. Since by (6) one ought not to be both certain of some truth and *ephektikos,* we can finally infer by (8) that one ought not to be *ephektikos* at all. Unfortunately for Augustine's argument, (7) is a bad epistemological principle and (8) is a bad deontic principle; and I do not see ways of dispensing with them on his behalf.

In any case we are looking in these later treatises for more than an argument against *epochē;* and Augustine does not indicate a route of advance from "ought not to be doubted" to "is known." The route which Descartes's "ergo" formulations misleadingly suggest—to exhibit a proof of "sum" in demonstration of its provability and so knowability—is not available from the starting point of doubt about "sum." For suppose a man follows the method apparently recommended by Descartes, and succeeds in doubting (and not believing) his own existence. At the time of doubting he does not know that he exists, for one of the conditions of knowledge, belief, is absent. But when the doubt is dispelled by recognition of its groundlessness, he no longer has the extra premise with which to pass by *modus ponens* from "If I doubt my existence, I exist" to "I exist." Moreover, this Cartesian characteristic of "sum" and "vivo" and "cogito" and "dubito," that doubts about them ensure their truth, is not shared by two other propositions put into the same bag by Augustine, "I want to be happy" and "I do not want to err" (*Trin.* XV 12.21). What all these do have in common is that *belief* in them ensures their truth; they cannot be believed erroneously. Two passages directed explicitly against the Academics make use of this feature. In *De Trinitate* Augustine bids us say "against the Academics not 'I know I'm not mad' but 'I know I'm alive.' So one who says he knows he is alive can never be deceived (falli) nor a liar (mentiri). Therefore let a thousand kinds of deceptive presentation be urged against one who says 'I know I'm alive'; none of them will frighten him, since even a man who is deceived is alive" (*Trin.* XV 12.21; cf. *DA* X 13). The other, and well-known, passage comes from the *City of God* and runs in part as follows:

Against these truths the arguments of the Academics are no terror, when they say "What if you are deceived?" For if I am deceived, I am. For one who is not, assuredly cannot be deceived; and because of this I am, if I am deceived. Because, therefore, I am if I am deceived, how am I deceived [in thinking] that I am, when it is certain that I am if I am deceived? Because, therefore, I who was deceived would be, even if I were deceived, it is beyond doubt that I am not deceived in that I know myself to be. [*CD* XI 26]

In these places, as G. B. Matthews has shown, Augustine is not "using *modus ponens* to establish the conclusion that he exists" (Matthews, p. 163); the conclusion is that he cannot erroneously believe he exists (or is alive). The argument for that conclusion contains an explicit premise "Si fallor, sum,"

(9) If Augustine believes something erroneously, he exists
(cf. *LA* II 3.7 for its contrapositive; both passages were alleged by Mersenne to anticipate Descartes: Gilson, pp. 191-192), and a tacit premise,
  (10) If Augustine exists, he does not believe erroneously that
       he exists.
From (9) and (10) it follows that if any of Augustine's beliefs are erroneous, belief that he exists is not; hence if that one is erroneous, it is not; hence it is not. The premises are generalizable and necessary. So the conclusion is generalizable and necessary: *no one can* believe erroneously that he exists (compare the similar reconstruction in Matthews, p. 162).

We may now finally ask, though Augustine himself does not ask, whether "sum" and the other examples in these passages satisfy Zeno's condition for knowledge. Of course if a proposition has the features that (a) it is believed by someone and (b) it cannot be erroneously believed by that person, then it is true: the features are jointly possessed by no falsehood. The question we have to consider, though, is whether the features can be a "distinguishing sign" of the truth of Augustine's examples. In order to be a sign, the features must be manifest in those examples; and in order to be a distinguishing sign in the required sense, it must be manifest that no falsehood possesses them. The former condition is fulfilled by anyone who recognizes the examples as (a) among his own beliefs, and sees the force of Augustine's proof that (b) he cannot believe them erroneously; and the latter condition is fulfilled by anyone who sees the force of the simple little proof just given that no falsehood can possess features (a) and (b) jointly. If anything can be manifest, these facts can be. Accordingly it would be unreasonable to deny that the examples can satisfy Zeno's conditions for knowledge. I conclude that Augustine eventually succeeded in meeting the Academics' challenge, in the form in which he set it up for himself.

HOW MUCH HAS BEEN RESCUED?

When Augustine's "Si fallor, sum" was brought to the attention of Descartes, Descartes commented that while each of them had proved the "certainty" of his own existence, they put the proof to very different uses (letter to Colvius, 14 November 1640, in Kenny, pp. 83-84). This is true of the two philosophers' answers to skepticism considered generally. Augustine claims in the *Contra Academicos* to have found a range of propositions that can be known. But unlike Descartes he does not seek to build any edifice on this foundation: in particular he does not seek to reinstate the multitudinous propositions which pass for known in scholarly circles, let alone in ordinary life. I suspect that the reason lies in the continuing influence on him of Neoplatonism. There is a passage in the *Retractationes* which takes a thoroughly Platonic line about ordinary claims to knowledge (I thank Professor Dewey Hoitenga for drawing it to my attention). In *De utilitate credendi* Augustine had written, "What we understand, we owe to reason, what we believe, to authority" (*UC* I 11.25). The *Retractationes* quote "understand (intelligimus)" as "know (scimus)" and go on:

This is not to be taken in such a way as to make us frightened in ordinary speech of saying that we know what we believe on adequate testimony. It is true that when we speak properly, we are said to know only what we apprehend with the mind's firm reason. But when we speak in language which is better suited to common use—as even the holy scripture speaks—we should not hesitate to say we know both what we have perceived by our bodily senses and what we believe of trustworthy witnesses, while understanding the distance between the latter and the former. [*R* I 14.3]

We may wonder whether Augustine continued to think that satisfaction of Zeno's definition was necessary for "apprehension by the mind's firm reason." I do not know the answer. But I think that he himself did not much care how extensive a title to knowledge he had acquired by "ridding his mind" of the Academic *argumenta*. The important thing for him was to have rid his mind.*

REFERENCES

Augustine's works are in *Patrologia Latina* (cited as *PL*), ed. J. P. Migne (Paris, 1844-1864), volumes 32-47. The following abbreviations are used in the text:

BV   *De beata vita.* A.D. 386 *PL* 32.
CA   *Contra Academicos.* A.D. 386. *PL* 32. Translated with introduction and notes by J. J. O'Meara, Ancient Christian Writers, no. 12 (Newman Press, 1951).
CD   *De civitate Dei contra paganos.* A.D. 413-427. *PL* 41. Edited and translated by W. M. Green, Loeb Classical Library, 7 vols. (Heinemann, 1967-1972).
Conf.   *Confessiones.* A.D. 397-401. *PL* 32. Many translations.
DA   *De duabus animabus.* A.D. 391-392. *PL* 42. Translated by A. H. Newman, Nicene and Post-Nicene Fathers, 1st series, volume 4 (reprint ed., Eerdmans, 1974).

*I wish to thank Anthony Long and, especially, Myles Burnyeat for comments and suggestions.

Ep   *Epistolae. PL* 33. A large selection translated by J. G. Cunningham, Nicene and Post-Nicene Fathers, 1st series, volume 1 (reprint ed., Eerdmans, 1974).

LA   *De libero arbitrio.* A.D. 388-395. *PL* 32. Translated by J. H. S. Burleigh, The Library of Christian Classics, volume 6 (SCM Press, 1953); also by M. Pontifex, Ancient Christian Writers, no. 22 (Newman Press, 1955).

R   *Retractationes.* A.D. 426 or 427. *PL* 32.

Sol.   *Soliloquia.* A.D. 386. *PL* 32. Translated by Burleigh (see *LA*).

Trin.   *De Trinitate.* A.D. 399-419. *PL* 42. Translated by Stephen McKenna, *The Fathers of the Church,* volume 45 (Washington: Catholic University, 1963).

UC   *De utilitate credendi.* A.D. 391-392. *PL* 42. Translated by Burleigh (see *LA*).

VR   *De vera religione.* A.D. 389-391. *PL* 34. Translated by Burleigh (see *LA*).

Other works cited:

Ackrill, J. L. "Anamnesis in the *Phaedo.*" In *Exegesis and Argument,* edited by E. N. Lee, A. P. D. Mourelatos and R. Rorty. Phronesis, supplement 1. Van Gorcum, 1974.

Bonner, Gerald. *St. Augustine of Hippo.* SCM Press, 1963.

Burnyeat, M. F. "Idealism and Greek Philosophy: What Descartes Saw and Berkeley Missed." In *Idealism: Past and Present,* edited by G. Vesey. Royal Institute of Philosophy Lectures, volume 13, 1982.

Cicero. *Academica.* Edited and translated by H. Rackham. Loeb Classical Library. Heinemann, 1933.

Descartes, R. *OEuvres de Descartes.* Edited by C. Adam and P. Tannery. Cerf, 1904. (AT)

Diogenes Laertius. *Lives of the Philosophers.* Edited and translated by R. D. Hicks. Loeb Classical Library. Heinemann, 1959.

Gilson, Etienne. *Études sur le rôle de la pensée médiévale dans la formation du système cartésien.* Vrin, 1951.

Grice, H. P. "Vacuous Names." In *Words and Objections,* edited by D. Davidson and J. Hintikka. Reidel, 1969.

Kenny, A. J. P. *Descartes, Philosophical Letters.* Edited and translated by A. J. P. Kenny. Oxford, 1970.

Matthews, G. B. "Si fallor, sum." In *Augustine: A Collection of Critical Essays,* edited by R. A. Markus. Doubleday, 1972.

O'Meara, J. J. See above under *CA*.

Plutarch. *Adversus Colotem.* Edited and translated by B. Einarson and P. H. de Lacy. *Moralia,* volume 14. Loeb Classical Library. Heinemann, 1967.

Sextus Empiricus. *Adversus Mathematicos* VII (= *Against the Logicians* I). Edited and translated by R. G. Bury. *Sextus Empiricus,* volume 2. Loeb Classical Library. Heinemann, 1935. (M)

Williams, Bernard. *Descartes.* Harvester, 1978.

9

The Rediscovery of Ancient Skepticism in Modern Times*

C. B. Schmitt

It is now apparent that the rediscovered skeptical texts of antiquity played an important role in the development of modern philosophy. During the past fifty years various studies have progressively clarified the role of skepticism in the intellectual climate of the sixteenth, seventeenth, and eighteenth centuries.[1] Although there is a certain amount of disagreement among scholars as to precisely what significance the skeptical movement had in the development of philosophy, theology, science, and literature during this period,[2] most interpreters agree that the recovery and assimilation of the teachings of the ancient skeptical school was of primary importance. In spite of the fact that some attention has hitherto been devoted to uncovering the precise details of the recovery of ancient skeptical doctrine by Renaissance thinkers, we still lack a comprehensive survey of the process whereby ancient skeptical ideas were assimilated into the early modern consciousness. While I cannot hope to deal with the matter exhaustively in this short paper, I can perhaps summarize some of its more important aspects, as well as call attention to some of the lesser known facts concerning the medieval and Renaissance diffusion of ancient skeptical doctrine before 1600.

Skepticism as a philosophical movement seems to have begun with Pyrrho of Elis (ca. 360-ca. 270 B.C.) and to have continued at least until

*An earlier version of this study appeared in *Rivista critica di storia della filosofia* 27 (1972), 363-384.

the time of Sextus Empiricus (A.D. ca. 160-ca. 210).³ During that five-century period skepticism developed significantly as a philosophical school, in addition to undergoing several internal reforms. The number of writings produced by the skeptical school must have been quite substantial, though the only primary sources still extant are the compendia of Sextus Empiricus, who seems to have been an accurate compiler, but to have contributed nothing original to the movement himself. Consequently, we now possess none of the original philosophical writings of the earlier skeptics. In addition to the compilations of Sextus, we have several other works of skeptical inspiration, as well as various testimonies concerning skeptical doctrine written by authors who had access to the now lost writings of the Greek skeptics. In the former group are included Cicero's philosophical dialogue *Academica*, in which one of the participants argues the skeptical position in convincing fashion, and Diogenes Laertius's *Life of Pyrrho*, which relates some of the founder of skepticism's characteristic teachings. Of the ancient and early Christian authors whose writings contain some information on Greek skepticism we might mention Plutarch, Galen, Ptolemy, Aulus Gellius, Lactantius, Jerome, Augustine, and Eusebius.

The Renaissance saw a resurgence of interest in the philosophical position of the skeptics. The recovery of ancient texts on the subject played an important role in this.⁴ Connected with the reassertion of interest in skepticism by Renaissance thinkers is the continued concern with and development of various protoskeptical movements of the Middle Ages. These two aspects are but parts of a unified whole and must ultimately be discussed as part of the same fabric. In the present paper, however, I shall deal primarily with the continuity of the influence of ancient sources, focusing especially upon what I take to be the three most important of these: Cicero's *Academica*, Diogenes Laertius's *Life of Pyrrho*, and Sextus Empiricus's collected writings.

Although there had been a quite significant development of the various skeptical schools in antiquity, the continuity of these with the Middle Ages was practically nil. Cicero could still speak of the Academic school —along with Epicureanism and Stoicism—as one of the three major philosophical groups. The force of Academic skepticism remained potent down to the time of St. Augustine, whose first extant work is the *Contra Academicos*. In this treatise the great theologian launched a vigorous polemic against the skeptical position, which was so eloquently presented in Cicero's *Academica*. Augustine's treatise, however, seems to be the last Western effort before the revival of skepticism in the Renaissance to deal with that philosophy as a living force.

Owing to a peculiar concatenation of circumstances, the central works of ancient skepticism were practically unknown through the Latin Middle

Ages. Some of these were never recovered, and others only came to light in the fifteenth and sixteenth centuries, when they once more became a center of focus and the major impetus from which modern philosophical skepticism developed. Of the three major ancient writings on skepticism still extant—Sextus Empiricus's *Opera*, Diogenes Laertius's *Life of Pyrrho*, and Cicero's *Academica*—the first and the third were known to a very few in the West during the Middle Ages, while the second was apparently wholly unknown. The writings of Sextus Empiricus,[5] by far the most important and most detailed of the three, exerted no visible influence during the Middle Ages, although we know of three early-fourteenth-century manuscripts of a complete Latin translation of the *Outlines of Pyrrhonism*.[6] Yet, no evidence has thus far appeared to indicate that anyone other than the translator actually read the work. Although Walter Burley's *Lives of the Philosophers* is somehow partially based on Diogenes Laertius's work, either proximately or remotely,[7] it does not have a chapter on the ancient skeptic Pyrrho of Elis, and I know of no evidence that the *Life of Pyrrho* was known to anyone in the Latin-speaking world before the fifteenth century.

Cicero was one of the most widely known and read ancient authors throughout the Middle Ages, but remarkably enough his *Academica* was little known during the period.[8] There are a few extant manuscripts of this work dating from before the fourteenth century, it is referred to by several medieval authors, and we know that copies of it were in several medieval libraries. Yet, its diffusion was not extensive and it certainly does not rank with the *De officiis* or *De amicitia* as one of Cicero's better known works. In fact, direct references to it in medieval writers are very few indeed, though a fairly wide range of thinkers knew of some of its doctrines through Augustine's *Contra Academicos*, a much better known work. In fact, the only writers before the time of Petrarca who seem to have made much of Cicero's work or the doctrines of the Academics found therein are John of Salisbury (ca. 1125-1180)[9] and Henry of Ghent († 1293).[10] The former admired the Academic philosophers as being more modest in their claims than the members of the various dogmatic schools. It seems clear, however, that John knew Cicero's work only through several intermediary sources including Augustine's work. On the other hand, there is good evidence to suppose that Henry of Ghent knew the *Lucullus* directly, for he quotes passages from it which are not available in Augustine's *Contra Academicos* or any other intermediary source which I have been able to discover. Henry takes some of the skeptical arguments seriously, and it is perhaps not without reason that he is the first of the great scholastics to begin his *Summa* with the basic epistemological question: "Utrum contingat hominem aliquid scire."

The ultimate outcome of this introduction of Academic skepticism into scholasticism is not clear at the moment, and further research is required. We do know that as significant a writer as Jean Buridan (fl. 1360) was concerned with a similar epistemological question,[11] and the most extreme of the Western medieval writers of protoskeptical orientation, Nicolas of Autrecourt (fl. 1347), was condemned for his troubles.[12]

While the sources of ancient skepticism were all but hidden from the view of western medieval thinkers, there were developing other tendencies, which must be accounted for in any comprehensive discussion of skepticism and its influence. If the carefully worked-out epistemological and logical arguments of the Greek skeptics were not available in the West during the Middle Ages, we do find the development of a certain native brand of doubt and anti-intellectualism.[3] This is to be found particularly in certain of the mystical movements, which emphasized faith and dependence on God at the expense of a concerted intellectual effort to attain truth. Such an orientation is evident in a twelfth-century writer like Hugh of St. Victor[14] or in the enormously influential *Imitatio Christi*,[15] which came into its own in the fourteenth century and maintained an undiminished popularity for hundreds of years afterwards. There also flowed into the West during the later Middle Ages a certain number of ideas of skeptical orientation from Hebrew and Arabic sources, including writers such as Al-Ghazzali (1059-1111)[16] and Jehuda Ha-Levi (ca. 1085-ca. 1147).[17]

It is, however, with the recovery of the ancient sources of skeptical thought that we are here primarily concerned. In the course of the fifteenth and sixteenth centuries, the three sources mentioned above were recovered and assimilated; during the seventeenth century skepticism emerged as an important philosophical movement, which had a significant impact not only on philosophical thought, but on theology, science, and literature as well. Though there was a continuity of what I have called the native medieval traditions, it is my belief that the recovery and the reassimilation of the ancient writings were the primary factor in the evolution of the modern skeptical attitude.

Here, with regard to skepticism, we see once again the enormous significance of the rebirth characteristic of the Renaissance. Although this aspect of the fifteenth and sixteenth centuries has been emphasized by historians for more than a century, in recent years many scholars have tended to stress the continuity of the Middle Ages and the Renaissance.[18] In the case of early modern skepticism, however, the major factor in its development was the recovery of the three texts mentioned above. Doubtless these materials were used to build upon the native tradition, but it seems clear that the writings of Sextus Empiricus contain a much more sophisticated and highly developed form of philosophical skepticism than anything found in medieval Christian writing. I should like to emphasize the word "philosophical" here, for as skepticism developed in the fifteenth and sixteenth centuries, it did not generally have the anti-religious connotations that it later attained. To put it another way, as the skeptical question was argued during the Renaissance, it nearly always revolved around whether man can attain reliable knowledge through natural means or not, and seldom, if ever, was it used to discredit religion. In fact, it was more often used in behalf of religion.[19] In later times —in the seventeenth, eighteenth, and nineteenth centuries—skepticism came to have an increasingly antireligious tinge, but such was not the case for the earlier period.[20] I would like to emphasize this fact very strongly, for I am often met—even by distinguished historians—by those who *begin* with the assumption that when we discuss skepticism we are necessarily dealing with some sort of antireligious attitude. Fideism—the position that faith alone provides the way to truth and that philosophical activity is of no avail—was a fairly common attitude among Renaissance skeptics. In fact, we can name at least several sixteenth-century thinkers who held that skepticism was the most acceptable philosophy for a Christian to hold, for it allowed him to have a more complete confidence in Scripture than did any of the dogmatic philosophical schools.[21]

Having said this much, I should now like to turn to a consideration of the Renaissance revival of the three major sources of ancient skepticism. Let us first look at Cicero's *Academica* and its influence in the context of the Renaissance. Although we find an increase of interest in this particular work in the fourteenth and fifteenth centuries, it is not until the middle of the sixteenth century that it begins to be taken more seriously. Petrarca knew the work and included it among his "favorite books,"[22] but its direct influence on his thought is rather meager. Coluccio Salutati[23] also used it in a discreet way, weaving it into a discussion of certitude here or a discussion of doubt there. Lorenzo Valla also made use of certain skeptical arguments derived partly from Cicero, but also from Lactantius and other sources.[24] In general, mining the fifteenth-century Italian humanists' works in search of influences from Cicero's work is very unrewarding. Knowing what we do of the importance of Cicero for the development of humanism, we would expect a priori that there would be an intense discussion of so fascinating a work as the *Academica*. Such, however, is not the case.

For reasons not entirely clear to me, the *Academica* is one of the most neglected of Cicero's works during the fifteenth and sixteenth centuries. Even after searching a good deal to find the reason for this, I have not been able to hit upon one which is entirely satisfactory. My hypothesis is that, given the fact that Cicero was generally praised as a superb orator and excellent philosopher (we must keep in mind that during the Renaissance Cicero was still considered to be an original philosopher of considerable stature and not merely a popularizer of important Greek philosophical ideas), the picture of Cicero in the *Academica* does not square with this overall evaluation. What we find in the *Academica*, especially in the final speech in the *Lucullus*, is that Cicero defends a rather unusual philosophical position, namely, Academic skepticism. While the men of the Renaissance knew very well that Plato and Aristotle were important philosophers and were generally to be praised unless one found adequate reason to do otherwise, such was not the case with the skeptics defended by Cicero in the *Lucullus*. In fact, Cicero's speech is largely devoted to arguing against traditional dogmatic philosophy—Platonic, Epicurean, Stoic, and Aristotelian. My contention is that the men of the Renaissance generally found this a bit disconcerting. Though they knew of Cicero's excellence in oratory and rhetoric, as illustrated in many of his works, and his general subtlety as a philosopher, as in dialogues such as *De officiis*, and *De natura deorum*, when they encountered him speaking out against the important philosophical schools, they didn't quite know how to interpret it. This, I feel, led them to turn aside from the *Academica* and to give it little serious consideration until after the middle of the sixteenth century, at which time the ideas of ancient skepticism had become better known and didn't have the peculiar aura about them which they had when first introduced. This interpretation cannot be documented, but it seems more plausible than any other which has come to my attention.

At all events, we do not find much concern, on a philological, historical, or philosophical level, with the *Academica* before 1536. Though the *editio princeps* of this and other philosophical works of Cicero appeared in 1471, it is not until the decade of the 1530s that we find any attempt at a commentary on the work. Indeed, even then, most of the sixteenth-century commentaries on it are of a philological rather than of a philosophical character. It seems as though Pier Vettori, in a volume appearing in 1536,[25] was the first to publish a series of annotations on the *Academica*. Before the end of the century at least a dozen more humanists annotated or commented on the work, but of all of these only one or two are of more than passing interest to the intellectual historian.[26] In addition there were several other works appearing in the second half of the sixteenth century which were inspired in one way or another by the *Academica* and which might engage our attention. In chronological order, the works of more than passing interest are (1) Omer Talon's *Academia* (1547, 1550) which was also accompanied by a commentary on Cicero's work; (2) Giulio Castellani's *Adversus Marci Tullii Ciceronis academicas quaestiones disputatio* (1558); (3) Joannes Rosa's commentary on the

Academica (1571); and (4) Pedro de Valencia's *Academica* (1596). Of the four, those of Talon and Pedro de Valencia are generally favorable to the Academic position, that of Castellani is critical, and Rosa's is favorable with reservations.

Talon, a close follower of Petrus Ramus, seems to have written his work[27] to show that there was an ancient precedent for rejecting dogmatic philosophy, as well as to elucidate certain philosophical alternatives to the Aristotelian scholasticism being taught at Paris in the middle of the sixteenth century. This work of Talon was used as a weapon for revolutionizing the university curriculum. Ramus and Talon were the revolutionaries of sixteenth-century Paris, and the changes they sought, at least as far as curriculum is concerned, were probably no less far-reaching in the context than those sought by the revolutionaries of our own universities.[28] They hoped to replace the scholasticism taught at Paris since the thirteenth century by a new humanistic curriculum in which "philosophy" would be joined to "elegance," reechoing the cry of Bruno, Valla, and other Quattrocento Italian humanists.[29] The *Academica* was important here, for it showed that no philosophical system, even that of the Peripatetics, could entirely escape the critique of the skeptics. In this, it prefigures Pierre Gassendi's *Exercitationes paradoxicae adversus Aristoteleos* of three-quarters of a century later, though the latter makes abundant use of Sextus Empiricus, a source presumably unknown to Ramus and Talon.[30]

The effort of the Ramists drew the ire of Pierre Galland, who, among other things, attacked them in a work published in 1551[31] for preaching a philosophy which does not lead to certitude. It also seems to have been the occasion for the work in French by Guy de Brues entitled *Les dialogues contre les nouveaux academiciens* published in 1553.[32] We should not make a mountain out of a molehill, as I feel Busson has done,[33] but these things do indicate that there was a certain revival of Academic skepticism at Paris in the middle of the sixteenth century. Further work is needed on this matter, and despite Ong's excellent book, the last word has not been said on Ramus, his circle, and the controversies which they started.[34]

A few years after the Paris outburst, a rather little-known Italian from Faenza named Giulio Castellani wrote his work which criticized the Academic position defended in Cicero's *Academica*.[35] What is significant about Castellani's attack is that he rejects the Academic philosophy not because it is a danger for religion, but because it undermines good philosophy. In attempting a point-by-point rebuttal of Cicero's skeptical argument *more peripatetico*, Castellani gives us one of the more significant antiskeptical works of the century.

A fascinating sidelight to the works of Talon and Castellani is that both discuss Cicero's reference in the *Academica*[36] to Hicetas of Syracuse, whose argument that the earth moves while other heavenly bodies are stationary takes on a special significance in view of Copernicus's work published in 1543. It should be noted that Copernicus himself also knew and cited Hicetas's position (probably from Cicero's work) in the *De Revolutionibus*.[37] This apparently gave him the support of a much-needed ancient authority for his novel contention. Castellani merely rejects Hicetas' position as not being in accord with what the senses tell us about the world.[38] Talon, on the other hand, actually mentions Copernicus approvingly as having followed *illam veterem opinionem*.[39]

The only other sixteenth-century attempt, as far as I have discovered, to use the *Academica* as a vehicle for teaching is to be found in Joannes Rosa's commentary printed at Frankfurt in 1571.[40] This was undoubtedly unsuccessful, for Rosa's book was never reprinted and today is very rare. Rosa's commentary is significant for a number of reasons. First of all, unlike the others I have mentioned, he was a Protestant, having been educated at Wittenberg, later teaching at the new University of Jena, where he also became one of the first Rectors. Rosa is a bit ambiguous in his attitude to the *Academica*. He sees it as having a certain value in the education of youth, for it instills in them the virtue of cautiousness and prevents them from uncritically becoming members of any particular dogmatic philosophical school as well as from becoming overly arrogant, when they have a bit of knowledge. On the other hand, the work has a certain inherent danger, he feels. Not only can it chill "all ardor for learning"[41] but it can bring about impiousness by encouraging one not to make use of the abundant gifts given us by God for the attainment of the truth.[42] This somewhat unusual concern for the *Academica* and for the ideas found therein which we find in Rosa apparently found no reflections in the German thought of the next generations. It must be noted, however, that thus far, scholars have paid scant attention to the diffusion of skeptical ideas in late sixteenth-century Germany, and systematic study of the extant materials may reveal unexpected finds.

One final thinker of the sixteenth century, who took the *Academica* seriously and hence deserves brief mention, is Pedro de Valencia, whose work with the same title as Cicero's dialogue appeared at Antwerp in 1596.[43] Pedro's *Academica* is basically a careful historical analysis of the development of ancient Academic skepticism. As such it retained a scholarly value until the nineteenth century[44] and was frequently reprinted and translated during the eighteenth century.[45] Only at the very end of the work does Pedro give a hint of his own position, when he emphasizes that the consideration of the Academic philosophy should make us realize that God is the only source of truth.[46]

The second important text from antiquity to be considered is Diogenes Laertius's *Life of Pyrrho*.[47] Of this we shall say little, not because it is unimportant, but because its diffusion and influence in the Renaissance have not yet been studied in detail.[48] Diogenes Laertius's work, however, was widely known after its first translation by Ambrogio Traversari, in the 1430s.[49] This is evidenced by the dozens of extant fifteenth-century manuscripts and the numerous early printed editions.[50] The precise role of this work in the Renaissance has yet to be evaluated. We do know, however, that Diogenes' material regarding skeptical doctrine was used in a variety of ways to amplify what was available from Latin sources before the works of Sextus Empiricus became generally available.[51] For example, various commentators and scholiasts on Cicero's *Academica* supplemented what was available in that work by using material from Diogenes.[52]

It also might be mentioned in passing that from all indications, Traversari's translation seems to be responsible for the introduction of the word *scepticus* into the Latin vocabulary. The only ancient use of the word listed in even the largest Latin dictionaries is in Aulus Gellius, and there the earliest manuscript evidence shows it to be consistently written in Greek characters.[53] The two medieval Latin manuscripts of Sextus Empiricus, which do contain the word, were of little, if any, influence.[54] So far as I have been able to discover, *scepticus* and other derivative cognates were not otherwise used during the Middle Ages, and only gradually did they come into more common usage in the course of the fifteenth century.[55] By the early sixteenth century it was fairly common—Luther could lash out at Erasmus with "Sanctus Spiritus non est scepticus"[56]— and by the end of the century it seems to have been firmly established in everyone's vocabulary.

The major source of ancient skepticism still extant, however, is to be found in the writings of Sextus Empiricus, far more substantial and detailed than what either Cicero or Diogenes Laertius have to say on the subject. As Popkin has rightly pointed out, the recovery of the writings of Sextus is the key to the development of later skepticism. Although practically unknown in the West during the Middle Ages[57] and seemingly unknown to both Arabs and Jews, Sextus's works were known by the Greek writers of the Byzantine Empire.

Apart from a partial translation of Sextus Empiricus into Latin, which had no noticeable influence,[58] there is little evidence of any direct knowledge of the Greek skeptical tradition in the West until Filelfo brought his manuscript to Italy. Before tracing the meager *fortuna* of ancient skepticism in medieval Western Europe I should like briefly to consider the continuity of interest in the subject among the Greek Christians of the Byzantine Empire. This should give us the background leading up to the early fifteenth century when the Greek manuscripts of Sextus Empiricus and other writers on skeptical topics came to the West culminating in a renewed interest in that philosophy.

It is probably impossible to determine precisely how widely skeptical materials were diffused in Byzantium from the coming of Christianity to the fall of Constantinople. Several things, however, are clear. First, names such as Pyrrho and Sextus Empiricus were better known in the East than in the West during the Middle Ages. Second, skeptical doctrines played at least some role in the theological and doctrinal discussions characteristic of Eastern Christianity. A full study of the continuity of skepticism in Byzantium is lacking, though undoubtedly such an investigation would be illuminating and rewarding. Here I can merely call attention to a few instances of an interest in skeptical ideas among the medieval Greeks.

The tone of opposition to Greek skepticism was set by Gregoy Nazianzen (ca. 330-389), writing about 379 in his *Oration XXI*. There he speaks of "Sextuses and Pyrrhos and an opposing voice have crept into our churches as some sort of fearful and malignant disease."[59] In Gregory's view the skeptics are to be lumped with Greek philosophers in general as being incompatible with Christianity,[60] a view endorsed also in one of the poems, where the Pyrrhonians are grouped with Aristotle as purveyors of intricate and confusing argument.[61] Such a interpretation, which contrasts markedly with the predominant Western Christian view before the seventeenth century, was apparently fairly widespread in later Greek Christianity.

In the next centuries Pyrrho was mentioned by Joannes Stobaeus (fifth century),[62] who perhaps derived his information directly from Sextus Empiricus, and Agathias (ca. 530-580) referred to both Pyrrho and Sextus in a passage which shows that he understood the basic skeptical position and was, indeed, in some measure sympathetic to the approach.[63] The fact that some skeptical texts now lost were still known to the Byzantines is clear from an entry on Aenesidemus in Photius's *Bibliotheca* (ninth century), which contains information not available in other extant sources.[64] During the twelfth century Nicholas of Methone and Georgios Tornikes also referred to Pyrrho and Sextus,[65] as did Georgios Kedrenos, who devoted a brief paragraph of his *Compendium historiarum* to a presentation of their basic doctrines.[66]

It was, however, in the fourteenth century that we find a renewed interest in ancient skepticism among a group of thinkers who were part of one of the most vivid intellectual flowerings of Byzantium. It is evident that these men had some access to the writings of Sextus Empiricus and to other ancient skeptical texts, which were at that time little known in the West.[67] Further research is still necessary before we can accurately determine the extent of this knowledge and the impact which it had on the Byzantine thought of the period. Theodoros Metochites (1260-1322), in his monumental *Miscellanea philosophica et historica*, severely criticized the contemporary revival of interest in the writings of Sextus Empiricus which he considered to be extremely harmful to the serious study of philosophy and theology.[68] The precise context from which Metochites' attack grew has not been uncovered, and it is difficult to know exactly how widespread was the contemporary interest in skeptical doctrine. What does seem evident is that after Metochites there was quite a flurry of interest in the subject for a generation or so. Nicephoros Gregoras (1290/1-1359/60), who was probably led to study the skeptical texts under the influence of Metochites, repeated word for word Gregory Nazianzen's dire warning of a millennium past.[69] Were it not for other contemporary evidence of a revived interest in skeptical texts and doctrines, his repetition of a well-known text could be interpreted as a mere literary figure reflecting the continued presence of a widely admired authority. However, there is evidence of a broader concern with skepticism found among at least two other contemporary authors, Gregory Palamas (1296/7-1359) and Nicholas Cabasilas (1322/3-1391?). Palamas showed himself aware of the problem,[70] while Cabasilas wrote a whole treatise entitled *Against Those Things Which Have Been Said Concerning the Criterion of Truth: Whether They Are from the Accursed Pyrrho.*[71] Only partially extant, this work contains the most detailed evidence of a continuing concern with the problems raised by Greek skepticism that has come to light from the Middle Ages. What influence Cabasilas's work had, or whether it was even read by contemporaries, is not yet clear. When taken in conjunction with other literary references to a skeptical threat, it indicates that Byzantine theologians and churchmen of various sorts saw traditional Greek skepticism as a serious challenge to the well-being of the Church.

The first Greek manuscripts came into Italy during the early fifteenth century, apparently brought back from Constantinople by Francesco Filelfo in 1427.[72] Later in the century, Greek texts of the work were known to Giovanni Aurispa,[73] Cardinal Bessarion,[74] Francesco Patrizi,[75] Angelo Poliziano,[76] Marsilio Ficino,[77] and Giovanni Pico della Mirandola.[78] Codices were also available in Medici Library,[79] the Vatican Library,[80] and the Library of S. Marco in Florence.[81] Moreover, Giovanni Lorenzi prepared a new partial translation, probably shortly after 1485.[82] A few years later Girolamo Savonarola advocated having a complete translation of Sextus made by several of his associates.[83] Whether such a translation was ever completed is not clear, but no trace of it seems to have survived. Thus, by the end of the fifteenth century there was a notable interest in the works of Sextus, at least in major Italian intellectual centers such as Rome, Venice, and Florence. On the other hand, there is no evidence of any knowledge of Sextus north of the Alps before the sixteenth century. Even the interest shown in Italy appears to have been primarily on a philological and historical, rather than a philosophical, level. The texts of Sextus were used almost exclusively as sources of historical and philological information about antiquity.[84] As yet no evidence has been produced to suggest that even this fairly widespread distribution of manuscripts produced anything approaching a "skeptical crisis" in the *Quattrocento*.

Leaving aside the effort of Savonarola, which apparently did not come to fruition, the first to take a serious interest in the destructive philosophical criticism contained in Sextus's works seems certainly to have been Gianfrancesco Pico della Mirandola (1469-1533), nephew of the previously mentioned Giovanni Pico.[85] Although already critical of the secular learning of the last years of the fifteenth century, the younger Pico sharpened his critique considerably during the first two decades of the next century. This came largely through a direct reading of the works of Sextus Empiricus, probably, as it now seems, in a codex in the possession of Giorgio Antonio Vespucci (ca. 1434-1514), an associate of Savonarola.[86] It is not clear precisely when Pico first came into contact with the works of Sextus and began to make use of their philosophical implications. By 1511 he was exploiting the writings of Sextus,[87] but it was only in the *Examen vanitatis* (completed in 1516, it would seem, but published in 1520) that his skeptical attack on ancient dogmatic philosophy came to full fruition. He was particularly intent upon applying Sextus's arguments against Aristotle in the name of Christianity. In brief, he maintained that the Aristotelian sense-based epistemology—that is, as represented by the slogan *nihil est in intellectu quod prius non fuerit in sensu*—could not be upheld in the face of the various difficulties raised by the skeptics' critique. For him, skepticism was a tool to be used in behalf of Christianity. With it he felt that he could cut out all hope of certitude from under the Aristotelian philosophers and thereby bring home to his readers that truth and reliability was to be found in Scripture alone. Although he employed various materials for his purpose, perhaps most striking is his use of Sextus Empiricus, whom he quotes often in Greek and from whom he also translates passages into Latin upon occasion. Pico thus seems to be the first Western thinker after antiquity to make serious philosophical use of the potent weapon of ancient skepticism.

Pico's *Examen vanitatis doctrinae gentium*, first published in 1520, caused little immediate reaction, though Castellani[88] devoted some pages to refuting it and Mario Nizolio (1488-1567),[89] the arch-Ciceronian, drew some arguments from it in attacking the Peripatetics. The next writer to make use of Sextus seems to have been Francesco Robertello (1516-1567),[90] best known today as an important commentator on Aristotle's *Poetics*, who quoted several Greek passages from a Sextus manuscript in clarifying certain texts dealing with skepticism found in Cicero.

The really important events in the popularizing of the skeptical ideas found in Sextus Empiricus occurred during the decade of the 1560s, when his writings first appeared in Latin translation. In 1562 Henri Estienne's translation of the *Outlines of Pyrrhonism* came from the presses,[91] and seven years later there appeared Gentian Hervet's translation of the *Adversus mathematicos*.[92] This is really the crucial event in the development of Renaissance and early modern skepticism, for now by far the most important work of ancient skepticism was generally available for the first time. One could still complain, as did Pedro de Valencia,[93] that he could not get his hands on the Greek text of Sextus, but at least something was in print, though at a distance of nearly a hundred years after the first printing of the less detailed compendia of skeptical doctrine by Cicero and Diogenes Laertius. It was not until 1621—nearly 200 years after Filelfo's first bringing of a Greek manuscript of the work back to Italy—that the *editio princeps* of Sextus was finally printed.[94] But once the translations were in print we see a direct development of skepticism as a more potent force in European life, and before the end of the century there emerged several skeptically oriented thinkers including Sanches (ca. 1550-ca. 1623), Montaigne (1533-1592), and Charron (1541-1603). These figures in turn point the way to the real "skeptical crisis" of the seventeenth century.

Among other things, we here see clearly just how the process of the recovery and assimilation of ancient skepticism took place. After Italian humanists expressed an initial interest in the skeptical texts, the works were accepted into the general European intellectual and cultural ambience, ultimately becoming far more influential in Northern Europe than in Italy. In fact, when we compare Northern Europe with Italy in this matter, we find striking differences. During the whole period—from Petrarca until the turn of the sixteenth century—when ancient skeptical writings were being recovered and assimilated in Italy, there was hardly a trace of knowledge of these materials north of the Alps. All of the incunabular editions of the Latin translation of Diogenes Laertius, as well as ten editions of an Italian translation, were printed in Italy.[95] Though Cicero's *Academica* was certainly known outside of Italy before 1500, there is clear evidence for its being read more frequently south of the

Alps. The same is also true, as we have seen, with regard to Sextus Empiricus, though little note was taken of his writings anywhere before Pico. Still, all references to Sextus and his writings which I have thus far come across dating from the fifteenth century are Italian. Consequently, we can readily see that in terms of being acquainted with and making use of the literary remains of ancient skepticism, Italy was far ahead of the rest of Europe until the early sixteenth century.

Somehow, during the period 1520-1550 all of this changed and an increasing interest in skeptical ideas was shown in the North, while Italian interest gradually waned. The *editio princeps* of the Greek text of Diogenes Laertius, which appeared in 1533, and the first printed Latin translations of Sextus Empiricus, which came from the presses in the decade of the 1560s, both were northern productions. Moreover, serious attention given to the study and interpretation of Cicero's skeptically oriented works was to be found increasingly in the North. This shift was not merely a temporary one, but one which was to have lasting consequences. While the concern with ancient skeptical doctrine gradually waned in Italy, it drew the attention of more and more thinkers of northern Europe in the course of the next century.

From our vantage point in the twentieth century we can see that already by the middle of the sixteenth century, skeptical ideas had taken root in the North to a degree that they were never to attain in Italy. It was during the next century and a half, however, that ancient skepticism truly became assimilated into western European thought as a philosophical position which time and again entered the mainstream of discussion. After the first printing of Sextus, we must wait but a few years for Montaigne's *Apologie de Raimond Sebond* (first published 1580), which still remains one of the most compelling expressions of the skeptical philosophy. From there we see a continuity of interest through Charron, Glanville, and many others down to Bayle, who codified the whole thing in his *Dictionaire* (first edition 1697), which took shape in the final decade of the seventeenth century. That century also saw the writings of Sextus Empiricus become available in several vernacular translations,[96] as well as the recovery of Ptolemy's Περὶ κριτηρίου, a further ancient source of importance for an understanding of skeptical ideas.[97] In short, the seventeenth century saw the establishment of the skeptical philosophy as a permanent feature on the intellectual map of modern Europe.

Here I have tried to sketch the present state of knowledge concerning the recovery and assimilation of ancient skeptical ideas by the Renaissance. Many of the individual thinkers I have mentioned and many of the avenues of the transmission of doctrine require much further study before we can give a more confident exposition of the situation. Now that serious work has begun on this subject, let us hope that it will not be too long before we have a much fuller understanding of matters such as the continuity of Greek skepticism in Byzantium and the impact of Greek ideas concerning skepticism on sixteenth-century religious controversy.[98] Though it is certainly too early in our work to hazard definitive answers to some of the key questions regarding the history of early modern skepticism, it might be well to end this study with some provisional conclusions both by way of generalization and as suggestions for further study.

First, I would like to say that nothing that I have read from the Renaissance period indicates to me that modern skepticism came through the Aristotelian tradition. Though one reads quite often in modern secondary literature about the "skepticism" of Pomponazzi or of the School of Padua, an investigation fails to reveal much that can be called "skeptical," except in the vaguest of senses. The skeptical and peripatetic schools were opposed in antiquity, and despite the writings of Owens, Busson, Allen, and a host of lesser writers we find little to indicate a skeptical influence on Renaissance scholasticism. One looks in vain through Pomponazzi or other "Paduans" for clear evidence of their even knowing of characteristic skeptical doctrines, let alone adopting them. When Aristotelians such as Jakob Schegk (1511-1587), who taught for forty-five years at Tübingen, do show themselves to be aware of some of the central teachings of the ancient skeptical school,[99] they were always, to the best of my knowledge, highly critical of skepticism. This seems to be uniformly the case, even though the adherents of Renaissance Aristotelianism were more open than is usually thought, absorbing important doctrines from time to time from Platonism, Stoicism, and even Atomism. With skepticism, however, they had little sympathy.

Second, and on this point I think we can speak with a little more confidence, the transmission of ancient skeptical ideas went from Italy to Northern Europe in the course of the sixteenth century. In this it follows the pattern of most other aspects of antiquity revived during the Renaissance. This consists in the recovery of the ancient texts in Italy during the fifteenth century and the transmission of these texts to the North during the next century. In the case of skepticism, all three of the key texts we have discussed were known much more generally in Italy than in Northern Europe during the fifteenth century. It remained, however, for the major influence, accompanied by a redevelopment of ancient skeptical ideas, to take place in France, Germany and the Low Countries in the sixteenth and seventeenth centuries, at a time when little interest was shown in the subject in Italy.[100]

Third, the investigations which we have carried out tend to indicate that the ancient skeptical texts were somewhat better known during the fifteenth and early sixteenth centuries (before the printing of Sextus Empiricus) than is generally realized. Though our work is still far from exhaustive, we have been able to uncover indications that Sextus Empiricus, for example, was somewhat better known than has previously been thought. The name of Sextus was, indeed, known to a circle of important fifteenth-century humanists, and some minimal use was made of his ideas. Moreover, ideas deriving from Cicero's *Academica* and other sources had a somewhat greater role in the religious controversies of the first half of the sixteenth century than has hitherto been believed. On the whole, however, skeptical tendencies were of relatively minor consequence until the last third of the sixteenth century. In no way was skepticism as important a movement as Platonism, Stoicism, Epicureanism, or other revived ancient philosophies. Moreover—and this needs to be emphasized—the continuity of the Aristotelian tradition was of such vigor that it remained the dominant philosophy of Western Europe until at least the second half of the seventeenth century.[101] Skepticism did come increasingly into its own during the period separating Montaigne and Bayle, but it represented a mere trickle alongside the veritable flood of Aristotelian doctrine.

Nevertheless, the development of skepticism in the early modern period certainly cannot be overlooked, as the research of the past thirty years by Richard Popkin amply demonstrates.[102] From the tentative beginnings of the fifteenth and early sixteenth centuries, it developed into quite a potent force in early modern philosophy. Sextus Empiricus was still a central source for the thought of David Hume. With Hume, of course, skepticism took a different direction; it became allied once and for all with the criticism of religious belief. Whereas it had been used in the service of religion by Lactantius, Savonarola, and Gianfrancesco Pico, among others, by the time we get to the eighteenth century the fideistic use of ancient skepticism had largely gone by the board. From Montaigne to Bayle—that is, essentially the seventeenth century—there is a gray area of shifting ground in which the religious affiliations of the skeptics were ambiguous to say the least. The reintroduction of the ancient skeptical texts had opened a veritable "Pandora's box." Even in antiquity there were ambiguities, but they were increased manyfold during the three centuries after the writings of Sextus Empiricus came to Italy in the form of a Greek manuscript during the early years of the fifteenth century. The stories we hear of the various ancient skeptics from Sextus or from Diogenes Laertius show that already in ancient times the skeptical school—if one can speak of such a heterogeneous group in this way—was anything but coherent and unified in its objectives. The variations increased many times during the sixteenth and seventeenth centuries, when figures such as G. F. Pico, Omer Talon, Francisco Sanches, Pedro de Valencia, Gentian Hervet, and Michel de Montaigne put skepticism to exceedingly different uses. In common with many other philosophical doctrines—the history of Platonism offers an excellent parallel example[103]—those of skepticism were interpreted, used, modified, and indeed perverted in many different ways. The Greek and Latin texts which have come down to us preserving at least some of the major teachings of the skeptics were capable of radically different interpretations. The history of early modern skepticism bears eloquent witness to this fact. Many thinkers used the basic materials in a highly creative and unconventional way. Pico used skeptical doctrine purely to bring down Aristotelian science on behalf of Christianity; a century later Pierre Gassendi found in skepticism the roots of a new probabilistic theory of scientific knowledge, meant above all to replace that of Aristotle which Pico had helped to demolish. Descartes saw the skeptical threat as something to be overcome and created a whole new philosophy to do just that. At the other extreme was his contemporary Isaac La Peyrère, who set about using skeptical tools to question not only human science but the Divine Science of Scripture as well. So it was that throughout the early modern period the surviving skeptical texts from antiquity provoked many different responses on the part of the protagonists of the intellectual history of Europe.

What is important to bear in mind is that under whatever variegated hues the texts were viewed, the point of departure in each instance was taken from ancient skepticism. The medieval tradition of criticism and logical analysis (*sophismata, insolubilia,* etc.), of course, had something in common with ancient skepticism, but was an independent development, not genetically tied to the literary remains of the ancients in any but the most indirect of ways. Rarely, if ever, did ancient skepticism and medieval criticism become fused before the advent of modern scholarship. Consequently, they functioned as two different historical strands.[104]

The revival of ancient skepticism was one of several long-forgotten traditions and sets of doctrines which were revived by the Renaissance. Before the process which I have described here took place, the fundamental tenets of the ancient skeptics were not known in the West. Thus skepticism, along with many other aspects of antiquity, was brought back to currency through the desire of the humanists of the Italian Renaissance to recover the literary and material sources of antiquity. The continuity of interest in the texts on the part of the Byzantine Greeks of the Middle Ages insured that when the time came, the appropriate manuscripts were to be had in Constantinople. It was only when these Greek materials came to Italy, especially the writings of Sextus Empiricus, that the new knowledge could be conjoined to the sparse information already available in Latin sources. After some delay, which has never been satisfactorily explained, skepticism as a serious philosophical position once again began to enter the mainstream at the time of Montaigne. From there it passed into the common currency of Western intellectual life.

NOTES

1. See especially Richard H. Popkin, *The History of Scepticism from Erasmus to Spinoza*, 3d ed. (Berkeley, Los Angeles, and London, 1979), pp. 300-326 for an extensive bibliography of further literature on the subject. Of other publications that deal directly with the same theme the following may be mentioned as being among the more important: Henry G. Van Leeuwen, *The Problem of Certainty in English Thought, 1630-1690* (The Hague, 1963); Don Cameron Allen, *Doubt's Boundless Sea: Skepticism and Faith in the Renaissance* (Baltimore, 1964); Craig B. Brush, *Montaigne and Bayle: Variations on the Theme of Skepticism* (The Hague, 1966); Charles B. Schmitt, *Gianfrancesco Pico della Mirandola (1469-1533) and His Critique of Aristotle* (The Hague, 1967); Benjamin Nelson, "The Early Modern Revolution in Science and Philosophy: Fictionalism, Probabilism, Fideism, and Catholic 'Prophetism,'" *Boston Studies in the Philosophy of Science*, vol. 3 (Dordrecht, 1967), pp. 1-40; Richard H. Popkin, "Scepticism, Theology, and the Scientific Revolution in the Seventeenth Century," in *Problems in the Philosophy of Science*, ed. I. Lakatos and A. Musgrave (Amsterdam, 1968), pp. 1-39; Charles B. Schmitt, *Cicero Scepticus: A Study of the Influence of the Academica in the Renaissance* (The Hague, 1972); J. P. Dumont, *Le scepticisme et le phénomène* (Paris, 1972). Among recent articles I should like to call attention to E. de Olaso, "Las Academica de Ciceron y la filosofia renacentista," *International Studies in Philosophy* 7 (1975), 57-68 and N. Jardine, "The Forging of Modern Realism: Clavius and Kepler against the Sceptics," *Studies in the History and Philosophy of Science* 10 (1979), 141-73.

2. See, for example, the paper by Nelson cited in the preceding note, as well as his exchange with Edward Grant in *Daedalus*, Summer 1962, pp. 599-616, and his " 'Probabilists,' 'Anti-Probabilists' and the Quest for Certitude in the 16th and 17th Centuries," *Actes du Xme Congrès international d'histoire des sciences* (Paris, 1965), I, 269-273. See also my review of Allen (above, n. 1) in *International Philosophical Quarterly* 5 (1965), 321-324 and Paul Oskar Kristeller, "The Myth of Renaissance Atheism and the French Tradition of Free Thought," *Journal of the History of Philosophy* 6 (1968), 233-243.

3. On ancient skepticism in general see, among others, Victor Brochard, *Les sceptiques grecs*, 2d ed. (Paris, 1933; 1st ed. 1887), which is still fundamental; A. Goedeckemeyer, *Die Geschichte des griechischen Skeptizismus* (Leipzig, 1905); Mario Dal Pra, *Lo scetticismo greco*, 2d ed. (Bari, 1975); Léon Robin, *Pyrrhon et le scepticisme grec* (Paris, 1944); Charlotte Stough, *Greek Skepticism: A Study in Epistemology* (Berkeley and Los Angeles, 1969); A. E. Chatzilysandros, *Ge-*

schichte der skeptischen Tropen (Munich, 1970); and K. Janáček, *Sextus Empiricus' Sceptical Methods* (Prague, 1972).

4. See the introductory material by J. A. Fabricius in his edition of *Sexti Empirici Opera* (Leipzig, 1718); Fabricius-Harles, *Bibliotheca Graeca*, editio nova (Hamburg, 1780-1809), vol. 5 (1796), pp. 527-535; Hermann Mutschmann, "Die Überlieferung der Schriften des Sextus Empiricus," *Rheinisches Museum für Philologie*, N.F. 64 (1909), 244-283, 478; Popkin, *History of Scepticism*; and my two books cited in n. 1 above.

5. The best edition is that in the Teubner series, ed. H. Mutschmann, J. Mau, and K. Janáček, 4 vols. (Leipzig, 1912-1962). See also the Loeb edition, which is accompanied by an English translation, ed. R. G. Bury, 4 vols. (London, 1933-1949).

6. This translation—extant in MSS Paris, Bibliothèque Nationale, lat. 14, 700, fols. 83-132; Madrid, Biblioteca national, 10, 112, fols. 1-30; and Venezia B. Marciana, lat. X 267 (3960)—seems to be attributable to the well-known translator of Galen, Niccolò da Reggio (active in Naples 1308-1347). It was made from a Greek manuscript no longer extant. For further details see the Introduction to vol. 1 of the Teubner ed. of Sextus, cited in the previous note; Mutschmann (above, n. 4); Popkin (above, n. 1); and H. Mutschmann, "Zur Übersetzertätigkeit des Nicolaus von Rhegium (zu Paris lat. 14,700)," *Berliner philologische Wochenschrift* 22 (1911), 691-692. For additional information on the translator see esp. L. Thorndike, "Translations of Works of Galen from the Greek by Niccolò da Reggio (c. 1308-1345)," *Byzantina Metabyzantina* 1 (1946), 213-235 and I. Wille, "Ueberlieferung und Uebersetzung: Zur Uebersetzungstechnik des Nicolaus von Rhegium in Galenos Schrift *De temporibus morborum*," *Helikon* 3 (1963), 259-277. It has only recently been shown that the Venice MS is also a copy of the same translation. See W. Cavini, "Appunti sulla prima diffusione in occidente delle opere di Sesto Empirico," *Medioevo* 3 (1977), 1-20, esp. 1-10.

7. See esp. *Gualteri Burlaei liber de vita et moribus philosophorum*, ed. W. Knust (Tübingen, 1886), in particular the introduction, where the problem of sources is discussed; V. Rose, "Die Lücken im Diogenes Laertius und die alten Übersetzer," *Hermes* 1 (1866), 367-397 and A. Biedi, *Zur Textgeschichte des Laertios Diogenes: Das grosse Excerpt: φ* (Vatican City, 1955).

8. Additional detail will be found in my *Cicero Scepticus* (above, n. 1), 33-42.

9. Ioannes Saresberiensis, *Policratici sive de nugis curialium et vestigiis philosophorum libri VIII*, ed. C. C. I. Webb (Oxford, 1909) I, 17; II, 93-99, 129, and *passim*; Étienne Gilson, *History of Christian Philosophy in the Middle Ages* (London, 1955), pp. 150-153, 624-625; Hans Liebeschutz, *Mediaeval Humanism in the Life and Writings of John of Salisbury* (London, 1950), p. 75; and M. Kerner, *Johannes von Salisbury und die logische Struktur seines Policraticus* (Wiesbaden, 1977), pp. 15-16, 183-184.

10. See the opening pages of Henry's *Summa quaestionum ordinariarum* (Paris, 1520; reprint ed., St. Bonaventure, New York, 1953).

11. E.g., "Quaestio III: Utrum metaphysica sit omnium scientiarum certissima," in Joannes Buridan, *In Metaphysicen Aristotelis Quaestiones argutissimae* (Paris, 1518; reprint ed., Frankfurt, 1968), fols. 4^r-5^r.

12. See especially Joseph Lappe, *Nicolaus von Autrecourt* (Münster, 1908), and Julius R. Weinberg, *Nicolaus of Autrecourt: A Study in Fourteenth Century Thought* (Princeton, 1948).

13. There is a large literature on the so-called "skepticism" of the Middle Ages. For a penetrating analysis of the situation, as well as for a critique and bibliography of earlier literature on the subject, see A. Maier, "Das Problem der Evidenz in der Philosophie des 14. Jahrhunderts," in her *Ausgehendes Mittelalters* (Rome, 1964-1977), II, 367-418.

14. For but one example see Cap. I: "De differentia mundanae theologiae atque divinae et de demonstrationibus earumdem," in Hugo de S. Victore, *Commentarium in Hierarchiam Caelestem S. Dionysii Areopagitae*, in *PL* 175, cols. 923-928.

15. A strong antiintellectual orientation is evident nearly everywhere in the work. I cite but one example from the first chapter, which reads, in part: "Not high-flown words, but a virtuous life, makes a man blessed and just. . . . If you were to know the entire Bible from the outside and the teachings of all the philosophers, what would it all profit you without God's love and grace? Vanity of vanities and all is vanity, except for loving God and serving Him alone." *Thomae a Kempis . . . Opera omnia* (Cologne, 1680), p. 269. For a detailed analysis of this tradition see Albert Hyma, *The Christian Renaissance: A History of the Devotio Moderna*, 2d ed. (Hamden, Conn., 1965) and R. R. Post, *The Modern Devotion* (Leiden, 1968).

16. Particularly important are his *Tahafut al-falasifah* (*Destructio philosophorum*). For further details see especially Farid Jabre, *La notion de certitude selon Ghazali dans ses origines psychologiques et historiques* (Paris, 1958); M. E. Marmuda, "Ghazali and Demonstrative Science," *Journal of the History of Philosophy* 3 (1965), 183-204; and the recent reprint of the Latin text, *Destructio Destructionum Algazelis in the Latin Version of Calo Calonymos*, ed. Beatrice H. Zedler (Milwaukee, 1961). The starting point of any study is still the annotated edition of the Tahāfut by M. Bouyges (Beirut, 1927).

17. Jehuda's *Kuzari* has a strongly skeptical orientation. On his life and works see the bibliography collected in Wilhelm Totok, *Handbuch der Geschichte der Philosophie* (Frankfurt am Main, 1964 ff.), II (1970), 299-300, which besides being up-to-date lists the scattered literature.

18. This has particularly been emphasized by Garin and Kristeller. See especially Eugenio Garin, *Medioevo e Rinascimento*, 2d ed. (Bari, 1961); idem, *Dall' umanesimo all'illuminismo* (Pisa, 1971); Paul Oskar Kristeller, *Renaissance Philosophy and the Mediaeval Tradition* (Latrobe, Pa., 1966). Instructive material is also found in Cesare Vasoli, "La cultura dei secoli XIV-XVI," in *Atti del primo convegno internazionale di ricognizione delle fonti per la storia della scienza italiana: i secoli XIV-XVI*, ed. C. Maccagni (Florence, 1967), pp. 31-105 and Charles H. Lohr, "Aristotle in the West: Some Recent Books," *Traditio* 25 (1969), 417-431.

19. Thus I feel that books such as John Owen, *The Sceptics of the French Renaissance* (London, 1893); idem, *The Sceptics of the Italian Renaissance* (London, 1893); Henri Busson, *Les sources et le développement du rationalisme dans*

la littérature française de la Renaissance (1533-1601) (Paris, 1922; slightly revised version with revised title, 1957); and Allen (above, n. 1) are somewhat mistaken in their approach. See my review of Allen cited in n. 2 above and chapter 1 of my *Cicero Scepticus*, as well as Popkin's "Scepticism, Theology and the Scientific Revolution" (above, n. 1); Kristeller's article cited in n. 2 above; and Lucien Febvre, *Le problème de l'incroyance au 16ᵉ siècle* (Paris, 1942; reprint ed., 1968). Neal W. Gilbert, "Renaissance Aristotelianism and Its Fate: Some Observations and Problems," in *Naturalism and Historical Understanding: Essays on the Philosophy of John Herman Randall,* ed. J. Anton (Buffalo, N.Y., 1967), pp. 42-52 offers an instructive exposé of some of the shortcomings of Busson's method.

20. In a forthcoming study I plan to deal with the history and evolution of the term "skepticism" in early modern philosophical vocabulary.

21. Gianfrancesco Pico and Pedro de Valencia are two examples. On the former see my *Gianfrancesco Pico* (above, n. 1) and on the latter see the text cited in Popkin, *History of Scepticism* (above, n. 1), 259 for example.

22. See B. L. Ullman, *Studies in the Italian Renaissance* (Rome, 1955), pp. 118-137.

23. See, e.g., Coluccio Salutati, *Epistolario,* ed. F. Novati (Rome, 1891-1905), III, 457-458, 602-603; idem, *De nobilitate legum et medicinae; De verecundia,* ed. E. Garin (Florence, 1947), pp. 136-138; idem, *De laboribus Herculis,* ed. B. L. Ullman (Zurich, 1951), p. 130. Salutati's manuscript of the *Lucullus* is now in Florence, Biblioteca nazionale, Mag. XXIX. 199 (Strozzi, 1066), fols. 60-90, which has some marginal annotations in Salutati's hand. On this see Eugenio Garin, "Un codice ciceroniano del Salutati," *Rinascimento* 1 (1950), 99-100 and B. L. Ullman, *The Humanism of Coluccio Salutati* (Padua, 1963), pp. 175-176, 223-224.

24. See L. Jardine, chap. 10 of this anthology, and L. Panizza, "Lorenzo Valla's *De vero falsoque bono,* Lactantius and Oratorical Scepticism," *Journal of the Warburg and Courtauld Institutes* 41 (1978), 76-107.

25. Petrus Victorius, *Explicationes suarum in Ciceronem castigationum* (Venice, 1536), fol. 71. Cf. Francesco Niccolai, *Pier Vettori (1499-1585)* (Florence, ca. 1907), pp. 198-220 on Vettori's edition of Cicero, one of the most important of the century.

26. A complete list of these will be found in my *Cicero Scepticus* (above, n. 1), p. 55.

27. Audomarus Talaeus, *Academia eiusdem in Academicum Ciceronis fragmentum explicatio* (Paris, 1547). In the edition published three years later, there was added a commentary on the *Lucullus.* For further details of the various editions see Walter J. Ong, *Ramus and Talon Inventory* (Cambridge, Mass., 1958), pp. 488-490. On Talon and his activities see, inter alia, Louis François Daire, *Histoire littéraire de la ville d'Amiens* (Paris, 1782), pp. 94-96; Busson (above, n. 19; 1957 ed.), pp. 235-237; Walter J. Ong, *Ramus: Method and Decay of Dialogue* (Cambridge, Mass., 1958), pp. 270-274 and *passim;* idem, *Ramus and Talon Inventory,* pp. 465-491; Popkin, *History of Scepticism* (above, n. 1), pp. 28-30.

28. On Ramus and his reform see especially the volumes of Ong cited in the previous note, which cite the earlier literature. Of recent publications of particular note are R. Hooykaas, *Humanisme, science et reform: Pierre de la Ramée*

(*1515-1572*) (Leiden, 1958); Neal W. Gilbert, *Renaissance Concepts of Method* (New York, 1960); J. J. Verdonk, *Petrus Ramus en de wiskunde* (Assen, 1966); Cesare Vasoli, *La dialettica e la retorica dell'umanesimo: "Invenzione" e "metodo" nella cultura del XV e XVI secolo* (Milan, 1968). Craig Walton, "Ramus and Socrates," *Proceedings of the American Philosophical Society* 114 (1970), 119-139 is of particular interest with regard to some of the points discussed here. See also P. Sharratt, 'Peter Ramus and the Reform of the University: The Divorce of Philosophy and Eloquence?" and C. J. R. Armstrong, "The Dialectical Road to Truth: The Dialogue," in *French Renaissance Studies, 1540-1570*, ed. P. Sharratt (Edinburgh, 1976), pp. 4-20, 36-51.

29. On this see Jerrold E. Seigel, *Rhetoric and Philosophy in Renaissance Humanism: The Union of Eloquence and Wisdom, Petrarch to Valla* (Princeton, 1968).

30. For Gassendi's clear statement of his indebtedness to Ramus see Pierre Gassendi, *Dissertations en forme de paradoxes contre les aristoteliciens*, ed. B. Rochot (Paris, 1959), p. 7, which is the Preface of his *Exercitationes paradoxicae adversus Aristoteleos*, first published in 1624. For the influence of skepticism on Gassendi see especially Henri Berr, *Du scepticisme de Gassendi* (Paris, 1960), which is a French translation of Berr's Latin thesis originally published in 1898; Tullio Gregory, *Scetticismo ed empirismo: Studio su Gassendi* (Bari, 1961); Popkin, *History of Scepticism*; and Oliver René Bloch, *La philosophie de Gassendi* (The Hague, 1970).

31. *Pro schola Parisiensi contra novam academiam Petri Rami oratio* (Paris, 1551). On Galland see especially Claude Pierre Goujet, *Mémoire historique et littéraire sur le collège royal de France* (Paris, 1758), I, 153-156; L. Froger, "Les hommes de lettres au XVIe siècle dans le diocese du Mans, II: Pierre Galland," *Revue de la Renaissance* 2 (1902), 189-191; Busson (above, n. 19; 1957 ed.), 269-273; Ong, *Ramus and the Decay of Dialogue*, 39-41; Sharratt and Armstrong (above, n. 28).

32. On this see the modern annotated edition with an illuminating introduction, *The Dialogues of Guy de Brués: A Critical Edition with a Study in Renaissance Scepticism and Relativism*, ed. Panos Paul Morphos (Baltimore, 1953).

33. See the publications by Febvre, Gilbert, Kristeller, Popkin, and Schmitt cited above in n. 19 above.

34. See the literature cited above in n. 28 above. I hope that chapter 4 of my *Cicero Scepticus* sheds some light on the situation.

35. *Iulii Castellanii Faventini adversus Marci Tullii Ciceronis academicas quaestiones disputatio* (Bologna, 1558). For a detailed discussion of this work and further bibliography see my *Cicero Scepticus* (above, n. 1), pp. 109-133.

36. For the original text see Cicero, *Academica* II, 123. On Hicetas as a "precursor of Copernicus" see G. V. Schiaparelli, *I precursori di Copernico nell'antichità*, Pubblicazioni del Reale Osservatorio de Brera in Milano, III (Milan, 1873), 1-11 and Thomas Heath, *Aristarchus of Samos* (Oxford, 1913), pp. 187-189.

37. *Nicolai Copernici. . .De revolutionibus orbium caelestium libri sex*, ed. F. & C. Zeller (Munich, 1949), pp. 5, 14, and the editors' comments on pp. 429, 423-433.

38. Schmitt, *Cicero Scepticus* (above, n. 1), p. 128.

39. Talaeus (above, n. 27; 1550 ed.), II, 104.

40. *In reliquas Academicarum quaestionum M. Tullii Ciceronis & eiusdem quinque libros de finibus Iohannis Rosae commentarius* (Frankfurt am Main, 1571). For further details on this nearly forgotten work and additional bibliography on Rosa see chapter 6 of my *Cicero Scepticus*.

41. Rosa (above, n. 40), fol. 92v.

42. Ibid., fol. 92v-93r.

43. *Academica sive de indicio erga verum, ex ipsis primis fontibus* (Antwerp, 1596). For further information on Pedro and his work see especially M. Serrano y Sanz, *Pedro de Valencia: Estudio biográfico-crítico* (Badajoz, 1910); Marcial Solana, *Historia de la filosofía española: Epoca del Renascimiento (siglo-XVI)* (Madrid, 1941), I, 357-376; and M. Menéndez Pelayo, *Ensayos de crítica filosófica*, Edicion nacional de la obras de Menéndez Pelayo, vol. 43 (Santander, 1948), pp. 235-256.

44. See the opinion of Reid in Cicero, *Academica*, ed. James S. Reid (London, 1885; reprint ed., Hildesheim, 1966), p. 72.

45. For details see Menéndez Pelayo (above, n. 43), pp. 252-256.

46. Petrus de Valentia (above, n. 43), pp. 123-124. Cf. Popkin, *History of Scepticism*, p. 259.

47. It is contained in Diogenes' *Lives of Eminent Philosophers* IX 11. 61-108. A convenient edition is the one edited with an English translation by R. D. Hicks (London, 1925), II, 474-519.

48. The article on this author for the *Catalogus Translationum et Commentariorum* is being prepared by Professor Grundy Steiner. When it has been completed we shall be in a much better position to evaluate the impact of the recovery of Diogenes Laertius on the Renaissance. As yet this has been but little studied.

49. For some information see R. R. Bolgar, *The Classical Heritage and Its Beneficiaries* (London, 1954), p. 472 and Eugenio Garin, "La prima traduzione latina di Diogene Laerzio," *Giornale critico della filosofia italiana* 38 (1959), 283-285.

50. I know of approximately seventy-five manuscripts, though my research in this matter has been far from complete. There are seven incunabular editions of Traversari's translation and ten editions of the Italian translations (for further details see *Gesamtkatalog der Wiegendrucke*, s. v.), in addition to numerous sixteenth-century editions of the Greek text (*editio princeps*, Basel, 1533) and various Latin and vernacular translations.

51. The entry in Niccolò Perotti's *Cornucopiae* (1st ed. 1489) used in Venice 1499 ed., 535-536) seems to be largely derived from Diogenes Laertius, but is not really very informative or profound.

52. For details see my *Cicero Scepticus*.

53. Aulus Gellius, *Noctes atticae*, ed. P. K. Marshall (Oxford, 1968), p. 341 (XI 5. 6), where manuscript variants are given. The context here also indicates that the use of the word is considered unusual.

54. The question of the translations of Sextus Empiricus and the influence of his work during the Middle Ages and Renaissance will be dealt with in a future

study. For evidence that the word was used in the medieval translation see the excerpts printed by Charles Jourdain, "Sextus Empiricus et la philosophie scolastique," in Jourdain's *Excursions historiques et philosophiques à travers le moyen age* (Paris, 1888), pp. 201-217, at 204; Clemens Baeumker, "Eine bisher unbekannte mittelalterliche lateinische Übersetzung der Πυρρώνειοι Ύποτυπώσεις des Sextus Empiricus," *Archiv für Geschichte der Philosophie* 4 (1891), 574-577, at p. 577; and Cavini (above, n. 6).

55. This seems to begin with Traversari's translation of the *Vita Pyrrhonis*. See Diogenes Laertius, *Vitae et sententiae philosophorum* (Venice, 1475; GW 8379), 153v-159v. Ficino, for example, used the word several times. See P. O. Kristeller, *Il pensiero filosofico di Marsilio Ficino* (Florence, 1953), p. 461 for a listing.

56. In the *De servo arbitrio* of 1525. See Martin Luther, *Werke: Kritische Gesamtausgabe* (Weimar, 1883 ff.), XVIII, 605.

57. See the literature cited in nn. 6 and 54 above, as well as Popkin, *History of Scepticism* (above, n. 1), p. 252 for the information available in printed sources.

58. See below for a discussion of this.

59. Ἀφ' οὗ δὲ Σέξτοι, καὶ Πύρρωνες, καὶ ἡ ἀντίθετος γλῶσσα, ὥσπερ τι νόσημα δεινὸν καὶ κακόηθες ταῖς Ἐκκλησίαις ἡμῶν εἰσεφθάρη ...
PG, 35, vol. 1096.

60. For a general analysis of Gregory's attitude towards Greek philosophy see R. R. Ruether, *Gregory of Nazianzenus: Rhetor and Philosopher* (Oxford, 1969), esp. pp. 167-175.

61. Πλέκων λαβυρίνθους δυσδιεξόδοις λόγοις Ἀριστοτέλους ἤ τινων Πυρρωννίων. *Carmina, sectio II: Poemata moralia*, no. X: *De virtute* (lines 48-49), in *PG*, 37, col. 684. A similar view is expressed in his poem *De si ipso et de episcopis* (*PG*, 37, col. 1188, line 303), where both Sextus and Pyrrho are mentioned.

62. In *Florilegium* 121, 28 as found in Joannes Stobaeus, *Florilegium*, ed. T. Gaisford (Oxford, 1822), III, 479.

63. *Agathiae Myrinaei Historiarum libri quinque*, ed. R. Keydell (Berlin, 1967), p. 79, line 8 (II, 29). For an analysis of the text see Averil Cameron, *Agathias* (Oxford, 1970), 104-105. As she notes, reflections of skeptical doctrine can also be found in the *Anthologia Palatina* VII, 576.

64. *Bibliotheca*, 212, in Photius, *Bibliothèque*, ed. R. Henry (Paris, 1959 f.), III, 119-123.

65. See G. Podskalsky, "Nicolaos von Methone und die Proklosrenaissance in Byzanz (11/12 Jh.)," *Orientalia Christiana Periodica* 42 (1976), p. 512, n. 5.

66. *PG*, 121, col. 320 (§283-284).

67. Much information on the Byzantine knowledge of Sextus Empiricus was already available in Fabricius, *Bibliotheca Graeca* (above, n. 4), though most later scholars who have worked on the history of skepticism in the West have not taken note of it. A useful general survey is found in D. M. Nicol, "The Byzantine Church and Hellenic Learning in the Fourteenth Century," *Studies in Church History* 5 (1969), 23-57, esp. 43.

68. Theodorus Metochites, *Miscellanea philosophica et historica*, ed. C. G. Müller and T. Kiessling (Leipzig, 1821; reprint ed., Amsterdam, 1966), pp. 370-377.

69. Nicephoros Gregoras, *Byzantina historia*, ed. L. Schopen (Bonn, 1829-1855), II, 930 (XIX, 1). See above, n. 59. Cf. Nicol (above, n. 67), p. 43 and R. Guilland, *Essai sur Nicéphore Gregoras, l'homme et l'œuvre* (Paris, 1926), pp. 206-207, both of whom cite the text, but do not point out its source in Gregory.

70. See Gregory Palamas, Συγγράμματα, ed. B. Bobrinsky et al. (Thessalonike, 1962), I, 258 and I. Ševčenko, "Nicolaus Cabasilas' Correspondence," *Byzantinisches Zeitschrift* 47 (1954), 49-59, at 51.

71. Fabricius (above, n. 4), V, 527-528 noted the text long ago. For an edition of what survives with a discussion of its significance see A. Elter and L. Radermacher, *Analecta graeca* (Bonn, 1899), §I, "Nicolai Cabasilae κατὰ τῶν λεγομένων περὶ τοῦ κριτηρίου τῆς 'αληθείας εἰ ἔστι παρὰ Πύρρωνος τοῦ καταράτου," and §II, "Analecta ad historiam litterarum Graecarum scr. A. Elter," esp. cols. 11-28. See also Ševčenko (above, n. 70) and, in general, P. Enepekides, "Der Briefwechsel des Mystikers Nikolaos Kabasilas," *Byzantinisches Zeitschrift* 45 (1953), 18-46; A. A. Angelopoulou, Νικλαος Καβασιλας χαριαετος (Thessalonike, 1970); and G. Podskalsky, *Theologie und Philosophie in Byzanz* (Munich, 1977), pp. 152-153.

72. R. Sabbadini, *Le scoperte dei codici latini e greci nei secoli XIV e XV* (Florence, 1905-1914; reprint ed., ed. E. Garin, Florence, 1967), I, 48, where references to Filelfo's letters are cited. On Filelfo's use of Sextus see also A. Calderini, "Ricerche intorno alla biblioteca e alla cultura greca di Francesco Filelfo," *Studi italiani di filologia classica* 20 (1913), 204-424, esp. 389-390. Besides lending his manuscript to Aurispa (see next note), Filelfo also sought in 1452 to get hold of Bessarion's in an effort to improve his own copy. See *Francisci Philelfi. . . Epistolarum familiarum libri XXXVII* (Venice, 1502), fol. 71. Cf. Calderini, p. 189.

73. See the letter to Aurispa dated 10 June 1441, where Filelfo agrees to lend his Sextus manuscript. The relevant section is printed in *Carteggio di Giovanni Aurispa*, ed. R. Sabbadini (Rome, 1931), p. 97.

74. H. Omont, "Inventaire des manuscrits grecs et latins donnés à Saint-Marc de Venise par le Cardinal Bessarion (1468)," *Revue des bibliothèques* 4 (1894), 165.

75. Francesco Patrizi, *De institutione reipublicae libri IX* (Strasbourg, 1594), p. 53. This work was written about 1471. It is not clear which work of Sextus Patrizi knew or whether his information was based on secondhand evidence. For further information see *Cicero Scepticus* (above, n. 1), pp. 49-51.

76. I. Maier, *Les manuscrits d'Ange Politien* (Geneva, 1965), pp. 117-123, 229. See also Angelo Poliziano, *Miscellaneorum centuria secunda*, ed. V. Branca & M. Pastore Stocchi (Florence, 1972), III, 103 (§47, 13).

77. Ficino cited Sextus in his commentary on Plotinus, *Enneades* IV, sec. 3, cap. 8.

78. P. Kibre, *The Library of Pico della Mirandola* (New York, 1936), nos. 673 and 1044 are the two copies of Sextus's works in Pico's library.

79. A text of Sextus was already in the hands of the Medici by 1459 when Guarino da Verona wrote to Piero di Cosimo de' Medici asking for a copy of the manuscript. See L. Capra, "Contributo a Guarino Veronese," *Italia medioevale e umanistica* 14 (1971), 193-247, esp. 244-247. Three Sextus manuscripts are cited in the inventory of the Medici Library made by Janos Lascaris sometime before

the death of Lorenzo de' Medici in 1492. See K. Müller, "Neue Mittheilungen über Janos Lascaris und die Mediceische Bibliothek," *Zentralblatt für Bibliothekswesen* 1 (1884), 333-412. There is but a single manuscript listed, however, in the inventory made on 20 October 1495. See E. Piccolomini, *Intorno alle condizioni ed alle vicende della Libreria Medicea privata* (Florence, 1875), p. lxxxiii, item 174 [also printed in *Archivio storico italiano*, 3d ser., 19 (1874) and 21 (1875)].

80. There was a manuscript in the Vatican Library as early as 1475. See R. Devreesse, *Les fonds grecs de la Bibliothèque Vaticane des origines à Paul V* (Vatican City, 1965), p. 55 and E. Muntz & P. Fabre, *La bibliothèque du Vatican au XVᵉ siècle d'après des documents inedits* (Paris, 1887), p. 232.

81. B. L. Ullman & P. A. Stadter, *The Public Library of Renaissance Florence: Niccolò Niccoli, Cosimo de' Medici and the Library of San Marco* (Padua, 1972), pp. 257 (no. 1142), 277 (M.94).

82. See my "An Unstudied Fifteenth-Century Latin Translation of Sextus Empiricus by Giovanni Lorenzi (Vat. Lat. 2990)," in *Cultural Aspects of the Italian Renaissance: Essays in Honour of Paul Oskar Kristeller*, ed. C. H. Clough (Manchester, 1976), pp. 244-261, where the details are given. Further information on other points raised in the present paper is also given.

83. The fullest discussion on this is now Cavini (above, n. 6), pp. 15-18.

84. This is evident in the texts of Filelfo, Patrizi, Poliziano, and Ficino cited above.

85. Dealt with in my *Gianfrancesco Pico* (above, n. 1). Also now see W. Cavini, "Un inedito di Giovan Francesco Pico della Mirandola: La 'Quaestio de falsitate astrologiae,'" *Rinascimento*, 2d ser., 13 (1973), 133-171 and Cavini (above, n. 6).

86. See Cavini (above, n. 6), pp. 15-18. For further information on Vespucci see A. C. de la Mare, *The Handwriting of the Italian Humanists*, vol. I, fasc. I (Oxford, 1973), pp. 106-138.

87. The earliest citation yet noted is in the *Quaestio de falsitate astrologiae*, datable no later than 1511. See Cavini (above, n. 85), pp. 140, 147, 148.

88. See above, n. 35.

89. See Schmitt, *Gianfrancesco Pico* (above, n. 1), pp. 161-163.

90. For details see my *Cicero Scepticus* (above, n. 1), pp. 69-71.

91. Sextus Empiricus, *Pyrrhoniarum hypotypōseōn libri III. . . latine nunc primum editi interprete Henrico Stephano* (Paris, 1562).

92. Sextus Empiricus, *Adversus mathematicos. . . graece numquam latine nunc primum editum, Gentiano Herveto interprete; Eiusdem Sexti Pyrrhoniarum hypotyposeon libri tres. . . interprete Henrico Stephano* (Paris, 1569).

93. Petrus De Valentia, ed. cit., p. 122.

94. Sextus Empiricus, *Opera omnia quae extant* (Geneva, 1621).

95. See *Gesamtkatalog der Wiegendrucke*.

96. On this see Popkin, *History of Scepticism* (above, n. 1), pp. 19-20, as well as his "Samuel Sorbière's Translation of Sextus Empiricus," *Journal of the History of Ideas* 14 (1953), 617-621. Further information in E. A. Strathmann, *Sir Walter Ralegh: A Study in Skepticism* (New York, 1951), pp. 224-253; S. E.

Spott, "Ralegh's Sceptic and the Elizabethan Translation of Sextus Empiricus," *Philological Quarterly* 42 (1963), 166-175; P. Lefranc, *Sir Walter Ralegh écrivain: L'œuvre et les idées* (Paris, 1968), pp. 66-67 and *passim*; C. B. Schmitt, "An Unknown Seventeenth Century French Translation of Sextus Empiricus," *Journal of the History of Philosophy* 6 (1968), 69-76.

97. The first printed edition is *De judicandi facultate et animi principatu*, ed. Isaac Bulliardus (Paris, 1663), though there were a significant number of manuscripts in circulation before the first printing. See the Introduction to the Teubner edition of the work, ed. F. Lammert (Leipzig, 1961), vol. III-2 of the Teubner Ptolemaeus, *Opera quae exstant omnia.*

98. For some information see Popkin (above, n. 1), esp. chap. 1, and some of the same author's various articles, esp. "Skepticism and the Counter-Reformation in France," *Archiv für Reformationseschichte* 51 (1960), 58-87 and "The High Road to Pyrrhonism," *American Philosophical Quarterly* 2 (1965), 1-15, as well as my *Cicero Scepticus*, pp. 58-66.

99. See, e.g., Jacobus Schegk, *De demonstratione libri XV* (Basel, 1564), p. 3.

100. One Italian writer of the period concerned with the skeptical problem, however, was Filippo Fabri, a Franciscan of Scotist orientation. See his *Disputatio secunda: Utrum aliqua veritas sincera et pura haberi possit ex puris naturalibus in hac vita absque speciali illustratione Dei et qua argumentum efficax contra Atheistas elicitur*, in Philipus Faber, *Adversus impios atheos disputationes quatuor philosophicae* (Venice, 1627), pp. 154-222. See my "Filippo Fabri and Scepticism: A Forgotten Defence of Scotus," in *Storia e cultura al Santo di Padova* (Vicenza, 1976), pp. 309-312.

101. I have tried to make this point in my *Critical Survey and Bibliography of Studies on Renaissance Aristotelianism, 1958-1969* (Padua, 1971).

102. Besides the *History of Scepticism* (above, n. 1) see also the studies now collected in his *High Road to Pyrrhonism*, ed. R. A. Watson & J. E. Force (San Diego, 1980).

103. For two different possibilities see my *Cicero Scepticus* and E. N. Tigerstedt, *The Decline and Fall of the Neoplatonic Interpretation of Plato* (Helsinki, 1974).

104. See *Cicero Scepticus*, pp. 8-10.

Note: Since this paper has been completed, the following relevant publications have come to my attention: R. H. and M. A. Rouse, "The Medieval Circulation of Cicero's *Posterior Academics* and the *De finibus bonorum et malorum*," in *Medieval Scribes, Manuscripts and Libraries. Essays Presented to N. R. Ker*, ed. M. B. Parkes and A. G. Watson (London, 1978), pp. 333-367; L. Cesarini Martinelli, "Sesto Empirico e una dispersa enciclopedia delle arti e scienze di Angelo Poliziano," *Rinascimento* 2ª ser., 20 (1980), pp. 327-358; and B. Faes de Mottoni, "Isidoro di Siviglia e gli accademici," in *Lo scetticismo antico*, ed. G. Giannantoni (Naples, 1982), pp. 395-414.

10

Lorenzo Valla: Academic Skepticism and the New Humanist Dialectic

Lisa Jardine

About the turn of the fifteenth century, the humanist program of classical studies which for a century or more had struggled in competition with high scholasticism finally established itself as a serious alternative to the Aristotelian curriculum in the universities of Northern Europe. A systematic program of reading in the great literary texts of Greece and Rome, coupled with a careful grooming in "eloquence" in the ancient languages, became an acceptable substitute for the meticulous study of logic and philosophy which medieval scholars had considered the necessary propaedeutic for all learning. At the heart of the humanist program was a new and deliberately independent course in the kind of ratiocination appropriate to the literary focus of the new arts course—a dialectic tailored to the needs of the graduate destined for a civic or legal career (the articulate civil servant).[1]

The history of the assessment of this new program in dialectic is a curious one. Essentially it has always been assumed that humanist revisions of dialectic were frivolous: humanists were, after all, anxious to pour scorn on the unnecessary quibbling of scholastic logic, and to assert its lack of relevance to eloquence and the classical tradition.[2] The standard account (as given, for instance, in William and Martha Kneale's *The Development of Logic*[3]) lays the blame for the neglect of formal logic which the humanist outlook fostered at the feet of Cicero and Quintilian:

In general education the writing of elegant Latin was now the chief accomplishment to be learnt, and for this Cicero and Quintilian were the authorities. From them the men of the Renaissance acquired the Roman attitude to scholarship, with the result that genuine logic was neglected for rhetoric and books which purported to be on logic quoted Cicero as often as Aristotle. Laurentius Valla, who exposed the forged donation of Constantine, and Rudolph Agrippa [Agricola] were two writers who started the corruption.[4]

Cicero and Quintilian—orators, not philosophers—seduced humanists away from the proper center of logical studies, the exploration of the principles of valid inference. As far as the Kneales are concerned, any treatment of ratiocination which is not centrally concerned with formal validity does not deserve the serious consideration of the historian of logic. They therefore condemn as entirely unproductive the shift in attention away from syllogistic and toward the analysis of active argument in orations and dialogues which characterizes the dialectic of Valla and Agricola. The brief sketch of the history of humanist intervention in logic studies which the Kneales give is perceptive (apart from the misnaming of Agricola); the interpretation they place upon it is the product of the particular view of logic which they make quite explicit in the introductory sections of their history.[5]

In recent years, however, there has been a shift in interest on the part of practicing logicians and philosophers of a kind very similar to that evidenced in humanistic treatises on the subject (if we read these with the care and serious attention they deserve). They have come increasingly to respect the importance for philosophy of forms of inference which do not readily lend themselves to formalization, and thus whose validity is at some level in doubt.[6] In this I suggest they are taking a direction anticipated by fifteenth-century humanists. I shall try to show here how intentionally innovative humanist dialectic actually was; how self-consciously and deliberately it took the steps which the conventional histories of logic attribute to logical ignorance and "Ciceronian" sloppy thinking. I shall further show how the role of Cicero himself within the story is more active and central (more than a name-tag denoting inferior intellectual achievement) than the traditional account allows. I shall argue that the development of discussion of dialectical inference forms other than the syllogism, and of associated semantic problems, is intimately related to the recovery by humanists of Cicero's skeptical thinking; if Cicero is viewed as consistently taking a skeptic's stand, it is possible to bring together his philosophical and oratorical works in one coherent reading. I shall argue that far from being an "interregnum" in the history of logic,[7] humanist dialectic, as developed by Lorenzo Valla in particular, deserves serious consideration as a significant strand in the emergence of modern philosophical method.

Suppose we begin by retracing our steps to the point at which the historian of logic designates humanist dialectic as "rhetoricizing." It is indeed the case that early humanist writers were particularly fascinated with the complex and sometimes elusive patterns of reasoning which the sophisticated protagonist in a Platonic dialogue or a Ciceronian oration deploys to establish a preferred position as more convincing than another. These are the areas highlighted in the flurry of intellectual activity which resulted from the recovery for the first time in intact form of literary and philosophical texts which had hitherto lain unread (often in corrupt form) in monastery libraries. And it is probably the case that this encouraged their interest in that part of the existing logic curriculum which gives systematic attention to the kinds of strategy used in such active debate: the kinds of strategy discussed in Aristotle's *Topica* and the Roman texts derived from it (Cicero's *Topica* and *De inventione;* the fifth book of Quintilian's *Institutio oratoria*), and most familiar to late medieval students in Boethius's seminal text, the *De differentiis topicis.*[8]

Where the treatise on syllogistics is plainly concerned with formalization and validity (the model treatment being Aristotle's *Analytica priora*), the treatise on *Topica*, as medieval logicians were fond of pointing out, was an *applied* work: it tackled the practical detail of employing ratiocination in debate and disputation, to enable the participant to arrive at a desired conclusion from acceptable premises. It is easy to be lured into the view (again, regularly expressed by medieval commentators) that "topics" means a weaker and less systematic version of the ideal arguments which the syllogistic logician studies for validity in his theoretical treatise.

Yet the form of the *Topics* treatise clearly allows discussion of nonsyllogistic inference and even of inference whose status is dubious.[9] Boethius, for instance, sets up his topics-logic as follows: Where a matter is in doubt, the object of the dialectician's activities is to select and arrange appropriately such material as will establish belief.[10] Topical "invention" is the process of selecting and classifying material appropriate to the case in hand for convenient recall. Dialectical "judgment" is its arrangement "ad fidem faciens" (to secure belief). The *De differentiis topicis* classifies procedures for dialectical invention in such a way as to take account of the varied possibilities of using the material to convince an adversary in debate. The classification is based on *topical maxims* (what Bird calls "inference warrants"[11]): general principles which hold regardless of the particular matter under consideration, and by means of which we can find our way to suitable arguments to support our case. Thus if the question is, "Whether it is preferable to rule as absolute head of state or as consul," we may argue as follows: "The rule of the absolute head of state is longer than that of the consul, both being desirable (*bonum*); therefore the rule of head of state is preferable to that of consul." Here the *maxim* is: "The good thing of longer duration is preferable to that of shorter duration."[12] Topical maxims are then grouped under *topical differences*: the boxes into which maxims can be sorted according to the nature of the rule they give, for convenient recall in the course of a debate. Suppose the question is, "Whether trees are animals," we construct the syllogism: "An animal is a sensible, animate substance; a tree is not a sensible, animate substance; therefore a tree is not an animal." The topical maxim is: "What does not match the definition of the genus is not a species of that genus," and that maxim is classified under the *topical difference definition*, which groups all maxims containing rules concerning the relation between definitions.[13] A number of the maxims which Boethius gives (e.g., relational and etymological maxims) are certainly not reducible to syllogistic form.[14]

Books I to III of the *De differentiis topicis* treat topical invention in dialectic; Book IV adds the distinct but similar procedures for rhetoric. Books I to III feature regularly in late scholastic university curricula as part of dialectic teaching; Book IV features in the rhetoric course.[15] So that as far as the medieval schoolmen were concerned, there was a recognizable difference between topical invention "ad fidem faciens," where the doubt is considered in a dialectical context, and that appropriate to rhetoric. If we insist on considering topics-theory as intrinsically unsuitable as a part of logical instruction (because of its evasiveness about validity), we immediately cut ourselves off from late medieval and early Renaissance thinking on the subject. It is surely more instructive to preserve the contemporary view that some treatment of topics-theory has a bearing on logic training, even if it is also adaptable to rhetoric (where plausibility is the order of the day, rather than conviction, and the topical maxims tolerated will reflect this). Having identified an ancient tradition of discussion of inference of *doubtful* validity (for this, as Agricola, for example, points out, is the importance of the topical maxims),[16] let us retain the title "dialectic" for its discussion until we find some real justification for discarding it in favor of the (inevitably derogatory) alternative, "rhetoric."

So we may begin by setting aside the notion that Lorenzo Valla and Rudolph Agricola introduced some curious perversion into logic teaching in the latter half of the fifteenth century, and take a fresh look at the impact of the two crucial works on dialectic which these authors produced: Valla's *Dialecticae disputationes* and Agricola's *De inventione dialectica*.[17]

Valla completed his *Repastinatio dialecticae et philosophiae*, which in printed editions came to be known as the *Dialecticae disputationes*, in

1439.[18] It is a contentious work, which sets its face resolutely against the Aristotelianism of late scholasticism. It combines iconoclastic rejection of the fundamental metaphysical assumptions of scholastic thought with selective discussion of topics drawn from Cicero and Quintilian to produce a determined shift of focus in treatment of dialectical instruction: a shift away from syllogism and formal validity, and toward a survey of the varied and variously reliable active techniques for settling a matter in dispute. Valla's avowed aim is to show that Cicero's and Quintilian's transmission of Greek philosophy and logic deserves a central place in our understanding of these fields. In his view the enlarged horizons of the renaissance in classical learning ought substantially to modify conventional approaches to the art of reasoning. Valla's own position as one of those brilliantly gifted linguists who contributed most fully to the early fifteenth-century recovery of ancient Greek and Latin texts, their editing, and their diffusion encouraged him to feel competent to take a strong stand on identifying the main currents in classical thought.[19]

Agricola was a second-generation humanist. He came from the Low Countries to study at Erfurt and Cologne in the 1450s, and in 1468 or 1469 went to Italy, drawn by the reputation of the Italian legal schools, to continue his arts training first at Pavia and then at Ferrara. There he came in contact with the enlightened schools of humanist textual exegesis and linguistic study, modeled on the approaches of Cicero and Quintilian, which the great classical scholars like Panormita and Guarino had founded a generation earlier.[20] Sometime around 1479 he completed his seminal dialectic textbook, the *De inventione dialectica*, which amalgamated his perceptions about the range and compass of intellectual debate as practiced in the Italian schools, with his northern commitment to clear and unpretentious instruction in the arts of discourse for the pious layman. The *De inventione dialectica* is openly influenced by Valla's more highbrow and polemical work.[21] But where Valla's text is compressed, intellectually taxing, and frequently obscure, Agricola's is a down-to-earth instruction manual, amply provided with worked examples, in "the art of discoursing on any given topic appropriately to secure belief."[22] The *De inventione dialectica* became the standard humanist handbook on dialectic (widely commented and epitomized throughout Europe)[23] whilst (as Valla himself recognizes in his prefaces and correspondence) the *Dialecticae disputationes* was bound to remain a set-piece of humanist iconoclasm (admired but relatively inaccessible), to be read alongside his key linguistic and philosophical writings, the *Elegantiae*, the *De vero falsoque bono* and the *De libero arbitrio*.[24]

Both the polemical treatise and the instruction manual make it clear that there is far more to humanist reform of dialectic than a simple revamping of the old tradition on pragmatic grounds of its limited relevance to newly eloquent orators. Both Valla and Agricola promote a reformed dialectic as the basis for a fresh outlook on learning as a whole. A thoroughgoing reassessment of the study which defines the humanist's commitment to language and eloquence as the source of authentic understanding—dialectic—must accompany the patient reconstructions of ancient literary texts, the training of grammarians and rhetoricians in the subtleties of the ancient languages, and the establishing of schools of liberal studies on the model of those of Greece and Rome.[25] Valla and Agricola chose dialectic as the point for their main assault on scholastic education not because the dialectic texts of high scholasticism sat uneasily in a secular arts program focused on legal and political studies (the justification conventionally given by historians of education and of logic), but because they believed that there was something intrinsically wrongheaded about fifteenth-century dialectic studies, which made them inherently incompatible with the humanist attitude toward the acquisition of knowledge.

It is the implicit dogmatic strain in high medieval logic which offends Valla and Agricola. Because of their preoccupation with the validity of syllogistic inference, fifteenth-century editions of thirteenth-century logic manuals, even more than the original texts, concentrate their intellectual energies on the formal analysis of the relations between terms in appropriately constructed propositions, and on instructions for checking syllogisms to ensure that their conclusions follow from their premises.[26] They devote comparatively little space to the ancient tradition in dialectic— the tactical application of ratiocination to specific debating questions, which allowed as subsidiary supports for syllogistic argument induction, curtailed syllogism or enthymeme, example (reinforcement by illustration), and a number of relational arguments and arguments by analogy whose validity is guaranteed by nonsyllogistic rule.[27] Although a standard scholastic manual like Peter of Spain's *Summulae logicales* includes for completeness an account of topics-theory, based on Boethius's *De differentiis topicis*, it is cursory and dismissive, and takes the view that dialectical ratiocination is simply a debased and unreliable version of formal syllogistic (a view which is strongly reinforced in the fifteenth century *scholia* which accompany Peter of Spain's text).[28] The effect is to disparage active grappling with problems, in favor of high technical skill with a syllogistic "machine language."

At a practical level, therefore, Valla and Agricola are justified in wishing to reestablish within the standard discussion of ratiocination some serious treatment of the kinds of *argumentatio* frequently (and successfully) used by Cicero and by Cicero's hero, Plato (who on the scholastic account employs no logical method in his dialogues).[29] But this is not the end of it. The heavy emphasis on formal validity in the medieval logic text, which led to its concentrating almost exclusively on the syllogism, tended to divert the student's attention away from the technical difficulties surrounding the establishing of independent premises which are *true*. It was therefore all too easy to persuade the student that if only an argument could be reduced to a series of well-formed syllogisms, the validity of the inference implied the necessary truth of the conclusion (since in a well-formed syllogism a true conclusion necessarily follows from true premises).

For Valla and Agricola the pursuit of truth is an elusive if not an impossible undertaking. Any study of ratiocination which restricts itself to, or even concentrates on, objective truth and techniques for arriving at it must be inadequate:

For the extent of those things which can be grasped by us as necessary and indubitable is not great, and if we are to believe the Academic philosophy, absolutely none at all. Which everyone accepts in the case of ethics and behavior; and likewise in the case of knowledge of natural things, there is nothing which may not be disputed, and debated on all sides with great virtuosity.[30]

The road to knowledge is dogged by uncertainty; and the techniques available for exploring that uncertainty are those customarily employed for arguing "in utramque partem" on open questions (as Agricola goes on to specify in the above passage), particularly by the great classical jurists. Valla turns to Cicero, Quintilian, Aulus Gellius, and the "last of the erudite,"[31] Boethius, for a philosophy which will countenance his lack of confidence in the attainability of certainty, and a dialectic rich enough to allow him to explore the relative probability of conflicting dogmas, while withholding overall assent.

There is a double advantage for the present purposes in bracketing together Valla's intellectually taxing manifesto and Agricola's widely disseminated manual as I have done here. In the first place, it is Agricola's work whose direct influence can readily be traced throughout the sixteenth century[32]—an influence which historians of logic like the Kneales consider such a harmful interruption of the development of logic as they understand it. To contribute to a deeper understanding of the motivation behind Agricola's manual is thus to add a dimension to the consideration of an evident shift in focus within dialectic studies during the latter half of the fifteenth century. In the second place, Agricola's more direct concern with the practical consequences of dialectic studies, coupled as it is with vigorous acknowledgment of the vital part Valla's work plays in considering the form such revisions should take, enables us to build back into the original text of the *Dialecticae disputationes* some of the assumptions and transitions which this rather virtuoso piece takes for granted. As we turn back to Valla's work we may keep Agricola's text at our elbow for cross-reference and elucidation.

But before we do, a brief excursus is necessary. The cornerstone in Valla's case against the "dogmatic" dialectic of scholasticism, and the basis for a reconstruction of an ancient "undogmatic" alternative is Ciceronian or Academic skepticism (as developed in the face of Stoic dogmatism). Valla treats Cicero as an authoritative philosopher of the New Academy, and his philosophical dialogues as embodying a skeptical method of inquiry which is also reflected in the pedagogic works on oratory. Now this is an interesting reading of Cicero, but not one which at first sight is likely to meet with much support from modern students of ancient philosophy. Cicero is respected as an *orator*, with a body of solid pedagogic works on oratory to his credit, but his philosophical dialogues are considered naive and uncritical: a clumsy attempt by a nonphilosopher to chronicle Greek philosophical debate whose key problems he failed to grasp. Consequently the terms "debased," "rhetoricizing," and "Ciceronian" are used virtually interchangeably in studies of humanist philosophy and logic, further supporting the traditional reading of its dismal history.[33]

Valla's reading of Cicero deserves attention, and we need to stop and consider it here if we are to take the force of his recommendations for radically reconstituting the art of ratiocination to overcome its dogmatic bias.

The principle difference between Academic skepticism (the sect of which Valla considers Cicero the spokesman) and Pyrrhonian skepticism (the more radical sect whose principles are preserved in the writings of Sextus Empiricus) is, on Sextus's own account, in the *end* it serves. For Pyrrhonians the methodical critique of and confrontation between the key beliefs of the Stoic, Peripatetic, and Epicurean schools of philosophy is an end in itself: it furthers the "suspension of belief" from all philosophical system-building, and encourages the "quietude" or "quiescence" which is the characteristic stance of the Pyrrhonist. For the Academic skeptic, on the other hand, such a critique is used to arbitrate between *levels* of probability in competing systems, and the subsequent ranking is then available as a basis for making specific decisions about conduct.

If with Valla we take the entire body of Cicero's pedagogic works as equally weighty components in his philosophical approach (and therefore collate remarks in the oratorical works with those in the explicitly philosophical dialogues), then it appears that Cicero believes that there is a strategy—a distinctive *ratio argumentandi* of Academic skepticism—

for determining which of two or more alternative beliefs is the more probable (though it will not be possible to decide if it is true, or closer to the truth). The Academic will then choose tentatively to act in ways which are consistent with the "more probable" alternative. His method therefore enables him to make positive decisions about action, whereas, by contrast (as Sextus emphasizes),[34] the "quiescence" of the Pyrrhonist leads him to comply with the first demand made on him for action (it simply makes no difference to him).

There are indeed several indications, if we collate the philosophical dialogues with the oratorical works as Valla does, that Cicero sees his oratorical method as deriving from the distinctive *ratio argumentandi* which for the New Academy is the focus of skeptical activity. In *Academica* II Cicero characterizes this method as a discourse *in utramque partem*:

The sole object of [Academic] discussions is, by arguing on both sides [in utramque partem dicendo], to draw out and give shape to some result that may be either true or the nearest possible approximation to the truth. Nor is there any difference between ourselves and those who think that they have positive knowledge except that they have no doubt that their tenets are true, whereas we hold many doctrines to be probable which we can easily act upon but can scarcely advance as certain.[35]

At the end of *Academica* I such discourse *in utramque partem* is explicitly linked with Plato and Socrates and leads to the claim (from Cicero speaking for once in his own *persona*) that they were the original Academic skeptics:

Accordingly Arcesilas denied that anything can be known, not even that dictum itself (which Socrates left himself). . . . His philosophical procedure was consistent with this view: he led many to share it by arguing against all points of view, so that when equally weighty reasons were found on opposite sides of the same subject, it was easier to withhold assent from either side. They call this school the New Academy, but to me it seems old, at all events if we count Plato as a member of the Old Academy, in whose works nothing is stated positively [nihil adfirmatur] and there is much arguing on either side [in utramque partem multa disserentur], all things are inquired into and no certain statements are made.[36]

(Sextus, on the other hand, rather than link Plato with the Academics, chooses to stress that his method is not authentically *Pyrrhonian*, because his method of doubt is a means to a *decision* between alternatives.)[37] In the *De oratore* and the *Tusculanae disputationes*[38] Cicero claims that the method of discoursing *in utramque partem* was developed separately by Academics and Peripatetics as a method of philosophical inquiry (one recalls Aristotle's characterization of his dialectical method in the *Topica* as "useful because, if we are able to raise difficulties on both sides, we shall more easily discern both truth and falsehood on every point").[39] Such a method is the ideal one for the *orator* to use, Cicero continues, since he is always concerned with *dubia materia*: questions about which there is uncertainty. The orator handles only doubtful matters because (he points out in the *De oratore*) controversy in law and politics only arises under such circumstances: points of fact and direct applications of laws are handled by legal specialists and political theorists.[40]

Once we become alert to this bracketing of the aims and achievements of *in utramque partem* discourse as practiced by the orator and employed by the philosopher, the *ratio disserendi* gains increasingly in stature as a philosophical tool. The introduction to the *De fato* characterizes the method of the *De divinatione* and the *De natura deorum* as "that of setting out a continuous discourse [oratio] both for and against [in utramque partem], to enable each student to accept for himself the view that seems to him most probable,"[41] while the opening exchanges of the *De fato* itself explicitly locate it as employing oratorical method for the exploration of philosophical systems:

"What now?" Hirtius remarked. "Since I am confident that you have not abandoned your oratorical exercises, even if you have undoubtedly subordinated them to philosophy, is it possible for me to hear something?"

"Certainly, you can either hear something or contribute yourself," I said, "for you are right in thinking that I have not deserted those oratorical studies. Indeed, I have kindled a similar enthusiasm for them in you also (however receptive you were from the outset). Nor have my present concerns diminished, but rather increased that faculty. For there is a close alliance between the orator and the kind of philosophy of which I am a follower: the orator borrows subtly from the Academy, and repays the loan by contributing richness of diction and ornament. So that since both fields are within our competence, you can choose today which you want to enjoy."[42]

Hirtius goes on to compound the deliberate confusion between oratorical and philosophical method by asserting: "I am acquainted with your rhetorical exercises [rhetorica], . . . and your commitment to the Academic custom of arguing against a proposition advanced is shown by the fact that you have adopted this practice in your *Tusculanae disputationes*."[43] For Valla there is ample textual evidence to show that in Cicero's scheme of things, Orator and Academic share a common purpose and pursue the most probable point of view using an identical method. Furthermore, because he is *aware* (as philosophers tend not to be) that he negotiates only for the position of greatest likelihood (rather than for truths) in his discourse, the orator, in Valla's opinion, is closer to wisdom than the philosopher: more *sophos* than the *philosophos*.[44]

It is not surprising, then, that a philologist like Valla is inclined to attach importance to terms which Cicero has coined in the philosophical dialogues to translate Greek skeptical terminology when they recur without gloss in the works on oratory. In *Academica* II Cicero uses the term *verisimile* ("like truth," "true-seeming") to distinguish what is selected by the Academic skeptic as close to truth from what is merely *plausible* on the scale of the probable: "For they hold . . . that some things can be determined as probable and, as it were, *veri simile* (like truth), and that this provides them with a basis for action and for inquiry and disquisition [et in agenda vita et in quaerendo ac disserendo]."[45]

In the *Partitiones oratoriae* he defines the proposition on which the orator's strategy for convincing his audience is to depend (*argumentum*) as "probabile inventum ad faciendam fidem" (something probable selected to secure belief)[46] and goes on to characterize the study of "those things which secure belief" as entirely concerned with *verisimilia* ("what is almost always the case"), together with the "characteristic marks of things."[47] Here the terminology is apparently confidently used as having the weight of the philosophical usage behind it (and retains a measure of this, I think, in Quintilian and Boethius):[48] *verisimilitude*, *probability*, *plausibility* are stages of demarcation within a methodology of approximation to truth. Ideally at least, oratory aspires to the verisimilitude at which Academic philosophy sets its mark (and this is the conclusion of the *De oratore*).[49] As Crassus says, in his final summing up of the debate in the *De oratore*:

If there ever existed anyone who was able to speak on either side on all matters, and to produce two speeches on contrary sides of the same case by knowing Aristotle's method, or who in the manner of Arcesilas and Carneades could argue against any proposition, and if in addition to knowing the method he was experienced and well-practiced in speaking [ad eam rationem adiungat hunc usum exercitationemque dicendi], he would be the one and only true and perfect orator.[50]

At a number of points (including this last passage) to which I have drawn attention, Cicero links a skeptical *ratio argumentandi* with Aristotle's dialectical method (the method of the *Topica*).[51] There is a passage in Book IV of the *De finibus* which suggests that Cicero's own *Topica* might provide the key to a distinctively skeptical method of inquiry. Criticizing the incompleteness of Stoic logic teaching (the propositional logic of Chrysippus), Cicero argues that there are concealed basic principles of Stoic philosophy which underpin Stoic dialectic. Foremost among these, according to Cicero, is the belief that a combination of sense perception (appearances) and reasoning will yield *truth*. It is as a direct consequence of this belief, Cicero argues, that Stoic logicians confined their attention to rules of inference, entirely neglecting *inventio*— choice of strategy for arguing a case *probabiliter*, or topics-theory:

[Stoic logicians] commence their deductions from what is self-evident, and then apply their rules of inference to conclude in a given case what is true [quid verum sit]. How varied are their rules of inference, and how far removed from paradoxes and sophisms! . . . And since two arts make up the perfect study of reasoning and oratory, one of *inventio*, the other of inference, although both Stoics and Peripatetics have explored the latter, the former, though excellently handled by the Peripatetics, the Stoics have not touched at all.[52]

It is to this neglected branch of logic that Cicero devotes his *Topica*, and the suggestion seems to be that this portion of the *ars disserendi* is of peculiar importance to the Academic skeptic. At the end of the *Partitiones oratoriae* Cicero concludes:

Now you have had set before you all the *partitiones oratoriae*, which indeed derive centrally from our Academy. Nor can they be discovered or understood or used without an understanding of that school. For the actual process of partition, and of defining and dividing ambiguous partitions, and of knowing the *loci* for *argumenta*, and of concluding the argumentation itself, and of recognizing what is assumed in a line of argument and what follows from what is assumed, and of discriminating and distinguishing true from false and true-seeming (*verisimilia*) from implausible, and of censuring what is wrongly assumed or ill concluded, and of discoursing on all these things either narrowly (as do those who are termed dialecticians) or broadly, as befits the orator, all come under the exercises mentioned and are part of the study of subtle debate and copious speech.[53]

Moreover, the familiar passage with which Cicero's *Topica* opens is a compressed version of the *De finibus* passage:

Every *ratio disserendi* consists of two parts, *inventio* and *iudicium* [topics-theory and rules of inference], both of which, it seems to me, Aristotle treated excellently. The Stoics, however, only handled one: they explored diligently the rules of *iudicium*, in the study which they call *dialectikē*, but they utterly neglected that art which is called *topikē*, which is more useful, and certainly prior in the order of nature.[54]

As I shall show, Valla turns to Cicero's pedagogic works on oratory because he believes that there and in Aristotle's *Topica* and Book II of the *Rhetorica* are to be found, "handled excellently," the basic skeptical techniques for arguing *in utramque partem*, and that this provides an alternative methodology (sanctioned by antiquity) to the "dogmatic" dialectic of the scholastics. Cicero's regular linking both of his oratorical method with the skeptical *ratio argumentandi*, and of each of these with Aristotelian topics-theory and dialectic, allows Valla to use Aristotle's *Topica* (and the section on topics-theory from Book II of the *Rhetorica*) and particularly Boethius's treatment of topics-theory based on the Ciceronian and Aristotelian traditions together, alongside Cicero and Quintilian as part of a coherent antidogmatist *ratio disserendi*. Within the framework of Ciceronian skepticism (provided in the *Dialecticae disputationes* by citation of Cicero's philosophical dialogues) elements of Aristotle's logic program can provide part of the *apparatus* for a distinctively skeptical dialectic. On the other hand, Valla studiously ignores late-scholastic treatments of *sophismata* which tackle this same material in the context of a "dogmatic" outlook on ratiocination as a whole.[55]

The first version of the *Dialecticae disputationes*[56] circulated widely among Valla's friends (we know that Tortelli read it, and that it was sent to Serra for prepublication approval).[57] It was, however, never published. Following his arraignment on charges of heresy, in which charges the reforms of dialectic and philosophy in the *Dialecticae disputationes* were explicitly included,[58] Valla twice emended and reworked the material. The first reworking, circa 1444, was subsequently published (the first printed edition appeared around 1500);[59] the second, like the original, exists only in manuscript. In the preface to the third book of the *Elegantiae* Valla remarks that his friends "prevailed upon him" to publish the *Elegantiae* rather than the *Dialecticae disputationes* (which apparently alarmed them). Possibly as a result, Valla makes his philosophical points cautiously in the published version. He regularly uses a strategy of loaded citation rather than open quotation—a favorite strategy amongst humanist authors. Instead of openly stating a position, a passage is cited (for which the full reference is invariably if occasionally inaccurately given) which makes the point strongly when the reader turns it up. Clusters of citations contribute to a particular sectarian point of view. In every case in which I shall derive Valla's philosophical bias from loaded quotation and clusters of citations in the published (historically influential) text, it is comforting to find that the first, suppressed version makes the same point more explicitly.[60]

This strategy can be clearly illustrated from the opening passages of the *Dialecticae disputationes*. In the preface to the first book Valla sets up his philosophical position by means of the traditional story of the coining of the name "philosopher" by Pythagoras: the true philosopher calls himself a "lover of wisdom," *philosophos*, rather than a "wise man," *sophos*, "because he believed that neither [his predecessors], nor he himself, nor

any man whatsoever, could attain to wisdom."[61] As a lover of the search
for wisdom he does not adhere dogmatically to any single sect, and
indeed denies that there can be any certainty in human knowledge:

And so no one after Pythagoras was called "wise," and the peculiar privilege of
philosophers was thenceforth to say what they felt: not just against the leaders of
other sects, but also against their own. . . . So that the recent Peripatetics are not
to be endured, who . . . deny others the right to dissent from Aristotle, as if he
were "sophos," not "philosophos," and as if no one before him had held any
other opinions. Those Peripatetics ignore the fact not only that some sects flour-
ished earlier than the Peripatetic, like the Pythagorean and Democritean, but also
that others arose later, like the Stoic and Epicurean, which Luke reports in the
Acts of the Apostles to have been (as it were) enjoying prosperity in that birth-
place of philosophy, Athens (Acts 17:18). Nor do they acknowledge that the
Platonists preceded the Peripatetics, and the Academics derived from the same
source. What should I add? Was not Theophrastus, Aristotle's successor, accustomed to dissent without fear from his master? . . . What of the Latins? Did they
regard Aristotle as "sophos"? On the contrary, they did not even regard him as
the greatest of all philosophers. Was Varro an Aristotelian? Not at all, but if we
are to believe Lactantius, he held a middle path between Plato and Aristotle.
Cicero was an Academic and emulator of Plato, to whom he always attributed
the highest role in philosophy; as did almost everyone. Plancus was part Stoic
and part Epicurean; Brutus and Seneca Stoics, which sect Jerome considered the
closest to the Christian religion; and Ambrose emulated the Stoics according to
the precepts passed on by Panaetius and Cicero, and even he was, as it were,
"Stoicized." Augustine openly admitted Plato to be the prince of philosophers.
Apuleius wished to be and be thought a Platonist. And Macrobius's greatest debt
was to Plato. Nor did that last of the erudite, Boethius, think otherwise: being
much more Platonist (as I see it) than Aristotelian (which authors he promises in
one place to show to differ little, in which I believe he followed Porphyry, who
held that the sects of Plato and Aristotle were one and the same).[62]

The philosopher's position is ideally one of utmost flexibility. Nonsectarian and exploratory, it negotiates a stand among the precepts of the
various doctrinaire schools (and this involves a method of intellectual
inquiry which Valla considers it to be the true function of the dialectician
to perfect). But this catalogue of significant thinkers (in Valla's eyes) who
declined to follow dogmatically the tenets of Aristotelianism (which have
rigidified scholastic dialectic) is more than a mere parade of erudition. It
is worthwhile studying the passage a little more closely.

The sources assembled in this passage all emphasize the theme of *doubt*
as the crucial stance to be adopted in the pursuit of knowledge: true wisdom is always inaccessible, all knowledge is provisional, philosophy is
the constantly renewed *search* for wisdom. Among these sources are
texts which we know Valla to have read carefully:[63] Cicero's *De officiis*,[64]
Augustine's *De civitate Dei* (and the *Contra Academicos*),[65] and the third
book "De falsa sapientia philosophorum" of Lactantius's *Divinae institu-*

tiones.[66] And in Cicero's *De officiis* and Lactantius a method of distinguishing between levels of probability, as a guide to conduct, is explicitly associated with the Academic school of philosophy. In what I take to be a synopsis of his argument in the *Hortensius*,[67] Cicero argues that the philosopher is "lover of wisdom," and philosophy a search for wisdom, and that the ideal method to employ in that search is the one he chooses as an Academic:

> For we Academicians are not men whose minds wander in uncertainty and never know what principles to adopt. For what sort of mental habit, or rather what sort of life, would that be which should dispense with all rules for reasoning or even for living? Not so with us; but, as other schools maintain that some things are certain, others uncertain, we, differing from them, say that some things are probable, others improbable.
>
> What, then, is to hinder me from accepting what seems to me probable, while rejecting what seems to be improbable, and shunning the presumption of dogmatism [affirmandi arrogantiam vitantem] which is diametrically opposed to wisdom? And as for the fact that our school disputes against everything, that is only because we could not get a clear view of what is "probable" unless a comparative estimate were made of the arguments on both sides [nisi ex utraque parte causarum esset facta contentio]. But this subject has been, I think, quite fully set forth in my *Academica.*[68]

Lactantius's use of this argument matches Valla's even more closely, and is probably his direct source.[69] Furthermore, if we excavate the cluster of allusions to classical authors who reject Aristotle as master philosopher, we find further corroboration for the view that skepticism and dialectical method are intimately linked: they lead us directly to Lactantius (rather contrivedly: the remarks on Varro are in fact in Augustine's *De civitate Dei*),[70] Augustine (both directly and as the source for the remark on Apuleius),[71] Macrobius, and Cicero's skeptical works (in which such rehearsals of the sects as part of a case for neutrality with regard dogma abound).[72] I take it that we are being asked to endorse Lactantius's argument for adopting the Academic position in philosophy as the opening thrust of Valla's *repastinatio* of philosophy and dialectic:

> Pythagoras, who first coined this name [philosophos] since he was a little wiser than those before him who thought themselves wise, understood that no human knowledge could attain to wisdom, and, therefore, that it was not appropriate to impose a perfect name on something uncomprehended and imperfect. And so when he was asked what he would declare himself, he answered: "a philosopher," that is, a seeker of wisdom.[73]

Fortunately the original, unprinted version of Valla's preface (written before the heresy charges against him had driven sensitive issues underground) shows the skeptical drive of the argument more clearly. Here

Valla says that after Pythagoras, all philosophers, of whatever sect, by adopting his name "philosopher" (lover of wisdom), assented to the view that "his words were not an oracle of Apollo, but a mortal opinion, and so like man might easily prove fallible."[74] And in contrasting this view with the dogmatism of the Aristotelians he adds: "How much superior was Socrates, that second father of philosophy, after whom all philosophers wished to be called Socratics: 'this much alone I know,' he said, 'that I know nothing.'"[75] Once one has detected Valla's strategy of citation, one perceives that his *Dialecticae disputationes* is packed with arguments borrowed and cited from the key available works on Academic skepticism.[76] (A letter to Tortelli survives in which Valla inquires eagerly after the four complete books of Cicero's *Academica* which had purportedly been discovered in Siena—the *Academica* was known to have gone through two editions of which only fragments of two books survive[77]—which provides independent evidence of his interest in skepticism as an argued philosophical position.) And if we need confirmation for the suggestion that the tissue of sceptical reference carried a strong enough message for contemporary readers, despite its enigmatic quality (at least for readers of our own period), that confirmation is provided when we turn to Agricola's openly derivative *De inventione dialectica,* and particularly to Alardus's careful commentary in what became the standard edition of that work.[78]

Like Valla, Agricola links an *ars disserendi* which is concerned with discriminating between the more or less probable position on any question and the Academic skeptic's view that we know (with certainty) only that we know nothing:

Since truly belief in a thing in doubt cannot be established out of itself alone, but we must build up certainty about each thing from other better known and better explored matters: and furthermore some, relying on mental acumen, will devise copious and more ready matter (or as Cicero puts it, what is selected as probable to secure belief); others, with a more sluggish mental power, will grope around things dully, and be able to discover what can be said concerning anything either too late or not at all. Therefore it seemed most useful for someone to devise certain seats of arguments which they call "places," alerted by which, as if by certain markers, we may run the mind over things themselves, and see clearly what things are probable and appropriate to be used in our discourse on anything. And it appears that this method of places will be of use . . . seeing that very many things remain in doubt, and open to controversy. For only a tiny portion of what we learn is fixed and unchangeable, and indeed if we are to believe the Academics, we know only that we know nothing.[79]

Alardus glosses this passage at length, and cross-references it with similar passages on Academic skepticism in the second book, which also link discourse "probabiliter" with this philosophical position, and stress the fact that all tenets of the dogmatic schools are "probable" only, when considered as the basis for dialectical disputation.[80]

But, of course, the important question is whether Valla (and then Agricola) carries his academic skepticism any further than the affiliation indicated in the preamble to his dialectic treatise. That is to say, whether we are able to point to a significant link between the exclusions from and additions to the dialectic curriculum which he proposes and the practice of the Academic skeptics (as reconstructed from his prime sources). If we are to take Valla's reforms of philosophy and dialectic seriously, he has to contribute more than the literary and philological insights of the grammarian and textual scholar.

In Book II of the *Dialecticae disputationes* Valla makes the distinction between propositions which are true (*verum*) and those which are true-seeming (*verisimile* or *credibile*) the basis for his approach to ratiocination. In his chapter on what standard scholastic texts call the "modals" (which in Valla's original text is entitled "De vero verisimilique et necessario") he develops a rudimentary scale of greater or less verisimilitude in ratiocination, combining the relative verisimilitude of the premises and the validity of the inference. *Necessity*, he maintains, is strictly a matter of validity of the inference-form: in a valid inference the conclusion *necessarily* follows from the premises. Those premises, on the other hand, are either *verum, verisimile, possibile* or *impossibile* (and these replace the six Aristotelian modals, necessary, contingent, possible, impossible, true, false).[81] In most cases the dialectician argues validly from "semi-verum" or "semi-certum" premises, and in such cases the conclusion is at best *verisimile* (or, as Valla glosses in the *third* version of the *Dialecticae disputationes*, "highly possible"), at worst *possibile* ("passably plausible").[82]

Valid inference from necessarily true premises is, for Valla, an open-and-shut case, of little interest to the dialectician. Valid inference from true-seeming premises, however, opens up wide vistas of possibilities for astutely combining varieties of inference with appropriately chosen premises, and apposite supporting material, "ad faciendam fidem" (to secure belief) when a matter is in doubt.[83] Like Cicero and Quintilian, Valla divides strategies which provide "medium inferens conclusionem" generally into two broad categories: *syllogisms* and *epicheiremes*.[84] The former conclude *necessario*, the latter *verisimiliter*.[85] Syllogism, following Aristotle's *Analytica priora* definition, also favored by Aulus Gellius, is *any valid deductive reasoning procedure* (and Valla expressly includes relational and other inferences not reducible to strict syllogistic form). It includes arguments like "*a* is twice *b*; *b* is twice *c*; therefore *a* is four times

c" (which is not reducible to strict syllogistic form), and "all as are bs; this is an a; therefore this is a b" (which, while a time-honored "example" of syllogism, is not actually in correct syllogistic form).[86] If, however, the premises in inferences such as these (or in syllogism proper, for that matter) are merely true-seeming, the ensuing argument is an *epicheireme*, since it must conclude "verisimiliter." Equally, where an argument depends on interpretation of words, or on etymology—on the *content* of the premises, rather than on the form of the inference—it falls within Valla's epicheireme category. Valla takes Quintilian's view that what distinguishes epicheireme from syllogism is the kind of ingenuity used in selecting the premises used in a chain of reasoning: careful choice of material with astute supporting argument and illustration converts the straightforwardly probative force of any syllogism (in the broad sense) into coercion to a desired conclusion.[87]

Arguments which are compelling, but whose inferential status is in some way unclear, hold a peculiar fascination for the Academic skeptic. On Valla's analysis this means all arguments which take a basically valid inference form and play about with it, either in the manner of selection of and support for premises, or in the kind of substitutions made for the variables in the valid form (substituting "is greater than" for the copula, to produce a relational inference, for example, or using two meanings of the same term in major and minor premise of a standard syllogism).[88] Here what we are talking about is really a question of attitude: the skeptic says, "If it works, use it," without anxiety about the consequences. Since the premises of a matter in doubt can at best be supported by probable reasoning, it is open to the skeptic to use *any* strategy for "securing belief" in his audience (it must not, of course, *fail*), whether it is readily reducible to a valid form, or otherwise compelling.[89] All the innovatory material which Valla introduces into the final book of the *Dialecticae disputationes* deals with material which, while treated as "syllogism," Valla considers to conclude "verisimiliter" rather than "necessario"—its forensic effectiveness cannot readily be formalized and explained. It is the inclusion of this material which becomes the recognizable mark of a humanist dialectic manual from Agricola's *De inventione dialectica* onward.

There are some arguments, says Valla, which depend upon the "(ambiguous) nature of words."[90] He takes his central examples from Cicero and Quintilian as follows:

Such is the type of argument in Cicero's *De natura deorum*, Book I: "That which employs reason is superior to [melius] that which does not use reason; nothing is superior to the world; therefore the world employs reason." And similarly in

Quintilian (though I think he took his example from another source): "All animate things are superior to inanimate things; nothing is superior to the world;
therefore the world is animate."[91]

As it occurs in the *De natura deorum* (actually in Book II), this argument
is advanced by Balbus, and treated as compelling.[92] But it is so only as
long as one does not inquire too closely into the meaning of "superior."
In the third book, Cotta proceeds to show that if you permit this argument, you must also concede that the world can read a book ("that which
is literate is superior to that which is not literate," etc.), is an orator, a
mathematician, musician, and flute-player:

When you say that nothing is superior to the world, what do you mean by superior? If you mean more beautiful, I agree; if more suited to our needs, I agree to
that, too [adsentior]; but if what you mean is that nothing is wiser than the
world, I entirely and absolutely disagree; not because it is difficult to sever the
mind from visual impressions, but because the more that happens, the less I am
able to comprehend your meaning.[93]

Valla means the reader to know he takes the force of this turning of the
argument upon itself, I think, since earlier he cites the relevant passage at
length where a much briefer citation would suffice in the context.[94] This
kind of "arguing in stages" or by degrees, Valla is apparently saying, is
effective in context, but also contains the possibility of reducing almost
any argument to absurdity if it is applied ruthlessly, as the Academic
Cotta does.

He also, I think, chooses his examples so as to draw our attention to
the close textual links between the Academic's strategy of arguing either
side of a question in order to arrive at the most plausible solution, and
the tradition of dialectical debate discussed in the Roman oratorical
works (which I described earlier). Valla cites his second example, "All
animate things are superior to inanimate things; but nothing is superior
to the world; therefore the world is animate," from Quintilian, adding
that he thinks that Quintilian "took this example from another source."
Quintilian in fact gives both this and Valla's preceding example as part of
his discussion of epicheireme, in which he analyzes the example worked
out in Cicero's *De inventione* to arrive at his own standard form.[95] So
Valla is cross-referencing the synopses of arguments in Cicero's "rhetorical" or oratorical works with the same arguments employed in Stoic/
Academic debate,[96] and thereby drawing attention to Cicero's own
reminders (prefixed to each book of the *De natura deorum*) that in his
philosophical dialogues he is testing a variety of "opinions" by conven-

tional standards of ratiocination: "Those who seek to learn my personal opinion on the various questions show an unreasonable curiosity. In discussion it is not so much weight of authority as force of argument that should be demanded."[97] If the "superior to" argument yields an absurd conclusion when provided with perverse, but "probable," premises, then the Stoic assertion that "the world possesses reason" (which has been affirmed by using this argument) falls.

Here the Academic characteristically chooses to have things both ways (and considers that this in no way undermines his own position). He can expose the absurdities consequent upon a particular strategy of argument within a conventional dialectical context, and thereby query the possibility of arguing cogently about such issues at all. At the same time, he does not claim to *rely* upon valid inference: it does not threaten his position to concede in the end that dialectic is an unsatisfactory means of establishing truth. As Cicero has it in *Academica* II: "This same science destroys at the end the steps that came before, like Penelope unweaving her web."[98] The central strategy which the skeptic uses and then overturns in this way, and one to which Valla devotes considerable attention, particularly in the earliest redaction of the *Dialecticae disputationes*,[99] is *sorites*.

Sorites is an argument form which draws attention to, and takes advantage of, the *vagueness* of some of our language usage. The classic example of sorites is as follows (the example from which the form takes its name):[100] "If a pile of salt is large enough to be fairly described as a heap, the subtraction of a single grain of salt cannot make a relevant difference: if $n + 1$ grains of salt constitute a heap, so do n grains. Thus one grain, and, indeed, zero grains constitute a heap." Sorites plays a crucial role in the Stoic/Academic confrontations in Cicero's philosophical dialogues (as indeed it does in Sextus Empiricus):[101] the skeptic argues that it entitles him to deny the possibility of distinguishing closely similar states of affairs; the Stoic refuses to accept it as a valid form of argumentation, because to do so would threaten his ability to discriminate clearly between (and therefore give his rational assent to) distinct sense-impressions.

In *Academica* II Cicero is quite explicit about the consequences of the sorites argument:

[The Stoic] school says that dialectic was invented to serve as a "distinguisher" or judge between truth and falsehood. . . . But since your school sets so much store by that science, take care it is not essentially entirely against you, when at the first stage it gaily imparts the elements of discourse, the solution of ambiguous propositions and the theory of the syllogism, but then by a process of small additions comes to the *sorites*, certainly a slippery and dangerous position, and a class of syllogism which you lately declared to be erroneous. What then? Is that an error for which we are to blame? No faculty of knowing absolute limits has been bestowed upon us by the nature of things to enable us to fix exactly how far to go in any matter; and this is so not only in the case of a heap of wheat from which the name is derived, but in no matter whatsoever—if we are asked by gradual stages, is such and such a person a rich man or a poor man, famous or undistinguished, are yonder objects many or few, great or small, long or short, broad or narrow, we do not know at what point in the addition or subtraction to give a definite answer.[102]

In any case in which we apply terms with some vagueness (like "rich" and "poor") the skeptic can make his interlocutor admit that he has "no good reason for" distinguishing between adjacent steps in a chain of examples (of the more or less rich, or more or less poor), and hence drive him to an absurd or unwelcome conclusion (that the man without wealth is "rich," or the millionaire "poor").[103]

In the first version of the *Dialecticae disputationes*, Valla devotes no less than three chapters of the third book to three (as he sees it) variations on the sorites argument. This in itself gives an idea of how powerful he considers the form, although he is careful to indicate that in his view it concludes "verisimiliter" rather than "necessario"—in other words, however compelling the stage-by-stage argument, it is not susceptible to the kind of limpid understanding the logician finds in more readily formalized arguments like the syllogism.[104] And in the shortened treatment included in the published *Dialecticae disputationes* Valla concludes his discussion by explicitly indicating the significance of sorites in challenging the possibility of sustaining the kinds of distinctions essential to the dogmatist: "This type of argument . . . arises in all sorts of contexts. Whence Cicero concludes in the *Academica*: 'Truly, nature has bestowed on us no knowledge of absolute limits to enable us to fix exactly how far to go in any matter; and this is so not only in the case of a heap of wheat from which the name is derived, but in no matter whatsoever . . . .'"[105] So Valla places inference which undermines the possibility of certainty in knowledge, squarely at the center of his treatment of ratiocination.[106] The skeptic takes particular delight in the sorites argument, as almost a paradigm for "uncertainty" or "acatalepsia"—and hence for the necessity of suspending belief.

In the first place, sorites receives extensive consideration by the Stoic logicians, who call it *aporos logos*—insoluble or puzzling. While they believe it to be invalid as a form of argument, they are in the severest difficulties in trying to justify this view. Thus their doctrinal need for a clear and unequivocal answer on whether any form of inference is valid or not is threatened, and with it the confidence in their ability to distinguish between truth and falsity.[107] Again, and more tellingly still (particularly in the eyes of modern philosophers), sorites can be used as *the* means of logically denying the clear boundaries between semantic usages which are essential to the logician if he is to sustain the linguistic distinctions necessary in the search for truth. If, for instance, we grade the colors from red to yellow along the spectrum, and make the steps along our scale sufficiently small, we may ask, "is this patch of color the same as the adjacent patch?" and always secure the answer "yes," leading to the conclusion that red and yellow are "the same" color.[108]

In the first version of the *Dialecticae disputationes* Valla distinguishes three types of what he calls "coagmentatio syllogistice," syllogistic cementing together, or sorites. In addition to sorites in its traditional form ("if one should not go to one's death for one person, neither should one for two, . . . nor for the whole state"; Valla also gives the standard example of the number of hairs in the tail of a horse),[109] Valla distinguishes two other cases. The first of these argues by gradual steps as follows: "What I want (whose wisdom is limited), my mother also wants (who is wiser than I), and also Themistocles (who is the wisest man in Athens [*De oratore* II 299]), so it must be wanted by the entire populace of Athens." The other is always propounded (for effectiveness) in question and answer form, and makes the transition by gradual stages from one case to a closely similar one, and finally to a controversial conclusion. The classic example of this is the one Cicero recapitulates in the *De natura deorum*,[110] and which Sextus gives in full in *Against the Physicists*: "If Zeus is a God, Poseidon also is a God. . . . And if Poseidon is a God, Achelous, too, will be a God; and if Achelous, Neilos; and if Neilos, every river as well; and if every river, the streams also will be Gods; and if the streams, the torrents; but the torrents are not Gods; neither, then is Zeus a God. But if there be Gods, Zeus would have to be a God. Therefore, there are no Gods."[111]

Valla associates this final form of sorites with "Socratic" induction— the rhetorical induction given by Cicero in the *De inventione* (and by Boethius in the *De differentiis topicis* and *In Topica Ciceronis*).[112] Cicero's familiar example runs as follows:

In a dialogue by Aeschines Socraticus, Socrates reveals that Aspasia reasoned thus with Xenophon's wife and with Xenophon himself: "Please tell me, madam, if your neighbor had a better gold ornament than you have, would you prefer that one or your own?" "That one," she replied. "Now, if she had dresses and other feminine finery more expensive than you have, would you prefer yours or hers?" "Hers, of course," she replied. "Well, now, if she had a better husband than you have, would you prefer your husband or hers?" At this the woman blushed. . . . In this instance, because assent has been given to undisputed statements, the result is that the point which would appear doubtful if asked by itself is through analogy conceded as certain, and this is due to the method employed in putting the question.[113]

Both the question-and-answer sorites and "Socratic" induction are concerned with clarification of concepts (although formally they have nothing in common). On the strength of this characterization of their comparable dialectical (polemical and persuasive) effectiveness Valla proceeds to reject the traditional distinction between induction and deduction as distinct types of ratiocination, in favor of a catchall "syllogistic" that includes *all* ratiocinative strategies which drive home a conclusion in debate.[114]

The final irony for the Academic skeptic is still to come. For having assiduously explored the strategies for upsetting that "certainty" on which dogmatic philosophy depends, he reinstates these along with more conventional forms of debate as part of the "ratio disserendi" which will now lead him with due caution to the "most probable" solution to any given question. To see how Valla's dialectic ties up with Cicero's "ratio disserendi" at this point it is appropriate to turn back to our parallel textbook, Agricola's *De inventione dialectica*.

The final chapters of Agricola's manual are devoted to tactics to be used in controversial debate: the "artificial" organization of discourse where a matter is in doubt. And the culmination of these is the strategy to be used where it is inconceivable that your adversary will accept your main premises (on ideological grounds) if these are openly stated. Once more Agricola associates this strategy directly with Socrates and his skepticism—Socrates, "who affirmed that he knew nothing, and that there was nothing which he could maintain as his opinion."[115] By using the "hidden weapons" of Socratic induction, argument from "ambiguous use of words," or argument employing the "superior to" or "better than" strategy (as described above), the desired conclusion can be arrived at against the better judgment of the adversary. For, says Agricola, "we believe many things, not because they are seen to be true, but [simply] because we believe them."[116] Suppose that the Academic wishes to convince the Epicurean (Agricola suggests by way of illustration) that whoever lacks virtue will be unhappy. It is no good his assuming that virtue is the *summum bonum* (since the Epicurean finds this no more plausible than the conclusion toward which we are arguing). Instead he must start "farther back":

He asks whether it is granted that the soul is superior to (melius) the body. But even this is reinforced with a Socratic induction. He must ask whether in driving a chariot, or steering a ship, or ruling a household, or leading the state, and in general, that which rules is considered to be of higher standing than what is ruled, and if the body is considered to be governed by the rule of the soul. If that is conceded, it must necessarily be conceded that the soul is superior to the body.[117]

After which he goes on to argue obliquely that "virtue," which is "superior to" pleasure, belongs to the soul (which is superior to the body). And so on, till he arrives at his conclusion, which cannot, under these circumstances, be denied by his adversary.[118] Skeptical "ratio disserendi" as a means of securing belief triumphs even when the opponent is committed to a diametrically opposed set of principles. And the heroes of this kind of debate, which "extorts by force the desired conclusion," are Plato (in his *Dialogues*) and Quintilian (in his *Declamationes*).

The achievement of Valla's *Dialecticae disputationes* (as borne out in Agricola's subsequent textbook treatment) is to shift the focus of dialectic from syllogism and validity into the murky waters of probable and convincing arguing of a case. But this does not imply that all systematic treatment has been abandoned for the exuberance of "rhetoric." To borrow Hamblin's formulation in his description of "the concept of argument" in *Fallacies*: "The modified criteria, which I shall call *dialectical* ones, are formulated without the use of the words 'true' and 'valid'; or of the word 'known,' which would imply truth. With this difference they run closely parallel to the epistemic criteria." And he goes on to set up the following principles, with which Valla would have been entirely in sympathy:

D1)   The premises must be accepted.
D2, 3) The passage from premises to conclusion must be of an accepted kind.
D4)   Unstated premises must be of a kind that are accepted as omissible.
D5)   The conclusion must be such that, in the absence of the argument, it would not be accepted.[119]

Valla regards this kind of treatment of "the concept of argument" as a more authentic reconstruction of ancient dialectic in its relation to language and meaning than the resolutely dogmatic explorations of validity found in late scholasticism. His dialectic text (and Alardus's commentary on Agricola) is awash with parallel citations from Plato, Cicero, Quintilian, Aulus Gellius, Augustine, Lactantius, Macrobius, and Boethius, supporting his alternative outlook on ratiocination and its probabilistic thrust. The final point I would wish to make here is that it is high time we took this view seriously as intellectual historians. How appropriate it would be, in this era of renewed enthusiasm for the dubious areas of philosophy of language which are one step off the well-worn track of standard treatments of logical validity, if we were to find that Valla had read his Cicero correctly.[120]

NOTES

1. On humanism and reforms of dialectic within the University curriculum see T. Heath, "Logical Grammar, Grammatical Logic, and Humanism in Three German Universities," *Studies in the Renaissance* 18 (1971), 9-64; L. Jardine, "The Place of Dialectic Teaching in Sixteenth-Century Cambridge," *Studies in the Renaissance* 21 (1974), 31-62; L. Jardine, "Humanism and the Sixteenth-Century Cambridge Arts Course," *History of Education* 4 (1975), 16-31.

2. Such attacks become a trope of humanist invective. See, e.g., J. L. Vives, *In Pseudodialecticos* (1520), ed. R. Guerlac (Dordrecht, Holland, 1979).

3. W. and M. Kneale, *The Development of Logic* (Oxford, 1962).

4. Ibid., p. 300.

5. Ibid., p. 33: "Aristotle's *Topics* . . . is avowedly a handbook for the guidance of those taking part in public debating contests. . . . As it stands, it is a number of not very well-ordered observations on matters logical, psychological, and linguistic. It may be said, however, to hold a logical theory in solution. . . . In the first place a *practical* interest in the winning of arguments leads to a *theoretical* interest in valid inference; for among honest men the surest way of winning argument is to present a train of valid reasoning. It is true that Aristotle points out devices that may also help in dishonest winning, e.g., the concealment of the direction of the argument, but this is part of the sediment which will drop from the solution."

6. See, e.g., J. Lear, "Going Native," *Daedalus*, 1978, pp. 175-188, particularly as he invokes Crispin Wright's discussion of *sorites* in the context of a theory of meaning. See C. Wright, "Language Mastery and the Sorites Paradox," in *Truth and Meaning*, ed. G. Evans and J. McDowell (Oxford, 1976), 223-247.

7. Ivo Thomas summarizes the prevailing attitude of historians of logic towards the logic of the Renaissance as follows: "The interregnum was characteristically sterile, a cause for despondency when one thinks of the large place logic continued to occupy in the educational curriculum and of the innumerable writers who put manuals of logic on the market" ("Logic, history of," *The Encyclopedia of Philosophy* [New York and London, 1967], IV, 534).

8. On the *De differentiis topicis* see E. Stump, *Boethius's De topicis differentiis* (Ithaca, N. Y., 1978); O. Bird, "The Tradition of Logical Topics: Aristotle to Ockam," *Journal of the History of Ideas* 23 (1962), 307-323; and "The Formalizing of Topics in Medieval Logic," *Notre Dame Journal of Formal Logic* 1 (1960), 138-149.

9. See W. and M. Kneale (above, n. 3), pp. 33-44.

10. Migne, *PL* 64. 1174; Stump (above, n. 8), p. 30.

11. Bird (above, n. 8), passim.

12. Migne, *PL* 64. 1185; Stump (above, n. 8), pp. 46-47.

13. Migne, *PL* 64. 1187; Stump (above, n. 8), p. 49.

14. E.g., relational and etymological maxims: Migne 64. 1187-88; 1193-95.

15. See, for instance, the fifteenth-century Oxford statutes in S. Gibson, *Statuta antiqua Vniversitatis Oxoniensis* (Oxford, 1931), p. 200.

16. See R. Agricola, *De inventione dialectica* (Coloniae, 1539), pp. 175-176, and Alardus's commentary, ibid., p. 177. Agricola favors omitting discussion of topical maxims and leaving them up to the common sense of the student.

17. Lorenzo Valla (1407-1457). On Valla see, in particular, G. di Napoli, *Lorenzo Valla: Filosofia e religione nell'umanesimo italiano* (Rome, 1971); S. I. Camporeale, *Lorenzo Valla: Umanesimo e teologia* (Florence, 1972); C. Vasoli, *La dialettica e la retorica dell'umanesimo* (Milan, 1968), pp. 28-77; F. Adorno, "Di alcune orazioni e prefazioni di Lorenzo Valla," *Rinascimento* 5 (1964), 191-225; L. G. Janik, "Lorenzo Valla: The Primacy of Rhetoric and the De-moralization of History," *History and Theory* 12 (1973), 389-404; P. O. Kristeller, *Eight Philosophers of the Italian Renaissance* (Stanford, 1964), pp. 19-36; G. Zippel, "L'Autodifesa di Lorenzo Valla per il processo dell'inquisizione napoletana (1444)," *Italia medioevale e umanistica* 13 (1970), 59-94.

Rudolph Agricola (1444-1485). On Agricola see Vasoli, *La dialettica*, pp. 147-182; W. S. Howell, *Logic and Rhetoric in England 1500-1700* (New York, 1961); N. W. Gilbert, *Renaissance Concepts of Method* (New York, 1960); W. J. Ong, *Ramus, Method, and the Decay of Dialogue* (Cambridge, Mass., 1958).

18. On the various versions of the *Dialecticae disputationes* and their dates of completion see G. Zippel, "Note sulle redazioni della 'Dialectica' di Lorenzo Valla," *Archivo storico per le provincie parmensi* 9 (1957), 301-315; Camporeale, *Valla, passim* (Camporeale prints a number of useful passages from the first and third, unpublished versions among his notes).

19. On Valla as textual scholar and "humanist" see F. Gaeta, *Lorenzo Valla: Filologia e storia nell'umanesimo italiano* (Naples, 1955), pp. 9-55. On the chronology of recovery of lost classical works see R. Sabbadini, *Le scoperte dei codici latini e greci nei secoli xiv e xv*, 2 vols. (Florence, 1905; reprint ed., 1967); L. D. Reynolds and N. G. Wilson, *Scribes and Scholars: A Guide to the Transmission of Greek and Latin Literature* (Oxford, 1968).

20. For a lively reconstruction of the humanist circle at Ferrara see Angelo Decembrio's *Politia literaria* (1462). See also A. della Guardia, *La Politia literaria di Angelo Decembrio e l'umanesimo a Ferrara nella prima meta del sec. XV* (Modena, 1910). On the school of Guarino see Sabbadini, *La scuola e gii studi di Guarino Guarini Veronese* (Catania, 1896). On characteristic attitudes of Italian humanists towards learning see Sabbadini, *Le scoperte* and *Il metodo degli umanisti* (Florence, 1922); G. Holmes, *The Florentine Enlightenment 1400-50* (London, 1969); E. Garin, *Prosatori latini del quattrocento* (Milan, 1952) for some original texts on humanism and learning; and the authoritative accounts of humanism and humanistic studies by Kristeller, e.g., *Renaissance Thought*, vol. I (New York, 1961). On the relation between humanism and legal studies in Italy at the time of Agricola's stay there see Vasoli, *La dialettica*, 151-158. On the history of legal studies see K. H. Burmeister, *Das Studium der Rechte* (Wiesbaden, 1974).

21. See Vasoli, *La dialettica*, p. 157; also Alardus's cross-references between the two works in his edition of the *De inventione dialectica* (Coloniae, 1539).

22. *De inventione dialectica* (Coloniae, 1539), p. 193.

23. See W. J. Ong, *Ramus and Talon Inventory* (Cambridge, Mass., 1958).

24. See, e.g., the so-called "epistola apologetica" to Serra, *Opera Omnia*, ed. Garin (Turin, 1962), II, 81-82, 390: "When once I had perceived the necessity for my writing a work *De elegantia linguae latinae* (which Latin language I saw for the most part corrupted and distorted), how then could that be done without my finding fault with those who had been the originators of that decadence, whether I wished to have regard for our own era or for the next? And just as those men know they are unjust when they calumniate me, and that they are thoughtless and destructive when they call me thoughtless and destructive, I say, and if possible I proclaim to the whole attendant crowd of slanderers the following: those books of mine which I have mentioned are worth more in regard to the Latin language than all those which have been written over the past six hundred years, be it on grammar, rhetoric, logic, civil or canon law, or on the signification of words. And if this is mere idle boasting, let them write against me, let them hurl weapons at me from all sides, barbed with poison. To come to my other books. I will say nothing of those which perhaps are not very relevant to this discussion. I have written three books *De vero bono*, the same number *De institutione dialectica ac philosophica*, one *De libero arbitrio*. In which, if my critics are in their right mind, they must infer that I have treated my subjects with the same intelligence and the same diligence as I did in those works above." See also the letter to Tortelli, II, 122 (Camporeale, 224-225); also the cross-references within the works themselves, e.g., *Dialecticae disputationes*, *Opera* I, 663; I, 670; *Elegantiae*, *Opera* I, 97; I, 216.

25. On humanist programs of education, and the place of dialectic within those programs see A. T. Grafton and L. Jardine, *From Humanism to the Humanities* (in preparation).

26. For the text of a typical fifteenth-century logic manual see Peter of Spain's *Summulae logicales*; there is a modern edition by L. M. De Rijk, *Tractatus Called Afterwards Summulae Logicales* (Assen, 1972), though it should be stressed that Renaissance editions of this text are extremely corrupt by comparison. J. P. Mullally, *The Summulae Logicales of Peter of Spain* (Notre Dame, Indiana, 1945) gives a summary of the content of the *Summulae*.

27. On the alternative forms of ratiocination offered by topics-logic see Stump (above, n. 8), pp. 179-204 *passim*.

28. As an example of the reinforcing of Peter of Spain's disparaging treatment of topics-logic in the *Summulae*, see the Cologne Thomists' commentary in *Textus omnium tractatuum Petri Hispani* (Coloniae, 1489): "This is the fifth tractate, in which after determining concerning simple and unrestricted syllogism Peter of Spain turns to determining concerning syllogism limited to probable material, that is, dialectical syllogism" (fo. xcix[V]). On Peter of Spain and Boethius see Stump, above, n. 8, 215-236.

29. See, e.g., G. Trapezuntius, *Comparationes philosophorum Aristotelis et Platonis* (Venetiis, 1523), where Trapezuntius, using the criteria of Aristotelian

logic, states categorically that Plato had no method comparable with that of Aristotle.

30. *De inventione dialectica* (Coloniae, 1539), p. 207.

31. Valla, *Opera* I, 644. Valla is less wholeheartedly in favor of Boethius's detailed approach to dialectic elsewhere in the *Dialecticae disputationes*, for instance on his treatment of induction, *Opera* I, 757, although at I, 760 he writes: "Although Boethius was distinguished both as orator and philosopher, he is more of a philosopher."

32. For the direct influence of Agricola's manual on subsequent treatments of dialectic see C. Prantl, *Geschichte der Logik im Abendlande* (Leipzig, 1870), IV, chap. 21; Vasoli, *La dialettica, passim*, and "La retorica e la dialettica umanistiche e le origini delle concezioni moderne del 'metodo,' " *Il Verri* 35/6 (1970), 250-306; Ong, *Ramus, Method;* L. Jardine, "Humanism and the Sixteenth-Century Cambridge Arts Course." For contemporary acknowledgment of Agricola's importance see, e.g., John Seton's introduction to his *Dialectica* (1545), (London, 1584 ed.), fo. A2^r.

33. See e.g., W. Risse, *Die Logik der Neuzeit*, vol. I (Stuttgart, 1964). Attempts have been made by historians of humanist dialectic to improve the reputation of their subject, but unfortunately they have tended to stress the rhetorical nature of humanist reforms, but to assert the importance of these for their own sake. See, e.g., Vasoli, "La logica europea nell'età dell'umanesimo e del rinascimento," *Atti del Convegno di Storia della Logica*, Testi e Saggi, 4 (Padua, 1974), pp. 61-94.

34. *PH* I 231.

35. *Acad.* II 7-8.

36. *Acad.* I 45-46.

37. *PH* I 225.

38. *De oratore* III 107: "Others on the contrary are noncommittal debates allowing copious arguments to be advanced both *pro* and *contra* in regard to the general question [in utramque partem disseri]. The latter exercise is now considered the special province of [the Peripatetics and the Academics]." *Tusculanae* II 9: "Accordingly these considerations always led me to prefer the rule of the Peripatetics and the Academy of discussing both sides of every question, not only for the reason that in no other way did I think it possible for the probable truth to be discovered in each particular problem, but also because I found it gave the best practice in oratory. Aristotle first employed this method and later those who followed him." See also *De finibus* V 10-11; *De oratore* III 80.

39. *Topica* I 2. 101a35-37. On Cicero and discourse "in utramque partem" see A. Michel, *Les rapports de la rhétorique et de la philosophie dans l'œuvre de Ciceron* (Paris, 1960). See also C. J. R. Armstrong, "The Dialectical Road to Truth: The Dialogue," in *French Renaissance Studies 1540-70*, ed. P. Sharratt (Edinburgh, 1976), pp. 36-51.

40. I 241: "And yet those cases which are such that the law involved in them is beyond dispute, do not as a rule come to a hearing at all. . . . Thus there are no judicial decisions in this branch of the law. And so the orator may safely disregard all this region of unquestionable law."

41. *De fato* 1. See also the vital quote from Seneca's *Epistulae* which associates "in utramque partem" argument with Protagoras's skeptical method: "Protagoras

declares that one can take either side on any question and debate it with equal success—even on this very question, whether every subject can be debated from either point of view" (LXXXVIII.43), cited by M. F. Burnyeat, "Protagoras and Self-refutation," *The Philosophical Review* 85 (1976), 44-69, at 61.

42. *De fato* 3.

43. Ibid.

44. *Contra calumniatores apologia, Opera* I, 799. G. Zippel, "L'Autodifesa" prints the original text of this defense by Valla against charges of heresy, in which the phrase occurs as follows: "Alie questiones, quae ut hereticus sum accusatus. ...Oratorem esse verum sapientem quantum in hominem cadit, hoc est plus quam philosophum, id est 'sophum.'" In the printed text this runs, "hoc est, plus esse quam philosophum et sophon," so the reading is not clear, but I think the sense requires, "hoc est, plus quam philosophum [oratorem] esse 'sophon.'"

45. II 32.

46. *Partitiones oratoriae* 5.

47. 34: "Inference is based entirely on probabilities [in verisimilibus] and on the essential characteristics of things. But let us for the sake of conveying our meaning define the term 'probable' as "that which usually occurs in such and such a way'—for example, that youth is more prone to self-indulgence; while an essential characteristic gives a proof that is never otherwise and that supplies an indication that is certain, as smoke is a certain indication of fire." This is in fact a translation of a passage in Aristotle's *Rhetorica* (1357a38-42).

48. E.g. *Institutio oratoria* II 17. 39; *In Topica Ciceronis*, Migne, *PL* 64. 1046-47. In the *De differentiis topicis* Boethius discriminates between arguments drawn from definition, genus, difference, and cause, which add greatly to the force of demonstrative syllogisms, and the remainder, which do so for syllogisms which are "verisimilis" and "dialecticus" (Migne, *PL* 64. 1195).

49. This is the reading at which one arrives if one treats the *De oratore* as a philosophical dialogue which incidentally contains pedagogic material illustrative of the particular intellectual stand taken by each of the participants.

50. III 80.

51. In addition to the passages cited in which Cicero links Academic and Peripatetic methods of arguing "in utramque partem," Cicero commends Aristotle as a teacher of oratory (and topics theory) in *Tusculanae disputationes* I 7; *De oratore* I 43, and III 71. In *De oratore* II 152 he says: "Aristotle, however, my own most particular admiration, set forth certain commonplaces, among which every line of argument might be found, not merely for philosophical debate, but also for our own contentions in the Courts."

52. IV 8-10.

53. 139.

54. II 6.

55. On the tradition of *sophismata* in the Middle Ages see the bibliography in E. J. Ashworth, "The treatment of Semantic Paradoxes from 1400 to 1700," *Notre Dame Journal of Formal Logic* 13 (1972), 34-52. Valla was trained using the manual of Paul of Venice (as he indicates in the *epistola apologetica*) and knew Albertus Magnus's works (Camporeale, *Valla*, pp. 122-124).

56. Valla refers to the work in a number of ways, but never as *Dialecticae dis-*

putationes. See Camporeale, *Valla,* p. 195; Zippel, "Note sulle redazioni," p. 301.

57. See the letter to Tortelli and *epistola apologetica* to Serra; Camporeale, *Valla,* pp. 221-228.

58. On the charges of the inquisition see *Antidoti in Pogium IV (Opera* I, 355-362); *Autodifesa* (ed. Zippel); *Contra calumniatores apologia (Opera* I, 795-800a).

59. Zippel, "Note sulle redazioni," 305-306, gives the first printing as 1509. I am grateful to E. J. Ashworth for bringing to my attention the earlier edition in Florence (Biblioteca Ricardiana R520), n.d., but catalogued as "Venice c. 1500," Its title page runs as follows: *Dialecticae Laurentii Vallae libri tres. Seu eiusdem Reconcinnatio totius Dialecticae: & fundamentorum Universalis Philosophiae: ubi multa adversus Aristotelem: Boetium: Porphyrium: aliosque recentiores philosophos acutissime disputantur. Logica Beati Augustini. Eiusdem Praedicamenta. Eiusdem Topica. Eiusdem Perihermenias.*

60. I am grateful to the Warburg Institute, London, for obtaining for me the microfilm of the Vatican manuscript (MS. Urb. lat. 1207) of the first version of Valla's *Dialecticae disputationes.* Camporeale prints useful passages from this version in the notes to his book, and collates them with the other extant manuscript from the Badia di S. Pietro, Perugia (CM53).

61. I, 644.

62. Ibid.

63. Most of our information about Valla's reading is drawn from his citations in the *Elegantiae.* I am not certain Valla knew Augustine's *Contra Academicos,* but since he certainly read Lactantius (Augustine's chief source besides Cicero) this is not vital. He had read the *De civitate Dei.*

64. II 2. 5-8. Pythagoras is not here mentioned by name, but philosophy is defined as "love of wisdom." Pythagoras is credited with the coinage in *Tusculanae disputationes* V 8-11. According to Boethius the same story is used in the lost *Hortensius:* "Philosophy is love of wisdom, which no one doubts ought to be studied; so philosophy ought to be studied. 'Interpretation of the name' gives this argument, not 'definition of the thing,' which argument Cicero also uses in defense of the same philosophy in *Hortensius" (De differentiis topicis,* Migne, *PL* 64. 1187-88).

65. *De civitate Dei* VIII 2 (Migne, *PL* 41.225): "For since before that those who seemed to surpass others in a certain manner of praiseworthy life were called 'sapientes' (wise men), when [Pythagoras] was asked what he professed he answered that he was a 'philosopher,' that is, a student or lover of wisdom, because it seemed most presumptuous to profess wisdom." *Contra Academicos* III 3.5 (Migne, *PL* 32.936), and III 9.20 *(PL* 32.922); II 3.7 *(PL* 32.922). Here again Pythagoras is not mentioned by name.

66. III 2 (Migne, *PL* 6.352-353); also Diogenes Laertius I 12 and VIII 8.

67. See II 6: "Sed haec, cum ad philosophiam cohortamur, accuratius disputari solent, quod alio quodam libro fecimus."

68. II 7-8.

69. On Valla's indebtedness to Lactantius see L. Panizza Jackson, "The Significance of the St. Paul-Seneca Correspondence for Stoic thought from Petrarch to Erasmus" (Ph.D. diss., University of London, 1975).

70. XIX 1-3 (Migne, *PL* 41.621-627).

71. VIII 12 (Migne, *PL* 41.237).

72. The two *Academica* fragments, the *De natura deorum*, the later letters to Atticus. The last is possibly the source for the Plancus remark, although this is the one allusion I have so far been unable to trace.

73. *Divinae institutiones* III 2 (Migne, *PL* 6.352-353).

74. "[Pythagoras] cum se non sapientem dicit palam declarat sua verba non Apollinis oracula esse, sed mortalis opinionem ideoque ut hominem facile falli posse" (Camporeale, *Valla*, p. 405).

75. Camporeale, *Valla*, p. 406.

76. I retain an open mind on the question of whether Valla knew the work of Sextus Empiricus. Greek manuscripts of Sextus were known to Giovanni Aurispa and Bessarion (both associates of Valla). On knowledge of Sextus in the Byzantine Empire in the fourteenth century see C. B. Schmitt, chap. 9 of this anthology.

77. "Now . . . I will write nothing more but what was enjoined on me by a friend as I was writing, that I ask if anyone amongst you has the four books of Cicero's *Academica*, recently discovered at Siena" (*Opera* II, 422). See Cicero, *Tusculanae disputationes* II 4; *Ad Atticum* XIII 19; *De natura deorum* I 11: "To those again who are surprised at my choice of a system to which to give my allegiance, I think that a sufficient answer has been given in the four books of my *Academica*."

78. On Agricola's editor and commentator, Alardus, see B. De Graaf, *Alardus Amstelredamus (1491-1544)* (Amsterdam, 1958).

79. *De inventione dialectica* (Coloniae, 1539), p. 2.

80. Ibid., p. 5. The cross-references are to *De inventione dialectica* II, chap. 2 and 6. Among the extremely full references to ancient sources on Academic skepticism which Alardus gives are Seneca's letters (with a quote) and the vital passage in Cicero's *Academica* II in which Cicero indicates that the sorites argument potentially undermines the possibility of certain knowledge in almost all areas of investigation (see below p. 272).

81. *Opera* I, 717.

82. *Opera* I, 717-719; the passage from the *third* version of the *Dialecticae disputationes* (which I have yet to see) is given by Camporeale, *Valla*, pp. 39-40. The relevant passage in the printed text runs: "But as long as the 'ratio' (way) is not plainly certain but semi-true and semi-certain, then the conclusion is not necessary but semi-necessary, which when it has much force is called 'verisimilis' or 'credibilis,' that is, exceedingly possible, and when it has scant force is called 'possibilis,' that is, scarcely 'verisimilis' or 'credibilis.' "

83. *Opera* I, 732.

84. Ibid.

85. The secondary literature has been so scathing of Roman discussion of epicheireme that it is almost impossible to gain a clear picture of what Cicero and Quintilian thought they were discussing under this heading. See, for instance, Hubbell's footnote to Cicero's remarks on epicheireme in the *De inventione* (Loeb Classical Library ed., p. 104), where he writes: "Cicero is in error here," and again, "It should be understood that Cicero was describing a rhetorical, not a logical kind of reasoning, and that his use of such terms [as induction and deduc-

tion] is loose, and, at times, careless" (p. 92). As far as I can judge, Valla's notion that epicheireme is any reasoning process which is acceptable (valid, or persuasive without being readily formalizable) but which employs premises that require support because they are "true seeming," rather than true is based on a fair reading of Cicero and Quintilian. See Cicero, *De inventione*, I 57 ff.; *Ad Herennium* II. 28 ff.; Quintilian, *Institutio oratoria*, V *passim*, and especially V 14.14: "There is no difference between the *epicheireme* and the *syllogism*, except that the latter has a number of forms and infers truth from truth, whereas the *epicheireme* is frequently concerned with statements that are no more than credible."

86. For relational syllogism, and singular syllogism see *Opera* I, 736.

87. *Institutio oratoria* V 14.14 ff.

88. I, 741.

89. Agricola, in particular, stresses repeatedly that the "ars argumentandi" of dialectic is "ars *probabiliter* disserendi," because, although the dialectician makes every effort to argue consistently, his *material* is never certain ("neque ullam certam sibi praefinire materiam"). See, e.g., *De inventione dialectica* (Coloniae, 1539 ed.), p. 17.

90. *Opera* I, 741: "Quaedam verba reddere numerosum ac multiplicem syllogismum."

91. *Opera* I, 741.

92. Which, of course, it is, if the disjunctions are exhaustive. It is the ambiguity of the premises which causes the problem.

93. *De natura deorum* III. 21.

94. *Opera* I, 662-663: "Neither does Aristotle alone attribute reason to dumb animals on some occasions, but others do also, amongst whom (if we leave out the Greeks) are Cicero and Quintilian. For in the *De natura deorum* the former writes: 'You say there is nothing in the universe superior to the world. No more is there anything on earth superior to our city; but you do not therefore think that our city possesses a reasoning, thinking mind? Or because it does not, you do not therefore consider, do you, that an ant is to be rated more highly than this supremely beautiful city, on the ground that a city does not possess sensation whereas an ant has not only sensation, but also a mind that reasons and remembers?' "

95. V 14.12; *De inventione* I 58.

96. The Loeb *De inventione* does *not* cross-reference the discussion correctly. Cicero's example of a five-part epicheireme is taken from *De natura deorum* II 21 (where it occurs in "Quintilian" tripartite form), with the additional supporting material for the premises supplied. Hubbell only cross-references the Socratic induction which supports the opening premise, and which occurs elsewhere in the *De natura deorum* (II 35).

97. I 10. See also the reminder which immediately precedes the examples discussed above: "Cotta having thus spoken, Velleius replied. 'I am indeed a rash person,' he said, 'to attempt to join issue with a pupil of the Academy who is also a trained orator. An Academic unversed in rhetoric I should not have been much afraid of, nor yet an orator, however eloquent, who was not reinforced by that system of philosophy'" (II 1).

98. II 95. Sextus has an appealing formulation of this position at the end of *Against the Logicians:* "Just as it is not impossible for the man who has ascended to a high place by a ladder to overturn the ladder with his foot after his ascent, so also it is not unlikely that the Skeptic after he has arrived at the demonstration of his thesis by means of the argument proving the nonexistence of proof, as it were by a stepladder, should then abolish this very argument" (*M* VIII 481).

99. MS. Urb. lat. 1207, chaps. 15-17: "De prima specie coagmentationis syllogistice"; "De secunda specie coagmentationis"; "De tertia specia coagmentationis." For a table of the different allocations of space in the third book of the *Dialecticae disputationes* in the first and second (printed) versions see Camporeale, *Valla*, pp. 117-119.

100. I take this formulation of sorites from C. Wright, "Language Mastery and the Sorites Paradox," in *Truth and Meaning: Essays in Semantics*, ed. Gareth Evans and John McDowell (Oxford, 1976).

101. *PH* II 253; III 80; *M* VII 416-421; IX 182-191.

102. *Acad.* II 91-92.

103. "Having no good reason for" distinguishing one case from that which precedes it is the criterion for assent suggested by M. Burnyeat.

104. MS. Urb. lat. 1207, fo.149^r.

105. *Opera* I, 744. The Loeb edition has "Rerum natura" for "Verum natura" at the beginning of the Cicero passage, which accounts for the slightly different versions in the two quotations above.

106. Diogenes Laertius reports that the Stoics defined dialectic as "the science of statements true, false, and neither true nor false" VII 42. Sextus gives the same definition in *PH* II 247. The section of *Academica* II which contains the crucial discussion of sorites as undermining certainty which Valla uses at the end of his own treatment also draws in the liar paradox (II 95) and "antistrephon" (II 98) to support the skeptic's viewpoint. Valla follows his treatment of sorites with a long chapter on these two forms.

107. See Diogenes Laertius VII 43-44; Sextus, *PH* II 253-255: "And if the Dogmatists of the School of Chrysippus declare that when the 'Sorites' is being propounded they ought to halt while the argument is still proceeding and suspend judgment, to avoid falling into absurdity, much more, surely, would it be fitting for us, who are Skeptics, when we suspect absurdity, to give no hasty approval of the premises propounded but rather to suspend judgment about each until the completion of the whole series which forms the argument. And whereas we, by starting undogmatically from the observation of practical life, thus avoid these fallacious arguments, the Dogmatists will not be in a position to distinguish the Sophism from the argument which seems to be correctly propounded, seeing that they have to pronounce dogmatically that the form of the argument is, or is not, logically sound and also that the premises are, or are not, true."

108. See C. Wright, "Language Mastery and the Sorites Paradox."

109. Horace, *Epistulae* II 1.45-47.

110. *De natura deorum* III 43-52.

111. SE *M* IX 182-190.

112. *De inventione* I 51-56, where Cicero links this kind of induction with Soc-

rates's skepticism in debate: "Socrates used this conversational method a good deal, because he wished to affirm nothing (nihil ipse afferre), but preferred to get a result from the material which the interlocutor had given him—a result which the interlocutor was bound to approve as following necessarily from what he had already granted," I. 53. Boethius, *De differentiis topicis*, Migne, *PL* 64.1183-84; *In Topica Ciceronis*, Migne, *PL* 64.1116-17. See also Quintilian, *Institutio oratoria* V 11.2-5 (which also associates this form of induction with Socrates).

113. *De inventione* I 51-53.

114. *Dialecticae disputationes*, first version, fo.166^r (MS. Urb. lat. 1207).

115. Coloniae, 1539 ed., p. 449.

116. Ibid., p. 446: "Credimusque multa, non quia uera uideantur, sed quia credimus."

117. Ibid., p. 447.

118. Agricola's strategy in this example is remarkably like that of which Hamblin gives an account in discussing the "obligation game" in medieval logical practice, and as a serious type of forensic discourse for modern logical consideration. See C. L. Hamblin, *Fallacies* (London, 1970), pp. 125-133, 260 ff.

119. Hamblin, *Fallacies*, p. 245. The numbers relate these "dialectical criteria" to the corresponding "alethic rules":

1. The premises must be true.
2. The conclusion must be implied by them (in some suitable sense of the word "implied").
3. The conclusion must follow reasonably immediately.
4. If some of the premises are unstated, they must be of a specified omissible kind (pp. 234-235.)

Hamblin maintains that "arguments which pass these alethic tests can be regarded as setting a certain theoretical standard of worth, corresponding to a certain conception of 'pure' Logic" (p. 256).

120. This paper is developed from an earlier one entitled "Lorenzo Valla and the Intellectual Origins of Humanist Dialectic," *Journal of the History of Philosophy* 15 (1977), 143-164. I am extremely grateful to M. F. Burnyeat for his advice on modifications to that paper and several subsequent drafts of this one.

11

Skepticism and Fideism*

Terence Penelhum

> To be a philosophical sceptic is, in a man of letters,
> the first and most essential step towards being
> a sound, believing Christian.

This extraordinary statement is the final moral which Hume puts into the mouth of Philo in the *Dialogues Concerning Natural Religion.* Understanding why Hume places it there is probably the most essential, even if it is not the first, step towards unraveling his final intentions in that work. Whatever these intentions were, one fact is clear: in making Philo say this, Hume is parodying an apologetic tradition with which he could assume his readers to be familiar, and is echoing its sentiments for his own purposes.

The tradition Hume parodies I shall call Skeptical Fideism. Its history in the early modern period has been traced for us with great erudition and finesse by Richard Popkin.[1] Its influence continues into our own

*Acknowledgments. Most of this essay was written during a period of leave supported by a Leave Fellowship from the Social Sciences and Humanities Research Council of Canada. Some of the material was included in two public lectures. The first was given at the University of London, King's College on May 22, 1978; the second to the Divinity Faculty at Cambridge University on January 28, 1980. I am grateful for the stimulus these occasions provided to develop the themes considered here. I wish also to express my gratitude to Myles Burnyeat for very enlightening lectures and discussions on classical Skepticism. Without these, most of the things I say about that tradition would certainly have been mistaken, and anything I happen now to have got right is the result of what I learned from them.

time. It is a tradition which tries to enlist the doubts and questions of the philosophical skeptic in the supposed interests of Christian faith. I shall use the title to include not only those thinkers who openly avow sympathy with philosophical skepticism, but also those who merely utilize specific skeptic arguments or attitudes in the interests of a faith which they see to be antithetical to it. I follow others in calling both groups fideists because in every case they judge it to be of the essence of religious faith that it cannot be justified by rational argument.

The influence of Skeptical Fideism should seem surprising. Faith, after all, seems to involve anyone who has it in the acceptance of transcendent realities; yet skepticism seems to entail doubts even about the familiar. Faith commits one to far more than the everyday affairs of life require one to accept; skepticism makes one feel sure of far less. How could movements of thought that pull in such opposite directions be thought to have anything in common? That these obvious appearances are the true guides is the view of Augustine, Luther, and Berkeley; but against them we have the opinions, or at least the statements, of Erasmus, Montaigne, Bayle, and even Pascal and Kierkegaard. After some preliminary historical comments about skepticism, I shall look at some of the arguments to be found in their works, and in those of more recent writers who have learned from them. Since I consider the arguments to be bad ones, I shall also attempt to indicate the sources of their appeal.

I

The Skeptical Fideist tradition in modern times was the result of the rediscovery of the writings of Sextus Empiricus in the sixteenth century, when the theological controversies of the Reformation were at their height. Even a brief glance at Sextus, or at the intellectual history of this period, makes it clear that Skepticism is not an anonymous position which live philosophers compete in refuting, but a significant school of thought of late antiquity whose ideas underwent a remarkable revival.

Like any other school, Skepticism had variations. Its questionings were varied in their sources and their targets. But they were, throughout, supposed to yield a spiritual benefit. Skepticism was a third, practically directed alternative to Epicureanism and Stoicism, offering, as they offered, a way of life that concentrated on the cultivation of an appropriate inner state that would prevent the vicissitudes of life from penetrating the soul of the practitioner and disturbing his peace. Its distinctive recommendations lay in the procedures it offered for the cultivation of this inner state. Instead of following the Epicurean in the pursuit of low-budget satisfactions, or following the Stoic in the passionless pursuit of ends set by the divine order, it recommended suspense of judgment, or noncommitment. The consolations of other philosophical systems depended upon the alleged acquisition of knowledge, both of fact and of value. But the very multiplicity of the competing knowledge-claims of these systems showed, in the Skeptic view, that the certainties from which these consolations are alleged to follow are unreal, and that the competition between contending dogmas is itself a source of confusion and anxiety. To avoid it one must decline to dogmatize on either side of controversies. The complex, and often tedious, batteries of Skeptic arguments, which range from accounts of the odd ways of exotic tribes to remarks about sticks looking bent in water and the world looking yellow to men who have jaundice, and which may be marshaled on either side of a dispute, are designed to induce this suspense of judgment by fair or foul means.

So much seems to be common to the Skeptic tradition throughout late antiquity. But a movement spanning several centuries inevitably involves development and disagreement, especially as it attempts to respond to hostile criticisms. The two most obvious objections to Skepticism are that it is impossible to live by it in practice, since action requires belief; and that it is incoherent because its own principles require commitment and not suspense from those who follow them. It is the way in which these criticisms are met that is traditionally taken to distinguish the Academic Skeptics (particularly Arcesilaus and Carneades) from the Pyrrhonians (particularly Aenesidemus and Sextus). As Sextus represents the matter,[2] the Pyrrhonians judged the Academics to have compromised the tradition begun by Pyrrho in two ways: first, by denying the possibility of real knowledge—which the Pyrrhonian sees as negative dogmatism; and second, by claiming that in spite of this, life can be pursued by the recognition of probabilities or likelihoods—which the Pyrrhonian sees as the abandonment of suspense.[3] The Pyrrhonian evades these difficulties in another manner. First, the Skeptic way is not recommended on the basis of theoretical generalizations or value judgments for which Sextus is proselytizing: it is rather a stance or attitude or habit of mind which he illustrates. Someone exemplifying it is driven by the assemblage of arguments on each side of a question to a point where their felt equivalence induces suspense of judgment in him; and from this suspense quietude (*ataraxia*) follows "as if by chance."[4] Second, neither the suspense nor the consequent quietude is understood in a way inconsistent with daily activities. The Pyrrhonian yields to appearances and to local opinion in order to carry on the affairs of the day in the least stressful manner. This is due to his yielding to them in an undogmatic (or belief-less) way. Sextus describes this practical accommodation as follows:

> Adhering, then, to appearances, we live in accordance with the normal rules of life, undogmatically, seeing that we cannot remain wholly inactive. And it would seem that this regulation of life is fourfold, and that one part of it lies in the guid-ance of Nature, another in the constraint of the passions, another in the tradition of laws and customs, another in the instruction of the arts. Nature's guidance is that by which we are naturally capable of sensation and thought; constraint of the passions is that whereby hunger drives us to food and thirst to drink; tradi-tion of customs and laws, that whereby we regard piety in the conduct of life as good, but impiety as evil; instruction of the arts, that whereby we are not in-active in such arts as we adopt. But we make all these statements undogmati-cally.[5]

However this is to be interpreted, it is clear that the Skeptic's suspense allows some level of involvement with day-to-day affairs, albeit with a good deal of *arrière-pensée*. In such circumstances[6] we would expect similar accommodation in the understanding of *ataraxia*:

> We do not suppose, however, that the Skeptic is wholly untroubled; but we say that he is troubled by things unavoidable; for we grant that he is cold at times and thirsty, and suffers various affections of that kind. But even in these cases, where ordinary people are afflicted by two circumstances,—namely, by the affections themselves and, in no less a degree, by the belief that these conditions are evil by nature,—the Skeptic, by his rejection of the added belief in the natural badness of all these conditions, escapes here too with less discomfort. Hence we say that, while in regard to matters of opinion the Skeptic's End is quietude, in regard to things unavoidable it is "moderate affection."[7]

It is essential to touch briefly upon some of the problems of interpreta-tion that Sextus presents, since it was the work of Sextus that was the major source of Skeptical thought in the early modern period. It is par-ticularly important here not to read him anachronistically in the light of the methodological Skepticism we encounter in Descartes.

There is, first of all, no trace in Sextus of the post-Cartesian identifica-tion of skepticism and solipsism. The problem of Other Minds hardly arises; and the Skeptic's suspense, while extending to all judgments con-cerning the extent to which realities correspond to appearances, does not embrace any proposition to the effect that there are external realities. The issue is always one of whether those realities, which are not accessible or evident, can be known by means of appearances, which are. Conversely, there is no Cartesian assurance that certain knowledge of inner realities is available to us directly; this is not because knowledge of inner realities is denied, but because the questions that concern Sextus are questions about alleged nonevident realities *beyond* appearances. It is these that concern him when he asks whether knowledge is possible, or, as he expresses it, whether Anything True Exists.[8] This has to be kept constantly in mind when determining Sextus's position on the Skeptic's practical accommodations.

The precise nature of these accommodations is important and difficult to determine: important because the practical viability of the Skeptic stance is crucial when its end is not theoretical enlightenment (as in the case of Cartesian skepticism) but spiritual liberation, and difficult to determine because of the obscurity of what Sextus says. What is it to be led by Nature and the passions and customs and the arts, but to be led by them without belief? If the only example of accommodation were adherence to customs, we might be tempted to conclude that the Skeptic settles for outward conformity and inner distance; but apart from the fact that this kind of settled hypocrisy is too close to a formal policy to fit the mood of the texts, it is of no value as an interpretation of the other modes of compliance that Sextus lists for us. The inclusion of Nature and the passions makes it clear that the Skeptic will yield to whatever feelings and choices arise in him from the demands of his organism, without making positive or negative value-judgments about them or about the objects with which they require him to deal: so following appearances here seems to be a matter of yielding to those passions that remain in us after we have shed the emotional turbulence that comes from seeking certainties and forming opinions. But here the inclusion of custom forces us to widen our understanding of what it is to follow appearances to include concurrence, at *some* mental level, in society's evaluations; and if we are to retain the suggestion of passivity and absence of belief here, we seem to be left with the elimination of all those elements of individual judgment which prevent the unhindered repetition of those sayings and doings that one is brought up conventionally to follow. The pursuit of the arts by the Skeptic seems easiest to understand: it will consist in the continued practice of those professional skills in which society has trained one, without any opinion at all about the worthwhileness of their products. So the Skeptic way of life is the deliberately unexamined life. One is inevitably reminded here of Pyrrho's pig[9] and Mill's comment about the dissatisfied Socrates.[10]

Adhering to appearances, therefore, is not to be taken as an ancient version of twentieth-century phenomenalism, but as a mode of thought and behavior that includes the unreflective use of skills and the unquestioning adherence to natural passion and ingrained convention. These latter, nevertheless, are understood on the model of sensory affection, as alterations brought about in us without our choice or control: how some matter appears to me is not understood to be a product of free reflection but to be a passive change in my experience. Hence the Skeptic is even said to be stating "what appears to himself" and to be "announcing his own impression in an undogmatic way" when he expounds the Skeptic practice. So once one has come to have the Skeptic attitude, one does not follow it as a policy, but merely yields to habit.[11] It is questionable whether the Skeptic can coherently say that he can yield to appearances (particularly social norms) without belief, or that his practice of the Skeptic way is itself a mere yielding to appearances. But if this is indeed the correct way to understand Sextus, it has two important consequences.

The first is that Sextus is not committed to any doctrine that belief is voluntary. It would be odd to say that one can suspend belief by choice and then labor mightily to produce batteries of countervailing arguments to produce this suspense: one could, after all, just practice it immediately to gain its promised rewards. Just as assent to appearances is involuntary, so also the onset of suspense is a passive outcome of the balanced arguments, and the lessening of perturbation a passive outcome of that.

The second consequence is that we must view the relation of the Skeptic attitude to unphilosophical opinion as a special kind of aloof conformity. While there is nothing in theory to prevent the Skeptic from finding that what his inclinations dictate for him is radical or minority action, it is obvious that the overwhelmingly likely result of the Skeptic attitude will be conservative habits of action. This is because the Skeptic will starve all tendencies he may have to evaluate the habits he has acquired. This does not mean, however, that the Skeptic is one whose stance is indistinguishable from that of unreflective common sense, or that he is committed to believing that ordinary folk live in a state of prephilosophical innocence. If this were true, the Skeptic's doubts would only be directed against competing philosophical schools and would pass the layman by. It is true that philosophical dogmatists, usually the Stoics, are his standard targets, but there can be no question that the unlettered are also considered to be the victims of dogmatism, and to be subject to perturbation and unhappiness because of the unfounded judgments they make. So although the Skeptic's practice may not differ outwardly from that of his unphilosophical fellows, he is someone who *returns* to common practice after extinguishing his wish to judge it, and who returns to a common practice that is disinfected of those underpinnings of belief and valuation that have given it meaning and helped to establish it for those with whose behavior he allows himself to conform. He is *in* their world, but not *of* it. One cannot throw away the Skeptic's ladder without first climbing it. In this, Skepticism resembles other antiphilosophical philosophies, like those of Hume and Wittgenstein.

II

The Skeptic attitude to religion is naturally of a piece with the Skeptic attitude toward all affairs of life. Sextus expresses it in the *Outlines* by prefacing his summary of dogmatic positions with this comment: "Although, following the ordinary view, we affirm undogmatically that Gods exist and reverence Gods and ascribe to them foreknowledge, yet as against the rashness of the Dogmatists we argue as follows."[12] The much lengthier theological discussions of *M* IX end, predictably, with the introduction of Skeptic suspense at 191, and the additional comment that such suspense is not only a response to the balanced arguments of theists and atheists, but a response to the divergency of the views of ordinary people. However we are, precisely, to determine the meaning of this combination of easy outward piety and inner suspension concerning the Gods' very existence, it is clearly a far cry from any dynamic faith, and is intended to be.[13] In particular, it cannot be equated with a combination of simple religious faith and abstinence from theological disputes, whatever the merits of the latter combination.

It is therefore surprising to see the extent of the attraction Pyrrhonism exerted on thinkers embroiled in the theological wrangles of the Reformation period. The two most important and well-known examples of this that are commonly cited are the position taken by Erasmus in his debate with Luther on free will, and the Catholic Pyrrhonism of Montaigne. Both appear to recommend the wholesale importation of Skeptic attitudes into Christian thought.

It is not at all clear that this was what Erasmus intended, although Luther had sufficient excuse for reading him in this way. No doubt Erasmus's main reason for publishing an argument on the Catholic side of the Reformation controversies was his conviction that the theological divisions on which Luther was insisting, and for which he himself felt such distaste, were destroying the unity of Christendom and endangering simple piety. He also says that to say the human will can achieve nothing for its own salvation is to undercut the moral effort on which such piety depends. His arguments are found in the *Diatribe Concerning Free Choice* of 1524.[14] This work is specifically a response to an earlier work of Luther's whose title begins with the word *Assertio*. In this work Luther had stated that free choice is a "fiction," and that the human will makes no contribution of its own to salvation, which is due wholly to the grace of God. Erasmus says at the outset that "so far am I from delighting in 'assertions' that I would readily take refuge in the opinion of the Skeptics, wherever this is allowed by the inviolable authority of the Holy Scriptures and the decrees of the Church, to which I everywhere willingly submit my personal feelings, whether I grasp what it prescribes or not."[15]

This is not an unambiguous endorsement of Skepticism, and the arguments which follow reflect its ambiguity.

We can find echoes of Skeptic themes when Erasmus insists that "Christian godliness" does not require us to engage in theological disputation about divine foreknowledge or the efficacy of the will, and that there are matters which God does not wish us to penetrate but only to "contemplate, as we venerate himself, in mystic silence."[16] To insist on exploring them is divisive, morally harmful, and generative of paradoxes. It is plausible to read Erasmus's total argument as a recommendation to do our Christian duty by striving to turn from evil to good, yet to attribute any good we achieve not to ourselves but to God—all while declining to worry about any inconsistencies that tiresome dialecticians can generate from this. This is close to the Skeptic recommendation to fall in with tradition while avoiding interpretation. But most of the detailed argument is explicitly in favor of one dogmatic solution—namely, a middle-of-the-road theology which states that the will is free but that it needs grace to stir it to decision and to make its decisions effective. While he marshals texts on both sides of the controversy in an apparent imitation of Skeptic practice, he does so only to reinterpret those which seem on the surface to support the Lutheran doctrine.

Faced with this uncertainty of method, Luther's singlemindedness has overwhelming dialectical advantages, since he is able to maintain that the weaknesses in Erasmus's arguments are the results of an attempt to combine Christianity and Skepticism when the two will not mix. It is not my purpose here to explore the grace and free-will controversy itself, but two of Luther's replies bear directly on Erasmus's attempt to combine the two traditions. First, Luther accuses Erasmus of contradiction in maintaining on the one hand that the free-will question is a theological matter that the simple believer does not have to settle, and saying on the other that godliness requires both effort of will and divine mercy.[17] Erasmus, in other words, has not avoided the theological problem but has committed himself to one solution of it while protesting indifference. Here Luther is not merely questioning his opponent's consistency, but denying the very possibility of engaging in the Christian life without theological commitment. He insists that such attempted disengagement would destroy faith altogether.[18]

Second, and more fundamentally, Luther declares that faith and Skepticism entail incompatible attitudes:

> For it is not the mark of a Christian mind to take no delight in assertions; on the contrary, a man must delight in assertions or he will be no Christian. And by assertion . . . I mean a constant adhering, affirming, confessing, maintaining, and an invincible persevering; nor, I think, does the word mean anything else either as used by the Latins or as used by us in our time.[19]

The Holy Spirit is no Skeptic, and it is not doubts or mere opinions that he has written on our hearts, but assertions more sure and certain than life itself and all experience.[20]

On this Luther is surely unanswerable, and understands both faith and Skepticism the better, whichever of them is right about grace and free will. Whether or not it is possible to have faith while avoiding theology, and whether or not it is possible to adhere to a tradition without believing the assertions that are uttered by those who practice it, a life without commitment is not a life lived in faith. Any simple attempt to graft Skeptic attitudes onto Christianity is bound to fail. And it is not surprising that others who have tried to follow in Erasmus's footsteps, however circumspectly, have been suspected of disguised apostasy.

The most famous of these figures is Montaigne, whose *Apology for Raimond Sebond*, published in 1580, became the most famous of all modern Pyrrhonist texts, and introduced dozens of the arguments and examples of Sextus to a wide literary audience. Montaigne's motives in writing it are not unlike those of Erasmus: to offer an antidote to violent sectarianism, both that of the Protestants and that of their overzealous Catholic persecutors. His method is far more radical: it amounts to nothing less than the explicit undermining of confidence in the power of reason to arrive at truth in any sphere whatever. Montaigne does not see clearly that by being as explicit as this about the impotence of reason (as indeed most of his subsequent fideist imitators have been also) he is shifting away from a strict Pyrrhonism toward the very sort of negative dogmatism he says he follows Sextus in rejecting.

The nominal structure of this enormous essay centers around two objections made by critics to the natural theology of the fifteenth-century Spanish thinker Raimond Sebond. Montaigne had translated Sebond into French at the request of his father. The oddity of the alleged defense arises from the fact that Sebond tried to prove the major articles of Christian faith by reason. The first objection Montaigne says he is meeting is the claim that faith should not be based on reason at all; his answer is that *within* faith reason can be of value—a manifestly irrelevant response which is coupled with the personal opinion that faith comes as a gift of divine grace. The second objection to Sebond is that his actual arguments are weak. Montaigne answers this by arguing at length, with assistance from Sextus, that the greatest human minds have been unable to find the truth about anything at all, so that there is no cause to be disturbed if the arguments of Sebond, which are as good as any, are not compelling! Sebond disappears from sight as Montaigne assembles arguments in Pyrrhonian fashion to undermine our confidence in the sciences, the senses, philosophy, and the rest. There are two morals that emerge from this, the first drawn in comments as the essay proceeds, and the second in conclusion. The first, and more explicitly Catholic, moral, rests upon man's incapacity to transcend the relativities in which he is placed by history and tradition: being so placed, man must recognize his inability to stand outside his own circumstances and must submit to the religious forms and teachings that surround him. The echo of Sextus here is obvious. Montaigne expresses this moral as follows:

> Now, from a knowledge of this volatility of mine, I have accidentally begotten in myself a certain steadfastness of opinion, and I have not much altered those that were original and native with me. For whatever semblance of truth there may be in a novel idea, I do not easily change, for fear of losing by the bargain. And since I am not capable of choosing, I take the choice of other men and keep myself in the station in which God has placed me. Otherwise I could not save myself from rolling perpetually. In this way I have, by the grace of God, with no perturbation and disturbance of conscience, preserved my faith intact in the ancient beliefs of our religion, amid so many sects and divisions that our age has produced.[21]

The second moral is more general, equally acceptable to the Protestant, and is the most familiar form of the Skeptical Fideist position. Since neither the senses nor reason can be judged reliable guides to reality, we have to accept that our own resources are inadequate to grasp it. To a man humble enough to recognize this impotence, divine grace may then vouchsafe access to the truth as a gift, in the form of faith:

> Nor can a man rise above himself and humanity; for he cannot see but with his eyes, nor take hold but with his own grasp. He will rise if God will extraordinarily lend him His hand; he will rise by abandoning and renouncing his own means and by suffering himself to be uplifted and upraised by means purely celestial.
> It belongs to our Christian faith, and not to his Stoical virtue, to aspire to that divine and miraculous metamorphosis.[22]

There is no reason to suppose that Montaigne was clearly aware of the fact that these two morals are distinct from each other. They are indeed only compatible if one follows him in equating the faith that comes from grace with the Skeptic's acquiescence in local tradition. In this he appears to have been followed by other Catholic Pyrrhonists such as Charron.[23] The objections to such a position are, as with Erasmus, easy to make. It assumes, to begin with, a readily identifiable local consensus which the hearer largely shares and from which he has only been temporarily disturbed; in an era like our own, when it is unlikely that he has such a relationship to any tradition, none can be represented to him as an easy refuge from intellectual indecision. It also assumes a faith so tepid that it can genuinely seem more easily conformist than its competition. Montaigne's own religion may well have been of this sort. Whether or not this is so, the confusing amalgamation of these two ill-matched recommendations serves to conceal what the most distinguished subsequent fideists saw more clearly—that if Skeptic argument is to serve religious ends, it must issue not in belieflessness but in belief: the precise contrary of the outcome of Skeptic reasoning in its original habitat. Once this is recognized, the function of rehearsing Skeptic argument changes. It is now rehearsed to make its hearer move toward belief in the very process of abandoning the search for grounds for it. So the theologies of groundlessness and paradox have a Skeptic ancestry.

III

Before proceeding to examine other forms of fideist argument, it is important to reflect on the phenomenon that Erasmus and Montaigne (and, I think, Bayle)[24] represent: the assimilation of faith and the Skeptic attitude. It is one thing to respond to the perceived impotence of reason by a leap of commitment rather than by suspense of judgment. It is quite another to respond by a commitment that one describes in Skeptic language. It is one thing to abandon the rational quest in the hope that divine grace will provide the solution that your own powers have failed to provide. It is quite another to identify the fruits of such grace with the halfhearted conformism that Sextus recommends. How could such a phenomenon arise?

Undoubtedly speculation about an answer has to include the fact that Skeptical Fideists saw themselves in opposition to radical enthusiasts, and believed humility and intellectual self-depreciation to be an urgent Christian need. But an explanation needs to go deeper than this. It lies, I think, in the recognition that the stances of faith and of Skepticism are indeed similar in certain vital respects. Both involve dissatisfaction with the disturbance and anxiety associated with the commitments of the world of secular common sense. Both recommend, as a cure for these anxieties, not physical disengagement from the commonsense world, but a kind of participation in it that requires inner detachment or otherness from it. It is, indeed, this key element of participation without identification that often encourages those of faith to accept the authenticity of other religious traditions, since they too incorporate this same element in their conceptions of the liberated personality. Of course in *religions* this detachment is to be understood as a consequence of a commitment to some end which transcends the sphere of secular common sense, whereas it is identified as itself the end in Pyrrhonism. But it is only too easy for the hard-pressed apologist not to scrutinize similarities when he finds them. In philosophy of all places we should know that my enemy's enemy may not be my friend; but it is an easy mistake.

I would suggest, then, that Skepticism was not universally perceived as an enemy of faith because it was also, in its enervating way, a saving mode of life. The analogy can be pressed further, to show that in quite a number of ways Skepticism and faith are mirror images of one another. This can be seen most easily if we consider the oldest of all criticisms of Skepticism: that it is not humanly viable.

The best-known expression of this criticism is the one we find in Hume. He can quite properly be called a Skeptic himself, since he accepts many of the classical Pyrrhonist arguments and adds to them. But he insists they are *vain* arguments. They do show our natural beliefs to be without foundation. But since these beliefs are entrenched in our natures by forces that have nothing to do with philosophical argument, philosophical arguments cannot dislodge them. So the Pyrrhonian's "cavils" can only produce a "momentary amazement and confusion," which we cannot sustain when we leave our studies. This is just as well, for if we could sustain it, the effect would not be liberating, but paralyzing and distressing. So Hume claims Pyrrhonism to be doomed to failure, and happily denies any power to his own negative arguments.[25]

This shows far less engagement with the actual detail of Sextus than one might expect, but one can certainly extract from Hume's understanding of belief the claim that beliefless participation in human affairs is impossible, so that one cannot live undogmatically. On the other hand, the references to momentary amazement and confusion, to say nothing of Hume's candid expression of his own skeptical perplexities, show a recognition that the Skeptic arguments have some force against our tendencies to believe. Hume's critique comes down to saying that Skeptic suspense cannot be *sustained*—that one is bound, human nature being what it is, to lapse from it. What does this show? Only that Pyrrhonian suspense can only stay with us by the repeated assemblage of reminders, which most people have no inclination to engage in, and which require the regular retreat to the study which only an intellectual elite can manage to arrange. The lapses into commitment that might occur in the marketplace would reinforce the need for such reminders. But they would not show that the suspense the Skeptic regularly reinstated in the study was not, overall, his real attitude, or that it did not serve to moderate the stresses of decision. One does not show oneself not to be an example of a way of life merely by lapsing from the pattern from time to time—as long as one has a fixed enough practice of *contending* with such lapses.

For this to be an answer to Hume it needs elaboration. Hume may not prove that concurring with appearances without belief is impossible; but undoubtedly the concept of such concurrence is unclear. In cases of sensory affection it is presumably a matter of acting as though the thing I see really is the way it looks to be, without any inner assent (or denial) that it really is the way it looks. Here, perhaps, the onus is on the critic to deny that we can act in this way. But, as Burnyeat has pointed out,[26] the onus is on the Skeptic to construe his own philosophical utterances (such as, "The arguments on each side of this question are equivalent") in a way which shows him to concur in *them* passively without believing them, for in such cases something's appearing to be so consists in nothing other than our *inclination to believe* it to be so. The more propositions there are with which one cannot concur without assent, the more propositions there are to which the Skeptic cannot apply his habit of suspension without explicitly dissociating himself from his own inclination to assent. I am not convinced, however, that this difficulty proves Pyrrhonism not to be viable, though it does indeed prevent the Pyrrhonist from treating all his philosophical pronouncements as expressions of appearance. Some now have to be expressions of a policy to which he commits himself, namely, that of cultivating a habit of suspense which undermines our inclination to share the beliefs that surround us. This policy is indeed one he can follow, and which will express his real stance in spite of those occasions when he may lapse into conviction like the rest of us. How often this is unavoidable for him will depend on the independent question of how far action in a given sphere requires inner assent as well as outward behavior—a question on which neither Hume nor Sextus is likely to be the best guide.

It is of great importance to note, as Burnyeat does, that if I withdraw at one level of myself from an assent I have given, or am inclined to give, at another, I am practicing a kind of self-distance: I am treating some action or passion within my own nature as though it is not part of my real or deepest or most considered self. (No doubt Hume's rejection of Pyrrhonism is, among other things, a consequence of his doctrinaire insistence that a science of human nature shows such talk to be absurd; I am no more than the sequence of passions that pass within me.) This device of externalizing some passion that one deems should be otherwise is characteristic of religious understandings of man and salvific modes of thought.[27] The most familiar Western example is St. Paul on the flesh and the spirit. In such understandings of human nature, the norm adopted is the total absence of the externalized lapse; the purpose of the externalizing device is the consolidation of the policy of combating it; and in the case of someone in whom the mode of thought is settled, the reality is a progressive reduction in the number of occasions when such lapses occur. But the speaker's description of the inclination as external to himself is an acceptable one when the reality has reached this stage. The norm is not proved incoherent, and his adoption of it is not put in doubt, by decreasing falls from grace.

Skepticism, then, can be defended against a Humean critique as a stance which can be sustained by the regular assemblage of arguments against the daily temptations to lapse into conviction. Its rewards are the progressive reduction of stresses to the available minimum, and the simple pleasures of destructive intellectual activity.

It can now be compared with faith. Faith, too, is a stance toward daily experience which has to be sustained by reminders, and which is claimed to yield spiritual strengths. These strengths are the reduction of anxiety and openness to love. The pressures of the world do not make these easy prizes, and they constantly threaten them when they are achieved. The reminders that help to sustain faith are primarily prophetic and sacramental, though there is in my view no good reason of principle why they should not also include philosophical reflections. These reminders serve to recall to the believer that which he holds to be true about his relation to God, and to enable him to reenact and renew his response to that supposed relationship. The source of that relationship as faith has traditionally perceived it is that God has intervened in history in a way that reassures his people that his Kingdom will ultimately triumph within it. The believer's relative freedom from the anxieties that would otherwise beset him is the fruit of that reassurance. He sees the world he shares with others as a world in which such anxieties would be inevitable *and reasonable* if this reassurance were unavailable. This involves an interpretation of daily experience which goes far beyond the appearances, and from which, therefore, the Skeptic would withdraw. But the two are offering competing ways of release from the strains of human anxiety.

I have suggested that the Skeptic suspense of judgment can be ascribed to someone even in the face of lapses into conviction. The converse is clearly true for the person of faith, whose conviction can still be acknowledged despite periods of doubt. For doubt can occur within faith, and need not destroy it. It will not destroy it if the doubter *contends* with the doubts that he has. This fact is seen, but misrepresented, in the classic account of faith we find in Aquinas. He tells us that faith is wholehearted in a way that opinion is not. On the surface this would seem to imply that it is impossible to have faith and doubt together. This is only true in perfect, or ideal, faith. In actual faith one can demonstrate the very existence of the faith one has by contending with the residual doubts and anxieties that still arise within it. Faith also is a normative notion, and one shows one deserves to be credited with having faith when one acknowledges that one does not have it strongly enough and accepts the obligation to deepen it. The norm excludes doubt, but the state does not, any more than the state of courage excludes all fear. And when Jesus spoke of the lilies of the field, he showed how the anxieties of the world can threaten the commitment that should otherwise liberate us from them.

In both lived Skepticism and lived faith, therefore, there is a crucial two-way relationship between reasoning and the emotional life. Reflection supports a mood which one may only have imperfectly, but has firmly enough to muster intellectual resources in its defense, to ward off judgments which might undermine it and generate anxiety and disturbance. So each appears from outside to be at odds with common sense, however much its possessor's behavior may conform to it. For the one seems from without to be obstinately doubting the indubitable, and the other seems from without to be obstinately believing the incredible. Given the notorious tendency of a religious establishment to construe faith in a manner that permits too extensive an outward accommodation with common sense, it is intelligible that their profounder differences would be overlooked. Let us now turn to those clearer versions of Skeptical Fideism which are not guilty of this confusion.

IV

If the Skeptical Fideist does not identify the Skeptic attitude with the faith he professes, he must see the Skeptic as a thinker who serves the faith in spite of himself. This, he will claim, the Skeptic does by showing us the impotence of reason in the search for truth. When the Skeptic's assemblage of arguments dispels our confidence in the power of reasoning to understand the world and identify the good life, we are freed from intellectual obstacles to the operation of grace. We do not find, as the Skeptic says he does, that the abandonment of reasoning turns out, accidentally, to *be* the very solution that we have sought. We find, rather, that when our mind has become a *tabula rasa* once again, grace will write upon it.

This position is, of course, essentially hostile to Skepticism taken as a whole, though it is compatible with the most extensive use of Skeptic argumentation. It is essential to it to maintain that the faith the fideist professes not be offered *for reasons*: for it is stated to be the result of recognizing that reason carries us nowhere; although the faith may well commit us to the most ontologically luxuriant doctrines. Within the theology that expresses that faith, the faith's existence is due to the action of God supervening when the human search has spent itself. But the same transition viewed from outside, and described in the language of apologetics, can only be called a motiveless leap or groundless choice: hence the paradoxical juxtaposition of the language of arbitrary voluntarism on the one hand and helpless passivity on the other in talking of the same events.

Skeptical Fideism in this form is not strictly refutable, since there is no incoherence in the concept of believing without reasons. But it does give rise to some obvious perplexities. The first arises from the fact that a leap of faith can be made to any one of an indefinite number of theological positions, each of them including the claim that it is the product of grace. Unless one simply assumes there is only one dogmatic option available, the adoption of one of them presents the familiar possibility of Skeptic questionings over the criterion of selection among them. The second difficulty, or group of difficulties, concerns the psychology of the transition. Is it, indeed, possible for us to believe something while holding there is no more reason to believe it than its contrary? Is the notion of a leap of faith psychologically intelligible at all, or is it perhaps only possible to speak of the transition in the in-group language of theology? A third, and deeper, question is that of the significance of the alleged fact from which Skeptical Fideism starts—namely, that there is no better reason to believe the propositions of the faith than their contraries. Is this just a bewildering brute fact that happens to be religiously advantageous to know, or does it have theological import? If the Skeptic is to be seen as the unwitting ally of faith, something must surely be found wanting in the work of those dogmatists who supposed that its allies were themselves. While the Fideist may be able, within the bounds of logical strictness, to avoid these questions, he will have to have some answer to them if what he says is to function as apologetic and not merely as assertion.

We can find profound and influential responses to all of them in Pascal. While seeing Skepticism, as he knew it through Montaigne, as the intellectual parent of an easygoing aristocratic libertinism, Pascal is fully aware of its power and absorbs much from it. For him there can, of course, be no question of following Montaigne in thinking (or pretending) that the path of faith can consist in social conformity. (He had his say about *that* sort of religion in the *Provincial Letters*.)[28] The moral he draws from Skepticism is that reason cannot take us to God, and indeed is powerless even to support the basic principles on which daily life depends.[29] He insists, however, that Skeptic suspense is impossible for our natures, and that in any case the uncertainties on which Skepticism trades can lead only to despair rather than unperturbedness, since our natures are created with the need for the kind of assurance which only faith can provide for us. This is why the life of genteel conformism is a life devoted so extensively to play and distraction.[30] The assurance is available; but only if we "listen to God."[31] To listen to God is to pass from the realms, or orders, of the senses and the reason to that of the heart. The illumination it will provide for us will not only overcome our corruption, but will in so doing give us something of that understanding which the dogmatic philosophers tried unsuccessfully to achieve, and explain their failure to achieve it. What has appeared to the Skeptic as the unknowability of God is then understood to be God's hiddenness:

> It is true then that everything teaches man his condition, but here must be no misunderstanding, for it is not true that everything reveals God, and it is not true that everything conceals God. But it is true at once that he hides from those who tempt him and that he reveals himself to those who seek him, because men are at once unworthy and capable of God: unworthy through their corruption, capable through their original nature.[32]
>
> What can be seen on earth indicates neither the total absence, nor the manifest presence of divinity, but the presence of a hidden God. Everything bears this stamp.[33]

God's hiddenness is offset by his revelation in Christ, which exposes man's fallenness and its remedy.

Pascal's answer to our first problem, then, consists in the claim that only the Christian revelation, with its doctrine of original sin, can respond to the ambiguity which generates Skepticism *and* explain it; for only it insists upon, and only it remedies, the corruption which prevents our recognizing the presence of God and our need for him. While we remain in this corrupted state, we will be unable to do better than vacillate between accepting and rejecting the facile arguments of deism, which seize on the indications of the God we need but encourage us to ignore the very evils which intensify that need and keep us from him.[34] His answer to the second problem is essentially the claim that faith can only come to us if we listen to God; this is something we cannot do in the context of the pleasantries of philosophical disputation, but can do if we abandon these in the light of the recognition of our own corruption. (He augments this response in the course of the "Wager" argument, which I discuss below.) The answer to the third problem is the famous doctrine of the Hidden God. If God only manifests himself to those who seek him, it is only *to be expected* that man's natural reason will not find him. Of the three interrelated answers it is this last that has been the most influential. While it has long been an apologetic commonplace that faith and knowledge are in some measure incompatible, we have here the much stronger thesis that if the Christian God exists he would not permit us to learn that he does by mere philosophical argument.

While apologists have made much of the concept of the hiddenness of God, philosophers have been most intrigued by the "Wager" argument.[35] It has been described recently as a substantial early example of decision theory.[36] It is also a sophisticated attempt to persuade someone intellectually inclined to Skepticism to take the path to faith, to listen to God. Like much of the *Pensées* it is in the form of an imagined dialogue between the author and a cultivated unbeliever. It is common ground between them in this passage that if God is, he is beyond our comprehension, and that in consequence Christians cannot give rational grounds for their beliefs. Either God exists or he does not; and reason cannot decide. The unbeliever says that in these circumstances he does not blame the Christian for making the affirmative rather than the negative choice: he rather blames him for making any choice at all. While the coin is being spun, one should decline to make any wager on how it will come down. Pascal's reply is, "Yes, but you must wager. There is no choice, you are already committed." Suspense is not an open option. We must wager; the stakes (our reason and will) are finite; the prize (eternal happiness) is infinite, but so is the penalty (eternal misery); the chances of winning and losing are equal. In such circumstances someone who wagers that God does not exist gains nothing if he wins and loses everything if he loses, whereas someone who wagers God does exist gains everything if he wins and loses nothing if he loses. So if the Skeptics are right and the arguments for and against God are equal, this creates a situation in which it is evidently wiser to wager that he does. But *how* does one wager? To wager is to believe something, and the unbeliever says that he is unable to believe merely through wishing that he could. Pascal's reply is psychologically and historically resourceful. It turns Montaigne inside out. He who wishes to believe but cannot, must conform with the practices of those who do: not with an inner distance from them, but from a desire to become one with them. Such conformity will enable one to pass from the Skeptic's paralyzed suspense to real faith. It will break down the passions which prevent him from listening to God.

Pascal's counter to Skepticism depends in part upon a different psychology of doubt and commitment from that of Sextus and Montaigne. Sextus takes it for granted that distress and anxiety will diminish as commitment does—paying, no doubt, far too high a compliment to the priority of the intellect over the emotions. Whether Pascal, and in this matter Hume also, are right in saying that indecision leads instead to despair is another matter. While this was no doubt an accurate reading of their own personalities, both had great vested interest in stressing the primacy of the heart (or the passions) over the reason in our natures. Perhaps the dull truth is that people differ in this. Some derive a pleasing sense of superiority from showing by intellectual means that the intellect can take us nowhere, whereas others are only downcast by such a conclusion.

Pascal's brusque assertion that we cannot not wager is widely accepted without argument, perhaps because it is too readily assumed to be of a piece with his insistence that Skeptical doubts are unnatural. It is of course a quite distinct argument, to the effect that refraining from the wager is equivalent in its consequences to wagering that God does not exist, since if he does exist one can only gain by wagering positively. This presupposes that if God does exist, he would reject the outward pieties that compose the classical Pyrrhonian solution to the problem of God. So the reasoning should at least be widened to take the form: if God exists and would reject mere outward conformity, Pyrrhonian avoidance of positive and negative dogmatism is equivalent to the negative in its long-term consequences. But its short-term consequences might well be different; in which case the choice would be one between a likely short-term quietude and a possible long-term bliss. At least the modalities make this choice more complicated than Pascal says it is.

The theme of the hidden God rests on an essentially Skeptic premise: creation's *ambiguity*. This is not the mere fact that one has no need to resort to theistic hypotheses to explain the world. It is the fact that much of the world seems to reveal God, yet much else of it seems to require us to deny him. To cease to seek the truth in the face of this ambiguity, as the Skeptic does, is in Pascal's eyes to indulge in a contemptible frivolity which he repeatedly denounces with passion. "Nothing is more cowardly than to brazen it out with God."[37] Again,

> The proofs lie before their eyes, but they refuse to look, and in this state of ignorance they choose to do everything necessary to fall into this calamity, if it exists, to wait for death before testing the proofs, while yet remaining highly satisfied in that state, professing it openly, and indeed with pride. Can we seriously think how important this matter is without being horrified at such extravagant behaviour?[38]

So much for the Skeptic solution. But the only humanly available alternative is despair:

> This is what I see and what troubles me. I look around in every direction and all I see is darkness. Nature has nothing to offer me that does not give rise to doubt and anxiety. If I saw no sign there of a Divinity I should decide on a negative solution: if I saw signs of a Creator everywhere I should peacefully settle down in the faith. But, seeing too much to deny and not enough to affirm, I am in a pitiful state....[39]

The antidote is the revelation in Christ, which enables man at once to see his own corruption and be rescued from it. It is only this redemptive act that enables men to resolve the ambiguity that would otherwise merely torment them.[40]

The obstacle to this knowledge of God is corrupt human passion. Philosophical theologies such as deism do nothing to remove this obstacle, so that deism is an abhorrent to Christianity as atheism is.[41] Indeed, no product of reason can save us, even though the blame for our blindness is wholly ours.[42] "God wishes to move the will rather than the mind. Perfect clarity would help the mind and harm the will."[43] There is no way to God except through Christ, who unites divine and human nature and thereby makes those who accept him capable of God.[44] But, for the same reasons as before, there can be no proofs of who he is, and anyone who wishes to do so can, faced with him, perpetuate the ambiguity which only he can resolve.[45]

The same theme is developed in closely parallel fashion, and with additional special references to Skepticism, in Kierkegaard's *Philosophical Fragments*.[46] The problem as Kierkegaard presents it is one of knowledge; and we might naturally expect a solution to it through philosophical reasoning. It is the problem that the classical Skeptic gives up, but one whose form he inherits from Socrates: how can a being living in a temporal sensory world come to knowledge of eternal and nonevident truths? The Socratic (or at least Platonic) solution is the doctrine of Recollection: that the only way this is possible is if the subject already has such eternal truths in his possession and merely needs to be reminded of them. In such a case the teacher's function is only to remind him, so the teacher contributes nothing by way of content or capacity and is merely an accidental instrument enabling the learner to fend for himself. Suppose, however, that the learner is, prior to the time of enlightenment, genuinely ignorant, so that, as Kierkegaard words it, the Moment is decisive. What does the teacher's role then become? It will involve more than the presentation of the Truth. It will involve also the creation of the capacity to recognize it. But we are here speaking not of the learner's general human potential for knowledge, but of a power that he acquires at the time of learning (else he would have the knowledge all along); and we must remember that in learning the learner is in some manner a free agent, contributing something essential on his own side. What the teacher has to do, then, is simultaneously present the Truth and eliminate barriers to its recognition—these barriers being themselves self-imposed ones. So acquiring knowledge of eternal truths is a passage from sinfulness to salvation. It is a conversion or new birth, at once a free choice and an act of divine grace. The Skeptic paradoxes of knowledge entail the miraculousness of learning.

How can God (the Teacher) perform such an act? To answer this, Kierkegaard tells the story of the king who loves a humble maiden and wishes his love to be returned freely. He must woo her in ways that conceal his royalty and his power, or else she will accept him from fear or ambition and not for himself. But this involves her not recognizing him or knowing his love for what it is. Similarly, God's love for men makes him wish to teach them the truths they seek, but in ways that preserve their freedom to find them for themselves or reject them. To teach in this manner is to teach as an equal could. This means that God must simultaneously take on real humanity while remaining God. This, itself paradoxical, means also that the man God becomes must be a man who is not *undeniably* God, or men's freedom would be taken away. So God as Teacher will not obviously be God, except to those made willing to recognize him.

From this it follows that Reason cannot attain eternal truths itself; not merely because the "wisdom in nature, the goodness, the wisdom in the governance of the world"[47] are not obvious enough, but because even if they were, proving God's existence from them would not produce the transformation that knowledge of him demands. It follows further that the conditions of God's teaching man are intellectually offensive, paradoxical, or absurd[48] and that reason will try to domesticate them and make them fit its canons. It follows, third, that a person close in space and time to the divine Teacher, since he is able to find him unremarkable if he chooses, has no spiritual advantage over those of other times or places who only learn of him by report, since these latter can, equally, recognize him for who he is if they choose to do so.

The common theme which this brief examination of the two greatest fideists reveals is one which resembles something Kant says, with typical pedantry and insight, about another matter—the analysis of the moral consciousness. At the end of the *Groundwork of the Metaphysics of Morals*, Kant remarks that while we cannot comprehend the practical unconditional necessity of the moral imperative, we can comprehend its incomprehensibility. It is this same fact, or alleged fact, that Pascal and Kierkegaard tell us we can comprehend in the knowledge of God that man has in faith. They see the perplexities of Skepticism as a step toward this comprehension, and therefore as superior to the friendlier-looking dogmatisms offered as substitutes for it by other philosophers.

V

The theme of the hiddenness of God is the most important legacy of Skeptical Fideism. Versions of it have appeared very recently, and others will no doubt continue to appear. I wish to suggest that the use to which this theme is put by Pascal and Kierkegaard and their successors is not one for which it is adequate.[49] They argue that the alleged ambiguity of the evidences of God are only to be expected, since man has alienated himself from God by his own spiritual corruption, which can only be overcome by a special revelatory act, of a kind which preserves man's freedom, and which he can therefore reject if he chooses. To seek to establish God's presence by reason is to attempt to bypass the spiritual regeneration which is the condition of recognizing it, and which requires response to his special revelation. The Skeptic, by using reason to undermine our confidence in its power to establish such a conclusion, performs faith a service, whether or not he wishes to do so, in making us recognize that this attempt is doomed to frustration.

This argument is sometimes reinforced by others, to the effect that faith is voluntary, whereas proof coerces; that if God's presence were evident and unambiguous we would be overwhelmed by it and forced into submission through fear instead of being drawn by love; that the demand for signs is rejected in the New Testament; or that faith requires contrary appearances in order to have occasions to be exercised. With or without these embellishments, however, the argument fails in its main purpose: to provide a rationale for the alleged impossibility of proving God's presence, and to show that faith requires the epistemic distance of God.

The fact that some truth is proved to me, or established for me beyond reasonable doubt, does not ensure that it costs me nothing to accept it, or that I cannot use my ingenuity to deceive myself and reject it and live my life as though it were false. (Think of the truths that I will die, or that my child has died, or that I am chronically lazy or cowardly or arrogant, or that my expenditure exceeds my income, or that I cannot eat my cake and have it too.) The fact that something has *not* been proved to me, and cannot be, does not guarantee that I will not be coerced into accepting it. (Think of the propositions that the hero of Orwell's *1984* ends by accepting.) The claim that man, to have faith in God, must not be overwhelmed or coerced by whatever assures him of God's presence, is not at all the same as a claim that to have faith in God, man must have less than adequate grounds for such assurance. It is true that the New Testament appears to reject men's demands for signs: "If they hear not Moses and the prophets, neither will they be persuaded, though one rose from the dead" (Luke 16:31). But this rejection probes men's motives in demanding signs, and treats the demand as a symptom of chronic unwillingness to accept God. This unwillingness, we are told, would not go away if the sign were given. But the very fact that the text says men would not be persuaded by something that put God's presence beyond reasonable doubt indicates that there is no theological necessity for his presence *not* to be beyond reasonable doubt. For even if it were beyond reasonable doubt, doubt would continue. So freedom and epistemic distance are not necessarily connected. If they have been thought to be, this is due to a confusion between questions about the epistemological grounding of beliefs and questions about the nonepistemic forces which are also at work when men accept or reject them. This is the very confusion which Pascal and Kierkegaard thought they were removing by arguing that proving God's existence by reason cannot bring us to God. If it cannot, this shows it to be religiously pointless and unable to yield conversion. This does not entail that God's existence is unprovable. We pay far too high a compliment to the powers of reason if we suggest that when something has been proved, it cannot be disregarded. And even if we agree that faith must run counter to appearances, it is quite common for us to know things that appearances contradict, when the truth has been made clear to us in some independent manner.

So nothing the fideist tells us can demonstrate that our supposed inability to establish facts about God by reason is not what it seems at first sight to be: unfortunate.

VI

We have so far scrutinized two main forms of Skeptical Fideism: the attempt to incorporate the Skeptic way within faith, and the attempt to view Skeptic argument as a preparation for it. Before concluding I must mention a third strand of Skeptical Fideist thought, which can be distinguished from the two we have so far examined, and which appears far more frequently than either in popular apologetic.

Historically this strand of thought seems to depend on a wider understanding of the scope of Skeptic questioning than was possible before Descartes. Descartes sought to refute Skepticism by carrying it further than it had been carried before him, and then discovering rational certainties buried at the heart of it. His famous method of doubt involves, first, the abandonment of any pretense that the exercise on which he is embarking is of more than theoretical interest; second, the determination to reject as *false* anything about which doubt is theoretically possible; and third, the extension of the subject matter of doubt to include states of the subject's own body and even the existence of real objects without us. He claims that this radical doubt reveals a core of certainty about the existence and nature of the doubting mind, and that this certainty, once attained, can be extended by reason to include many of the propositions doubted at the outset.

I am not concerned here with attempts to show that Descartes had failed to refute Pyrrhonism, or with the effects on epistemology down to our own time of the changes that Descartes brought about in the understanding of the Skeptic challenge. One effect on Skeptical Fideism, however, is of importance. We can find it in Pascal, together with arguments examined already. Pascal[50] develops the famous doctrine of the heart, in a way that bears upon general issues in epistemology as well as upon theological matters. His position appears to be that Descartes is mistaken in attempting to respond to Skepticism by appealing to the reason, since it is through the heart that we know first principles (that there are three spatial dimensions and an infinite series of numbers, or that we are not dreaming), and that reason only holds sway within a framework that it receives from the heart: "Principles are felt, propositions proved, and both with certainty though by different means. It is just as pointless and absurd for reason to demand proof of first principles from the heart before agreeing to accept them as it would be absurd for the heart to demand an intuition of all the propositions demonstrated by reason before agreeing to accept them."[51] The argument is developed further (in Fragment 131/434) when it is said that we cannot be sure of these principles apart from faith. The claim, therefore, seems to be that we should not attempt to respond to Skeptic doubt by reason, but accept that reason in its turn requires faith: we cannot guarantee our reason by first using it to prove God, but must accept that our rational knowledge of our world requires faith of the same order that reveals God to us.

There is an abundance of argument of this form in apologetic literature and sermons, all with the common theme that the faith which is being urged upon the listener is something which he has to show in his daily living and can have no consistent reason to refuse to extend to the religious sphere. We cannot wait to refute the Skeptic before we act on the assumption that we are awake, or that the sun will rise tomorrow, or that there are other minds, so there can be no good reason for hesitation about the presence of God.

It is indeed true that there are some matters on which Skeptic noncommitment is far more unnatural than others, and the significance of this fact must be assessed in any attempt to come to terms with the tradition. It is also true that philosophers are not at all prone in commonsense matters to suggest that lay commitment should await their refutation of Skepticism, though they are quite likely to say precisely this about commitment in religious matters. I do not wish to deny the importance of arguments purporting to show the rational status of (say) belief in other minds to be on a par with the belief in God as creator. But any simple assimilation of common sense to faith runs into three major difficulties. First, if it proves anything it proves too much, since there are a great many actual forms of faith equally able to recommend themselves in this manner. Second, the fact that our natures urge all of us to believe the propositions of common sense but leave us divided on those of faith demands explanation, and it is implausible to insist that only in the religious case does our nature have a vested interest in doubt. Third, faith is a state which it requires persistent efforts of attention and will to sustain, whereas (by definition) the convictions of common sense require comparable efforts of skeptical reflection to resist.

VII

I claimed at the outset that in the concluding Part of the *Dialogues Concerning Natural Religion* Hume gives us a parody of Skeptical Fideism. I will now make a brief attempt to show this.[52]

It is instructive to begin by noticing affinities between Hume and Pascal. Both are sensitive to the power of Pyrrhonist argument, but both reject the recommendation to suspend judgment. Hume insists, indeed, that we are unable to refrain from belief except for brief periods, and follows Pascal once again in holding that the attempt to practice Skeptic recommendations leads only to despair. A further, and vital, area of agreement is to be found in their joint rejection of the Cartesian attempt to refute the Skeptic by reason: both insist that the propositions the Skeptic questions are beyond its powers, and only become objects of human assent through the operation of other principles in our natures. Both see these principles to be at work in the life of the passions; but whereas Pascal sees the passions that dominate our fallen nature as obstacles preventing the heart from bringing men to God, Hume sees in our passions, as they are, an essentially beneficent force which rescues us from the dangers of doubt and dogmatism together.

Since our natural beliefs are the products of our passions, and not of reason, the reasonings of the Skeptic cannot dislodge them (even though he exposes their groundlessness) and the reasonings of the Dogmatist cannot establish them (even though he correctly sees they are inescapable). We are not creatures of reason in the way both these traditions assume us to be. The passions do not merely supply us with the beliefs we need to act in the world; they also supply us with the motivations necessary for the action in the world and the pursuit of objects of individual and social utility. Our natures have been endowed, by Darwinian good fortune, with a capacity for commitment and a suitability for society to which philosophers can only erect temporary hindrances.

Notoriously Hume believed that philosophical errors were merely ridiculous, and could be avoided, by most of us, simply by not taking philosophy too seriously. Equally notoriously, he believed that religion was a more sinister force than this, liable to overturn the accommodations of human society for much deeper reasons. But a philosophical system based upon the primacy of passion faces an obvious difficulty if it seeks to undermine the power of religion by reasoning. Just as a fideist like Pascal has a problem assimilating faith and common sense sufficiently, so a secularizer like Hume has a problem dissociating them.

Hume's solution is twofold. The first part is to be found in the *Natural History of Religion*, where he points out that religion is not universal in the way that commonsense beliefs are, since some nations appear to have been without it, and goes on to argue, in effect, that the forces which have established religion in most of the world, and in particular the forces at work in the development of Christian monotheism, are pathological forces from which the enlightened readers of his own day can (it is assumed) free themselves. The second part is to be found in the conclusion of the *Dialogues*. Here Hume argues, with only apparent inconsistency, that although we cannot help believing, this has no practical consequences.

Throughout Parts II to XI Cleanthes has been attempting to establish the intelligence and goodness of God through the argument from Design. Philo, the "careless skeptic," has attempted to refute Cleanthes' arguments, and to show that there is as much, or as little, support to be found for alternative explanations of the natural order, such as Epicurean atomism. The orthodox conservative theologian, Demea, who has been present throughout, is significantly absent when the concluding discussion takes place. The surprising feature of the concluding discussion, especially for those of us who are convinced by Norman Kemp Smith that Philo most nearly represents Hume, is the apparent assumption that *Philo* makes that "the cause or causes of order in the universe probably bear some remote analogy to human intelligence."[53] This, as has often been said, is much less than Cleanthes argues for; but it is also much more than Philo can possibly be said to have agreed to previously. The solution, I suggest, is that Hume is conceding here that the Design Argument, which he has until this point shown again and again to provide no good *reasons* for accepting the existence of a cosmic intelligence, is nevertheless a symptom of a tendency in our natures to accept a vaguely personal teleology in the universe as a whole. He is once more recognizing the powerlessness of his own skeptical arguments. But this, if correct, is still only part of the story. Most of the interchange between Philo and Cleanthes in Part XII consists of discussion about whether the actual practices of the church can or cannot be reconciled with "true religion," which both are assumed to espouse—a question on which Philo takes the negative. He also insists that the vague deism which he has conceded to be true ascribes no moral properties to God and does not imply any moral consequences for human conduct that cannot be established independently of it. The "religion" which Philo concedes to be inescapable is thoroughly unreligious in all respects.

It is, however, a position he can represent on the surface as in agreement with that of Cleanthes, who here has to be taken as the liberal theologian who will adopt no moral stance at odds with secular practice, and is prepared to concede that the actual doings of the church have to be evaluated by standards which he and Philo have in common. What Hume offers us is the nearest he can come to a Sextus-like adoption of the nominal pieties of the church's moderate wing, a stance which preserves social conformity (in contrast with the disruptive atheism of the continental *philosophes*) while avoiding the darker enthusiasms of orthodoxy (in the manner of his Scots Calvinist opponents).

It is not, however, very near at all. Its ambiguity is reinforced by two features of Philo's concluding comments. Hume reinforces the skepticism of the character of Philo by dissociating his position from that of the "haughty dogmatist" who is "persuaded that he can erect a complete system of theology by the mere help of philosophy." Skeptical argument may not prevent us from some degree of assent, but will indeed prevent us from becoming theologians. He goes on to say, however, that faced with the "obscurity" of natural theology, a "well-disposed mind" will "fly to revealed truth with the greatest avidity" in order to rescue itself from its ignorance! We can see how seriously to take this when we reflect on his treatment of revealed religion in the *Natural History* and his discussion of miracles in Section X of the first *Enquiry*, and when we see that Philo follows his comment by expressing the hope that some revelation will be vouchsafed to us![54]

Scholars will never agree entirely about the intent of Part XII. Nor is it clear that if I have reconstructed Hume's position there correctly, it is a fully coherent one. But I think it can be said with confidence that Hume is attempting to reconcile his theory of the role of the passions in human nature with his secularism, and to achieve this by resorting to the social conformism which he inherits from the Pyrrhonian tradition. A consequence of this is the importation of the verbal features of Skeptical Fideism, which thinly mask his real intentions, perhaps even from himself.

VIII

I have suggested that there is a major division within Skeptical Fideism, between that form of it which has sought to import the Skeptic Way as a whole into Christian thought, and that which has sought to interpret

Skeptic attacks on reason as a preparation for a groundless leap of faith. It is not surprising that the latter division has been the source of the more interesting arguments and has been more fertile in apologetic devices, though I have tried to expose the arguments as weak and the devices as specious. They will always appeal to those who see the task of Christian thought as that of re-Hebraicizing its thought forms and eliminating its dogmatic dependence on philosophical support. Apologists of this persuasion will always be tempted to represent the unprovenness of God's existence as some kind of theological advantage, instead of the pity that it is. (It is indeed a pity, for as long as it remains a fact, or is thought to be one, unbelievers are not merely the prisoners of their own passions but have at least one good reason for their hesitations.) In our own day, however, there have been at least two developments which represent an unknowing return to positions uncannily reminiscent of the former kind of Skeptic Fideism. In both cases, what is offered as faith seems to many observers, as before, to be rather less than the genuine article.

(1) We are far past the point in our culture where social and religious conformity can be equated to any significant degree. In our secularized age, no one seeking to respond to questionings of religious dogma in the manner of Sextus or Montaigne could find a convenient religious consensus ready to hand. Philosophical divisions about religion merely reflect equally extensive lay disagreements. This coincides with a frequent consensus among professional philosophers that philosophical divisions on other matters, at least when properly understood, are concerned with conceptual or second-order questions which do not impinge on the lay consciousness at all.

The deep influence of Wittgenstein has resulted in the view that Skepticism (known in essentially its Cartesian form of generalized doubts about the external world or other minds or waking-hour dreams) has been shown to be incoherent, and that philosophical dogmatism (often supposed, ironically, to be primarily a response to Skepticism, as Descartes indeed offered it) is a pointless and idle exercise, frequently incoherent in its turn. The proper task of the philosopher is to treat dissatisfactions with our perceptual and intellectual skills and conventions by exposing the conceptual confusions on which skeptical criticisms of them are thought to be based. This process will enable us to return to them fully reconciled to their actuality, from which in practice no one can genuinely depart, and to make this return without resorting to those metaphysical fantasies which post-Cartesian thinkers erected to support them.

The objective of philosophical analysis on this view is the return to undogmatic participation in common life, improved by some conceptual insights gleaned along the way. The assumption of the procedure is that common life is free of dogmatism before the philosopher finds it and after he returns to it. This assumption is not, of course, made in classical Skepticism, which saw itself as at odds with the lay values to which it told its practitioners to conform. But the dogma-free life of the enlightened philosopher is precisely the Skeptic objective, democratized by being held to be the stance of the layman also. Wittgenstein refutes Skepticism by incorporating it.

What of religion? Given its controversial status among nonphilosophers, those who have followed Wittgenstein's philosophical method have naturally responded in two ways. The majority have seen religion as itself a form of dogmatism. They have then either attacked it as a source of useless or dangerous fantasies and have construed its obscurities and paradoxes as special kinds of logical incoherence; or they have sought to defend it as one form of dogmatism which has healthy sources. An interesting minority has taken another route. Its members have construed faith itself as a form of life free of dogma, and have argued that philosophical attacks on faith and philosophical defenses of faith have alike been concerned with metaphysical importations from which the actual life of faith is free. This position has for some years been known as "Wittgensteinian Fideism,"[55] though its analogies with classical Skepticism have not, I think, been noted. It is close in many respects to some forms of liberal secularism in theology, which interpret faith as a transformation of the personality in its affective and conative aspects without the prior judgments to which such transformations are usually thought to be the responses.

Such a picture of faith takes us a long way from the psychology of the New Testament, where the serenity and dedication and liberatedness never appear sheerly as spiritual prizes to be sought for their own value. When Jesus chides his hearers for their lack of faith, he seems to say that if they recognized the Lordship of God in the way that they say they do, they should be free of the anxieties that they still allow to fetter them. The natural way to understand this is that the liberation of the personality from such anxieties, however desirable we can all see it to be even if we do not acknowledge the Lordship of God, is in fact a consequence of that acknowledgment completely and sincerely made, and cannot be expected without the reassurance that acknowledgment makes possible, and which he himself had come to bring. Faith, thus depicted, has a cognitive core and could not survive its abandonment.

(2) The introduction of the concept of beliefless faith occurs in another context, which is assuming more and more importance in contemporary religious thought. Increasingly, Christian religious thinkers are taking seriously the variety and the spiritual strength of other major religious

traditions that are doctrinally different from theirs, or even doctrinally opposed to Christian teachings in major respects. Those who are not inclined on that account merely to dismiss them, or to follow the Skeptic way and see their variety as cause for suspending judgment about them all, have been forced to attempt theological reconciliations of ways of life that incorporate irreconcilable beliefs. One way of attempting this reconciliation is to treat the *doctrines* of each tradition as culturally relative responses to the impact of one transcendent Power or Spirit, while viewing faith as an essentially identical response in all traditions, however their indigenous beliefs vary.[56] Such forms of theological reflection are full of obvious difficulties and are at a very early stage. But one consequence of them seems clear already. A second-order theological judgment that *one's own* tradition is culturally relative in these respects is bound to lead to inner reservation and self-distancing from its doctrines, at least those in which it differs significantly from the faiths of other cultures. So whatever becomes of the affective and conative aspects of religion in the wake of such movements of thought, they are bound to generate an undogmatic faith, or faith-with-inner-reservation that has an embarrassing resemblance to the Skeptic's surface pieties. The question will remain: Is the kind of faith which a Skeptic form of thought permits, whatever its merits, recognizably identical with that which it is invented to defend? Or is faith not, after all, essentially dogmatic?

NOTES

1. Richard H. Popkin, *The History of Scepticism from Erasmus To Spinoza* (Berkeley, Los Angeles, and London: University of California Press, 1979). See also the essays collected in his *The High Road to Pyrrhonism* (San Diego: Austin Hill Press, 1979).

2. *PH* I 226. References to Sextus are to the *Outlines of Pyrrhonism* (*PH*) and *Adversus Mathematicos* (*M*); quotations are from the Loeb Classical Library translation by J. B. Bury (London: William Heinemann; Cambridge, Mass.: Harvard University Press, 1933-1949).

3. *PH* I 228-229.

4. *PH* I 29.

5. *PH* I 23-24.

6. Pyrrho, to whom Aenesidemus and Sextus trace their tradition, was reputed to have been much less accommodating to appearances. Diogenes Laertius says, "He led a life consistent with this doctrine [viz., that no single thing is in itself any more this than that], going out of his way for nothing, taking no precaution, but facing all risks as they came, whether cats, precipices, dogs, or what not, and generally leaving nothing to the arbitrariment of the senses; but he was kept out of harm's way by his friends . . ." (DL IX 62, tr. Hicks).

7. *PH* I 29-30.

8. *M* VIII 2.

9. "When his fellow-passengers on board a ship were all unnerved by a storm, he kept calm and confident, pointing to a little pig in the ship that went on eating, and telling them that such was the unperturbed state in which the wise man should keep himself" (DL IX 68).

10. See Mill's *Utilitarianism*, the section entitled "What Utilitarianism Is."

11. On this see Burnyeat, chap. 6 of this anthology.

12. *PH* III 2.

13. The sort of faith it might permit has, perhaps, provoked biblical comment. See *Revelation* 3:15.

14. The text of the Erasmus-Luther debate I cite here is *Luther and Erasmus: Free Will and Salvation*, ed. E. G. Rupp and P. S. Watson (Philadelphia: Westminster Press, 1969).

15. Erasmus, *Luther and Erasmus*, p. 37. The full title of the earlier work of Luther's to which Erasmus alludes here is *Assertio omnium articulorum M. Lutheri per Bullam Leonis X novissimam damnatorum* (1520).

16. Erasmus, *Luther and Erasmus*, p. 39.

17. Luther, *Luther and Erasmus*, p. 114.

18. Luther, *Luther and Erasmus*, p. 122.

19. Luther, *Luther and Erasmus*, p. 105.

20. Luther, *Luther and Erasmus*, p. 109.

21. Quoted from *The Essays of Michel de Montaigne*, trans. and ed. Jacob Zeitlin (New York, Alfred A. Knopf, 1935), II, 233.

22. Ibid., p. 269.

23. For a brief account of the role of Charron, see Popkin, *The History of Scepticism*, chap. 3, pp. 55-62.

24. I have had to resist the temptation to discuss Bayle, but it is impossible not to mention him. For a very plausible interpretation of his position, see Popkin's introduction to his translation of Selections from the *Historical and Critical Dictionary* (Indianapolis: Bobbs-Merrill, 1965).

25. For a much fuller version of these assessments of Hume see my essay "Hume's Skepticism and the *Dialogues*," in *McGill Hume Studies*, ed. D. Norton, N. Capaldi, and W. Robison (San Diego: Austin Hill Press, 1979); also chap. 1 of my *Hume* (London: Macmillan, 1975). The key passages in Hume himself are the Conclusion (Section VII) of Part IV of Book I of the *Treatise of Human Nature*, and Section XII of the *Enquiry Concerning Human Understanding*.

26. Chap. 6 above, pp. 137 ff.

27. I have tried to explore the notion of rejecting tendencies that are part of oneself in "Human Nature and External Desires," *The Monist* 62 (1979).

28. On this work see the valuable study by Walter E. Rex, *Pascal's Provincial Letters: An Introduction* (London: Hodder and Stoughton, 1977).

29. Fragments 131/434 and 449/556. In what follows all citations are from the translation of the *Pensées* by A. J. Krailsheimer in the Penguin Classics (1966). This translation follows the Lafuma classification of the fragments; the second number is in each case that of the same fragment in the Brunschvicg classifica-

tion. The recently published short volume *Pascal* by Krailsheimer (Oxford, 1980) is a valuable aid to understanding Pascal's intentions.

30. 136/139.

31. 131/434.

32. 444/557.

33. 449/556.

34. 449/556.

35. 418/233.

36. See Ian Hacking, *The Emergence of Probability* (Cambridge: at the University Press, 1975), chap. 8.

37. 427/194.

38. 428/195.

39. 429/229.

40. 446/586; 443/783.

41. 449/556.

42. 236/578.

43. 234/581; see also 446/586.

44. 449/556.

45. 228/751; 237/795.

46. Søren Kierkegaard, *Philosophical Fragments*, trans. David Swenson, rev. H. V. Hong (Princeton: Princeton University Press, 1967).

47. Ibid., p. 52.

48. Ibid., pp. 55-66.

49. The themes of this section are also developed in my *Problems of Religious Knowledge* (London: Macmillan, 1971), esp. chap. 3.

50. See, for example, Fragments 109/392; 110/282; 131/434.

51. 110/282.

52. See also "Hume's Skepticism and *Dialogues*."

53. See the next of the *Dialogues* edited by Norman Kemp Smith (Indianapolis: Bobbs-Merrill, 1947), p. 227.

54. Basil Willey sums up Hume's hope as "Oh for a revelation! but not, if you please, the one we are supposed to have had already." *The Eighteenth Century Background* (London: Chatto and Windus, 1940), p. 135.

55. The term is Kai Nielsen's. See his essay of this title in *Philosophy* 42 (1967). The best-known exponent of the view he criticizes is D. Z. Phillips, in such works as *The Concept of Prayer* (London: Routledge, 1965), *Faith and Philosophical Enquiry* (New York: Schocken, 1971), and *Religion Without Explanation* (Oxford: Blackwell, 1976).

56. See John Hick, *God and the Universe of Faiths* (London: Macmillan, 1973) and Wilfred Cantwell Smith, *Faith and Belief* (Princeton: Princeton University Press, 1979).

12

Gassendi and Skepticism

Ralph Walker

Skepticism has had a long history, and in the modern period its influence has been felt in a variety of intriguingly different ways. Descartes and Gassendi saw skepticism differently and reacted to it differently, though at the same time they were the first two significant philosophers among the moderns to treat the problems of skepticism as serious problems for the epistemologist. Valuable and illuminating work has recently been done on the influence of ancient skepticism in the sixteenth century and before, and the importance of this influence is not to be underestimated. But the skepticism of the sixteenth century was the skepticism of Cicero or of Montaigne—the recognition of the limitation of one's cognitive powers, the rejection of dogmatic certainty. It was not seen as posing a critical epistemological problem which urgently demanded a new solution; the thinkers of the sixteenth century did not feel themselves caught by it in the fashion Hume was to describe so effectively, unable either to resolve their doubts or to deny the absurdities into which they led. Usually, like Carneades and the New Academy, they saw skepticism not as all-destroying but as a weapon against the comfortable certainties of their opponents, leaving the ordinary beliefs of everyday life more or less intact so long as too great a confidence was not placed in them. And even those who went further, as Montaigne did, saw it not as providing a philosophical problem to be tackled but as removing the traditional authority of reason and the senses and thereby, perhaps, making way for faith. Bayle said that until Gassendi's work was published, the name of Sextus

Empiricus was scarcely known and his views were "no less unknown than the Terra Australis";[1] this is a considerable exaggeration, but all the same, Gassendi and Descartes were the first to respond to Sextus as he himself would have intended—as philosophers wrestling with the fundamental and inescapable issues of epistemology.

We are all familiar with Descartes's idea of skepticism and with his reaction to it, however contentious some of the details may be. He starts by adducing familiar reasons for doubting the deliverances of the senses; argues that all our sensory beliefs may be mistaken; and then, through the hypothesis of the *malin génie*, generalizes this doubt into a doubt about human cognitive faculties in general, which he ultimately resolves by relying on the certainty of truths that are so clearly and distinctly perceived by the intellect as to leave us unable to doubt them. Gassendi's approach is the other way around, and so is his solution, which is why much of the discussion between them is so curiously at cross-purposes. Most of us were introduced to Descartes very early, and his influence upon us has been enormous, so that we tend to see the issues rather as he did. At first reading, therefore, one may get the impression that in his attacks on Descartes Gassendi is very far from taking skepticism seriously: he seems to have as little sympathy for Descartes's problem as Dr. Johnson had for Berkeley, though this appears to contrast sharply with the enthusiasm for the ancient skeptics which is expressed in his (much earlier) *Exercitationes Paradoxicae adversus Aristoteleos*.[2] The impression is misleading, however. What Gassendi lacks sympathy with is not skepticism in general but the Cartesian approach. To doubt the reliability of our senses on particular occasions he considers reasonable, but to question their reliability in general he regards as wildly absurd: we have nothing firmer to fall back on than our sense-experience.[3] The skeptics' most important contribution, he thinks, lies in their attack on the supposed powers of the human intellect. We tend to make inferences about the nature of things which far outrun what is attested by the empirical evidence, and we lay claim to a knowledge of abstract truths that is allegedly provided by reason itself. The skeptics pointed to the fallibility of our reasoning powers, and our complete inability to justify the assumption that because a principle strikes some human being as having a certain kind of compelling force, it must actually be true. From Gassendi's point of view the person who fails to take skepticism seriously is Descartes: radically to doubt the senses, and then to accept certain intellectual truths because they are so compellingly clear and distinct, is to miss the point in a manner that is simply perverse. True, Descartes does attempt a kind of vindication of his reliance on clear and distinct ideas, but Gassendi was among those of his critics who saw his argument for a God who is no deceiver as blatantly circular.[4] No defense of reason by relying on reason will be an adequate counter to skepticism: what is required rather is that we should limit our claims to experience, or at any rate (for as we shall see, Gassendi is by no means as clear as we should like at this critical point) that we should keep them as close to experience as possible and avoid rash speculations and putatively a priori claims.

Much of Gassendi's criticism of Descartes is acute, though his quibbling style and the vituperative tone of the exchange combine to obscure the fact. And certainly here he has put his finger on a point of fundamental importance for Descartes's program. This is not the place to consider how vicious the Cartesian Circle is, or whether its true shape is something less than circular, but prima facie there is a substantial case for Descartes or any other rationalist to answer. What grounds are there to suppose that our habits of thinking correspond to the way things really are? What warrants us in using human reason to draw conclusions which go beyond what we can see and feel? Philosophers of an empiricist turn of mind have always argued in this way, though they have differed over how much to include in "experience" and have generally allowed to reason some ancillary role within the field of experience. But however satisfactory the negative part of his work may be, Gassendi shows up less well when it comes to the positive statement of his own alternative position. In the history of modern empiricism his place is an early one, so that these shortcomings are not surprising, but he confuses himself badly through his own unclarity as to what "experience" is supposed to include; and though he never quite denied, and increasingly came to recognize, that sense-experience requires supplementation by the mind, he gave no adequate account of the distinction between what is legitimately and what is illegitimately inferred from the sensory given.

It is his confusion over what counts as sense-experience that allows Gassendi to miss the point of Descartes's skepticism about the external world as completely as he himself considered Descartes to have missed the point of skepticism about our intellectual powers. The task of the senses, he thinks, is to "apprehend appearances," and not to make judgments on the basis of these appearances about how things actually are; this latter function belongs not to the senses but to the intellect. He concludes that although the intellect can err, there is no way in which the senses can.[5] Now if by "apprehending appearances" he meant simply receiving data without making any kind of judgment about them, he would no doubt be right in this. He would be right also—or at any rate would be plausibly held by quite a few philosophers to be—if his intention was to assign to the senses judgments of the form of "It seems to me now that I am tasting sweet honey," in contrast with objective judgments like "Honey is sweet." But in fact, although it may at first sight seem to a modern reader that he is getting at something like this, his point is actually quite different. He standardly uses examples like Timon's "Honey tastes sweet to me," in which it is taken for granted that there is something perfectly real and objective, the honey, which is being tasted, and the skeptical problem he sees regarding perception is simply this: that if honey tastes sweet to me and bitter to you—or sweet to me now and bitter at some other time—it is not clear how we are to determine what honey is really like. We cannot just dismiss the testimony of the abnormal or the sick, for instance, for

who can be certain that the constitution that you call unsound gives rise to appearances that are less true than the ones framed by the constitution you consider legitimate and sound? Just as there are certain mad people who see things more clearly than those of sound mind, so those whose constitution departs from the normal pattern perhaps perceive things more clearly and truly than others.[6]

What Gassendi wants to maintain is that we have no way of knowing what honey is really like in itself—this is the sort of thing that God knows about it and that a completed science would no doubt include—but also that for most purposes we do not have to: it is enough if we know how honey *appears* under different circumstances. "All we can know is how a thing appears to different people" he says in the *Exercitationes*, in his most skeptical vein, and this he takes to be the traditional opinion of the skeptics (setting aside a few more radical individuals like Gorgias, who are not to be taken seriously).[7]

It is easy for us to think in reading him that he must have been intending some such distinction as we might make, between the passive data of sense and our judgments about them, but this would be entirely wrong. The senses are by no means incapable of reaching an assessment of what is given to them, and deciding that the honey tastes sweet or that the stick in the water looks bent; where the fallible intellect comes in, according to Gassendi, is in judging "whether such a thing is or is not as it appears to be."[8] This being so, however, he is wrong to suggest that error about "appearances" is not possible and that they are therefore not subject to skeptical doubt; error about appearances is perfectly possible, and in two ways. In the first place, if I think that honey tastes bitter to you now, or that it regularly tastes bitter to people who have been drinking Sauternes, I may be quite straightforwardly wrong about that.[9] In the second place, even if I confine my judgment to my own present case there remains the possibility that this thing that I am tasting is not honey, or even that I am not tasting anything at all (I only think I am). Gassendi is helped to overlook these possibilities by his use of words like "appearances" and "apprehension," which encourages the confusion of an awareness that is not subject to error with the knowledge of public facts about how objects look and taste to different observers or under different circumstances.

Rather surprisingly, Gassendi goes on to say that everyday objective perceptual judgments like "That tower is square" and "That stick is bent" are also judgments about appearances and therefore not open to serious doubt. To doubt whether the tower is round or square may be all very well when the tower is at a distance, he says against Descartes, but we all know how to settle doubts like that.[10] Initially this appears inconsistent with the position outlined above, according to which there was a major skeptical problem in telling whether the honey was really sweet or not; he now seems to be saying that the problem is easily resolved. His idea must be that such statements as these can be taken in two different ways. In one acceptation they say something about the real intrinsic character of the honey, the stick, or the tower; this is the usage metaphysicians and perhaps scientists are primarily concerned with, and here skeptical doubt is very much in place. But the ordinary man is not interested in the real intrinsic characters of things, and when he says that the stick is bent or that the tower is square, the truth or falsity of *his* claim can be established fairly readily by making a few observations. In other words, his assertion has different truth-conditions from that of the metaphysicians, though both may use the same words. And though he does not say it very clearly, it is presumably Gassendi's view that the ordinary man's claim is to be analyzed in terms of how the object feels, looks, etc., to various observers.[11] That is what must be meant by saying that he is still judging "about appearances," and it explains why judgments of this type should be thought not to give rise to skeptical problems: they inherit their unproblematic character from the immediate experiential judgments on which they are based.

Gassendi criticizes Descartes for arguing that the senses are untrustworthy in general because they are found to deceive us on occasion. In this he anticipates a great many subsequent critics, but also (if the above interpretation is correct) does a little better than they generally do. For as it is usually presented, the objection is beside the point: Descartes is not drawing a universal conclusion from a particular premise, nor does he have to assume that some of our perceptions are veridical in order to find that others are illusory. The commonsense hypothesis that the senses give us accurate information about how things are destroys itself, in his opinion, since the deliverances of sense conflict—not all of them can be veridical together; and if we know they are not all reliable, we can only justify confidence in particular instances by applying some test which will distinguish trustworthy from untrustworthy cases.[12] As Descartes sees the matter, no such test lies readily to hand; it is easy enough to separate perceptions into groups in a variety of ways, but to find a reason for singling any group out as veridical is not so easy (and takes him until *Meditation* VI). For Gassendi, however, the perceptual judgments that the ordinary man makes about the stick or the tower are bound to be true if they accord with the majority, or with the claims of normal people under normal circumstances (or something of the kind: the details of this phenomenalistic aspect of his thought are not worked out). They are bound to be true of these objects because that is all it is for such predications to be true, in the sense in which the ordinary man intends them. And if truth in such cases, truth "among appearances," consists in something like accordance with the majority of mutually consistent perceptual judgments, evidently the discovery of occasional illusion cannot cast doubt on the reliability of perception in general. The illusion on this view is necessarily only occasional, or only in abnormal circumstances; there may be practical difficulties in determining whether such circumstances obtain in a given case, but in principle they must be resoluble by considering the perceptual evidence. It is in this way that the phenomenalist can avoid the problem about the trustworthiness of the senses which faces the rest of us, though it must be stressed that Gassendi's affinities with phenomenalism are limited. It is only for the *predications* "is round," "is straight," "is sweet" that he suggests an analysis that might be called phenomenalistic; the possibility that we might be in error about the *subjects* of these predications—that we might be mistaken in thinking we were perceiving the tower, the stick, the honey—does not occur to him, and to this (considerable) extent he fails to see Descartes's point. Moreover, the phenomenalistic analysis applies only to one of the meanings that such predications have, the one intended by the ordinary man; Gassendi thinks they also have another and metaphysically more significant sense in which they are concerned with the real intrinsic characters of things, and this other sense is not susceptible of any such analysis and must therefore leave room for skeptical doubt.

There is an additional contributory cause for his brusque dismissal of Cartesian skepticism with regard to the senses. There has never been a philosopher who was more of a pedant than Gassendi, and he clearly feels a considerable irritation at Descartes for misunderstanding the classical authorities. The skeptics, he says with some asperity, were not interested in questioning the ordinary deliverances of sense-experience, but concerned with our inability to discover the real natures of things.[13] It is almost as though he is so obsessed with scholarship as to be unable to see that a philosophical point can stand on its own merits without a classical background. He recognizes, of course, that the traditional skeptics included a few extremists who tried to push skepticism to its limits, thereby calling in question sense-experience as well as everything else, but these he regards as very minor figures, foolish logic-choppers who are not in need of much refutation. He does make one or two points against them in passing which are interesting and which could have been developed into more elaborate and perhaps valuable arguments: thus against Gorgias, whom he takes to have doubted absolutely everything, he says not only that at least one thing must exist for him to think and reason as he does, but also that "it is at least true and certain that a man who says he is speaking is telling the truth, and that if he concludes he is speaking his conclusion is true."[14] Again, and perhaps more suggestively, he says that someone totally lacking in knowledge "would very probably think nothing more than this: I, I, I; because you would not be able to attribute anything to yourself in your thought, for neither would you know any attribute nor would you know the force of the word 'am,' since you would not know what being is or the difference between being and not being."[15] These ideas are not developed, however, because he does not think it worthwhile to mount a full-scale attack on the more extreme forms of skepticism, including the kind that has apparently seduced Descartes. And he thinks that no one of any importance among the ancient skeptics took these extreme views seriously, either. They did not doubt of "appearances," in the sense in which he understands that word, but only questioned whether they gave us an adequate guide to the real natures of things.

In this, it may be noticed, he is not entirely fair at least to Sextus Empiricus. He was thoroughly familiar with Sextus's work, but he was still sufficiently blinkered by the standard interpretation of him to fail to see that his doubts about the senses go significantly further than Gassendi's own. The stock arguments which he adduces (and takes from his predecessors) can be used to make the limited point that with such variations among percipients there is a problem in determining what the real taste of honey is, and Gassendi copies them for that purpose. But Sextus also sees that the doubt they raise need not stop here. When he reflects upon the matter, which is by no means all of the time, he recognizes that all objective claims are similarly open to question: I may be mistaken in thinking I am tasting honey at all, or in supposing that I know how it tastes to you or to myself under different conditions. The only things beyond doubt are the *phantasiai* that I have, and they can enjoy that status only because they are no more than modifications of my own mind;[16] any further claims I may make, as for example that there is such a thing as honey in the world, must be based on the *phantasiai* and arrived at by a kind of inference, through the use of "signs," and can therefore be called in doubt by the skeptic who mistrusts inference and regards the use of "signs" as lacking in justification. Admittedly, though, Sextus is not as clear and consistent as one would like; he treats "Honey tastes sweet" as a direct report of a *phantasia,* and so tends to slip into thinking that skeptical difficulties arise only over the objectivity of the sweetness and not over that of the honey. Descartes did rather better, but even so, clarity on the matter only began to be within reach after the concept of an idea had been refined through the work of Arnauld, Locke, and their successors. Indeed it is not an area in which clarity is at all easy to obtain, as is made evident by the disagreements in recent years over what, if anything, may be regarded as directly given in experience and consequently immune from doubt. Gassendi is not to be blamed too greatly for being rather unsatisfactory on the subject.

And it is much to his credit that despite the inadequacy of his conception of the empirically given, he came to recognize that an acceptable epistemology must allow for the fact that we regularly go beyond it. His inclination was to be as radically empiricist as possible, and it is true that in his early work against the Aristotelians he often seems to be suggesting that even judgments which we would normally take to involve a considerable amount of inference must really, so far as they are legitimate, be a matter of directly apprehending "appearances" that are empirically given; he says, for example, that by reading the label on a box one can come to "see" that it contains a cure for snakebite, and that in the same sort of way a mathematical argument can bring one to "see" that the internal angles of a triangle are equal to two right angles. "The mathematician does nothing more than to advise you to look more closely to see what you did not notice at first glance."[17] But in his later writings, and particularly in the *Syntagma,* he is well aware that in cases of these kinds we have to make judgments which go well beyond what is empirically given to us. Some commentators have claimed to find a considerable difference of position between his earlier and his later works, the former being negative in intention and skeptical in character, the latter being constructively Epicurean and more dismissive of skepticism. More recently it has been argued that there is a change of presentation only and no real change of view.[18] I think this goes too far, but what development there is in Gassendi's thought is largely on the present issue. He continues to agree with the skeptics' attack on all those theories (like Descartes's) which hold that the human mind can by reflection come to know about the essential natures of things, but it becomes increasingly clear to him that the mind must be capable of making some kinds of reliable inference on the basis of what is given to the senses. In the classical terminology which he takes over, this means that he is faced with the problem of "signs"—of just when it is that one is entitled to draw a conclusion to the unobserved from what is before one's senses, taking the latter as a sign of something hidden and not observable directly.

Sextus had distinguished between indicative signs (*endeiktika sēmeia*) and commemorative signs (*hypomnēstika sēmeia*). When A and B have regularly been observed together in the past, the presence of A may allow us to infer the presence of B on an occasion when B cannot itself be perceived directly, and A is then called a commemorative sign; thus smoke may be a commemorative sign of the presence of fire.[19] In general, though he is not quite precise about this, it would seem that whenever B may be inferred from A by straightforward induction from past experience, A is a commemorative sign of B, and whenever B is inferred from A by any other means, A is being used as an indicative sign of B.[20] If the movements of the body are taken as signs of the soul (Sextus's own example) they can only be indicative signs, since the soul cannot be discovered by induction and observation; or again (to take an ancient example which Gassendi frequently cites), if the existence of pores in the skin is postulated as necessary to account for sweating, the sweat is treated as an indicative sign of the pores.

Although he is not entirely unaware that there are problems about induction, Sextus regards the use of commemorative signs as legitimate and does not raise skeptical doubts about it. Indicative signs, however, he rejects: he does not think there is any way of vindicating their use which does not rely on a circular argument. Gassendi disagrees; he thinks this is much too sweeping; some uses of indicative signs, in his view, must surely be legitimate, though he is not very clear about how to separate the legitimate ones from those that are not. He does recognize the need to make this separation, though, and to justify those uses of signs that he considers proper, and in effect he makes two suggestions. One, which is not presented in a very explicit form, is that indicative signs may be allowable where they are used to reach conclusions which *can* be directly established by observation even though they have not been yet; this test would be passed by the theory of pores in the skin, since (as Gassendi points out) the microscope makes it possible to see what the ancients could only infer, but it would presumably be failed by those metaphysical conjectures about the real nature of things which Gassendi wishes to repudiate.[21] The other suggestion, which is more explicit but even more inchoate, is that it is legitimate to use indicative signs when, and only when, the inferences in question are so self-evidently correct that they force themselves upon us.[22]

Interesting though it is, the first suggestion will not really do, for two reasons. To start with, it evidently requires some qualification: to admit as legitimate *every* inference to a conclusion verifiable by direct observation would be absurd. It may be that Gassendi means to admit only those in which the conclusion appears the only way of accounting for the observed data, for he takes this to be the case with the example of the pores and with the other instances he mentions.[23] But then he has to face the skeptic, who is not prepared to accept without proof the legitimacy of moves of this kind. Obviously we very often do rely upon such arguments; but Gassendi, like Descartes, has set out to take skepticism very seriously, and his own argument against the metaphysicians who purport to know the hidden natures of things is just that their claims cannot be defended against such skeptical doubt. So it looks as though he must fall back upon his second suggestion, and hold it to be self-evident that moves of this kind are correct. The other reason why the first suggestion will not do is that it does not cover all the cases he wants to allow. These include—very importantly for his Epicurean account of the physical world—the inference from the observed movements of bodies to the existence of atoms and the void; powerful microscopes could arguably enable us to observe very tiny particles (in Gassendi's broad sense of "observe"), but they could hardly enable us to detect by sheer observation that the intervening space was genuinely empty. Moreover, he wants to include not only the inference to the soul from the movements of the body but also the inference to God from "his effects perceived by the senses."[24] So it must be on his second suggestion that his case depends.

This second proposal was that these inferences may be accepted as valid when they force themselves upon us as self-evident, and not otherwise. Thus "the truth of the demonstration by which it is established that there are pores shines forth by itself: that is, it is firmly grounded upon propositions which are known in their own right (*per se notae*) and which the intellect cannot reject; so that argument must come to a stop here."[25] Antiskeptical argument cannot go on for ever; justification has an end. But in ending it with so straightforward an appeal to self-evidence Gassendi turns out (as Brush remarks[26]) to be adopting a position surprisingly similar to that of Descartes, which he had so forcefully criticized. His argument against Descartes was that he had no reply to the skeptic who called in question his belief that whatever he clearly and distinctly perceived was true, because the defense that he does offer—the attempt to prove there is a God who is no deceiver and who guarantees that what seems to us very clear and evident must actually be the case—is bound to be circular. Any such defense must rest upon premises of which nothing better can be said than that they seem thoroughly clear and distinct, and the question can again be asked why this should be sufficient to show them to be true.[27] And in case it should be thought that such skeptical doubt is altogether idle and frivolous, he points out that something can appear extremely clear and distinct and yet turn out to be false after all, and that two men may be prepared to die for opposite opinions which each of them regards as wholly evident.[28] The mistake of the rationalist is the gratuitous trust he places in the human mind; he relies entirely upon the power of the human intellect, whereas in reality our minds are weak and may convince themselves as easily to adopt principles that are false as to accept those that are true.[29] But Gassendi now appears to have rendered himself as liable to these criticisms as Descartes.

Inevitably, of course; anyone who accepts the legitimacy of inferences which go beyond what is given in experience must be committed to regarding the human mind as reliable when it carries these inferences out. And when it is suggested that our intellect is not a reliable guide to the way things are, he is bound to find himself in some difficulty. Naturally there are various responses he can make, such as arguing that the skepticism he is faced with is self-defeating, or contending, in a Kantian vein, that without relying in this way upon reason, no experience would be possible at all. Gassendi does not attempt any such defense. The only thing he says that can be construed as a reply to any of the points he made against Descartes is that we need not worry about "the very great diversity among intellects," because the man to trust is the one "who, having weighed all considerations, presents an argument that cannot be legitimately contradicted, such as the one concerning the existence of pores."[30] He does, admittedly, add that the search for more and more ultimate justification must eventually have an end, but that provides no good reason for bringing it to rest in a trust of our intellectual powers and our intuitions of self-evidence.

There are other disadvantages in his proposal, besides his own refutation of it. Much scientific theory of the most useful kind is excluded if the only legitimate inferences beyond sense-experience are those that force themselves upon us as self-evidently correct: the theory of pores is allowed because it so obviously must be true, given the observed phenomena (or so Gassendi thinks); but if it had just seemed likely to be the simplest or the neatest or the most convenient explanation, we would not have been entitled to adopt it. So the proposal seems too restrictive; but it is also perhaps not restrictive enough for Gassendi's purposes. For he does want to repudiate the possibility of our ever knowing about the real natures of things, and it is difficult to see why it should not in principle be possible to find out about these real natures in much the same way as we found out about the pores. It is true that like Locke, who inherited so much from him, he vacillates somewhat on whether our lack of knowledge about the real character of things is due to a necessary or a contingent limitation of our cognitive powers, but his dominant view seems to be that such knowledge is more than contingently beyond our reach.[31] Still, these are minor difficulties compared with the main one, which is that he has opened himself to his own skeptical attack.

In getting into this position Gassendi has discovered what many more philosophers with empiricist sympathies have discovered after him, that the weapon the empiricist uses against those he considers unduly rationalistic or metaphysical has an awkward tendency to turn against himself. His plausible and persuasive argument, that the rationalists have no right to rely upon a human faculty which can only be judged if its own trustworthiness is assumed, has certainly turned out to be two-edged; for unless the empiricist is content to confine himself to judgments about what is empirically given, he must also rely on the intellect for the inferences that he makes beyond it or the construction that he puts upon it. More recently, empiricists have sometimes tried to dismiss their opponents' remarks as meaningless, only to find that the criteria they propose for meaningfulness rule out what they themselves want to say; and here the problem is essentially the same: their opponents' offense was to make claims which could not be supported in the proper way by experience, but it turns out to be remarkably difficult to avoid saying things that are equally hard to justify empirically. The difference between Gassendi and most of his successors is that his empiricism is more radical than theirs. Impressed by the apparently overwhelming power of the skeptical attack upon human reason, he would have liked to admit as legitimate knowledge only what could be discovered directly by empirical observation, without the mediation of inference or any kind of theory-construction, and the inadequacy of his conception of experience at first prevented him from seeing how little would be left of knowledge if this program were carried through. Once he had recognized this, it is true that he could have taken a step that would have rendered his empiricism more radical still, for he could have accepted the limitation of knowledge and refused to grant the legitimacy of indicative signs (allowing, perhaps, the inductive use of commemorative signs, since the induction is in principle subject to empirical test). But this would have meant ruling out scientific theories he regards as important, like the theory of atoms and the void, unless of course it had occurred to him to give them a purely instrumental interpretation. More decisively perhaps, it would have meant ruling out the theory that other people have minds as well as bodies that move and talk, for though their bodies may be observable their minds or souls are not.

There are also two other respects in which Gassendi is a more radical empiricist than some who have claimed that title. For one thing he anticipates Locke in a wholesale rejection of innate ideas, and suggests—without developing it in the detail Locke adduces—how the mind can come to abstract from experience even such very general concepts as that of a thing.[32] He also, and more strikingly, anticipates Mill and Quine with an equally vigorous repudiation of a priori knowledge. He makes no exception for analytic or verbal truths; even those truths which seem to us most evidently necessary, like the elementary laws of logic and mathematics, appear so only because all our experience has told in their favor and none against. "Thus, to consider the proposition everyone continually cites, that every whole is greater than its parts: we assent to it at once because right from the start . . . we have never compared a whole with one of its parts without noticing that it contains other parts as well and is therefore larger and greater than it."[33] We have seen that by its use of indicative signs the mind is capable of discovering truths other than those it can learn by direct observation, but it can proceed only by drawing conclusions from data that are empirically given. There are no truths which it can detect by the natural light of reason independently of all experience.

However, he is not quite as thoroughgoing in this as he might have been—or else not quite as consistent. For what is the status of the knowledge *that* these inferences, made by the use of indicative signs, are legitimate? Sometimes he appears to think it is empirical, but this it can hardly be: since the whole point of the inferences is to take us beyond experience, experience itself cannot vindicate them. And since he defends them by an appeal not to experience but to the capacity of the intellect, to its inability to do otherwise than accept them, he seems committed to the view that in this area, genuinely a priori knowledge is possible after all, though about one thing only, the legitimacy of inferences from experience.

Quine is more radical here, or perhaps just more clearheaded. He admits no a priori knowledge of any kind, not even of this latter kind. The consequence, which he accepts, is that the search for a justification of those claims that go beyond experience must be abandoned. The task of justification must be replaced by that of simply describing our practice; the theory of knowledge as it has been traditionally conceived must give way to naturalized epistemology, which is the scientific study of how we actually proceed in forming and defending our claims to know things. Naturalized epistemology cannot tell us which of the inferences we make are the right ones and which are the wrong ones (except, no doubt, insofar as they may have empirically testable consequences); it can tell us only which of them are in accordance with the normal practice of human beings. This is not to say that the proponent of naturalized epistemology does not take skepticism seriously. As Quine says, the position is essentially Hume's,[34] and not many philosophers have taken skepticism as seriously as Hume did. But while in one sense it admits the skeptic's case, in another it seems to destroy it: in demanding justifications for our beliefs and proofs of legitimacy for our forms of argument, the skeptic was requiring us to meet a standard which we cannot ever attain but never need to reach. The very impossibility of satisfying the skeptic's demand shows (or so it may be held) that the demand itself was out of place. What can properly be asked for in connection with a knowledge claim is not the sort of justification that the skeptic has in mind, but at most the sort of argument to which the word "justification" is applied in common talk: an argument, that is to say, which purports to sustain the claim in question, and which is of a type that finds favor with the many or with those whom the many regard as authoritative where arguments are concerned—and about which no more can be said than that.

But the proponent of naturalized epistemology has to proceed very carefully here. For as Stroud has pointed out,[35] if he is to confine himself to describing how we argue he cannot also reject as *illegitimate* the claims to a priori knowledge or the attempts at genuinely normative justifications that traditional epistemologists have made. To declare them illegitimate is itself to adopt a normative position, and therefore to go beyond the official program of sticking to pure description. He may be able to observe that certain of the justifications traditionally offered contradict themselves or fail to achieve what they set out to do, but he cannot mount any general attack on the traditional conception of justification nor, therefore, any general defense of his own nonnormative approach; to do that he would have to do more than just describe. And to the contention that knowledge is possible a priori he can only reply by showing —or trying to show—that he can account for all that we believe we know without having need of that hypothesis. He cannot show that a priori knowledge is not possible; he can only argue that we do not, in fact, possess any.

Quine is not always consistent in his adherence to this position, and does at times allow himself to make the normative remarks for which he has officially no place.[36] That only serves to emphasize how revolutionary naturalized epistemology is. Originally he rejected a priori knowledge for reasons rather similar to Gassendi's: claims to such knowledge could not be defended except by relying on circular argument. But whereas Gassendi ultimately finds himself allowing a kind of a priori knowledge after all—namely, that which has to do with the justification of inferences—Quine will permit no such exception, and so finds himself no longer able consistently to hold the view that there is anything wrong in principle with the idea of a priori knowledge.

The advantage of Gassendi's position is that he goes as far as he can go without proceeding to this extremity. The disadvantages we have seen: his argument against Descartes tells equally against himself, and it appears arbitrary to accept one sort of a priori knowledge and rule out the rest. If the use of reason requires no defense from skeptical attack, or if the kind of circular defense of itself that it can itself provide is considered to be adequate, one would have thought it legitimate to trust reason not only when it tells us that certain forms of inference are valid but also when it enunciates self-evident truths like the axioms of logic and arithmetic. If on the other hand no answer can be given to the skeptic who calls in question the use of our reason, Gassendi will hardly be offering a satisfactory defense of the inferences he approves of when he says that they are obvious to all rational men.

But it might be possible to retain the benefits of Gassendi's approach without the disadvantages. One could do this if one could find a way to justify roughly that class of inferences which he wanted to defend while continuing to reject roughly those claims and those arguments that he wanted to reject. Exactly what was accepted and what was rejected would have to depend, of course, on exactly how this was done, and one might very well find oneself drawing the line at a slightly different point from Gassendi; that, as we have seen, might not necessarily be a bad thing. But it would certainly be a bonus from Gassendi's point of view if the result were such as to exclude the possibility of our knowing about things as they are in themselves. Kant, in fact, was to put forward a line of thought which at least in his own opinion met the relevant requirements, and which I cannot help thinking Gassendi would have found rather congenial—by which I do not, of course, mean to suggest that there was any direct influence of Gassendi on Kant or any serious anticipation by Gassendi of the characteristically Kantian solution. What repelled Gassendi about the complete and total skepticism he ascribed to Gorgias was the utter absurdity of it; it was for the same reason that he gave up the view (if he ever unambiguously held it) that all inferences beyond the experientially given are equally illegitimate; on the other hand, he saw no such absurdity in denying that reason is capable of providing us with substantive knowledge about the world in a purely a priori fashion. Reflection on this absurdity might have led him—though it did not—to the idea that the legitimate use of reason could be defended against skeptical attack on the grounds that without it no experience, or no coherent experience, would be possible at all, while no such defense could be provided for the use he wanted to reject.

Kant, of course, thought that by this means he could establish more than the legitimacy of certain uses of indicative signs. He thought he could show that we must possess certain a priori concepts, and that these concepts must find application in our experience in such a way as to give rise to quite legitimate claims to synthetic a priori knowledge. Gassendi would have found these conclusions less acceptable, for as we have seen, he considered that all our concepts are derived from experience and that the claims Kant calls synthetic a priori must likewise be accounted empirical. Kant also finds room for the a priori knowledge of analytic truths, and this again Gassendi would have considered highly uncritical. But at a more fundamental level they are in agreement, for they share the feeling that the human mind has an indispensable and entirely legitimate role to play in interpreting what is given in experience, but goes beyond the limits of its proper use when it purports to give us information, a priori and without relation to experience, about the nature of things as they are in themselves.

Their objection to this transcendent use of reason is also similar: it cannot be defended against skeptical attack. Its title cannot be vindicated, and we have therefore no good grounds for supposing that what it tells us is correct. We saw how this objection turned against Gassendi himself when he tried to justify the legitimate use. Kant evidently saw no danger of anything similar happening to him; in view of Gassendi's example we may wonder whether he was right. The answer is not, I think, quite obvious. But it is certainly another story.

Gassendi was not the most farsighted of thinkers, and he was not helped by his inadequate conception of experience. Largely because of this, he failed to see the point of many of Descartes's arguments and concerns, or to realize how closely related they were to his own. All the same, he did have a propensity to ask the right questions and a serious appreciation of the philosophical importance of skepticism. One must stress "philosophical": he was not just interested in it as a weapon of theological debate, but well aware that any epistemology worth considering must deal with the problems that skepticism raises. His own attempt to deal with those problems ran into difficulties, as others have subsequently done; but it does manage, in a number of ways, to foreshadow one of the most promising attempts to have been made so far, that of Kant.

No one could be a Gassendist nowadays. But then no one could be a Cartesian either; and it is eminently possible to be a follower of Kant.

NOTES

1. P. Bayle, *Dictionaire historique et critique*, art. *Pyrrhon*, note B; p. 2430 in the Rotterdam edition of 1702.

2. This work has been reprinted with a French translation by B. Rochot (Paris:

Vrin, 1959), as has Gassendi's attack on Descartes, the *Disquisitio Metaphysica* (Paris: Vrin, 1962). Excerpts from both of these and from other works of Gassendi, notably the *Syntagma Philosophicum*, are available in English in *The Selected Works of Pierre Gassendi*, ed. and trans. C. B. Brush (New York: Johnson Reprint Corp., 1972). In giving references I shall cite first the six-volume 1658 Lyons edition of Gassendi's *Opera Omnia*, by volume, page number, and column, and then give the page number in Brush's book where appropriate. Rochot's editions carry the Lyons pagination in the margins.

3. *Disquisitio Metaphysica*, *Opera* III, 281B ff. = Brush, pp. 168 ff.; *Opera* III, 388a-b = Brush, p. 267; *Opera* III, 389b-390a. The second of these is also to be found in *Oeuvres de Descartes*, ed. C. Adam and P. Tannery (Paris: Cerf, 1897-1913) (henceforth referred to as "AT") VII, 333, or in English in E. S. Haldane & G. R. T. Ross, *The Philosophical Works of Descartes* (Cambridge: at the University Press, 1931-1934) (henceforth referred to as "HR") II, 193.

4. *Disquisitio Metaphysica*, *Opera* III, 316a = Brush, p. 204; *Opera* III, 360a-b = Brush, p. 231.

5. *Disquisitio Metaphysica*, *Opera* III, 388a = Brush, pp. 266 f. = AT VII, 332 = HR II, 192 f. *Syntagma*, *Opera* I, 53a-b; *Opera* I, 85a = Brush, p. 345.

6. *Exercitationes*, *Opera* III, 197b = Brush, p. 88. In quoting Gassendi I rely on Brush's translation where it is available, but modify it as seems appropriate.

7. *Exercitationes*, *Opera* III, 203a = Brush, p. 96. See A. A. Long, *Hellenistic Philosophy* (London: Duckworth, 1974), chap. 3, esp. p. 83, in support of this interpretation of Pyrrho and Timon.

8. *Syntagma*, *Opera* I, 53a.

9. Gassendi seems to recognize the former possibility in the *Exercitationes* at *Opera* III, 199b-200a = Brush, p. 92.

10. *Disquisitio Metaphysica*, *Opera* III, 281b-282a = Brush, pp. 168 f.; *Opera* III, 388a-b = Brush, pp. 266 f. = AT VII, 332 f. = HR II, 192 f.

11. Cf. *Syntagma*, *Opera* I, 70a = Brush, p. 294; and cf. his use of the dictum *id apparet, quod cuique apparet*, *Disquisitio Metaphysica*, *Opera* III, 314b = AT VII, 277 = HR II, 151. And see further O. R. Bloch, *La philosophie de Gassendi* (The Hague: Nijhoff, 1971), pp. 94 ff.; Bloch remarks on the affinities with Kant.

12. *Meditation* I.

13. *Disquisitio Metaphysica*, *Opera* III, 286a-b = Brush, pp. 176 f.; *Opera* III 384a = Brush, p. 264. *Syntagma*, *Opera* I, 80b = Brush, p. 329.

14. *Syntagma*, *Opera* I, 80a = Brush, pp. 328 f.

15. *Disquisitio Metaphysica*, *Opera* III, 320a = Brush, p. 207. Actually this is directed against Descartes.

16. *PH* I 22, II 72-73. Cf. also *PH* III 38 ff. and *M* VII 293 ff.

17. *Exercitationes*, *Opera* III, 208b = Brush, pp. 106 f.; cf. also *Disquisitio Metaphysica*, *Opera* III, 384a = Brush, p. 265.

18. See for example H. Berr, *An jure inter Scepticos Gassendus numeratus fuerit* (Paris: Hachette, 1898), trans. B. Rochot as *Du scepticisme de Gassendi* (Paris: A. Michel, 1960); B. Rochot, *Les travaux de Gassendi sur Épicure et sur l'atomisme* (Paris: Vrin, 1944); R. H. Popkin, *The History of Scepticism from Erasmus to Descartes*, rev. ed. (New York: Harper, 1968), chaps. 5 and 7; and,

most usefully, Bloch, *La philosophie de Gassendi*, part I.

19. "Commemorative sign" is Bury's translation, in the Loeb edition of Sextus Empiricus. Gassendi's term is *signum commonefactivum* (*Syntagma, Opera* I, 81a), and this is less felicitously rendered as "empirical sign" by Brush (p. 332). See *PH* II 100-101 and *M* VIII 151-156.

20. Provided, at any rate, that B is "naturally nonevident." On this, and for the examples cited in the next sentence, see *PH* II 97-102 and *M* VIII 145-155.

21. *Syntagma, Opera* I, 82a = Brush, pp. 334 f.

22. *Syntagma, Opera* I, 85b-86a = Brush, pp. 346-348.

23. Cf. *Syntagma, Opera* I, 81a ff. = Brush, pp. 332 ff.

24. *Syntagma, Opera* I, 82b = Brush, p. 336. Thus Gassendi is not averse to proving the existence of God, as is sometimes said; he is only averse to attempts at an a priori proof. On the soul, see *loc. cit.* and also slightly further on, *Opera* I, 83a = Brush p. 337; but note that at the foot of p. 335 Brush mistranslates *Opera* I, 82b, for Gassendi does not deny that the *operationes* constitute an indicative sign of the soul. (In fact Brush misreads *indicatorium* as *indicativum.*)

25. *Syntagma, Opera* I, 85b = Brush, p. 347.

26. Brush, p. 347 n.

27. *Disquisitio Metaphysica, Opera* III, 279b-280a = Brush, pp. 166 f.; *Opera* III, 316a = Brush, p. 204; *Opera* III, 360a-b = Brush, p. 231.

28. *Disquisitio Metaphysica, Opera* III, 315a = AT VII, 278 = HR II, 152; *Syntagma, Opera* I, 90b = Brush, p. 364.

29. *Disquisitio Metaphysica, Opera* III, 280a = Brush, p. 167.

30. *Syntagma, Opera* I, 86a = Brush, p. 347.

31. For a review of the texts see Bloch, *La philosophie de Gassendi*, pp. 101 ff.

32. *Disquisitio Metaphysica, Opera* III, 318a-b = AT VII, 280 f. = HR II, 153 f.; *Opera* III, 319b-320a = Brush, pp. 205 f.; and cf. *Opera* III, 326a ff.

33. *Syntagma, Opera* II, 458a.

34. W. V. O. Quine, "Epistemology Naturalized," in his *Ontological Relativity and Other Essays* (New York: Columbia University Press, 1969), p. 72. This essay gives the clearest statement of Quine's position.

35. B. Stroud, "The Significance of Naturalized Epistemology," in P. A. French, T. E. Uehling, and H. K. Wettstein, eds., *Midwest Studies in Philosophy* VI: *The Foundations of Analytic Philosophy* (Minneapolis: University of Minnesota Press, 1981).

36. Even in "Epistemology Naturalized": cf. pp. 75, 80 f., 86, 89.

13

Descartes's Use of Skepticism

Bernard Williams

Descartes was not a skeptic. One has to take a distant and inaccurate view of his writings to suppose that he was. One of his principal complaints against Bourdin, who produced the *Seventh Objections*, was that Bourdin seemed only to have studied the passages of the *Meditations* in which Descartes raised the doubt, and not those in which he answered or dispelled it; as he complained in his letter to Father Dinet (VII, 574), "Who has ever been so bold and shameless in calumny, that he blamed Hippocrates or Galen for having set out the causes from which illnesses arise, and concluded from that, that they have never taught anything except the method of falling ill?"

The point of reading Hippocrates or Galen was, presumably, to learn how to recover from illness, and there is a well-known asymmetry to this in the practice of philosophy, lying in the fact that the illness is in that case self-inflicted and of the same general nature as the cure. This asymmetry pressed hard on the conception of philosophy offered by "therapeutic positivism" and similar outlooks, which diagnose as the illness not merely deformations such as philosophical skepticism, but the disposition to philosophy itself. Such a program needs, and characteristically lacks, a theory of the origins and nature of the philosophical neurosis.

That same problem does not apply to Pyrrhonism, where skepticism is the cure—a cure, first of all, for an uncertainty which flows from the unsatisfiable desire for knowledge. Nor does it apply to Descartes, whose aim is precisely to replace uncertainty with knowledge. For him, skepticism was two things. It was the extreme dramatization of uncertainty, an uncertainty which, largely independent of any philosophical discipline or exercise, already existed, and which Descartes felt he had to confront. It was, second, part of his method for overcoming uncertainty and attaining knowledge.

In his mature works he presents himself as, from the beginning of his enquiry, adopting skepticism as a method. In the fourth part of the *Discourse on the Method* (VI, 31-32) he writes:

For a long time I had remarked that so far as practical life is concerned, it is sometimes necessary to follow opinions which one knows to be very uncertain, just as though they were indubitable . . . , but because I wanted to devote myself solely to the search for truth, I thought that it was necessary that I should do just the opposite, and that I should reject, just as though it were absolutely false, everything in which I could imagine the slightest doubt, so as to see whether after that anything remained in my belief which was entirely indubitable.

A similar introduction to the method of doubt occurs in the *First Meditation* (VII, 18):

Reason persuades me already, that I should withhold assent no less carefully from things which are not clearly certain and indubitable, as from things which are evidently false; so that if I find some reason for doubt in each of them, this will be enough for me to reject them all. It does not follow that I should have to go through them one by one, which would be an endless task; if the foundations are undermined, anything built on top of them falls down by itself, so I shall attack directly those principles which supported everything I have up to now believed.

That this is Descartes's starting point implies from the beginning a certain *control* of skepticism. He does not merely encounter skepticism as an outside force and survive it, like the knightly hero of some romance, and he does not even present himself as so doing. His tone differs in this from that of a work such as Ayer's *Problem of Knowledge*, which chronicles a series of successes by the knower against various applications of skepticism. Such a work makes it seem as though the supports and nature of skepticism could be encountered first, quite independently of the view of knowledge which will help to overcome it; and since in fact the solutions merely adopt standards of knowledge which bypass the problem (indeed, virtually constitute an assertion of customary practice), the battle seems either lost, or all the time a sham, and the supposed solutions factitious. The Cartesian, however, resembles the Pyrrhonist, in deploying a skepticism which he has intelligibly shaped to his own purposes, in the one case of satisfying the desire for knowledge, in the other of banishing it.

Descartes thought that the skepticism he deployed, though he carefully used it for his own methodical purposes, was at least as extreme as that deployed by those who called themselves skeptics. He boasted that he was the first of all to overthrow the doubts of the skeptics (*Seventh Replies*: VII, 550). In these words, as elsewhere, he construes the doubt that he constructs and overcomes as belonging to a tradition. Exactly how much he knew of that tradition and through what writers, remains, to some degree, uncertain: "I had long ago seen several books written by the Academics and Skeptics," he wrote (*Second Replies*: VII, 130), and he says in the *Seventh Replies* that the "Sect of the Skeptics still flourishes" (VII, 548-549). He seems to have been familiar with the works of Montaigne and Charron, among other skeptical writers.[1] Insofar as he deploys doubt both in that tradition and against its contemporary representatives, his doubt can be seen as preemptive. It is designed to head off any subsequent recurrence of skepticism, and his claim that he has taken doubt to its extreme, as far as any doubt could be taken, is central to his claim that what he recovers from the process is a foundation of knowledge. Thus his two claims, that he takes traditional skepticism to an extreme, and that he refutes it, are connected. If the ancient skeptics had persisted far enough in their doubt, they could have transcended it: as he puts it (letter of 1638: II, 38-K 53), "although the Pyrrhonians reached no certain conclusion from their doubts, this is not to say that no one could."[2]

The fact that doubt is used as a tool and as part of a method—the method referred to in the title of the work which is called, in correct translation, the *Discourse on the Method*[3]—radically affects the character of the doubt. It conditions the structure of the skeptical arguments themselves and prescribes a particular attitude toward them. The Method is deployed in the course of an intellectual project, which has the feature that if doubt can possibly be applied to a class of beliefs, then that class of beliefs must, at least temporarily, be laid aside. One question raised by that project is what it is for; one answer to that question is the one already implied in saying that the doubt is preemptive—namely, that if the project can generate knowledge or permit knowledge to be generated, then we know that the skeptics are wrong, who claim that such a project can generate nothing but doubt. But there is also a distinct aim, in relation to which the inquiry can be seen not just as banishing doubt and establishing the possibility of knowledge, but as concerned with the content of that knowledge, and as helping to generate the most fundamental kind of knowledge, absolute knowledge. I shall come back to that wider objective later.

In the *Meditations* Descartes proceeds—and does so, it is clear, self-consciously—through three levels of doubt. The first is associated with the common illusions of the senses. Descartes uses these examples only to loosen everyday convictions in a preliminary way, and does not claim that reflection on these cases has any tendency to cast doubt on *each* case in which one thinks that one is perceiving a material object. He makes the transition to the idea that on each occasion of supposed perception one can properly think "I might be mistaken *now*" very clearly in *Discourse* Part iv, in the *First Meditation,* and also in the *Recherche de la Vérité* (X, 510 ff.), by moving from the occasional errors of the senses to the phenomenon of dreaming.

The difference between the two cases, for Descartes, consists in the fact that errors which depend on such things as bad light, distance, illness, and so forth, resist generalization, in the sense that they depend on special misleading conditions, and reflection on those conditions can arouse suspicion even at the time. But dreams take one in completely, and reflection cannot get a grip within the situation to reveal that situation as special: the beliefs one might bring to bear on it are themselves affected by dreaming.[4] In this case, correction is unequivocably retrospective. But, if it is, how does one resist the thought that one might, now, be dreaming?

Descartes's own eventual answer to that question is not totally satisfactory. The answer refers to the coherence of our waking experience under natural laws, which helps to form a general rational picture of the world in which dreaming is "placed" relative to waking. We need that picture, in fact, even to understand his introduction of dreaming in the first place (as opposed, for instance, to madness, which he notably dismisses in the *First Meditation* from the discussion of skepticism), but he does not give us the means to focus that understanding of dreaming on answering the skeptical question when it is raised on a particular occasion. This is partly because his conception of dreaming is itself inadequate.

However, his very passing reference to this problem at the end of his inquiry makes perfectly good sense in terms of what, by then, he thinks that he has achieved. Once we have acquired the well-founded picture of the world, we do not have to go back and answer every skeptical question, because we do not have to go on asking them. Having eventually come through and out of the general doubt, we are provided not only with answers to general and philosophical doubts, if someone still raises them, but also with methods of answering particular doubts when, in a nonphilosophical way, they present themselves. In addition to that, we will have been given the grounds of a confidence that we need not raise such doubts, nor try to answer them, when they do not present themselves in practical life or in the course of some more limited scientific inquiry. The prereflective confidence in waking experience as waking experience is in fact well founded, and the best witness to that fact, most of the time, will be that very confidence.

The distinction between everyday errors of the senses on the one hand, and dreaming on the other, is used by Descartes to mark the distinction between the undeniable fact that we are sometimes deceived, and the stronger possibility that *on any given occasion* of apparent sense-perception we may be deceived. He goes further, however, to a more radical consideration (which he recognizes to be more radical) that not only on any given occasion may one be deceived, but that it is possible that one may be deceived on every occasion and the "external world" not exist at all. In the *Meditations* he achieves this final level of doubt by invoking the fiction of the *malin génie*, the malicious demon "of the highest power and intelligence, who devotes all his efforts to deceiving me" (*First Meditation*, VII, 22).[5] This device provides a thought experiment which can be generally applied: if there were an agency which was indefinitely powerful and acted purposely and systematically to frustrate inquiry and the desire for truth, would *this* kind of belief or experience be invalidated? It is obvious how far such a conception goes beyond the old material about the illusions of the senses, and, correspondingly, how clearly removed it is from any idea that if skepticism is a rational attitude, then it is so because it is *supported* by the facts of sense-deception or of dreaming.

The fully "hyperbolical" doubt, as Descartes calls it, which is introduced with the demon, does not only permit, for the first time, the idea that every supposed sense-perception may be illusory. It also obliterates the past, and God. Moreover, it casts some shadow over the reliability of purely intellectual processes. The exact extent and depth of that shadow has been extensively discussed, but the answer to the question, as we shall see later, is bound to be in a way indeterminate.

Toward the end of the *First Meditation*, Descartes says (VII, 21): "I am forced to admit that there are none of the things I used to think were true, which may not possibly be doubted, and not because of carelessness or frivolity but for sound and well-considered reasons (*non per inconsiderantiam vel levitatem, sed propter validas & meditatas rationes*)." Thus the doubt, even the hyperbolical doubt, is in some sense serious and well founded. Yet Descartes also says, and with great and repeated emphasis, that the doubt is not to be carried into everyday life, and indeed that the existence of the external world is something which "no one of sound mind ever seriously doubted" (*Synopsis* of the *Meditations*, VII, 16; cf. *Fifth Replies*, VII, 350; *Principles* i 1-3; letter of August 1641, III, 398-K 110). That judgment, moreover, is not simply retrospective, something to be recovered when one has come out at the other end; rather, it is an observation about the nature of the project.

What then are, or could be, the "sound and well-considered reasons"? This phrase gets its content from what it is contrasted with, its force being that the doubt is not a matter of "carelessness or frivolity." The reasons are systematic, arrived at as part of Descartes's sustained intellectual project: they are *validae* because *meditatae*, sound just because they are well considered. It is not that, by practical standards, the doubt is as reasonable as its opposite. It is extremely important in this connection that so little use is made of the empirical material deployed by Montaigne or Charron or indeed Sextus. "Reasons for doubt" which relied on empirical content would not, beyond an early stage, be "serious" in Descartes's context. In the empirical context, his doubts are unserious; they are serious in the context of the problem, and in that context the reasons that do the work are not those with the most empirical content, but rather the utterly abstract conception of the demon. The other considerations are helpful in the business of getting used to thinking about corporeal things (in particular) in a certain way, and that is why Descartes devoted a whole *Meditation* to those doubts, and, as he put it, reheated with some distaste the stale cabbage of the Academics and Skeptics (*Second Replies*, VII, 130).

Descartes's distance from the empirical materials of skepticism means also that the traditional Pyrrhonist claim (or weapon) of *isostheneia*, although it has an application to Cartesian skepticism, has it only in an indirect and refined way. The "equally plausible argument to the opposite effect" takes the form, in Descartes's procedure, of a consideration which removes all effect both from the original argument and from its normal contraries. There is thus no place for the states of mind which Pyrrhonists thought to be the appropriate reaction to lack of real knowledge. Those states of mind, for the Pyrrhonists, while not the conclusion of philosophical reflection, were *at* the conclusion of it; but the hyperbolical doubt could not possibly, for Descartes, have constituted the conclusion of anything.

If the Cartesian inquiry had been disappointed, there would have been no question of staying in a state of hyperbolical doubt. It would rather be a question of giving up science, and returning to an operationalist outlook and everyday standards of reasonable belief. (This is of course a point about Cartesian, as opposed to Pyrrhonist, *inquiry*. What Descartes himself would have done if so disappointed is an empty question; we are concerned with the Descartes given by his writings, and what we are given leaves no room for such a disappointment.)

It is important that, for Descartes, to fall back on everyday empirical standards of belief would be to *give up* science. Unlike Mersenne, Gassendi, and others who tried to give an operationalist style of answer to skepticism, he shared with the ancients the idea that the coherence of appearances in itself provided no foundations for a real science; and although at the practical level some bets about appearances were no doubt better than others, he thought that arguments which had pretensions to being scientific but which operated merely at the level of appearances really were subject to *isostheneia,* and were no better and no worse than one another. This attitude evidently emerged at the very beginning of his career, in the incident when he spoke against a speech by Chandoux, to the approval of Cardinal Bérulle.[6] In his mature work this attitude comes out in the belief that rival hypotheses, until properly criticized, may all share some profound and equally vitiating misconceptions —misconceptions, above all, about appearances themselves and the respects in which they may or may not be systematically misleading. The doubt is an instrument to uncover such misconceptions, and it is reflection encouraged by the doubt that leads Descartes to isolate, first in the *Second Meditation,* a nonsensory conception of matter as extension, which not only becomes the central concept of his physics but also enables him to revise radically everyday ideas about the relation of sense-perception to knowledge.

Descartes's undertaking of applying successively three levels of doubt yields, correspondingly, three levels at which our thought might be affected by error: the merely local; systematically, as in our conception of nature; and universally, the imagined result of the malicious demon. The last, which would undercut the other two altogether, is eventually shown to be baseless by appeal to the existence and benevolence of God. The second turns out to be real, but corrigible by the progress of the sciences. The first kind of error is at the limit, ineliminable, but it can be contained and allowed for, particularly granted the systematic understanding gained at the second level. The fact that there is need for theoretical correction of systematic prereflective error at the second level means (as Margaret Wilson rightly emphasizes)[7] that the doubt is, in a sense, correct: *we are* systematically deceived by our senses. It also illustrates the need for the sciences to be given "foundations." That does not mean that they are to be provided with axioms, from which all scientific truth can be deduced. It means that they have to be purged of false presuppositions, and put on a sound basis of method.

The *Synopsis* to the *Meditations* states quite clearly that we can doubt of all things, particularly material things, "so long as we have no foundations of the sciences other than the ones we had before." It says also (VII, 12) that the process of doubt delivers us from all sorts of prejudices; detaches the mind from the senses; and puts us finally in a situation where we no longer have any doubt about what we discover to be true. All these three are important to the method of doubt, and the first two, as we have seen, are connected. The third, Descartes's search for "something firm and enduring" (*First Meditation*, VII, 17), raises further issues. Descartes insists that no *cognitio* which can be rendered doubtful "should, it seems, be called *scientia*" (*Second Replies*, VII, 141; cf. *Fifth Meditation*, VII, 70), and this is connected by him with having a kind of reason "so strong that it cannot be knocked out by any stronger reason." In considering Descartes's emphasis on this, it is important to bear in mind the extent and chaotic character of the disagreements that obtained in the early seventeenth century, both in religious matters and in the understanding of nature. There was little effective agreement at a theoretical level and, correspondingly, little understanding of where disagreement might explicably arise. A probabilistic and corrigibilist conception of the scientific enterprise, in any specifically modern sense, did not yet exist.

Descartes's belief that there is nothing between agreed certainty and a chaotic disagreement in which anything goes is not simply or even mainly the product of reflection on the concept of knowledge. It is, rather, an effect produced jointly by the historical situation of scientific understanding in his time, and a very natural interpretation of what scientific knowledge should be. That interpretation takes scientific knowledge to be a system which represents the world as it is independently of any inquirer, using terms which to the greatest possible extent display that independence. This objective of *absolute* knowledge, as it may be called, is not peculiar to Descartes. Indeed, it can be seen as implicit in a natural conception of knowledge itself, and the fact that this ideal is, in particular, an ideal for scientific knowledge implies the idea that scientific knowledge peculiarly realizes, or seeks to realize, the ambitions for knowledge *tout court*. What is more peculiar to Descartes is the connection that he makes between the objective of absolute knowledge and an ideal of certainty, and that connection is the product of his historical situation, which encouraged him and others to think that if a claim to knowledge—at least, to the most basic and general kinds of knowledge—was not certain, then it must be *relative*, the product, to an undetermined degree, of one's peculiar circumstances. Those two ideas could perhaps be separated only when the existence of scientific institutions gave practical substance to the idea that claims even to the most fundamental kinds of scientific knowledge need to be tested and can be corrected. It could then be seen that a respectable claim to scientific knowledge does not need to be certain (indeed, according to some, its respectability depends on its not being so). At the same time, the methods of testing such claims, and the theories for their correction, themselves reflect the idea of absolute knowledge; and the understanding of disagreement, in particular insight into reasons that make disagreement in certain cases entirely natural, prevent disagreement generating skepticism.[8]

For Descartes, however, *scientia*, real knowledge, would have to be immune both to disagreement and to being recalled into doubt. There were two steps that Descartes had to take in order to replace disagreement, and skepticism associated with disagreement, with *scientia*. The first was to find a class of truths which, when they were carefully considered, commanded assent from anyone who so considered them. The second step was to provide a way of safeguarding those truths against skeptical attack at times when they were not being carefully considered: that is to say, to permit the project of acquiring knowledge to go on in a settled and cumulative manner, and not constantly be thrown off balance by recurrent skeptical doubt.

So far as the basic truths were concerned, he believed that he could identify these, and, further, that the skeptics, if not merely pretending, could never have perceived these things clearly, or they would no longer be skeptics (*Seventh Replies*, VII, 477); as he wrote to a correspondent in August 1641 (III, 434-K 119): "Certainly I have never denied that the Skeptics themselves, so long as they clearly perceive some truth, spontaneously assent to it, nor do they remain in that heresy of theirs, of doubting everything, except just in name, and possibly in intention and resolve. . . ."

Despite some mild ambiguities about the role of the will, Descartes fundamentally regards these propositions as *irresistible*. This is made clear in the *Fifth Meditation* (VII, 65, 69) and frequently elsewhere—for instance, in the *Second Replies* (VII, 145-146), and at *Principles* i 43—and he must so regard them, if the method of doubt is not to leave him with assent suspended forever. In connection with this notion of irresistibility, it is important what is meant by the idea of a proposition's being "carefully considered." It is natural to say that a proposition is irresistible if it cannot come before the mind without, in Descartes's phrase, being clearly and distinctly perceived, and thus (in these cases) believed; as Descartes says in the *Second Replies* (VII, 145-146) of the things about which we can be perfectly certain, "we cannot think of them without believing them to be true," and he there claims that we cannot doubt them without thinking of them. From those premises it follows, as he correctly points out, that we cannot doubt them. Yet it seems that there is something which counts as doubting even those propositions, so it must be possible for such a proposition to be sufficiently "before the mind" for one to entertain a doubt about it, but not be so clearly in view that one's belief in it is activated. This is not a very deep or difficult problem. All that is required is some way of referring to or indicating a proposition or idea of this kind without bringing it clearly to mind. A standard way of doing that will lie in deploying a word or sentence which expresses that idea or proposition, without, however, concentrating closely on what that word or sentence expresses. One can, granted this, entertain a doubt about an irresistible proposition, but only by not thinking about it clearly (cf. *Seventh Replies*, VII, 460, 546; to Clerselier, IX-I, 204-205).

A more serious problem, however, has been thought to arise at this point. There is no great difficulty in admitting that one can refer to an idea without clearly and distinctly perceiving it, but Descartes also (*Seventh Replies*, VII, 511) claims that many people think that they have clearly and distinctly perceived an idea when they have not done so. This is a more alarming consideration, since it suggests that the notion of irresistibility may ultimately be vacuous: it may turn out that these ideas or propositions are irresistible only because one does not count as having clearly and distinctly perceived them unless one assents to them.

However, what Descartes says need not really weaken his position. His point basically concerns a *practice* of clear intellectual concentration, and the people he has in mind are those who, while they may claim clearly to see certain truths, show by their whole practice of argument that they do not separate one item from another nor concentrate intently on any one question or consideration. When the matter is seen in this way, the decision whether an objector has clearly and distinctly considered a given proposition does not turn, vacuously, simply on the issue of whether he agrees with that proposition. The first question is whether a given person is one who in general, by careful intellectual consideration, can isolate an idea or proposition and concentrate on it. Such a capacity, Descartes believes, is innate in every nondefective human being, though it needs eliciting by practice—practice which need not involve standard academic education, and may well be impeded by it.

Two such people will, Descartes believes, almost always agree about the truth of a simple proposition if—by the ordinary criteria of concentration—they concentrate on it. If, exceptionally, they do not agree, then one of them after further concentration will eventually come to agree with the other. Descartes thought that constant disagreement and hence skepticism obtained because people addressed large and contentious issues in a confused manner, without subjecting them to analysis, and because they had not acquired practice in analyzing them into intellectually simple elements. The ability to do that is one that almost everyone displays in some familiar connections, but conventional education and styles of learning actually discourage one from applying it in the right way to the fundamental issues of scientific and metaphysical inquiry.

Thus Descartes supposed that conditions of proper concentration would produce clear and distinct perception, and clear and distinct perception would of course produce agreement. Moreover, that agreement would be agreement to *truth*. Descartes says in the *Third Meditation* (VII, 35): "I seem to be able to take it as a general rule that everything that I very clearly and distinctly perceive is true." However, the indeterminate shadow of the *malin génie* can in certain circumstances be taken to threaten this assurance, and Descartes thinks that he has eventually established it only by proving the existence of God, whose benevolent purpose as the creator of intellectual beings assure that they cannot be mistaken in what they clearly and distinctly perceive. Since, however, the existence of God is itself proved only by reliance on clear and distinct perceptions, this claim has famously elicited the charge of circularity, first in the *Second* and *Fourth* sets of *Objections* (VII, 125, 214).

It has sometimes been asked whether Descartes regards clear and distinct perception as the *criterion* of truth. The answer to this depends on what is meant by the claim that it is such a criterion. If that claim means that the idea of a proposition's being true is the same idea as that of someone's clearly and distinctly perceiving it, then Descartes's answer is certainly "no." If it means that one can on a given occasion decide that a proposition is true on the basis of noting that one is then clearly and distinctly perceiving it, then the answer is again "no," since we are here dealing with propositions that are irresistible, and with them there is no gap between clear and distinct perception and deciding that the proposition is true: if one is actually clearly and distinctly perceiving such a proposition, by that very fact one believes it to be true. If the claim means, again, that it is itself certain as a general proposition that anything clearly and distinctly perceived is true, then indeed Descartes accepts that claim; but if it means, lastly, that no justification could appropriately be given for that general proposition, then Descartes once more rejects such a claim, since he gives precisely such a justification, in the existence and benevolence of God.

There are obviously some parallels here to ancient discussions of *katalēpsis*, just as there are some parallels with regard to the notion of irresistibility, the Stoics finding some difficulty, it seems, in saying under what conditions propositions would "drag us by the hair to assent."[9] But the fundamental difference is, of course, that the Stoic kataleptic presentations were paradigmatically some particular kinds of sense-perception. No sensory item, at least when regarded as a perception of the world rather than as a purely psychological datum, can for Descartes carry this kind of kataleptic certainty. For him, the kataleptic impression is intellectual. However, that does not exclude its giving information of reality outside the mind, for—whatever view one takes on the vexed question of the status that Descartes gives to "eternal truths" which make no claim of existence—the existence of God is thought by Descartes to be something that we can come to know through such impressions, and that is a vital feature of his system.

The Stoics have been accused[10] of not distinguishing issues of truth and issues of knowledge. There have, similarly, been strains in the criticism of Descartes and in the exposition of him[11] which represent him as equally running these matters together. This representation of him can be itself a reaction against the charge of circularity. It is thought, roughly, that he can be protected from the charge of getting something for nothing only if it turns out that all he gets is the coherence of knowledge.

The clearest and simplest way of representing Descartes's position, however, seems to me to free him from this charge. It is essential to Descartes's system that he supposed that he could argue from thought to independent reality, in particular to the existence of God. In the ontological proof in the *Fifth Meditation*, he argues to God's existence from the content of his idea of God, while the causal proof in the *Third Meditation* proceeds to the same conclusion from the factual existence of that idea as an item in his thought (the kind of fact guaranteed in the *cogito*). These arguments are not valid, and there is no historical reason to think that they commanded even in the seventeenth century the kataleptic assurance for which Descartes hoped. But the fault in Descartes's answer to skepticism lies in the faults of these arguments themselves and not in his general procedure. Granted those arguments, there is no reason to accuse him of confusing knowledge and truth nor of arguing in a circle.

The exact nature of the answer that Descartes gives to the charge of circularity has been much disputed.[12] Descartes certainly held that unless one knew of the existence of God, one could have no perfect assurance or *scientia* about anything; he also held that, in some sense, this point applied only with respect to conclusions which recur in memory when we are no longer attending to the arguments on which they are based. One of Descartes's strongest, and also most helpful, statements of his position occurs in the *Second Replies* (VII, 141):

That an atheist can clearly know that the three angles of a triangle are equal to two right angles, I do not deny; I merely say that this knowledge of his (*cognitio*) is not true science (*scientia*), because no knowledge which can be rendered doubtful should, it seems, be called science. Since he is supposed to be an atheist, he cannot be certain that he is not deceived even in those things that seem most evident to him, as has been sufficiently shown; and although this doubt may never occur to him, nevertheless it can occur to him, if he examines the question, or it may be suggested by someone else, and he will never be safe from it, unless he first acknowledges God.

My own interpretation of Descartes's position, in brief summary, is as follows. His aim is to build up a systematic body of knowledge (*scientia*) which will be immune to being recalled into doubt. He starts from what he takes to be a fact, that there are some propositions which, when clearly considered, are irresistible, and are so to the skeptic himself. Among these are the proofs of the existence and benevolence of God. So long as an inquirer is clearly considering, or (in a Cartesian phrase) intuiting, any irresistible proposition, he cannot doubt it and is not open to entertaining skeptical doubts; equally the skeptic himself must, in such a moment, lay aside his doubts. But no one who is going to develop a systematic body of knowledge can spend all his time intuiting one proposition, not even that of the existence of God, and when he is not considering such a proposition, some skeptic might make him doubt it. He might doubt some particular proposition, because he is not properly considering it, or he might entertain very general or hyperbolical doubt, and indeed wonder, in the abstract, whether anything that he clearly and distinctly perceived was true. Here, according to Descartes, it makes a difference whether the inquirer believes in God—the believer has a general answer to the general doubt, while the atheist does not. The atheist can only cite some clear and distinct propositions, and get the skeptic to assent, temporarily, to those propositions. The believer, however, has a general and systematic answer to a general and systematic doubt—an answer that rests in the existence and benevolence of God. Of course, the skeptic may doubt that, but he cannot doubt it while he intuits the proofs of it. So the believer can always recall the skeptic, unless the skeptic is willfully obstinate, to considering the existence and benevolence of God, and if the skeptic concentrates on those proofs, he will believe not only those propositions themselves but also something that follows from them —namely, that clear and distinct perceptions are reliable, and hence skepticism is unjustified. If the skeptic, ceasing to intuit the proofs, then reverts to objecting merely because he is no longer intuiting, we can point out that the use of propositions one is not at that instant intuiting is a minimal structural condition on getting on at all in the acquisition of systematic knowledge, and that just as it would be unreasonable to spend all one's time rehearsing one intuition, so it would be unreasonable to spend all one's time rehearsing the proofs of the general answer to skepticism, an answer which we nevertheless possess.

This interpretation of Descartes's answer involves three distinctive features of his position, besides his crucial acceptance of the proofs of God. One is his distinction between the situation in which one is actually intuiting an irresistible proposition and that in which one is merely remembering that one has done so; this has the consequence, of course, that one can entertain a doubt at the latter time which is impossible at the former. Another is the distinction between particular doubts about particular propositions, and the general doubts of the skeptic, at the limit of which is Descartes's own ultimate and hyperbolical doubt. The third feature is an element very characteristic of Descartes's general outlook which has nevertheless been neglected by commentators.[13] This is a pragmatic consideration, to the effect that the aim is to get on and construct *scientia*, engage in an ongoing scientific inquiry, and that it is *practically* unreasonable to spend one's time repeatedly answering skepticism. If skepticism can be answered, at the general level required by the hyperbolical doubt, then there are other things to do, and we have an assurance that we can do them. The skeptic has no reasonable claim, in terms of practical reason, to make us spend time on going round and round his problems, rather than making genuine progress (as we are now assured that we can) with the problems of science.

Descartes thought that he had put us in a position, once and for all, to have that assurance. He probably also thought that it was worthwhile for each of us, or at least some of us, to relive the process of doubt and recovery from it that is enacted so vividly in the *Meditations*, but he did not suppose that it was sensible to spend too much time on such inquiries. He not only converted skepticism from being an obstacle to metaphysical inquiry to being a tool of it, but characteristically placed both skepticism and metaphysical inquiry as essentially preliminaries relative to the real business of scientific investigation.

NOTES

References to Descartes's writings are made, by volume and page, to the standard edition of Charles Adam and Paul Tannery (most recent edition, Paris, 1964-1975). In the case of some letters, a page reference, preceded by the letter K, has been given to Anthony Kenny, *Descartes: Philosophical Letters* (Oxford, 1970).

1. For detailed discussion of Descartes's acquaintance with ancient and contemporary skepticism, see Richard Popkin, *The History of Scepticism from Erasmus to Spinoza* (Berkeley, Los Angeles and London, 1979), a revised edition of his *History of Scepticism from Erasmus to Descartes* (Assen, 1960).

2. This point is very clearly made by Myles Burnyeat in his "Idealism and Greek Philosophy: What Descartes Saw and Berkeley Missed," in *Idealism Past and Present*, ed. G. Vesey (London, 1982), where he quotes this passage.

3. The title of this famous work is very often mistranslated. See my *Descartes: The Project of Pure Enquiry* (Harmondsworth, 1978) (subsequently referred to as *PPE*), pp. 18-19, n. 4.

4. This is how Descartes represents the matter. He assumes that the pure intellectual power of judgment is not affected in sleep, and this assumption makes it harder for him to dispose of skepticism based on dreaming. For further discussion, see *PPE*, Appendix 3.

5. Popkin (*History of Scepticism*, pp. 180-181) interestingly speculates that the origin of this idea may lie in the famous trial at Loudun, concerned with demoniac possession. It should be noticed, however, that the trial was in 1634, three years before the publication of the *Discourse*, in which the idea does not occur. It does not appear until the *Meditations*, in 1641. The idea may go back to a passage in Cicero reporting arguments used by Academic skeptics about the powers of the gods (*Academica* II 47), though, if it does, Descartes's use of it (as of other ancient material) goes far beyond anything envisaged by the ancients themselves. E. M. Curley (*Descartes against the Skeptics* [Oxford, 1978]) points toward sources in Montaigne, but his evidence relates more to Descartes's account of God's relation to the eternal truths than to the (admittedly associated) issue of the *malin génie*.—On the Ciceronian material, see Burnyeat, "Idealism and Greek Philosophy."

6. See Popkin, *History of Scepticism*, pp. 174 ff., and notes, pp. 285-286.

7. Margaret Dauler Wilson, *Descartes* (London, 1978). It will be evident that I agree with Wilson when she says (p. 8) "While Descartes is, no doubt, concerned with the problem of certainty—of traditional skepticism—in its own right, he is also concerned to *use* this problem to present convincingly an anti-empiricist metaphysics, a form of (rationalist) 'scientific realism'" (emphasis in original).

8. A striking characteristic of contemporary science, which links the various features mentioned here, is the high degree of convergence that it displays. Some philosophers, however, regard this appearance of convergence as a cultural artifact. Richard Rorty, in his *Philosophy and the Mirror of Nature* (Princeton, 1980), seems to express this view, though in a notably self-destructive way. See, e.g., pp. 344-345: "It is less paradoxical . . . to stick to the classic notion of 'better describing what was already there' for physics. This is not because of deep epistemological or metaphysical considerations, but simply because, when we tell our Whiggish stories about how our ancestors gradually crawled up the mountain on whose (possibly false) summit we stand, we need to keep some things constant throughout the story. . . . Physics is the paradigm of 'finding' simply because it is hard (at least in the West) to tell a story of changing physical universes against the background of an unchanging Moral Law or poetic canon, but very easy to tell the reverse sort of story." The force of "simply because" in this passage would repay some exegesis. The fundamental difficulty is that, if the story that Rorty tells were true, then there would be no perspective from which he could express it in this way. If, for whatever reasons, we need to describe physics as an activity of finding out how nature already is, then the correct thing for everyone to say, including Rorty, is that physics is an activity of finding out how nature already is. This is just one example of a persistent confusion in Rorty's book between what might be called empirical and transcendental pragmatism.

9. Cf., e.g., J. M. Rist, *Stoic Philosophy* (Cambridge, 1969), pp. 133-151.

10. See Julia Annas, "Truth and Knowledge," in *Doubt and Dogmatism,* ed. M. Schofield, M. Burnyeat, and J. Barnes (Oxford, 1980). It must be said, however, that Annas does not succeed in distinguishing the two issues at all satisfactorily by means of her two questions (p. 100) "Are there any experiences whose veridicality can be guaranteed?" and "Can we know that there are any experiences whose veridicality can be guaranteed?" *Guarantee* is surely itself an epistemological notion.

11. Most recently by H. Frankfurt in *Demons, Dreamers and Madmen* (New York, 1970). For criticism, see *PPE,* pp. 35-36, n. 2, and pp. 197 ff.; and Curley, *Descartes against the Skeptics,* pp. 104-114 and elsewhere.

12. See *PPE,* pp. 188-207, and Curley, *Descartes against the Skeptics,* chap. 5 and references.

13. Curley's interesting treatment (*Descartes against the Skeptics*) rightly draws attention to the requirement that the skeptic should have to bring forward some grounds for doubt, a requirement which the classical skeptics accepted: it underlies, as Curley points out, the idea of *isostheneia.* He then bases his construction of Descartes's argument on the principle that what counts as a ground for doubt at one stage of the proceedings may not still count as one at a later stage. However, unless one appeals to a pragmatic dimension of the exchange with the skeptic, there is nothing to stop him from recalling the argument to an earlier stage. Curley's treatment is based, in effect, on the idea that a proposition can acquire more strength in the course of Descartes's inquiry, so that more strength will be needed in any consideration that could raise a doubt against it. But the claim that a given proposition has acquired a given degree of strength can itself have a doubt brought against it, which will be removed only by going back and intuiting the proposition and its supports once more. So the pragmatic dimension is needed, against constant recursion; and once we have that dimension, we do not need, for this problem at least, such an elaborate account as Curley offers of what a reason for doubt at any given stage needs to be.

14

Locke and Pyrrhonism: The Doctrine of Primary and Secondary Qualities

Martha Brandt Bolton

I

In the middle sections of the chapter in the *Essay* on primary and secondary qualities, Locke seems to argue for his distinction by citing some familiar facts about the variability of the sensible qualities of things.[1] He describes some familiar experiences of secondary qualities: the fact that the red and white colors of porphyry disappear in the dark, that pounding an almond changes its taste and color, that water may feel hot to one hand at the same time that it feels cold to the other. These facts are supposed to show, as Locke puts it, that the colors, tastes, and warmth we feel are not really in the stone, the almond, and the water; or, those objects do not resemble the ideas of colors, tastes, and warmth. These passages do not contain Locke's only argument for the doctrine of qualities, and they are not concerned to support the distinction as he initially states it. Still, the reasoning is especially interesting, because it depends on observations about sense experience. Reflection on the variability of a thing's perceived qualities is supposed to show something about what the thing is really like.

Locke's premises, but not his conclusions, bear a striking similarity to a pattern of reasoning typically used by skeptics of the Pyrrhonian school and found among the traditional "ten *tropes,* or modes." The *tropes,* recorded for instance by Sextus Empiricus, are a series of strategies for achieving suspense of judgment about the sensible qualities of things.

Now the strategy typically begins, as do Locke's arguments, by citing situations in which a thing appears first to have one sensible quality and then another. For instance, honey tastes sweet and pleasant to some, bitter and unpleasant to others; but, the skeptics say, there is no reason to prefer one appearance to the other, and so we cannot say what the real nature of the honey is; to do so is to be dogmatic.[2] Locke, of course, aims at no such skeptical suspense of judgment. His conclusion is a dogmatic thesis about what bodies really are, and are not, like. So far, this quick comparison of Locke's reasoning with a certain skeptical strategy suggests that Locke begins by citing the very sort of "variability" of sensible qualities that is thought by the skeptics to frustrate attempts to say what sensible things are really like, and ends with an antiskeptical conclusion about the properties of things. And this suggests the further possibility that Locke's arguments, as well as his distinction between primary and secondary qualities, are propounded to amend an error in the Pyrrhonians' reasoning about the sensible qualities of a thing.

The suggestion of this sort of link between Locke and Pyrrhonism seems to be well worth examining. So far as I know, it has not previously been discussed. In this section, I want to offer some historical evidence in support of it. I will point out that Locke had access to Pyrrhonian views and thus could hardly have been unaware of the contrast between his own treatment of the variability of appearances and theirs. Further, Pierre Bayle, a contemporary of Locke, links Pyrrhonism and the distinction between qualities in his famous *Dictionaire*. Finally, although recent work has emphasized the influence of Robert Boyle, I will argue that the text does not support the contention that Boyle's was the sole influence on Locke's doctrine of qualities. If the doctrine is not wholly derived from Boyle's theory of matter, then we may well look for influences from other sources. In section II, I will defend an interpretation of the arguments about porphyry, and the rest, which fits well with the suggested Pyrrhonian influence, as opposed to that of Boyle. And in section III, I will argue that Locke's doctrines are relevant to a certain Pyrrhonian strategy; in fact, Locke's views about primary and secondary qualities (if they are correct) show that two crucial assumptions of a typical skeptical way of reasoning are incorrect.

Before proceeding to the historical evidence, however, I want to correct some widely held assumptions about those arguments concerning porphyry, the almond, and the water. Most commentators regard them as weak and ill conceived. I want to urge, however, that they should not be dismissed on the easy grounds they often are. This point has no direct relevance to the suggested link between Locke and Pyrrhonism. Although the suggested link places a great deal of importance on those arguments, the suggestion may be correct regardless of their strength. But, because much of my discussion focuses on these arguments, I would like at the outset to clear the air by briefly considering three grounds on which they are often too readily dismissed.

In the first place, these arguments cite facts about the "variability" of colors, tastes, and so forth, in support of the contention that secondary qualities are importantly different from primary ones. As Berkeley pointed out, perceptions of the primary qualities of a thing are "variable," too. Berkeley, among others,[3] concluded that Locke simply overlooked this obvious fact and that it completely undermines his distinction. It is, however, very implausible that Locke made such an elementary error.[4] Others have concluded that Locke does not after all *argue* for his claims about secondary qualities from the "variability" of colors and the like.[5] But this view contradicts what seems obvious from the passages about porphyry, and the others. There is a third alternative which has so far been overlooked. It is that Locke cites "variability" of colors, and the like, in arguing for his thesis about secondary qualities, and *his point* is in part that a similar conclusion does not follow from the similar "variability" in perceptions of shape, motion, solidity, and the like. I will defend this interpretation in section II.

A second problem, also related to Berkeley's attack on the distinction between primary and secondary qualities, is widely thought to defeat Locke's attempts to argue for it. These arguments *assume* one matter of central interest to Berkeley: that there are bodies distinct from sensory ideas and corresponding to them. If Locke's arguments for his distinction between qualities are made to bear the weight of establishing this claim about existence, they are bound to fail.[6] In fact, although Locke states his doctrine about qualities in terms which assume that bodies exist independently of perception, his doctrine can be separated from that assumption. As we will see, in the arguments which concern us, Locke's main contention is that it is impossible that bodies should resemble the ideas of colors, tastes, and so forth; by implication, it is possible that bodies should resemble ideas of shapes, motions, and the rest. Locke typically *states* his position in terms that imply that bodies exist;[7] for instance, there is nothing in bodies like our ideas of colors and tastes. But the main claim, concerning the *possibility* of resemblance, is independent of the assumption about existence. Locke makes no attempt to argue for the existential assumption in his discussion of qualities, and perhaps he nowhere successfully defends it.[8] But that, in itself, does not vitiate his arguments in support of the basic distinction between primary and secondary qualities.

There is a third reason why Locke's arguments are often dismissed.

They are supposed to show that certain ideas do not resemble bodies, but it is difficult to explicate clearly Locke's notion of resemblance. Some philosophers reject it out of hand, on the grounds that it could only make sense on the discredited view that ideas are immediate objects of perception.[9] Even if such objects of perception are allowed, it is difficult to say how ideas are to be compared to bodies. In what sense is an idea supposed to "have" properties like warmth and coldness, motion, solidity, or shape? What is it about an idea that is supposed to be compared to a body? But, whatever the problems with the notion, resemblance is central to Locke's doctrine of qualities. It is virtually certain that Locke was aware of certain difficulties in the view that ideas can resemble bodies; this was debated within Cartesian circles, and there is good evidence Locke studied the controversy during his travels in France.[10] It hardly seems likely that Locke would have chosen to state his position in controversial terms, had he not thought his own use of them an appropriate way to express his view.

I want now to turn to the evidence for a link between Locke and Pyrrhonism. The immediate textual support rests on the fact that both Locke's arguments and Pyrrhonian *tropes* draw their conclusions from facts about the "variability" of perception. It is likely that Locke was fully aware of this, for there is reason to think he was familiar with Pyrrhonian ways of arguing. Locke does not mention the skeptical view in his discussion of primary and secondary qualities; in fact, he identifies the position against which he is arguing as the *common* view of qualities.[11] This is easy to understand within the framework of my suggestion. I am not proposing that Locke aims to refute skepticism about qualities by an explicit attack of the sort he launches against the doctrine of innate ideas. My suggestion is rather that Locke's aim is to preclude the Pyrrhonian reasoning and the impasse about a thing's qualities to which it leads. What Locke identifies as the common view of qualities is presupposed in the typical pattern of skeptical reasoning (as we will see). To frustrate this way of reasoning, it is enough to expose an error in the common view and to replace it with an account of qualities not open to the typical skeptical argument. Locke might well have thought it unnecessary to mention the skeptics or rehearse their reasoning in order to achieve this end.

There is reason to think Locke knew that others drew a skeptical conclusion from the "variability" of perception. His collection of books included Diogenes Laertius's *Lives*, where one version of the ten *tropes* is sketched, and Michel de Montaigne's *Essais*, in which versions of these strategies are used.[12] There is good evidence that Locke studied works by Pierre Gassendi in which the *tropes* are recorded at length;[13] and it is not unlikely that he knew about the use of such arguments by his contemporary Joseph Glanville.[14] There is also some textual evidence outside of the discussion of primary and secondary qualities that Locke was familiar with Pyrrhonian arguments about qualities. In another context, Locke introduces the possibility that different people may be affected with different sorts of color sensations when presented with the same object (whatever causes ideas of yellow in one may produce ideas of blue in another, and vice versa); this suggestion is very likely to have come from a skeptical source.[15] Moreover, Locke's reason for posing this skeptical suggestion is to make an antiskeptical point dependent upon his account of qualities. Even if the color sensations of two people are systematically different, Locke claims, both have "true" ideas of a thing's color, understood in accord with Locke's account of secondary qualities as powers.

Through Gassendi's work, Locke not only had access to Pyrrhonian views, but also knew that philosopher's antiskeptical program. In *Syntagma*, which Locke seems to have studied, Gassendi presents the *tropes* in lengthy detail and then goes on to reply to the skeptical view. Gassendi's general influence on Locke has long been recognized (although given surprisingly little attention).[16] It is thus possible that part of his influence was to enlist Locke's interest in propounding views able to withstand the Pyrrhonian attack on claims about sensible qualities. Furthermore, it is likely that Locke's exposure to Gassendi's view, and to views of others influenced by Pyrrhonism, was most intense during the years he spent in France. These contacts have special interest because of their relation to Locke's first formulation of the doctrine of primary and secondary qualities. Although Locke wrote two drafts of the *Essay* in 1671, before his extended stay in France (1675-1679), these early drafts make no mention of the doctrine. It first appears in the draft of 1685.[17] There are, then, historical facts that make it entirely possible that the Pyrrhonian tradition, possibly through Gassendi's work, was a significant influence on Locke's doctrine of qualities.

Further historical evidence comes from the *Dictionaire* of Pierre Bayle. It indicates a connection between Pyrrhonism and the "moderns" who make a distinction between colors and so forth, on the one hand and shape, motion, and so forth on the other. Bayle apparently has the Cartesians in mind, but he would probably have included Locke among them in this connection. The article in Bayle's *Dictionaire* on Pyrrho says:[18]

One hardly knew the name of Sextus Empiricus in our schools [and] the methods he proposed so subtly for bringing about suspense of judgment . . . , when Gassendi gave us an abridgement of it, which opened our eyes. Cartesianism put the final touches on this, and now no good philosopher any longer doubts that the skeptics were right to maintain that the qualities of bodies that strike our senses are only appearances. Every one of us can justly say, "I feel heat in the presence of fire," but not "I know that fire is, in itself, such as it appears to me." This is the way the ancient Pyrrhonists spoke. Today the new philosophy speaks more positively. Heat, smells, colors, and the like, are not in the objects of our senses. They are modifications of my soul. I know that bodies are not at all as they appear to me. They would have wished to exempt extension and motion, but they could not. For if the objects of our sense appear colored, hot, cold, odoriferous, and yet they are not so, why can they not appear extended and shaped, in rest and in motion, though they are not so?

The Pyrrhonians, Bayle says, disclaim knowledge of whether, for instance, the heat one feels is in the fire itself. The moderns take the dogmatic view that heat is a modification of the mind and, on Cartesian principles, thereby not a quality of body.[19] Apparently, the moderns overcome the web of skeptical strategies aimed at suspense of judgment about the qualities of the fire. (Bayle seems to think that if their reasoning works for odors, colors, and heat, it works *in the same way* for extension and motion; I return to this criticism, as it applies to Locke's view, at the end of section II.) This passage shows that a contemporary of Locke took the modern distinction between qualities to be opposed to the Pyrrhonian view about sensible qualities, and that is the sort of connection between Locke and the skeptics which I am suggesting.

A final indirect argument for my suggestion is, as I have said, the inadequacy of the usual account of the historical influence on Locke's doctrine of qualities.[20] On this account, Locke adopted his doctrine from the "natural philosophy" of Robert Boyle. According to Boyle's theory, the real properties of matter are the mechanical affections (primary qualities); sensory ideas, like all phenomena, are produced by the sizes, shapes, and motions of (often insensible) particles. Large portions of the works in which Boyle expounds this "corpuscular hypothesis" consist of reports of laboratory experiments. His argument for the theory is the sort of inductive one by which we expect a theory to be confirmed: his experimental results and observations are best explained on the corpuscular view. Following Boyle, Locke is supposed to be propounding the same hypothesis and to argue for it, to the extent he does so, by pointing out its explanatory power. Locke's point about the qualities of porphyry and the rest is supposed to be that they can be explained by attributing nothing but primary qualities to bodies. By and large, on this account, Locke makes little effort to support this claim. Locke's purpose in urging a doctrine supported, not by his own arguments, but by the work of others, is supposed to have been to report upon the accomplishments of the new "experimental philosophy."[21]

There is no doubt that in the course of his discussion, Locke appeals to

Boyle's hypothesis; and I think it is correct and useful to emphasize the influence of the corpuscular theory on Locke's thought.[22] But there is reason to doubt that Locke's doctrine is identical with Boyle's and that his interest in it was the same as that of the "natural philosophers." For one thing, Locke's discussion of porphyry, and the rest, takes quite a different turn from that suggested on this account. A comparison of a rather similar passage from Boyle's *Origin of Forms and Qualities* illustrates the point. Boyle touches on the question, as does Locke, whether "there is in bodies anything . . . like our ideas" of colors and the like; his answer is that it is not *necessary* to suppose there is, because we can explain what we observe solely in terms of primary qualities.[23] *Locke's* response to the question is that it is *impossible* that bodies should be like those ideas. (It is true that Locke then adds that bodies have particles whose primary qualities cause those ideas; but this is a further point.) Locke makes very little of what the corpuscular theory can explain; he mentions it explicitly only once.[24] As I will argue in section II, his arguments against resemblance are of quite another sort.

Another objection to taking Boyle's concerns to have been the main influence on Locke comes from Locke's explanation of his reasons for discussing the corpuscular hypothesis. He explains, near the end of his treatment of qualities:[25]

I have . . . been engaged in Physical Enquiries a little farther than, perhaps, I intended. But it [was] necessary, to make the Nature of Sensation a little understood, and to make the difference between *Qualities in Bodies, and the* Ideas *produced by them in the Mind,* to be distinctly conceived, without which it were impossible to discourse intelligibly of them; . . .

Locke says here that his main aim was *not* to discuss "physical enquiries," the sort of question answered by the corpuscular hypothesis. Physical considerations were only mentioned as a means to clarify the difference between qualities (in general) and ideas, a point needed for *intelligible discourse* on qualities. In the remark that follows, Locke asks pardon again for introducing natural philosophy, excusing himself by saying it was necessary in order to distinguish those ideas that resemble bodies from those that do not. Here, again, the apology indicates that Locke's aim in making the claim about resemblance is not primarily to instruct his readers about natural philosophy. No doubt Locke shared with Boyle a keen interest in the natural philosophy of qualities. But these remarks show that indulging that interest is not the *main* reason for Locke's discussion of qualities. The way is open then to look to the Pyrrhonian tradition to account, at least in part, for Locke's interest in sensible qualities.

II

My aim in this section is to defend an interpretation of Locke's arguments from "variable" perceptions which favors the suggestion of Pyrrhonian influence rather than that of Boyle. But before turning to the arguments about porphyry, and the others, we need quickly to review the points Locke makes before coming to these arguments. They occur in the middle sections of the chapter on qualities, and several important claims are made in the earlier sections.

Even before distinguishing between primary and secondary qualities, Locke gives a general explanation of what qualities are: "powers in bodies" to produce "ideas in the mind." He stresses that it is a confusion to take an idea to be a quality—for instance, to take the ideas of whiteness or roundness to be *in* a snowball. (He himself admits to sometimes speaking of "ideas in things," when he means "qualities.")[26] After this general account of qualities, Locke argues that the qualities he labels "primary" (extension, motion, solidity, etc.) are "inseparable from bodies in what state so ever they be." In contrast, those he calls "secondary" are declared to be "nothing in the bodies but powers to produce ideas by the primary qualities of the insensible parts."[27] This first statement of the distinction (in which the intended contrast is not entirely clear) is said to imply a second thesis, the one about resemblance: the ideas of primary qualities *resemble* bodies, but the ideas produced by secondary qualities do *not*.[28] Our observations about porphyry, almonds, and water occur in the subsequent discussion of the resemblance claim. The basic argument against resemblance is the same in all three cases; but each successive version of it makes a somewhat different point.

(i) The porphyry example

The fullest statement of the basic argument is in section 19:

> Let us consider the red and white colours in *Porphyre*: Hinder light but from striking on it, and its Colours Vanish; it no longer produces any such *Ideas* in us: Upon the return of Light, it produces these appearances on us again. Can any one think any real alterations are made in the *Porphyre*, by the presence or absence of Light; and that those *Ideas* of whiteness and redness, are really in *Porphyre* in the light, when 'tis plain *it has no colour in the dark*?

The question is evidently intended as an argument in support of the claim, as Locke puts it here, that "the ideas of whiteness and redness are [not] really in porphyry." Strictly speaking, his own distinction between qualities and ideas has it that *no idea* is in a body; Locke considers it more accurate to say that the ideas are not *like* any quality in the stone. Apparently, Locke is opposing what he identifies as the common view that colors as they appear to us are genuine qualities of bodies.

I suggest that the argument implied by the rhetorical question is this:[29]
(1) Porphyry looks red in the light, but its color disappears in the dark (i.e., it does not produce ideas of red in the dark).
(2) The "real" qualities of porphyry are the same whether it is in the light or in the dark.
(3) It is inconceivable that the porphyry should have a property resembling the idea of red at the same time that its color has disappeared (i.e., it is not producing the idea of red).
(4) Therefore, the porphyry does not have a "real" quality resembling the idea of red.

The force of the whole argument turns on premise (3). The first premise simply records a certain "variability" in perception of the colors of porphyry. The second involves Locke's notion of a "real" quality. The most conspicuous element in this notion is that a thing's real qualities are ones it has "whether our senses perceive them or no";[30] they are stable with respect to the conditions of perception and presence of perceivers. The force of premise (2) is, then, that the temporary absence of light does not affect the stone's stable, perceiver-independent properties. Now it would be a mistake, I think, to suppose that Locke covertly appeals to the corpuscular hypothesis in this description of the real properties of porphyry. Locke's contention is simply based on common conceptions. After all, it is commonly supposed that the presence or absence of light does not create a stone's qualities or destroy them; light only allows us to see what is supposed to be there all along. So, premise (2) is nothing more than common sense; the burden of Locke's argument against the common view rests on premise (3).

The third premise also bears the weight of differentiating the primary qualities of porphyry from its colors. Locke maintains that nothing is wrong with the resemblance view of porphyry's shape, motion, and the like, so there must be some stage in the argument where he thinks those qualities part company with colors. As I have said, it is most implausible to suppose Locke thought premise (1) was the crucial one in this regard; it is evident that the primary qualities of the stone are "variable" in just the same way its colors are. And the second premise does not concern colors, as opposed to shapes or motions. So, it is the third premise that makes the important difference in Locke's eyes. To uphold the distinction between colors and the primary qualities, then, Locke is committed to yet another claim:

(3') It is conceivable that porphyry should have a property resembling the idea of a shape, e.g., a cube (a motion, a position, extension, solidity, etc.) at the same time that its shape (or whatever) has disappeared.

In order to understand Locke's argument, and the basis of his distinction between primary qualities and secondary ones, we need to see why he thought (3) and (3′) are true.

It seems we will have to get clear about idea/body resemblance before we know how to understand these claims. As I have said, Locke had studied disputes among Cartesians on the related issues of what ideas are, how they represent, and whether they can resemble bodies. Nevertheless, he offers no technical explanation of these points. He seems to think that the rough notion of a sensory idea, on which he relies throughout the *Essay*, suffices to clarify the claims about resemblance that arise in his attack on the common view of qualities. I will suppose without further explanation that sensory ideas have distinctive contents. An idea of red, for instance, I will take to be a sensory awareness of something's redness; that is, something's redness as it appears to us is the content of an idea of red. Now the common view is that porphyry is red whether in the light or dark and its redness is that color *as it appears.* Commonly, when we think of the color of the stone in the dark, we think of the stone as if it were appearing red; but, as Locke stresses, no appearance actually exists in the dark. To conceive the stone to be in the dark *and* to have the quality that is the content of an idea of red, we must manage to conceive the stone to have *that* quality even though its color does not appear. We must, in other words, find something in the content of the idea that we can conceive to be a feature of the unperceived stone. Locke questions whether we can do so, and this is his question about resemblance between the idea and the stone. Idea/body resemblance is a matter of the unperceived body having a feature that is (at least part of) the content of the idea. Resemblance enters into Locke's attack on the common view; for, if an idea of red cannot be conceived to resemble an unperceived stone, then it is inconceivable that the stone is red as it appears when it is not appearing red.

Locke seems to think that inspection of the idea of red suffices to show that its content has no salient features that can be conceived to characterize the unperceived stone. He offers no argument for this. If I understand him correctly, however, one sort of consideration that supports claim (3) is our apparent inability to describe an idea of red. If we cannot say what is distinctive of the content of the idea, then we cannot describe anything common to it and an unperceived stone. Neither can we explain how something that is unperceived and red as that color appears differs from something that is unperceived and green. Again, if we cannot conceive anything to be distinctive of the porphyry's redness as it appears *except* its sensory appearance, then we cannot conceive what it is for the porphyry to have that quality (redness as it appears) when unperceived, and we cannot understand how porphyry in the dark differs from things with other colors. To be sure, we may suppose that red things have a distinctive physical property such as reflecting light-waves of a particular sort the problem is in understanding that physical property to be the stone's redness as it appears. Merely superficial predicates common to the stone and the content of the idea will not suffice. For instance, the fact that both porphyry and the color red are mentioned in the *Essay* is not to the point. What is required is, roughly speaking, a feature common to the content of an idea of red and the unperceived stone which is part of the intrinsic character of each.

Locke considers the claim in (3') to be just as evident as the contrasting claim in (3). As I understand it, (3') is the contention that the content of an idea of the square shape of a surface, for instance, has features readily conceived to be shared by the stone when unperceived. Having a surface bounded by four straight lines, or described by a certain algebraic equation, or with infinitely many lines of symmetry through an interior point are examples of such features, I suppose. The important fact about the contents of ideas of shape, size, motion, position, and solidity is that there are various ways of describing them and distinguishing among them. We can understand what distinguishes a square as it appears (visually, say) and an oval as it appears in a way that allows us to conceive how a square surface differs from an oval one even when the surfaces are not appearing.

I want to make a couple of observations about Locke's position on (3) and (3'). Those claims, as I understand them, are based on features of what is perceived when one sees something red, as compared with something square. They do not involve the view that what is perceived has the metaphysical status of a modification of mind. So, for instance, it is not Locke's argument that the content of an idea of red is a sensation and, as such, incapable of belonging to a body or existing unperceived. It is also important to see that Locke does not covertly presuppose a Boylean conception of body. It is not that he assumes bodies to have shape, position, and so forth, and thus to resemble contents of the sensory ideas of shape, and the rest. Instead, Locke's position rests on intrinsic features of sensory ideas of colors and shapes and the resources they supply for conceiving their contents to characterize unperceived things. Finally, however, although Locke's claim about colors is initially plausible, it is not entirely convincing. It rests on an argument from ignorance, or perhaps on the false assumption that whatever is distinctive of ideas of various colors is manifest. In fact, even if we have failed to notice a distinctive, separable feature of the content of an idea of red, one which could belong to something unperceived, there may still be one.[31]

To summarize: the basis of Locke's claims (3) and (3') is the view that

the content of an idea of red, unlike the contents of ideas of primary qualities, has no distinctive feature it could conceivably share with a body
when unperceived. Thus, to suppose that the unperceived porphyry had
the stone's redness as it appears, we would have to make the absurd supposition that the stone is appearing red when it is unperceived.
(ii) The almond example
     The second of Locke's arguments based on the "variability" of quali-
ties is:

Pound an Almond, and the clear white *Colour* will be altered into a dirty one,
and the sweet *Taste* into an oily one. What real Alteration can the beating of the
Pestle make in any Body, but an Alteration of the *Texture* of it?

Jonathan Bennett has urged that the argument is fallacious: "the assumption that pounding can cause only primary quality changes in the object
pounded is false, as is shown by what happens when an almond is
pounded with a pestle."[32] Bennett overlooks the fact that Locke has the
common view of secondary qualities under attack. Locke certainly does
not deny that pounding changes an almond's color and taste. His point
concerns the nature of the change. It is not the sort of real change in the
almond it is commonly supposed to be.
     Locke's question about what happens when an almond is subjected to
the pestle is meant to bring out that the nut's texture, color, and taste are
altered, and that of these qualities only texture is real. Now these claims
are implied by the corpuscular hypothesis, and it might seem that Locke's
only support for them is a tacit appeal to that theory. On this view,
Locke's question is quite without force as an argument against the common view of the almond's color and taste; its polemical value depends
entirely on prior acceptance of Boyle's physics, a circumstance that
makes it unnecessary to argue for the Boylean account of qualities. On
the contrary, I think Locke's question *is* intended to give a reason to
reject the common view of colors and tastes, quite independently of the
corpuscular theory. We would *commonly* suppose that pounding an
almond mainly affects its texture, color, and taste; and we would suppose the almond's texture to be real. Locke assumes all this, not because
it is Boylean theory, but because it is the common view.
     He wants to challenge the further common view that the color and
taste of the almond are real, that is, qualities the almond has whether or
not it is perceived. From this point, it seems to me the reasoning proceeds
as in the porphyry case. We can conceive an *unperceived* almond to have
powers to produce ideas of a clear white color and a dirty one, a sweet
taste and an oily one; Locke urges that we ought to think of it that way.

Of course, this is to reject the common view that the nut has its colors and tastes *as they appear to us* whether or not it is perceived. To conceive what happens to the nut in accordance with the common view, we would need to find features in the contents of the ideas of a change from clear white to dirty color, and from sweet to oily taste, which we could understand to be features of the almond when unperceived. Locke is convinced that inspection of these ideas shows such features do not exist, and thus grounds his attack on the common view.

(iii) The example of water that feels hot and cold

Locke's third case is the water that feels hot and cold at the same time:

> *Ideas* being thus distinguished and understood, we may be able to give an Account, how the same Water, at the same time, may produce the *Idea* of Cold by one Hand, and of Heat by the other: Whereas it is impossible, that the same Water, if those *Ideas* were really in it, should at the same time be both Hot and Cold. For if we imagine *Warmth*, as it is *in our Hands*, to be *nothing but a certain sort and degree of Motion in the minute Particles of our Nerves*, . . . we may understand, how it is possible, that the same Water may at the same time produce the Sensation of Heat in one Hand, and Cold in the other; . . .

Here Locke does refer to the explanatory potential of a theory about primary qualities of insensible particles, but it is easy to exaggerate his claims about what such a theory explains as well as the role of such claims in his actual argument. It is important to notice that the resemblance view of the ideas of heat and cold is rejected on the grounds that it is *impossible*. An impossible theory, to be sure, does not adequately explain the phenomenon. But failure of the resemblance view in the area of explanation is not the reason Locke gives for rejecting it.

Locke takes it to be evident that it *is* impossible that the water should be like the ideas of heat and cold. The argument is, I think, a variation on the previous two. In this case, Locke assumes, the common view has it that both the water's warmth and its coldness as they appear are real qualities of the water. It is interesting that he disallows the view that the water really has one of these qualities, but not the other. Here Locke seems to depart from the common view and tacitly to follow instead the skeptical suggestion that neither appearance is preferable to the other. Now if the water is warm as it appears, there is a feature distinctive of the content of an idea of its warmth which the water has and by which it is distinguished from (even unperceived) things that are cold. At the same time, if the water is cold as it appears, it also has a feature distinctive of the content of an idea of its coldness, and the water shares this feature with all those things (perceived or not) that are cold. The water is thus distinguished from things that are cold at the same time that it has what is distinctive of such things. This seems impossible, and that is Locke's complaint against the common view of the water's qualities.

Locke does favor the corpuscular account of warmth and coldness. But the advantage of the corpuscular account over the common view is not, in the first instance, that the preferred account offers better explanations. It is merely that the corpuscular theory is possible. Moreover, Locke says that the theory that ideas of heat and cold are caused by changes in the motions of particles of the nerves "may account" for the water's feeling both hot and cold. He does not say that this very general proposal actually does explain the case. What I want to bring out is that it is not clear that Locke's talk about "explanatory power" goes beyond the claim that it is *possible* that the phenomenon might be explained in terms of a corpuscularian account.

If I am right, the claim about primary qualities for which Locke mainly contends is that it is *possible* that they are real and that things are like our ideas of them. His position on the matter of whether objects really *do* have primary qualities is significantly illuminated by the way he continues the passage I have just quoted. He goes on to say that if we suppose a corpuscularian account,

we may understand, how it is possible, that the same Water may at the same time produce the sensation of Heat in one Hand, and Cold in the other; which yet Figure never does, that never producing the *Idea* of a square by one Hand, which has produced the *Idea* of a Globe by another.

Now I take it to be most unlikely that Locke denies or overlooks the obvious fact that objects *do*, in some cases, appear spherical under certain conditions and cubical under others. With this in view, Locke's remark that such contrary appearances do *not* occur in certain circumstances becomes unexpectedly significant. It then suggests that if certain experiences of that sort were to occur, they would refute the common view that bodies have real qualities like our ideas of shape, size, motion, solidity, and the rest. As it happens, however, we do not find that these refuting experiences occur. All in all, Locke's position seems to be that the cases of contrary appearances of a thing's primary qualities which do occur are compatible with the common view, but that that view is open to falsification by hypothetical cases such as he describes.

No, details are provided. Locke gives no account of how we arrive, in actual cases, at an opinion about the shape of a thing, consistent with the common view that it resembles various *contrary* ideas of its shape. (It has, however, been noticed by a few commentators that Locke is not committed to an exact resemblance between object and idea.[33] So, to take the standard example of the tower, it is open to Locke to say that its real shape is like the idea of a circle in one way and like the idea of a square in another. Given the many respects in which an unperceived object can conceivably resemble the contents of ideas of shapes, a resemblance in different respects to ideas of contrary shapes is easily conceivable.) By the same token, Locke does not say why we would be *unable* to suppose his hypothetical object has a shape like both the ideas of a sphere and a cube. My suggestion is that what is crucial in the description of the hypothetical case is that the contrary ideas occur under identical conditions. Of course, if the situation actually occurred, we would *look for* a difference, say, in the neural processes begun in the two hands; but that is exactly why Locke's omission of any difference seems to be the important feature of his case. When an object pressed firmly against one's hand produces the idea of a cube, the common view will have it that the object *is* a cube; in Lockean terms, we suppose the idea and object resemble each other in respect of a feature distinctive of cubes (having twelve edges equal in length, for instance). But when under the very same conditions the object produces the idea of a sphere, the common view will be that the object is also a sphere. Just as the water cannot be like the ideas of warmth and coldness, the object cannot have features distinctive of both the contents of ideas of a cube and a sphere. So, should this hypothetical situation occur, Locke seems to think, we would be forced to retract the opinion that shape is a real quality of the object felt.

In spite of the lack of detail in Locke's account, I think this remark helps to clarify his views on the difference between primary and secondary qualities. In an important passage I quoted earlier, Pierre Bayle poses a challenge to the distinction between primary and secondary qualities as he understood it: "If the objects of our sense appear colored, hot, cold, odoriferous, and yet they are not so, why can they not appear extended and shaped, in rest and in motion, though they are not so?" Locke's response is that, indeed, objects might appear extended, shaped, and so on, and not be so. Experience could lead us to this conclusion although so far it has given us no reason to deny that objects have extension, shapes, and so on. But the possibility that objects which cause ideas of primary qualities might not really have such qualities does not collapse the distinction between them and the secondary ones. For it is also possible that objects *should* have primary qualities in accordance with the common view, whereas it is *not possible*, according to Locke, that objects should really be like the ideas of colors, odors, and the like.

III

In the last section, I urged an interpretation of Locke's arguments from "variable" perceptions, and I tried to show that Locke's main concern is not the same as Boyle's. As I have said, if Locke's doctrine of qualities shows an influence that was not from Boyle, then it may well have been from the Pyrrhonians. My suggestion is that Locke's dogmatic doctrine of qualities was formulated in response to a line of argument from the *tropes.* In this section, I want to show that Locke's views on primary and secondary qualities, if correct, pose two problems for the skeptics' reasoning.

In general, Pyrrhonians aim to avoid making judgments about how a thing is and to assert only opinions about how it *seems* to be. The basic strategy is this: any proposed judgment about how a thing is can be opposed by a contrary competing claim, and skeptics suggest that neither opinion can reasonably be preferred above the other; neither can then be asserted without dogmatism. The traditional ten *tropes* are ways of executing this strategy on judgments about sensible qualities. Roughly speaking, each *trope* cites a way of varying percipients or circumstances so that a thing seems first to have one quality and then an opposing one.

The various *tropes* are developed somewhat differently by the authors I have mentioned, but they follow a more or less common pattern. The following argument sketch is based on a frequently used example and follows the pattern of the "fourth *trope*" in the usual listing. It serves to give a general idea of one strain of argument found in the *tropes*:[34]

(1) The air in the bath hall feels hot to a person who enters the room from the cold outside.

(2) The air in the room feels cool to a person who steps into the room from a hot bath.

(3) It seems there is no way to settle whether the impression of the air's warmth or that of the air's coolness is to be preferred.

(4) Therefore, it seems that although we can say how the air seems to each person to be, we cannot say what its "real nature" is.

A number of interesting points about the argument require study. But for our purposes, it is especially important that premise (3) presupposes an opposition between the sensory experiences reported in (1) and (2). These reports must be understood as making, or at least supporting, contrary claims about the properties or nature of the air.[35] As a result, premise (1), for instance, cannot be understood as saying merely that the air *feels* hot, or presents a certain sensory appearance; for, if (2) is also understood that way, the opposition between the two premises is lost. The contrary claims are that the air *is* hot and that the air *is* cold. In other words, the premises must be understood as reports that it feels to a perceiver as if the air *is* hot (cold). To bring out the opposition between (1) and (2) more clearly, they might be restated:

(1') It seems to a person coming from the outside that (A) the air in a certain room is hot.

(2') It seems to a person coming from a hot bath that (B) the air in the room is cold.

Without the opposition brought out in these two statements, the skeptical thesis in (3) would have no point.

Locke's claims, explicit and implicit, about primary and secondary qualities challenge the skeptics' assumptions about premises like (1') and (2'). In a word, his rejection of the common, resemblance view of secondary qualities challenges the assumption that claims like (A) and (B) (about *secondary* qualities) are opposed. And his implied contention that actual experiences do not lead us to attribute contrary primary qualities to a thing challenges the supposition that where premises like (1') and (2') about *primary* qualities are concerned, *both* such premises are true. I will explain more fully the details of these two different challenges.

Before proceeding, however, I want to make an observation about the background of Locke's position as compared to the skeptics'. Locke's whole discussion of primary and secondary qualities presupposes his initial contrast between "qualities in bodies" and "ideas in the mind." The contrast between ideas and qualities lets Locke describe a thing's sensory appearance without thereby attributing to it anything but the power to produce certain ideas. At the outset of the skeptical argument, no such distinction is in view, but something like it emerges at the end. The argument starts with the presumption that what we perceive (at least sometimes) reveals the nature of a thing; the whole point is that this presumption leads to an impossible choice among diverse and opposing appearances. The outcome, that we have no way of knowing whether what we perceive reveals the real nature of an object, suggests a distinction between a thing's appearance and its real nature not unlike Locke's contrast between idea and quality. But, of course, Locke insists that at least we know the object to have the power to appear in various ways. Moreover, Locke goes beyond the skeptical appearance/reality contrast to ask whether it is *even possible* that an object should really be like certain of its appearances.

I said that if Locke's arguments about the ideas of color and so on are sound, then claims like (A) and (B) (about secondary qualities) are *not* opposed. There are, Locke maintains, two views about such claims. On the common, resemblance view, (A) for instance is understood as:

(A1) The air in the room resembles the idea of heat.

Now this claim is opposed to the claim that the air resembles the idea of cold in some distinctive way. But if Locke is right, the claim in (A1) is inconceivable, for there is no respect in which we can understand the air to be like the distinctive content of the idea of its heat. On the alternative view of (A) which Locke proposes, it is:

(A2) The air in the room has the power to produce the idea of heat (by the primary qualities of its insensible parts).

On this sort of reading of (A) and (B), there is no opposition between the two. By exposing the inconceivability of the common view, Locke's position undermines the skeptical reasoning where secondary qualities are concerned. Without opposing claims about the qualities of a thing, there is no material for the argument of the *tropes*.

If the Lockean thesis does frustrate the skeptical argument, however, it is only when the thesis is isolated from other skeptical strategies. Pyrrhonians unquestionably have resources for replying to the charge that a version of the *tropes* presupposes an incoherent view about secondary qualities. The reply would consist of urging that the charge is to be neither accepted nor rejected; the argument, neither conceded nor defended. Certainly Locke's thesis is open to treatment by a variety of techniques toward this end. For instance, there is the fact that Locke rejects the commonly accepted view of colors; no matter how plausible his argument against that view may be, his conclusion is opposed to the common view, and there is room for a skeptic to urge that there is no way to settle the dispute. Now it may well be that Locke, for his part, has a general strategy for defending his views from this sort of skeptical attack. I do not, however, want to consider that aspect of Locke's epistemology here.[36] If he does have such a strategy, it is not part of his doctrine of primary and secondary qualities. The objection that doctrine poses to the *tropes* is clearly not a general antiskeptical defense of claims about secondary qualities. Still, if it is accepted (pending the outcome of all-out debate about Pyrrhonism), it keeps a skeptic from employing our version of the *tropes* as it stands. It forces the skeptic either to espouse an incoherent view of secondary qualities or to urge suspense of judgment on grounds which do not presume that reports of a thing's "variable" secondary qualities are mutually inconsistent. In fact, this limited result fits well with Locke's remark that his purpose was to make it possible to "discourse intelligibly" about qualities.

Locke's treatment of the primary qualities is, of course, quite different. He allows that the common view of them may be correct; his view poses no objection to the assumption that claims like (A) and (B) about a thing's *primary* qualities are opposed. But Locke's implicit contention about primary qualities, based on his remark about the hypothetical object that feels like both a sphere and a cube, poses a different problem for the skeptic's reasoning. Locke's implicit contention is that *actual* experiences do not support contrary beliefs about the primary qualities of a thing (although certain possible experiences would do so). Thus, in pairs of premises like (1') and (2') about primary qualities, it actually turns out that at least one premise or the other is false.

Take the familiar example of the tower. On Locke's view, the tower causes the ideas of a circle and a square; but this does not mean that a perceiver is thereby inclined to think that the tower is circular or to think that it is square. In other words, although the tower *looks* circular and *looks* square, it does not follow that it seems to a perceiver as if the tower *is* circular and square. I suggested earlier that Locke might give as a reason for this, that the perceiver takes the conditions of perception into account in judging the primary qualities of a thing. Realizing that the tower looks circular *from afar*, the perceiver will not judge that it *is* circular (nor, presumably, that it is square either). Although Locke does not develop this sort of point, it is suggested by his remark about the hypothetical object we would be inclined to think was both a cube and a sphere.

Locke's remark calls attention to the fact that the premises of the skeptical argument should not be granted simply on the grounds that there are "variable" perceptions of an object's primary qualities. It is not that the opposing pair of premises the skeptical argument requires *cannot* be supplied. Locke admits, indeed points out, that our experiences *could* support contrary beliefs about something's shape. The force of the point is in showing how far the familiar instances of "variability" are from being of this sort. The skeptic is called up on the presumption that the way something appears to the senses is the way it seems to a perceiver to be, and this poses a challenge for the skeptical way of arguing from the *tropes*.

In conclusion, what can be said of the suggestion that Locke propounded his doctrine of primary and secondary qualities to forestall the Pyrrhonian way of arguing? I think it has considerable plausibility. The fit between Locke's doctrine and the skeptical reasoning seems to be a very good one. That is, the Pyrrhonian argument I sketched presumes that reports of "variable" perceptions of something's qualities are mutually incompatible; and I have argued that Locke's views raise two sorts of barriers against this presumption. Moreover, in moving against the skeptics' assumption, Locke can be seen to be pursuing his stated purpose of making distinctions needed for intelligible discourse about qualities. To be sure, the fact that Locke's views constitute a certain reply to the Pyrrhonians does not show that Locke intended them as such. But I have argued that Locke would have been aware of the relation between his doctrine of qualities and the skeptics' views. There is a genuine historical possibility of Pyrrhonian influence on Locke, and it can account for certain main points of Locke's doctrine of qualities which are not explained by the influence of Boylean physics.[37]

NOTES

1. II viii 19-21. References to the *Essay* and quotations are taken from *An Essay Concerning Human Understanding*, ed. Peter H. Nidditch (Oxford, 1975).

2. See, e.g., Sextus Empiricus, *PH* I 36-163. The taste of honey is perhaps the most familiar example, but others standardly given include cases like those cited by Locke.

3. George Berkeley, *The Principles of Human Knowledge*, secs. 14-15, and *Three Dialogues*, in *Berkeley's Philosophical Works*, ed. D. M. Armstrong (London, 1965), pp. 151-158. Also see R. I. Aaron, *John Locke* (Oxford, 1937), pp. 105-118 (esp. p. 117); J. D. Mabbot, *John Locke* (London, 1973), pp. 25-28.

4. This has been argued by E. M. Curley in "Locke, Boyle and the Distinction between Primary and Secondary Qualities," *Philosophical Review* 81 (1972), 438-464 (esp. sec. VI). Also see Peter Alexander, "Boyle and Locke on Primary and Secondary Qualities" in *Locke on Human Understanding*, ed. I. C. Tipton (Oxford, 1977), p. 74. However, I disagree with these authors' accounts of Locke's aim and argument in II viii 19-21.

5. Especially Alexander, "Boyle and Locke," pp. 70-73; also Curley, "Locke, Boyle." In addition, see Maurice Mandelbaum, *Philosophy, Science and Sense Perception* (Baltimore, 1964), chap. 1 (esp. pp. 27 f.) and J. L. Mackie, *Problems from Locke* (Oxford, 1976), pp. 22-23.

6. See, e.g., Aaron, *Locke*, p. 108. Mandelbaum, *Philosophy*, stresses Locke's lack of concern about demonstrating the existence of bodies, urging that Locke is preoccupied with issues in the natural science of his time.

7. At least three claims can be distinguished in II viii 19-21; (1) that it is impossible that ideas of color etc. resemble bodies, whereas it is possible that ideas of shape etc. resemble bodies; (2) that bodies, i.e., perceiver-independent objects characterized by primary qualities, exist; (3) that sensory ideas of all sorts are caused by the motions and other primary qualities of bodies. I maintain that (1) is Locke's main contention in these sections, because it is prominent in his discussion and it is the only one for which he offers arguments.

8. In Book IV, Locke argues that we *know* there are objects that have powers to produce the ideas we receive by sense, but he does not claim we know these objects to be characterized by primary qualities; see IV ii 14; IV iv 4; and IV xi. This is brought out by Curley, "Locke, Boyle." I suggest below that Locke's view is that experience supports the belief that objects have primary qualities, but experience could also falsify that belief.

9. See Jonathan Bennett, *Locke, Berkeley, Hume: Central Themes* (Oxford,

1971), secs. 5 and 23; also Robert Cummins, "Two Troublesome Claims about Qualities in Locke's Essay," *Philosophical Review* 84 (1975), 401-418.

10. Relevant books Locke is known to have had in France include: Nicholas Malebranche, *Recherche de la vérité*, vols. I, II, and III; Simon Foucher, *Critique de la recherche de la vérité* and *Réponse pour la critique de la recherche de la vérité*; Robert des Gabets, *Critique de la critique de la recherche de la vérité*. (See John Lough, "Locke's Reading during His Stay in France," *The Library* 8 [1953], 229-258.) For an account of the issue in dispute among these French philosophers, see Richard Watson, *The Downfall of Cartesianism, 1673-1712* (The Hague, 1966), chaps. 4 and 5.

11. II viii 16 and 24 f.

12. See John Harrison and Peter Laslett, *The Library of John Locke* (Oxford, 1971).

13. For evidence that Locke knew *Syntagma Philosophicum*, see Aaron, *Locke*, pp. 33-38; also Gabriel Bonno, "Les relations intellectuelles de Locke avec la France," *University of California Publications in Modern Philology* 38 (1955).

14. See Aaron, *Locke*, p. 26; cf. James Gibson, *John Locke's Theory of Knowledge and Its Historical Relations* (Cambridge, 1917), pp. 259 f.

15. See *Essay* II xxxii 14-16. The suggestion is found in Gassendi's *Syntagma Philosophicum*, Pt. I, Bk. II, chap. 3 (in *Selected Works of Pierre Gassendi*, ed. and trans. Craig B. Brush [New York: Johnson Reprint, 1972], pp. 91 f.); it is also in Glanville's *The Vanity of Dogmatizing* (1661; reprint ed., New York, 1931), pp. 218 f.

16. See G. W. v. Leibniz, *Nouveaux Essais*, Bk. I, chap. 1; the point has recently been reiterated by some scholars, notably Aaron, *Locke*, pp. 33-38.

17. See my "The Origins of Locke's Doctrine of Primary and Secondary Qualities," *Philosophical Quarterly* 26 (1976), 305-316.

18. Pierre Bayle, *Historical and Critical Dictionary, Selections*, trans. Richard H. Popkin (Indianapolis, 1965), p. 197. On the Cartesian background of the distinction between primary and secondary qualities, see E. A. Burtt, *The Metaphysical Foundations of Modern Physical Science*, rev. ed. (Garden City, N.Y., 1953).

19. Jacques Rohault, in his widely read work on Cartesian physics, *Traité de physique* (1683), argues: "The heat of the fire, and the cold of ice, being properties or qualities belonging to bodies which everyone acknowledges to be inanimate, they cannot be like the sensations which we feel by their means, because these sensations belong to us as animate creatures" (Pt. I, chap. 23, sec. 9). Quoted from the English translation, *A System of Natural Philosophy*, trans. John and Samuel Clarke (1723; reprint ed., New York: Johnson Reprint Corp., 1969).

20. The influence of Boyle on Locke's doctrine of qualities has recently been greatly emphasized by Curley, "Locke, Boyle," Mandelbaum, *Philosophy*, and Alexander, "Boyle and Locke."

21. See esp. Alexander, "Boyle and Locke," pp. 70-73.

22. As Mandelbaum, *Philosophy*, emphasizes, Locke's focus on the corpuscu-

lar theory accounts for his assumption throughout II viii of claims (2) and (3) (see above, n. 7) without pretense of argument.

23. *Robert Boyle: The Works,* ed. Thomas Birch (Hildesheim, 1965), III, 23 f.

24. II viii 21. The argument of this section is treated in detail below, pp. 365-367.

25. II viii 22; concern for intelligible discourse about qualities is also expressed in II viii 7.

26. III viii 8.

27. II viii 9-10.

28. II viii 15.

29. The suggestion was made to me that Locke begs the question by saying "'tis plain porphyry has no color in the dark"; certainly he does, if by "color" he means "property *like* the ideas of red and white." Unfortunately, it is not easy to settle what Locke does mean. If by "color" he means "quality," then it is *false* that the stone has no color (power to produce ideas of red and white) in the dark; on the other hand, if he means the term to stand for ideas of red, etc., then on his own showing it is *illicit* to suggest that a stone might have a color (idea) at all. I suggest that the way out of this difficulty is to take Locke's own gloss on the earlier statement that the stone's "color vanishes"; that is to say, in the dark porphyry does not produce ideas of red and white (even if you look at it). It *is* plain (granting Locke's theory of ideas) that in the dark the stone does not produce ideas of red and white. Part of the *argument* is that given this, it is inconceivable that in the dark porphyry should resemble the ideas of red and white.

30. II viii 17, 22 and 23. Some commentators say it is central to Locke's notion of a "real" quality that it is nonrelational; see, e.g., Cummins, "Two Troublesome Claims," and Reginald Jackson, "Locke's Distinction between Primary and Secondary Qualities," reprinted in *Locke and Berkeley: A Collection of Critical Essays,* ed. C. B. Martin and D. M. Armstrong (Garden City, N.Y., 1968), pp. 53-77. The passages in which Locke uses the expression "real qualities" provide no basis for this, and elsewhere he indicates that real qualities do essentially involve relations (II xxi 3; also II iv 1 f.). It is true that real qualities do not essentially involve relations *to perceivers.*

31. Leibniz insisted against Locke that ideas of color, etc. do resemble their causes (*Nouveaux Essais,* esp. II viii), but he seems nowhere to have tried to explain the basis of the resemblance.

32. Bennett, *Locke, Berkeley, Hume,* p. 103.

33. See Mandelbaum, *Philosophy,* pp. 16 ff.; contrast the account given by Aaron, *Locke,* pp. 107 f.

34. This sketch follows most closely the text of Sextus Empiricus, *PH* I 112-117. For this type of argument in the skeptical authors found in Locke's library, see: DL IX 79-88; Michel de Montaigne, *Essais,* trans. George B. Ives (New York, 1939), I, 807. Also see Pierre Gassendi, *Syntagma Philosophicum,* Pt. I, Bk. 2, chap. 4 (Brush [see above, n. 15], p. 306).

35. See *PH* I 88. Of course, a skeptic does not hold dogmatically that such claims are contraries, although the argument presupposes that they are.

36. So far as I know, the only study of whether Locke's epistemology deals with Pyrrhonism is by Henry G. van Leeuwen, *The Problem of Certainty in English Thought, 1630-1690* (The Hague, 1963), chap. 5.

37. In preparing this paper I profited from discussion with Robert Bolton, Jane Duran, Margaret Gilbert, Ann Jacobson, and Margaret Wilson. I also want to express my thanks to R. S. Woolhouse for comments on the paper.

15

Berkeley and Pyrrhonism*

Richard H. Popkin

Berkeley laid great stress on the vital importance of refuting skepticism in his *Philosophical Commentaries (Commonplace Book)*, *Principles of Human Knowledge*, and *Dialogues between Hylas and Philonous*, but very little attention has been given to this aspect of his thought. In this paper, I shall try to show that the exploration of this theme sheds some light on the aims, import, and possible origins of some of Berkeley's ideas.

The complete title of the *Principles* is *A Treatise Concerning the Principles of Human Knowledge, Wherein the chief causes of error and difficulty in the Sciences, with the grounds of Scepticism, Atheism, and irreligion, are Inquired into.*[1] The complete title of the *Dialogues* is *Three Dialogues between Hylas and Philonous. The design of which is plainly to demonstrate the reality and perfection of human knowledge, the incorporeal nature of the soul, and the immediate providence of a Deity: in opposition to Sceptics and Atheists. Also to open a method for rendering the Sciences more easy, useful, and compendious.*[2] The introductions to each work, as well as various remarks in the *Philosophical Commentaries*, explain at greater length the author's intention of refuting the skeptics and atheists. In the initial section of the introduction to the *Principles*, Berkeley had said that the attempt to understand the nature of things had led men into all sorts of "uncouth paradoxes, difficulties, and

*Originally published in *The Review of Metaphysics* 5 (1951); reprinted with permission.

inconsistencies, . . . till at length, having wander'd through many intricate mazes, we find ourselves just where we were, or, which is worse, sit down in a forlorn scepticism."[3] And a few sections later, Berkeley stated that his intention was to discover the sources of the absurdities and contradictions that have entered philosophy, and to eliminate them.[4]

The Preface to the *Dialogues* is almost entirely devoted to stating and restating that the author's intention is to destroy atheism and skepticism. Skepticism arises from distinguishing the real nature of things from their apparent nature, and such a distinction leads to all kinds of paradoxes and perplexities. Berkeley's principles will rescue mankind from these difficulties. *"If the principles, which I here endeavour to propagate, are admitted for true; the consequences which, I think, evidently flow from thence, are, that* atheism *and* scepticism *will be utterly destroyed, many intricate points made plain, great difficulties solved, several useless parts of science retrenched, speculation referred to practice, and men reduced from paradoxes to common sense."*[5]

In his notebooks, the *Philosophical Commentaries*, Berkeley noted several times that skepticism was the view he was opposing, or, that it was the direct opposite of what he was advocating. "The Reverse of the Principle [Berkeley's] I take to have been the chief source of all that scepticism and folly, all those contradictions and inextricable puzzling absurdities, that have in all ages been a reproach to Human Reason."[6] "I am the farthest from Scepticism of any man."[7] And finally, in a letter Berkeley wrote to Sir John Percival on September 6, 1710, regarding the initial reaction to the *Principles*, he said "whoever reads my book with due attention will plainly see that there is a direct opposition between the principles contained in it and those of the sceptics."[8]

In the letter to Percival quoted above, Berkeley revealed that one of his great fears when he published the *Principles* was that he might be considered a skeptic. Percival's letter of August 26, 1710, indicated that such a consideration was already being presented.[9] And, of course, it is ironic but true that many times in the eighteenth century Berkeley was interpreted as the greatest skeptic of them all, by figures like Andrew Baxter and David Hume.[10]

With all this emphasis on the skeptics and skepticism, it seems reasonable to inquire why Berkeley was so upset about such a view. Whom was he attacking? Why do such people require such a strong refutation?[11] Some scholars, like G. A. Johnston, have stressed the fact that Berkeley wanted to prove that Locke and Descartes, and possibly Malebranche, were skeptics.[12] But apparently little or no attention has been given to the questions of what skepticism represented for Berkeley, why he considered it so horrendous, why he considered it to be in complete opposition to common sense, what part the identification of Cartesianism and Lock-eanism with skepticism played in Berkeley's thought, and what the rela-tion of the Berkelian concept of an attitude towards skepticism was to the conception of skepticism in Berkeley's time. In this paper I shall try to answer these questions at least in part. The answer that I shall offer is a way of interpreting Berkeley in the light of his views about skepticism and the development of Pyrrhonian skepticism at the time. Such an inter-pretation makes it possible to explain rather than ignore the emphasis on skepticism in the *Principles, Dialogues,* and *Philosophical Commen-taries*. It seems probable that an author who devotes so much time to dis-cussing such a view must have some reason for so doing. In offering my explanation of this reason, I shall also present a hypothesis regarding part of the development of Berkeley's views, in terms of his having had what Pierre Villey has called "la crise pyrrhonnienne"[13]—the realization of the force and consequences of Pyrrhonism. Such a crisis, I believe, must have happened to Berkeley on reading certain passages in Pierre Bayle's *Dictionary,* and led Berkeley to discover his "refutation" of skep-ticism.

First of all, what did Berkeley mean by skepticism? This doctrine is de-fined either explicitly or implicitly in the *Philosophical Commentaries,* the *Principles,* and the *Dialogues*. Altogether Berkeley attributes three doctrines to the skeptics: (1) the skeptic doubts everything;[14] (2) the skep-tic doubts the validity of sensible things;[15] (3) the skeptic doubts the exis-tence of real objects like bodies or souls.[16] These three different views constitute the core of the skeptical view for Berkeley. The second and third are corollaries of the first, and were for Berkeley the most interest-ing features of the position.

Before considering Berkeley's analysis of skepticism at length, let us see how it is related to the discussions of skepticism in the seventeenth and eighteenth centuries.

There are two articles in Pierre Bayle's *Dictionaire historique et cri-tique* which seem to form the basis, or at least part of the basis, of Ber-keley's conception of skepticism. These are the articles on Pyrrho of Elis and on Zeno the Eleatic. There is much evidence in the *Philosophical Commentaries* that Berkeley was acquainted with these articles. If we ex-amine some of the material in these articles and the way in which Berke-ley apparently used this material, and the evidence that Berkeley was referring to this material in the *Philosophical Commentaries,* I believe we shall have found the key to Berkeley's interest in skepticism, and will then be able to interpret Berkeley's discussions and refutations of skepti-cism in the *Principles and Dialogues*.

The first passage from Bayle that is relevant here is in the famous remark B in the article on Pyrrho, where Bayle related a discussion between two abbots about the dangers of Pyrrhonism to religion. One of the abbots is showing the force of Pyrrhonism against Christian theology, and digresses to show the further support that Pyrrhonists might gain from the new Philosophers, and the relation of Pyrrhonism and modern philosophy. Since the development of Cartesianism, we are told,

none among good Philosophers doubt now but the Sceptics are in the right to maintain, that the qualities of bodies which strike our senses are only meer appearances. Every one of us may say, *I feel heat before a fire*, but not *I know that fire is such in itself as it appears to me*. Such was the style of the ancient Pyrrhonists. But now the new Philosophy speaks more positively: heat, smell, colours, etc. are not in the objects of our senses; they are only some modifications of my soul; I know that bodies are not such as they appear to me. They were willing to except extension and motion, but they could not do it; for if the objects of our senses appear to us coloured, hot, cold, smelling, tho' they are not so, why should they not appear extended and figured, at rest, and in motion, though they had no such thing. Nay, the objects of my senses cannot be the cause of my sensations: I might therefore feel cold and heat, see colours, figures, extension, and motion, tho' there was not one body in the world. I have not therefore one good proof of the existence of bodies.[17]

Then, after referring to Malebranche for support of this last point, the abbot goes on to demolish the Cartesian argument for the existence of bodies from the fact that God is not a deceiver. Thus, all qualities, both primary and secondary, are reduced to mere appearances, subjective conditions of the mind. The reality of sensible things is denied. Further, since there is no need for real bodies to produce appearance, and there is no proof of the existence of real bodies, the reality of bodies is denied. And this is what Bayle offered as Pyrrhonism developed from the new philosophy, or the new philosophy developed from Pyrrhonism.

In the article on Zeno, in remark G Bayle argues against the real existence of extension. Once again, he claimed that the sort of Pyrrhonism or skeptical arguments that led philosophers to deny the reality of secondary qualities should lead them to deny the reality of primary qualities.

Add to this [a set of previous arguments], that all the *ways of suspension* which destroy the reality of corporeal qualities, overthrows the reality of extension. Since the same bodies are sweet to some men, and bitter to others, it may reasonably be inferred that they are neither sweet nor bitter in their nature, and absolutely speaking: The modern Philosophers, though they are no Sceptics, have so well apprehended the foundation of the epoche [*epochē*, suspense of judgment] with relation to sounds, odours, heat, and cold, hardness, and softness, ponderosity, and lightness, savours and colours, etc., that they teach that all these qualities are perceptions of our mind, and do not exist in the objects of our senses. Why should we not say the same thing of extension? If a being, void of colour, yet appears to us under a colour determined as to its species, figure and situation, why cannot a being, without any extension, be visible to us, under an appearance of determinate extension, shaped, and situated in a certain manner? Observe, also, that the same body appears to us little or great, round or square, according to the place from whence we view it: and certainly, a body which seems to us very little, appears very great to a fly. It is not therefore by their proper, real, or absolute extension that objects present themselves to our mind: whence we may conclude that in themselves they are not extended. Would you at this day argue thus: *Since certain bodies appear sweet to one man, sowre* [sic] *to another, and bitter to another, etc. I must affirm, that in general they are savoury, though I do not know the savour proper to them, absolutely, and in themselves?* All the modern philosophers would explode you. Why then would you venture to say, *since certain bodies appear great to this animal, middle sized to that, and very little to a third, I must affirm, that in general they are extended, though I do not know their absolute extension.*[18]

This same theme was discussed again in remark H in the article on Zeno, where Bayle asserted:

There are two Philosophical axioms which teach us, one that nature does nothing in vain; the other, that things are done in vain by more means which might have been as commodiously done by fewer. By these two axioms the Cartesians, whom I am speaking of [Malebranche, Fardella, etc.], may maintain that no such thing as matter exists; for whether it doth or doth not exist, God could equally communicate to us all the thoughts which we have. To say that our senses assure us, with the utmost evidence that matter exists, is not proving it. Our senses deceive us with respect to all the corporeal qualities, not excepting the magnitude, figure, and motion of bodies, and when we believe them, we are persuaded that out of our mind there exists a great number of colours, savours, and other beings, which we call hardness, fluidity, cold, heat, etc. yet it is not true that any such thing exists out of our mind. Why then should we rely on our senses with respect to extension? It may very well be reduced to appearance in like manner with colors.[19]

Bayle then went on to cite passages from Malebranche and Fardella in support of this thesis, and as evidence that the Cartesian proof of the existence of an external world is invalid. Next, Arnauld's objections to Malebranche were considered in which Arnauld charged Malebranche with holding *"some extravagant propositions, which strictly taken, tend to the establishment of a very dangerous Pyrrhonism."*[20]

These three passages in Bayle present a basis for a skepticism which denies both the reality of sensible objects, that is, the independent existence of sense objects, and also the reality of the sort of real objects posited by the "new" philosophies of Descartes and Locke, that is, objects consisting of primary qualities. All qualities, whether primary or secondary, are reduced to the status of appearances or modifications of the soul.

A world of real objects which produces the world of appearances is unknown, and possibly unknowable. There is no rational evidence for the
existence of an independent reality.

This presentation of Bayle's was apparently intended to offer a new
version of Pyrrhonian skepticism, developed from the arguments of the
seventeenth-century rationalists. An earlier version had appeared in the
writings of Montaigne and Gassendi, based on the classical statement of
Pyrrhonism of Sextus Empiricus. In these presentations, the Pyrrhonist
was said to believe that only appearances were known, that we had no
means of discovering the nature of reality, and that all that was known
was only an affection of the mind.[21] Rationalists like Descartes had tried
to found their certitude about the nature of the real world on the basis of
this new Pyrrhonian theory about appearances, by introducing the distinction between primary and secondary qualities; real qualities of real
objects and apparent qualities of unreal objects. The "new" philosophy
was thoroughly in keeping with seventeenth-century Pyrrhonism about
secondary qualities, and employed many of the stock Pyrrhonian arguments from the ten tropes of classical Pyrrhonism to defend this denial of
the reality of secondary qualities. The "new" philosophy was opposed to
what Hume later called "the most extravagant scepticism," the view that
there is nothing that can be said of real objects with continued and independent existence outside of our minds,[22] since this "new" doctrine
always maintained that there was a real external world composed of
objects possessing primary qualities.

Bayle's novel presentation of seventeenth-century Pyrrhonism is original mainly in that the great skeptic had made all the "new" philosophers
his allies in Pyrrhonism. The same sort of skeptical arguments that they
accepted about secondary qualities applied to the allegedly real primary
qualities as well; and hence the "new" philosophy, in spite of all its brave
attempts, was just a disguised form of that most extravagant skepticism
—Pyrrhonism.[23]

Malebranche, Fardella, Lannion, and others had already shown that
there were grave difficulties in the Cartesian attempt to establish a
demonstration of the existence of a real physical world. However, they
had not been willing to accept the skeptical conclusion. Bayle, armed not
only with their arguments, but also with his great discovery of the equal
ontological status of primary and secondary qualities, was ready to her-
ald and propound the triumph of seventeenth-century Pyrrhonism, that
no external reality can be known, and that all that we know is only a set
of modifications of our own mind.

Bayle had succeeded in showing that those who denied the reality of
sensible things were really complete Pyrrhonists, since once the objects of

our perception are denied any reality, the alleged real world of primary qualities is also denied and destroyed.

I believe it can be shown in two ways that Bayle's type of Pyrrhonism was what Berkeley had in mind when he set out to refute the skeptics: (1) by examining Berkeley's refutation, and (2) by producing evidence that Berkeley had knowledge of, and was aroused by, Bayle's skepticism.

One of Berkeley's themes in the *Philosophical Commentaries, Principles,* and *Dialogues* is that he has discovered the source of skepticism, and can show us how to avoid falling into such a horrendous view. His own position he presents as that one which is farthest from skepticism.[24] The skeptics doubt that we can know if anything really exists. All we can ever be acquainted with are appearances, which are "in the mind." Berkeley claims to have found the basis for this extravagant theory in the distinction between appearances and real objects, or between what is perceived and what exists. And finally, Berkeley tries to show us that all philosophers who believe in the absolute existence of matter will be reduced to skepticism, since their views are always based on such a distinction.

At the beginning of the third dialogue between Hylas and Philonous, Berkeley presents us with the picture of the man who has arrived at "la crise pyrrhonienne." Hylas starts the discussion with a pitiful picture of the limits of human knowledge. He is "plunged into the deepest and most deplorable *scepticism* that ever man was."[25] Hylas informs Philonous that we can know of nothing in this world, we can know naught of the real nature of things, not even if real objects exist. As far as we can tell, it is impossible for real objects to exist in Nature. All that we are ever acquainted with are ideas or appearances in our own minds, and no real object could exist with the qualities that we perceive in the appearances.[26]

The dangers of falling into the sort of skeptical despair in which we find poor Hylas are that it is a flagrant violation of our ordinary commonsensical views and practices, and that it paves the way of doubt of the principles of religion. The normal members of the human race have no skeptical doubts of the real existence of the objects they perceive. Every sane man would consider a skeptical view like Hylas's as ridiculous.[27] Thus the philosopher who ends as a skeptic is making a farce of his profession by spending his life *"in doubting of those things which other men evidently know, and believing those things which they laugh at, and despise."*[28] If philosophy is to be more than a useless comedy, it must return to the views of the vulgar and reject as absurd any view that ordinary mortals could not possibly believe. Otherwise, Berkeley believes, philosophy will have no contribution to make to the actual life of man.[29]

In addition there is the danger that the skeptic who doubts if anything exists will lead people to doubt the principles of true religion. When people see the most learned men professing an ignorance of everything, or advancing absurd theories, this may lead to a suspicion that the most sacred and important truths are dubitable. The same sort of reasoning that has ended in skepticism has also led to atheism.[30]

The error on which skepticism is always based, Berkeley claims, is the distinction between ideas and things, between *percipi* and *esse*. It is this which leads the skeptic to declare that the absolute existence of any object apart from the mind is unknowable.

All this scepticism follows, from our supposing a difference between *things* and *ideas*, and that the former have a subsistence without the mind, or unperceived. It were easy to dilate on the subject; and show how the arguments urged by *sceptics* in all ages, depend on the supposition of external objects.
So long as we attribute a real existence to unthinking things, distinct from their being perceived, it is not only impossible for us to know with evidence the nature of any real unthinking being, but even that it exists. Hence, it is, that we see philosophers distrust their senses, and doubt of the existence of heaven and earth, of every thing they see or feel, even of their own bodies.[31]

Berkeley's point here is that the classical Pyrrhonian arguments about illusions, the round tower, the bent oar, the pigeon's neck, etc. are decisive if ideas are distinguished from things. Our ideas vary, and if the variations are attributed to an external reality, contradictions follow. Our ideas are the only things we know; hence we cannot tell what things are like, or if they exist.[32]

All modern philosophy, from Descartes to Locke and Malebranche, reduces to skepticism. This *does not* mean that modern philosophy is skeptical, since Berkeley is well aware that Descartes, Locke, and Malebranche all hold that an unperceived external world of things exists. They all deny the reality of sensible things, but maintain that a real corporeal world of objects composed of primary qualities actually exists. However, the distinction between primary and secondary qualities is untenable; and besides, not a shred of evidence or meaning can be given to the contention that an unperceived corporeal world exists. Thus, in spite of the titanic efforts of Descartes, Locke, and Malebranche to support their denial of the existence of sensible qualities without advocating the Pyrrhonian doubt if anything exists, by means of appealing to God's perfection, a *je ne sais quoi*, or the authority of Scriptural revelation, they are all turned into advocates of Pyrrhonism.

This transformation of dogmatists into skeptics is accomplished not by sleight of hand, but by Berkeley's appealing to Baylean-type arguments about primary qualities, and Malebranchian-type attacks on Descartes's proof of the existence of an external world. Besides contending that no one has an abstract general idea of primary qualities, Berkeley attempts to show that the same type of skeptical arguments about the variability of appearances that have led all modern philosophers to deny the real existence of secondary qualities will lead them to deny the reality of primary ones. Figures, extension, solidities, and motions all vary according to our state and circumstances. Things appear large to a mite which can hardly be seen at all by us, objects appear to be moving to one observer, and to be stationary to another, etc. "In short, let anyone consider those arguments, which are thought manifestly to prove that colours and tastes exist only in the mind, and he shall find they may with equal force, be brought to prove the same thing of extension, figure and motion."[33]

Hence, as Bayle had already pointed out, the "new" philosophy, in building on the Pyrrhonian arguments about secondary qualities, would be forced into an unholy alliance with the skeptics on the status of primary qualities. Everything would become only appearance.

To show that there is no evidence or meaning to the claim that material substance exists, Berkeley develops the thesis that matter is undefinable and the contention of Malebranche and Bayle that there is no demonstration of the existence of matter. To show that we can have no idea of matter, Berkeley first appeals to the fact that material substance conceived of as a substratum supporting qualities and causing our perceptions makes no sense if primary qualities have been shown to be mental in the same sense as secondary ones. How can matter "support" extension if it cannot be extended (because extension is "in the mind, too")? How can matter cause perceptions if it does not move (since motion is "in the mind")? Thus, the Baylean claim that there is no difference in ontological status between primary and secondary qualities destroys the conception of matter of the new philosophy. Further, since matter is not perceived, we know nothing of it.[34]

Finally, Berkeley shows that we cannot know of an external material reality by reason. Here he builds on the type of argument of Malebranche and Bayle that the existence of matter is not demonstrable. From this, Berkeley goes on to point out that there is no classification into which matter falls, neither accident, occasion, instrument, etc.[35] When Hylas says that all this does not prove the impossibility of matter's existence, Philonous replies sharply,

You are not therefore to expect I should prove a repugnancy between ideas where there are no ideas; or the impossibility of matter taken in an *unknown* sense, that is no sense at all. My business was only to shew, you meant *nothing*; and this you were brought to own. So that in all your various senses, you have been shewed either to mean nothing at all, or if anything, an absurdity. And if this be not sufficient to prove the impossibility of a thing, I desire you will let me know what is.[36]

At this point the skeptic seems to have triumphed in casting in doubt the view that a real world exists. Once a distinction has been made between appearance and reality, the Pyrrhonist is able to conquer all by showing that anything that we ever come to know is appearance. Rather than trying, as his predecessors did, to stem the onrushing tide of Pyrrhonism by stoutly defending an unperceived reality as a last bulwark against the menace of skepticism, Berkeley follows the sage political advice of our day, "If you can't beat them, join them." After joining forces with the Pyrrhonists, Berkeley is able to show that their attack is innocuous if *esse est percipi*. The others who tried to oppose skepticism by denying the reality of sensible things have been captured by the skeptics.

In order to accomplish this revolution from within, of changing the Pyrrhonian denial of the reality of anything into an affirmation of the reality of the entire sensible universe, Berkeley merely places together two views, one of the vulgar and the other of the seventeenth-century Pyrrhonists which the new philosophers had accepted—"the former being of opinion that *those things they immediately perceive are the real things;* and the latter, *that the things immediately perceived, are ideas which exist only in the mind.* Which two notions put together, do in effect constitute the substance of what I advance."[37] Once Berkeley's criterion of reality is joined to the skeptic's thesis, the latter is completely overturned, and a commonsensical realism results.[38] And from this Berkeley derives, by means of his causal theory of perception, his entire theory of immaterialism.[39]

Thus, the skeptical overthrowing of the believers in material substance is only half the tale. Once the unseen material world is removed, then we can find the real world right before us where previous philosophers had simply failed to look. The world of sensible things really exists, even though the skeptics have shown that it is only in the mind. The world of appearance is the world of reality. And thus Berkeley can say in triumph in his notebooks, "I am more for reality than any other Philosophers, they make a thousand doubts and know not certainly but we may be deceiv'd. I assert the direct contrary," and "In ye immaterial hypothesis, the wall is white, fire hot, etc."[40] Only Berkeley with his insistence that the world of appearance is the real world could defend commonsense realism and challenge Pyrrhonism on its own battlefield, the world of sensible things. Only Berkeley could accept the skeptical arguments and not their nihilistic conclusions and thus overcome "la crise pyrrhonienne." In this way Berkeley overturns the arguments from illusion or variety of experience. Berkeley sees that the Pyrrhonian tropes are only forceful if one assumes a real world apart from sensation. If, instead, one adopts the view that *esse est percipi*, then there are no examples of sense illusions. The only possibility of error with regard to perception is the inference that is drawn from experience. The experiences of the bent rod or the tower that is round at a distance are not illusory experiences, but sensible things. If we infer from these experiences that we will perceive other sensible things, then we may make an incorrect inference. In this manner, what was traditionally the strongest part of Pyrrhonism is rendered harmless by Berkeley's revolution within the citadel of Pyrrhonism.[41]

The secret of this conquest of skepticism, Berkeley is always willing to admit, is the examination of the nature of existence. All previous philosophers, skeptical or otherwise, distinguished things and ideas, *esse* and *percipi*. Hence when the skeptics showed that sensible things were ideas, this appeared to be a devastating result. However, once we understand that *esse est percipi*, Berkeley claimed no skeptical objections can be dangerous. Thus he could make his remark in his notebooks,

Mem: Diligently to set forth that many of the Ancient philosophers run into so great absurdity as even to deny the existence of motion and those other things they perceiv'd actually by their senses, this sprung from their not knowing w^t existence was and wherein it considered this is the source of all their Folly, 'tis on the discovering of the nature & meaning & import of existence that I chiefly insist. This puts a wide difference between the Sceptics & me. This I think wholly new. I am sure 'tis new to me.[42]

This discovery of the source of the strength of seventeenth-century Pyrrhonism, I believe, follows out of the discoveries of Bayle and Malebranche. All modern philosophers prior to Berkeley had fallen into the skeptic's trap, and had distinguished appearance from reality. Berkeley alone had been able to accept the skeptics at their word and still offer a theory of the reality of sensible things. Descartes, Locke, and Malebranche had all reduced the sensible world to appearance and had struggled valiantly, albeit unsuccessfully, to defend a theory of the real existence of a material world. Berkeley had refused to follow their lead after seeing that the Baylean and Malebranchian type of analysis reduced such attempts to skepticism. Instead Berkeley chose to turn the Baylean type of Pyrrhonism inside out, and use it to defend the reality of sensible things, rather than of an unperceived material substance. Bayle had shown that we only know the existence of sensible things. This, Berkeley showed, was knowing the existence of a real world. This dialectical victory over Pyrrhonism is neatly put in the closing passages of the *Dialogues*. Hylas says, "You set out upon the same principles that Academics, Cartesians, and the like sects, usually do; and for a long time it looked as if you were advancing their philosophical *scepticism*; but in the end your conclusions are directly opposite to theirs."

Philonous replies in his closing speech, "You see, Hylas, the water of yonder fountain, how it is forced upwards, in a round column, to a certain height; at which it breaks and falls back into the basin from whence it rose: to ascent as well as descent, proceeding from the same uniform law or principle of *gravitation*. Just so, the same principles which at first view lead to *scepticism*, pursued to a certain point, bring men back to common sense."[43]

Descartes had accepted a partial Pyrrhonism, a denial of the reality of sensible things, to defend his view of the true nature of things. Bayle, employing his discovery about primary qualities and Malebranche's view about the evidence for the existence of a material world, had unleashed a new "crise pyrrhonienne" by showing that this partial Pyrrhonism quickly becomes a complete skepticism, a denial of all reality. Berkeley with his new principle was able to overcome the crisis by following Bayle to a certain point and then adding a new ending to the skeptic's tale.

Seeing Berkeley in relation to Pyrrhonism also aids in observing the originality of his metaphysics. In his *Berkeley and Malebranche*,[44] A. A. Luce defends the originality of Berkeley's immaterialism, maintaining that such a view was not "in the air" at the beginning of the eighteenth century, but that materialism was. This view has been attacked recently by Anita D. Fritz, in her article, "Malebranche and the Immaterialism of Berkeley,"[45] her main argument being that Malebranche's principles logically imply an immaterialist theory, which was developed by Berkeley. In terms of the interpretation of Berkeley's views on skepticism that I have been presenting in this paper, I think a more precise delineation of Berkeley's originality can be given. At the beginning of the eighteenth century two types of theories were current, one advocating that some sort of material reality existed (Descartes, Locke, and Malebranche), the other doubting whether anything outside the mind really existed (Baylean Pyrrhonism). Malebranche's "seeing all things in God" tended in the direction of ignoring rather than denying materialism, and making the real world one of essences in God's Mind. Berkeley's immaterialism is a radical innovation in this battle of ideas, based on the Malebranchian theory that God's Mind is the source of all that exists, and the Pyrrhonian insistence that we only know appearances. The innovation is that the real world, produced and sustained by some spiritual substance or substances, is the world of appearance. Though Berkeley and Malebranche might agree that the source of all was immaterial, and that only spirit can be efficacious in this universe, they would never agree on the status of appearance. Malebranche's *esse est concepi* is from another universe than Berkeley's *esse est percipi*. The immaterialism Malebranche was tending to was one of essences supported by Spirit, while Berkeley pictured a world of appearances supported by Spirit. Malebranche saw reality as radically different from appearance, and hence relegated appearances to being mere "modifications of the soul" unlike the real natures that existed in God's Mind. Berkeley refused to give up the Pyrrhonian thesis that all we can ever know is appearance, and in offering a foundation for appearance, offers one that makes appearance real, not unreal. In his notebooks, Berkeley insists that he, unlike Malebranche, has no doubts of the existence of bodies.[46] Malebranche's doctrines may lead logically to a type of immaterialism, but certainly not to Berkeley's, since the former is still in the Pyrrhonian trap of distinguishing the real from the perceived. The uniqueness of Berkeley's immaterialism is that it provides a basis for the Pyrrhonian world of appearances in the mind.

Reading Berkeley as a challenge to Bayle's Pyrrhonism gives some basis for Berkeley's claim to being the refuter of skepticism. If the passages that I quoted from Bayle's *Dictionary* were known to Berkeley, they might have led him to see that Bayle's monumental discovery about primary qualities and Malebranche and Bayle's destruction of the arguments to prove that a real external world exists, meant that if one denied the reality of sensible things, the reality of all things would follow therefrom. Hence Descartes, Locke, and Malebranche would be forced into skepticism. And this in turn might have led to Berkeley's analysis of the sources of skepticism, and his discovery of the new principle by which he escaped the Pyrrhonian conclusion.

When one comes to proving historically that this is what happened, one finds that there is much evidence to make this probable, if not certain. Two great experts on Berkeley, A. A. Luce and T. E. Jessop, have examined the evidence that links Bayle and Berkeley and have apparently come to a growing recognition that it is more than probable that there was a direct connection between Bayle's *Dictionary* and Berkeley's philosophy. In his *Berkeley and Malebranche*, published in 1934, A. A. Luce pointed out that a copy of Bayle's *Dictionary* was sold at the auction of Berkeley's library; Luce said that "I suspect that Bayle exerted considerable influence upon Berkeley, but I cannot prove it."[47] After discussing some of the evidence, Luce concluded his discussion of Bayle by suggesting that Bayle was probably one of Berkeley's important sources ranking next in importance after Malebranche and Locke.[48] In 1944, Luce stated in a note to his edition of the *Philosophical Commentaries* that Berkeley was probably influenced by Bayle, especially by the articles on Pyrrho and Zeno.[49] More recently, in his notes to the *Philosophical Commentaries* in a different edition, Luce states categorically that Bayle's *Diction-*

ary, and especially the articles on Pyrrho and Zeno, "had considerable influence on Berkeley's thought."[50] No reason is offered for coming to this definite conclusion of the matter. Jessop, in his notes to the *Principles*, suggests three places where Berkeley may have been influenced by Bayle's articles on Pyrrho and Zeno.[51]

What evidence there is supports Luce's more definite stand on the matter. As far as I know, Berkeley mentions Bayle only three times in his writings. There are two almost identical references to Bayle in the *Philosophical Commentaries*, entries 358 and 424, which read, "Malebranche's & Bayle's arguments do not seem to prove against Space, but onely Bodies," and "Bayle's Malebranche's etc. arguments do not seem to prove against space, but only against Bodies."[52] In *The Theory of Vision Vindicated*, Bayle is referred to along with Hobbes, Leibniz and Spinoza as a dangerous enemy of religion.[53] This last reference is of little value here since it appears in a work written long after the *Principles* and the *Dialogues*. It does suggest, however, that Berkeley had Bayle in mind when he listed as one of the dangers of skepticism that it leads to a denial of the principles of religion.

The two entries in the *Philosophical Commentaries* can easily be read as references to Bayle's discussion in the Pyrrho and Zeno articles, in which case the coupling of the names of Bayle and Malebranche would make sense, since Bayle introduces Malebranche's arguments in both articles.[54] Also, in the Zeno article the discussion starts off with Zeno's arguments about space, before it arrives at a discussion of the status of primary qualities and the existence of bodies; and the arguments of Bayle and Malebranche there relate only to bodies and not to space.

Further evidence in the *Philosophical Commentaries* that Berkeley had read Bayle's articles on Pyrrho and Zeno can be found in entry 79 referring to Fardella, and many of the entries on infinite divisibility, e.g. number 26. Besides the few entries that seem almost certainly to refer to Bayle's articles, there are a tremendous number that are in agreement with Bayle's text. The Fardella entry states "Mem. that I take notice that I do not fall in wth Sceptics Fardella, etc., in y^{t} I make bodies to exist certainly, wch they doubt of."[55] There is no evidence that Berkeley read Fardella, and he is quoted in Bayle's article on Zeno, Remark H, in a context that could lead to his being coupled with skeptics.[56] As to infinite divisibility, almost all of Berkeley's arguments on the subject appear in Bayle's article on Zeno. In entry 26 Berkeley connects the problem of infinite divisibility with the problem of external existence, just as Bayle does in the Zeno article.[57]

The last piece of direct evidence linking Bayle and Berkeley is one that neither Luce nor Jessop seems to have noticed—that is, that the same type of illustrations are used by both Bayle and Berkeley on the primary quality issue. In showing that the extension of things varies as color does, both philosophers appeal to what objects will look like to tiny animals, flies or mites, and how objects appear under magnification. They also both appeal to the change in size and shape of objects as we change position.[58] It might be a coincidence that Bayle and Berkeley discovered the same fact about primary qualities, but it could hardly be a coincidence that they used the same type of illustrations to prove their case.

Thus, considering the popularity of Bayle's *Dictionary*, the fact that a copy was auctioned off from Berkeley's library, the two references in the notebooks to Bayle, the mention of Fardella in the notebooks, the same arguments about infinite divisibility in the notebooks and in the Zeno article, the same theory about primary qualities, and the similarity of illustrations on the matter, I think that we have more than just probable evidence of a historical connection between Berkeley's philosophy and Bayle's *Dictionary*.

As a last bit of evidence in support of interpreting Berkeley as an antagonist of Baylean Pyrrhonism, I should like to appeal to the way it was read by Andrew Baxter and Thomas Reid. Baxter sees Berkeley as a terrible Pyrrhonist, in a class with Bayle or Pyrrho. Berkeley's type of reasoning in denying the material world would lead in turn to denying the spiritual world, too, and thus to complete Pyrrhonism. Berkeley's attempt to refute skepticism only leads to the "wildest and unbounded skepticism." Baxter treats Berkeley's view as being a denial that there is a real world anywhere, and such a view he places in the Pyrrhonian tradition. Thus Baxter considers that Berkeley's skepticism is no antidote but actually a worse form of the disease. He says of Berkeley's claim to have refuted skepticism, "This is, I think, as if one should advance, that the best way for a woman to silence those who may attack her reputation, is to turn a common prostitute. He puts us into a way of denying all things, that we may get rid of the absurdity of those who deny some things."[59] Throughout his answer to Berkeley, Baxter keeps developing the relation of Pyrrhonism to modern philosophy, and placing Berkeley in the absurd position of the man who tried to answer Pyrrhonism by advocating it.[60]

Reid is careful never to accuse Berkeley of being a skeptic like Hume, but treats him as the first to see that the systems of Descartes and Locke lead to skepticism, and that this may be avoided by eliminating the material world from the system. Unfortunately, Reid observes, Hume showed that Berkeley's system, in spite of all attempts to avoid it, led to skepticism, too. So Reid sees Berkeley's historical role in the collapse of the Cartesian type of philosophy as that of one who saw that it was tending to skepticism and who thought he could avoid it by his immaterialism.[61]

Thus both of these readings, Baxter's and Reid's, place Berkeley in the context of an opponent of the skeptical tendencies in modern philosophy, and both of these see him, unfortunately, plunging headlong into the greatest of all skeptical debacles.

The contention of this paper is, then, that Berkeley set out to refute skepticism because of "la crise pyrrhonienne" that Bayle had just brought to light. Bayle, like his later follower, Hume, had turned the whole enterprise of modern philosophy into a new Pyrrhonism—a doubting of the real existence of everything, and an asserting that all that we could ever be acquainted with were mental appearances. This Baylean type of Pyrrhonism was in flagrant violation of common sense, and led, even in the hands of its creator, to free thought and doubt of Christian principles. Berkeley saw, as Reid later did, too, that this type of Pyrrhonian skepticism reaches its disastrous conclusions through a distinction between the real and the perceived. The Pyrrhonian contention that all that we ever came in contact with was a set of appearances in the mind, Berkeley believed, was undeniable. But one could avoid the horrendous consequence of this by a new theory of the nature of reality. The theory of the "new" philosophers, that real objects were constituted of primary qualities, was shown to be untenable by Bayle's argument. Their contention that a world of reality was inferable from the world of appearances was shown to be untenable by Malebranche's, Fardella's, and Bayle's arguments. Hence the skeptical challenge had to be met by a new theory of reality— the world of appearance is the real world. This thesis coupled with the theory of immaterialism to explain the cause and status of the world of appearance, would provide a new foundation for human knowledge. Baylean Pyrrhonism destroyed the world of the seventeenth-century philosophers. Berkeley tried to construct a new world out of Baylean Pyrrhonism, with skepticism paving the way of truth. Unfortunately, Hume turned the skeptical attack against the new realism of Berkeley and reduced it again to Pyrrhonism, and Reid followed once again with an attempt to find a more material reality safe from the attacks of the skeptics.

NOTES

1. George Berkeley, *The Principles of Human Knowledge* (hereafter referred to as *Principles*), in *The Works of George Berkeley, Bishop of Cloyne*, ed. A. A. Luce and T. E. Jessop, vol. II (London and Edinburgh, 1949), p. 1. (All references to Berkeley's *Principles, Dialogues, Philosophical Commentaries*, and *Theory of Vision Vindicated* are to the text in this edition.)

2. George Berkeley, *Three Dialogues between Hylas and Philonous*, p. 147. (This work is hereafter referred to as *Dialogues*.)

3. Berkeley, *Principles*, Introduction, par. 1, p. 25. In the original draft of this introduction, Berkeley had said, "[men] are often by their principles lead into a necessity of admitting the most irreconcilable opinion or (which is worse) of sitting down in a forlorn scepticism." Ibid., p. 121.

4. Ibid., Introduction, pars. 4-5, p. 26.

5. *Dialogues*, Preface, p. 168. See also p. 167. The point is reiterated again on p. 168 when Berkeley claimed that the main virtue of his theory, if it is correct, would be that *"the discouragements that draw* to scepticism [would be] *removed."*

6. George Berkeley, *Philosophical Commentaries (Commonplace Book)*, in *Works of Berkeley*, vol. I (London and Edinburgh, 1948), p. 52, entry 411.

7. Ibid., p. 70, entry 563. See also p. 15, entry 79, p. 38, entry 304, and pp. 61-62, entry 491.

8. Benjamin Rand, *Berkeley and Percival: The Correspondence of George Berkeley and Sir John Percival* (Cambridge, 1914), p. 83.

9. Ibid., pp. 80-83.

10. Cf. Andrew Baxter, *An Enquiry into the Nature of the Human Soul*, vol. II, 2d ed. (London, 1737), sec. II, especially pp. 258-260, 267, 270-272, 279-280, 284, and 310; and David Hume, *An Enquiry Concerning Human Understanding*, Open Court edition (La Salle, Ill., 1949), sec. XII, p. 173 n.

11. The same problems could be raised with regard to atheism and atheists, but these are not the concern of this paper.

12. See for example, G. A. Johnston, *The Development of Berkeley's Philosophy* (London, 1923), pp. 57-59 and 70.

13. Cf. Pierre Villey-Desmeserets, *Les Sources et l'Évolution des Essais de Montaigne*, vol. II (Paris, 1908), p. 230. This is what he believes happened to Montaigne on reading Sextus Empiricus.

14. Rand, *Berkeley and Percival*, p. 83, "the sceptics, who are not positive as to any one truth." Also, in the *Dialogues*, p. 173, Hylas explains that what he means by a skeptic is "one that doubts of everything."

15. Cf. *Philosophical Commentaries*, p. 61, entry 491. Also in the *Dialogues*, p. 173, Hylas offers as a second definition of a skeptic, "What think you of distrusting the senses, of denying the real existence of sensible things, or pretending to know nothing of them. Is not this sufficient to denominate a man a *sceptic*?" And, in the letter to Percival referred to above, Berkeley stated that he did not wish to be confused with the skeptics, who doubt of the existence of things (Rand, *Berkeley and Percival*, p. 83).

16. Cf. *Philosophical Commentaries*, p. 15, entry 79, "Mem. that I take notice that I do not fall in wth Sceptics Fardella etc. in y^t I make bodies to exist certainly, wch they doubt of." See also entries 304-305, p. 38. This meaning of skepticism is made most clear in the *Principles*, pars. 86 ff., pp. 78-79.

17. Pierre Bayle, *The Dictionary Historical and Critical*, 2d ed. (London, 1737), IV, 654. The reduction of primary qualities to the same status as secondary qualities had already been suggested, as Bayle noted here, by the Abbé Foucher in his *Critique de la recherche de la vérité* (Paris, 1675), pp. 44-80, esp. pp. 78-80. In Foucher the point is not made as clearly as in Bayle's writings, nor is as

sweeping a conclusion drawn. Foucher's intention was to show how easily the Academic and Pyrrhonian skeptics could destroy Malebranche's and Descartes's philosophy. Bayle's aim was to reduce all modern philosophy to Pyrrhonism.

18. Ibid., V, 612.

19. Ibid., V, 614.

20. Ibid., V, 615.

21. Cf. Sextus Empiricus, *PH* I 19-24 and II 22-79, esp. 72; Michel de Montaigne, "Apology for Raimond Sebond," in *The Essays of Montaigne*, trans. E. J. Trechmann (New York and London, n.d.), 'ii, 16-17 and 45-50; and Petrus Gassendi, *Syntagma philosophicum, De Logicae fine*, Caput III, "Modi Epoches Scepticorum circa Veritatem, ipsiusque Criteria," in *Opera*, vol. I (Lyon, 1658).

Seventeenth-century Pyrrhonism is a movement that has been almost completely neglected.

22. Cf. David Hume, *A Treatise of Human Nature*, ed. Selby-Bigge (Oxford, 1949), pp. 214 and 228. Arnauld, in *La logique ou l'art de penser* treated this doubt of whether a real world exists as one of the more fantastic features of Pyrrhonism. See the 1724 edition, pp. xx-xxi.

23. Cf. Francisque Bouillier, *Histoire de la philosophie cartesienne*, 3d ed., vol. II (Paris, 1868), p. 487; François Picavet, "Bayle," in *La Grande Encyclopédie*, vol. V (Paris, 1888), p. 951; Jean Delvolvé, *Religion, critique et philosophie positive chez Pierre Bayle* (Paris, 1906), pp. 252-253 and 256; and F. Pillon, "Le scepticisme de Bayle," *L'anneé philosophique* 6 (1895), 193-194.

24. Berkeley, *Principles*, par. 40, p. 57.

25. *Dialogues*, p. 229.

26. Ibid., pp. 227-228.

27. Cf. ibid., pp. 172, 211, 229, 237, and 246.

28. Ibid., Preface, p. 167.

29. See, e.g., ibid., Preface, pp. 167-168.

30. See ibid., pp. 171-172, and *Principles*, pars. 92-93, pp. 81-82.

In Baxter, *Enquiry*, the author, who interprets Berkeley as a skeptic, feels that one main reason for refuting him is that skepticism leads to irreligion. Cf. pp. 280 and 293.

31. *Principles*, pars. 87-88, p. 79. See also par. 86, p. 78, par. 92, p. 81, par. 101, p. 85; *Dialogues*, pp. 228-229, 246, and 258; and *Philosophical Commentaries*, entry 606, p. 75. The latter states, "The supposition that things are distinct from Ideas takes away all real Truth, & consequently brings in Universal Scepticism, since all our knowledge & contemplation is confin'd barely to our Ideas."

32. See *Dialogues*, pp. 174-207 and 258.

33. *Principles*, par. 15, p. 47. See also the first *Dialogue*, pp. 188-192, and *Principles*, pars. 10-14, pp. 45-47.

34. Cf. *Principles*, pars. 16-18, pp. 47-48, and *Dialogues*, pp. 198 and 215-217.

35. Cf. *Principles*, pars. 18-20, pp. 48-49, and *Dialogues*, pp. 217-225. See also Nicolas Malebranche, *De la recherche de la vérité*, ed. Geneviève Lewis (Paris, 1945), III, Éclaircissement vi, pp. 24-33; Nicolas Malebranche, *Dialogues on Metaphysics and Religion*, trans. Morris Ginsberg (New York, 1923), I, v, pp. 75-77, and VI, v-vi, pp. 167-168; and Pierre Bayle, *Dictionary*, art. *Pyrrho*, Remark B, and art. *Zeno*, Remarks G and H.

36. *Dialogues*, p. 226.

37. Ibid., p. 262.

38. That Berkeley's theory is a defense of commonsense realism has been most forcefully pointed out in F. J. E. Woodbridge's essay, "Berkeley's Realism," in *Studies in the History of Ideas*, vol. I, edited by the Department of Philosophy, Columbia University (New York, 1918), pp. 188-215.

39. See, e.g., *Dialogues*, pp. 211 ff.

40. *Philosophical Commentaries*, entry 517a, p. 64, and entry 19, p. 10. See also *Principles*, pars. 3-4, p. 42, pars. 34-35, p. 55 and par. 40, p. 57; *Dialogues*, pp. 229-230, 237-238, 244, 249, 260 and 262; and *Philosophical Commentaries*, entry 305, p. 38.

41. Cf. *Dialogues*, p. 238.

42. *Philosophical Commentaries*, entry 491, pp. 61-62.

43. *Dialogues*, pp. 262-263.

44. A. A. Luce, *Berkeley and Malebranche* (London, 1934), pp. 47-48.

45. Anita Dunlevy Fritz, "Malebranche and the Immaterialism of Berkeley," *Review of Metaphysics* 3 (1949-50), 59-80.

46. *Philosophical Commentaries*, entry 686a, p. 84, and entries 800-801, p. 96. In connection with this difference between the views of Berkeley and Malebranche, and what I claim is the originality of the former, some mention must be made of the thesis of John Wild concerning the nature of Berkeley's philosophy. Professor Wild, in his interesting work, *George Berkeley* (Cambridge, Mass., 1936), attempted to show that Berkeley's philosophical career represented the development of a "concrete logic," which discarded abstractions and fragmentary pictures of reality, and pointed to a transcendental reality toward which reason was constantly groping. In this interpretation the *Siris* is seen as the culmination of the Neoplatonic or Hegelian philosophy which Berkeley was creating through his dissatisfaction and disillusionment with the philosophy of the times. It is impossible in the scope of this paper to do justice to Wild's views, but in terms of my contention regarding Berkeley's relation to Pyrrhonism, I think that Wild's interpretation gives too little importance to Berkeley's major contribution to the seventeenth- and eighteenth-century war against Pyrrhonism. Rather than applying a "concrete logic" to the issue. Berkeley advanced a commonsense realism, and came out with the startling discovery that in this way the Pyrrhonian arguments could be accepted and rendered innocuous. The Malebranchian philosophy, by rejecting such a realism, could never defeat the skeptical menace. Berkeley certainly deserves recognition for offering this new way out of some of the basic difficulties of modern philosophy.

Berkeley's views about the nature of the reality behind the commonsense world, or on which the commonsense world depended, may have led him on to his later views in the *Siris*. This, however, does not destroy or detract from the initial originality of the *Principles* and the *Dialogues*. Regardless of what Berkeley's views may have later become, or how his later views may be related ones, one of his main contributions to eighteenth-century philosophy was his new way of dealing with old problems through admitting the force of skepticism, and then showing the harmlessness of the attack if the sense world is the real world.

47. Luce, *Berkeley and Malebranche*, p. 53.

48. Ibid., p. 55.

49. George Berkeley, *Philosophical Commentaries*, ed. A. A. Luce (London, 1944), note to entry 358, p. 388.

50. *Philosophical Commentaries*, in *Works of Berkeley*, vol. I, note to entry 358, p. 122.

51. *Principles*, notes on pp. 44, 76, and 95.

52. *Philosophical Commentaries*, pp. 43 and 53.

53. George Berkeley, *The Theory of Vision Vindicated*, in *Works*, I, 254. Luce hints in *Berkeley and Malebranche* that Bayle's antireligious views may be responsible for the almost complete omission of Bayle's name in Berkeley's writings.

54. In Mrs. Fritz's article, "Malebranche and the Immaterialism of Berkeley," it is suggested that Berkeley is referring to Bayle's *Recueil de quelques pièces curieuses concernant la philosophie de Monsieur Descartes*. See Fritz, p. 77. However, I think this is unlikely, since Bayle's interest in that work is in the religious opposition to Descartes, and Bayle makes no arguments there to which Berkeley's remarks are appropriate.

55. *Philosophical Commentaries*, p. 15.

56. Bayle, *Dictionary*, V, 614.

57. *Philosophical Commentaries*, p. 10, and Luce's note in his 1944 edition of the *Philosophical Commentaries* to entries 26 and 258, pp. 325 and 388.

58. Bayle, *Dictionary*, art. *Zeno*, remark G, vol. V, 612; and *Dialogues*, pp. 188-189.

59. Baxter, *Enquiry into the Nature of the Human Soul*, II, 284. The discussion of Berkeley occurs in Section II, pp. 256-344.

60. A somewhat similar point is made in James Beattie's *An Essay on the Nature and Immutability of Truth, in Opposition to Sophistry and Scepticism*, in *Essays* (Edinburgh, 1776), Part II, chap. ii, sec. 2, pp. 187-189.

Also, in Jean Pierre de Crousaz's *Examen du Pyrrhonisme* (La Haye, 1733), p. 97, and *A New Treatise of the Art of Thinking* (London, 1724), I, 42. Berkeley was apparently alluded to by the remark, "Un auteur moderne prétend renverser le Pyrrhonisme, en niant l'Existence des Corps, & n'admettant que celle des Esprits." This view is then shown to be fantastic and unbelievable.

61. Cf. Thomas Reid, *Inquiry into the Human Mind*, I, v and vii, and VII; and Thomas Reid, *Essays on the Intellectual Powers of Man*, II, 10-11. It is interesting to note what Hume says of Berkeley in a footnote after stating Berkeley's argument against abstract general ideas. "This argument is drawn from Dr. Berkeley; and indeed most of the writings of that very ingenious author form the best lessons of scepticism, which are to be found either among the ancient or modern philosohers, Bayle not excepted. He professes, however, in his title-page (and undoubtedly with great truth) to have composed his book against the sceptics as well as against the atheists and free-thinkers. But that all his arguments, though otherwise intended, are, in reality, merely sceptical, appears from this, *that they admit of no answer and produce no conviction.* Their only effect is to cause that momentary amazement and irresolution and confusion, which is the result of scepticism." David Hume, *An Enquiry Concerning Human Understanding*, sec. XII, part I, Open Court edition, p. 173 n.

16

The Tendency of Hume's Skepticism

Robert J. Fogelin

During his lifetime Hume was thought to be a skeptic and (both inconsistently and falsely) an atheist. In time the charge of atheism has fallen away, but for most of the two hundred years since his death, Hume's position as the leading (and almost only) British skeptic has seemed secure. Things have changed. Starting with the claim made early in this century by Norman Kemp Smith that Hume was not simply, or even primarily, a skeptic, but a naturalist instead, we now find interpreters of Hume arguing (or simply assuming) that skepticism has little or no role in Hume's philosophical position.[1] I think that this new way of reading Hume is, first of all, one-sided in ignoring a great many important texts. More deeply, I think that interpreters of Hume who downplay the skeptical moment in his position misunderstand the fundamental tendencies of his philosophy, including the naturalistic themes that they bring to prominence.

Part of the difficulty of fixing issues here is that no clear sense is attached to the claim that a philosopher is or is not a skeptic. In common parlance, skepticism is concerned with *doubt*: to say that one is skeptical about something is to express doubt concerning it. Furthermore, skepticism suggests rather strong doubt. A skeptic, then, is one who entertains strong doubts—usually about many things. In contrast, if we turn to the philosophical literature (both ancient and modern), skepticism has a different focus. A philosophical skeptic deals in *arguments* and, in particular, with arguments that call in question the supposed grounds for some system of beliefs. The system of beliefs may be more or less wide and the

form of challenge may vary with the subject matter. Diversity of opinion
provides a specific reason for raising skeptical doubts concerning morality, but it is less effectively invoked as a skeptical challenge to mathematics. Other skeptical challenges are perfectly general—that is, they
apply to any system of beliefs whatsoever. The so-called argument from
the criterion (of truth) falls into this category—as does Hume's skepticism with regard to reason.

There seems to be an obvious connection between the common notion
that skepticism concerns doubt and the philosophical notion that skepticism shows the groundlessness of systems of belief: when a system of
belief is shown to be groundless, then we ought not to adopt beliefs of
that kind.[2] But even if this connection seems obvious, it will be important
for our purposes to distinguish between principles of the following kind:

I. There are no rational grounds for judgments of kind A.

II. One ought not to assent to judgments of kind A.

I shall say that a position that embodies the first principle expresses a *theoretical* skepticism and that a position that embodies the second principle
expresses a *prescriptive* or *normative* skepticism. A prescriptive skepticism may be based upon a theoretical skepticism, but it need not be. A
person may recommend the suspension of belief on scriptural rather than
theoretical grounds.[3] Similarly, one can be a theoretical skeptic without
recommending suspension of belief. It might be argued that there is nothing wrong with holding beliefs for which there is no theoretical justification, or it might be argued that beliefs are not in our control and that
therefore recommendations concerning them are idle.[4]

Although the difference between a theoretical skepticism and a prescriptive skepticism is perfectly clear, criticisms of skepticism have the
tiresome habit of ignoring it. Hume captures this tendency in the *Dialogues Concerning Natural Religion* by having Cleanthes address Philo in
these words:

Whether your scepticism be as absolute and sincere as you pretend, we shall learn
by and by, when the company breaks up: We shall then see, whether you go out
at the door or the window; and whether you really doubt, if your body has grav-
ity, or can be injured by its fall; according to popular opinion, derived from our
fallacious senses and more fallacious experience. [*Dialogues Concerning Natural
Religion*, p. 382][5]

Actually, this passage involves a double confusion. It first confuses theoretical skepticism with prescriptive skepticism, and then, by citing Philo's
own behavior as evidence, it confuses prescriptive skepticism with what
we might call *practicing skepticism*. After all, a person may sincerely
believe that he ought not to believe something, yet believe it. This is just

a special case of a person believing that he ought not to do something, yet doing it.

With the distinction between theoretical and prescriptive skepticism in hand, it is possible to summarize the main tendencies of Hume's skepticism. (I) His theoretical skepticism is, I shall argue, *wholly unmitigated.* (II) Hume's prescriptive skepticism is less easily described because it is variable. In moments of intense skeptical reflection he comes as close as possible to holding that we ought not to believe anything whatsoever, and indeed he finds himself (for a time, at least) in a state of radical doubt. But the more normal tendency of Hume's philosophy is to put forward a more moderate or mitigated prescriptive skepticism of an Academic rather than a Pyrrhonian cast. Both in daily life and in the pursuit of science we ought to limit our inquiries to matters suited to our limited faculties, and in these modest inquiries we ought always to adjust our beliefs to probabilities established upon experience.[6] (III) The final point I wish to make about Hume's presentation of skepticism is that he offers no independent *arguments* for the moderate skepticism that generally characterizes his position. Instead, his moderate skepticism is quite literally a mitigated Pyrrhonian skepticism. Here Hume's skepticism and naturalism meet, for the state of moderate skepticism is viewed as the result of two causal factors: radical Pyrrhonian doubt on one side being moderated by our natural (animal) propensities to believe on the other. This causal explanation of moderate skepticism as the natural terminus of philosophical reflection is, I believe, Hume's major contribution to the skeptical tradition.

In what follows I shall show that the above claims can be easily documented in the text of the *Treatise.* I shall then show that the same views persist, without essential change, in Hume's later writings, including the *Enquiry Concerning Human Understanding* and the *Dialogues Concerning Natural Religion.*

HUME'S SKEPTICISM WITH REGARD TO REASON

Each Book of Hume's *Treatise* has at least one skeptical episode. Most famously, Book I successively puts forward a skepticism concerning induction, a skepticism with regard to the senses, and, finally, a skepticism with regard to reason. Book II, which concerns the passions, provides fewer targets for skeptical tropes, but even here we find Hume insisting that reason is incapable, of itself, of influencing the passions (and therefore "ought always to be the slave of the passions"). Finally, in his treatment of morals, in Book III, we find Hume introducing skeptical arguments intended to show that reason—in a broad sense including both demonstrative and empirical reasoning—cannot determine the moral qualities of agents or actions.

In what follows I shall lay more stress than is usual on Hume's skepticism with regard to reason. There are both textual and systematic reasons for doing this. Textually, Hume's skepticism with regard to reason reveals his skeptical commitments in their most radical form. It also provides the occasion for Hume to write most explicitly about the nature and significance of his skepticism. For example, it is precisely the impact of this argument that throws Hume into his (real or feigned) funk in the concluding section of Book I: "The intense view of these manifold contradictions and imperfections in human reason has so wrought upon me, and heated my brain, that I am ready to reject all belief and reasoning, and can look upon no opinion as more probable or likely than another" (*Treatise*, pp. 268-269).[7] Systematically, the argument is important because it transcends its specific target, reason, and yields a skepticism that is wholly general. This follows at once from the general form of the argument, which has two parts. Hume first argues for the reduction of all knowledge to probability and then argues that, upon reflection, we see that any probability, however high, must reduce to "nothing." But if we begin, as Hume does, with an exhaustive distinction between knowledge and probability, reduce the first to the second, and then argue that, upon reflection, all probabilities must be reduced "to nothing," we arrive at a skepticism unlimited in its application and wholly unmitigated. We arrive at a skepticism on a par, in its way, with the classical skeptical argument from the criterion (of truth).

The first part of Hume's argument—the reduction of knowledge to probability—is launched by the following consideration:

Now as none will maintain, that our assurance in a long numeration exceeds probability, I may safely affirm, that there is scarce any proposition concerning number, of which we have a fuller security. For 'tis easily possible, by gradually diminishing the numbers to reduce the longer series of addition to the most simple question, which can be form'd, to an addition of two single numbers; and upon this supposition we shall find it impracticable to shew the precise limits of knowledge and probability, or discover the particular number, at which the one ends and the other begins. But knowledge and probability are of such contrary and disagreeing natures, that they cannot well run insensibly into each other, and that because they will not divide, but must be either entirely present, or entirely absent. [P. 181]

Hume adds to this the further consideration that if there be no error in the simple parts of a complex sum, there could be no error in the whole.

By this argument Hume intends to show that the probability of error which (as no one denies) infects large computations, must—*at least to some degree*—infect our beliefs in the most simple mathematical truths.[8]

Hume offers a *causal* account of this tendency of the human mind to fall into error: "Our reason must be considered as a kind of cause, of which truth is the natural effect; but such-a-one as by the irruption of other causes, and the inconstancy of our mental powers, may frequently be prevented" (p. 180). This, in turn, leads Hume to assert that we must take into account the possibility of such an "irruption of other causes" in deciding upon the credibility of any knowledge claim. Such an assessment is a matter of probabilities (not simply a matter of "comparing ideas"), and thus we arrive at Hume's first major conclusion: ". . . by these means all knowledge degenerates into probability; and this probability is greater or less, according to our experience of the veracity or deceitfulness of our understanding, and according to the simplicity or intricacy of the question" (p. 180). Notice that Hume is not maintaining the weaker and certainly more plausible thesis that the consideration of the propriety of a knowledge claim will always lead us to raise probabilistic questions. He is asserting instead that the knowledge is itself reduced, by these means, to probability. I do not think that he gives any reason for offering the stronger rather than the weaker thesis. Indeed, his argument seems to muddle them together.

The second part of Hume's argument is a morass. He notices that the point made about knowledge holds for probabilities as well; that is, when we make a probabilistic judgment, we must consider the possibility that here our faculties have erred. This leads him to lay down the following principle: "In every judgment which we can form concerning probability as well as knowledge, we ought always to correct the first judgment deriv'd from the nature of the object, by another deriv'd from the nature of the understanding" (pp. 181-182). Now suppose that we have made a probabilistic judgment in the common way and then, following Hume's instructions, we have added to it a further judgment concerning the probability that the first judgment is correct. What next? Obviously, this new (second-order) judgment is itself susceptible of error, and it too must be evaluated before it is accepted. In Hume's words, ". . . we are obliged by our reason to add a new doubt deriv'd from the possibility of error in the estimation of the truth and fidelity of our faculties" (p. 182). The infinite regress is now fair before us, but Hume gives this ancient trope a twist of his own by suggesting that these successive evaluations must progressively drive the probability of the *original* judgment down to "nothing." Hume continues his argument in these words:

This doubt, which immediately occurs to us, and of which, if we would closely pursue our reason, we cannot avoid giving a decision. But this decision, tho' it should be favourable to our preceding judgment, being founded only on probability, must weaken still further our first evidence, and must itself be weakened by a fourth doubt of the same kind, and so on *ad infinitum*, till at last there remain nothing of the original probability, however great we may suppose it to have been, and however small the diminution of every new uncertainty. No finite object can subsist under a decrease repeated *in infinitum*; and even the vastest quantity, which can enter into human imagination must in this manner be reduc'd to nothing. [P. 182][9]

So Hume concludes that "all the rules of logic require a continual diminution, and at last a total extinction of belief and evidence" (p. 183). This conclusion and the argument leading up to it establish my claim that, in the *Treatise* at least, Hume accepts a *theoretical* skepticism that is wholly unmitigated.

Furthermore, Hume understands the radical character of his position with complete clarity. This comes out most forcefully in the way he deals with the old trick of trying to refute the skeptic by turning his arguments back upon themselves—the so-called *peritrope*. He responds to this challenge in these words:

If the sceptical reasonings be strong, say they, 'tis proof, that reason may have some force and authority: if weak, they can never be sufficient to invalidate all the conclusions of our understanding. This argument is not just; because the sceptical reasonings, were it possible for them to exist, and were they not destroyed by their subtlety, wou'd be successively both strong and weak, according to the successive dispositions of the mind. [P. 186]

That is, skeptical arguments are self-refuting, but this only puts us on a treadmill, since setting aside our skepticism and returning to the canons of reason inevitably puts us on the road to yet another skeptical impasse. For Hume, skepticism is completely immune to rational refutation. Indeed, it is the fated end of all reasoning pursued without restraint.[10]

Turning next to the *prescriptive* skepticism of the *Treatise*, we can quickly tell a familiar tale. Hume does not recommend a radical suspension of belief because he thinks that it is not in the power of human beings to achieve this state. Hume develops this side of his theory by asking himself the following question: "How it happens, that even after all we retain a degree of belief, which is sufficient for our purposes, either in philosophy or common life." Of course, most people have never heard of Hume's skeptical argument and it is the process of going through it—and not just its soundness—that induces a skeptical response. But Hume has gone through the argument and we want to know how *he* (or anyone else who appreciates its force) can retain a degree of belief sufficient for our purposes either in philosophy or in common life. Hume responds:

I answer, that after the first and second decision; as the action of the mind becomes forc'd and unnatural, and the ideas faint and obscure; tho' the principles of judgment, and the balancing of opposite causes be the same as at the beginning; yet their influence on the imagination, and the vigour they add to, or diminish from the thought, is by no means equal. . . . The attention is on the stretch: The posture of the mind uneasy; and the spirits being diverted from their natural course, are not governed by the same laws, at least not to the same degree, as when they flow in their usual channel. [P. 185]

Later, now speaking generally about all skeptical arguments, he adds: "'Tis happy, therefore, that nature breaks the force of all sceptical arguments in time, and keeps them from having any considerable influence on the understanding" (p. 187).

Hume returns to this argument and gives it special prominence in the concluding section of Book I.

I have already shewn, that the understanding when it acts alone, and according to its most general principles, entirely subverts itself, and leaves not the lowest degree of evidence in any proposition, either in philosophy or common life. We save ourselves from total scepticism only by means of that singular and trivial property of the fancy, by which we enter with difficulty into remote views of things and are not able to accompany them with so sensible an impression, as we do those, which are more easy and natural. [Pp. 267-268]

What, for Hume, is the point of this excursion into skepticism? In the *Treatise*, Hume's stated reason for dabbling in these skeptical arguments is that they confirm his theory of belief.

My intention then in displaying so carefully the arguments of that fantastic sect, is only to make the reader sensible of the truth of my hypothesis, *that all our reasonings concerning causes and effects are deriv'd from nothing but custom; and that belief is more properly an act of the sensitive, than of the cogitative part of our natures.* [P. 183]

Hume's central idea seems to be this: If belief were fixed by processes of reasoning, then the skeptical argument just presented would drive all those who have considered it to a state of total suspension of belief. Indeed, in our closet, such skeptical reflections can come very close to inducing this extreme state. Yet when we return to the affairs of daily life, our ordinary beliefs come rushing back upon us and our previous state will now strike us (perhaps with some lingering jitters) as amusing. But this restoration of belief is not a matter of reasoning and therefore cannot be explained on any of the traditional theories of belief formation where it is assumed that the mind comes to its beliefs by a process of reasoning. Hume's own causal theory of belief formation suffers no such embarrassment. He does not, however, attempt to show that his approach is *unique* in this regard.

There is a final feature of Hume's treatment of skepticism that is at least broached in the *Treatise* and becomes an important theme in his later writings. Skeptical doubts, no matter how intense, are no match for the beliefs that come back upon us when we return to daily life, but not all the beliefs that antedated our Pyrrhonian catharsis have a like tendency to be restored. Those, for example, that are the product of mere education, indoctrination, fashion, and so forth, will not inexorably force themselves back upon us. For this reason, Pyrrhonian exercises will have a tendency to curb the *enthusiasm* that Hume so much despised. The outcome, then, of this philosophical progression, is a person who shares the opinions of the vulgar on the common topics of life—with them, he leaves by the door and not by way of an upstairs window. He may also carry his reflections beyond common life, but here he moves with caution, always adjusting his beliefs to probabilities grounded in experience. For matters that lie beyond experience, he suspends inquiry altogether. We have thus arrived at a position very close to academic skepticism, and arrived at it, not by means of argumentation, but as a natural consequence of the interaction of philosophical reflection carried to its extreme with daily life carried on in a normal way.

SKEPTICISM IN HUME'S DIALOGUES
CONCERNING NATURAL RELIGION

At no place in Hume's later writings do we find a commitment to skeptical principles as explicit as that found in the opening and closing sections of the fourth part of Book I of the *Treatise*. Yet if we keep in mind the distinctions introduced at the beginning of this essay, I think that we may also say that he never recants the central features of his skeptical position. In particular, he never explicitly rejects the unmitigated *theoretical* skepticism of the *Treatise*. Indeed, though his emphasis may change, particularly in the *Enquiry Concerning Human Understanding*, there is abundant textual evidence to show that (even in the *Enquiry*) he continues to accept a radical theoretical skepticism. But before turning to the *Enquiry*, I shall first look at Hume's skepticism as it emerges in the *Dialogues Concerning Natural Religion*.

Because of its form, the *Dialogues* present problems for the interpreter.

Hume never speaks directly in his own person—not even in the introductory remarks which are spilt from the pen of Pamphilus—and as his correspondence indicates, he made a conscious effort to lend plausibility to the positions of the two main protagonists of the dialogue, Cleanthes and Philo. At the close of the dialogue, Hume seems to hint at his own preference by having Pamphilus aver that one of the protagonists, Cleanthes, has gotten the better of the debate, but he gives no reasons for saying so. Pamphilus shows a similar preference for Cleanthes in his prefatory remarks where he describes him as a "careful thinker." By way of contrast, Demea is said to be a man of "rigid orthodoxy" and Philo is called a "careless sceptic." These remarks at the beginning and end of the *Dialogues* together with the fact that Cleanthes does, in fact, present his position from within an empiricist (and probabilistic) framework have led some commentators—I do not think the majority—to hold that Cleanthes represents Hume's position or at least comes closest to doing so. This, I think, is just wrong, and though it pretends to be daring, it entirely misses the underlying logic of the *Dialogues*. Cleanthes is a civilized "naturalist" who has never thought his principles through to the Pyrrhonian crisis they entail. Philo views the world from the other side of that gulf. Demea, of course, knows nothing of all this, and his occasional invocation of skepticism *cum fideism* is wholly superficial and does not cohere with other things he says. Except for one place where he gets in a telling blow against Cleanthes, Demea is presented as a stooge.

Perhaps another, more plausible view, is that Hume sorts his views out between Philo and Cleanthes, assigning to Philo a more radical skepticism than he himself would accept while making Cleanthes, however inconclusive his positive arguments are, closer in general orientation to his own position. I think that this is also mostly wrong, for in no place in the *Dialogues* does Philo express skeptical commitments that Hume himself had not expressed in the *Treatise*. More to the point, *the fine details* of Philo's skepticism mirror exactly the ideas developed in that earlier book. On the other hand, Cleanthes rarely expresses views that reflect the more sophisticated aspects of Hume's philosophy. The one exception to this is Cleanthes' rejection of the ontological proof offered by Demea; and here, as Cleanthes himself remarks, he is not disagreeing with Philo, merely beating him to the punch.

To see that Philo's position reflects the "fine-grained" features of the *Treatise*, we may notice first that in a single paragraph Philo alludes directly to the skepticism concerning *reason* and then repeats the claim of the *Treatise* that it is only the mind's natural incapacity to sustain subtle inquiry that saves us from a total lack of assurance and conviction on *any subject*.

All sceptics pretend that, if reason be considered in an abstract view, it furnishes invincible arguments against itself, and that we could never retain any conviction or assurance, on any subject, were not the sceptical reasonings so refined and subtle, that they are not able to counterpoise the more solid and more natural arguments, derived from the senses and experience. [P. 385]

Here, of course, the word "pretend" is used in its eighteenth-century sense, and the skeptical pretensions expressed are precisely those of the author of the *Treatise*.

But Philo not only invokes the radical (theoretical) skepticism of the *Treatise* in a general way, he also shows genuine sophistication concerning it. This comes out, for example, in his response to an attack upon skepticism offered by Cleanthes. Skeptical reflections generate uneasiness when they are undertaken and have no lasting effects (good or bad) when they are terminated. So Cleanthes asks for what reason the skeptic imposes "on himself such a violence," adding that "this is a point, in which it will be impossible for him [the skeptic] ever to satisfy himself, consistently with his sceptical principles" (p. 383). Philo's response does not deny the uneasiness that skeptical reflections may produce; instead it rejects the claim that skeptical reflections will have *no* lasting effect. His answer involves a comparison with the effects of the teachings of Stoicism which, traditionally, have been subjected to the same complaint that they lose all efficacy when confronted with genuine problems of life.

Though the mind cannot, in Stoicism, support the highest flights of philosophy, yet even when it sinks lower, it still retains somewhat of its former disposition, and the effects of the Stoic's reasoning will appear in his conduct in common life, and through the whole tenor of his actions.... In like manner, if a man has accustomed himself to sceptical considerations on the uncertainty and narrow limits of reason, he will not entirely forget them when he turns his reflection on other subjects; but in all his philosophical reasoning, I dare not say, in his common conduct, he will be found different from those, who either never formed any opinions in the case, or have entertained sentiments more favourable to human reason. [Pp. 383-384]

Once more, Hume describes himself.

There are a number of other places in the text where Philo expresses fine points of Hume's own position,[11] but the most striking instance of Philo's adherence to the central features of Hume's skeptical position occurs, oddly enough, at the one place in the text where Cleanthes is able to silence him. Having been badly mauled by Philo's objections to the inductive inference from the supposed order in nature to the existence of an intelligent creator, Cleanthes shifts his tactics (and with it his grounds) and responds to Philo in these words:

The declared profession of every reasonable sceptic is only to reject abstruse, remote, and refined arguments; to adhere to common sense and the plain instincts of nature; and to assent, wherever any reasons strike him with so full a force that he cannot, without the greatest violence, prevent it. Now the arguments for natural religion are plainly of this kind; and nothing but the most perverse, obstinate metaphysics can reject them. Consider, anatomize the eye; survey its structure and contrivance, and tell me, from your own feeling, if the idea of a contriver does not immediately flow in upon you *with a force like that of sensation.* [Pp. 402-403]

This passage has a number of remarkable features. In the first place, Cleanthes here shows a more sympathetic understanding of skepticism by dropping the spurious criticism that it has disastrous consequences for daily life ("Will you leave by the door or window?"). More significantly, Cleanthes shifts the grounds of his position by no longer arguing that the signs of order in the world provide *evidence* for an inductive argument showing that the world must have an intelligent being for its cause. He now puts forward a causal thesis to the effect that the contemplation of the exquisite organization of the eye, for example, immediately induces in us the idea of a being who contrived it. Hume underscores this shift in position by having Cleanthes acknowledge that this new argument is of an "irregular nature" (p. 403). More importantly, once the position is put on this footing, it becomes completely immune to the pattern of skeptical argument found in the *Treatise.* Hume's theoretical skepticism concerns arguments. In its various manifestations it shows the groundlessness of given beliefs. It is not aimed at nor does it have any tendency to diminish the force of those beliefs that spring up in us naturally. So if our conception of an intelligent creator of the universe flows immediately in upon us "with a force like that of sensation," then the groundlessness of the belief is admitted, and no argument presents itself as a target for skeptical attack. The skeptic can only affirm or deny the fact. I think that we can now understand why at this point in the *Dialogues* Hume has Pamphilus tell us that Philo falls silent: "Here I could observe, Hermippus, that Philo was a little embarrassed and confounded; but, while he hesitated in delivering an answer, luckily for him, Demea broke in upon the discourse and saved his countenance" (p. 403).

We may also be able to make some sense out of the most problematic feature of the *Dialogues.* At the close of the *Dialogues* Philo seems to undergo a remarkable conversion where he seems to agree with Cleanthes—despite the fact that he has quite demolished every particular argument that Cleanthes has presented. This seeming reversal is, it seems to me, quite inexplicable, unless we assume that Philo is here admitting that the contemplation of the wonderful contrivances of nature naturally induces in us the thought of a divine contriver. That is, it is Cleanthes' irregular argument that Philo cannot refute and may, consistently with his stated principles and consistently with the principles of the *Treatise* as well, accept. These considerations remove some of the shock from Philo's claim that "to be a philosophical Sceptic is, in a man of letters, the first and most essential step toward being a sound believing Christian" (p. 467). A man of letters will find the *reasons* adduced for religion less than compelling. More to the point, the kind of deity presented by the arguments of natural religion is hardly a fit object for our religious sentiments. This is the one forceful point that Demea makes in the *Dialogues*, and it is aimed against Cleanthes. The arguments of natural religion are not only weak, as Philo shows, but present an inappropriate object for our religious sentiments, as Demea rightly protests. The skeptic, then, is better placed to accept the doctrines of *received* religion than is the proponent of natural theology. That, I think, is what Philo is saying.

The *Dialogues* remain a problematic text, for the interpretation sketched out here is subject to criticism.[12] This much, however, does seem to be beyond dispute: the *Dialogues Concerning Natural Religion* are written in the framework of the radical theoretical skepticism of the *Treatise*, and the central core of the work is lost if this fact is ignored or suppressed.

SKEPTICISM IN THE ENQUIRY CONCERNING HUMAN UNDERSTANDING

I said at the beginning of this essay that Hume never—to my knowledge —retreats from the unmitigated theoretical skepticism of the *Treatise*. The discussion in the closing section of the *Enquiry* may seem to belie this claim, for there he comes out quite explicitly for a mitigated as opposed to a Pyrrhonian skepticism. I shall argue that no such change takes place, although there is, I think, an important shift in emphasis.

Before going into this matter directly, it will be useful to give a quick survey of the differences between the *Treatise* and the *Enquiry* on the range of skeptical discussions. The one important addition to the skeptical topics discussed in the *Treatise* is, of course, the essay on miracles. That essay has the skeptical conclusion that, by the nature of the case, we can never have sufficient inductive evidence to establish the occurrence of a miracle. The skepticism concerning induction is carried over from the *Treatise* although in a simplified, perhaps even different, form. The skeptical arguments concerning the senses are carried over exactly from the *Treatise* to the *Enquiry*, although to see this, one must look in the right place, namely, at the discussion entitled "Of the Modern Philosophy" and not at the discussion mislabeled "Of the Scepticism with regard to the Senses." The argument, which is as old as skepticism itself, calls in question inferences from our perceptions to the existence of the external world. Here, at least, there is no retreat from an unmitigated theoretical skepticism:

> This is a topic . . . in which the profounder and more philosophical sceptics will always triumph when they endeavour to introduce an universal doubt into all subjects of human knowledge and enquiry. Do you follow the instincts and propensities of nature . . . in assenting to the veracity of sense? But these lead you to believe that the very perception or sensible image is the external object. Do you disclaim this principle, in order to embrace a more rational opinion, that the perceptions are only representations of something external? You here depart from your natural propensities and more obvious sentiments; and yet are not able to satisfy your reason, which can never find any convincing argument from experience to prove, that the perceptions are connected with any external objects. [P. 126]¹³

The most curious feature of the treatment of skepticism in the *Enquiry* is the handling of skepticism with regard to *reason* as it appears in the second part of Section 12. It is strange in two ways: (i) the argument of the *Treatise* which, as we saw, was intended to reduce all knowledge claims to probabilities and then drive all probabilities down to "nothing" is nowhere to be found, and (ii) in its place Hume puts ancient puzzles that he claimed to solve in the *Treatise*. In particular, Hume simply trots out standard puzzles about infinity and infinite divisibility in order to show that even abstract reasoning, when left to itself, will be led into intractable difficulties. He then suggests in a footnote that it may not be impossible to avoid these absurdities.

So our comparison between the *Treatise* and the *Enquiry* comes to this. The theoretical skepticism concerning induction and the theoretical skepticism concerning the existence of the external world is the same in both. The skeptical argument concerning miracles is new to the *Enquiry*. Only the skepticism concerning reason has been modified—and that by omission.

I think that we are now in a position to understand the "mitigated scepticism or academical philosophy" that Hume recommends at the close of the *Enquiry*. Let me comment on its nature, then on its source. In the first place, the mitigated skeptic is a fallibilist and a probabilist: "In general, there is a degree of doubt, and caution, and modesty, which, in all kinds of scrutiny and decision, ought for ever to accompany a just reasoner" (p. 132). But Hume also speaks of another *species* of mitigated skepticism which calls for "the limitation of our enquiries to such subjects as are best adapted to the narrow capacity of human understanding" (pp. 180-181). Taking the phrase from Alexander Pope, I shall call this *man's middle-state skepticism*, for it reflects the same sentiment as the following lines from his "An Essay on Man":

> Placed on this isthmus of a middle state,
> A being darkly wise, and rudely great:
> With too much knowledge for the Sceptic side,
> With too much weakness for the Stoic's pride. . . .

A similar sentiment is expressed in *Paradise Lost*, where Milton has Raphael warn Adam not to enquire into the deep mysteries of the universe, but, instead, study to become "lowly wise." Indeed, Hume here adopts one favorite religious use of skeptical arguments, namely, to curb the extent of man's inquiries and restrict it to topics fit for his state.[14] This middle-state skepticism with its call for a restriction upon the range of inquiry was characteristic of the eighteenth century; and here, at least, Hume reveals himself a man of his time.

One last question: How does one attain this state where we are suitably cautious in our assent and modest in our inquiries? Hume's answer is that this is brought about by reflection on Pyrrhonian arguments. "To bring us to so salutary a determination, nothing can be more serviceable, than to be once thoroughly convinced of the force of the Pyrrhonian doubt, and of the impossibility, that anything but the strong power of natural instinct, could free us from it" (p. 181). The clear implication of this passage is that there are no arguments that will refute Pyrrhonian skepticism and thus there can be no arguments that will justify a more mitigated version of skepticism. The mitigated skepticism that Hume recommends is thus the causal consequence of the influence of two factors: Pyrrhonian doubt on one side and natural instinct on the other. We do not argue to mitigated skepticism, we find ourselves there.

In sum, Hume's skepticism and his naturalism meet in a causal theory of skepticism itself.

NOTES

1. Nicholas Capaldi's *David Hume* (Boston: Twayne, 1975) represents the extreme version of this new dispensation, but he has been followed, in varying degrees, by others.

2. As W. K. Clifford put it, "it is wrong always, everywhere and for anyone, to believe anything upon insufficient evidence."

3. See, e.g., Ecclesiastes 3:11.

4. Thomas Reid, whose commonsense philosophy involves a theoretical skepticism every bit as radical as Hume's, adopts the first alternative. Hume, as we shall see, largely adopts the second.

5. All citations to the *Dialogues Concerning Natural Religion* are to vol. II of *David Hume: Philosophical Works*, ed. Green and Grose (London, 1886).

6. Notice that this moderate skepticism has two sides: (1) a limitation upon the *range* of inquiry, and (2) a limitation upon the degree of assent. The second limitation amounts to a *probabilism* or *fallibilism* and is, of course, a standard feature of Academic skepticism. The first limitation, which concerns the permissible range of human inquiry, has a long association with religious thought and may, indeed, lay claim to a scriptural basis. I shall examine such calls for limitations upon the range of permissible investigation when I consider the distinctive features of Hume's skepticism as it appears in the *Enquiry*.

7. All citations to the *Treatise of Human Nature* are to the Selby-Bigge edition (Oxford: At the Clarendon Press, 1888).

8. Actually, this is not much of an argument, for the source of error in performing a large sum is not likely to be a momentary lapse where we suddenly believe, say, that three plus four equals eight. Error typically arises from such external difficulties as forgetting what number we are carrying along or not being able to read our own writing. None of this touches upon the possibility of falling into error when contemplating simple mathematical propositions.

9. The closing sentence of this passage contains an obvious mistake. Hume doesn't realize that an infinite series of finite diminutions can sum to a finite limit. Beyond this, the proper analysis of Hume's argument—which involves taking probabilities on probabilities—is far from obvious and may lie outside the range of standard probability theory.

10. Hume also notices the practical difficulties that would attend the lot of a person who attempted to carry his philosophical skepticism over into life. But this does not provide a reason for rejecting skeptical principles, for these pragmatic considerations are themselves subject to skeptical doubt.

11. Of particular interest is a passage that appears in the final dialogue where Philo remarks "that the Theist allows that the original intelligence is very different from human reason: The atheist allows, that the original principle of order bears some remote analogy to it. Will you quarrel, Gentlemen, about the degrees, and enter into a controversy which admits not of any precise meaning, nor consequently of any determination?" (p. 459). This passage, I believe, gives Hume's own assessment of the debate, i.e., that it concerns only matters of degree, and is therefore incapable of resolution. In the fourth appendix to the *Enquiry Concerning the Principles of Morals*, Hume discusses this topic under the title of "Verbal Disputes." An examination of that essay will again show that Philo serves as the vehicle for expressing some of Hume's most sophisticated thoughts. A similar line of argument is pursued in Hume's famous discussion of personal identity in the *Treatise* (p. 262).

12. Although I give more stress to the skeptical themes carried over in detail from the *Treatise*, much of what I have said here is a simplified borrowing from

Nelson Pike's careful and insightful commentary on the *Dialogues*. See, in particular, Section Four of his edition of the *Dialogues Concerning Natural Religion*
(Indianapolis: Bobbs-Merrill, 1970).

13. All citations to the *Enquiry Concerning Human Understanding* are to vol.
4 of *David Hume: Philosophical Works*, ed. Green and Grose (London, 1886).

14. In passing, this is the central theme of a remarkable Pyrrhonistic work by
Bishop Huet entitled *A Philosophical Treatise Concerning the Weakness of
Human Understanding*. Huet is cited in the *Dialogues* (p. 388).

17

Kant and Skepticism

Barry Stroud

Pyrrhonists are reputed to have suspended judgment on every question as to how things are, and thereby to have achieved contentment. It is not easy to determine whether and how that goal is to be reached with complete generality. Certainly there is no more to be said on one side than on the other of some of the questions that arise from time to time in our daily lives, so the proper response is to suspend judgment, at least for the time being. More frequently it happens that we are more disposed toward one side than the other, even if we are not completely free of doubt or hesitation. But in the overwhelming majority of ordinary, humdrum cases, things are so obvious and uncontroversial as to leave us in no doubt or suspense at all. We often find we simply cannot withhold judgment or even seriously entertain doubts about the way things are—at least not in the ordinary way, or for the usual sorts of reasons—and it would be foolish or perverse to believe or even to suspect anything to the contrary.

Modern philosophers influenced by the skeptical tradition have not ignored these facts of our daily life. Descartes, for example, distinguishes between those situations in which we can easily be deceived by our senses, and so can reasonably doubt or withhold assent from what they seem to inform us of—when what we are looking at is too small to be seen properly, for example, or too far away—and those in which it is normally impossible to doubt, where doubt or denial would be nothing short of madness. On first reflection Descartes finds that if, when sitting by the fire with a piece of paper in his hand, he were to doubt or deny that he is sitting by the fire with a piece of paper in his hand, he would appear to be no less mad than those paupers who assert that they are kings or those madmen who believe they are pumpkins or are made of glass.[1]

Descartes nevertheless goes on to find what he regards as very good reason to doubt even those apparently certain and obvious things that he had thought he knew through the senses. But his reason for that general doubt is not simply that there are *some* things about which the senses are not fully reliable, or that the senses have *sometimes* deceived him, or that *sometimes* he can reasonably doubt or suspend judgment about what the senses appear to inform him of. The uncertainty or suspension of judgment that is sometimes appropriate in special circumstances is not directly transferable without further argument to *every* case of sense perception.

This same cautious and apparently completely reasonable attitude is also present in philosophers strongly opposed to the skeptical tradition. G. E. Moore, for example, would agree that the uncertainty present in some cases cannot be directly transmitted to them all, but he would see no chance of ever going on, as Descartes did, to find additional reasons for doubting, and hence denying that we know, even what seemed at the outset to be the most obvious and most certain propositions about the way things are. It is simply incorrect, Moore thought, to say that we never know any such proposition to be true. Just as the best refutation of someone who says there are no chairs in the room would be to point out to him a particular chair that is in the room, so the best refutation of someone who says that nothing of a certain sort is known would be to point out to him some particular thing of that sort that *is* known. Moore thought it was easy to do that. In objecting to what he called Hume's skeptical philosophical "principles," for example, he appealed not to a fire and a piece of paper, but to a pencil. And he found that for proving Hume wrong "there really is no stronger and better argument than the following. I *do* know that this pencil exists; but I could not know this, if Hume's principles were true; *therefore,* Hume's principles . . . are false. I think this argument really is as strong and good a one as any that could be used: and I think it really is conclusive."[2]

Of course, philosophers do not simply adopt such "principles" or dogmatically assert such startling conclusions; they give what they think are good arguments for them. But precisely because they are arguments against the knowledge or certainty that we have in the obvious and uncontroversial cases that Moore would cite, he thought those arguments could never succeed. He once held up his finger before his philosophical audience and announced:

This, after all, you know, really is a finger: there is no doubt about it: I know it, and you all know it. And I think we may safely challenge any philosopher to bring forward any argument in favour either of the proposition that we do not know it, or of the proposition that it is not true, which does not at some point, rest upon some premiss which is, beyond comparison, less certain than is the proposition which it is designed to attack.[3]

His confidence in issuing this challenge clearly rested on his certainty that there was a finger before him. He thought that nothing could be more certain than that is, so he was confident that no "premisses" put forward by a philosopher could be more certain than that is. By whatever route Descartes might try to reach his general negative conclusion, we know in advance, according to Moore, that he cannot reach it. On Moore's view, no argument could ever establish the general skeptical conclusion that we know nothing, or that we can always reasonably suspend our judgment, about the way things are.

Many have found the response of Moore and other commonsense philosophers convincing, and there has been a corresponding lack of interest in philosophical skepticism in recent years. But that is to take it for granted that there is a direct and unproblematic relation between the particular cases a Moore-like critic would cite and the general conclusions a philosophical theorist of knowledge accepts. Since at least the time of the *Critique of Pure Reason,* if not earlier, there has been no excuse for making that simple assumption. In this paper I try to sketch part of what I think Kant contributes to our understanding of the complex relation between the philosophical theory of knowledge, on the one hand, and the inquiries and claims to knowledge that we make in everyday and scientific life that are presumably its subject matter, on the other.

It is important to understand the special nature of Kant's contribution, for he too argues that Descartes's attempt to bring everything about the world around us into doubt or suspension of judgment must fail; but he does so in a way that also shows that the kind of objection Moore relies on could never succeed against philosophical skepticism either, and in fact could never refute or support any philosophical account of our knowledge of the world at all. Our ordinary assertions of knowledge and certainty, and the familiar procedures we employ in arriving at them in everyday life, are shown to be no refutation of philosophical skepticism. Descartes also would find Moore's counterassertions ineffectual because of his own conception of his special philosophical enterprise and its relation to the ordinary assertions and beliefs of everyday life. But Kant's understanding of what is required for the philosophical investigation of human knowledge amounts to a radical break even with Descartes and other pre-Kantian philosophers of the modern skeptical tradition. To understand that radical break we must understand something as complicated as the distinction between the "transcendental" and the "empirical" in Kant's philosophy. That is not easy to do.

"EMPIRICAL REALISM"

Reflecting on Descartes's appeal to the possibility of dreaming and of an evil demon is supposed to leave us certain only of our own existence and of that of our experiences, but uncertain of everything about the way things are beyond that—for example, about the existence of any things around us in space. Even such certain and obvious matters as my sitting by the fire with a piece of paper in my hand are seen to be uncertain when I realize that I could be having my present experiences even if I were simply dreaming that I am sitting by the fire with a piece of paper in my hand. The modern problem of the external world, perhaps formulated for the first time in its present form by Descartes,[4] is therefore to show how I can come to know about the existence of things around me in space on the basis of my experiences. Simply posing the problem in this way is perhaps almost enough in itself to convince us that it could never be solved.

It would seem that any attempted solution would have to represent our knowledge of things around us as at best indirect and therefore to some degree problematic. If objects in space are never given directly in experience, then we can know of them, if at all, only by inference from something we are directly and unproblematically aware of. Kant thinks that on any such view, and on Descartes's in particular, the existence of things in space would therefore always be to some degree uncertain. We would always have to admit that our perceptions *might* be due to something other than the external objects we believe to exist, and so we could never completely eliminate the possibility that they have a purely "internal" source and are nothing more than "a mere play of inner sense" (A368).[5] That is why Kant identifies all such views as forms of "idealism"—"problematic" idealism because they leave the existence of things in space problematic or uncertain for us, or "sceptical" idealism because they leave things in space doubtful or insufficiently justified (B274; A377). All such views imply that the existence of things around us in space is "incapable of proof" (A377).

Against all forms of what he calls "idealism" Kant argues that "realism" is the only correct account of our position in the world. That is the view according to which objects exist in space completely independently of human or other perceiving beings and are directly and unproblematically knowable by perception. It accords to material things "a reality which does not permit of being inferred, but is immediately perceived" (A371). "In order to arrive at the reality of outer objects," Kant says, "I have just as little need to resort to inference as I have in regard to the reality of the object of my inner sense, that is, in regard to the reality of my thoughts" (A371). In both cases, he thinks, "the immediate perception (consciousness) of [things of those kinds] is at the same time a sufficient proof of their reality" (A371). "All outer perception, therefore, yields immediate proof of something real in space" (A375).

Kant's realism would therefore deny what has come to be called the "epistemic priority" of perceptions, sensations, or other experiences, as well as perceivers themselves, over those things that exist in space. Any view that makes one's inner states, or oneself, more certain or more directly knowable or in any other way "epistemically prior" to objects existing outside oneself in space is committed to what Kant calls "idealism" and hence is to be opposed. No such view can admit that the existence of external objects is "known through immediate perception" or that we can ever be "completely certain as to their reality" (A368-369).

But Kant does not oppose Descartes's view and other forms of "idealism" simply on the grounds that they have that unfortunate consequence. He does not argue, as Moore does, that we sometimes *are* certain and *do* know that we are sitting by a fire with a piece of paper in our hands, and that "problematic idealism" therefore must be incorrect. Nor does he simply announce that we sometimes do immediately perceive a fire and a piece of paper without relying on any intermediate object, and that therefore "realism" must be true. Of course Kant thinks that we often are certain and do know such things, and that we usually do perceive the objects around us directly, but he does not use such facts to oppose the philosophical theories that he thinks are incorrect. The "refutation of idealism" and the corresponding "proof" of "realism" is considerably more complicated than that. And if it were successful, it would show that no such straightforward appeal to particular cases in which we do perceive or know something about the things around us could possibly refute philosophical skepticism.

Kant thinks the refutation of idealism and the proof of realism "must . . . show that we have *experience*, and not merely imagination of outer things; and this, it would seem, cannot be achieved save by proof that even our inner experience, which for Descartes is indubitable, is possible only on the assumption of outer experience" (B275). He claims to have shown in his refutation that inner experience is possible only on the condition that we sometimes have "*immediate* consciousness of the existence of outer things" (B276n); so when he contrasts "*experience*" with "mere imagination," Kant obviously means to contrast direct or immediate perception of things in space with mere imagination. To establish such access to objects in space would be to establish "the reality of outer intuition" (Bxl) or "the reality of outer sense" (Bxli) and thereby to show that realism is the correct account of our position in the world. As he puts it in the Fourth Paralogism in the first edition of the *Critique*, if "all outer perception . . . yields immediate proof of something real in space," then "empirical realism is beyond question" (A375).

This does not imply that each and every time we have an "outer perception" we are at that moment immediately perceiving something that exists outside us in space. We can and sometimes do make mistakes, or sometimes cannot be sure, about the reality of this or that thing. In dreams or delusions, for example, our perception is "the product merely of the imagination" (B278). But if particular questions arise about the reality of something, they are to be settled, if they can be, in ordinary, recognized ways. "Whether this or that supposed experience be not purely imaginary, must be ascertained from its special determinations, and through its congruence with the criteria of all real experience" (B279). Kant says very little about what these "criteria" of reality are. He recommends that in order to avoid being deceived by illusions we must proceed according to the rule "*Whatever is connected with a perception according to empirical laws, is real*" (wirklich) (A376), but he does not go into detail about how we actually distinguish reality from appearance on particular occasions on which the question arises. Beyond remarking, in effect, that we establish something's reality by fitting it coherently into the rest of reality as characterized by known laws of nature, he scarcely discusses the question.

Kant's desultory treatment of this issue should not be construed as a shortcoming of his realism, or of his argument for it. If realism required that we must independently establish the reality of each item that we experience, then obviously Kant as a realist would have to explain very carefully how, and with what warrant, we can do that. But Kant's realism does not require that in each case or in general we must independently determine whether there is an external reality corresponding to the perceptions we know we are having. To that question he concedes that problematic or skeptical idealism could be the only answer, and so reality would always be at best uncertain. But the question itself rests on a belief in the epistemic priority of perceptions over external reality, a belief that our inner states, and ourselves, are more certain or more directly knowable than objects outside us in space, and that is precisely what the statement of Kant's realism denies. If it is true that "inner experience in general" is possible only if "outer experience in general" is possible, and "outer experience" is the immediate, direct perception of external things, then in

order to know of the existence of things around us it is not required that
we determine in each case or in general that there is an external reality
corresponding to our perceptions. An "outer perception" will often be
"an immediate consciousness of the existence of . . . things outside me"
(B276), and so no further inference to the existence of something outside
me is either required or possible. That of course does not imply that every
particular "outer perception" involves the existence of an outer thing, but
it does imply that there is no completely general skeptical threat in the
fact that there are sometimes illusions or mere plays of the imagination.
The kind of doubt or uncertainty about reality that is sometimes appropriate in special circumstances cannot be extended to every case of sense
perception. If it could be, there would always have to be an inference involved in arriving at knowledge of things around us in space, and that
would be a version of what Kant calls "idealism." The realism that he
wishes to show is the only correct view would deny the inferential and
therefore problematic character of our knowledge of things around us in
space. That is precisely why it is the only correct view; it is the only view
that is incompatible with skeptical idealism, and hence the only view that
can explain how our knowledge of the world is possible.

"TRANSCENDENTAL IDEALISM"

Kant's rejection of all forms of skepticism nevertheless comes out of a full
acknowledgment of its powerful appeal. He thinks the constant threat of
skepticism is a good thing in philosophy; it drives us "by main force" to
the correct view we would never arrive at without its help (A378). We
have seen that for Kant the correct view of our position is the realism I
have already sketched. But that form of realism must be established;
Kant demands that it be "proved." And he finds that there is only one
"refuge still open" for proving it and thereby explaining how immediate
perception and direct knowledge of things around us in space are possible. We must accept what he calls "the ideality of all appearances"
(A378). What we perceive must be in some way dependent on our own
sensibility and understanding. That is the point of Kant's so-called
"Copernican revolution" in philosophy. We can never explain how our
knowledge of the world is possible on the assumption that our perception
and knowledge of things simply conform to the constitution of the
objects known, so we must adopt the revolutionary idea that "objects
must conform to our knowledge" (Bxvi) or to "the constitution of our
faculty of intuition" (Bxvii). To avoid skeptical idealism and thereby
explain how noninferential knowledge of things around us is possible, we

must view "all our perceptions, whether we call them inner or outer, as a consciousness only of what is dependent on our sensibility," and all "the outer objects of these perceptions . . . only as representations, of which . . . we can become immediately conscious" (A378). And to adopt that view is to adopt a form of idealism. It says that the objects we perceive around us in space are dependent on our sensibility and our understanding. It is only because that is true that we can perceive those objects directly and therefore can be noninferentially certain of their reality. So some form of idealism is required, after all, in order to explain how our knowledge of the world is possible.

It is well known that Kant thinks this same form of idealism is also required to account for the necessary and therefore a priori character of our knowledge of space, as embodied in geometry, and, through time, of our knowledge of arithmetic. Space and time must be regarded as no more than "forms of sensibility" and not as things existing on their own, independently of our sensibility. And therefore all the things we perceive to exist in space or time—which exhausts all the things we perceive— must likewise be seen as having no existence independent of thought and experience. If this idealist view were not correct, Kant thinks, there would be no explanation of how our knowledge of mathematics or our knowledge of the world around us is possible.

So for Kant skepticism or idealism must be avoided as an account of human knowledge, and it can be avoided only by adopting idealism after all; the desired "refutation of idealism" can succeed only if idealism is true; the things we directly perceive can be shown to be spatial things and independent of us only if they are all appearances and dependent on us. But for Kant there is no conflict or paradox here. The idealism that must be accepted is "transcendental" idealism, and the realism that is the correct account of our position in the world is "empirical" realism. What is to be refuted is "empirical" or skeptical idealism, and only the truth of "transcendental" idealism can secure that result. Space and the things in space are to be seen as "empirically" real but "transcendentally" ideal. Although idealism and realism are incompatible, they do not conflict if the one is understood "transcendentally" and the other "empirically." That is precisely Kant's solution to the problem of how human knowledge is possible.

The distinction is perhaps best understood as a distinction between two different ways of speaking or two different points of view from which things can be said.[6] The expression "independent of us," for example, can be used in two different ways. To use it "empirically" is to pick out a class of things that can be found in experience to differ from another class of things to which the term does not truly apply. There is a significant contrast to be drawn within our experience between those things whose existence and nature are to some extent dependent on those who perceive them, and those whose existence and nature are fully independent of all perceivers. Stones and trees and pencils and pieces of paper fall into the latter class—they are independent of us and of our understanding and sensibility—whereas pains, afterimages, dreams, and the like depend for their existence on the person who experiences them. If the expression "independent of us" is taken "empirically," as a way of picking out a class of things to be encountered in experience, then to say "We are aware of things that are independent of us" is to say only that when we apply to all the things we are aware of the empirical distinction between things that are not dependent on us and things that are, we find that there are in fact many things in the former class. That is not the way it is, for example, with the empirical distinction we can recognize between human beings who are born green all over and those who are not. When we apply that particular distinction to all the things that fall within our experience, we find that as a matter of fact nothing belongs to the former class. So from the mere fact that we recognize an empirical distinction between two sorts of things it does not follow that there are things of both sorts. For some empirical distinctions that is true, and for others it is not. In each case the issue can be settled by experience. And in the case of the "dependent on us—independent of us" distinction, we find that in fact it has instances on both sides. Realism is in part the view that objects exist in space independently of human or other perceiving beings, so it is quite obvious that at least that part of realism, understood "empirically," is true.

But Kant does not accept realism, understood "transcendentally." For him it is not true "transcendentally" that we are aware of things that are independent of us. The correct "transcendental" position is idealism: what we perceive and know are all "appearances," things that are dependent on us. But how are we to understand the "transcendental" employment of the expression "independent of us"? If it does not serve to pick out a subclass of all the things we can encounter within our experience, as it does in its "empirical" employment, how can it have any intelligible use at all?

The question is difficult, and cannot be given a short answer. But we know at least that for Kant what holds "empirically" does not determine what holds "transcendentally." From the fact that we are aware of things that are independent of us, "empirically" speaking, it does not follow that we are aware of things that are independent of us, "transcendentally" speaking. Kant's own combination of "empirical" realism and "transcendental" idealism is an example of the failure of that inference.

So the two ways of speaking or the two different points of view from which things can be said are independent of each other at least to that extent. A "transcendental" doctrine cannot be established or refuted "empirically."

How then is a "transcendental" doctrine, and in particular Kant's transcendental idealism, to be established? We know at least that transcendental idealism is not to be taken as a doctrine about a realm of entities that transcend our ordinary earthbound perceptual experience. It does not state truths about a domain existing somehow behind or beyond the possibility of all human sensory perception, and when Kant accepts transcendental idealism he does not claim to be doing so on the basis of some extrasensory access to such a transcendent domain. "Transcendental" for Kant does not mean the same as "transcendent" or "having to do with a world beyond." A statement or question is transcendental if it has to do with the general conditions of our knowledge of objects. "I entitle *transcendental*," Kant says, "all knowledge which is occupied not so much with objects as with our knowledge of objects insofar as this knowledge is to be possible *a priori*" (A11-12, altered slightly from Kemp Smith). A transcendental investigation examines the necessary conditions of knowledge in general; it is the search for an understanding of how any knowledge at all is possible. And for Kant that amounts to an investigation of what we must know a priori if any knowledge of objects is to be possible.

Kant holds, as we have seen, that the only explanation of the a priori character of our knowledge in geometry and arithmetic is the truth of idealism. Only if space and time are "forms of our sensibility" is it possible for us to have the a priori knowledge that we do have of them. And Kant also insists on an idealist answer to the question of how our knowledge of things *in* space and time is possible. The idealism in each case is to be understood "transcendentally," since it is required by the only explanation of how our knowledge, including our a priori knowledge, is possible. It is the result of an investigation into what we must know a priori if we are to know anything at all. And that investigation itself must be a priori for Kant; its results could not be reached empirically (A14-B28), since "experience teaches us that a thing is so and so, but not that it cannot be otherwise" (B3).

For Kant, therefore, the very enterprise of examining philosophically the conditions of human knowledge in general also requires the truth of transcendental idealism. We could discover a priori, independently of experience, what the general conditions of knowledge are, he thinks, only if those conditions were in some sense "supplied by us" or had their "source" somehow "in us," the knowing subjects, and not simply in an independently existing world. That is precisely the "Copernican" point.

If perception were to involve thought or the understanding, and the principles of the understanding were "in us" independently of our having experience and were necessary even to "constitute" objects for us, then it would be possible for us to gain a priori or transcendental knowledge of those principles which make our knowledge possible. If that were not so, we could not examine human knowledge philosophically or a priori at all; we could at most gain empirical knowledge of the way human knowledge contingently happens to be. So transcendental idealism is required by the philosophical enterprise as Kant sees it.

This shows in another way that Kant does not accept his transcendental doctrines on the basis of some supersensible access he thinks he has to a transcendent domain in which he discovers that there are in fact no objects existing independently of us. Rather he rejects transcendental realism, and accepts transcendental idealism, on the only sorts of grounds on which any transcendental doctrine can be rejected or accepted, namely, because it explains how knowledge in general is possible. Realism, understood transcendentally, is completely unsatisfactory in that respect. "If," in an attempt to explain how knowledge in general is possible, "we treat outer objects as things in themselves, it is quite impossible to understand how we could arrive at a knowledge of their reality outside us, since we have to rely merely on the representation which is in us" (A378). That is why realism must be rejected, and idealism must be accepted, transcendentally speaking. Any other choice would lead directly back to skepticism (A369), and therefore to no explanation at all of how our knowledge is possible.

Although this perhaps serves as a warning against a possible misunderstanding of Kant's views, it still does not tell us what "transcendental" means. So far I have indicated only that for Kant there is a distinction between the empirical and the transcendental employment of the same form of words, that what is true empirically does not determine what is true transcendentally, and that transcendental truths do not describe, nor are they discovered by an inspection of, some world or domain lying behind or beyond the empirically knowable world of familiar objects. But that is not enough to give us a positive and informative characterization of the transcendental. We know that transcendental knowledge is the upshot of an investigation into the conditions of knowledge in general; but since it seems that there is, or could be, an empirical investigation into the conditions of knowledge in general, we will understand the transcendental only when we understand how that special a priori investigation that Kant has in mind is possible. But its possibility was seen to require the truth of transcendental idealism, so we will understand it only if we have some prior grasp of the distinction between the transcendental and the empirical. That is one thing that makes it difficult to get an independently clear grasp of the transcendental.

There are other, even apparently Kantian, reasons for finding the notion of the transcendental difficult to understand. If, as Kant maintains, human thought and discourse are possible only about that to which the categories apply, and the categories apply only within the limits of possible experience, then how can there be intelligible thought and discourse in terms whose employment is not determined by empirically ascertainable conditions holding within our experience? How can there be a meaningful nonempirical or transcendental employment of our terms at all? And if the transcendental employment of terms *is* intelligible to us, and we follow Kant in adopting idealism at the transcendental level, why is that "refuge" any more attractive than adopting idealism at the empirical level? Our knowledge would still be restricted to what we would understand to be only appearances, or things that are dependent on us, and that seems to be just the position we were trying to avoid at the outset. Of course, Kant would reply that there is no such option as adopting idealism at the empirical level. Empirical idealism is not compatible with the possibility of thought and experience. And the point of recommending transcendental idealism is to guarantee the immediacy and certainty of the everyday and scientific knowledge with which we began. But, given Kant's conception of the transcendental, there remains a serious question about the source of that guarantee. To say that transcendental idealism must be true if there is to be any knowledge of things around us is to say that, unless we regard the things around us in space as appearances, or as dependent on us, transcendentally speaking, we cannot explain how our knowledge of things in space is possible. And how does that differ from saying that if we did not adopt the transcendental doctrine that things in space are appearances, we would be left with no explanation of how our knowledge of things in space is possible? Does that in itself amount to an independent argument in favor of transcendental idealism? Or is it nothing more than an expression of the apparently still-unsupported assumption or hope that we do have knowledge of things in space and that there simply must be some nonskeptical explanation of how that knowledge is possible?

For my purposes in this paper I do not want to go further into Kant's answers to these difficult questions. My concern is with the special nature of his transcendental theory and with the way in which transcendental idealism is supposed to be incompatible both with Cartesian skepticism and with Moore's commonsense attack on it. I think it is in the nature and implications of the transcendental-empirical distinction itself, and not primarily in the details of the arguments used to reach the positive transcendental conclusions, that Kant's special contribution to the problems of knowledge is to be found.

THE SPECIAL NATURE OF KANT'S THEORY

I have said that Kant's special contribution lies in his original conception of the complex relationship between the philosophical investigation of knowledge on the one hand and everything that goes on in ordinary and scientific life that is presumably its subject matter, on the other. I do not mean to imply that Descartes does not also understand that relation to be more complex than Moore did, but there remains a way in which Descartes and Moore, for all their differences, both take the relation to be straightforward and unproblematic in a way that Kant would reject. The novelty and uniqueness of Kant's theory can therefore perhaps best be explained by contrasting it with what those two very opposed philosophers nevertheless retain in common.

Moore appealed to particular cases of ordinary certainty or knowledge to oppose the general proposition that nothing of a certain sort can be known for certain. He thought that in his own assertions of knowledge and certainty he was expressing the very things that all of us say and believe many times a day in ordinary or scientific life. His citing of such cases was to serve as a reminder to philosophers who in his eyes had gone so far as to deny that anything of that sort can be known. Clearly, Moore thought that if what he said in his reminders (e.g., "I know that this pencil exists"), and therefore what all of us say on many occasions in everyday life, is true, then what philosophers say when they claim that no one knows whether there are any external things must be false. The particular cases which we are all familiar with would be negative instances of the general proposition about knowledge.

Descartes shares that assumption with Moore. He examines all of our knowledge of the world, and arrives at a general negative conclusion about it, by considering, in effect, one particular case—what must be conceded to be the best possible kind of case—of knowing something for certain about the world around us. He starts out by taking it as certain or beyond reasonable doubt that he is sitting by the fire with a piece of paper in his hand, but he then finds good reason to doubt it. Since that particular case is typical of the best position he can ever be in vis-à-vis things around him, he concludes that he has found good reason to doubt *everything* he previously regarded as certain and obvious about the world around him. That too is to take what is said or believed in the particular ordinary case as a straightforward instance of the general conclusion about knowledge or certainty. It is to grant that *if* what Moore says when he says "I know that this pencil exists" or what Descartes says when he initially says "I cannot reasonably doubt that I am here by the fire with this paper in my hand" is true, *then* what Descartes says when he says "The existence of things around us cannot be known, or can be reasonably doubted" is false. Both Descartes and Moore accept that conditional proposition; the dispute between them is over the truth values of its components. For Descartes the consequent, and therefore the antecedent, is false, and so Moore does not really know what he claims to know. Even what had seemed most certain and obvious to Descartes himself on first reflection, he finds, *can* reasonably be doubted, and he would extend that verdict to every particular case of someone's claiming in everyday life to know or to be unable reasonably to doubt the existence of things around him. Moore would argue from the truth of the antecedent to the truth of the consequent of the conditional he shares with Descartes. Since he thinks he does know and cannot reasonably doubt that this pencil exists, he thinks nothing could ever show that he does not know it; that is why he believes that any reasoning used to reach Descartes's general negative verdict will have to contain at least one premise that is less certain, and therefore more reasonably to be rejected, than the particular ordinary assertion that this pencil exists or that he knows that it does. But both agree that the particular cases in ordinary life and the philosopher's general proposition stand or fall together. That is what I mean by saying that they both take the relation between the two to be straightforward and unproblematic. And that is one thing Kant has in mind in calling Descartes an "empirical idealist"; his negative conclusion is skeptical, or in Kant's terms "idealist," and its generality consists in saying of every case of putative knowledge of the world around us just what is said of particular cases in everyday life in which we find we do not know, or can reasonably doubt, something about the way things are.

To say that Descartes's general skepticism is related to the particular claims to knowledge and certainty that we make in everyday life in the same straightforward way in which a universal generalization is related to its instances is not necessarily to say that the general verdict can be directly and empirically refuted simply by citing a negative instance as a counterexample, as Moore tried to do. Descartes would not be impressed by any such attempted refutation. If he had understood his conclusion at the end of the first *Meditation* to be so easily refutable he would never have reached it. He too, like Moore, begins with certainty about several particular things around him, and therefore with equal certainty about the general conclusion that things around us can be known, but he then subjects that certainty or apparent indubitability to philosophical scrutiny, and he finds it wanting. He does not conclude that his philosophical reasoning must be defective because it conflicts with his unshakable certainty about the fire and the piece of paper. Rather he finds that his certainty about the fire and the piece of paper is shakable, that the existence of those things can reasonably be doubted, and in fact that there is nothing about the existence of things around him in general that he cannot now doubt, and "for reasons that are very powerful and maturely considered."[7] So if there can be a legitimate inquiry of the sort Descartes pursues into the grounds or bases of ordinary certainty or knowledge, then a simple assertion of that apparent certainty or indubitability is not enough in itself to refute the general negative verdict Descartes reaches as a result of that enquiry.

The examination to which he subjects his ordinary beliefs is not one they would normally be subjected to in everyday life. His investigation, Descartes insists, is directed not toward conduct but only toward "the truth,"[8] and therefore it carries within it standards or procedures that are not necessarily appropriate, or even desirable, for arriving at conclusions in practical life. It is only from the purely "theoretical" point of view that all our ordinary assertions of knowledge and certainty about things around us are found wanting. That alone does not imply that we should refrain from making them, or should make them more tentatively, when we are actually engaged in the questions of conduct and inquiry that naturally arise in the living of our lives. There are other relevant reasons for investigating and asserting things, and accepting the assertions of others, in everyday life than the purely "theoretical" considerations involved in the pure search for truth that Descartes as a philosophical theorist of knowledge engages in.[9] Nor does it mean that there is no point to Moore's saying what he says. If he is reminding us that we are often absolutely certain in practical life, perhaps even that we must be, then what he says is perfectly correct, and there is no need for Descartes to disagree. That is a fact about our practical attitudes, and it is quite consistent with the conclusion that, even while we are expressing those practical attitudes, we do not really know the things we confidently claim to know in everyday life, and that, contrary to what we normally believe, what we are absolutely certain about in everyday life is not beyond all reasonable doubt.

So although Moore's assertions, and those of the rest of us in everyday life, do not directly *refute* Descartes's negative verdict, they are nevertheless understood by Descartes (and by Moore) to *conflict* with that verdict. If the negative "theoretical" conclusion arrived at at the end of the first *Meditation* is true as Descartes understands it, then all the positive assertions of knowledge, certainty, and indubitability that we make in everyday life about the things around us are, strictly speaking, false. What we are saying on those occasions might well be acceptable and not even rationally criticizable on the standards appropriate in everyday or scientific life, but what we are saying is not literally true if Descartes's philosophical conclusion as he understands it is true. What we say or believe about the things around us is, strictly speaking, deficient; it goes beyond what we can see to be the truth about our position when we view it from the purely contemplative or purely theoretical standpoint. It is precisely because the theoretical conclusion conflicts with ordinary assertions and beliefs that Descartes sees that conclusion as, strictly speaking, refuting or undermining those ordinary claims to knowledge and certainty.

Descartes, then, unlike Moore, does have a distinction of sorts between two different standpoints, or between what is appropriate or relevant in the philosophical investigation of our knowledge or certainty about things around us on the one hand, and what is appropriate or relevant in gaining or assessing knowledge or certainty about things around us in everyday life, on the other. The philosophical investigation takes the ordinary assertions and beliefs as its subject matter, and it can reveal our position with respect to those assertions and beliefs to be inferior to what we unreflectively take it to be when we remain within the practical standpoint and concern ourselves only with the questions of conduct and inquiry that naturally arise there. So for Descartes it is at least possible for philosophical reflection to reveal that our epistemic position in the world is not as secure as our confident assertions of knowledge and certainty would suggest. Moore would disagree. For him nothing at all can undermine our everyday knowledge or certainty, and so any philosophical reflection that might seem to do so must be wrong. That is why he thought Descartes could not extend the uncertainty or reasonable doubt that is admittedly present in some cases to all cases of knowledge or certainty about the things around us. In fact, for Moore, unlike Descartes, there is no special philosophical standpoint and no uniquely philosophical reflection on human knowledge at all. In these respects Descartes can be said to take philosophical skepticism seriously in a way that Moore never did.

But although Descartes does have the conception of a special philosophical standpoint, or a special philosophical enterprise of examining human knowledge, and Kant also stresses the special character of the philosophical task, the two conceptions are very different. Descartes's inquiry and his conclusion remain "empirical" in Kant's sense, and therefore philosophically unsatisfactory from his point of view in being incapable of going deeply enough into the conditions of knowledge. Kant is akin to Descartes and not Moore in taking philosophical skepticism seriously. And since, like Descartes, he thinks our ordinary claims to knowledge and certainty are subject to a certain kind of philosophical scrutiny, he would agree that assertions of knowledge or certainty like those of Moore and the rest of us in everyday life do not directly refute philosophical skepticism. Both philosophers, unlike Moore, stress the need for a special philosophical legitimation of our ordinary beliefs. Descartes attacks their legitimacy in his first *Meditation*. And Kant thinks it was a "scandal to philosophy and to human reason in general" that until the *Critique of Pure Reason* the attack had never been properly repulsed and that "the existence of things outside us . . . must be accepted merely on *faith*, and that if anyone thinks good to doubt their existence we are unable to counter his doubts by any satisfactory proof" (Bxl). But Kant would also hold that if the attack is allowed to get even as far as Descartes thought he had carried it by the end of his first *Meditation*, then it could never be successfully met. We could never hope to reinstate the full certainty and knowledge we enjoy in everyday life, or explain how it is possible. We would be stuck with what Kant calls "idealism."

Kant's refutation of idealism is meant to prove that if Descartes's negative conclusion were true it would violate one of the conditions that make any experience at all possible. That conclusion says that things around us cannot be known, or are open to reasonable doubt, and it rests on the alleged discovery that we can know or be certain only about the contents of our own experiences and not about the existence of any external thing that is fully independent of us, since we are never directly aware of any such external things in experience. But that in turn implies the existence of at least "inner" experience, so it could not possibly be true if the refutation of idealism is correct. If we have any experience at all, we must be capable of direct experience of "outer" things that exist quite independently of us in space, so our access to, and hence our knowledge about, things in space must be direct and unproblematic in a way that is invulnerable to philosophical attack of the sort Descartes tries to mount.

This is a stronger conclusion than Moore's claim that we often do in fact perceive, and therefore know of the existence of, things around us. It says that it is *necessary* if we are to have any experience at all that we be (or be capable of being) directly aware in experience of things around us in space. If that is so, no philosophical investigation of knowledge could possibly establish that we can never perceive external things. Of course, we know that there are occasions on which what we are aware of in experience does not in fact exist independently of us in space, but those occasional illusions or delusions could not possibly pose a threat to our knowledge of external things in general if Kant's proof is successful.

What is true in those particular cases could not possibly be true of every case of putative knowledge of things around us.

So Kant's special philosophical investigation of human knowledge is an investigation of what must be the case, and for him what must therefore be knowable a priori to be the case, if any experience or knowledge is to be possible at all. According to Kant, if Descartes had examined what we can know a priori about our epistemic position, he could never have reached his skeptical "idealist" conclusion. This conception of a purely a priori or transcendental investigation of human knowledge is what Kant himself sees as his unique contribution to philosophy. It is what enables us finally to remove the "scandal to philosophy and to human reason in general" posed by the problem of our knowledge of the external world. It makes possible a philosophical critique of pure reason that sets philosophy distinctly apart from all other kinds of human knowledge, not just with respect to its subject matter, or with respect to its purely "theoretical" character, as in Descartes, but with respect to its very content.

By that I mean that although Kant claims to be examining our ordinary and scientific knowledge of the world, his own positive philosophical account of it expressed in his transcendental idealism does not stand to our ordinary claims to knowledge and certainty in the same straightforward relation as Descartes's philosophical account stands to them. Our direct and unproblematic access to objects around us in space is possible, according to Kant, only because the things we are directly aware of in experience are appearances and are dependent on us. That idealist thesis in turn implies that we can have knowledge only about those things that are dependent on us. But when we say or believe in everyday life that we see a pencil or a piece of paper and thereby know that it is there, and we also believe that pencils and pieces of paper are things that are not dependent on us, we are not saying or believing anything that contradicts those idealist theses. Not only do those ordinary assertions or beliefs not refute Kant's idealism; their literal truth and full legitimacy do not even conflict with it. That is the deeper reason why Moore's assertions, and those of the rest of us in everyday life, could not refute Kant's philosophical position. Not only are they subject to philosophical scrutiny and therefore not to be taken at face value as invulnerable to philosophical attack; the philosophical scrutiny to which Kant subjects them reinstates them as literally true, fully legitimate, and in no way deficient. It guarantees that those assertions can be taken at face value after all, but only by showing that what they say does not conflict with the idealist truth that guarantees their truth and legitimacy. So Kant does not share with Descartes and Moore the conditional proposition that if what we say in everyday life when we say "I know that this pencil exists" is true, then what the philosopher who says "we can have knowledge only about things that are dependent on us" is saying must be false. Kant rejects that conditional. In fact he claims that it is only because the consequent is false that the antecedent can be true.

Descartes's philosophical examination of our ordinary assertions and beliefs about the things around us inquires into the credentials of those assertions and beliefs—whether and how they can ever be completely certain or express reliable knowledge. Kant's philosophical investigation and subsequent legitimation of our ordinary empirical assertions and beliefs is by contrast an investigation into the conditions that make any such assertions or beliefs even so much as possible at all. It is concerned with the system of all of our ordinary beliefs as a whole, and it is intended to show that their not being *in general* deficient or vulnerable to skeptical attack is a condition of our having any experience at all, and hence of our being able to make any such empirical judgments in the first place. In speaking of their invulnerability to skeptical attack I mean that *all* of our empirical judgments could not possibly be shown to be deficient or unwarranted in the way that this or that particular assertion of knowledge or certainty can be shown to be defective or false on a particular occasion in everyday life because of the possibility that it is based on nothing more than an illusion or a dream or some other "mere play of inner sense." Kant's guarantee of the general invulnerability of our knowledge of the world is therefore secured a priori; it is a transcendental guarantee, and not something, as it is on Descartes's view, that must be secured on each and every occasion if we are to assert truly that we know or are certain about the world around us.

On Kant's view, when we make an ordinary assertion of knowledge or certainty about things around us, we are not implicitly asserting or committing ourselves to the falsity of those things Descartes believes we must know to be false (e.g., that we are dreaming) if we are to know anything at all about the world around us. In our ordinary empirical judgments about reality we do not commit ourselves one way or the other on the question whether reality in general matches up with or corresponds to the way it is perceived to be; so in claiming knowledge or certainty about the world we do not commit ourselves to the falsity of philosophical skepticism. Therefore we do not have to show on each occasion how we know that philosophical skepticism is false in order for our ordinary assertions of knowledge and certainty to be true and fully legitimate. We are taking no stand one way or the other on the truth of any philosophical view when we say, for example, that we see a pencil and thereby know that it exists and is independent of us. As we have seen, Kant's own transcendental idealist theory and that ordinary assertion do not conflict, even though the philosophical theory is naturally expressed in words that seem on the face of them to say the opposite of what is asserted in the everyday judgment. But the way in which the ordinary judgments are in general legitimized secures the result that, in making them, we are saying nothing about the way things are, transcendentally speaking. Kant's idealism is not "empirical."

NEO-KANTIANISM

The idea of philosophy as an a priori discipline examining the possibility of all fields of human knowledge (including itself) has dominated philosophy in one form or another since Kant's time. It survives in the conception of philosophy as "conceptual analysis" or "the logic of science." Of course, most post-Kantian philosophers nowadays would claim to have dismissed the explicitly transcendental aspects of Kant's philosophy, even though they retain the antiskeptical conclusions to be derived from the idea of a split between what is said in philosophy and what is said, even in the same words, in ordinary or scientific life. But it remains an important and still unanswered question whether those reassuring antiskeptical results can be achieved if Kant's notion of the non-"empirical" or the transcendental is repudiated entirely.

Most recent antiskeptical philosophers have relied heavily in one way or another on the notion of meaning. Logical positivism or logical empiricism, for example, which has been the dominant Kantian philosophy of this century, used its famous verifiability principle of meaningfulness to guarantee the general invulnerability of ordinary empirical judgments to skeptical attack.[10] If a form of words is meaningful and expresses something only if it is in principle possible for us to verify or confirm in experience that what it says is true, or that what it says is false, then there is no possibility of there being anything meaningful whose truth value we could not ascertain. On a particular occasion we might speak falsely in claiming to know something, but the error we fall into on that occasion must always be in principle eliminable, and it could not possibly be extended to all of our empirical judgments as a whole. If it were not possible for us to know their truth value, they would be meaningless and therefore not judgments or assertions at all. Hence no philosophical skepticism to the effect that we can never know anything about the world around us could possibly be correct. If our talk about the world around us is even meaningful at all, then the verifiability principle of meaningfulness guarantees that we must be capable of ascertaining whether or not what we say about the world around us is true. So when we speak meaningfully about the things around us and of their independence from us, we are employing purely "empirical" concepts of "external thing," "independence," and so on—concepts whose application we must be able to determine empirically if they are intelligible to us at all.

This view is Kantian in its general guarantee of the legitimacy of our ordinary assertions, and in its derivation of that guarantee from the necessary conditions of our making any such assertions at all. It is Kantian also in its conception of the complex relation between ordinary assertions and beliefs on the one hand and philosophical skepticism on the other. For the verificationist, the skeptic is stating no intelligible possibility when he says that the world around us might be different from what we could ever ascertain it to be, or that there might be no external world at all, even given the complex course of experience that we are all familiar with. Philosophical skepticism, like all philosophical theories, is therefore literally meaningless. But meaningless nonsense cannot conflict with meaningful assertions that are either true or false. Therefore when we say in everyday life, for example, "I know that this pencil exists," we are not saying anything that conflicts with what a philosopher says when he says "No one can ever know anything about the world around him." Such a philosopher says nothing. So the verificationist is Kantian in also rejecting the conditional proposition endorsed by both Descartes and Moore.

It is therefore not much of an exaggeration to say that the verifiability principle of meaningfulness has come to play the same antiskeptical role in guaranteeing the general legitimacy of our ordinary and scientific knowledge-claims about the world around us that transcendental idealism plays in Kant's philosophy. I alluded earlier to some of the difficulties we face in gaining a clear understanding of the status of Kant's transcendental idealism and of whether and how it can be independently established. The verifiability principle was attacked by metaphysically or theologically inclined critics in the 1930s and 1940s on what then seemed the rather tedious ground that it itself was neither analytic nor empirically confirmable, and so, by its own lights, was meaningless. But if the verifiability principle is doing the job of Kant's transcendental idealism, the question of its status and of how it is to be established without any transcendental proof is perhaps of greater interest and importance than it then seemed. Until the question has been answered we cannot be sure we are entitled to the comfortable antiskepticism it would provide. But since the time of Kant it should have been clear that we are even less entitled to that antiskepticism solely on the basis of the confident assertions of knowledge and certainty that we unquestioningly make in everyday life.[11]

NOTES

1. *The Philosophical Works of Descartes,* trans E. S. Haldane and G. R. T. Ross (New York: Dover Publications, 1955), I, 145. Hereafter cited as *Descartes.*

2. G. E. Moore, *Some Main Problems of Philosophy* (London: Allen and Unwin, 1958), pp. 119-120.

3. G. E. Moore, *Philosophical Studies* (Paterson, N.J.: Littlefield, Adams & Co., 1959), p. 228.

4. For the idea that the problem of the external world as we know it today was never asked before the time of Descartes see M. F. Burnyeat, "Idealism and Greek Philosophy: What Descartes Saw and Berkeley Missed," in *Idealism Past and Present,* ed. G. Vesey, Royal Institute of Philosophy Lectures, vol. 13 (1982).

5. References in parentheses in the text are to *Kant's Critique of Pure Reason,* ed. and trans. N. Kemp Smith (London: Macmillan, 1953).

6. Here I am indebted to the illuminating, if rather unsystematic, discussion of the distinction and some of its implications in Graham Bird, *Kant's Theory of Knowledge* (London: Routledge and Kegan Paul, 1962).

7. *Descartes,* I, 148.

8. *Descartes,* I, 148, 219-220; II, 44, 206. The importance of this distinction for the proper understanding of Descartes's philosophy is admirably explained and stressed in Bernard Williams, *Descartes: The Project of Pure Enquiry* (Harmondsworth: Penguin, 1978), esp. chap. 1.

9. For the idea that it was the purely theoretical and completely nonpractical character of his investigation which enabled Descartes to take his doubts further than any skeptics had done before him and thereby raise in absolutely general terms the problem of the external world in its modern form, see Burnyeat, "Idealism."

10. For early applications of the verifiability principle to the problem of the external world see, e.g., R. Carnap, *Pseudoproblems in Philosophy* (1928), §§7-10, in R. Carnap, *The Logical Structure of the World* and *Pseudoproblems in Philosophy,* trans. Rolf A. George (London: Routledge and Kegan Paul, 1967); Moritz Schlick, "Positivism and Realism" (1932), in *Logical Positivism,* ed. A. J. Ayer (Glencoe, Ill.: The Free Press, 1959). Both Carnap and Schlick distinguish between an "empirical" and a "philosophical" or "metaphysical" concept of reality, and argue that only the former makes sense. Explicit comparisons with Kant are made by Schlick who, in summing up the consequences of accepting the verifiability principle, concludes that "whoever acknowledges our fundamental principle must be an empirical realist" ("Positivism and Realism," p. 107).

11. I am grateful to Janet Broughton, Graciela De Pierris, and Barbara Winters for helpful comments on an earlier version of this paper, and to Thompson Clarke for my appreciation of the importance for epistemology of something like Kant's distinction between the transcendental and the empirical.

Index

Designer:	University of California Press Staff
Compositor:	Janet Sheila Brown
Printer:	Vail-Ballou Press
Binder:	Vail-Ballou Press
Text:	10/12 Paladium, Compuwriter II
Display:	Paladium Bold